JONATHAN SWIFT
AND
THOMAS SHERIDAN

The
Intelligencer

Edited by
JAMES WOOLLEY

CLARENDON PRESS · OXFORD
1992

Oxford University Press, Walton Street, Oxford OX2 6DP

Oxford New York Toronto
Delhi Bombay Calcutta Madras Karachi
Petaling Jaya Singapore Hong Kong Tokyo
Nairobi Dar es Salaam Cape Town
Melbourne Auckland

and associated companies in
Berlin Ibadan

Oxford is a trade mark of Oxford University Press

Published in the United States
by Oxford University Press, New York

British Library Cataloguing in Publication Data
(data available)
ISBN 0–19–812670–0

Library of Congress Cataloging in Publication Data
(data available)

Set by Joshua Associates Ltd, Oxford
Printed and bound in
Great Britain by Biddles Ltd,
Guildford and King's Lynn

Preface

In 1728 and 1729, Jonathan Swift and Thomas Sheridan collaborated on the *Intelligencer*. Often in these Dublin essays and poems the two authors can be seen working near the top of their form—in Swift's well-known defence of satire and *The Beggar's Opera*, in his neglected but defiantly incisive exploration of Ulster emigration, and in his satiric political dialogue *Mad Mullinix and Timothy*, a poem critics will enjoy discovering. To this list must be added Sheridan's vivid depiction of poverty in the Irish countryside and his anecdotal distinction between good story-tellers and bad.

Behind the variety and vibrant unevenness that periodical writing brings—the authors on camera live, no retakes—there hovers the spirit of Swift's *Short View of the State of Ireland*, relentlessly and sardonically demonstrating Britain's economic exploitation of Ireland and the systematic acquiescence of Irish leaders in it. Because the Irish establishment centred in Dublin, the *Intelligencer*'s discussions of Irish politics and economics focussed, like the rest of the periodical, on Dublin—on its social life high and low, its morality, its failures of initiative, its hypocrisy and self-deception. While evoking the Drapier's Letters, Swift and Sheridan were not speaking to the 'whole people of Ireland'; rather they addressed those occupying some place in the administrative, legislative, mercantile, and social matrix of life in the capital city. Amidst customary misery, self-congratulation, and mediocrity, the *Intelligencer* offered a fresh minority voice of critical and unsentimental intelligence.

Yet these papers, lively though they are, belong to that class of works most valued because they cast sidelights on greater writings. They embody concerns—manners and morals, rewards and punishments, liberty versus slavery—that animate *Gulliver's Travels*, *A Modest Proposal*, and many of Swift's later poems. The *Intelligencer*, moreover, is a significant document in Irish social history and in the history of Swift's relationship with Sheridan, who shows in these essays a seriousness not evident in his better-known poetic and epistolary trifles. The power of the *Intelligencer* to illuminate Swift's other writings contextually has been inhibited, however, because not much has been known about it as a literary enterprise, not even precisely when Swift and Sheridan published its twenty numbers in Dublin.

This is the first collected edition of Swift and Sheridan's periodical to appear since 1730. I have tried to site the *Intelligencer* in its original chronological circumstances, starting from a fresh effort to date the papers. Where possible, I have recovered contemporary reactions to them. The commentary draws not only on Swift's and Sheridan's own writings but on contemporary manuscripts, pamphlets, and newspapers as well. Thereby the edition sheds new light on the life and writings of Swift's closest Irish friend and on the response of both authors to the growing Irish crisis immediately prior to *A Modest Proposal*.

I have established the text from Sarah Harding's printings of the original numbers, collating them against any later printings that Swift or Sheridan might have revised. The work of collation has been assisted by optical comparison devices such as the Hinman Collating Machine and by computer collating techniques. From collating every known copy of the Harding *Intelligencers* has come discovery of concealed editions and impressions. Because they came from the shop that produced the Drapier's Letters and *A Modest Proposal*, a similar study of such other Harding imprints would now seem desirable.

It is a pleasure to acknowledge my indebtedness, for various kinds of help, to a great many people, among whom I must particularly mention Judson Boyce Allen, C. J. Benson, Anthony J. Camp, Bryan Coleborne, Maurice Craig, W. H. Crawford, Eveline Cruickshanks, Michael Crump, Carl P. Daw, J. A. Downie, Irvin Ehrenpreis, Richard Everett, Arthur Friedman, Holden Furber, Bertrand A. Goldgar, Eric P. Hamp, David L. Hayton, Mervyn Jannetta, Maurice Johnson, Paul J. Korshin, David L. Kuebrich, William Kupersmith, William LeFanu, F. P. Lock, Edward McParland, Allison Mankin, K. I. D. Maslen, George P. Mayhew, Joan Mayhew, M. Pollard, Janet K. Price, Hermann J. Real, Nancy Lee-Riffe, Edward W. Rosenheim, A. H. Scouten, J. G. Simms, Sujay Sood, James E. Tierney, Heinz J. Vienken, and Margaret Weedon. Beate Maria Weckermann, whose *Staatsexamen* thesis at the University of Münster was an edition of the *Intelligencer*, very kindly made a copy of her work available to me.

The present edition has everywhere benefited from the scholarship of Susan Overath Woolley. The suggestion that I edit the *The Intelligencer* came from my friend David Woolley, who along with A. C. Elias, Jr, and John Irwin Fischer generously improved this book with advice and criticism from a wealth of Swiftian learning. The errors that remain are all my own.

For their kind assistance and hospitality I am grateful to the staffs of the Bodleian Library; the British Library; the Department of Irish Folklore Archives, University College, Dublin; the Dublin City Libraries; the Eighteenth-Century Short Title Catalogue; the English Faculty Library, Oxford; the Folger Shakespeare Library; the Free Library of Philadelphia; the Genealogical Office, Dublin Castle; the Guildhall Library, London; the Historical Society of Pennsylvania; the Huntington Library; the India Office Library and Records; the Institute of Historical Research, London; the Library Company of Philadelphia; the Library of Congress; the National Library of Ireland; the New York Public Library; the Newberry Library; the Pierpont Morgan Library; the Public Record Office, London; the Public Record Office of Ireland; the Registry of Deeds, Dublin; the Representative Church Body Library, Dublin; the Royal Irish Academy; the Royal Society of Antiquaries of Ireland; the Society of Genealogists, London; the State Historical Society of Wisconsin; the Thesaurus Lingua Latina; the University Library, Cambridge; and the libraries of Christ Church, Oxford; Cornell University; Harvard University; the King's Inns, Dublin; Lafayette College; the National Portrait Gallery; the Osborn Collection, Yale University; Princeton University; Trinity College, Cambridge; Trinity College, Dublin; the Victoria and Albert Museum; Yale University; and the Universities of Chicago; Illinois (Urbana); Kansas; London; Pennsylvania; and Wisconsin.

For permission to quote from manuscripts or to print photographic reproductions of materials in their care I am indebted to the Bodleian Library, Oxford; the British Library; the Governing Body of Christ Church, Oxford; Dublin Corporation (Gilbert Library); the Houghton Library, Harvard University; the Huntington Library; the Osborn Collection, Yale University; Princeton University Library; the Public Record Office of Ireland; the Representative Body of the Church of Ireland; the Director and University Librarian of the John Rylands University Library of Manchester; the Master and Fellows of Trinity College, Cambridge; the Board of Trinity College, Dublin; the Syndics of the University Library, Cambridge; and the Victoria and Albert Museum. Quotations from Crown-copyright records in the India Office Records appear by permission of the Controller of Her Britannic Majesty's Stationery Office.

Portions of the introduction first appeared in *Studies in Eighteenth-Century Culture*, 9 (1979), and in *Proceedings of the First Münster Symposium on Jonathan Swift* (Munich, 1985). They are revised here by contractual arrangement with the University of Wisconsin Press and Wilhelm Fink Verlag respectively.

The groundwork for this edition was laid with the help of a Summer Stipend for Younger Humanists from the National Endowment for the Humanities. Research continued with one of the Research Fellowships for Recent Ph.D. Recipients awarded by the American Council of Learned Societies; with a grant from the Penrose Fund of the American Philosophical Society; and with summer fellowships and grants from the University of Pennsylvania and Lafayette College. For such generous support, I am deeply grateful.

Readers wishing to use the *Intelligencer* texts in machine-readable form may write to the Oxford Text Archive (Oxford University Computing Service, 13 Banbury Road, Oxford OX2 6NN, England).

J.W.

Contents

Illustrations   xi

Abbreviations and Short Titles   xii

General Introduction   1
  Characteristics and Emphases   1
  Publication and Reception   3
  Sheridan's Life   6
  Sheridan the Writer   16
  Swift, Sheridan, and the *Intelligencer*   20
  Dates of the *Intelligencers*   26
  A Note on the Annotation   33

Textual Introduction   35

THE INTELLIGENCER, NOS. 1–20   45

Appendices
  A. Archbishop King on the Taxation of Ireland   227
  B. Unpublished Contemporary Comment   230
  C. William Duncombe's Essay on *The Beggar's Opera*   234
  D. Commentary in *Mist's* and *Fog's*   236
  E. *The True Character* and *On Paddy's Character*   244
  F. Building in Dublin *c.* 1728   249
  G. Published Replies to No. 16   251
  H. The Spurious No. 20   261
  I. The Bowyer–Davis Preface   267
  J. Intended Papers: Swift's Manuscript Hints   269
  K. *To the Author of Those Intelligencers Printed at Dublin*   276
  L. Unauthorized Titles of the *Intelligencers*   283

Textual Notes   285
  Conventions   287
  General Bibliographical Note   288
  Nos. 1–20 and Appendices A–L   298
Index   341

Illustrations

Fig. 1. *Intelligencer* 5, p. 3, from the Rothschild *28b* copy. Reproduced by permission of the Master and Fellows of Trinity College, Cambridge. 37

Fig. 2. The Monkey Who Had Seen the World. Engraving by Gerard van der Gucht from a design by John Wooton. Reproduced by permission of the Syndics of the University Library, Cambridge, from *Fables. By Mr. Gay* (London: J. Tonson and J. Watts, 1727), 46. 130

Fig. 3. Swift's manuscript hints for *Intelligencer* papers, reproduced from John Rylands University Library of Manchester MS Eng. 659, items 9–10, by permission of the Director and University Librarian. 273–4

Fig. 4. Printer's ornaments used in the Harding editions. Items a, d, e, h, and i are reproduced from the Rothschild copies of no. 3 (*28d*), no. 5 (*28a*), no. 2 (*28d*), no. 1 (*28d*), and no. 10 (*28a*), respectively, by permission of the Master and Fellows of Trinity College, Cambridge. Items b, c, and g are reproduced from no. 20, by permission of the Huntington Library, San Marino, California. Item f is reproduced from no. 1 (*28d*) by permission of the Syndics of the University Library, Cambridge. 290–1

The sigla used here are explained in the General Bibliographical Note and textual notes to individual *Intelligencers*, below.

Abbreviations and Short Titles

Account Books	*The Account Books of Jonathan Swift*, ed. Paul V. Thompson and Dorothy J. Thompson. Newark, Del., 1984.
Alumni Dublinenses	*Alumni Dublinenses*, ed. G. D. Burtchaell and T. U. Sadleir. London, 1924.
BJRL	*Bulletin of the John Rylands Library*; later *Bulletin of the John Rylands University Library of Manchester*.
BL	British Library.
Boulter	*Letters Written by His Excellency Hugh Boulter, D.D.*, 2 vols., Dublin: Faulkner and Williams, 1770.
Chicago	The University of Chicago.
Commons J. Ireland	*The Journals of the House of Commons of the Kingdom of Ireland*, vol. iii. Dublin: Grierson, 1796.
Corresp.	Swift, *Correspondence*, ed. Harold Williams, rev. David Woolley, 5 vols., Oxford, 1965–72.
Corresp. ed. Ball	Swift, *Correspondence*, ed. F. Elrington Ball. 6 vols., London, 1910–14.
Craig	Maurice Craig, *Dublin, 1660–1800: A Social and Architectural History*. 1952; reissued with corrigenda, Dublin, 1969; further corrigenda 1980.
Cullen, *Anglo-Irish Trade*	L. M. Cullen, *Anglo-Irish Trade, 1660–1800*. New York, 1968.
Cullen, *Econ. Hist.*	L. M. Cullen, *An Economic History of Ireland since 1660*. London, 1972.
A Discourse	Swift, *A Discourse of the Contests and Dissentions between the Nobles and the Commons in Athens and Rome*, ed. Frank H. Ellis. Oxford, 1967.
DNB	*Dictionary of National Biography*.
Drapier's Letters	Swift, *The Drapier's Letters to the People of Ireland against Receiving Wood's Halfpence*, ed. Herbert Davis. Oxford, 1935; corrected impression 1965.
Ehrenpreis	Irvin Ehrenpreis, *Swift: The Man, His Works, and the Age*. 3 vols., London, 1962–83.
Enquiry	Swift, *An Enquiry into the Behavior of the Queen's Last Ministry*, ed. Irvin Ehrenpreis. Bloomington, 1956.
Ferguson	Oliver W. Ferguson, *Jonathan Swift and Ireland*. Urbana, 1962.

Forster   Forster Collection, Victoria and Albert Museum.

Foxon   D. F. Foxon, *English Verse, 1701–1750: A Catalogue of Separately Printed Poems.* 2 vols., London, 1975.

GEC   G. E. C[okayne], *The Complete Peerage*, new edn., rev. Vicary Gibbs *et al.* 13 vols., London, 1910–59.

Gilbert   Gilbert Collection, Dublin City Libraries.

Gilbert, *Dublin*   John T. Gilbert, *A History of the City of Dublin.* 3 vols., 1854; reprinted Dublin, 1978.

Goldsmiths'   Goldsmiths' Library of Economic Literature, University of London.

Hdbk Brit. Chron.   *Handbook of British Chronology*, 3rd edn., ed. E. B. Fryde, D. L. Greenway, S. Porter, and I. Roy. London, 1986.

Hervey   John, Lord Hervey, *Some Materials towards Memoirs of the Reign of King George II*, ed. Romney Sedgwick. 3 vols., London, 1931.

Hore   Philip H. Hore, *History of the Town and County of Wexford: Ferns . . . Enniscorthy . . . Gorey and Newtownbarry . . .* London, 1911.

Huntington   Henry E. Huntington Library.

Illinois   University of Illinois, Urbana.

James   Francis Godwin James, *Ireland in the Empire, 1688–1770.* Cambridge, Mass., 1973.

Johnson   Samuel Johnson, *A Dictionary of the English Language.* 2 vols., London: Strahan, 1755.

Journal to Stella   Swift, *Journal to Stella*, ed. Harold Williams. 2 vols., Oxford, 1948.

L'Estrange's Aesop   Sir Roger L'Estrange, *Fables of Aesop and Other Eminent Mythologists: with Morals and Reflections.* London: Brown *et al.*, 1724.

Lib. Mun. Pub. Hib.   *Liber Munerum Publicorum Hiberniae*, comp. Rowley Lascelles. 2 vols., n.p., [1852].

Loeb   Loeb Classical Library translation.

London Stage   *The London Stage, 1660–1800.* Part 1: 1660–1700, ed. William Van Lennep. Carbondale, 1965. Part 2: 1700–1729, ed. Emmett L. Avery, 2 vols., Carbondale, 1960.

Loveday   John Loveday of Caversham, *Diary of a Tour in 1732 through Parts of England, Wales, Ireland and Scotland.* Edinburgh, 1890.

McCracken	John Leslie McCracken, 'Central and Local Administration in Ireland under George II'. Ph.D. thesis. The Queen's University, Belfast, 1948.
Mayhew, 'Dramatizations'	George Mayhew, 'Some Dramatizations of Swift's *Polite Conversation*', *Philological Quarterly*, 44 (1965), 51–72.
Mayhew, *Rage or Raillery*	George P. Mayhew, *Rage or Raillery: The Swift Manuscripts at the Huntington Library*. San Marino, Calif., 1967.
Molyneux	William Molyneux, *The Case of Ireland Stated*, intro. J. G. Simms. Irish Writings from the Age of Swift, v. Dublin, 1977.
New Hist. Ire.	*A New History of Ireland*, ed. T. W. Moody *et al.*, Oxford, 1976– .
NLI	National Library of Ireland.
OED	*Oxford English Dictionary.*
OED Suppl.	*A Supplement to the Oxford English Dictionary.*
OEFL	English Faculty Library, Oxford.
Plumb	J. H. Plumb, *Sir Robert Walpole.* 2 vols., London, 1956–60.
POAS	*Poems on Affairs of State: Augustan Satirical Verse, 1660–1714.* New Haven, 1963–75. Vol. v, 1688–1697, ed. William J. Cameron (1971); vol. vi, 1697–1704, ed. Frank H. Ellis (1970); vol. vii, 1704–1714, ed. Frank H. Ellis (1975).
Poems	*The Poems of Jonathan Swift*, ed. Harold Williams, 2nd edn. 3 vols., Oxford, 1958.
Pol. State	*The Political State of Great-Britain.*
Pope, *Corresp.*	Alexander Pope, *Correspondence*, ed. George Sherburn. 5 vols., Oxford, 1956.
Pope, *Prose Works*	*The Prose Works of Alexander Pope.* Vol. i: ed. Norman Ault. 1936; reprinted New York, 1968. Vol. ii: ed. Rosemary Cowler. Hamden, Conn., 1986.
PQ	*Philological Quarterly.*
PRO	Public Record Office, London.
PRO Ire.	Public Record Office of Ireland.
Prose	Swift, [*Prose Writings*], ed. Herbert Davis *et al.* 14 vols., 1939–68. Vol. xi rev. 1959. Various re-impressions, sometimes with corrections, Oxford, 1964–69.
RIA	Royal Irish Academy, Dublin.

Rogers	Swift, *The Complete Poems*, ed. Pat Rogers. Harmondsworth, Mddx., 1983.
Rothschild	Rothschild Collection, Trinity College, Cambridge (see *The Rothschild Library*, Cambridge, 1954).
Rylands	John Rylands University Library of Manchester.
Scott (1814)	Swift, *Works*, ed. Walter Scott. 19 vols., Edinburgh, 1814.
Scott (1824)	Swift, *Works*, ed. Sir Walter Scott, Bt. 19 vols., Edinburgh, 1824.
Temple Scott	Swift, *Prose Works*, ed. Temple Scott. 12 vols., London, 1897–1908.
Sedgwick	Romney Sedgwick, *The House of Commons, 1715–1754*. 2 vols., London, 1970.
Sheridan, *Library*	*A Catalogue of Books, the Library of the Rev. Dr. Sheridan, Deceased.* Dublin: Rider, 1739. Copy: NLI.
Spectator	*The Spectator*, ed. Donald F. Bond. 5 vols., Oxford, 1965.
Swift vs. Mainwaring	*Swift vs. Mainwaring: The Examiner and The Medley*, ed. Frank H. Ellis. Oxford, 1985.
Tale	Swift, *A Tale of a Tub*, 2nd edn., ed. A. C. Guthkelch and D. Nichol Smith. Oxford, 1958.
Taylor	Robert H. Taylor Collection, Princeton University.
TCD	Trinity College, Dublin.
TE	*The Poems of Alexander Pope*, ed. John Butt *et al.* The Twickenham Edition. 11 vols., New Haven, 1939–69.
Teerink	Teerink Collection, University of Pennsylvania.
Tilley	Morris P. Tilley, *A Dictionary of the Proverbs in England in the Sixteenth and Seventeenth Centuries.* Ann Arbor, 1950.
T–S	Teerink–Scouten, i.e., H. Teerink, *A Bibliography of the Writings of Jonathan Swift*, 2nd edn., ed. Arthur H. Scouten. Philadelphia, 1963.
ULC	University Library, Cambridge.
Weckermann	'Thomas Sheridan. *The Intelligencer*', ed. Beate Maria Weckermann. Staatsexamen thesis. Westfälische Wilhelms-Universität, Münster, 1981.
J. Woolley, 'Friends and Enemies'	James Woolley, 'Friends and Enemies in *Verses on the Death of Dr. Swift*'. *Studies in Eighteenth-Century Culture*, 8 (1979), 205–32.

General Introduction

THE *Intelligencer* began in 1728, Swift blandly recalled, because 'two or three of us had a fancy . . . to write a Weekly paper'.[1] What provoked this fancy we can only guess, but a good guess might be that at first the *Intelligencer* was for Swift a diversion from the loss of Esther Johnson and from his failure to establish the rapport he wished with the court of the new king, George II, both within the previous year.[2] Out of Sheridan's frustrations as well as Swift's, the new periodical addressed its weekly audience with commentary that was pointed, often personal in its reference, and seldom dull.

Characteristics and Emphases

Swift and Sheridan were not very concerned to imitate such well-established models of the periodical essay as the *Tatler* or the *Spectator* or even the *Examiner*. The *Intelligencer* almost disregarded the character of Mr Intelligencer, there was only a perfunctory nod to the idea of a sponsoring society or club, and there was very little fair-sexing.[3] The *Intelligencer* was never merely polite or genteel, nor did it, like the *Examiner*, write in triumphal advocacy of a political programme.[4] Rather the *Intelligencer* simply offered its authors a set of weekly occasions for a wide range of trenchant discourses and poems. Its name suggests its essential character, in so far as it has one.

Since the seventeenth century, *Intelligencer* had been a popular name for newspapers, an intelligencer being literally a newsgatherer or spy. In his introductory essay Swift stresses the truth-telling, reportorial function of the new periodical. Its numbers were to be based on '*Facts, Passages,* and *Adventures*'—that is, on 'Information of all *Important Events* and *Singularities,* which this famous *Metropolis* [Dublin] can furnish'. The *Intelligencer* would report the deeds of '*Lords, Ladies, Squires, Madams, Lawyers, Gamesters, Toupees, Sots, Wits,*

---

[1] Swift to Pope, 12 June 1732, in *Corresp.* iv. 30.

[2] On Swift's aspirations at the accession of George II, see J. Woolley, 'Friends and Enemies', 210–21.

[3] As to the latter point, in sharp contrast with its summer replacement the *Temple-Oge Intelligencer.*

[4] *Swift vs. Mainwaring,* xxxv–xxxviii.

Rakes, and *Informers'*. In short, its mission was, Swift announced, 'to *Inform*, or *Divert*, or *Correct*, or *Vex* the Town'.

The *Intelligencer*'s factuality, or at any rate its insistently tough-minded reference to the contemporary Dublin context, accounted for much of its interest in 1728, and it still does. Among the *Intelligencer*'s subjects are *The Beggar's Opera* and its satire, the vulgarity and incorrigibility of upstarts, fashionable gambling among Dublin ladies, and the value of story-telling in good conversation. While most of these subjects do not sound particularly Irish, and while Swift, owing to his acquaintance with the wider world of London, wrote some essays that could well have appeared there, inspection will almost always reveal a Dublin occasion or stimulus. *The Beggar's Opera* was playing to packed Dublin houses while an Irish bishop condemned its morality, and the Irish peerage was even more decadent than the English. Although it may be true, as the London editions of the *Intelligencer* insinuated, that Sheridan's characteristically scatalogical 'Tale of a T—d' satirizes Walpole as an upstart, the upstarts it more immediately attacks are the vulgar and opportunistic English colonizers coming to Ireland as functionaries.[5]

Anger being always a great stimulus to both Swift and Sheridan, they used the *Intelligencer* as a vehicle for lampoons, making scoundrels of such Irish dignitaries as Abel Ram, Richard Tighe, and Jonathan Smedley. Swift and Sheridan took a political position clearly opposed to the establishment represented by Walpole and Dublin Castle. Most importantly, their scrutiny of Irish life was intensified, perhaps more than they knew, by the famine then entering its third year—a circumstance that threw nearly every Irish social and economic problem into starker relief.[6]

Swift and Sheridan discuss Ireland's exploitation by the English and by its own landlords; Swift writes a story about how a dull and 'discreet' clergyman rises while one cursed with wit and intellect fails. The personal resonance here for these two priests of the Church of Ireland helps explain the keenness of their interest in what they saw as the British exploitation of their country: the establishment condoned and even perpetrated injustice, to persons as well as nations.

Sheridan's *Intelligencer* 2, about Abel Ram's churlishness toward Swift in violation of ancient ingrained Irish traditions of hospitality, was printed in full by Walter Scott, who admired it so much that he

---

[5] See Appendix I.   [6] Cullen, *Econ. Hist.* 48–9.

thought Swift must have helped write it.[7] Herbert Davis judged excellent Sheridan's *Intelligencer* 6 on poverty in Ireland.[8] Swift's *Intelligencers* 3 (on *The Beggar's Opera*), 8 (*Mad Mullinix and Timothy*), and 9 (on the education of the nobility) have all recently been anthologized. Such instances suggest at least that, occasional though it is, the *Intelligencer* is accessible to later readers.

Publication and Reception

How, then, does it happen that the *Intelligencer* has always been one of Swift's least known publications?[9] Much of the blame is chargeable to the negative tone of Swift's defensive account to Pope in 1732:

The whole Volume (it was re-printed in London and I find you have seen it) was the work only of two, my self and Dr. Sheridan. . . . In the Volume you saw . . . , the 1, 3, 5, 7, were mine. Of the 8th I writ only the Verses (very uncorrect, but against a fellow we all hated) the 9th mine, the 10th only the Verses, and of those not the four last slovenly lines; the 15th is a Pamphlet of mine printed before with Dr. Sh[eridan]'s Preface, merely for laziness not to disappoint the town. . . .

Swift also claimed no. 19 (on poverty and famine in the north of Ireland), though describing it as 'only a parcel of facts relating purely to the miseries of Ireland, and wholly useless and unentertaining'[10]—yet Irvin Ehrenpreis assesses its writing as 'typical of Swift's best prose'.[11] Swift told Pope that the *Intelligencer* did not sell, and once in a nasty mood he blamed Sheridan for making 'sorry work' of it.[12] These dour remarks need to be examined and qualified.

[7] Scott (1814), i. 367–72 n.

[8] *Prose*, vol. xii, p. xv. See, however, Davis's comparison between Sheridan's essay and Swift's no. 15 (*A Short View of the State of Ireland*): 'The Conciseness of Swift', in J. Sutherland and F. P. Wilson (eds.), *Essays on the Eighteenth Century Presented to David Nichol Smith* (Oxford, 1945), 24–6; repr. in *Eighteenth-Century English Literature*, ed. James L. Clifford (New York, 1959), 93–5; and in Davis, *Jonathan Swift* (New York, 1964), 226–8.

[9] Previous discussions of the *Intelligencer* include Richard Robert Madden, *The History of Irish Periodical Literature* (1867; repr. New York, 1968), i. 297–303; Robert Munter, *The History of the Irish Newspaper, 1685–1760* (Cambridge, 1967), 163–4; Elizabeth A. Kraft, 'The Intelligencer', in Alvin Sullivan (ed.), *British Literary Magazines: The Augustan Age and the Age of Johnson* (Westport, Conn., 1983), 169–72; and Ehrenpreis, iii. 559, 580–6. Swift's papers have been edited, most notably in Temple Scott, in *Prose*, and in *Poems*.

[10] Pope, *Corresp.* iii. 292, using an earlier copy-text than Swift, *Corresp.* iv. 30–1.

[11] Ehrenpreis, iii. 585.

[12] Swift to Pope, 12 June 1732, *Corresp.* iv. 30; Swift to Pope, 6 Mar. 1728/9, *Corresp.* iii. 314.

Swift and Sheridan had hoped sales would permit hiring a young editor who would do much of the writing from their hints. But the publisher's profits did not permit it, and they found the weekly deadlines increasingly onerous.[13] For circulation's sake, the periodical should have been begun during a parliamentary session, when Dublin was full. But in fact, no. 1 did not appear until five days after the 1727–8 session had ended. Week by week, more people left Dublin, either to return to London in the viceroy's entourage, or to go into the country, depleting the pamphlet-buying public.[14] Further, the Irish economy was depressed from two years of famine, and it is hard to believe that that did not adversely affect publishing. Against these disadvantages the *Intelligencer* did better than Swift was willing to concede to Pope. Collation of all known copies of the original pamphlets shows several concealed impressions and editions of some of the early numbers, suggesting continued demand. Assuming that the number of surviving copies of each issue is a rough index to the sales of that issue, we find that from a relatively strong beginning, the circulation held its own or increased for a few numbers, then declined. Comparing the incidence of reprinting with this index of sales leads to the conclusion that the *Intelligencer* was constantly gaining new readers but—with the normal summer departures from town—losing old ones faster. That Sheridan continued to gain readers in a decreasing market, with Swift toward the end offering him little help, is an achievement Swift seems ungenerously to have ignored. Not all readers would have been purchasers: the references to Lucas's Coffee House suggest an active coffee-house readership.

The extent of the *Intelligencer*'s circulation outside Dublin is unclear, although we have testimony that the original numbers, printed in Dublin by Sarah Harding, were read in New York.[15] The papers were frequently reprinted in London newspapers, especially the Jacobite *Mist's Weekly Journal* and its look-alike successor *Fog's Weekly Journal*.[16] Through *Mist's* the *Intelligencer* reached provincial audiences,[17] and at least one *Intelligencer*, no. 14, was brought to colonial notice by the *Maryland Gazette*.

---

[13] *Corresp.* iv. 30.

[14] As early as 25 May, *Mist's Weekly J.* reported from Dublin that since the Lord Lieutenant and Members of Parliament had left 'the Place was become very empty and quiet'.

[15] Appendix K.   [16] See Appendix D.

[17] To judge from a letter in *Brice's Weekly J.* (Exeter, 30 Aug. 1728; copy: BL) against *Mist's* reprint of no. 9; see Appendix D.

But of these reprinters, only the *Maryland Gazette* identified its source as the *Intelligencer*, and London newspapers often hinted that the papers were by Swift whether they were or not. Indeed, it was one of the vagaries of anonymous publication that the personal letters Swift received complimenting the *Intelligencer* dwelt upon the papers he had *not* written, one of them even a spurious number bawdily urging sexual calisthenics for adolescent girls.[18] But the imposture provides a glimpse of local interest in the *Intelligencer*, as does a lampoon abusing Sheridan for his role in the paper.[19] All this confirms the evidence of Sarah Harding's reimpressions, namely, that the *Intelligencer* by no means fell stillborn from the press, no matter what Swift told Pope.

The *Intelligencer* finally established itself, though still without identifying its authors clearly, when it was handsomely reprinted in London. There were editions of a thousand copies apiece in both 1729 and 1730.[20] Unfortunately these editions were advertised as 'by the Author of the Tale of a Tub', denying Sheridan any recognition, but at a minimum they show that the *Intelligencer* found its audience in London.

Swift's letter to Pope deprecating the *Intelligencer* is best viewed in the context of his tendency to undervalue his own work, especially when writing to Pope. Then he would disparage his own writing, his printing, his publishing, his Irish friends, and Ireland itself, wishing to deflect Pope's critical gaze from his work, I think, and also to pay a deferential compliment to the English circle with whom Pope shared his letters.[21] Not much reliance should be placed on this strain of discourse, when we can find from other sources that the *Intelligencer* was much more nearly successful than Swift admitted, and when we can find from Swift himself that its faltering and cessation were due not to small sales *per se* but to the desire of the authors to escape the deadlines.

Yet partly because of Swift's negative comments, partly because the London editions of the *Miscellanies* and of Swift's works often fail to identify the *Intelligencer* papers as such, and partly because even George Faulkner, late in his distinguished career as the printer of Swift's works, published an inaccurate account, scholars have been

[18] See Appendices B and H.   [19] Appendix E.
[20] See the General Bibliographical Note, below.
[21] On the latter point, see Archibald C. Elias, Jr, 'Jonathan Swift and Letter-Writing: The Natural and the Playful in His Personal Correspondence', Ph.D. thesis (Yale, 1973), chs. 5–8.

confused about what the *Intelligencer* was, when it was, and by whom it was written.[22] There are other difficulties. Not a single surviving copy of the original numbers is annotated, or even priced and dated by some Dublin Narcissus Luttrell. Very few Dublin newspapers from the months of the *Intelligencer*'s publication survive, so that it is that much harder to ascertain its original contexts and the reactions of its original audience. The loss of the holdings of the Public Record Office of Ireland when it was burned in 1922 deprived scholars of resources for biographical, political, economic, and even bibliographical background. Moreover, biographical information is scarcer than usual for both Swift and Sheridan in 1728.

Sheridan's Life

On the whole, none the less, Swift has been well served by biographers, beginning in the eighteenth century and culminating in the three volumes by Irvin Ehrenpreis. By contrast, his collaborator has been so little known that a full account is necessary. Thomas Sheridan (1687–1738) was a classicist, schoolmaster, translator, priest, poet, essayist, and wit. He was Swift's closest Irish friend and his partner in language games and metrical *jeux d'esprit*. Some scholars have suggested that he was merely a jester, with whom Swift regrettably wasted a great deal of time; others, taking a similarly theatrical view, remember that this was the grandfather of Richard Brinsley Sheridan, and see him as a genial but improvident Charles Surface, more lovable by far than the dean of St Patrick's. The difficulty is to get beyond the half-truth of such stereotypes to a balanced yet sympathetic understanding of what Swift saw in Sheridan and his writings.

Of Sheridan's early life we know nothing more than is recorded in the muniments of Trinity College, Dublin. He was born in County Cavan in 1687, the son of Patrick Sheridan, about whom no reliable information seems to exist.[23] Thomas studied under the Dublin

[22] Faulkner's note, which first appeared in his 18° edition of Swift's *Works*, 1762, claims that 'the Rev. Dr. SHERIDAN, and some other Gentlemen' wrote the *Intelligencers* other than Swift's nos. 3, 5, 7, and 9 (i. 261). More recent inaccuracies: T–S, pp. 330–1; *Poems*, ii. 457; R. L. Munter, *A Handlist of Irish Newspapers, 1685–1750* (London, 1960), 19–20, mistakenly listing the *Intelligencer* as a newspaper; his error is perpetuated in *The New Cambridge Bibliography of English Literature*, ii. 1384.

[23] *Alumni Dublinenses*. Sheridan's birthdate is confirmed by his saying on 1 Jan. 1733/4 that he is 'in [his] forty seventh' year (Sheridan to J. Oughton, Osborn Collection, Yale University). Conceivably this Patrick Sheridan is the same identified in the TCD muniments as *colonus* (farmer), the father of two other Sheridans, Anthony and

schoolmaster Dr John Jones, according to John Dunton 'the most Eminent School-master in all *Ireland*'. This is the same John Jones who had been Swift's college classmate and who had been punished for writing a notorious 'Tripos'.[24] From Dr Jones's school Sheridan went to Trinity College, perhaps after some delay, for he entered as a pensioner (the ordinary tuition-paying student) in his twentieth year, three or four years older than the usual entering student. At Trinity he would have met such important future members of Swift's circle as Dr Richard Helsham, then Physic Fellow, and Dr (then Mr) Patrick Delany, then a Fellow of TCD, whom Sheridan himself later introduced to Swift.[25] Sheridan distinguished himself sufficiently that in his second year he won a prize.[26] He received his BA, according to the college records, on 9 February 1710/11, and it is probable that he immediately took holy orders as a deacon in the Church of Ireland.[27] Archbishop William King ordained him as a priest in January 1711/12. A bishop's licence was required in order to teach, and it may be that Sheridan sought this licence in 1713, since a testimonium of his BA

John (see *Alumni Dublinenses*). Efforts to assert Patrick Sheridan's kinship with Bishop William Sheridan or Bishop Patrick Sheridan have proved mistaken or at best without support. J. Edgar Bruns offers some alternative speculations about Patrick's ancestry: 'The Genealogy of the Sheridans', *Irish Genealogist*, 3 (1961), 219. An incomplete listing of Sheridan's writings appears in *New Camb. Bibl. Eng. Lit.* ii. 567. Writing *about* Sheridan includes, in addition to works mentioned in subsequent notes, Samuel Whyte, *Poems on Various Subjects*, 3rd edn. (Dublin: Marchbank, 1795), 362–3; *Brookiana*, ed. C[harles] H[enry] W[ilson] (London, 1804), i. *passim*; Richard Ryan, *Biographia Hibernica* (London, 1821), ii. 504–6; Alicia LeFanu, *Memoirs of the Life and Writings of Mrs. Frances Sheridan* (London, 1824), 17, 32–5; James Wills, *Lives of Illustrious and Distinguished Irishmen* (Dublin, 1842), IV. ii. 443–9; [R. S. Brooke], 'A Pilgrimage to Quilca', *Dublin University Mag.* 40 (1852), 509–26; Stanley Lane-Poole, 'Dr. Sheridan', *Fraser's Mag.* NS 25 (1882), 156–72; Percy Fitzgerald, *The Lives of the Sheridans* (London, 1886), i. 8–15; Daniel Hipwell, 'Sheridan Family', *Notes and Queries*, ser. 7, 7 (1889), 75; W. B. Stanford, *Ireland and the Classical Tradition* (Dublin, 1976), 32–3; *Account Books*, pp. xliii–xlv; Ehrenpreis, iii. 62–8, 358–68; Bricriu Dolan, 'Tom the Punman: Dr. Thomas Sheridan, the Friend of Swift', *J. of Irish Literature*, 16, no. 1 (Jan. 1987), 3–32. Sheridan is usually discussed in biographies of Richard Brinsley Sheridan. Fanciful assertions abound.

[24] Dunton, *The Dublin Scuffle* (London: Baldwin, 1699), 131; John Barrett, *An Essay on the Earlier Part of the Life of Swift*, in Swift, *Works*, ed. John Nichols (London, [1808]), vol. i, pp. lxxxii–lxxxviii; George Mayhew, 'Swift and the Tripos Tradition', *PQ* 45 (1966), 98–9.

[25] T. Percy C. Kirkpatrick, *History of the Medical Teaching in Trinity College, Dublin* (Dublin, 1912), 73, 79–80; *Corresp.* ed. Ball, iii. 18–19n.

[26] The prize (an 'exhibition') carried with it an annual stipend of £3, which Sheridan drew for more than a year after he took his BA. TCD muniments, Board's Register, MUN V 5/2, p. 430; and Quarterly Account Book 1697–1721, MUN V 57/1, pp. 361–440.

[27] Board's Register, TCD, MUN V 5/2, p. 435.

was issued to him on 25 May 1713.[28] Before taking his MA in 1714, he seems to have begun his career as a teacher, in what were known as classical schools—schools which emphasized the Latin classics and prepared boys to be gentlemen. He published a Latin grammar in 1714 ('by *Thomas Sheridan* M.A.'), the preface of which suggests that he already had been teaching for some time: 'The hasty Performance of this Work . . . proceeded from my Zeal to *Rescue* young *Boys* from that *miserable Toil and Trouble* which I saw the reading of a *Latin Grammar* involv'd them in'.[29]

A student of Sheridan's intelligence might ordinarily have expected to compete for a fellowship at Trinity, and having won it, to stay on indefinitely. But college statutes did not permit married fellows.[30] Perhaps as early as 1710, while still an undergraduate, Sheridan had married Elizabeth, daughter and sole heir of Charles and Anne McFadden of Quilca (Cuilcagh), near Virginia in County Cavan.[31] We have Sheridan's word that it was a supremely unhappy marriage from the very first week. Sheridan calls his wife 'a clog bound to me, by an iron chain, as heavy as a mill-stone', and says, 'How terrible a thing it is y^t a man should suffer all his life, for the phrenzy of Youth. I was in the mad years of life when I marryed & mad to marry, & almost mad after I had marry[d.]'[32] A fair example of Swift's esteem for Mrs Sheridan is his poem *A Portrait from the Life*:

> Come sit by my side, while this picture I draw:
> In chatt'ring a magpie, in pride a jackdaw;
> A temper the Devil himself could not bridle,
> Impertinent mixture of busy and idle.

---

[28] Registers of Testimonials [degree certificates], TCD, MUN V 17/1; *Corresp.* ed. Ball, iii. 18n.; Church of Ireland, *Constitutions and Canons Ecclesiastical* (Dublin: Grierson, 1729), published with the Book of Common Prayer (Dublin: Grierson, 1730), Canon xcvii. One of the rubrics in the Book of Common Prayer's 'The Form and Manner of Making of Deacons' provides that the candidate for priesthood should ordinarily have spent a year as a deacon.

[29] *An Easy Introduction of Grammar in English. For the Understanding of the Latin Tongue* (Dublin: Tompson, 1714), p. viii.

[30] Constantia Maxwell, *A History of Trinity College, Dublin, 1591–1892* (Dublin, 1946), 151.

[31] The date 1710 occurs in William Hale's Exchequer bill, filed 30 Apr. 1740; the original in the Public Record Office of Ireland was destroyed in the Four Courts fire of 1922, but a transcript is among Henry C. S. Torney's papers on Sheridan genealogy, PRO Ire., M 4855, pp. 46–7. Compare Sheridan's statement in 1735 that he had been 'linked to the Devil for twenty-four years' (*Corresp.* iv. 315).

[32] *Corresp.* iv. 315; Sheridan to J. Oughton, 1 Jan. 1733/4 and 3 Nov. 1736.

As rude as a bear, no mule half so crabbed;
She swills like a sow, and she breeds like a rabbit:
A house-wife in bed, at table a slattern;
For all an example, for no one a pattern.
Now tell me, friend Thomas, Ford, Grattan, and merry Dan,
Has this any likeness to good Madam Sheridan?[33]

Sheridan shared this opinion of Elizabeth. In his will he cut his 'unkind wife' off with five shillings.[34] She is supposed to have brought with her a dowry of £500, and through her Sheridan inherited the lands of Quilca, where Swift spent many months, some of them at work on *Gulliver's Travels.* The couple had seven or eight children, one of whom, Thomas, was especially dear to his father; he later was a notable actor, theatre manager, and elocution teacher, and was the father of Richard Brinsley. Mrs Sheridan's frequent pregnancies made Swift regard her husband as a typical clergyman who married and had a large family too early, in consequence never managing to become financially secure.[35]

Sheridan succeeded as a schoolmaster if not as a husband and father. Swift praises him for his methods of teaching; and his concern for pleasure and speed in learning is evident in the preface to his grammar, when he decries teaching Latin by forcing boys to learn grammar rules in Latin and then making them quote the rules for each construction as they read.[36] A conventional measure of Sheridan's success as a teacher is the number of students he enrolled in Trinity College. During the ten-year period 1718–29, he was conspicuously the college's greatest source of new students. In one year (1720–1), thirty-six schoolmasters sent eighty-six new students; Sheridan alone was responsible for fifteen of them. A 1725 class list preserved in one of his notebooks shows, when compared with *Alumni Dublinenses*, that twenty out of the twenty-four boys in his top three classes entered TCD—a very high proportion.[37]

[33] *Poems*, iii. 955.

[34] The actual will was destroyed in the Four Courts fire of 1922, but abstracts remain: PRO Ire., Betham Abstracts, BET I/62, p. 95; PRO Ire., Thrift Abstracts 1687. In seeking to have the will thrown out Sheridan's widow unsuccessfully contended that this provision proved his insanity; see *Corresp.* ed. Ball, vi. 212.

[35] Swift, 'Character of Doctor Sheridan', in *Prose*, v. 217. A generally unnoticed version of the obituary, softened for publication, appears in Faulkner's *Dublin Journal*, 14 Oct. 1738 (copy: Linenhall Library, Belfast).

[36] *Intelligencer* 9 (the teacher alluded to is Sheridan).

[37] I have analysed the TCD entrance registers, MUN V 23/1–2, for the years 1713–40. Sheridan's boast in 1724 that he had sent over 150 boys to TCD is hyperbolic; by my

Swift took an interest in Sheridan's school. At times, when Sheridan had to be away, Swift came and heard the recitations. And he 'was always one of the Examiners at the Public Quarterly Examinations'. He found the boys' papers amusing in the same way that Sheridan must have: when bored, he wrote, 'Pray send me a large Bundle of Exercises, bad as well as good, for I want something to read.'[38] In an obituary Swift calls Sheridan

doubtless the best instructor of youth in these kingdoms, or perhaps in Europe. . . . His chief shining quality was that of a schoolmaster; here he shone in his proper element. He had so much skill and practice in the physiognomy of boys, that he rarely mistook at the first view. His scholars loved and feared him. He often rather chose to shame the stupid, but punished the idle, and exposed them to all the lads, which was more severe than lashing. Among the gentlemen in this kingdom who have any share of education, the scholars of Dr. Sheridan infinitely excel, in number and knowledge, all their brethren sent from other schools.[39]

In the cultural life of Dublin, Sheridan's school was particularly noted for its performances of plays, usually Latin, Greek, or Shakespearian. It was a part of his pedagogical method for the boys 'to act plays first and understand them after'. Archbishop King reports, 'I was invited to see Hippolytus acted in Greek by Mr. Sheridan's scholars, and was prevailed on to go there. They did it very well, and having read it before and a book in my hand, I went along with the actors, whom otherwise I should not have understood.' Among the earliest evidence of Sheridan's contact with Swift is a notation in Swift's account book for December 1717 of his having attended 'the Greek play'.[40]

count the figure as of the 1724–5 academic year was 94. (I am crediting to Sheridan the anti-Tisdall pamphlet, *Letter from a Dissenting Teacher to Jet Black* (Dublin, 1724), 11; copy: RIA). The undergraduate enrolment seems to have ranged from 220 to 600; for the basis of this estimate, see John William Stubbs, *The History of the University of Dublin* (Dublin, 1889), 143, 154, 316; see also R. B. McDowell and D. A. Webb, *Trinity College Dublin, 1592–1952* (Cambridge, 1982), Appendix 2. The class list is Gilbert MS 125, back flyleaf. A contemporary letter shows the guardian of little Sir Edward O'Brien, Bt., scolded for not sending him to Mr Sheridan's school: 'I see my lord Mountcashell is well treated & does well there, & he sends the best schollars to the colledge.' J. Davoren to Mrs Catherine O'Brien (5 Feb. 1718), in *The Inchiquin Manuscripts*, ed. John Ainsworth (Dublin, 1961), 134.

[38] Thomas Sheridan the younger, *The Life of the Rev. Dr. Jonathan Swift* (London: Bathurst, 1784), 374; Swift to Sheridan, 29 June 1725, *Corresp.* iii. 69.

[39] *Prose*, v. 216–17.

[40] *Corresp.* ed. Ball, iii. 125 n.; Mayhew, 'Dramatizations', 57 n.; William Smith Clark, *The Early Irish Stage: The Beginnings to 1720* (Oxford, 1955), 165; *Account Books*, 190.

Though the school flourished, Sheridan found that when his promising young gentlemen finished Trinity they would be unlikely to find places commensurate with their abilities: Englishmen occupied such places. He complains that many of his students are 'laid aside, after passing their Studies in our *College*, with the closest Application, to qualify themselves for the Service of their Religion, their King, and their Country, as if they had neither Head, nor Hands', and he goes on to lament their being banished to curacies 'of forty Pounds a Year'.[41]

By far the greatest portion of Sheridan's income seems always to have come from his teaching; during his best years—the 1720s—he earned £800 per year from his school alone. His wife's portion was worth £500 (the value is sometimes expressed in terms of the income, £40 per year), but according to Swift, 'The portion he got proved to be just the reverse of 500*l*. for he was poorer by a thousand.' This is confirmed by an Exchequer bill filed against Sheridan's estate after he died: he evidently had inherited many of his father-in-law's debts. Sheridan's other primary source of income was rents—as much as £400 per year.[42]

Though a priest, Sheridan had no benefice until 1725, but ran his school as a private enterprise. His thoughts of gaining preferment may have had something to do with his taking divinity degrees: the BD in 1724, three years after he became eligible, and the DD as soon as he became eligible in 1726.[43] At Swift's intercession, the new Lord Lieutenant, Lord Carteret, in 1725 gave Sheridan the living of Rincurran, in County Cork, and also made him one of his domestic chaplains, an appointment which ordinarily led to some preferment of importance.[44] But when Sheridan travelled down to County Cork to take possession of his living, he stopped to visit his old schoolfellow Thomas Russell, archdeacon of Cork, who invited Sheridan to preach

[41] Sir John Davies's *Historical Relations: or, A Discovery of the True Causes Why Ireland Was Never Entirely Subdued*, ed. Sheridan (Dublin: Hyde, 1733), dedication; this was published with Sheridan's edition of Davies, *A Poem on the Immortality of the Soul* (Dublin: Hyde and Dobson, 1733). See also *Intelligencer* 17.

[42] Sheridan the younger, *Life of Swift*, 384; [Theophilus] Cibber [i.e., Robert Shiels], *The Lives of the Poets* (London: Griffiths, 1753), v. 67; Hale, Exchequer bill, 30 Apr. 1740.

[43] In effect, twelve years post-MA seem to have been required for the DD, seven post-MA for the BD; compare Stubbs, 46, and *A Translation of the Charter and Statutes of Trinity-College, Dublin*, tr. Robert Bolton (Dublin: Nelson, 1749), 147–8; see also *Alumni Dublinenses*.

[44] On Sheridan's preferments, see *Corresp.* iii. 57n., 99; *Lib. Mun. Pub. Hib.* II. v. 124; W. Maziere Brady, *Clerical and Parochial Records of Cork, Cloyne, and Ross* (London, 1864), i. 234.

for him. On Sunday morning he forgot this obligation until the parish clerk came to say that the service had already begun and the congregation was waiting. In haste he grabbed up one of the two sermons he had brought with him, rushed into the church, entered the pulpit, and began to preach, taking as his text the verse, 'Sufficient unto the day is the evil thereof.' He had neglected to observe that the day was 1 August, the anniversary of the Hanoverian Succession to the throne.[45] This appearance of disloyalty was officially brought to the attention of the Lord Lieutenant by Richard Tighe, a member of the privy council. The appointment to Rincurran had already raised many eyebrows. John Pocklington, Baron of the Exchequer, had reported to Archbishop William Wake of Canterbury that 'one Mr Sherridon (a Schoolmaster in Town and second to Swift in the Battle about the halfpence) has gott a Living, which last is surprising to all here'; and Timothy Godwin, bishop of Kilmore, had told Wake that it was remarked in Dublin on this occasion 'that neither Bishop, Deans or Rectors preferr'd by his Exc. ever went under the Denomination of Whiggs'.[46] After Sheridan's débâcle Carteret therefore had little choice; though he could not remove him from the living to which he had been instituted, he removed him from the list of chaplains and forbade him the Castle. Archdeacon Russell generously sought to set matters right by giving Sheridan a lease of the manor of Drumlane, worth £250 per year.[47]

Sheridan's erudition had helped him get the living of Rincurran and the chaplaincy at Dublin Castle. Carteret, himself learned, had taken an interest in Sheridan's performance of one of Sophocles' plays, and

[45] Swift, *A Vindication of his Ex—y the Lord C—, from the Charge of Favouring None but Toryes, High-Churchmen, and Jacobites*, in *Prose*, xii. 162–4; Sheridan the younger, *Life of Swift*, 380–4; Marmaduke Coghill to Edward Southwell, 9 Oct. 1725, in Richard Caulfield (ed.), *The Council Book of the Corporation of Kinsale, from 1652 to 1800* (Guildford, 1879), p. lxxiv. Swift errs in 'The History of the Second Solomon' in saying the débâcle occurred on King George's birthday (*Prose*, v. 223). The view of some writers that Sheridan's sermon was bold Jacobite defiance goes against Swift's informed acceptance of the choice of text as inadvertent (*Corresp.* iii. 94) and does not offer a plausible motive for Archdeacon Russell's consolatory gift to Sheridan of £250 per year.

[46] Pocklington to Wake, July 1725; T. Kilmore to Wake, 14 July 1725; in Wake MS 14, fos. 274, 276–7, Christ Church, Oxford.

[47] The gift, reported in the younger Sheridan's life of Swift, 383–4, is doubted by Ehrenpreis, iii. 363 n., but although the details, especially the amount, may be incorrect, various documents in the Registry of Deeds, Dublin, show that Sheridan later held a lease of Church lands from Russell and that he held a lease of Church lands in the manor of Drumlane, suggesting at least some grains of truth in the son's account. See Memorials 68-201-47659, 71-259-50623, 76-479-55495, 82-432-58467, and 97-293-68386, all summarized in the Torney papers, PRO Ire. M 4856.

Sheridan had dedicated to Lady Carteret his translation of Sophocles' *Philoctetes*.[48] But in the quest for patronage he otherwise met with no striking success. Like many who had attended Trinity College in the first decade of the century, Sheridan had been a High Tory and High Churchman. He was unlucky enough to dedicate his grammar (1714) to Thomas Lindsay, the Tory archbishop of Armagh, just as Queen Anne died and Lindsay lost his political influence. Sheridan next cultivated Lady Mountcashel, whose sons he taught—the second Viscount, who died in childhood, and the third Viscount, whom Sheridan sent to Trinity College in 1727.[49] To this young man Sheridan dedicated his translation, *The Satyrs of Persius*.[50] Sheridan's edition of Sir John Davies's *Nosce Teipsum* and other writings seems intended as a further compliment to the Mountcashel family, since they were (erroneously) believed to be descended from Davies. Unfortunately the young lord died in 1736 before he could become helpful to Sheridan.[51]

Though Swift once advised Sheridan, for the sake of his ecclesiastical career, to 'talk a little Whiggishly', he hooted at Sheridan's attempt to pay court to the establishment by writing the official birthday ode to Queen Caroline in 1729.[52] Perhaps it was too unsubtle a gesture from a Tory, although one may suspect that Swift's animus was aroused partly because of his own ill feeling toward the Queen.[53]

Sheridan made another public effort at patronage-seeking with the dedication of *A Poem on the Immortality of the Soul* (1733) to the young Earl of Orrery. In Orrery Sheridan seems to have placed a great deal of hope: this is evident from the references to him in Sheridan's letters to Thomas Carte.[54] But there were no tangible benefits at the time, and in his *Remarks on the Life and Writings of Dr. Jonathan Swift*, Orrery treats Sheridan roughly.[55]

[48] (Dublin: Hyde and Dobson, 1725).

[49] *Alumni Dublinenses* under Davys; GEC under Mountcashell.

[50] (Dublin: Grierson, 1728).

[51] Davi[e]s, *A Poem on the Immortality of the Soul*; see Aaron Crossly, *The Peerage of Ireland* (Dublin: Hume, 1725), 146; *The Irish Compendium: or, Rudiments of Honour*, 2nd edn. (London: Nutt, 1727), iii. 220–1.

[52] Swift to Sheridan, 18 Sept. 1728, *Corresp.* iii. 298; Sheridan, *An Ode to be Performed at the Castle of Dublin, March the 1st, 1728–9. Being the Birth-day of Her Most Serene Majesty Queen Caroline* (Dublin, 1728/9).

[53] See J. Woolley, 'Friends and Enemies', 210–21.

[54] Bodleian MS Carte 227, fos. 47ʳ, 48ʳ, 99ʳ; see also Sheridan's poem, 'A Letter of Advice to the Right Hon. John Earl of Orrery', *Gentleman's Mag.* 5 (1735), 378.

[55] (London: Millar, 1752), 84–7. For some of the information and imagery in his character of Sheridan, Orrery draws upon [William Tisdall's] lampoon, *Tom Pun-sibi*

Not only did these efforts to seek patronage meet with no further results, but during the 1730s Sheridan's enrolments seem to have fallen, so that he became gradually poorer.[56] Though it is not to be supposed that he spent a great deal of time in Rincurran parish (Swift condoled with him for being given the farthest possible living from his lands in County Cavan), Sheridan in 1730 found it convenient to exchange that living for another, becoming vicar of Dunboyne and Kilbride in County Meath, not far from Dublin and on the road to Quilca. But Dunboyne was worth only £80 a year, whereas Rincurran was supposed to have been worth £150.[57] Finding his school less lucrative as well, in 1735 Sheridan exchanged the living of Dunboyne for the Royal School in Cavan, closing his school in Dublin. The Cavan school carried with it a salary of £80 a year, in addition to the fees he might charge, but it lacked a suitable school building.[58] We find Sheridan on various occasions mortgaging his estate at Quilca to Swift for £300, selling land to Swift, and having great difficulty collecting his rents.[59] He avoided Dublin because of his indebtedness, and was unable to find £14 to keep his son Tom at Westminster School in London.[60]

To increase his income, Sheridan considered setting up a school in England. He wrote melodramatically to Thomas Carte, 'I would rather be a flea-catcher to a dog in England than a privy-counsellour here. . . . A very small prospect shall incline me to breath[e] in an air of Liberty.'[61] He also tried to become dean of Kilmore, to get a sinecure from the Lord Lieutenant, to become master of Armagh Royal School, to become a justice of the peace, and to publish his collection of *bons mots* and his annotated translation of Guarini's *Pastor Fido*. These schemes all came to nought.[62]

In 1737 Sheridan turned fifty. His family had become, except for

---

Metamorphosed: or, The Giber Gibb'd (Dublin, 1724): see Orrery's interleaved copy of the *Remarks*, Harvard MS Eng. 218.14, pp. 84–7; see also Appendix E.

[56] Sheridan the younger's *Life of Swift*, 385, is supported in this respect by the TCD entrance registers.

[57] *Corresp.* iii. 66; iv. 310; *Prose*, v. 217–18; *Lib. Mun. Pub. Hib.* II. v. 125.

[58] Faulkner's *Dublin Journal*, 3 May 1735; *Prose*, v. 217–18; *Corresp.* iv. 447.

[59] Torney papers, PRO Ire., M 4856, p. 27; *Corresp.* iv. 357n.; Gerald Y. Goldberg, *Jonathan Swift and Contemporary Cork* (Cork, 1967), 58.

[60] 'Non reddebam ad Dublinum apis causa debebam nummum, & ego habebam id non ad cicerem' ('I did not return to Dublin bee cause I owed a bit of money, and I did not have it to pea [pay]'). Sheridan to Swift, 22 June 1737, *Corresp.* v. 49; *Prose*, v. 217.

[61] 28 Nov. 1732, Bodleian MS Carte 227, fo. 287ʳ.

[62] *Corresp.* iv. 246, 454, 497, 513, 521; Sheridan to J. Oughton, 12 July 1735, Osborn Collection, Yale University; Faulkner's *Dublin Journal*, 23 May 1738.

Tom, less a comfort to him than ever. One of Sheridan's daughters, with her mother's connivance, had made a marriage of which he strongly disapproved (she, too, inherited only five shillings).[63] Sheridan's asthma worsened. As medicine he took 'whisky ... with an agreeable mixture of garlic, bitter orange, gentian-root, snake-root, wormwood, etc.' at the rate of one-half pint per twenty-four hours.[64] In Cavan he found 'the air ... too moist and unwholesome, and he could not bear the company of some persons in that neighbourhood'. After three increasingly difficult years, he sold his school for £400 and left his native county to resume teaching in Dublin. Illness must have hindered his teaching, however, and to raise money he had to pawn his library.[65] On 10 October 1738 he died at Rathfarnham, County Dublin, of 'a dropsy and asthma' (according to Swift) or of 'a polypus in the heart' (according to his son).[66] He is traditionally supposed to have died estranged from Swift.[67] An affectionate obituary by 'a very young Gentleman, who received Part of his Education from the said Doctor, by whose Death he had not an Opportunity of finishing his Studies' has this conclusion: 'And it was remarked, that none of his Scholars, was ever an Athiest, or a Free-thinker; and to sum up all, he was the best natured Man in the World.'[68]

Sheridan's library was sold at auction 'for upwards of £700'. The executors, 'to befriend' Thomas the younger, let him have his father's manuscripts in exchange for his note for only £50. They reopened the subscription for Sheridan's translation of *The Faithful Shepherd* in 1739. In January 1740, this play was performed at the Smock Alley Theatre, Dublin, having been 'fitted for the Stage by his Son'. The younger Sheridan issued proposals in Dublin in 1743 for publishing his father's works in four volumes, and in 1744–5 he issued proposals in London for one volume, to be published by Dodsley. No such edition ever appeared, though some of the Swift and Swift-related manuscripts

---

[63] *Corresp.* ed. Ball, v. 155.

[64] Sheridan to Mrs Whiteway, perhaps Apr. 1736, in *Corresp.* ed. Ball, v. 461; first published in Swift, *Works*, 12° edn., xix (Dublin: Faulkner, 1768), 74.

[65] William Hale, Exchequer bill of amendment filed 2 July 1741, abstracted in Torney papers, PRO Ire., M 4855, pp. 47–8; *Prose*, v. 218; Faulkner's *Dublin Journal*, 2 May 1738; Irish Privy Signet accounts, BL MS Add. 34775, fo. 176ᵛ. A. C. Elias, Jr, has suggested to me that the *Dublin Journal* paragraph—not a paid advertisement—of 30 Sept. 1738, announcing an auction of the 'Houshold Goods of a Gentleman in Big Butter-Lane' 3 Oct., refers to Sheridan's property; compare *Dublin Journal*, 2 May 1738.

[66] *Prose*, v. 216; Sheridan the younger, *Life of Swift*, 393.

[67] Ball discusses this point sensibly (*Corresp.* ed. Ball, vi. 210–12).

[68] *Dublin Journal*, 17 Oct. 1738.

Sheridan had left behind him were published as Swift's *Three Sermons* (Dodsley, 1744) and as *Miscellanies* x (Dodsley, 1745) and xi (Hitch, Davis, Dodsley, and Cooper, 1746).[69]

Sheridan the Writer

Prior to the *Miscellanies*, Sheridan was little known to readers in England.[70] His grammar never had a London edition; the London editions of *Ars Pun-ica* identified Pun-sibi as Swift. And London reprints of the *Intelligencer*, both in other periodicals and in the collected editions, appeared with the implication that Swift was the author.

In Dublin, on the other hand, Sheridan was well known both as a teacher and as a writer. Swift said that Sheridan 'had a very fruitful invention, and a talent for poetry. His English verses were full of wit and humour, but neither his prose nor verse sufficiently correct: However, he would readily submit to any friend who had a true taste in prose or verse.' As for his verses, they are almost all either *jeux d'esprit* or occasional pieces, many of them addressed to Swift.[71] Some of the better ones are readily available in Williams's edition of Swift's *Poems*: *Ballyspellin* (ii. 438–40), *A New Simile for the Ladies, with Useful Annotations* (ii. 613–16), *To the Dean of St. Patricks*, *1724* (iii. 1039–41), *To the Dean When in England, in 1726* (iii. 1042–4), and *Tom Punsibi's Letter to Dean Swift* (iii. 1045–8). In the same edition, Sheridan is one of the primary contributors to the 'Trifles' (iii. 965–1039).

Sheridan was better known in Dublin for his facetious *Ars Pun-ica, sive Flos Linguarum: The Art of Punning; or The Flower of Languages; in Seventy Nine Rules: for the Farther Improvement of Conversation, and Help of Memory. By the Labour and Industry of Tom Pun-sibi* (Dublin: Carson,

---

[69] Hale, Exchequer bill, 30 Apr. 1740; Faulkner's *Dublin Journal*, 12 Jan., 26 Jan., and 2 Feb., 1739/40; 15 Mar. 1743; 17 Nov. 1744; 'Memoirs of the Late Thomas Sheridan, Esq.', *European Mag.* 14 (1788), 210–12 and n.; *Daily Advertiser* (London), 21 Jan. 1745; Sheridan the younger, ed., Swift's *Works* (London: Bathurst *et al.*, 1784), x. 1 n.; Esther K. Sheldon, *Thomas Sheridan of Smock-Alley* (Princeton, 1967), 7, 17–18; Mayhew, 'Dramatizations', 58 n.; Leland D. Peterson, 'A Variant of the 1742–46 Swift–Pope *Miscellanies*', *Papers Bibliog. Soc. America*, 66 (1972), 304–5. Dodsley paid the younger Sheridan £50 in 1744 'for Sermons, Poems, &c., of the Dean of St. Patrick' (receipt listed in lot 274 of the John Wilks sale, Sotheby, 22 Mar. 1855).

[70] His Persius was posthumously reissued in London by D. Browne in 1739, probably without authority from Sheridan or his executors.

[71] *Prose*, v. 216. See Robert Hogan's compilation, 'A Selection of Dr. Sheridan's Poems', in *J. of Irish Literature*, 16, no. 1 (Jan. 1987), 33–60; no. 2 (May 1987), 19–54; no. 3 (Sept. 1987), 25–39.

1719). This mock-scholarly treatise has a subscription list at least partly facetious and prefatory verses by the author in praise of himself. The manipulation of language through paronomasia creates teetering absurdities, in a world where (as Delany's prefatory poem expresses it) 'a *double Meaning* is of *double use*'. Burlesque quotations of Latin, Greek, and even Hebrew authorities abound. The rules themselves are only a framework for the punning jests used to illustrate them; some of these witticisms have been attributed to Swift. The conclusion of the treatise is Another Preface. Not the least remarkable thing about this effervescent whimsy is that it evoked a ponderous, deadly reply, *The Folly of Punns, or, False Witt Disclosed. Shewing the Ill Tendency of a Book Lately Published, Entituled, The Art of Punning* (Dublin: Hume, 1719).

The name *Pun-sibi*, which Sheridan adopts as a *nom de guerre*, was sometimes used for Swift in England, since *Ars Pun-ica* was falsely attributed to him in its English editions. There is evidence that by 1732, *pun-sibi* simply meant a punster: in the *Universal Spectator* the writer of a punning letter signs himself 'Joseph Punsibi' (4 March). These misuses of the term only show that its origin and meaning were not understood, for *pun-sibi*, which I take to mean 'a pun on himself', refers to the surname *Sheridan*. It was interpreted to mean, in Irish, one who is 'still [constantly] Rhyming'. The (humorous?) supposition was evidently that the name—commonly spelled *Siridan* in this period—was formed from the Irish (*go*) *sír* (always) and *dán* (poetry, poem), *sír* being pronounced approximately like English *sheer*.[72]

The essentially comic persona of Pun-sibi well conveys Sheridan's good humour—a toleration of himself as impractical, childlike, and impulsive, and an incessant versifier. In his *Letter from a Dissenting Teacher to Jet Black*, Sheridan says he is 'all Day . . . as laborious as a Bee, and at Night as cheerful as a Grashoper, which made one of [my] Friends write a Poem, call'd, *The Grashoper*. If Merriment or an easy Conscience be a Sin, there lives not a greater Criminal' (10–11).

Yet Sheridan thrived on controversy; hardly anything he wrote failed to elicit a reply or rejoinder, not even his grammar, his Persius,

---

[72] Sheridan's rival teacher John Greer gives this interpretation in *Bathyllus Redivivus: An Essay Proving That the Grammar, Call'd Sheridan's, is a Transcript from The Royal-Grammar* (Dublin, 1718; copy: NLI), 9; for assistance with Irish etymology I am grateful to Eric P. Hamp. I should note that while Sheridan's grammar is in some respects a compilation, Greer's charge of plagiarism was not generally taken seriously; even one of Sheridan's enemies called Greer 'Envy . . . in humane Shape': *A Letter to Tom Punsibi. Occasion'd by Reading His Excellent Farce, Call'd, Alexander's Overthrow* [Dublin, 1721], 2 (copy: Newberry).

or his sermon on St Cecilia's day. We have a lampoon against him, 'Upon Mr Sheridan's turning Auth^r, 1716', though we have nothing he wrote in 1716.[73] When the *Intelligencer* began to appear in 1728, William Tisdall's lampoon *Tom Pun-sibi Metamorphosed* (1724) was trotted out again as *The True Character of the Intelligencer*.[74] The volume of the attacks on Sheridan seems to owe something to his physical oddity as well as to his combative attitude. He was short and thin, with a high voice which may have been one reason the frequently deaf dean enjoyed his company.[75] Lampoons often compare him to such small animals as parrots and spaniels. Even Swift says he has the voice of a cricket, the thighs of a fly, the hands of a mouse, and the shanks of a heron. His nicknames—Tom Titt, Tom Dingle—are diminutive.[76]

Among the merry writing for which Sheridan was sometimes ridiculed was a great quantity of doggerel, crambos, riddles, and Anglo-Latin language games, the latter no doubt the by-product of a language teacher's constant traffic with false cognates, literal translations of idioms, and other confusions and howlers. Sheridan also had at least two farces performed in Dublin. *Punch Turn'd School-master* (1721), presumably with some autobiographical reference, had actors playing puppets. In the same year Sheridan's *Alexander's Overthrow* was produced. Perhaps mercifully, it, like *Punch Turn'd School-master*, is now lost, but a fragment of its dialogue purports to be given in *S—'s Master Piece, or, Tom Pun-sibi's Folly Compleat, Alexanders Overthrow, or the Downfall of Babylon as It Was Acted at Mr. Lyddals in Damestreet, Decemb. 11th. 1721* ([Dublin, 1721]; copy: ULC).[77]

Sheridan spent several years gathering a collection of *bons mots*, *contes à rire*, and apothegms, of which some sign is visible in *Intelligencer* 13. He hoped to make money from them, but they never appeared in print,

---

[73] MS bound with printed halfsheets, TCD, Press A.7.6., no. 38, fo. 2; the MS is not earlier than 1733.

[74] Appendix E.

[75] See *Corresp.* iii. 43: 'I can hear nothing but Trebbles.'

[76] 'Sed levitate umbram superabis, voce cicadam: | Musca femur, palmas tibi Mus dedit, ardea crura.' *Ad Amicum Eruditum Thomam Sheridan*, in *Poems*, i. 213; see also *Mary the Cook-Maid's Letter to* [Mr.] *Sheridan*, in *Poems*, iii. 985–7; *A New Gingle on Tom Dingle* [Dublin, ?1726]; Delany, *The Pheasant and the Lark*, in *Poems*, ii. 511, lines 111–12.

[77] Some of the exchanges between Sheridan and Swift have been published in *Poems* and *Correspondence*. See also George P. Mayhew, 'Jonathan Swift's Games with Language', Ph.D. thesis (Harvard, 1952), ch. 7 and appendix; Mayhew, 'Swift's Games with Language in Rylands English MS. 659', *BJRL* 36 (1954), 413–48; and Mayhew, *Rage or Raillery*, ch. 7. Sheridan's prologue to *Punch Turn'd School-master* survives in [Matthew] Concanen (ed.), *Miscellaneous Poems . . . by Several Hands* (London: Peele, 1724), 398–400; see *Poems*, iii. 1102–5.

although he had arranged for Lord Orrery to see to their publication in England. Swift thought he had looked at 'about thirty' manuscript volumes of this material. They have been supposed lost, but nine of them survive among the Gilbert manuscripts in the Dublin City Library. They appear to justify Swift's unfavourable estimate of them in his obituary of Sheridan, but conceivably these nine are the dregs —what was left over after the best material had been sent to a publisher.[78] In any case, the collection shows Sheridan's fascination with the brief narratives—anecdotes, fables, jokes—which must have made him an attractive conversationalist and teacher. Swift probably designed both *Bons Mots de Stella* and his translation of the *Epigram on Fasting* for Sheridan's project.[79]

In addition to the translations of Sophocles, Persius, and Guarini, already mentioned, Sheridan translated some of Tasso. Moreover, Orrery reports a translation of Montaigne. In 1732 Sheridan sent an unidentified translation to Pope, who had previously vetted the Persius, and he is usually, though without good grounds, credited with a translation of Juvenal.[80] Sheridan's readiness as a translator is visible throughout his writings, including *Intelligencer* 4, which renders a passage from Horace into English verse.

Even Dublin readers familiar with Sheridan as a humorist, a classicist, and a poet may not, however, have realized the extent of his assistance to the Drapier in the campaign against Wood's halfpence (1724–5).[81] The two writers collaborated again to address public issues, but with a much larger role for Sheridan, in the *Intelligencer* papers.

---

[78] *Corresp.* v. 49; *Prose*, v. 216; Gilbert MSS 123–31. One of Swift's letters of 1730 seems to contain an early reference to the project: *Corresp.* iii. 411.

[79] *Prose*, v. 237–8; *Poems*, iii. 949. The French epigram appears untranslated in Gilbert MS 126, pp. 125–6; Swift's translation appears on the flyleaf in the handwriting of Bishop Percy, who once owned the notebooks.

[80] Orrery to Thomas Southerne, 17 Jan. 1735/6, *The Orrery Papers*, ed. Emily, Lady Cork and Orrery (London, 1903), i. 144; Sheridan to Thomas Carte, 28 Nov. and 24 Dec. 1732, Bodleian MS Carte 227, fos. 47ᵛ, 287ᵛ. The anonymous translation of Juvenal (London: D. Browne, Feb. 1738/9) is often bound with Browne's presumably unauthorized edition of Sheridan's Persius (Apr. 1739); see *London Mag.* (1739), 104, 207. (I assume that Browne supplied the two new items in his 1739 edn.—a translation of 'Auli Persii Flacci Vita' and a subject index. Another 1739 edition (London: Millar) lacks them.) There is no other authority for attributing the Juvenal to Sheridan. ULC has a copy in eighteenth-century binding with the label 'Dunster's Juvenal', perhaps an equally groundless attribution to Samuel Dunster.

[81] *Drapier's Letters*, pp. xxxiii, lxii; Ehrenpreis, iii. 308–10.

Swift, Sheridan, and the Intelligencer

How Sheridan had met Jonathan Swift, an exalted figure twenty years his senior, is not certain, but the acquaintance probably began in 1718.[82] Early in their friendship Swift addressed admiring Latin verses to him ('Deliciae *Sheridan* Musarum, dulcis amice') commending particularly his genius as a teacher:

> Aureus at ramus venerandae dona Sibyllae,
> Aeneae sedes tantùm patefecit Avernas:
> Saepè puer, tua quem tetigit semel aurea virga,
> Coelumque terrasque videt, noctemque profundam.[83]

Swift was impressed by Sheridan's wide classical learning, and got Sheridan to tutor him in Greek. When a dispute arose over the qualifications of the teacher of Hebrew at Trinity College, Sheridan was one of the 'Gentlemen skilled in that Language' who adjudicated the matter. He also knew Spanish, French, and Italian, and took some interest in Arabic and the ancient Near Eastern languages. Swift wrote that Sheridan was 'as great a master of the Greek and Roman languages' as anyone in Great Britain or Ireland.[84] Sheridan's library included, moreover, not only the usual divinity and a large collection of the classic authors, but also contemporary plays and popular fiction. The library was twice as large as Swift's, and the possibility that Swift used it deserves investigation.[85]

Swift and Sheridan had much in common. Both were graduates of Trinity College, Dublin, with doctorates in divinity. Both were High Churchmen. Both were sufficiently disenchanted with Ireland to try to leave it. Both were disappointed in their hopes, and both felt betrayed by the false friendship of others (Sheridan: 'As for my *Quondam* friends, as you stile them, *Quon-dam* them all').[86] There were other connections between the two. Both enjoyed good wine. Both enjoyed language games, punning, and other wordplay. Both had an eye for the

---

[82] *Account Books*, pp. xliii–xliv.

[83] 'But while the golden bough, gift of the revered sibyl, opened up no more than hell for Aeneas, often a boy once touched by your golden rod sees heaven, earth, and the deep night.' *Ad Amicum Eruditum Thomam Sheridan*, in *Poems*, i. 214. The date assigned in *35* ('*Oct. Ann. Dom.* 1717') cannot be confirmed, and Paul V. and Dorothy Jay Thompson have cast doubt on it (*Account Books*, ibid.).

[84] Sheridan the younger, *Life of Swift*, 371 (compare *Poems*, iii. 989n.); Faulkner's *Dublin Journal*, 26 May 1733; *Turco-Judaeo-Machia* (Dublin, 1733; copy: King's Inns, Dublin); *Prose*, v. 216; xiv. 37.

[85] Sheridan, *Library*.

[86] *Corresp.* iv. 454 (hyphen added).

absurd. Both wrote satiric verse. They shared enemies: William Tisdall, Smedley, Tighe, and Richard ('Sweats worth') Bettesworth, among others. Though divines, they wrote little on religious subjects. Sheridan often stimulated Swift to write in other veins, however, and he was active in preparing Faulkner's edition of Swift's *Works* (1735).[87]

Yet they differed strikingly. Sheridan, unlike Swift, was of Irish stock and never left Ireland. Swift, almost obsessive about his own financial security, could not understand Sheridan's carelessness about money and repeatedly criticized his 'inadvertency'. Swift is supposed to have had little appreciation of music and with his impaired hearing can have had little use for Sheridan's violin playing or his private concerts.[88] For his part, Sheridan lacked Swift's great self-consciousness and the minor virtues of tact, decorum, and rhetorical skill that commonly go with it.

Swift and Sheridan often mauled one another in verse 'trifles' —impromptu crambos and doggerel epistles the more outrageously rhymed the better. Theophilus, Lord Newtownbutler (whose family is well represented in the subscription list to *Ars Pun-ica*) collected them in his manuscript 'The Whimsical Medley', now in the library of Trinity College, Dublin. From that or some other copy, many of them—though not conceivably intended for publication—were first printed by Samuel Fairbrother in his rare fourth volume of Swift's *Miscellanies* (1735); Sheridan lampooned him to Swift as 'Fowlbrother' for his pains.[89] These sports might occasionally subside into something more frankly affectionate, as in this fragment from Swift's pen:

> Altho a great Dunce I be
> Happy if once I be
> with my Friend Punsiby[90]

And we must not forget that Swift wept when Sheridan moved to Cavan in 1735.[91]

---

[87] Sheridan the younger (ed.), Swift's *Works* (London: Strahan *et al.*, 1784), ii. sig. A2ᵛ; see also *Corresp.* iv. 531.

[88] For Sheridan's musical enterprises see his son's *Life of Swift*, 384–5; Sheridan's *A Sermon Preached at St. Patrick's Church on St. Caecilia's Day* (Dublin: Powell, for the Author, 1731); John Waldron, *A Poem upon Musick* (Dublin: Hoey, 1733), p. v; and *Poems*, iii. 1027, line 4; see also *Poems*, ii. 521–2.

[89] *Corresp.* iv. 474, 484. John Irwin Fischer has suggested to me that Sheridan may have been trying to excuse his indiscretion in having somehow made these private communications with Swift available to Fairbrother.

[90] Princeton University, John Wild autograph collection, vol. i, fo. 89.

[91] Sheridan the younger, *Life of Swift*, 385.

Sheridan must sometimes have reminded Swift of John Gay, an improvident but good-natured younger poet who had been an unsuccessful courtier. Indeed Sheridan himself suggests the comparison.[92] Much as Gay was near the centre of Swift's circle of English friends, Sheridan knew most of his Irish friends: Dr Delany, Dr Helsham, the Grattans, the Rochforts, the Worralls, Tickell, Orrery, Mrs Sican, and Mrs Whiteway. But Sheridan's intimate association with Swift is nowhere more significantly indicated than in his close friendship with Esther Johnson. The same cannot be said for Pope, Gay, or any of Swift's English friends. It was Sheridan who reported to Swift on Stella's last illness, until Swift couldn't stand the painful news and asked Worrall to 'hinder Dr. *Sheridan* from writing to me any more'. Sheridan also wrote the tender verses to Stella, signed by her friends. The manuscript is in his handwriting, and there is a space at the bottom of the list of signatures, between Rebecca Dingley's and Sheridan's, in which it would appear that Swift was to add his signature and return the poem for presentation to Stella. (Why did he not do so?) Sheridan 'gave her constant attendance' during her last days; he was one of her executors and her will was in his handwriting.[93]

But the slight awkwardness that this suggests—Sheridan performing a role Swift might more appropriately have played—hints at a distance between the two men which at times lengthened greatly. Swift more than once analysed Sheridan's character and failings in writing. Some of Swift's complaints suggest, as Irvin Ehrenpreis has pointed out, that Sheridan was a model for some features of the Laputan king in *Gulliver's Travels*.[94] After the sermon at Cork, Swift called Sheridan 'a Man of intent and abstracted thinking, enslav'd by Mathematicks, and Complaint of the World'; and Sheridan seems to echo this description when he writes, 'How is Imagination lost in the Reflection, considering the Nature of infinite Space, whose Centre is every where, and Circumference no where.'[95] Swift comments at more length in a letter to Thomas Tickell: 'His Books, his Mathematicks, the Pressure of his Fortunes, his Laborious Calling and some naturall

[92] *Poems*, iii. 1049.

[93] *Corresp.* iii. 156, 221; v. 239–40; BL MS Add. 5017(2), fo. 75; Sheridan the younger, *Life of Swift*, 362 (some details of this account are dubious). The original of Esther Johnson's will was destroyed in the Four Courts explosion of 1922, but a photograph of one page had been printed in a Dublin magazine, *The Lady of the House* (Christmas number, 1908). A transcript of the entire will may be read in W. R. Wilde, *The Closing Years of Dean Swift's Life* (Dublin, 1849), 94–7.

[94] *The Personality of Jonathan Swift* (1958; reissued New York, 1969), 109–15.

[95] *Corresp.* iii. 94; Davi[e]s, *A Poem on the Immortality of the Soul*, p. xxvi.

Disposition or Indisposition give him an egarement d'esprit [mental aberration] as you cannot but observe. But he hath other good Qualityes enough, to make up that Defect[:] Truth, Candor, good Nature, pleasantness of Humor, and very good Learning, and it was upon these Regards I was bold to recommend him, because I thought it was for the generall good that he should have some Encouragement to go on with his Drudgery.'[96]

In 1729 Swift composed a formal rebuke, ironically titled 'The History of the Second Solomon'. The strain in the friendship at this time may offer an explanation for the curious cessation of the *Intelligencer* in 1729. Swift begins at the beginning, complaining that Sheridan lampooned him—in a funeral elegy for Swift's muse—when they had been acquainted only three months. He disparages Sheridan's wife, his Cork sermon, his real estate transactions, and in particular his failure to keep up his property. 'You cannot make him a greater compliment', Swift charges, 'than by telling instances to the company, before his face, how careless he was in any affair that related to his interest and fortune'; 'he values himself thereupon as if it were the mark of a great genius, above little regards or arts, and [maintains] that his thoughts are too exalted to descend into the knowledge of vulgar management'. The indictment continues: Sheridan reacted unreasonably when Swift burlesqued his 'Ballyspellin', he was foolish to print his ode on the Queen's birthday, his head is turned by women, he fails to take advice, and he is stubborn and opinionated. In sum, 'He is a generous, honest, good-natured man; but his perpetual want of judgment and discretion, makes him act as if he were neither generous, honest, nor good-natured.'[97]

In a moment of sufficient detachment, Sheridan would probably have agreed with Swift's harsh assessment. In his 'Essay upon the Immortality of the Soul', he for once attempts to express his sense of frustration in philosophical terms. Without being overtly autobiographical, he catalogues the evils of this world, as part of an argument that a good God must have made 'a State for Man after this':

They who pursue the most rational Delights, of acquiring Knowledge, find it Vanity and Vexation of Spirit. . . . And after all our Labour and Acquirements, What are Languages, Arts and Sciences, but a fantastick Circle, through which the Learned have been running for several Ages, beginning at Ignorance,

---

[96] *Corresp.* iii. 97–8.
[97] *Prose*, v. 222–6; see also Swift's character of Sheridan as Lilly, in *Poems*, iii. 1012–13.

and ending at last in the same Point? This the truly Knowing will confess, while Fools rest contented in their vain Opinions.

· · · · ·

Scarce any one lives for the Present, but is ever impertinently employed about the Past, or Future. And if . . . some external Amusements did not call him abroad, how extreamly wretched would he be by too much Reflection. What a Contradiction is this, that a Man, who loves nothing so much as himself, cannot bear his own silent Conversation! but must gad abroad, or he is miserable. . . . Thus we live in the midst of Anxieties innumerable, with a few flying Pleasures among Legions of real Woes. . . .[98]

Sheridan's argument is standard in such discourses, but its particular congruity with his own life (and the length at which he pursues it —much abbreviated here) suggests that he speaks from experience. His statement of the need for 'external Amusements' explains and sufficiently defends Swift's *Vive la bagatelle*. Swift rightly called Sheridan 'My Viceroy Trifler'.[99] Though they knew the uses of play, their lively sense of the evils and absurdities of existence could emerge in serious works like the *Intelligencer*.

Of Sheridan's original compositions, none demonstrates more clearly than the *Intelligencer* the range of social and political concerns he shared with Swift. Their most ambitious joint enterprise, this periodical develops some ideas which bear crucially upon *A Modest Proposal* (1729). Though the initial plan seems to have been for Swift and Sheridan to alternate, each contributing an essay or poem every other week, both the schedule and the pattern of alternation went somewhat awry; Sheridan wrote nos. 2, 4, 6, 11, 13, 14, 16, 17, and 18. Both Swift and readers in Dublin seem to have recognized Sheridan as 'the Intelligencer', the editor or manager of the periodical.[100]

Sheridan writes on provincial inhospitality in Ireland (2), fashionable gaming (4), the life of the Irish peasantry (6), and the hypocrisy of Jonathan Smedley (11), among other topics. In nos. 2 and 18 he promotes the cult of the Drapier, patriot hero and potential martyr. To Sheridan more than Swift goes the credit for turning the *Intelligencer*'s attention toward Ireland and its problems—not only in his nos. 6, 16, 17, and 18, but also in reprinting their inspiration, Swift's *A Short View of the State of Ireland*, as no. 15. Sheridan's no. 6 is one of the

---

[98] Davi[e]s, *A Poem on the Immortality of the Soul*, pp. xxvi–xxviii.

[99] *Corresp*. iv. 367.

[100] See Appendix E; Swift implies that the *Intelligencer*'s printer, Sarah Harding, would recognize Sheridan as 'the Author of the Intelligencer' (*Corresp*. iii. 308).

more graphic and interesting descriptions we have of the Irish countryside in this period of famine and emigration. He discusses buildings in ruins, people scantily clothed and barefoot, shabby live-stock and produce, 'tattered Families flitting to be shipped off to the *West-Indies*', windows without glass, and inns without signs—or with signs 'taken from their Post to prevent the shaking of the House down by the Wind'. Like Swift, he ridicules the idea that Ireland is a rich nation, and expresses a '*sincere Compassion* for the Natives, who are sunk to the lowest Degree of Misery and Poverty, whose Houses are Dunghills, whose Victuals are the Blood of their Cattle, or the Herbs in the Field; and whose Cloathing to the Dishonor of God and Man is Nakedness'. Sheridan's eighteenth paper foreshadows the *Modest Proposal* by quoting ominously from Fynes Moryson's seventeenth-century account of the English oppression of Ireland: it led to the eating of babies.

Not all Sheridan's *Intelligencers* are so grim. He uses vivacious hudi-brastics to parody Jonathan Smedley's proposals for a Bible commentary he was incompetent to write. Smedley was all the more attractive a target, in that he had recently published *Gulliveriana*, where he attacks Sheridan as well as Swift. Thus, in the twentieth paper, Swift gives Smedley's fatuous lapidary panegyric on himself similar treatment.[101]

During much of the *Intelligencer*'s run Swift was with Sir Arthur and Lady Acheson in Market Hill, while Sheridan was in Dublin: the collaboration did not entail any sustained, intimate consultation. Yet it is reasonable to think that they had worked out a list of promising topics—what Swift called 'hints'.[102] Their essays usually reflect interests that they shared. Both were clergymen whose indiscreet writings impeded their careers; Swift writes to point out that the establishment favours those who are dull and discreet, while those who commit the sin of wit are suppressed (5, 7). Sheridan was devoted to drama;[103] Swift writes on *The Beggar's Opera* and its humour and satire (3). Swift and Sheridan were both interested in polite conversation; Sheridan conveys something of their concerns in his essay on story-telling (13).[104] Richard Tighe had persecuted Sheridan for his

[101] The attribution to Swift is discussed in the introductory note to no. 20.

[102] *Corresp.* iii. 297–8; iv. 30; *Prose*, xii. 306–7; compare Appendix J.

[103] See Sheldon, *Sheridan*, 6–8; and Mayhew, 'Dramatizations', 56–8. (The 'Mr. Sheridan' whom Mayhew identifies, p. 57 n. 21, as Dr Thomas Sheridan is probably rather a professional actor with the same surname.)

[104] See Ann Cline Kelly, 'Swift's *Polite Conversation*: An Eschatological Vision', *Studies in Philology*, 73 (1976), 204–24.

'Sufficient unto the day' sermon; Swift attacks Tighe in *Mad Mullinix and Timothy* (8) and *Tim and the Fables* (10). Sheridan was a schoolmaster who had educated a promising young viscount; Swift in *Intelligencer* 9 is able to praise both Sheridan and Lord Mountcashel while simultaneously casting aspersions on the Irish peerage.[105] Both writers despair over the present state of Ireland: there was a famine; Irish places and preferments were going to Englishmen; young Irishmen could not find employment worthy of their abilities; Great Britain's colonizing tendencies were proceeding apace; and Ireland was more a mock kingdom than ever.

Dates of the Intelligencers

Dating the *Intelligencers* adds significantly to the meagre supply of information we have about Dublin and about these authors at this time. More importantly, it may illuminate contexts that scholarly neglect of the *Intelligencer* has obscured.

Such dating must rest on several facts and inferences. Except for no. 1—labelled '*Saturday May* 11*th*, 1728. To be continued Weekly'— the *Intelligencer* papers at most carried only the year of publication on their title-pages, not the specific date of publication. But other facts of chronology are nevertheless apparent: that no. 10 prints a letter dated 4 July, purporting to reply to no. 8; that no. 19 prints a letter dated 2 December 1728; that no. 20 prints a 'proclamation' dated 7 May 1729; and that with only twenty weekly numbers, the *Intelligencer* was *not* published weekly during its entire year of existence. It can also be regarded as certain that the papers were published in the numbered sequence and that the original undated Dublin numbers were published before the reprints of them in London newspapers.

Further information can be gleaned from a letter of Dr Marmaduke Coghill, judge of the Prerogative Court in Dublin, to Edward Southwell, the Secretary of State for Ireland. He writes on Tuesday, 18 June 1728, from Dublin:

Swift has published a paper to day which I am sorry for, it being to keep up that faction I mentioned to you in my last, & makeing that division amongst us

---

[105] Sheridan had denigrated the Irish peers in his poem *To the Right Honourable the Lord Viscount Mont-Cassel* (Dublin: Harding, 1727; copy: BL). Persius' satires, which he translated and dedicated to Mountcashel, were themselves written against noblemen; thus all these cases stress the contrast between Mountcashel and the peerage as a whole.

that must do us mischeif, those he writes against are too close united allready, & this will make them more so, whereas the happinesse of this country must subsist by the good agreement & harmony amongst us all whether English or Irish protestants, the paper if I can gett itt, I will enclose it[.][106]

This condemnation of polarizing rhetoric almost certainly refers to the *Intelligencer*, since at the moment Swift was publishing nothing else. And of the *Intelligencers* published anywhere near Tuesday, 18 June, only no. 6 is a reasonable candidate, despite its in fact being by Sheridan, since it condemns the colonizing exploitation being practised by English officials in Ireland. (Nos. 4, 5, and 7 contain nothing that should have aroused official concern.) For *Intelligencer* 6 to have been published on a Tuesday suggests either that it was late, that the *Intelligencer* had changed its regular day from Saturday to Tuesday, or that its interval of appearance was only approximately a week—as seems permitted by the absence of a precise date on the pamphlet itself.[107] (To allow for the latter two possibilities, I have put ranges of dates, or the word *about*, into the list below, from no. 6 on.)

Several reasonable assumptions can be brought to bear on these facts. The *Intelligencer* almost certainly never appeared *more* often than weekly. Not only did no. 1 announce itself as a weekly, but Swift remembered the *Intelligencer* as 'a Weekly paper'. Swift and Sheridan appear to have had difficulty in producing material to meet this schedule. As noted earlier, no. 15, a reprint of Swift's *A Short View of the State of Ireland*, was issued 'merely for laziness not to disappoint the town', and in the same letter Swift implied that he and Sheridan had found the routine onerous.[108] Short papers such as Swift's *Tim and the Fables*, the reprints of matter published elsewhere (no. 12, from the *Craftsman*, as well as no. 15), and one or two weak papers by Sheridan all suggest that the writers felt burdened by a schedule they were determined to meet. Further, the rule of periodical publishing, despite doubtless hundreds of instances to the contrary, is to establish a schedule of publication with an audience that expects the periodical at the stated times; editors who value their audiences avoid disappointing them.

---

[106] Huntington MS HM 28675, postmarked 'DUBLIN' and '25 | IV'. In a letter of 5 November, Coghill reminded Southwell that he had previously sent him an *Intelligencer* (Huntington MS HM 28678). On Southwell, see McCracken, 172, 370.

[107] Yet although the *Temple-Oge Intelligencer*, discussed below, appeared without precise dates, in its reprint the author indicates that it appeared regularly on Wednesdays. It is of course possible that Coghill misdated his letter or that he was mistaken about when the pamphlet was published.

[108] *Corresp.* iii. 296; iv. 30.

For the same reasons that the *Intelligencer* probably adhered fairly closely to its weekly schedule, it also probably held interruptions of the schedule to the minimum—that is, I shall argue, to only one before no. 19, with a further hiatus between nos. 19 and 20. Swift himself envisaged an interruption that, in early August, he expected to last 'till the middle of Winter' 1728/9, when he intended to return to Dublin from Market Hill.[109] In September he told Sheridan, who seems to have written once more asking for contributions or ideas for a second series of papers, 'I told you I would think no more of it, neither do I conceive the World deserves so much Trouble from you or me.'[110] Sheridan decided to go ahead without Swift—one reason, probably, that Swift felt Sheridan had 'made but sorry work' of the *Intelligencer*—and it must be remembered that Swift probably wrote this comment while he was estranged from Sheridan in 1729.[111]

It seems likely that the *Intelligencer* was issued in what may conveniently be termed three series—Series 1 beginning with no. 1, Series 2 ending with no. 19, and Series 3 ending abortively (as I shall suggest) after one number. The probable publication dates for nos. 1–19 are most easily deduced by first dating the end of Series 2. It becomes a matter of counting by weeks—forward from 11 May and backward from the end, and then deciding when Series 1 ended and Series 2 began.

Series 2 can be dated once it is recognized that no. 18, Sheridan's paper calling for an enthusiastic celebration of Swift's birthday, was written for publication on or very shortly before his birthday, 30 November, which in 1728 fell on a Saturday. This inference accords with the date of the letter in no. 19: 2 December (a Monday). Most probably, therefore, no. 19 was published not later than the following Saturday, 7 December.[112] No. 18 would not have been published after 30 November, and it can hardly have been published more than a

---

[109] *Corresp.* iii. 296.

[110] *Corresp.* iii. 297; it may be inferred that Sheridan had also solicited contributions from Swift in July; see Swift to Sheridan, 2 Aug. 1728, *Corresp.* iii. 296.

[111] *Corresp.* iii. 314.

[112] A report from Dublin of Tues., 3 Dec., in the *Universal Spectator and Weekly J.* (London, 14 Dec. 1728) may suggest that Swift was anticipated on one or two points he raises in no. 19. It seems possible, however, that the *Universal Spectator* paragraph is a hasty and embroidered report of no. 19—and if so, confirming Tuesday as the *Intelligencer*'s day of publication: 'There's an Account from the Country, that Change for Gold is grown so scarce that Dealers are often forced to give 1 *s. per Pound* for Silver to change; and that it was proposed to cut Moidores through the Crosses in the Middle, into Quarters, and to pass them in Change by Weight at 7 *s.* 6 *d.* as in the Proclamation, giving the current Allowance of 2 *d. per* Grain.'

week before then. To suppose it was published even that early requires supposing also that between nos. 18 and 19 more than a week intervened, which is improbable in itself for the reasons already mentioned. Sheridan's advertisement in no. 18 soliciting Christmas gifts for the printer, Mrs Harding, also implies the latest possible date for no. 18—that is, 30 November—and this dating is particularly plausible since in 1728 the day following 30 November was the first Sunday in Advent. Probable dates of publication for Series 2 are therefore to be found by starting with 30 November for no. 18 and counting back week by week. (The list below expresses the dates as ranges from Tuesday to Saturday, however, on the chance that Coghill's Tuesday might have become the regular day.)[113]

No. 10, if part of Series 2, would have been published in early October. No. 9, however, cannot have been published later than 3 August, the Saturday before it was reprinted in London in *Mist's Weekly Journal*, 10 August 1728. If there were only two weekly sequences, then, no. 9 belongs to the first, since it cannot belong to the second. And if no. 9 was published on schedule, it appeared on 6 July or shortly after. No. 12, reprinting an anti-Walpole poem from the London *Country Journal: or, The Craftsman* of 3 August, cannot have been published earlier than that, and, allowing for time in the post, it cannot have been published in Dublin until about a week later, at the earliest. It follows that if there were only two sequences, no. 12 must be a member of the second, and that the gap between the sequences must have come somewhere after no. 9 and before no. 12.

No. 12 would not have opened the new series. As a reprint of a poem from London, it is pretty clearly filler material, and there would have been no point in beginning a series with a filler. No. 11, Sheridan's parody of Smedley, would therefore also belong to the second series and would have been published 12 October or shortly before. This satire on Smedley may well have been a retaliation against Smedley's *Gulliveriana*, published in London 13 August.[114] It attacked Swift, Pope, and even Sheridan. This would explain why Sheridan reached back to burlesque a newspaper essay several months old.[115]

Tim and the Fables, no. 10, if in the first series, would have appeared

---

[113] It also seems possible that the *Temple-Oge Intelligencer*, published on Wednesdays, may have imitated the *Intelligencer* in day of appearance as well as in its title.

[114] Advertisement, 'This Day is Published . . .', *Daily Journal*, 13 Aug. 1728.

[115] Though *Gulliveriana* was published anonymously, I presume that word of Smedley's role as compiler would have travelled.

in mid-July; if in the second, early October. It is a sequel to *Mad Mul-linix*, no. 8, and its prefatory letter dated 4 July suggests publication not long thereafter, though the evidence here, as with no. 11, is not as strong as might be wished.

Swift was away from Dublin from about June 1728 until about February 1728/9. If we assume, as I think we must, that in his absence the *Intelligencer* was managed entirely by Sheridan, and that in Sheridan's own absence from Dublin it would not have appeared at all, we are led to essentially the schedule already described. Swift tells us that Sheridan was away from Dublin for forty days, presumably beginning in mid-July, and that his school was on holiday during September.[116] Sometime during this interval, he was at Ballyspellan spa, writing his Ballyspellan ballad.[117] He had been away from his school so much that he found it necessary in September to publish a newspaper advertisement insisting that he had not given it up.[118]

The extant evidence, then, confirms that the *Intelligencer* was published in two series, nos. 1–10 running from mid-May until mid-July, and nos. 11–19 running from mid-October until early December.[119] The August–September break was, of course, quite in keeping with established vacation patterns, and during its own vacation the *Intelligencer* was in effect given a rather frivolous and doubtless unauthorized summer replacement in the *Temple-Oge Intelligencer*, Templeogue being a popular spa just south of Dublin. The *Temple-Oge Intelligencer* was written by John Browne of the Neale and appeared on seven consecutive Wednesdays from 7 August to 18 September, with the *Intelligencer* itself resuming about three weeks later.[120]

Though no. 19 terminates the second series, it gives no sign of having been meant as an ending, even though it brought Sheridan reasonably near the end of the year and up to an interval of vacation. He had managed to get through the second series without much help

---

[116] *Corresp.* iii. 296–7. See also *Corresp.* ed. Ball, iv. 41 n.

[117] *Poems*, ii. 437–40.   [118] *Dublin Intelligence*, 14 Sept. 1728.

[119] The July–Oct. period was also a slack season for printing and publishing in London, and for similar reasons: those who could left town for the country.

[120] Some original issues of the *Temple-Oge Intelligencer* can be found at the Royal Irish Academy and at Trinity College, Dublin; it was reissued in *The Lucubrations of Sallmanazor Histrum, Esq;* (Dublin: Powell, 1730; copy: NLI). Here it is also described as the *Plain Dealer's Intelligencer*, the *Plain Dealer* being a single-essay periodical Browne published in 1729 and 1730. On Browne, perhaps erroneously called 'Sir' John Browne, see the headnote and notes to no. 15.

from Swift, though the series is centred in Swift and his concerns, particularly those about Ireland. At this time Swift seems to have been blissfully happy at Market Hill, and his writing there was largely for Lady Acheson, not for the *Intelligencer*.[121] When Swift at last wrote a Market Hill poem he wanted to publish, *The Journal of a Dublin* [or *Modern*] *Lady*, he sent it to Sarah Harding for the *Intelligencer*, unaware that the *Intelligencer* had suspended publication. Mrs Harding published the poem separately in late January or early February 1728/9, mentioning in her colophon that at her shop 'Gentlemen may be furnished with the *Intelligencer*, from No 1, to No 19.'[122]

She had made no such announcement before, and it has an air of finality. On 6 March 1728/9 Swift described the *Intelligencer* as having been dropped.[123]

Subsequently, Swift and Sheridan apparently changed their minds and planned a third series of the *Intelligencer*. Holograph leaves of Swift's unused hints for *Intelligencers* survive in the John Rylands University Library of Manchester.[124] One hint refers to an event that took place in March of 1728/9.[125] Thus this leaf of hints was written out after no. 19 and probably before no. 20. The twentieth paper itself seems to expect further *Intelligencers*; its 'proclamation' invites communications from readers (though curiously the imprint fails to give an address) and promises retaliation if Irish dunces persist in writing. Except for Swift's remarks already quoted, we have no obvious explanation for the failure of Series 3 to develop: his exasperation with Sheridan, expressed about this time in 'The History of the Second Solomon', may hold a clue.[126] To judge from the number of surviving copies, the sale for no. 20 was about the same as the typical sale for Series 2.

Probable dates for the twenty *Intelligencers* can be conveniently summarized in a list:

---

[121] *Corresp.* iii. 297.
[122] Swift to John Worrall, 13 Jan. 1728/9, *Corresp.* iii. 308; for date of publication, see Foxon S863.
[123] *Corresp.* iii. 314. In 1732 he put a different construction on the project's cessation: *Corresp.* iv. 30.
[124] Appendix J(b).
[125] See introduction to Appendix J, esp. n. 5.
[126] *Prose*, v. 222–6. Deane Swift, who first published the 'History' in 1765, said it was written in 1729: Swift, *Works*, viii, pt. 1 (London: Johnson, 1765), 250; T–S 87, p. 86.

DATES OF THE INTELLIGENCERS

[Series 1]

1. Saturday, 11 May 1728, on the evidence of the title-page. By Swift.

2. Probably Saturday, 18 May. Not earlier than that; not later than about Tuesday, 21 May, a week before the latest date for no. 3. By Sheridan.

3. Probably Saturday, 25 May. Not earlier than that; not later than about Tuesday, 28 May, a week before the latest date for no. 4. By Swift.

4. Probably Saturday, 1 June. Not earlier than that; not later than about Tuesday, 4 June, a week before the latest date for no. 5. By Sheridan.

5. Probably Saturday, 8 June. Not earlier than that; not later than about Tuesday, 11 June, a week before the date for no. 6. By Swift.

6. Tuesday, 18 June, inferred from Marmaduke Coghill to Edward Southwell, 18 June 1728. By Sheridan.

7. Probably 22–5 June. Not earlier than Saturday, 22 June; not later than about Thursday, 27 June, a week before the latest date for no. 8. By Swift.

8. *Mad Mullinix and Timothy.* Probably 29 June–2 July. Not earlier than Saturday, 29 June; not later than 4 July, the date of the reply in no. 10. By Swift, with Sheridan's introduction.

9. Probably 6–9 July. Not earlier than Saturday, 6 July; not later than about 3 August, the Saturday before it was reprinted in London in *Mist's Weekly Journal*, 10 August 1728. By Swift.

10. *Tim and the Fables.* Probably 13–16 July. Not earlier than Saturday, 13 July; not later than 5 October, one week before the latest date for no. 11. The prefatory letter dated 4 July suggests publication not long thereafter. By Swift, with Sheridan's introduction and concluding quatrain.

[Series 2]

11. Probably 8–12 October. Not later than Saturday, 12 October; not earlier than 20 July, a week after the earliest date for no. 10. By Sheridan.

12. *The Progress of Patriotism. A Tale.* Probably 15–19 October. Not later

than Saturday, 19 October; not earlier than about 10 August, the first Saturday after the publication of the London *Country Journal* of 3 August, from which it reprints. Unknown author; Sheridan's introduction.

13. Probably 22–6 October. Not later than Saturday, 26 October; not earlier than about 17 August, a week after the earliest date for no. 12. By Sheridan.

14. Probably 29 October–2 November. Not later than Saturday, 2 November; not earlier than about 24 August, a week after the earliest date for no. 13. By Sheridan.

15. *A Short View of the State of Ireland.* Probably 5–9 November. Not later than Saturday, 9 November; not earlier than about 31 August, a week after the earliest date for no. 14. Swift's pamphlet reprinted with Sheridan's introduction.

16. Probably 12–16 November. Not later than Saturday, 16 November; not earlier than about 7 September, a week after the earliest date for no. 15. By Sheridan.

17. Probably 19–23 November. Not later than Saturday, 23 November; not earlier than about 14 September, a week after the earliest date for no. 16. By Sheridan.

18. Probably 26–30 November. Not later than Saturday, 30 November, Swift's birthday; not earlier than about 21 September, a week later than the earliest date for no. 17. By Sheridan.

19. Probably 3–7 December 1728. Not earlier than 2 December, when the letter it publishes is dated; not later than 28 December 1728, when a spurious *Intelligencer XX* was published in Dublin (see Appendix H). By Swift.

[Series 3]

20. *Dean Smedley Gone to Seek His Fortune.* Perhaps Saturday, 10 May 1729. After Wednesday, 7 May, when the 'proclamation' is dated, and before Tuesday, 20 May, since the dunces are presumed to have heard the 'proclamation' before then. By Swift.

A Note on the Annotation

I have tried, using contemporary sources where I could, to identify persons, things, places, or works named, quoted, or alluded to, to gloss words not presently in general use, and to recover contexts that would have been familiar to the *Intelligencer*'s original Dublin readers. Where events were changing rapidly, I have tried not to annotate using later materials. My first effort has been to show what Swift and Sheridan knew when they wrote the *Intelligencers* and what their readers would have known as they read them in 1728. A case in point would be that I do not use the extensive printed and manuscript discussion of Irish emigration in 1729 to annotate the *Intelligencer*'s references to it in 1728, nor do I generally use Prior's *A List of the Absentees of Ireland* (1729) to annotate the *Intelligencer*'s references to absenteeism in 1728.

In citing pre-1801 printed sources, I have included the name of the printer or bookseller, since such information can be meaningful to specialists. For printed sources believed to survive in only one or two copies, I have given the location of the copy consulted.

The notes are designed to meet the needs of a variety of readers, specialist and non-specialist. Notes are, as Samuel Johnson remarked, 'necessary evils', and where they are more evil than necessary, the arrangement of this volume permits the reader to disregard them.

Textual Introduction

To print and publish their new periodical Swift and Sheridan chose Sarah Harding, a Dublin pamphlet printer distinguished neither for typography nor for business success. But she was the widow of John Harding, a newspaper printer who had printed the Drapier's Letters. They had both been imprisoned for printing the fourth Drapier's Letter, *A Letter to the Whole People of Ireland* (1724).[1]

John had died in 1725, before the Wood's halfpence controversy was resolved.[2] That he died while in prison is an oft-repeated claim[3] that I have failed to substantiate, though it seems to have originated in John T. Gilbert's *History of the City of Dublin*. He quotes a halfsheet poem, *A Poem to the Whole People of Ireland, Relating to M. B. Drapier, by A. R. Hosier*, seeking charitable donations for Sarah Harding, John's 'poor Widow . . . who, by the Death of her Husband, is reduc'd to a helpless Condition; but might, by a small assistance, from each well-wisher of *Ireland*, be enable to Dye [drapers need dyers, i.e., printers] again for her Country's Service, if it shou'd ever be in Need.'[4] The poem includes these lines:

> To hearten him, the DRAPIER sent to him in Jail,
>   To tell him, he'd quickly get home to his Wife;
> But, scarce cou'd he find one, to stand for his *Bail*,
>   Which struck to his Heart, and depriv'd him of Life.
>
> He left with his Widow, two Children behind,
>   And little, God help her, to keep them from Starving;
> But hoped, for the DRAPIER's Sake friends she wou'd find,
>   Or, for his own merit, they'd think her deserving.
>
> But, alas, She's forgot! there's not one among all,
>   That ever thinks on her, or, her Childrens Case,
> Tho' her Husband helped to hinder their Fall,
>   And she suffer'd by it much shame, and Disgrace.

'Scarce cou'd he find one, to stand for his *Bail*' implies, I think, that he *did* find one; and indeed Swift himself implies that he was released.[5]

---

[1] *Drapier's Letters*, 99, 201. [2] *Corresp.* iii. 93.
[3] Most recently by Ehrenpreis, iii. 308.
[4] Gilbert, *Dublin*, i. 59–60. The halfsheet imprint is [Dublin]: Elizabeth Sadleir, 1726; TCD Press A.7.4/47. The poem is here quoted from the halfsheet.
[5] *Drapier's Letters*, 99–100; 289.

But in any case he was viewed as a martyr for the Drapier's cause. Had the Wood's halfpence controversy continued, Sarah would have continued printing for the Drapier.[6] That her suffering for his cause continued to be a mark of distinction is suggested by the advertisement following *Intelligencer* 18.

Sarah Harding was arrested for printing *On Wisdom's Defeat in a Learned Debate* (1725), which Swift may have written;[7] she issued Swift's *A Short View of the State of Ireland* and *An Answer to a Paper, Called A Memorial* in 1728 and *The Journal of a Dublin Lady* and *A Modest Proposal* in 1729. For Sheridan she published, among other pieces, *To the Right Honourable the Lord Viscount Mont-Cassel* in 1727. She was active as a printer only from 1725 to 1729, and during this period her total output was small.[8] It was typically badly printed in small octavo halfsheets using ancient battered type and ornaments (see Fig. 1).

It might be supposed that the *Intelligencer* was deliberately sent into the world in shabby guise—that the authors were masquerading, like Swift as the Drapier. What argues against this supposition is the relatively careful typography of the first edition of no. 1, with a split title-page layout that took some trouble to produce, running heads, spacing between paragraphs, and the first word of each paragraph raised to all caps.[9] Subsequent numbers and editions did not attempt such niceties, but I assume the first more nearly reflects authorial intentions and that relaxed standards later were tolerated. This is not to say that the authors were ever greatly concerned about typography or that Mrs Harding's printing was the worst that Dublin could produce. In fact, the *Intelligencers* for all their shabbiness are within the normal range of contemporary Dublin ephemeral printing. For book printing, Sheridan turned elsewhere—most recently to George Grierson, who produced his translation of

[6] *Corresp.* iii. 93.

[7] Ehrenpreis believes he did (iii. 314–16); see also *Drapier's Letters*, lxvi; *Poems*, iii. 1117–18; Swift, *Poetical Works*, ed. Herbert Davis (London, 1967), p. xiv (one 'of the more likely Attributions'); Rogers, 751.

[8] During her husband's lifetime she published over her own name when he was imprisoned, e.g., *The Present Miserable State of Ireland* (London Printed: And Re-printed in Dublin by Sarah Harding in Molesworth's-Court in Fishamble Street, 1721; T–S 1583, p. 310). She may, after his death, have worked for others; her ornaments appear in some imprints of William Wilmot, who died in 1727; for Wilmot, see H. R. Plomer, G. H. Bushnell, and E. R. McC. Dix, *A Dictionary of the Printers and Booksellers Who Were at Work in England, Scotland and Ireland from 1726 to 1775* (Oxford, 1932), 407.

[9] For the title-page see the photograph in *Prose*, vol. xii, facing p. 29, showing the NLI copy.

The *Intelligencer*.

 HERE is no *Talent* so useful towards rising in the World, or which puts Men more out of the rech of Fortune, than that Quality generally possessed by the Dullest sort of People, and is in common Speech, called *Discretion*, a species of lower Prudence, by the assistance of which, People of the meanest Intellectuals, without any other Qualification, pass through the World in great Tranquility, and with Universal good Treatment, neither giving nor taking Offence. *Courts* are seldom unprovided of Persons under this Character, on whom, if they happen to be of greatQuality, most Employments, even the gratial naturally fall, when Competitors will not agree ; and in such Promotions, no Body rejoyces or grieves. The Truth of this I could prove by several Instances, within my own Memory (for I say nothing of present Times.)

And indeed as Regularity and Forms are of great use in carrying on the Business of the World, so it is very convenient, that Persons endued with this kind of Discretion, should

Fig. 1. *Intelligencer* 5, p. 3, from the Rothschild *28b* copy.

Persius in 1728.[10] I think that because of Mrs Harding's background, political affiliation, loyalty, and known association with them, Swift and Sheridan wanted to give the *Intelligencer* to her and believed her work would be adequate. She could not have printed a book—so far as I know, she never attempted it—but the *Intelligencer* seemed within her abilities.

The *Intelligencer* was her biggest single project. Her address during most of its run—that is, during 1728—was 'next Door to the *Crown* in *Copper-Alley*'.[11] In *A Modest Proposal*, published in October 1729, the imprint gives her address as 'opposite the *Hand and Pen* near *Fishamble-Street*, on the *Blind Key*'. After *A Modest Proposal* she drops from sight, and George Faulkner becomes Swift's regular printer. Barry Slepian has surmised that Swift made the change because she died.[12] A contemporary halfsheet suggests rather that she married another printer, Nicholas Hussey.[13] The new alliance seems to have formed early in 1729, before *Intelligencer* 20 was published—which may explain why it carries no imprint. She was in Copper Alley at least as late as February, publishing there the first edition of *The Journal of a Dublin Lady*. The second edition, however, identifies itself as 'Re-printed by Nicholas Hussey on the Blind-Key'. In other imprints the address is given more fully as 'Opposite the Hand and Pen on the Blind-Key'. This is, of course, the address Harding gives for herself in *A Modest Proposal*. Swift may have wanted the Harding name on its title-page as a sign of his authorship, and indeed the imprint of a London edition of *A Modest Proposal* mentioned her, suggesting that her name carried significance.[14] Both *Intelligencer* 20 and *A Modest Proposal* diverge somewhat in their typographical style from the manner of earlier Harding printing such as the *Intelligencer*, suggesting

[10] In 1726 Swift had co-operated with John Hyde's Dublin edition of *Gulliver's Travels*; see David Woolley, 'Swift's Copy of *Gulliver's Travels*: The Armagh *Gulliver*, Hyde's Edition, and Swift's Earliest Corrections', in C. T. Probyn (ed.), *The Art of Jonathan Swift* (London, 1978), 141–4, 148.

[11] This was—is—a narrow walkway just north of the Castle. She had used the address 'on the Blind-Key' in 1725—e.g., in *On Wisdom's Defeat* and in ?Sheridan's *To the Honourable Mr. D. T.* (Foxon T373).

[12] 'When Swift First Employed George Faulkner', *Papers Bibl. Soc. Am.* 56 (1962), 354–6.

[13] *A Hue and Cry after the Letter to the Lord-Mayor of the City of Dublin* (Dublin: E. Waters, 1729) reprints *A Letter from a Country Gentleman, to the Honourable the Lord-Mayor of the City of Dublin* with this note: 'N. B. *That I have taken the above scurvy Letter, exactly from Mrs. Hussey, alias Harding's Print.*' BL C.121.g.8 (171).

[14] Dublin, Printed by S. Harding: London, Re-printed; and sold by J. Roberts in Warwick-lane, and the Pamphlet-Shops (T–S 677, p. 337); it is highly unusual for London reprinters to mention the name of the original printer.

a different shop and different printers. Like *Intelligencer* 20, Sheridan's *Ode to be Performed at the Castle of Dublin, March the 1st, 1728–9. Being the Birth-Day of . . . Queen Caroline* names no printer in its imprint, but its tailpiece is the Harding cock, familiar from John Harding's earlier printing (Fig. 2). This, too, was probably produced in the new Hussey–Harding shop. Hussey's signed output sometimes uses Harding ornaments and what would seem to be Harding type.[15] It may be that Sarah fades from the bibliographical scene in 1729 because she had become Mrs Hussey, and it may be also that Swift felt freer to turn to Faulkner, as he did in 1730, knowing that she was no longer alone.

Very little more can be known about Sarah Harding,[16] then, than that, recommended by her suffering, she was chosen to print the *Intelligencer*. Her original printings, rare today, offer the best text of it, despite their occasional corruption.

In the case of Sheridan's *Intelligencers*, only her original pamphlet editions have authority. For Swift's contributions, the Harding editions are, I believe, the best texts, though certainly not the only authoritative ones.

Faulkner's edition of Swift's *Works* (Dublin, 1735) was produced with Swift's co-operation, and many of its variants must result from authorial intervention. Directly or indirectly, Faulkner had access to Swift's marked copies of his works, such as the copy of the 1732 *Miscellanies* now in the Rothschild Collection at Trinity College, Cambridge. But probably most of Faulkner's new readings developed during the sessions he describes, in which he would read copy aloud to Swift.[17] I cannot believe that under such circumstances Swift gave any significant attention to capitalization and spelling, though I assume he advised Faulkner about pause, emphasis, and insinuation, and that this advice is reflected in Faulkner's punctuation, italics, and small caps.[18]

For the *Intelligencer* Faulkner goes when he can to the 1732 *Miscellanies* (*32*), and that text in turn derives from the 1729 Bowyer–Davis

[15] e.g., Joseph Trapp, *Sermon Preach'd before the Rt. Honourable the Lord Mayor and Aldermen of the City of London . . . January 30, 1729* (Dublin: Hussey, 1729/30); copy: BL 1606/79.

[16] I have, of course, not attempted to provide a complete list of her printing.

[17] *Prose*, xiii. 202.

[18] For observations about Faulkner's text as a source of information about Swift's pauses and emphases, I am indebted to A. C. Elias's unpublished paper, 'George Faulkner and the Sanctity of Swift's Texts'. See also Phyllis J. Guskin, 'Intentional Accidentals: Typography and Audience in Swift's *Drapier's Letters*', *Eighteenth-Cent. Life*, 6 (1980), 80–101.

edition of the *Intelligencer* (*29*). By acquiescing in Faulkner's use of *32*, Swift has imputed a certain authority to *29* and *32*, though they lack it in themselves. In a very few cases, it seems likely that the 1730 Bowyer–Davis edition and the 1732 *Miscellanies* incorporate authorial alterations.[19]

The present edition rests on the original Harding periodical pamphlets. It aims to reconstruct the text as it was intended to appear in those printings. One result of Mrs Harding's generally untidy presswork, however, is that marks of punctuation and other small pieces of type sometimes fail to print or else print very faintly. Where there is space for the missing character, and where I have seen it in other copies, I have not considered its lack in a particular copy to be a variant. The hundreds of such instances mean that there can never be a satisfactory facsimile of the original *Intelligencer* and suggest more immediately that no single copy of a Harding edition is likely to conform in every last comma with the text as here presented.

I have accepted later readings, where authorial, if they correct an error but not if they embody revisions and second thoughts. The *Intelligencer* papers, like most of Swift's work, are animated by topical and occasional concerns. These essays and poems are at their liveliest and best in their earliest form, responding directly to the contexts which engendered them. The Faulkner revisions sometimes blur the original controversy, and at other times they are deaf to the original wit or cadence.

The capitalization may seem chaotic to the reader familiar with the period's dominant style, in which all nouns are capitalized. The Harding editions use (not quite systematically) a different system, in which capitals reflect emphasis or parallelism rather than parsing. This system, endorsed by John White, is explained by James Greenwood: '*Emphasis* ... is usually express'd by putting such Kind of Words into another Character, as the *Italick*, &c. Some do also express it by beginning the Word with a *Capital* or great Letter: Wherefore for the better keeping up the Use of *Distinction Emphatical*, one ought not promiscuously to write every *Noun* with a great *Letter*, as is the Fashion of some now adaies.' Similarly, Thomas Tuite says, 'Any word shou'd begin with a capital letter, when there's a force, emphasis, or considerable stress of the author's sense laid on it.' He adds, ''Tis no more common than wrong, and unnecessary, among *English*

---

[19] See, for example, the variants for no. 5.

printers, to begin every substantive with a capital letter; because it hinders that expressive beauty, and remarkable distinction intended by a capital.'[20]

Punctuation is not necessarily used to mark grammatical units, as is common today, but rather to signal the length of pause if the text were being read aloud—the comma marking the shortest pause, the period the longest.[21] Illogical commas, such as those between subject and verb, often mark an emphatic pause and thus convey meaning.

Many seemingly misspelled words use spellings that were old-fashioned in 1728: collonel, heroe, houshold, interfaring (= *interfering*), intreigue, litle, mony, nit (= *knit*), oportunity, suddainly, etc. I have not emended a spelling for which the *OED* offers a seventeenth-century witness; and I have let stand a few otherwise unattested spellings which seem to offer phonetic evidence, e.g. filsh (= *filch*).

Even though such capitalization, punctuation, and spelling can be seen in Swift's and Sheridan's manuscripts, one cannot assert that Harding's accidentals *are* Swift's and Sheridan's. It is likely that Swift's papers were copied by an 'unknown hand' before being sent to the printer, as were the Drapier's Letters and as he ordered done with *The Journal of a Dublin Lady*, intended for the *Intelligencer*.[22] Moreover, the accuracy of Harding's typesetting, where it can be judged, does not achieve literal perfection.[23]

Nor do Swift and Sheridan—in stark contrast to Pope—seem to

[20] White, *The Country-Man's Conductor in Reading and Writing True English* (Exeter: Farley, 1701), 3; Greenwood, *An Essay towards a Practical English Grammar* (London: Tookey, 1711), 226–7; Tuite, *The Oxford Spelling-Book; Being a Complete Introduction to English Orthography* (London: Hazard, 1726), 6–7. On the history of capitalization in 17th- and 18th-cent. English texts, see D. F. Foxon, 'Pope & the Early Eighteenth-Century Book-Trade' (typescript, 1975), BL Dept. of Printed Books X.902/2958), chs. 4–6. See also Guskin, 'Intentional Accidentals'.

[21] On this system of punctuation see J. Jones, MD, *Practical Phonography* (London: Smith, 1701), 141–2; and [?Charles Gildon and John Brightland], *A Grammar of the English Tongue* (London: Brightland, 1711), 149–50.

[22] *Drapier's Letters*, 99; *Corresp.* iii. 308; compare iv. 82.

[23] Nos. 11, 12, 15, and 20 transcribe printed sources; see the recorded variant readings for an indication of the divergence. The changes made in transcribing her own printing of *A Short View* (no. 15) seem particularly instructive and may reflect the habits of different compositors, a possibility I have not attempted to explore. I have also examined her printing of Richard Savage's *The Bastard: A Poem* (1728; copy: RIA), which agrees in nearly every case with the other Dublin edition (Printed by S. Powell, for T. Benson and P. Crampton, 1728) against the original London edition (see Foxon S90–6). Assuming that the Harding and Powell printings do not derive from an intermediate printing unknown to Foxon, I infer that the Harding is printed from the Powell. Her accuracy is generally excellent, certainly excellent compared to Powell's, but she does allow two or three unintelligent miscopyings to stand.

have had clear expectations about the style the printer would apply in setting from manuscript.[24] They do not seem to have read proof carefully (though Swift did complain once about mistakes).[25] Even so, the evidence would suggest that the accidentals are accurate in the vast majority of cases and that the Harding printings are as close as we can come to Swift's and Sheridan's manuscripts. It is difficult not to conclude that the Harding printings are very substantially what their authors intended. At all events, the accidentals convey emphasis and therefore meaning (in contrast to a more regular system of capitalizing nouns, which merely conveys grammatical knowledge), and even if it is the meaning of a contemporary copyist or compositor, it deserves preservation for the reader who wishes to understand the *Intelligencer* in its original context. The reader who would like to consult Faulkner's text of Swift's *Intelligencers* can do so in *Prose*, xii.

The lists of variant readings include all emendations from the copytext. They also include all accidentals and substantives from the variant Harding printings, where they exist, since there is some possibility in these cases that one of the authors made the change. (Typographical errors that make obvious nonsense are not generally recorded.) But for all later editions, I record substantive variants only, and these only in texts with any likelihood of having received Swift's own attention: Faulkner's editions of 1735 and 1738 (an octavo and a duodecimo in both years). I record variants in the same way for the texts upon which Faulkner's edition may rest—the 1729 *Intelligencer* and the 1732 *Miscellanies* (the latter text in several editions)—and for the 1730 *Intelligencer* because some few of its readings seem authorial. At a minimum, the variants sometimes have interest as emendations proposed by a reader of the time—a compositor or press corrector. I have occasionally included a selection of substantive variants from other texts where these have seemed especially interesting.

Not-quite-substantive variants have been recorded where (in the editor's arbitrary judgement) italics, small caps, capitals, or marks of punctuation signal tone or emphasis (as where the pointing marks an emphatic pause), where spelling indicates a difference in pronunciation (except for verbs in *-ed/-'d*), and, for verse, where punctuation makes a significant difference in rhythm or caesura. All variants in proper names and in blank-filling are recorded.

Ambiguous end-line hyphenation in the copy-text is listed among

---

[24] Foxon, 'Pope & the Early Eighteenth-Century Book-Trade', chs. 4–6.
[25] *Corresp.* iii. 308.

the variants. Typesetting for the present edition has introduced no new word-breaks: any end-line hyphens come from the copy-text.

There is no reason to believe that any manuscript survived to enter the textual history at a late stage; and there is little reason to suspect authorial or editorial care at *any* stage, aside from Pope's not always careful intervention in *32*.

For the Harding printings, I have collated every copy known to me. For the later editions, I have collated at least two copies of each.[26] This comparison has led to the discovery that there are, particularly among the earlier numbers of the *Intelligencer*, numerous impressions. There are three distinct editions of no. 3 and a second, corrected impression of no. 6. It would appear that Mrs Harding found it desirable to print small batches, perhaps because she was too poor to buy paper in large quantities.[27] She often left the text type standing but removed the ornaments and display type for use in other jobs. Her impression size may have been smaller than the standard minimum of 250, given poverty and probable inefficiency.[28]

The precise Harding impression used as copy-text is specified in the textual notes to the individual numbers.

Where textual corruption required emending, I have often accepted an emendation made in early collected editions of the *Intelligencer*, the *Miscellanies*, or Swift's *Works*.

---

[26] I have used proof-read photocopies and Copyflo reproductions along with, at various times, the Hinman Collating Machine, the Lindstrand Comparator, and the British Library comparator. The two latter devices accommodate reproductions larger or smaller than actual size, as 'actual-size' reproductions from microfilm very often are. I am indebted to Philip Gaskell for facilitating the comparison of copies in Trinity College, Cambridge and the University Library, Cambridge.

[27] Examination of watermarks reveals that Mrs Harding sometimes used more than one kind of paper in a given impression. TCD has a 12° copy of no. 17—that is, with horizontal chain lines; it may be the third of a 12° sheet partly used in another job. These details suggest that she was printing on leftovers. If paper expense was a problem, it may have been a factor in the *Intelligencer*'s downfall toward the end. Most numbers were half sheets, but nos. 9, 11, 13, 14, 15, and 19 occupied full sheets. I do not know whether the usual $\frac{1}{2}d$. price was doubled for full-sheet numbers or whether—as often seems to have happened with Dublin printing—costs were partly subsidized by the authors.

[28] This 'standard' figure is taken from the average number of subscribers required in eighteen Dublin subscription proposals: 'Half called for 200 subscribers each, while the lowest number demanded was 150 and the highest 500, averaging 250 for the eighteen works.' I am greatly indebted to M. Pollard for this information from her unpublished paper 'Publishing and the Supply of Books in Eighteenth Century Dublin'. For other evidence of such very small editions in 18th-cent. Dublin publishing, see James W. Phillips, 'A Bibliographical Enquiry into Printing and Bookselling in Dublin from 1670 to 1800', Ph.D. thesis (TCD, 1952), 449–51.

THE INTELLIGENCER

In this introductory essay Swift outlines the plan 'to *Inform*, or *Divert*, or *Correct*, or *Vex* the Town'. The 'Town' (Dublin) emphasis is carried out in subsequent numbers—in the attack on Abel Ram, a Dublin banker (no. 2), in the discussion of *The Beggar's Opera*, then being performed in Dublin (no. 3), in the indictment of fashionable gambling (no. 4), in the lampoon on Richard Tighe (no. 8), and in the coffee-house reaction to it (no. 10), in the passing references to Trinity College in nos. 9 and 17, in the attacks on Smedley, who had until recently been a Dublin wit (nos. 11 and 20), and in the praise of the Drapier (nos. 15 and 18). With Sheridan's nos. 6, 16, 17, and 18, and Swift's no. 19, the *Intelligencer* turns its attention more toward Ireland at large, as was natural since both writers travelled into the country in mid-1728.

'*Facts*, *Passages*, and *Adventures*' do, as claimed, make up a large part of the *Intelligencer*, and the emphasis, as claimed, is on '*Folly* and *Vice*'. The promise is to report virtuous acts seldom, since there are few to report: 'the *Readers* of these *Papers*, need not be in pain of being over-charged, with so dull and ungrateful a Subject.' But Sheridan's no. 18, on Swift, deals with acts of virtue.

The claim that the *Intelligencer*'s intelligence comes from 'a *Society* lately established' to gather it is, of course, a fiction, but Swift and Sheridan may not have been alone in planning the periodical: 'Two or three of us had a fancy . . . to write a Weekly paper, and call it an Intelligencer' (*Corresp.* iv. 30). It is unlikely, however, that the *Intelligencer* had been planned in detail at the time Swift wrote no. 1, though Swift and Sheridan probably had generally agreed upon its emphases and methods.

NUMB. I.

For *Saturday May* 11*th*, 1728.
To be continued Weekly.

I T may be said, without offence to other *Cities*, of much greater consequence in the World, that our Town of *Dublin* doth not want it's due proportion of *Folly*, and *Vice*, both Native and Imported; And as to those Imported, we have the advantage to receive them last, and consequently after our happy manner to improve, and 5 refine upon them.

But, because there are many Effects of *Folly* and *Vice* among us, whereof some are *general*, others confined to smaller Numbers, and others again, perhaps to a few *individuals*; There is a *Society* lately

10 established, who at great expence, have Erected an *Office of Intelligence*,
from which they are to receive Weekly Information of all *Important
Events* and *Singularities*, which this famous *Metropolis* can furnish.
Strict injunctions are given to have the truest Information: In order to
which, certain qualified Persons are employed to attend upon Duty in
15 their several Posts; some at the *Play-house*, others in *Churches*, some at
Balls, *Assemblees*, *Coffee-houses*, and *meetings* for *Quadrille*; some at the
several *Courts of Justice*, both *Spiritual* and *Temporal*, some at the
College, some upon my *Lord Mayor* and *Aldermen* in their publick
Affairs; lastly, some to converse with *favourite Chamber-maids*, and to
20 frequent those *Ale-houses*, and *Brandy-Shops*, where the *Footmen* of
great Families meet in a Morning; only the *Barracks* and *Parliament-
house* are excepted; because we have yet found no *enfans perdus* bold
enough to venture their Persons at either. Out of these and some other
Store-houses, we hope to gather Materials enough to *Inform*, or *Divert*,
25 or *Correct*, or *Vex* the Town.

But as *Facts*, *Passages*, and *Adventures* of all kinds, are like to have
the greatest share in our *Paper*, whereof we cannot always Answer for
the Truth; due Care shall be taken to have them applyed to feigned
Names, whereby all just Offence will be removed; for if none be guilty,
30 none will have cause to Blush or be Angry; if otherwise, then the guilty
Person is safe for the future upon his *present* Amendment, and safe for
the *present*, from all but his *own Conscience*.

There is another Resolution taken among us, which I fear will give a
greater and more general discontent, and is of so singular a Nature,
35 that I have hardly confidence enough to mention it, although it be
absolutely Necessary by way of Apology, for *so bold and unpopular an
Attempt*. But so it is, that we have taken a desperate Counsel to
produce into the World every distinguished Action, either of *Justice*,
Prudence, *Generosity*, *Charity*, *Friendship*, or *publick Spirit*, which comes
40 well attested to us. And although we shall neither here be so daring as
to Assign Names, yet we shall hardly forbear to give some hints, that
perhaps to the great displeasure of such deserving Persons may
endanger a Discovery. For we think that even *Virtue it self*, should
submit to such a *Mortification*, as by it's *visibility* and *example*, will
45 render it more useful to the World. But however, the *Readers* of these
Papers, need not be in pain of being over-charged, with so dull and
ungrateful a Subject. And yet who knows, but such an occasion may be
offered to us, once in a Year or two, after we shall have settled a
Correspondence round the *Kingdom*.

But after all our boasts of *Materials*, sent us by our several 50
Emissaries, we may probably soon fall short, if the Town will not be
pleased to lend us further Assistance towards entertaining it self. The
World best knows it's own *Faults* and *Virtues*, and whatever is sent
shall be faithfully returned back, only a little Embellished according to
the Custom of AUTHORS. We do therefore *Demand* and *Expect* 55
continual *Advertisements* in great Numbers, to be sent to the *PRINTER*
of this *Paper*, who hath employed a *Judicious Secretary* to Collect such
as may be most useful for the *Publick*.

And although we do not intend to expose our own Persons by
mentioning Names, yet we are so far from requiring the same Caution 60
in our *Correspondents*, that on the contrary, we expressly *Charge* and
Command them, in all the Facts they send us, to set down the Names,
Titles, and Places of Abode at length; together with a very particular
Description of the *Persons*, *Dresses*, and *Dispositions* of the several
Lords, *Ladies*, *Squires*, *Madams*, *Lawyers*, *Gamesters*, *Toupees*, *Sots*, 65
Wits, *Rakes*, and *Informers*, whom they shall have occasion to mention;
otherwise it will not be possible for us to adjust our Style to the
different Qualities, and Capacities of the Persons concerned, and
Treat them with the *Respect* or *Familiarity*, that may be due to their
Stations and *Characters*, which we are Determined to observe with the 70
utmost strictness, that none may have cause to Complain.

HEADING. *To be continued Weekly*: For the schedule of publication, see the section 'Dates
  of the *Intelligencers*' in the General Introduction, above.
16. *Assemblees*: Elegant social gatherings; see *OED Suppl.*, citing *Journal to Stella*, ii. 460.
16. *Quadrille*: A highly fashionable card game; see introductory note to no. 4.
22. *enfans perdus*: 'Men ... appointed to give the first on-set in Battel ... so call'd
  because of the eminent danger they are expos'd to. In English they are commonly
  called, *The Forlorn.*' *A Military Dictionary. Explaining All Difficult Terms in Martial Discipline, Fortification, and Gunnery* (London: Nutt, 1702). (Weckermann.)
26. *Passages*: A passage was 'something that "passes", goes on, takes place, occurs, or is
  done; an occurrence, incident, event; an act, transaction, proceeding' (*OED*, sense
  13).
26. *Adventures*: Probably 'chance occurrence[s]' (*OED*).
28–9. *feigned Names*: An established if commonly violated ideal of satire was to avoid
  naming names; see Martial, *Epigrams*, x. xxxiii. 9–10; Ben Jonson, *Works*, ed. C. H.
  Herford and Percy Simpson, iv (Oxford, 1932), 319–20; Dryden, 'Discourse Concerning the Original and Progress of Satire' (1693) in his *Poems*, ed. James Kinsley
  (Oxford, 1958), ii. 645–6; Addison's *Spectator* 35; and perhaps most appositely,
  Swift's *Verses on the Death of Dr. Swift*, in *Poems*, ii. 571, lines 459–60: '"Yet, Malice
  never was his Aim; | He lash'd the Vice but spar'd the Name."' In the *Intelligencer*
  Swift significantly seems to reserve the right to break this rule if he can 'Answer for
  the Truth' of the allegations.
57. *a Judicious Secretary*: A fiction, or a hope. Swift told Pope in 1732, 'If we could have

got some ingenious young man to have been the manager, who should have published all that might be sent to him, it might have continued longer, for there were hints enough' (*Corresp.* iv. 30).

65. *Madams*: Gentlewomen; the term is apparently used as Robert Forby found it in 19th-cent. East Anglia: 'In a village, the Esquire's wife . . . must have *madam* prefixed to her surname. The parson's wife, if he be a doctor, or a man of considerable preferment and genteel figure, must be *madam* too' (*The Vocabulary of East Anglia* (London, 1830), ii. 203).

65. *Toupees*: A toupee was 'a new Name for a modern Periwig, and for its owner; now in Fashion, Dec. 1, 1733.' Presumably Swift's note, to *An Examination of Certain Abuses*, in *35* (*Prose*, xii. 219).

66. *Informers*: Swift despised an informer. While admitting that 'it is not impossible, but an honest Man may be called by that name', he preached an entire sermon against informers ('On False Witness', *Prose*, ix. 180–9) and in his 'Letter . . . to Mr. Pope' (1721) called them 'the most accursed, and prostitute, and abandoned race, that God ever permitted to plague mankind' (*Prose*, ix. 32–3). In *Gulliver's Travels*, i. 6, Lilliput's laws provide the death penalty for lying informers; British informers are severely ridiculed in iii. 6 (*Prose*, xi. 58, 191–2).

This essay is virtually the only primary source for the 'fact' about Swift that it recounts. His encounter with Abel Ram took place during a journey with Sheridan along the south-east coast of Ireland at least as far as the town of Wexford. They would have passed through Bray, Wicklow, Arklow, Gorey (Newborough), and Enniscorthy, perhaps travelling beyond Wexford, which was on the way to Sheridan's parish of Rincurran, near Kinsale, Co. Cork. Or perhaps, since they were travelling 'for their Health', their destination was Wexford, which had a spa frequently mentioned in the *Journal to Stella.* Ball's speculation (*Corresp.* ed. Ball, iv. 33 n.) that the journey took place during the spring of 1728 may be correct, but in *Intelligencer* 6, Sheridan describes a journey which he calls his 'last', and says it took place 'last year'.

Abel Ram of Ramsfort and Clonattin (1669–1740), the landlord of Gorey, was the son of the Dublin goldsmith and private banker Sir Abel Ram; he inherited his father's banking business. He moreover represented Gorey in the Irish House of Commons (1692–1740) and had been high sheriff of Co. Wexford in 1709, sovereign of Gorey in 1716, and deputy governor of Co. Wexford in 1721. As colonel of militia dragoons, he had hunted Jacobites in 1714. See *Burke's Genealogical and Heraldic History of the Landed Gentry in Ireland*, 4th edition, ed. L. G. Pine (London, 1958), 593; Hore, 616–35; C. M. Tenison, 'The Old Dublin Bankers', *J. Cork Hist. and Archaeol. Soc.* 3 (1894), 120; and McCracken, 358.

The story of Swift and Ram passed into oral tradition. Folklorists have recorded several versions, testimony not only to the imaginative power of the 'fact' but probably also to the circulation of Sheridan's original essay. Mackie L. Jarrell has examined the folk narratives in '"Jack and the Dane": Swift Traditions in Ireland', *J. of American Folklore*, 77 (1964), 111–12.

NUMB. II.

Occursare capro, cornu ferit ille, caveto.

Vir.

MY design, in Writing this *Paper*, being chiefly to expose such *Barbarians*, who think themselves exempt from those Laws of *Hospitality*, which have, through all Ages and Countries, been observed by the best and most distinguished part of Mankind; I hope I shall, *even in my own Country*, find Persons enough, 5 to joyn with me in a hearty detestation of a certain *Country-Squire*, at

the Relation of the following *Fact*, which I shall tell without the least
Aggravation, or Partiality.

Two *Clergy-men*, of some Distinction, Travelling to the Country for
their Health, happened to set up together in a small Village, which was
under the Dominion of a certain *Animal*, dignified with a *brace of
Titles*, that of a *Militia-Collonel*, and a *Squire*. One of these Gentlemen
standing in the Street, and observing *a Coach-man* driving his *Coach
and four Horses* furiously against him, turned into the close Passage
between his *Inn* and the *Sign-post*, but the *Coach-man*, instead of
driving through the middle of the Street, which was the usual and
most commodious way, turned short, and Drove full upon the
Gentleman, without any Notice, so that he was on a sudden enclosed
between the *fore-horses*, and if his Friend and another Gentleman, who
were in the middle of the Street, had not suddenly cryed out to stop
the *Coach*, he must have unavoidably been trodden under the Horses
Feet, and his Body bruised to Death by the Wheels running over
him. His Friend who saw with Terror what had like to have befallen
him, full of Indignation, repaired immediately to the aforesaid *Squire*
or *Collonel* (to whom he was told the *Equipage* belonged) with a
Complaint against his *Coach-man*. But the *Squire* instead of
expressing any Concern, or offering any Redress, sent the Doctor
away with the following Answer. *Sir, I have a great Regard for your Cloath,
and have sent my Coach-man to ask your Friend's Pardon; for one of your
Servants this moment, told me what had happened.* But, Sir, said the *Doctor*,
do you think *that is sufficient*? I dare venture to affirm, if the like had
befallen you, within the Liberties of my Friend, and you were brought
to the same Danger by his Servant, he would not only have him
Punished, but at the same time, he would discharge him his Service.
Sir, (said the *Collonel*) *I tell you again, that I have sent my Coach-man to
ask his Pardon, and I think that is enough*, which he spoke with some
sturdiness; and well he might; for he had two *Cannons* at his Back.
Good God, said the *Doctor* to himself, (when he had got out of Gun-
shot) what a *Hottentot* have I been talking to! who so little values the
Life of a Gentleman, and as it happen'd that very Gentleman, to whom
the Nation hath in a particular manner been obliged. Back he went full
of Resentment, for the slighting Treatment his Friend met with, and
very Candidly reported all that passed; who being a Man of a different
Spirit from that wretched *Collonel*, ordered one of his Servants to
Write the following Letter.

SIR,

M Y *Master commanded me to tell you, That if you do not punish and turn*
off that Villain your Coach-man, he will think there was a Design upon
his Life, I put this in Writing for fear of mistakes,
    I am your humble Servant to command   50

                    A. R.

The Superscription was, FOR SQUIRE WETHER, *or some such*
Name.

This *Letter* was delivered, and away went the *Travellers*. They had
not Rode far, before they fell into the Company of a Gentleman, a 55
degree above the common Level, and who seemed to be a Man of
Candor and Integrity, which encouraged them to recount what had
happened. He said in Answer, that they had a narrow escape; and it
was a Wonder that the whole Town did not fall upon them at once,
and worry them; for the People there, had little or no *Devotion*, besides 60
what was engaged to the *Squire*, as an Effect of the Terrors, they lay
under from their *Landlord*, who Rode them all down, as poor as his
Fox-hunters. After this he took occasion with great Modesty, and
Decency, to draw his *Character*, which was to the following purpose.
That the *Squire* had about *fifteen hundred Pounds* a Year, and lived in a 65
long White-Barn; where no Man living was one *Farthing* the better for
him. That his *Piety* consisted in Six *Psalms* every Day after Dinner,
without one Drop of Wine. That he had once reduced a certain
Reverend Dean, plumper than any two of his *Brethren*, to be as slender
about the Waste as a Weazle by a Fortnight Scouring of bad Ale, to 70
which the *Dean* was not accustomed. That his *hospitality* was within
the enclosure of a *Rampart*, with a Draw-bridge. That if any
Gentleman was admitted by chance, his entertainment was *lean Salt-
beef, sour Beer*, and *Muddy Ale*. That his *Charity* was as much upon the
catch as a *Pick-pocket*; for his method was to bring others to erect 75
Charity-Schools, by promising his Assistance, and so leaving them in
the Lurch.

That without the least Tincture of Learning, he was a great
pretender to *Oratory* and *Poetry*, and eminently bad at both, which (I
hope I shall be excused the Digression) brings to my Memory a 80
Character, given by *Julius Capitolinus* of the Emperor *VERUS*. *Melior*
quidem Orator fuisse dicitur, quam Poeta; imo (ut verius dicam) pejor Poeta
quam Rhetor, (viz.) *He was a better Orator than Poet, but, to speak the thing*
more properly, He was a viler Poet than an Orator. But to give you a

85 Specimen of his *Genius*, I shall repeat an *Epigram* of his own Composition (and I am very sure it is every Line his own, without any help) which is drawn by a Sign-Dawber on the Cross-board of a Ferry-boat, in Characters that have hitherto stood the Fury of all Weathers.

90
> *All you that are*
> *To* Andrew *Heir,*
> *And you that him attend*
> *Shall Ferry'd be,*
> *Oe'r* Carrick *free,*
> *For* Blank'*s the Boatman's Friend.*
95

The behaviour of this *Squire* being of the most Savage kind, I think my self obliged out of the tender Regard, which I bear to all Strangers, and Travellers, to animadvert upon him in as gentle a manner as the occasion will allow. And therefore I shall first lay down a few 100 Postulatums. *That every Travelling-Gentleman is presumed to be under the Protection of the Governing-Mayor, Sovereign, Portriff, or Squire of the Town or Village, which he happens to make his Stage. That the Laws of Humanity, Hospitality and Civility, oblige him, if there be no Accommodation in the Publick Houses, fit for a Person of Distinction, to invite him to his own, or supply the* 105 *Deficiencies as well as he can. That if any Insult or Injury be offered either to such a stranger, or his Servants, the Squire is obliged to justify, vindicate, and espouse their Cause.* This was the method observed among the civilized People of the old *Jewish*, and *Heathen* World; Where we find some of the *Patriarchs* themselves condescending to wash the Feet of such 110 Travellers, as they entertained. And so sacred was the Regard for Strangers among the *Heathens*, that they dignifyed their Supreme GOD with the Title of *Jupiter Hospitalis*. Nothing was thought so monstrous as to offer any Violence to Sojourners among them, which was so religiously observed, that it became the glory of the 115 most distinguished Heroes, to destroy and extirpate such as were remarkable for their Cruelty to Strangers. This it was, which added so much glory to the character of *Theseus*, for the Punishments he inflicted on *Sisiphus*, *Procrustes*, &c. It was owing likewise to a generous Indignation, That *Hercules* threw *Diomede* (The *Collonel* and 120 *Squire* of that Age) to be devoured by those Horses, which he fed with the Flesh of poor Travellers, and I find upon enquiry that they were *Coach-Horses* too. I shall make no farther remark upon this, nor Application, but say to the Squire, That it is very happy for him the present Age has not one *Hercules* left, or a Week would not pass, before he should feel the weight of that *Heroe's Club,* or be thrown by way of 125 Reprizal under his own *Horses* feet. And I may farther add, that in this whole Kingdom, from one end of it to the other, another *Squire* could not be found, who would behave himself in the same manner to the same Person; but Hundreds, who on the Contrary, would have given all the Satisfaction, that Gentlemen of Justice, Humanity, and 130 common Benevolence ought to do, upon the like accident, although they had never seen him before. I confess this *Paper* contains nothing besides a dry Fact, and a few occasional Observations upon it. But in the former I told my READERS, that Facts would be the chief part of the *Entertainment*, I meant to give them. If what I have said, may have 135 any Effect on the Person concerned, (to whom care shall be taken to send this Account) or if it helps to revive the old spirit of *Hospitality* among us, or at least begets a Detestation of the like inhuman *Usage* in others; one part of my design is answered. However, it cannot be unseasonable to expose Malice, Avarice, Brutality, and Hypocrisie, 140 wherever we find it.

MOTTO. *Eclogues*, ix. 25: 'Have a care not to get in the he-goat's way—he butts with his horn' (Loeb). This essay's punning references to Abel Ram offer almost the only hint in the *Intelligencer* that its authors were master punsters.

5. *even in my own Country*: Sheridan's italics probably signal an ironic reference to Gaelic Ireland's extraordinary traditional hospitality. Lawrence Eachard, *An Exact Description of Ireland* (London: Salusbury, 1691) observed that the 'Wild Irish' were 'kind and courteous to strangers' (15–16). On the tradition's survival among the eighteenth-century Anglo-Irish, see Katharine Simms, 'Guesting and Feasting in Gaelic Ireland', *J. Royal Soc. Antiquaries Ire.* 108 (1978), 93–5; and Loveday, 58.

9. *Two Clergy-men, of some Distinction*: Swift and Sheridan, on internal evidence, confirmed by Francis Geoghegan to Swift (Appendix B).

10–11. *a small Village . . . a certain Animal*: Gorey, Co. Wexford, and its landlord Abel Ram, for whom see the introductory note.

47–8. *turn off that Villain your Coach-man*: See Geoghegan's comments, Appendix B.

51. *A. R.*: Swift is not known to have had a servant with these initials.

65–6. *a long White-Barn*: Ramsfort, the Ram seat near Gorey; see Hore, 635.

74–5. *upon the catch*: 'On the watch for an opportunity of catching or seizing something' (*OED*, 'catch', *sb.* 1. b).

75–6. *his method was to bring others to erect Charity-Schools*: Charity schools were designed to bring up some of the poor children with a modicum of English literacy and with allegiance to the established Church. Since the first decade of the 18th century, the Irish charity school movement had grown rapidly. But Swift charged that 'very often the richest Parishioners contribute the least' (*Prose*, ix. 202). In 1716 Ram had led in founding a charity school society in Dublin, but in the printed records he never appears as a patron; perhaps more significant, there was as late as 1728 no charity school in his own town of Gorey. See Seán de Peitid, 'The Rev. Henry Maule of Shandon, and the Charity School Movement', *J. Cork Hist. and Archaeol. Soc.* 77

(1972), 110, 112; *Methods of Erecting, Supporting & Governing Charity-Schools: with An Account of the Charity-Schools in Ireland*, 2nd edn. (Dublin: Hyde, 1719); Thomas [Wilson], Lord Bishop of Sodor and Man, *The True Christian Method of Educating the Children Both of the Poor and Rich* (London: Downing, 1724 (the 60-page edn.)), p. 54; and the *Account of the Charity Schools* published periodically in London in the early 18th century. On Swift's support of the charity school movement, see Louis A. Landa, 'Jonathan Swift and Charity', *JEGP* 44 (1945), 342–6.

80–1. *a Character... of the Emperor VERUS*: In a life of Verus in the collection traditionally known as *Historiae Augustae Scriptores Sex.*

91, 94, 95. *Andrew ... Carrick ... Blank*: The reference to Carrick provides hitherto unnoticed information about the route of Swift's journey. The Ferry Carrick crossed the River Slaney about two miles west of the town of Wexford. See Samuel Lewis, *A Topographical Dictionary of Ireland* (London, 1837), i. 279–80, and the map of Co. Wexford in the accompanying atlas. Abel Ram had inherited the ferry from his father's brother Andrew Ram (whose surname fills the 'blank'), according to the terms of his will, dated 20 Apr. 1697 and proved in the Prerogative Court 8 Nov. 1699. See 'Abstracts of Wills', *Irish Ancestor*, 5 (1973), 58–9.

101. *Sovereign, Portriff* [*portreeve*]: Titles used for the mayor of some towns in Ireland; see *OED*.

109. *Patriarchs*: Compare Gen. 18: 4; 19: 2; 24: 32.

112. *Jupiter Hospitalis*: Hospitality in the ancient world was a sacred, reciprocal, and hereditary relation between private persons and between citizens of one state and another, under the auspices of Jupiter.

117–18. *Punishments* [*Theseus*] *inflicted on Sisiphus, Procrustes, &c.*: By their own methods, Theseus killed the murdering bandits Procrustes (who cruelly fitted his guests to their beds), Sciron (who ambushed travellers near the edge of a cliff and forced them to wash his feet, then knocked them over the edge as they bent to do so), and Sinis (who tore his victims limb from limb by tying them to two bent-over pine trees and then suddenly releasing the trees). Sheridan seems to have confused either Sciron or Sinis with Sisyphus, who does not enter the story of Theseus. See Apollodorus, iii. 16; Diodorus Siculus, iv. 59.

119–20. *Hercules threw Diomede... to be devoured*: Diomedes, king of Thrace, fed travellers to his team of man-eating horses, to seize which was the eighth of Hercules' twelve labours. He fed Diomedes to them, whereupon they grew tame and obedient. See Diodorus Siculus, iv. 15.

Swift apparently never saw a performance of Gay's *The Beggar's Opera* (1728), although he read it in a six-penny Dublin edition (*Corresp.* iii. 269) and was easily aware that it was the hit of the theatrical season in both London and Dublin. Swift had suggested the subject to Gay, and his energetic defence of the play may reflect a pride in its origins. ''Twas writ in the same house with me and Dr. Swift', Pope told Spence.

> Dr. Swift had been observing [in 1716] to Mr. Gay, what an odd pretty sort of a thing a Newgate Pastoral might make. Gay was inclined to try at such a thing for some time, but afterwards thought it would be better to write a comedy on the same plan. . . . He began on it, and when first he mentioned it to Swift the Doctor did not much like the project. As he carried it on he showed what he wrote to both of us, and we now and then gave a correction or a word or two of advice, but 'twas wholly of his own writing. When it was done, neither of us thought it would succeed.

(Joseph Spence, *Observations, Anecdotes, and Characters of Books and Men*, ed. James M. Osborn (Oxford, 1966), i. 57, 107; see also *Poems*, iii. 1131.)

In fact, from Swift's letters it appears that he left England before the script was finished in 1727, but whatever his apprehensions, the letters show the liveliest interest in the play and its contribution to Gay's fortune. Swift's friendship with Gay had strengthened in 1727. He saw in Gay a principled and gifted writer victimized, like himself, by the false friendship and ingratitude of Queen Caroline and her dresser Mrs Howard, later Lady Suffolk. Both were, he suspected, influenced by Walpole against him and Gay. Thus Gay's case seemed parallel to his own disappointment at not having been offered English preferment in the late summer of 1727. For these reasons Swift stresses a biographical and satirical interpretation of *The Beggar's Opera*. When the *Opera* had begun to be performed in London, he wrote to Gay, 'Does W— think you intended an affront to him in your opera. Pray God he may' (*Corresp.* iii. 267).

Intelligencer 3 has become the most influential of the Opposition interpretations, which were designed to stress the play's innuendo against Walpole, though Swift's essay was preceded by an excellent piece in the same vein in the *Country Journal; or, The Craftsman* (17 February 1727/8). Walpole's supporters rejoined with a different sort of moral argument—namely, that the play glorified criminal behaviour. See William Eben Schultz, *Gay's Beggar's Opera: Its Content, History & Influence* (1923; reprinted New York, 1967), chs. 17, 21; and Bertrand A. Goldgar, *Walpole and the Wits: The Relation of Politics to Literature, 1722–1742* (Lincoln, Neb., 1976), 66–74.

Swift's view of *The Beggar's Opera* was strongly influenced by his view of Gay's career as a patronage-seeker. As Swift reported to Lady Betty Germain,

... there came out a libel against Mr. Walpole [Swift ignores Walpole's knighthoods], who was informed it was written by Mr. Gay; and, although Mr. Walpole owned he was convinced that it was not written by Gay, yet he never would pardon him, but did him a hundred ill offices to the Princess. Walpole was at that time very civil to me, and so were all the people in power. He invited me and some of my friends to dine with him at Chelsea [in March or April 1726]. After dinner I took an occasion to say, what I had observed of Princes and great Ministers, That, if they heard an ill thing of a private person, who expected some favour, although they were afterward convinced that the person was innocent, yet they would never be reconciled. Mr. Walpole knew well enough that I meant Mr. Gay. I afterwards said the same thing to the Princess, with the same intention, and she confessed it a great injustice. But Mr. Walpole gave it another turn: For he said to some of his friends, and particularly to a Lord, a near relation of yours, That I had dined with him, and had been making apologies for myself: It seems for my conduct in her late Majesty's reign. . . .

(*Corresp.* iv. 98–9; see also Swift's note to *Verses on the Death of Dr. Swift*, *Poems*, ii. 560 n. 2; and *Corresp.* iii. 128n., 131–5.) The lampoon against Walpole, if it survives, cannot now be identified.

In 1727 Gay published his *Fables*, 'invented for [the] amusement' of 6-year-old Prince William; they began with 'The Lyon, the Tyger, and the Traveller', advising William that

> Princes, like Beautys, from their youth
> Are strangers to the voice of truth:
> Learn to contemn all praise betimes;
> For flattery's the nurse of crimes.
> Friendship by sweet reproof is shown,
> (A virtue never near a throne;)
> In courts such freedom must offend,
> There none presumes to be a friend.

See John Gay, *Poetry and Prose*, ed. Vinton A. Dearing (Oxford, 1974), ii. 302; courtiers are also alluded to in 'The Spaniel and the Camelion', ii. 304–5, 'The Courtier and Proteus', ii. 345–7, and perhaps other fables (see Edwin Graham, 'John Gay's Second Series, the *Craftsman* in Fables', *Papers on Lang. and Lit.* 5 (1969), 18 n.). Such references as these may have kept Gay from being rewarded with a place at court, since the prince seems to have been an astutely chosen dedicatee: he was not only the favourite son of his mother Princess Caroline, but was also regarded with great affection by his grandfather George I, who had in 1725 installed him as Principal Companion of the Order of the Bath, even though the courts of the king and the prince of Wales were politically at odds.

George II was proclaimed king 15 June 1727, and according to Swift, 'In a few weeks, the Q—n said to Mrs. Howard (alluding to one of Mr. Gay's Fables) that she would take up the Hare' (Gay had described himself in 'The Hare and Many Friends' as befriended by all and assisted by none). During the first weeks or perhaps months of the new reign, Swift and his friends regarded Mrs Howard as having great influence at court, and her comment to Gay in October—'by my consent you shall never be a *hare* again'—has been interpreted as confirming Swift's report. But it appears rather to relate to her advice that Gay 'mind the main chance', that is, work for the success of *The Beggar's Opera*. See *Corresp.* iv. 99; Gay, *Poetry and Prose*, ii. 368–70; *Letters to and from Henrietta, Countess of Suffolk*, ed. [John Wilson Croker] (London, 1824), i. 283–4. In October 1727 Gay declined the queen's offer of a place as gentleman-usher to her infant daughter Louisa; Swift approved his refusal. Whether Gay should reasonably have considered the offer satisfactory, unsatisfactory, or downright insulting is debatable; J. H. Plumb agrees with Swift that it was 'a joke'. See *Corresp.* iii. 246, 250, 471; *Poems*, ii. 531; Whitwell Elwin's note in Pope, *Works*, vii (London, 1871), 103; Plumb, ii. 175.

One particular impetus for Swift's essay may have escaped notice. William Duncombe's anonymous essay against *The Beggar's Opera* in the *London Journal*, 20 April 1728, was reprinted without acknowledgement in the *Dublin Weekly Journal*, 4 May 1728. It discusses low humour, wit, the power of drama to touch its audience, and the morality of *The Beggar's Opera*—all topics which engage Swift's attention. And assuming Swift saw this essay, as he was about to write his own, he would have been jarred by its implication that Gay (and probably also Swift and Pope, whom Gay had joined in the recently published *Miscellanies*) was guilty of ingratitude; in Swift's view Gay had been its victim. Because of the likelihood that Swift was in part responding to Duncombe's essay, it is reprinted in Appendix C.

Intelligencer 3 contains important statements on satire and on the relation between wit and humour. In the Apology (1710) prefixed to *A Tale of a Tub*, Swift had written, 'As Wit is the noblest and most useful Gift of humane Nature, so Humor is the most agreeable, and where these two enter far into the Composition of any Work, they will render it always acceptable to the World. Now, the great Part of those who have no Share or Tast of either, but by their Pride, Pedantry and Ill Manners, lay themselves bare to the Lashes of Both' (*Tale*, 18–19). This remark does not really distinguish humour from wit, and seems to imply that some people have no taste for humour, whereas in the present essay he maintains that people naturally have a taste for humour.

Swift makes a clearer and more useful distinction in *To Mr. Delany* (1718), where he describes wit and humour as contributing to the raillery which for him marks good conversation:

> [Wit], as boundless as the Wind;
> Is well conceiv'd thô not defin'd;

> For, sure, by Wit is onely meant
> Applying what we first Invent:
> What Humor is, not all the Tribe
> Of Logick-mongers can describe;
> Here, onely Nature acts her Part,
> Unhelpt by Practice, Books, or Art.
> For Wit and Humor differ quite,
> That gives Surprise, and this Delight:
> Humor is odd, grotesque, and wild,
> Onely by Affectation spoild,
> Tis never by Invention got,
> Men have it when they know it not.   (*Poems*, i. 215–16)

In the present essay Swift uses some traditional ideas of humour: it is natural, individual, and peculiar; it appears ridiculous, and it is therefore the proper basis for characterization in satiric comedy. See Dryden, 'The Author's Apology for Heroic Poetry and Poetic License' (1677), in *Of Dramatic Poesy and Other Critical Essays*, ed. George Watson (London, 1962), i. 199; Sir William Temple, 'Of Poetry' (1690), in J. E. Spingarn (ed.), *Critical Essays of the Seventeenth Century* (reprinted Bloomington, 1957), iii. 104; and William Congreve, 'Concerning Humour in Comedy' (1695), in Spingarn, iii. 245–8. Maurice Johnson has observed that the ideas of humour in *To Mr. Delany* and *Intelligencer 3* converge upon characterization. In conversation one might be humorous by 'acting in character' (35)—by being willing to pose as odd. But in good conversation the poses both of oddness and of raillery evoke an underlying community, whereas the ridicule of satiric comedy less ambiguously distances the butt from the laughers. See Johnson, *The Sin of Wit: Jonathan Swift as a Poet* (Syracuse, 1950), 32–105; and see also Addison's *Spectator* 47.

The relationship of humour to wit was much discussed by contemporary critics; see Stuart M. Tave, *The Amiable Humorist* (Chicago, 1960), 91–120 and especially 115–16. Among previous critics, John Dennis had argued clearly and influentially that humour was more important than wit in comedy. See his 'A Large Account of the Taste in Poetry' (1702), in his *Critical Works*, ed. Edward Niles Hooker (Baltimore, 1939), i. 281 and n. Tave regards Swift's high estimate of humour as significant in the development of 'amiable' humour (267n.).

NUMB. III.

Ipse per Omnes ibit Personas,
Et turbam reddet in uno.

THE *Players* having now almost done with the Comedy, called
the *Beggars Opera*, for this Season, it may be no unpleasant
Speculation, to reflect a little upon this *Dramatick Piece*, so
singular in the Subject, and the manner, so much an Original, and
which hath frequently given so very agreeable an Entertainment.   5

Although an evil *Tast* be very apt to prevail, both here, and in
London, yet there is a point which whoever can rightly Touch, will
never fail of pleasing a very great Majority; so great, that the Dislikers,
out of Dulness or Affectation will be silent, and forced to fall in with
the Herd; the point I mean, is what we call *Humour*, which in its 10
Perfection is allowed to be much preferable to *Wit*, if it be not rather
the most useful, and agreeable Species of it.

I agree with Sir *William Temple*, that the Word is peculiar to our
English Tongue, but I differ from him in the Opinion, that the
thing it self is peculiar to the *English Nation*, because the contrary 15
may be found in many *Spanish*, *Italian*, and *French* Productions,
and particularly, whoever hath a *Tast* for *True Humour*, will find a
Hundred Instances of it in those Volumes Printed in *France*, under the
Name of *Le Theatre Italien*, to say nothing of *Rabelais*, *Cervantes*, and
many others. 20

Now I take the *Comedy* or *Farce*, (or whatever Name the *Criticks* will
allow it) called the *Beggars Opera*; to excell in this Article of *Humour*.
And, upon that Merit, to have met with such prodigious success both
here, and in *England*.

As to *Poetry*, *Eloquence*, and *Musick*, which are said to have most 25
Power over the minds of Men, it is certain that very few have a *Tast* or
Judgment of the Excellencies of the two former, and if a Man succeeds
in either, it is upon the Authority of those *few Judges*, that lend their
Taste to the bulk of Readers, who have none of their own. I am told
there are as few good Judges in *Musick*, and that among those who 30
Crowd the Operas, Nine in Ten go thither meerly out of *Curiosity*,
Fashion, or *Affectation*.

But a Taste for *Humour* is in some manner fixed to the very Nature
of Man, and generally Obvious to the Vulgar, except upon Subjects
too refined, and Superior to their Understanding. 35

And as this *Taste* of *Humour* is purely Natural, so is *Humour* it self, neither is it a *Talent* confined to Men of *Wit*, or *Learning*; for we observe it sometimes among common Servants, and the meanest of the People, while the very Owners are often Ignorant of the Gift they
40 possess.

I know very well, that this happy *Talent* is contemptibly Treated by *Criticks*, under the Name of *low Humour*, or *low Comedy*; but I know likewise, that the *Spaniards* and *Italians*, who are allowed to have the most Wit of any *Nation* in *Europe*, do most excell in it, and do most
45 esteem it.

By what Disposition of the mind, what Influence of the Stars, or what Situation of the *Clymate* this endowment is bestowed upon Mankind, may be a Question fit for *Philosophers* to Discuss. It is certainly the best Ingredient towards that kind of Satyr, which is most
50 useful, and gives the least Offence; which instead of lashing, Laughs Men out of their Follies, and Vices, and is the Character which gives *Horace* the Preference to *Juvenal.*

And although some things are too Serious, Solemn, or Sacred to be turned into Ridicule, yet the Abuses of them are certainly not, since it
55 is allowed that Corruption in *Religion*, *Politicks*, and *Law*, may be proper *Topicks* for this kind of Satyr.

There are two ends that Men propose in Writing Satyr, one of them less Noble than the other, as regarding nothing further than personal Satisfaction, and pleasure of the Writer; but without any View towards
60 *Personal Malice*; The other is a *Publick Spirit*, prompting Men of *Genius* and Virtue, to mend the World as far as they are able. And as both these ends are innocent, so the latter is highly commendable. With Regard to the former, I demand whether I have not as good a Title to Laugh, as Men have to be Ridiculous, and to expose Vice, as another
65 hath to be Vicious. If I Ridicule the Follies and Corruptions of a *Court*, a *Ministry*, or a *Senate*; are they not amply payed by *Pensions*, *Titles*, and *Power*, while I expect and desire no other Reward, than that of Laughing with a few Friends in a Corner. Yet, if those, who take Offence, think me in the Wrong, I am ready to Change the Scene with
70 them, whenever they please.

But if my Design be to make Mankind better, then I think it is my Duty, at least I am sure it is the Interest of those very *Courts* and *Ministers*, whose Follies or Vices I Ridicule, to reward me for my good Intentions; For, if it be reckoned an high point of Wisdom to get the

Laughers on our side, it is much more easy, as well as Wise to get 75
those on our side, who can make Millions Laugh when they please.

My Reason for mentioning *Courts*, and *Ministers*, (whom I never
think on, but with the most profound Veneration) is because an
Opinion obtains, that in the *Beggars Opera* there appears to be some
Reflections upon *Courtiers* and *States-Men*, whereof I am by no means 80
a Judge.

It is true indeed that Mr. *GAY*, the Author of this Piece, hath
been somewhat singular in the Course of his Fortunes, for it hath
happened, that after Fourteen Years attending the *Court*, with a large
Stock of real Merit, a Modest, and Agreeable Conversation, a *Hundred* 85
Promises, and five *Hundred Friends*, he hath failed of Preferment, and
upon a very Weighty Reason. He lay under the Suspicion of having
Written a Libel, or Lampoon against a great M——— It is true that
great M——— was demonstratively convinced, and publickly owned
his Conviction, that Mr. *Gay* was not the Author; but having lain 90
under the Suspicion, it seemed very just, that he should suffer the
Punishment; because in this most reformed Age, the Virtues of a great
M——— are no more to be suspected, than the Chastity of *Cæsar*'s
Wife.

It must be allowed, That the *Beggars-Opera* is not the first of Mr. 95
Gay's Works, wherein he hath been faulty, with regard to *Courtiers*
and *States-Men*. For, to omit his other Pieces, even in his *Fables*,
published within two Years past, and Dedicated to the *D. of
Cumberland*, for which he was PROMISED a Reward; he hath been
thought somewhat too bold upon *Courtiers*. And although it is highly 100
probable, he meant only the *Courtiers* of former times, yet he acted
unwarily, by not considering, that the Malignity of some people might
misinterpret what he said to the disadvantage of present *Persons*, and
Affairs.

But I have now done with Mr. *Gay* as a Politician, and shall 105
consider him henceforward only as Author of the *Beggars Opera*,
wherein he hath by a turn of *Humor*, entirely New, placed Vices of all
Kinds in the strongest and most odious Light; and thereby done
eminent Service, both to *Religion* and *Morality*. This appears from
the unparallel'd Success he hath met with. All *Ranks*, *Parties* and 110
Denominations of Men, either crowding to see his *Opera*, or reading it
with delight in their Closets, even *Ministers* of State, whom he is
thought to have most offended (next to those whom the Actors more
immediately represent) appearing frequently at the *Theatre*, from a

115 consciousness of their own Innocence, and to convince the World how unjust a Parallel, *Malice*, *Envy*, and *Disaffection to the Government have made.*

I am assured that several worthy *Clergy-Men* in this *City*, went privately to see the *Beggars-Opera* represented; and that the *fleering* 120 *Coxcombs* in the *Pit*, amused themselves with making Discoveries, and spreading the Names of those Gentlemen round the Audience.

I shall not pretend to vindicate a *Clergy-Man*, who would appear openly in his Habit at a *Theatre*, among such a vicious Crew, as would probably stand round him, and at such lewd *Comedies*, and prophane 125 *Tragedies* as are often represented. Besides I know very well, that Persons of their Function are bound to avoid the appearance of Evil, or of giving cause of Offence. But when the *Lords Chancellors*, who are Keepers of the King's Conscience, when the *Judges* of the Land, whose Title is *Reverend*, when *Ladies*, who are bound by the Rules of 130 their Sex, to the strictest Decency, appear in the *Theatre* without Censure, I cannot understand, why a young Clergy-man who goes concealed out of Curiosity to see an innocent and moral Play, should be so highly condemned; nor do I much approve the Rigor of a great P——te who said, *he hoped none of his Clergy were there.* I am glad to hear 135 there are no weightier Objections against that Reverend Body, planted in this City, and I wish there never may. But I should be very sorry that any of them should be so weak, as to imitate a COURT-CHAPLAIN in *England*, who preached against the *Beggars-Opera*, which will probably do more good than a thousand Sermons of so 140 stupid, so injudicious, and so prostitute a Divine.

In this happy Performance of Mr. *Gay*, all the Characters are just, and none of them carried beyond Nature, or hardly beyond Practice. It discovers the whole System of that Common-Wealth, or that *Imperium in Imperio* of Iniquity, established among us, by which neither our 145 Lives, nor our Properties are secure, either in the High-ways, or in publick Assemblies, or even in our own Houses. It shews the miserable Lives, and the constant Fate of those abandoned Wretches; for how little they sell their Lives and Souls; betrayed by their *Whores*; their *Comrades*; and the *Receivers* and *Purchasers* of these Thefts and 150 Robberies. This *Comedy* contains likewise a *Satyr*, which, although it doth by no means affect the present Age, yet might have been useful in the former and may possibly be so in Ages to come. I mean where the Author takes occasion of comparing those *common Robbers to Robbers of the Publick*; and their several Stratagems of betraying, undermining,

and hanging each other, to the several Arts of *Politicians* in times of 155
Corruption.

This *Comedy* likewise exposeth with great Justice, that unnatural
Taste for *Italian* Musick among us, which is wholly unsuitable to our
Northern *Climat*, and the *genius* of the People, whereby we are over-
run with *Italian-Effeminacy*, and *Italian* Nonsense. An old Gentleman 160
said to me, that many Years ago, when the practice of an unnatural
Vice grew so frequent in *London*, that many were Prosecuted for it, he
was sure it would be a Fore-runner of *Italian-Opera*'s, and Singers;
and then we should want nothing but Stabbing or Poysoning, to make
us perfect *Italians*.   165

Upon the Whole, I deliver my Judgment, That nothing but servile
Attachment to a Party, affectation of Singularity, lamentable Dullness,
mistaken Zeal, or studied Hypocrisy, can have the least reasonable
Objection against this excellent Moral-performance of the
CELEBRATED MR. GAY.   170

MOTTO. Manilius, *Astronomica*, v. 480ᵇ–81, describing an actor: 'Solusque per omnis |
ibit personas et turbam reddet in uno' (freely, 'He will go through all the roles, one
man representing a multitude of characters'). The motto, which Swift could have
found in his copy of Michel Maittaire, *Opera et Fragmenta Veterum Poetarum Latinorum
Profanorum & Ecclesiasticorum* (London: Nicholson, Tooke, and Tonson, 1713), i. 784,
seems chosen to commend the accuracy of Gay's mimesis. We have no other evidence that Swift knew Manilius (and of course Sheridan may have picked the motto).
The Bowyer–Davis editions of the *Intelligencer*, like certain early editions of Manilius, emend *uno* to *unam*, changing the meaning: 'He will go among all the characters and will restore the mob to unity.' The Bowyer–Davis editions also correctly
rearrange the motto into hexameters (see variant readings).
1–2. *The Players having now almost done with . . . the Beggars Opera*: Writing to Pope (Fri-
day, 10 May 1728), Swift reports that 'Mr. Gay's Opera hath been acted here twenty
times, and my Lord Lieutenant tells me it is very well perform'd; he hath seen it
often, and approves it much' (*Corresp.* iii. 285). Because so few Dublin newspapers
have survived from 1728, a complete schedule of the Dublin run of *The Beggar's
Opera* is unavailable. The second performance was Saturday, 16 Mar.; others are
recorded on Thursday, 21 Mar.; Saturday, 23 Mar.; Thursday, 10 Apr. (tenth
performance); Saturday, 13 Apr. (eleventh performance), with a total run of twenty-
three nights (reported in *Mist's Weekly J.*, 6 July) or of twenty-four nights (reported
in the *Dunciad Variorum*, TE v. 190). All this suggests a schedule of performances
every Thursday and Saturday, with one or two extras. In that case, the players
should have been *entirely* done with *The Beggar's Opera* by 25 May, when *Intelligencer* 3 was probably published, but performances may have been less frequent
toward the end of the season. On 23 Mar. it was reported that 'Boxes &c. are
bespoke for 16 or 18 Nights to come' (*Dublin Intelligence*, 23 Mar. 1728), implying that
a run until 25 May was then expected. See Schultz, *Beggar's Opera*, 38–42; T. J.
Walsh, *Opera in Dublin, 1705–1797* (Dublin, 1973), 34–5.
10. *Humour*: See introductory note.
15. *peculiar to the English Nation*: Swift, in disagreeing with Temple that humour is

peculiarly English, rejects a notion that English critics had prided themselves on since Temple proposed it in 'Of Poetry' (Spingarn, *Critical Essays*, iii. 103–5); see Tave, *Amiable Humorist*, 94–6 and nn.

19. *Le Theatre Italien*: A compilation in which the Harlequin Evaristo Gherardi attempts to put the *commedia dell'arte* into writing (Paris, 1694); Swift owned a 6-vol. Amsterdam edn. (Braakman, 1701). An important treatment of this work's influence on Swift is included in Mackie Langham Jarrell's 'Swift's "Peculiar Vein of Humour"', Ph.D. thesis (Univ. of Texas, 1954).

19. *Rabelais, Cervantes*: Swift had known since Jan. 1728, if not earlier, that Pope intended to associate him with these authors in the *Dunciad* (*Corresp.* iii. 246, 261). On Swift's admiration for them see Spence, *Observations*, i. 55, 308; *Corresp.* iii. 407; Harold Williams, *Dean Swift's Library* (Cambridge, 1932), 50, 79–80; *Dunciad*, TE v. 62. In announcing his approval of Rabelais Swift again finds occasion to disagree with Temple's 'Of Poetry' (Spingarn, *Critical Essays*, iii. 101–2).

21–2. *Comedy or Farce, (or whatever Name the Criticks will allow it)*: For the controversy Swift here avoids, see Leo Hughes, 'Attitudes of Some Restoration Dramatists toward Farce', *PQ* 19 (1940), 268–87.

23–4. *such prodigious success both here, and in England*: The *Dublin Intelligence* reported, 'The New Opera which is again to be Play'd to Night, was On Thursday more Crowded with Spectators than ever, & really it is now so far the Topick of General Conversation here that they who have not seen it are hardly thought worth Speaking to by their Acquaintance, and are only admitted into Discourse on their Promise of going to see it the first Opportunity, which is so advantagious to Our Commedians, that we are told Boxes &c. are bespoke for 16 or 18 Nights to come' (23 Mar. 1727/8). Swift heard about the play's success in London directly from Gay (*Corresp.* iii. 265–6, 272); see also Schultz, *Beggar's Opera*, 1–42.

25–6. *Poetry, Eloquence, and Musick, which are said to have most Power over the minds of Men*: 'Nor is it any great Wonder that such Force should be found in Poetry, since in it are assembled all the Powers of Eloquence, of Musick, and of Picture, which are all allowed to make so strong Impressions upon Humane Minds' (Temple, 'Of Poetry', in Spingarn, *Critical Essays*, iii. 77). That Swift omits Picture from the discussion of a theatrical piece is perhaps a natural consequence of his not having seen it performed.

34. *generally Obvious to the Vulgar*: Swift's interest in writing accessible to all readers was nourished by his work as a writer (and critic) of sermons: see *A Letter to a Young Gentleman, Lately Entered into Holy Orders*, in *Prose*, ix. 65–7, 75–7. According to Faulkner, Swift tried his writings out on 'two Men Servants present for this Purpose . . . for [he said] I write to the Vulgar, more than to the Learned' (*Prose*, xiii. 202–3).

42. *low Comedy*: Dryden opposed low comedy in his preface to *An Evening's Love* (1671); Dennis, however, maintained 'that low Comedy is to be preferred to the high' (i. 281).

46–8. *By what Disposition of the mind . . . this endowment is bestowed upon Mankind*: Temple attributes the English propensity to humour to 'the Native Plenty of our Soyl, the unequalness of our Clymat, as well as the Ease of our Government, and the Liberty of Professing Opinions and Factions' ('Of Poetry', 104).

51–2. *gives Horace the Preference to Juvenal*: The Horace–Juvenal distinction was stated most influentially in Dryden's 'Discourse Concerning the Original and Progress of Satire' (1693). Apropos of Swift's discussion here, William Kupersmith has noted that Horatian satire's seeming mildness 'provided ideal camouflage for the political satirist' ('Vice and Folly in Neoclassical Satire', *Genre*, 11 (1978), 56–8).

55–6. *Corruption in Religion, Politicks, and Law, may be proper Topicks for this kind of Satyr*: 'Had the Author writ a Book to expose the Abuses in Law, or in Physick, he believes the Learned Professors in either Faculty, would have been so far from resenting it, as to have given him Thanks for his Pains, especially if he had made an honourable Reservation for the true Practice of either Science: But Religion they tell us ought not to be ridiculed, and they tell us Truth, yet surely the Corruptions in it may; for we are taught by the tritest Maxim in the World, that Religion being the best of Things, its Corruptions are likely to be the worst.' 'An Apology', *Tale*, 6–7.

68. *Laughing with a few Friends in a Corner*: In a remark Swift himself had edited, Temple had grudgingly restricted satire: to 'bring every Thing to Burlesque ..., if it be allowed at all, should be so only to wise Men in their Closets, and not to *Witts*, in their common Mirth and Company' (Temple to Lord Lisle, Aug. 1667, in Temple's *Letters* (London: Tonson *et al.*, 1700), i. 116). Similarly, in their preface to the *Miscellanies* of 1727, Pope and Swift described that volume's satiric poems as not originally intended for publication but rather the product of youthful folly and the 'Gaiety of our Minds at certain Junctures, common to all Men' (Pope, *Prose Works*, ii. 91).

69–70. *I am ready to Change the Scene with them, whenever they please*: The remark has autobiographical resonance, and its defiant tone offers some measure of the degree to which Swift had put behind him his recent hopes of preferment in England, under the patronage of Queen Caroline. See J. Woolley, 'Friends and Enemies', 210–21.

84. *after Fourteen Years attending the Court*: Typically Swift is not quite accurate about dates. Gay began paying his court to Princess Caroline in 1714, and—according to Swift's interpretation—'failed of Preferment' in 1727. See Vinton A. Dearing's introduction in Gay, *Poetry and Prose*, i. 7–13.

88–90. *that great M[inister] ... publickly owned his Conviction, that Mr. Gay was not the Author*: See introductory note. By 'publickly' Swift means before other witnesses; the admission occurred at a dinner to which Walpole invited Swift in Mar. or Apr. 1726 (the later meeting between them seems to have been private).

93–4. *no more to be suspected, than the Chastity of Cæsar's Wife*: Proverbial, from Plutarch, *Life of Caesar*, x; *Life of Cicero*, xxviii–xxix.

97–9. *his Fables ... Dedicated to the D. of Cumberland*: For the *Fables* see the introductory note. Prince William, the second son of George II, was at the age of five (1726) created Duke of Cumberland by his grandfather; he was later famous for leading the English forces at the Battle of Culloden, 1746.

99. *for which he was PROMISED a Reward*: See introductory note.

112–14. *even Ministers of State ... appearing frequently at the Theatre*: Swift alludes not only to the frequent attendance of the Lord Lieutenant at the Dublin performances but also to the London audiences: 'We hear a million of Storys about the opera, of the ancore at the Song, *That was levelled at me*, when 2 great Ministers were in a Box together, and all the world staring at them' (Swift to Gay, 28 Mar. 1728, *Corresp*. iii. 276). A more circumstantial account, though possibly derived from Swift, is given by William Cooke, *Memoirs of Charles Macklin, Comedian* (London, 1804), 53–4. See also Hervey, i. 98.

113–14. *(next to those whom the Actors more immediately represent)*: This innuendo that the actors represented government ministers was softened in 1735; see textual variants.

118. *I am assured*: Swift apparently did not see *The Beggar's Opera* performed. Whether he absented himself because of deafness or by reason of the scruples he mentions here—certainly he was no longer a 'young Clergy-man'—his writings reveal familiarity with the theatre. In the *Journal to Stella* he describes attending a rehearsal of Addison's *Cato*: 'We stood on the Stage. ... Bp of Cl[ogher] was there too, but he stood privatly in a Gallery' (ii. 654). It was particularly improper for the clergyman to attend in his clerical garb. Arthur Bedford wrote that 'it is universally reckoned a Scandal for any Clergyman to be seen in [theatres]' (*A Sermon Preached in the Parish-Church of St. Butolph's Aldgate... Occasioned by the Erecting of a Play-House in the Neighbourhood* (London: Ackers, 1730; reprinted New York, 1974), 25. And in

1758 Thomas Sheridan the younger noted that during his management of the Smock Alley theatre in Dublin (1745–58) there were 'sometimes more than thirty Clergymen in the Pit at a time, many of them Deans and Doctors of Divinity, though formerly none of that Order had ever entered the Doors, unless a few who skulked in the Gallery disguised' (*An Humble Appeal to the Publick* (Dublin: Faulkner), 20. The deans and doctors of divinity may have been present as early as the second night of the Dublin *Beggar's Opera*, when 'above half the People in the Gallery, were Persons of Distinction in Disguise' (*Dublin Intelligence*, 19 Mar. 1727/8).

126–7. *Persons of their Function are bound to avoid the appearance of Evil, or of giving cause of Offence*: In 'The Form and Manner of Ordering Priests' in the Book of Common Prayer, the bishop exhorts those about to be ordained 'to beware, that neither you yourselves offend, nor be occasion that others offend'; they are to 'set aside . . . all worldly cares and studies'. Swift alludes also to 1 Thess. 5: 22, 'Abstain from all appearance of evil'. No regulation against attending the theatre appears in the canons of the Church of Ireland.

127–8. *Lords Chancellors . . . Conscience*: So John Chamberlayne, *Magnae Britanniae Notitia*, 29th edn. (London: Midwinter, 1728), i. 113; compare *Prose*, vii. 10. The Lord Chancellor of England was Peter King, Baron King of Ockham; of Ireland, Thomas Wyndham, Baron Wyndham.

128–9. *the Judges . . . whose Title is Reverend*: A somewhat unusual usage, but see *Tale*, 181; and *Magnae Britanniae Notitia*, i. 111.

137–8. *a COURT-CHAPLAIN in England*: A future archbishop of Canterbury, Thomas Herring was already well on his way up the ecclesiastical ladder. As preacher to the Honourable Society of Lincoln's Inn, in Mar. 1728 he inveighed against *The Beggar's Opera*, which, being performed at the Lincoln's Inn Fields Theatre, no doubt drew a substantial portion of its audience from the Inns of Court. Though Herring's sermon does not survive, at least not the part of it particularly directed against *The Beggar's Opera*, it may well have been revised as his anti-decadence *Sermon Preached at Kensington* (London: Say, 1747), as Edmund Pyle claimed. Herring's opposition to *The Beggar's Opera* attained fame and notoriety. William Duncombe won Herring's friendship for praising the sermon in the *London Journal* (see Appendix C), while a miscellany of the time described Herring as 'a mighty weak sucking Priest, who to show his Theological Capacity, preached a Sermon at *Lincoln's Inn*-Chapel against the *Deism* of the Age, and the *Beggars Opera*.' As for Herring's being prostitute, he was at this time a chaplain-in-ordinary to the king and enjoyed the patronage of Bishop Fleetwood and Sir Philip Yorke, then Attorney-General and later Lord Hardwicke. Swift knew at least something of the controversy which Herring had touched off (see introductory note), but his comment here seems to echo Gay's letter of 16 May: 'I suppose you must have heard that I have had the honour to have had a Sermon preach'd against my works by a Court Chaplain, which I look upon as no small addition to my fame' (*Corresp.* iii. 288). If Gay's letter did prompt this sentence in the *Intelligencer*, it is further evidence that the essays were composed very shortly before publication. See Schultz, *Beggar's Opera*, 226–32; Aldred W. Rowden, *The Primates of the Four Georges* (London, 1916), 169–72; Herring, *Seven Sermons on Public Occasions* (Dublin: Faulkner, 1763), pp. iii–xviii; *Letters from . . . Thomas Herring . . . to William Duncombe* (London: Johnson, 1777), 1–7, 179–88; *Memoirs of a Royal Chaplain, 1729–1763: The Correspondence of Edmund Pyle* (London, 1905), 120; *The Twickenham Hotch-Potch, for the Use of the Rev. Dr. Swift, Alexander Pope, Esq; and Company. Being a Sequel to the Beggars Opera, &c. . . . Written by Caleb D'Anvers* (London: J. Roberts, 1728), 40.

157–60. *unnatural Taste for Italian Musick . . . whereby we are over-run with Italian-Effeminacy*: Italian opera, sung in English, Italian, or a mixture of the two, was introduced to

London in 1705; Swift had scoffed at it in 1709. It was produced sporadically and with varying financial success until the Royal Academy of Music, from its foundation in 1719 to 1728, gave the city nine straight seasons of opera. The performance of Italian music drew Italian singers, many of them castrati, to London. See *Prose*, vol. ii, pp. xxv–xxvii; and *London Stage*, II. i. lxxi–lxxx. For a succinct account of the opposition to Italian opera, see E. N. Hooker's note in Dennis's *Critical Works*, i. 522–3. Dublin's limited offerings of Italian music are chronicled in Walsh, *Opera in Dublin*.

162. *many were Prosecuted*: Homosexuals were extensively prosecuted in London *c.* 1699 and again *c.* 1707 and in 1726. See Alan Bray, *Homosexuality in Renaissance England* (London, 1982), 90–103, 132–9; two poems, *The Women-Hater's Lamentation* (London: Robinson, 1707; copy in Guildhall Library, London); and John Dunton, 'The He-Strumpets: A Satyr on the Sodomite-Club', 4th edn., in *Athenianism: or, The New Projects of Mr. John Dunton* (London: Darrack, 1710), i². 93–7; and Thomas Bray's sermon *For God, or for Satan* (London: Downing, 1709), 30.

163. *a Fore-runner of Italian-Opera's*: As early as 1706, John Dennis wrote that Italian opera was 'so prodigiously unnatural, that it could take its beginning from no Country, but that which is renown'd throughout the World, for preferring monstrous abominable Pleasures to those which are according to Nature' (*Critical Works*, i. 392). [Henry Carey], in his poem *Faustina: or The Roman Songstress, a Satyr, on the Luxury and Effeminacy of the Age*, linked foppery—'this damn'd, *Italian* Pathic Mode, | To *Sodom* and to *Hell* the ready Road'—with the enthusiasm for Italian opera (London: J. Roberts, [1726]), 5. Like Defoe in *The True-Born Englishman* (*POAS* vi. 268), Swift associates Italy—not opera specifically—with homosexuality, both in *Tale*, 41, and in his marginalia to Davila (Hermann J. Real and Heinz J. Vienken, '"A Pretty Mixture": Books from Swift's Library at Abbotsford House', *BJRL* 67 (1984), 537). The association was old, however: see Lawrence Stone, *The Family, Sex and Marriage in England, 1500–1800* (New York, 1977), 492; and Randolph Trumbach, 'London's Sodomites: Homosexual Behavior and Western Culture in the 18th Century', *J. of Social History*, 11 (1977), 10.

164. *nothing but Stabbing*: '*Stabbing* in *England* is much more seldom than in *Italy*', according to *Magnae Britanniae Notitia* (1728), i. 190.

Sheridan's essay against gaming, though largely conventional in its moral position, bore particular relevance to the current devotion to quadrille, then a craze among Dublin's fashionable ladies. *The Ladies Opera*, a Dublin halfsheet probably of 1728, refers to Dawson Street as 'Quadrill-Row' (Foxon L15). Although Sheridan is addressing female behaviour in a way the *Intelligencer* seldom attempts, Swift wrote a poem on much the same theme. *The Journal of a Dublin Lady* (or *The Journal of a Modern Lady*, as it is known from *Poems*, ii. 443–53) would have been published in the *Intelligencer* if it had not suspended publication after no. 19. This poem is the best single commentary on no. 4. See also Swift's remark that '*Quadrille* . . . bears some Resemblance to a State of Nature, which we are told is a State of War, wherein every Woman is against every Woman' (*Prose*, iv. 115).

Sheridan's essay was four times appropriated by reprinters for their own purposes (see textual notes).

NUMB. IV.

Quando alea hos animos?
Juv.

AMONG all the *Amusements*, invented by the idle part of
Mankind, to pass away their Time, there is not one, which is
attended with so many Evil Consequences as that of *Gaming*,
nor indeed any so much below the Dignity of Human-Nature, it being
5 an Employment so Trifling in Appearance, that a Man with a *Box* and
Dice, is hardly distinguishable from a Child with it's Rattle, nor when
he Diverts himself with a few scraps of Painted Paste-board, does he
make one whit a better figure.

But setting Appearances of this kind aside, which can make even
10 the Wisest look Ridiculous, I shall chiefly Dwell upon the more solid
Evils, that attend all intemperate practitioners in this way, and these
I shall Sum up in the following Losses, *viz. Loss of Time; Loss of
Reputation; Loss of Health; Loss of Fortune; Loss of Temper; and what is often
the Effect of it, the Loss of Life it self.*

15 *First*, That it is a *Loss of Time*, is plain, because our Time may be
employ'd to more advantage; for by Six Hours in the twenty four, I can
make my self *Wiser*, and *better*, and *Richer*; whereas on the Contrary,

by *Cards* or *Dice*, I do Infallibly grow more *Stupid*, and *Worse*; and a Hundred to One against me I grow *Poorer*.

Secondly, That it is a *Loss of Reputation*, and Esteem in the World, is 20 easily proved, because no Man of *Reputation* or *Esteem* was ever called a *Gamester*; Eo. *vice versa*, No *Gamester* can be called a Man of *Reputation* and *Esteem*. For in giving the best Characters to Men or Women, we never use the Word *Gaming* as an *Epithet*. We say, for Instance, *A great and Glorious King*; *A wise and a good Governor*; *A learned* 25 *and a Pious Bishop*; *An unbiassed and just Chancellor*; *a Virtuous and a Modest Lady*, and so through the best Degrees of Men and Women. But how odly would it sound, if we should take out the latter *Epithet* from each of these, and put in their stead the Word *Gaming*. And say, *A Wise and a Gaming King*; *A Learned and a Gaming Bishop*; *An unbiassed* 30 *and Gaming Chancellor*; *A Virtuous and a Gaming Lady*, &c. From which it is plain, that *Gaming* must stand and agree with the worst Characters; For it Sounds very well to say, *A Profligate Gaming Spendthrift*; *A Notorious Gaming Sharper*; *A Swearing Gaming Bully*. And the same *Epithet* will agree as well with *Pick-pockets*, *Rakes*, *Highway-* 35 *men*, and others of that distinguished Race of Mankind.

Thirdly, That it is *a Loss of Health* follows from the Sedentary Life, to which those who follow *Gaming* are confined; whence, as I am told by a knowing *Physician*, proceed *Dropsies*, *Gouts*, *Gravel*, and *Stone* in the Men; and in the Women, *Tympanies* of both kinds, *Hystericks*, *Vapours*, 40 and a load of bad *Humours*, for want of those Exercises, which produce *Perspiration*, and *Evacuations* necessary to Invigorate, Strengthen, and preserve the *Animal Oeconomy*, free from those Numerous Distempers, which *Laziness* and *Sloth* produce.

Fourthly, That it is *a Loss of Fortune* is out of all Dispute, from the 45 Numberless Instances, I cou'd give of *Lords*, *Ladies*, and *Squires*, some of whom have lost their whole Estates; others the most part; others again have laid themselves under such difficulties, that their Annual Income has fallen very short to supply them with the Common Necessaries of Life; so that they have been obliged to live upon the 50 Credit of the ensuing Year.

And as for Ladies whose Pride would not permit them to be so obliged to their Creditors, they either pawn their Houshold Moveables, or Sell (what next to *Gaming*, goes nearest to their Heart) their very *Parapharnalia*; but this I must Remark, has happend chiefly 55 among those who have been seduced as *Cullies* to the Fashionable *Game* of *Quadrill*. It will not be here Foreign to my purpose, to Write down some few *Inventories* of *Goods*, lately hawked about by trusty *Chamber-maids.*

60   Belonging to Lady *FLAVIA* near *Stephen's-Green.*
1 *Diamond Necklace,* 1 *Pair of Diamond Ear-Rings,* 3 *Diamond-Rings, and a Gold Watch with Trinckets.*

To Mrs. *DORINDA* of *Dawson-Street.*
2 *Large Silver-Cups,* 3 *Salvers,* 2 *Pair of Candlesticks,* 1 *Silver Sauce-Pan.*

65   To Madam *CHLOE* in *Jervice-Street.*
2 *Birth-Day Suits,* 1 *Piece of* French *Damask, Broad Green Stripe, with White Flowers, Pawned for Nine Pounds,* 4 *Damask Table-Cloaths, and a Dozen of Napkins.*

To Madam *LIBERIA* of *College-Green.*
70 *A fine wrought Coverlet of a Bed, A picture of her Husband's Father and Mother set in Gold, A Gold Snuff-box,* 1 *Dozen of Silver-spoons, A Child's Bells and Coral.*

I have had an Account of many more, but this is full enough to answer my Design, for I intend only by this discovery that their
75 Husbands should add a little more to their Pin-money, and thereby enable them to pay their Debts of Honour, in a less Scandalous way.

Indeed it would not be amiss, if Husbands should make use of their Authority, at least to regulate one Circumstance, that is, to bring their Wives to be content with two Hours Play, instead of twelve in the four
80 and twenty; because some Inconveniences attend it. The Servants having all that Time to themselves, to Intreigue; to Juncket; to Filsh and Steal; to pawn the Inferior Moveables of the Pantry, and Kitchen; and lastly to Corrupt the Children; by teaching them Cursing, Swearing, Lying, and Lewdness, which in all probability may bring
85 both Ruin and Disgrace to their Family.

It is very well known that among the great and fashionable People of former ages, they very rarely had recourse to *Gaming.* We read that *Artaxerxes*, *Cato*, and *Augustus*, did sometimes Divert themselves this Way, but I cannot recollect that ever the *Ladies* entered into it at all,
90 their Amusements being rather the *Needle* and the *Loom*; for which their Perfections are Celebrated by the Oldest and best Poet of the World. The Men of any Consequence, passed their Evenings in Learned and agreeable Conversation, such as tended to make them wiser and better, for which I appeal to the *Symposiacks* of *Plato*, the
95 *Feast* of *Xenophon*, and those Accounts given by *Macrobius*. And to

bring the matter nearer our own Times, the People of the greatest
Consequence, in these *British Isles*, have chosen rather to pass away
their Evenings in Polite Discourses with one another; and I should
think that I failed in a due Veneration for their Memories, if I should
pass their Names over in Silence. The Celebrated Lord *Falkland*, 100
Earl *Carnarvan*, *Endymion Porter*, Mr. *Waller*, Sir *John Sucklin*; and
among the conversible Ladies, The Countesses of *Bedford*, *Carlisle*,
Devonshire, and several others. This way of Improvement is elegantly
described by *Horace*.

$$\text{————————} Ergo \qquad\qquad 105$$

Sermo oritur, non de villis domibusve alienis:
Nec male necne Lepos Saltet: sed quod magis ad nos
Pertinet, et nescire malum est agitamus: utrumne
Divitiis homines, an sint virtute beati:
Quidve ad amicitias, Usus, rectumne trahat nos: 110
Et quæ sit natura boni, summumq; quid ejus.

Thus after plain Repast, each cheerful Guest,
With useful Conversation, Crowns the Feast,
Not Trifling Chat, on this, or tother Place,
Or *Lepos* Dancing with a better Grace;   115
But what is more Concern to Humane kind,
To mend our Manners, and improve the mind.
On *Philosophick Questions* wisely bent,
As whether Wealth or Virtue gives content,
What Cause directs us in the Choice of Friends,   120
Our private Int'rest, or more Noble Ends.
What Road to chuse, what End we should pursue,
And how to keep the Good Supreme in View.

For my own Part I could rather Wish, and I believe many Husbands
would agree with me, That the Ladies would rather employ 125
themselves, as *Juvenal* Describes those in his Time, in Fighting Prizes
upon a Publick Stage, whereby they would at least discover their
Activity, and their Courage, in a much more becoming manner, than
(according to the present Practice) pulling of Coifs upon a wrangle at
Quadrill.   130
The Ancients did so far abhor any Excess in Gaming, That *Aristotle*
in his 4th Book of *Ethicks*, at the latter end of the 1st. Chap. places
Tyrants, *Gamester's* and *Robbers* in one Class, their Dispositions being

exactly the same: For who ever yet knew a right Gamester, that was not
135 apt to insult upon Success, or to pillage all before him upon every
Advantage. The Author I have now mentioned Stiles them very justly
αἰσχροκερδεῖς (I wish the *Ladies* understood *Greek*) We have no
English Word expressive enough to explain it. The nearest meaning I
can think of is *base-gainers*. And what can be baser, than to sit down
140 deliberately with a Friend, either at his House, or my own, with an
Intention to pick his Pocket, by a lucky Throw of a Dye, or a Cast of a
Card. This has been frequently the Practice. However I shall content
my self with a Relation of one Fact, because it is somewhat singular in
it's kind.
145 BRYANIA the *Virago* one Evening, invited the beautiful *Morisda* to
a game of *Cards* at her House, which the latter declined, as having
neither Skill, nor Inclination, nor Money for Play; yet by much
Importunity was prevailed on to sup with her. Soon after *BRYANIA*
calls for a *Pack of Cards*, and told the poor innocent Lady, she would
150 instruct her in a Game, which a Child of four Years old might learn in
four Minutes; to this the complying good-natured *Morisda* willingly
consented, upon her Friend's telling her she might lose very little by
low playing at this Game. Accordingly they fixt upon three-pence a
Counter. They had not played above three Hours, when the poor
155 *Cully* was told she had lost about a trifle of twenty Guineas. Being not
able to command twenty Shillings in the world, she took her leave in
great Confusion, and Grief, promising to discharge the Debt in a litle
Time. The unmerciful *BRYANIA* dunned her the Day following, and
so continued for a Week. This put the poor indigent *Lady* upon trying
160 all Friends. In the mean Time, the following Letter was written to her,
which I have Transcribed with the strictest Justice to the Writer.

MADDUM,

I donat undarstand youar tretmint in giuin me they troble off Sendin so offen
forr that trifil wich youe losst too me tuther nit If youe doo nott sende itt bye
165 they berer I a shuar youe I wil rite too youar husbund forr itt, Maddum I amm
&c.

This terrible Letter put the poor *Lady* to her last Shifts (nor is it a
wonder it should, her Husband being the greatest Bear living) which
was to borrow the Money of a certain *Collonel*, and this, uncharitable
170 People did misinterpret *for a Valuable Consideration*.
The fifth *Loss*, I mentioned, was that of *Temper*. If any one doubts
the Truth of this Position, I refer him to the *Groom Porters*, and *Lucas's-*

Coffee-House, where the only Virtuosi of the Gaming Science are Daily and Nightly to be seen. If *Blaspheming, Cursing, Swearing, Duelling, Runing of Heads against the Wall, Throwing Hats and Wigs in the Fire,* 175 *Distortions of the Countenance, Biting of Nails, Burning of Cards, Breaking of Dice-Boxes,* can be called a *Loss* of Temper, they are found in the aforesaid places, in the highest degree of Perfection. And to make out the last and greatest Loss, which is, *The Loss of Life.*

I have, according to the best of my Memory, heard of no less than 180 seven or eight worthy Gentlemen of the Trade, within a very few Years, upon some hasty Words and Blows, given at some of these Gaming-Tables, retire from their Company, and one of them bring in the News of the other's Death in about Six Minutes.

Upon the whole, I cannot but remark, That Gaming proceeds from 185 three Qualities of the basest kind, *Avarice, Laziness* and *Ignorance*; For it must undoubtedly be a thirst for Gain, which is a motive to high playing; and as for the Lazy and Ignorant (if they play low) I am more willing to indulge them, because they have naturally better Talents for *sitting* and *trifling*, than wholsome bodily Exercise, or spending the 190 Evenings in a way of Conversation, agreeable to *Rational Creatures.*

I shall end this Paper with a very useful Remark. *Plato* is my Author, that the *Demon* THEUTH was the Inventor of *Dice* (The *Ladies* know well enough, that the *Devil* and *Demon* are the same) and the Vulgar have it by Tradition, that *Cards* are the Devil's own Invention, for 195 which reason, time out of mind, they are and have been called *the Devil's Books*, therefore I cannot but say after this Information given, if Gamesters will not desist, they are undoubtedly at the *Devil's Devotion.*

MOTTO. Correctly 'alea quando | hos animos?' *Satires*, i. 88–9 ('When was gambling so reckless?').

15. *Loss of Time*: The argument is anticipated in Owen Feltham, *Resolves*, 10th edn. (London: Clark and Harper, 1677), 280–2, which Sheridan owned (Sheridan, *Library*, 470).

21. *no Man of Reputation*: Sheridan soon contradicts himself.

22. *Eo.*: Ergo.

39. *a knowing Physician*: Not identified, though his theories, largely those of Thomas Sydenham, MD (1624–89), would have been propagated in Dublin by Sydenham's correspondent Dr (later Sir) Thomas Molyneux (1661–1733); see Sydenham, *Works*, ii (London, 1850), 129, 139–40, 148–53, 164–5; and Kenneth Dewhurst, *Dr. Thomas Sydenham* (London, 1966), 54, 57. See also Sir Richard Blackmore, *A Treatise of Consumptions and Other Distempers Belonging to the Breast and Lungs*, 2nd edn., corr. (London: Pemberton, 1725), pp. xx, 125–9; Blackmore, *Dissertations on a Dropsy, a Tympany, the Jaundice, the Stone, and a Diabetes* (London: Knapton, 1727), 71–2, 87–8, 103, 172–3, 177; and Francis Fuller's popular *Medicina Gymnastica* (London: Matthews, 1705), which by 1728 had reached its sixth edition.

40. *Tympanies*: A tympany was a 'Turgency, or a hard Inflation of the Abdomen, braced in some Measure like a Drum' (Blackmore, *Dissertations*, 87). The 'Kinds' are presumably intestinal and uterine. (Weckermann.)

43–4. *Distempers, which Laziness and Sloth produce*: Cf. *Prose*, ix. 193.

52. *Ladies*: These are the usual injunctions against women's gambling; compare [Edward Ward]'s 'Bad Luck to Him Who Has Her', in *The Modern World Disrob'd* (London: G. S., 1708), 51–7.

55. *Parapharnalia*: A wife's clothing—and (sometimes) jewellery and 'the Furniture of her Chamber'—title to which passed to her upon her husband's death. Since there were no Irish statutes governing paraphernalia, the English law was applicable, for which see Thomas Wood, *An Institute of the Laws of England*, 4th edn. (Dublin: Watts, 1724), 63.

63. *Dawson-Street*: One of Dublin's most fashionable new streets (Craig, 106–7, 111). See introductory note.

66. *Birth-Day Suits*: Clothing worn at Court on the king's birthday.

75. *Pin-money*: The recent custom of a husband's making his wife an annual allowance had been opposed by Addison in *Spectator* 295 (7 Feb. 1712); Swift in his hints for *Intelligencer* papers approves, however (Appendix J). See also Susan Muller Okin, 'Patriarchy and Married Women's Property in England', *Eighteenth-Century Stud.* 17 (1983–4), 136.

88. *Artaxerxes*: Plutarch, *Artaxerxes*, xvii.

88. *Cato*: Plutarch, *Cato the Younger*, vi, quoting Cicero's remark that Cato spent whole days in gaming; Erasmus in his *Apophthegms*, however, considers Cicero's comment ironic praise of Cato's industry.

88. *Augustus*: Suetonius, *Augustus*, lxxi.

91. *Oldest and best Poet*: See *Odyssey*, ii. 93–110; vi. 53–5; iv. 120–35.

95. *Macrobius*: In the *Saturnalia*.

96–7. *People of the greatest Consequence, in these British Isles*: While the moderns named— mostly seventeenth-century royalist literati—may be called 'conversible', Sheridan's claim that they preferred conversation to gaming seems in some cases to be unsupported speculation.

100. *Falkland*: Lucius Cary, 2nd Viscount Falkland (1610?–43), educated at TCD and hence particularly significant to Sheridan; Secretary of State 1642–3. He was of 'inimitable sweetness and delight in Conversation'; 'he contracted familiarity and friendship with the most polite and accurate Men of [Oxford] University; who . . . frequently resorted, and dwelt with him, as in a College situated in a purer Air; so that his House was a University in a less volume', according to Clarendon's *History*, ii (Oxford: at the Theatre, 1703), 270–1; Swift marked this passage in his copy (see *Prose*, v. xxxix–xl, 304).

101. *Carnarvan*: Robert Dormer, 1st Earl of Carnarvon (d. 1643), royalist general praised for his 'wit' and 'Fancy' in Francis Wortley's *Characters and Elegies* (1646), 36. Even though Carnarvon cautioned against gaming, he himself 'affected [it] inordinately', according to Da[vid] Lloyd, *Memoires* (London: Speed *et al.*, 1668), 369.

101. *Porter*: Endymion Porter, groom of the bedchamber to Charles I, friend of Herrick, and patron of Davenant. Davenant's 'A Journey into Worcestershire' recounts Porter's sociability: *Shorter Poems*, ed. A. M. Gibbs (1972), 26. That Porter gambled little seems confirmed: Gervas Huxley, *Endymion Porter* (London, 1959), 222.

101. *Waller*: The poet Edmund Waller (1606–87) was a friend of Lord Falkland, Lady Carlisle, and Lady Devonshire, among many others. 'King *Charles*, in his Diversions . . . always made Mr. *Waller* a Party', despite Waller's refusing to drink. 'He . . . whom his very Enemies cannot but extol for his Wit and Eloquence, must have been a Man of so agreeable a Conversation, that we may despair of producing such

another' (*Poems*, 8th edn. (London: Tonson, 1711), pp. xlvii, lxiv). See also the note on Lady Devonshire below.

101. *Sucklin*: Sir John Suckling, the poet (1609–41), praised for his conversation in Dryden's *Essay of Dramatick Poesie* and elsewhere. His notoriety as a gambler, though well known since the 19th century, was recorded in documents almost wholly inaccessible to Sheridan; they are thoroughly discussed in Herbert B. Berry's 'A Life of Sir John Suckling', Ph.D. thesis (Univ. of Nebraska, 1953), esp. ch. 3. See also Thomas Clayton (ed.), *The Works of Sir John Suckling: The Non-Dramatic Works* (Oxford, 1971), pp. xxxiv–xxxv, lxiv–lxxiv.

102. *Bedford*: Lucy Russell, Countess of Bedford (d. 1627), a member of James I's court; addressee of poems by Donne, Jonson, Davies, Drayton, and others.

102. *Carlisle*: Lucy, Countess of Carlisle (1599–1660). Donne, Carew, Davenant, Suckling, and Waller wrote poems to or about her; according to Sir Tobie Mathews, 'She more willingly allowes of the conversation of Men, than of Women. . . . Amongst men, her person is both considered and admired; and her Wit, being most eminent, among the rest of her great abilities, She affects the conversation of the persons, who are most famed for it' (*A Collection of Letters* (London: Herringman, 1660), sig. A5).

103. *Devonshire*: Christian, Countess of Devonshire (d. 1675) was praised for 'Conversation [that] was wise, and profitable, witty, and innocent' in Thomas Pomfret's *Life* of her (London: Rawlins, 1685), 38–40. Lord Lisle wrote in 1667, 'Old Lady *Devonshire* keeps up her Feasts still; and that hath been of late Mr. *Waller*'s chief Theatre' (Temple, *Letters*, ed. Swift (London: Tonson *et al.*, 1700), i. 448).

104. *Horace*: Satires, II. vi. 70–6; the translation is Sheridan's. Compare *Mad Mullinix and Timothy*, lines 259–76, in *Intelligencer* 8.

126. *Juvenal*: Satires, vi. 246–67.

131. *Aristotle*: Nicomachean Ethics, IV. i. 41–3.

145. *BRYANIA . . . Morisda*: Though these names seemingly denote real people (Bryan/ MacBryan/O'Brien and Morris/MacMorris), no real-life counterparts have been identified.

172. *Groom Porters*: At Dublin Castle, as at the London court, the Groom Porter presided over legal gaming. About 1725 a new Groom Porter's house was erected adjoining the chapel in Dublin Castle, occasioning a poem that has erroneously been attributed to Swift (*Poems*, iii. 1124).

172–3. *Lucas's-Coffee-House*: In Cork House, on Cork Hill, Lucas's was the scene of 'too splendid Dress', according to Francis Hutcheson (*Dublin Weekly J.*, 12 Feb. 1725/6); James Arbuckle, commenting on this remark, called Lucas's 'the gayest Coffee-House in *Dublin*' (*A Collection of Letters and Essays . . . Lately Publish'd in the Dublin [Weekly] Journal* (London: Darby and Browne, 1729), i. 393n.). An earlier poem describes Lucas's as 'the Thoughtless Place: | Where *Sucking Beaux*, our *future Hopes*, are bred, | The *Sharping Gamester*, and the *Bully Red*' (?William King of Christ Church, *The Swan Tripe-Club in Dublin: A Satyr* (London: the booksellers, 1706), 5).

192. *Plato*: Phaedrus 274 C–E.

197. *Devil's Books*: Proverbial; see Tilly; Swift, *Poems*, iii. 905; and *Polite Conversation*, in *Prose*, iv. 194.

Swift and Sheridan must often have pondered the opposition between discretion and wit in clerical careers. Swift had written to Charles Ford two decades earlier, 'I am not grown great, nor like to do so very soon: for I am thought to want the Art of being thourow paced in my Party, as all discreet Persons ought to be' (8 March 1708/9, *Corresp.* i. 125). On the other hand, he had written to Lord Bolingbroke, 'There is a lower kind of discretion and regularity, which seldom fails of raising men to the highest stations, in the court, the church, and the law' (19 Dec. 1719, ibid., ii. 332).

From his own career, damaged by the reputation of having written *A Tale of a Tub*, as well as from Sheridan's, it was not difficult to conclude that for a clergyman, 'nothing is so fatal as the Character of Wit'. 'S—— had the Sin of Wit no venial Crime', he had written in *The Author upon Himself* (1714; *Poems*, i. 193); and he later told Delany that 'A Genius in the Rev'rend Gown, | Must ever keep it's Owner down' (*To Doctor D—l—y* (1730), *Poems*, ii. 502). On Sheridan's indiscretion, see the General Introduction, and also Swift's description of Sheridan's 'perpetual want of . . . discretion' ('The Second Solomon' (1729), *Prose*, v. 225; compare v. 217).

NUMB. V.

Describ'd it's thus: Defin'd would you it have?
Then the World's honest Man's an errant Knave.

BEN. JOHNSON

THERE is no *Talent* so useful towards rising in the World, or which puts Men more out of the reach of Fortune, than that Quality generally possessed by the Dullest sort of People, and in common Speech, called *Discretion*, a species of lower Prudence, by
5 the assistance of which, People of the meanest Intellectuals, without any other Qualification, pass through the World in great Tranquility, and with Universal good Treatment, neither giving nor taking Offence. *Courts* are seldom unprovided of Persons under this Character, on whom, if they happen to be of great Quality, most
10 Employments, even the greatest naturally fall, when Competitors will not agree; and in such Promotions, no Body rejoyces or grieves. The Truth of this I could prove by several Instances, within my own Memory (for I say nothing of present Times.)

And indeed as Regularity and Forms are of great use in carrying on

the Business of the World, so it is very convenient, that Persons 15
endued with this kind of Discretion, should have that share which
is proper to their Talents in the Conduct of Affairs, but by no
means to meddle in matters which require *Genius*, *Learning*, *strong
Comprehension*, *quickness of Conception*, *Magnanimity*, *Generosity*,
Sagacity, or any other superior Gift of Human minds. Because this sort 20
of *Discretion*, is usually attended with a strong desire of Money, and
few Scruples about the way of obtaining it, with servile Flattery and
Submission, with a Want of all publick Spirit or Principle, with a
perpetual wrong Judgment when the Owners come into Power, and
High Place, how to dispose of Favour and Preferment, having no 25
measure for Merit, and Virtue in others, but those very Steps by which
themselves ascended; Nor the least Intention of doing Good or Hurt
to the Publick, further than Either one or t'other, is likely to be
subservient to their own Security or Interest. Thus being void of all
Friendship and Enmity, they never complain nor find Fault with the 30
Times, and indeed never have reason to do so.

Men of eminent Parts and Abilities as well as Virtues do sometimes
rise in *Courts*, sometimes in the *Law*, and sometimes even in the
Church. Such were the Lord *Bacon*, the Earl of *Strafford*, Arch-bishop
Laud in the Reign of King *Charles* I. and others in our own times 35
whom I shall not Name: But these and many more under different
Princes, and in different Kingdoms, were *Disgraced* or *Banished*, or
suffered Death, meerely in Envy to their Virtues and Superior *Genius*,
which emboldned them in great Exigencies and distresses of State
(wanting a reasonable Infusion of this Aldermanly Discretion) to 40
attempt the Service of their Prince and Country out of the common
Forms.

This evil Fortune, which generally attends extraordinary Men in
the Management of great Affairs, hath been imputed to divers Causes,
that need not be here set down, when so obvious a One occurs. For, 45
if what a certain Writer observes, be true, *when a great Genius appears
in the World, the Dunces are all in Confederacy against him*: And thus
although he imploys his *Talents* wholly in his Closet, without
interfaring with any Man's Ambition or Avarice; what must he expect
when he ventures out to seek for Preferment in a Court, but Universal 50
Opposition, when he is mounting the Ladder, and every hand ready to
turn him off, when he is at the Top? And in this point Fortune
generally Acts directly contrary to Nature, For in Nature we find, that
Bodies full of Life and Spirit mount easily, and are hard to fall,

55 whereas heavy Bodies are hard to rise, and come down with greater
Velocity, in Proportion to their weight. But we find Fortune every Day
Acting just the reverse of this.

This Talent of *Discretion*, as I have described it in it's several
Adjuncts and Circumstances, is no where so serviceable as to the
60 *Clergy*, to whose Preferment, nothing is so fatal as the Character of
Wit, Politeness in Reading, or Manners, or that kind of Behaviour
which we contract, by having too much Conversed with Persons of
high Stations and Eminency, these Qualifications being reckoned by
the *Vulgar* of *all Ranks* to be marks of *Levity*, which is the last Crime
65 the World will pardon in *a Clergy-Man*. To this I may add a free
manner of speaking in mixt Company, and too frequent an
Appearance in places of much resort, which are equally Noxious to
Spiritual Promotions.

I have known indeed a few Exceptions to some parts of these
70 Regulations. I have seen some of the Dullest Men alive aiming at Witt,
and others with as little Pretensions, affecting Politeness in Manners
and Discourse, but never being able to persuade the World of their
Guilt, they grew into considerable Stations, upon the firm Assurance
which all People had of their *Discretion*, because they were a Size too
75 low to deceive the World to their own Disadvantage. But this I confess
is a Tryal too dangerous often to engage in.

There is a known Story of a *Clergy-Man*, who was recommended for
a Preferment by some great Man at Court, to *A.B.C.T.* His Grace said,
he had heard that the *Clergy-Man* used to play at Whisk and
80 Swobbers, that as to playing now and then a Sober Game at Whisk for
pastime, it might be pardoned, but he could not digest those wicked
Swobbers, and it was with some pains that my Lord *S——rs* could
undeceive him. I ask, by what Talents we may suppose that great
Pr—— ascended so high, or what sort of Qualifications he would
85 expect in those whom he took into his Patronage, or would probably
recommend to Court for the government of *Distant Churches*.

Two *Clergy-Men* in my Memory stood Candidates for a small *Free-
School* in ——*Shire*, where a Gentleman of Quality and Interest in the
Country, who happened to have a better understanding than his
90 Neighbours, procured the place for him who was the better Schollar,
and more Gentlemanly Person of the two, very much to the Regret of
all the Parish; The other being disappointed, came up to *London*,
where he became the greatest Pattern of this lower *Discretion*, that I
have known and possessed with as heavy Intellectuals, which together

with the coldness of his Temper, and gravity of his Deportment, 95
carried him safe through many Difficulties, and he lived and dyed in a
great Station, while his Competitor is too obscure for Fame to tell us
what became of him.

This Species of *Discretion* which I so much celebrate, and do most
heartly recommend, hath one Advantage not yet mentioned, that it 100
will carry a Man safe through all the Malice and Variety of Parties, so
far, that whatever Faction happen to be uppermost, his Claim is
usually allowed for a share of what is going. And the thing seems to be
highly reasonable. For in all great Changes, the prevailing side is
usually so Tempestuous, that it wants the balast of those whom the 105
World calls moderate Men and I call *Men of Discretion*, whom People
in Power may with little Ceremony load as heavy as they please, drive
them through the hardest and deepest Roads without danger of
Foundring, or breaking their Backs, and will be sure to find them
neither Resty nor Vicious.   110

In some following Paper, I will give the Reader a short History of
two *Clergy-Men* in *England*, the Characters of each, and the Progress
of their Fortunes in the World. By which the force of worldly
Discretion and the bad Consequences from the want of that Virtue
will strongly appear.   115

MOTTO. The concluding couplet of Epigram 115, 'On the Townes Honest Man', in
   Jonson's folio *Workes* of 1640, which Swift owned: 'Describ'd it's thus: Defin'd
   would you it have? | Then, *The towns honest man's* her errant'st knave.' 'It' is a man
   who is all things to all people. Swift's copy, STC 14753, is TCD Press C.5.8.
34–5. *the Lord Bacon, the Earl of Strafford, Arch-bishop Laud*: 'Think upon Lord Bacon,
   Williams, Strafford, Laud, Clarendon, Shaftesbury, the last Duke of Buckingham;
   and of my own acquaintance, the Earl of Oxford and yourself: All great geniuses in
   their several ways; and, if they had not been so great, would have been less unfortunate.' Swift to Bolingbroke, 19 Dec. 1719, *Corresp*. ii. 333. Swift refers to Strafford, who was executed, as a man of 'exalted Abilities' who, when 'called to public
   Affairs', was 'drawn into Inconveniencies and Misfortunes, which others of Ordinary Talents avoid' (*An Enquiry into the Behaviour of the Queen's Last Ministry*, in *Prose*,
   viii. 138).
37. *Disgraced or Banished*: Faulkner in his 18° edition of Swift's *Works* (1762) finds a reference to 'Dr. ATTERBURY, Bishop of *Rochester*, who was tried and banished by the
   Parliament of *Great Britain* in the Year 1722' (i. 269n.).
40. *this Aldermanly Discretion*: 'A small infusion of the *Alderman* [is] necessary to those
   who are employed in publick Affairs.' *An Enquiry*, in *Prose*, viii. 139.
41–2. *the common Forms*: 'I take the Infelicity of such extraordinary Men to have been
   caused by their Neglect of common Forms' (*An Enquiry*, in *Prose*, viii. 138–9). Swift
   attributes to himself, but with complex implications, the maxim 'That common
   Forms were not design'd | Directors to a noble Mind' (*Cadenus and Vanessa*, *Poems*,
   ii. 706; compare *Tale*, 171).

46. *a certain Writer*: Swift himself, in 'Thoughts on Various Subjects', dated 1 Oct. 1706 and first published in his 1711 *Miscellanies*; see textual variants.

54. *Bodies full of Life and Spirit*: An ancient idea; see Aristotle, *De Caelo*, iv; Lucretius, an author Swift knew well, asserted that velocity was proportional to weight (*De Rerum Natura*, ii. 231).

78. *A.B.C.T.*: Thomas Tenison (1636–1715) became archbishop of Canterbury in 1694/5. The incident Swift recounts, if it is not apocryphal, would have occurred between 1695 and 1700, when Tenison headed a royal commission 'to recommend fit persons to all ecclesiastical preferments'. During this period he also attempted to upgrade clerical morality, and he actively supported the Societies for the Reformation of Manners (Edward Carpenter, *Thomas Tenison* (London, 1948), 167–76, 286–7). He was famous for moderation toward Dissenters and was commonly described by enemies as 'grave', 'dull', and a 'tool'. See *POAS* v. 134; vi. 16, 654–5; vii. 159; Carpenter, 405; Thomas Hearne, *Remarks and Collections*, ed. C. E. Doble *et al.*, ii (Oxford, 1886), 107; *Bishop* [Gilbert] *Burnet's History of His Own Time* (Oxford, 1823), iv. 238n. In 1708 Swift may have believed that Tenison favoured him for the bishopric of Waterford (*Corresp.* i. 68n.), though Ehrenpreis thinks otherwise (ii. 217). Swift suspected that Tenison conspired against his candidacy for an English deanery—those of Wells, Ely, and Lichfield all went to other candidates in 1713; see *The Author upon Himself*, in *Poems*, i. 195, line 47; C. H. Firth, 'Dean Swift and Ecclesiastical Preferment', *RES* 2 (1926), 13–14; and Ricardo Quintana, *The Mind and Art of Jonathan Swift* (London, 1936), 226; Ehrenpreis sees no 'serious' role for Tenison (ii. 632). In Swift's marginalia on Burnet, he calls Tenison 'the dullest, good for nothing man I ever knew' (*Prose*, v. 271 and also 260).

79–80. *Whisk and Swobbers*: Or whist. Despite the oft-quoted pronouncement in *The Whole Art and Mystery of Modern Gaming* (London: J. Roberts, 1726) that '*Whisk* is a Tavern Game' (96), it was fashionable enough to have been played regularly at the Dublin court on 'Castle-Nights' Tuesdays and Fridays (*The Ladies Opera*, [Dublin, ?1728]). Swift played it; see *Account Books*, 97, 116, 142; *Poems*, i. 315; iii. 943. Johnson, citing this passage, defines *swobber* as one of 'four privileged cards that are only incidentally used in betting at the game of whist'. From Fielding's *Life of Jonathan Wild* (1743), it is clear that 'whisk and swobbers' denoted the game as a whole.

82. *S——rs*: John, Baron Somers of Evesham (1651–1716), Lord Keeper (1693) and Lord Chancellor (1697) under William III and a leader of the Whig Junto in Queen Anne's reign. Somers, though allegedly a deist or atheist, exercised considerable patronage over ecclesiastical preferments and consulted closely with Tenison about them. In 1701 Swift defended Somers against impeachment in *A Discourse of the Contests and Dissentions*, and he dedicated *A Tale of a Tub* to him in 1704. See William L. Sachse, *Lord Somers* (Manchester, 1975), 102–3 and n. 87; Carpenter, 179n.; G. V. Bennett, 'King William III and the Episcopate', in Bennett and J. D. Walsh (eds.), *Essays in Modern English Church History* (London, 1966), 124; *A Discourse*, 15. On Swift's relations with Somers, see Ehrenpreis, ii. 81, 83–4, 121–4; and Robert M. Adams, 'In Search of Baron Somers', in P. Zagorin (ed.), *Culture and Politics from Puritanism to the Enlightenment* (Berkeley, 1980), 185–9, 200–2. See also the notes to no. 9.

83–4. *that great Pr[elate]*: Rumours were current that William III had made Tenison archbishop of Canterbury for his docility and stupidity; see *POAS* v. 469; and *The Diary of Dudley Ryder, 1715–1716*, ed. William Matthews (London, 1939), 167–8.

87–8. *Two Clergy-Men . . . in ——Shire*: Faulkner's editions read '*Yorkshire*', suggesting that Swift had a specific person in mind for the clergyman who 'lived and dyed in a great Station'—perhaps a bishopric. The likeliest candidate would seem to be John Sharp (1645–1714), archbishop of York, about whom there survived a tradition that *c.* 1667 he was an unsuccessful candidate for the curacy of Wibsey, near Bradford,

Yorkshire (William Cudworth, *Round about Bradford* (Bradford, 1876), 41); there-after he came to London as chaplain to Sir Hineage Finch and became rector of St Giles-in-the-Fields (A. Tyndal Hart, *The Life and Times of John Sharp, Archbishop of York* (London, 1949), 52–61). The Wibsey story could have provided Swift with a sufficient narrative frame for the hostility he felt toward Sharp, his 'mortall Enemy', for blocking his promotion to one of the English deaneries in 1713 (*Journal to Stella*, ii. 665).

100. heartly: An obsolete form of *heartily*; see *OED*.
111. *some following Paper*: No. 7.

For reprinting no. 6 the printer of *Mist's Weekly Journal* was arrested in London (see Appendix D); and the paper evoked a hostile reaction when it reached New York (see Appendix K).

Sheridan reflects on a journey northward out of Co. Dublin, doubtless via Glasnevin and Naul, through the edge of Co. Meath to Drogheda, and thence to Dundalk in Co. Louth—probably via Dunleer but perhaps by one of the more easterly roads north. And although Sheridan speaks of a journey from Dublin to Dundalk, he probably continued northward. The evidence is his account of being able to see the countryside from a mountaintop outside Dundalk; this would be from the north of the town. Further, he speaks of his journey as 'sixty Miles riding'. From Dublin to Dundalk was about forty Irish miles (1 Irish mile = $1\frac{3}{11}$ English miles). Since 'sixty' could not therefore be the length of either the outward journey or the outward and return journeys combined, the implication is that Sheridan continued another twenty miles beyond Dundalk. Though there are certainly other possibilities, one may speculate that he is describing a trip to Markethill in Co. Armagh, since that was almost precisely sixty miles from Dublin via Dundalk and Newry. (These distances come from [George] Taylor and [Andrew] Skinner, *Maps of the Roads of Ireland*, 2nd edn. (1783; reprinted Shannon, 1969).) Swift went to visit Sir Arthur and Lady Acheson at Markethill, probably early in June, and Sheridan may have escorted him there, then more or less immediately returned to Dublin and written *Intelligencer* 6 as an account of the journey. If so, the essay would reflect Swift's insights as well as Sheridan's own, and they as well as the timing would account for the apparent freshness of its observations. If these speculations are correct, Sheridan's statement that the journey took place 'last Year' must be considered fiction (or a hasty error)—leaving intact the hypothesis that Swift and Sheridan's journey to Gorey and Wexford took place in the spring of 1728 (see introductory note to no. 2).

Ruins, which Sheridan views as the malignant legacy of the Commonwealth era, had long been a feature of the Irish landscape, nor was it novel to take them as a symptom of spiritual and cultural decadence. From documents since destroyed in the Irish Public Record Office fire of 1922, St John D. Seymour showed that the Cromwellians 'frequently repaired' the Irish churches: claims of Cromwellian damage and destruction appear to have been much exaggerated (*The Puritans in Ireland (1647–1661)* (Oxford, 1921), 45–7). Seymour's findings have been sustained by T. C. Barnard, who shows that many churches had been in poor repair before 1640 (*Cromwellian Ireland* (London, 1975), 168–70).

But there is sufficient evidence that the Parliamentary forces damaged, profaned, or failed to maintain a great many churches. Much of the evidence has been collected and analysed by F. R. Bolton, *The Caroline Tradition of the Church of Ireland* (London, 1958), 206–9, 267–8. Beyond that, Gruffith Williams, bishop of Ossory, reported that St Canice's cathedral and the bishop's palace were in ruins when he returned to Kilkenny after the Restoration: 'They have utterly defaced, and ruined, thrown down all the *Roof* of it, taken away five great, and *goodly* Bells, broken down all the Windows, and carryed *away* every bit of the Glass, that, they say, was worth, a very great deal; and all the doors of it, that the *Hogs* might come, and *root*, and the *Dogs gnaw* the Bones of the dead; and they brake down a most *exquisite Marble Font* (wherein the Christians Children were *regenerated*) all to pieces, and threw down the many *many* goodly *Marble Monuments* . . .' ('To the King's Most Excellent Majestie, and to the Now-Convened Parliament, and all Posterity, the Humble Remonstrance of Gruffith Williams', in his *Seven Treatises* (London: for the Authour, 1661), sig. c1^v–2^r; and Williams's *The Persecution and Oppression . . . of John Bale . . . and of Gruffith Williams* (London: for the Author, 1664), 16). See also James Graves and John G. Augustus Prim, *The History, Architecture, and Antiquities of the Cathedral Church of St. Canice, Kilkenny* (Dublin: Hodges, Smith, 1857), 42–6, 128–9; and the various claims of Francis Grose, *The Antiquities of Ireland* (London: Hooper, 1791), i. preliminary leaves and 4, 19, 34–5; ii. 5–6, 8, 29–30. For St Patrick's cathedral, Monck Mason assembles evidence of Cromwellian neglect (*The History and Antiquities of the Collegiate and Cathedral Church of St. Patrick* (Dublin, 1820), 194, 197).

Perhaps the most dramatic and certainly the best documented instance is that of Drogheda, which Sheridan emphasizes. In the Siege of Drogheda in 1649, Cromwell burned the steeple of St Peter's Church, where about a hundred of the Royalist forces were garrisoned, and by a mortar attack did extensive damage to St Mary's Church, another Royalist stronghold, in capturing it. Cromwell's own cheerfully horrific description of the burning Royalists had been printed in *Letters from Ireland* (London: Field, 1649) and elsewhere.

In any case the belief that the Puritans profaned churches was current in Sheridan's time. Aubry de La Mottraye reported that 'since *Cromwell* melted the Bells of the Churches [in the City of Cork], and sent them to the Founderies to be cast into Canon, there have been no Rings of them' (*The Voyages and Travels*, iii (London: Symon *et al.*, 1732), 290). Swift himself, in his sermon 'Upon the Martyrdom of King Charles I' (1726), described the iconoclasm and desecrations of the Puritans in English churches, adding, 'In this kingdom those ravages were not so easily seen; for the people here being too poor to raise such noble temples, the mean ones we had, were not defaced, but totally destroyed' (*Prose*, ix. 225; on the dating of the sermon, see E. W. Rosenheim, Jr, 'Swift and the Martyred Monarch', *PQ* 54 (1975), 194). Or more flamboyantly, in 'On the Bill for the Clergy's Residing on Their Livings' (1732): 'Many of the Churches [have been] levelled to the ground, particularly by the fanatick zeal of those rebellious Saints who murdered their King, destroyed the Church, and overthrew Monarchy ...; so, in order to give a tolerable maintenance to a Minister, and the Country being too poor, as well as devotion too low, to think of building new churches, it was found necessary to repair some one Church which had least suffered, and join sometimes three or more, enough for a bare support to some clergyman, who knew not where to provide himself better' (*Prose*, xii. 184). With this may be compared Swift's soberer remark, in his 1710 'Memorial' to Robert Harley about the first-fruits: 'Five or six [parishes] are often joyned ... but these have seldom above one Church in repair, the rest being destroyed by frequent Wars &c.' (*Journal to Stella*, ii. 677).

On the other hand, many damaged churches had been repaired after the Restoration, and since then many churches had been ruined, either through the course of nature, in the Jacobite wars, or by deliberate policy in which two or more parishes were united and a single church built for the new parish. Thus at least some and perhaps most of the ruins Sheridan inveighed against were not the fault of the Cromwellians.

Herbert Davis has assessed the merits of the essay in his important paper 'The Conciseness of Swift', cited in the General Introduction.

NUMB. VI.

O patria! o divum domus!

WHEN I Travel through any part of this unhappy Kingdom (and I have now by several Excursions, made from *Dublin*, gone thro' most *Counties* of it) it raises two Passions in my Breast of a different kind; An Indignation against those vile betrayers 5 and Insulters of it, who Insinuate themselves into Favour, by saying, It is a Rich Nation; and a *sincere Compassion* for the Natives, who are sunk to the lowest Degree of Misery and Poverty, whose Houses are Dunghills, whose Victuals are the Blood of their Cattle, or the Herbs in the Field; and whose Cloathing to the Dishonour of God and Man 10 is Nakedness. Yet Notwithstanding all these Dismal Appearances, it is the Common Phrase of an upstart Race of People, who have suddenly sprung up like the *Dragons* Teeth among us: That *Ireland was never known to be so Rich as it is now*; by which as I apprehend, they can only mean Themselves, for they have Skipt over the Channel from the 15 Vantage Ground of a Dunghill upon no other Merit, either Visible or Divinable, than that of not having been born among us.

This is the Modern way of Planting Colonies—*Et ubi Solitudinem faciunt, id imperium vocant.* When those who are so unfortunate to be born here, are excluded from the meanest Preferments, and deem'd incapable of being entertain'd, even as common Soldiers, whose poor 20 stipend is but Four pence a Day. No Trade, no Emoluments, no Encouragement for Learning among the Natives, who yet by a perverse consequence are divided into Factions, with as much Violence, and Rancour, as if they had the Wealth of the *Indies* to contend for. It puts me in mind of a *Fable* which I Read in a *Monkish* 25 Author. He quotes for it one of the *Greek Mythologists*, That once upon a Time a Colony of large Dogs (called the *Molossi*) Transplanted themselves from *Epirus* to *Ætolia* where they seized those parts of the Countries, most fertile in Flesh of all kinds, obliging the Native Dogs to retire from their best Kennels, to live under Ditches and Bushes. 30 But to preserve good Neighbourhood, and Peace, and finding likewise, that the *Ætolian* Dogs might be of some use in the low Offices of Life, they passed a Decree, That the Natives should be entituled to the *Short-Ribs*, *Tips of Tails*, *Knuckle-Bones*, and *Guts* of all the Game, which they were obliged by their Masters to Run Down: 35 This Condition was accepted, and what was a little Singular, while the *Molossian* Dogs kept a good understanding among themselves, living in Peace and Luxury, these *Ætolian Curs* were perpetually snarling, growling, barking, and tearing out each others Throats. Nay, sometimes those of the best Quality among them, were seen to 40 Quarrel with as much Rancour for a Rotten Gut, as if it had been a fat haunch of Venison. But what need we wonder at this in *Dogs*, when the same is every Day practised among *Men*.

Last Year I Travelled from *Dublin* to *Dundalk*, thro' a Country esteemed the most Fruitful part of this Kingdom, and so Nature 45 intended it. But no Ornaments or Improvements of such a Scene were visible. No Habitations fit for Gentlemen. No Farmers Houses. Few Fields of Corn, and almost a bare Face of nature, without new Plantations of any kind, only a few miserable Cottages, at least three or four Miles distance, and one Church in the Centre between this *City* 50 and *Droghedah.* When I arriv'd at this last Town, the first mortifying Sight, was the Ruins of several Churches, batter'd down by that *Usurper Cromwell,* whose *Fanatick Zeal* made more Desolation in a few Days, than the Piety of succeeding Prelates, or the Wealth of the Town have, in more than sixty Years attempted to repair. 55

Perhaps the Inhabitants, through a high strain of Virtue, have in Imitation of the *Athenians* made a Solemn Resolution, never to rebuild

those sacred Edifices, but rather leave them in ruins, as Monuments,
to perpetuate the detestable memory of that hellish Instrument
60 of Rebellion, Desolation and Murther. For, the *Athenians* when
Mardonius had ravaged a great part of *Greece* took a formal Oath at the
Isthmus to lose their Lives rather than their Liberty. To stand by their Leaders to
the last. To spare the Cities of such Barbarians as they conquered. And, what
crowned all, the Conclusion of their Oath was, *We will never repair any of*
65 *the Temples, which they have burned and destroyed, that they may appear to*
Posterity as so many Monuments of these wicked Barbarians. This was a
glorious Resolution. And I am sorry to think, that the Poverty of my
Country-men will not let the world suppose, they have acted upon
such a generous Principle, yet upon this Occasion I cannot but
70 observe that there is a fatality in some Nations, to be fond of those,
who have treated them with the least humanity. Thus I have often
heard the memory of *Cromwell*, who has depopulated and almost
wholly destroyed this miserable Country, celebrated like that of a
Saint; and at the same time the Sufferings of the Royal Martyr turned
75 into Ridicule, and his Murder justifyed even from the Pulpit, and all
this done with an intent to gain favour under a *Monarchy*, which is a
new strain of Politicks that I shall not pretend to account for.

Examin all the Eastern Towns of *Ireland*, and you will trace this
horrid Instrument of Destruction, in the defacing of Churches, and
80 particularly in destroying whatever was Ornamental, either within or
without them. We see in the several Towns a very few Houses
scattered among the Ruins of thousands, which he laid level with their
Streets. Great Numbers of Castles! the Country Seats of Gentlemen
then in Being, still standing in ruin, habitations for *Bats*, *Daws*, and
85 *Owls*, without the least Repairs or Succession of other buildings. Nor
have the Country Churches, as far as my Eye could reach, met with
any better Treatment from him, nine in ten of them lying among their
Graves, and God only knows when they are to have a Resurrection.
When I passed from *Dundalk* where this cursed *Usurper*'s handy-work
90 is yet visible, I cast mine Eyes around from the Top of a Mountain,
from whence I had a wide and a waste Prospect of several venerable
Ruins; It struck me with a Melancholy, not unlike that expressed by
Cicero in one of his Letters which being much upon the like Prospect,
and concluding with a very necessary Reflection on the uncertainty of
95 things in this World, I shall here insert a translation of what he says. *In*
my Return from Asia, *as I Sailed from* Agina, *towards* Megara, *I began to*
take a prospect of the several Countries round about me. Behind me was Agina:

Before me Megara: *On the right Hand the* Piræus: *and on the left was* Corinth: *Which Towns were formerly in a most flourishing Condition; now they lye prostrate and in Ruin.* 100

Thus I began to think with my self. Shall we who have but a trifling Existence express any resentment, when one of us either dies a natural Death, or is Slain, whose Lives are necessarily of a short Duration, when at one view I behold the Carcases of so many great Cities. What if he had seen the Natives of those free Republicks, reduced to all the miserable consequences of a 105 conquered People, living without the common defences against *Hunger and Cold, rather appearing like Spectres than Men?* I am apt to think that seeing his Fellow-Creatures in Ruin like this, it would have put him past all patience for Philosophick Reflections.

As for my own Part, I confess, that the Sights and Occurrences 110 which I had in this my last Journey, have so far transported me to a mixture of Rage and Compassion, that I am not able to decide, which has the greater Influence upon my Spirits; For this new Cant of *a rich and flourishing Nation*, was still upper-most in my Thoughts; Every Mile I travelled, giving me such ample Demonstrations to the 115 Contrary. For this reason, I have been at the pains to render a most exact and faithful Account of all the visible Signs of Riches, which I met with in sixty Miles riding through the most publick Roads, and the best part of the Kingdom. First, As to Trade, I met nine Carrs loaden with old musty shrivel'd Hydes, one Car-load of Butter. Four 120 Jockeys driving eight Horses, all out of Case. One Cow and Calf, driven by a Man and his Wife. Six tattered Families flitting to be shipped off to the *West-Indies.* A Colony of a hundred and fifty Beggars, all repairing to people our Metropolis, and by encreasing the number of Hands, to encrease it's Wealth, upon the old Maxim, that 125 People are the Riches of a Nation. And therefore ten thousand Mouths with hardly ten pair of Hands, or any Work to employ them, will infallibly make us a rich, and flourishing People. 2dly, Travellers enough, but seven in ten wanting Shirts and Cravats; nine in ten going barefoot, and carrying their Brogues and Stockens in their Hands. 130 One Woman in twenty having a Pillion, the rest riding bare-backed. Above two hundred Horsemen, with four pair of Boots amongst them all. Seventeen Saddles of Leather (the rest being made of Straw) and most of their Garrons only shod before. I went into one of the principal Farmer's Houses, out of Curiosity, and his whole Furniture 135 consisted of two Blocks for Stools, a Bench on each side the Fireplace made of Turf, six Trenchers, one Bowl, a Pot, six Horn-Spoons,

three Noggins, three Blankets, one of which served the Man and Maid Servant; the others the Master of the Family, his Wife and five
140 Children. A small Churn, a wooden Candlestick, a broken Stick for a pair of Tongs. In the publick Towns, one third of the Inhabitants walking the Street barefoot. Windows half built up with Stone, to save the expence of Glass, the broken Panes up and down supplied by brown Paper, few being able to afford white; in some places they were
145 stopped with Straw or Hay. Another mark of our Riches, are the Signs at the several Inns upon the Road, *viz.* In some a Staff stuck in the Thatch, with a Turf at the End of it; a Staff in a Dunghill with a white Rag wrapped about the Head; A Pole, where they can afford it, with a Beesom at the Top. An Oatmeal Cake on a Board in a Window; And,
150 at the principal Inns of the Road, I have observed the Signs taken down and laid against the Wall near the Door, being taken from their Post to prevent the shaking of the House down by the Wind. In short, I saw not one single House, in the best Town I travelled through, which had not manifest Appearances of Beggary and Want. I could give
155 many more Instances of our Wealth, but I hope these will suffice for the End I propose.

It may be objected, What use it is of to display the Poverty of the Nation in the manner I have done. In answer, I desire to know for what Ends, and by what Persons, This new Opinion of our flourishing State
160 has of late been so Industriously advanced. One thing is certain, that the Advancers have either already found their own Account, or have been heartily promised, or at least have been entertained with hopes, by seeing such an Opinion pleasing to those who have it in their power to reward.

165 It is no doubt a very generous principle in any Person, to rejoice in the felicities of a Nation, where themselves are Strangers, or Sojourners. But if it be found that the same Persons on all other Occasions express a hatred and contempt of the Nation and People in General, and hold it for a Maxim—*That the more such a Country is*
170 *humbled, the more their own will rise*, it need be no longer a Secret, why such an Opinion and the Advancers of it are encouraged. And besides, if the Bayliff reports to his Master, that the Ox is Fat and Strong, when in reality it can hardly carry it's own Legs, is it not natural to think, that command will be given, for a greater load to be put upon it.

MOTTO. Virgil, *Aeneid*, ii. 241 ('O my country! the home of the gods!'). The Virgilian context suggests a similitude between Sinon, whose lies betrayed Troy, and the 'vile betrayers and Insulters' of Ireland. Sheridan cites this passage in his *An Easy Introduction of Grammar* (Dublin: Tompson, 1714) as an example of exclamation (321).

8. *whose Victuals are the Blood of their Cattle*: 'Among the Poor of the Kingdom of *Ireland* . . . it is customary . . . to bleed their Cattle for Food in Years of Scarcity'. [Patrick Delany], *The Doctrine of Abstinence from Blood Defended* (London: Rivington, 1734), 124 n. Swift refers to the custom in 'The Answer to the Craftsman' (*Prose*, xii. 178).

11. *an upstart Race of People*: Presumably Sheridan means those Englishmen preferred to Irish posts. David Hayton has pointed out to me, however, that the phraseology of this passage, e.g., 'from the Vantage Ground of a Dunghill', echoes anti-Cromwellian Tory rhetoric of Queen Anne's reign, an association strengthened by the references to Cromwellian vandalism later.

12. *like the Dragons Teeth*: Legendary and probably proverbial; both Cadmus and Jason sow dragon teeth from which armed men grow (e.g., Apollodorus, i. 9. 23; iii. 4. 1).

12–13. *Ireland was never known to be so Rich*: Representations of Ireland as flourishing were said to be falsely made in order to tax Ireland more heavily. They had previously been countered by Swift in *A Short View of the State of Ireland* (reprinted as *Intelligencer* 15) and, before him, by Archbishop King (see Appendix A).

17. *Colonies*: Compare the sarcasm against British colonizers in *Gulliver's Travels*, in *Prose*, xi. 294–5.

17–18. *Et ubi Solitudinem faciunt, id imperium vocant*: 'And when they make a wilderness they call it sovereignty', adapting Tacitus, *Agricola*, xxx: 'Ubi solitudinem faciunt, pacem appellant' ('When they make a wilderness they call it peace'). Tacitus refers to the Roman invasion of Britain.

19. *excluded from the meanest Preferments*: Similar complaints are voiced in nos. 15 and 16. See also *A Letter to the Intelligencer* in Appendix G.

19–21. *deem'd incapable of being entertain'd, even as common Soldiers, whose poor stipend*: As recently as 1727, the policy of not recruiting Irishmen for the forces on the Irish Establishment had been confirmed (James, 179; see also Charles Dalton, *George the First's Army*, ii (London, 1912), p. xxxv). The ordinary private foot-soldier on the Irish establishment was paid 4*d.* per day subsistence in 1726 (Tyrawley Papers, BL MS Add. 23636, fo. 43, and see fo. 48ᵛ). This 4*d.* was presumably the nominal 5*d.* given in an Army List *c.* 1728 (BL MS Add. 21188, fos. 61ᵛ–62) and in *The Quarters of the Army of Ireland in 1744* (Dublin: Faulkner, 1744), 18, less approximately 1*d.* 'stoppages' 'to answer the captain's outlay on necessaries'. See Alan J. Guy, *Oeconomy and Discipline: Officership and Administration in the British Army, 1714–63* (Manchester, 1985), 67–9; I owe to Guy the Tyrawley Papers reference.

25–6. *a Monkish Author*: Not identified; one of Sheridan's personae?

26. *one of the Greek Mythologists*: By 'mythologists' Sheridan would mean fabulists, e.g., Aesop or Aelian, but the fable does not appear in their collections.

27. *the Molossi*: Dogs bred in Molossia, a district of Epirus in Greece, were ancestors of the modern mastiff.

44. *from Dublin to Dundalk*: See introductory note.

50–1. *the Centre between this City and Droghedah*: Naul.

52–3. *Churches, batter'd down by that Usurper Cromwell*: See introductory note.

60–1. *the Athenians when Mardonius had ravaged a great part of Greece*: The Greeks gathered at the Isthmus of Corinth in 479 BC to attempt the final expulsion of the Persian forces commanded by Mardonius. Sheridan translates the account of Diodorus Siculus, xi. 29; compare Lycurgus, *Against Leocrates*, 81.

75. *even from the Pulpit*: Cf. Swift in his sermon 'Upon the Martyrdom of King Charles I': 'Of late times, indeed, and I speak it with grief of heart, we have heard even sermons of a strange nature; although reason would make one think it a very unaccountable way of procuring favour under a monarchy, by palliating and lessening the guilt of those who murdered the best of Kings in cold blood, and, for a time, destroyed the

very monarchy itself' (*Prose*, ix. 226–7). See also E. W. Rosenheim, Jr, 'Swift and the Martyred Monarch', *PQ* 54 (1975), 178–94.

89–90. *Dundalk where this cursed Usurper's handy-work is yet visible*: 'It is remarkable how extensive was the extirpation of the founding families of the town', according to Harold O'Sullivan, 'The Cromwellian and Restoration Settlements in the Civil Parish of Dundalk, 1649 to 1673', *J. County Louth Arch. and Hist. Soc.* 19 (1977), 30–1. O'Sullivan cites a 1667 grant to Viscount Dungannon of 391 forfeited properties in Dundalk, including 151 'wast' or 'ruinous' ones, their condition presumably a consequence of war.

93. *Cicero in one of his Letters*: Actually Servius Sulpicius Rufus to Cicero, Mar. 45 BC, in *Epist. ad Fam.* iv. 5.

118. *sixty Miles riding*: See introductory note.

119. *Carrs*: 'There are no Carts or Waggons here, they have Carrs, wch are a Kind of Sledges, set on two solid wooden Wheels straked wth Iron, & drawn by a single horse; they carry great Burthens, some 600 Weight.' Loveday, 59.

122–3. *flitting to be shipped off to the West-Indies*: Archbishop Boulter wrote to the Duke of Newcastle, 23 Nov. 1728, 'Above 4200 men, women, and children have been shipped off from hence for the *West Indies* within three years, and of these above 3100 this last summer. Of these possibly one in ten may be a man of substance, and may do well enough abroad, but the case of the rest is deplorable' (Boulter, i. 210). See also the introductory note to no. 19.

124. *Beggars*: In 1726 Swift had written of beggars, and the social problems they represented and caused, in 'Upon Giving Badges to the Poor', *Prose*, xiii. 172–3; and he raised the same questions in his sermon 'Causes of the Wretched Condition of Ireland', *Prose*, ix. 205–9 (probably mid-1720s; for the date, *Prose*, ix. 136). See also Swift's undated 'Considerations about Maintaining the Poor', *Prose*, xiii. 176–7; *A Modest Proposal* (1729), in *Prose*, xii. 109–18; *A Proposal for Giving Badges to the Beggars in All the Parishes of Dublin* (1737), in *Prose*, xiii. 131–40; Louis A. Landa, 'Jonathan Swift and Charity', *JEGP* 44 (1945), 338–41; and the notes to no. 17.

126. *People are the Riches of a Nation*: A principle of mercantile economics which did not apply in Ireland, as Swift pointed out in *A Short View of the State of Ireland*, *Maxims Controlled in Ireland*, and *A Modest Proposal*; see Louis A. Landa's discussion in '*A Modest Proposal* and Populousness', *Mod. Philol.* 40 (1942), 161–70 (but *Maxims Controlled in Ireland* was written in 1729, not 1724; *Prose*, vol. xii, p. xxiii, where the *Intelligencer* hints ('fragments') referred to date from 1729, not 1728: see Appendix J). See also F. V. Bernard, 'Swift's Maxim on Populousness: A Possible Source', *Notes and Queries*, 210 (1965), 18.

134. *Garrons*: See textual variants.

As early as 1777, John Nichols asked, 'Are the characters of *Eugenio* and *Corusodes* . . . real or imaginary?' (*Gentleman's Magazine*, 47: 419). In 1728 *Fog's Weekly Journal* had said they were 'feigned Names' (see Appendix D). Identifications have never been offered. Eugenio is presented as a virtual anonymity and at any rate as little more than a type—the well-born, educated, witty, and unrewarded cleric embodying, with exaggeration, Swift and Sheridan's sense of their own neglected merit. Eugenio (or Eugenius) is a stock name: it occurs a number of times in seventeenth-century literature. Corusodes on the other hand seems to be a name invented for the occasion, and its specific reference to a running nose is one of a number of details suggesting that Corusodes is identifiable. In his own copy of the 1732 *Miscellanies*, moreover, Swift when he came upon the phrase 'the arts he used to obtain a Mitre' inserted '(in which he Succeeded)'. This again suggests that he had a particular person in mind.

No Anglican bishop alive in 1728 perfectly fits the particulars of Corusodes's career: farmer's son, Oxford graduate and fellow, chaplain in a noble house, London preacher and rector, country rector, chaplain-in-ordinary, dignitary, bishop. Possibly, however, Swift misremembered or otherwise distorted some of the facts about a real-life model—in which case that model may have been White Kennett.

Kennett, born in 1660, was educated at St Edmund Hall, Oxford, graduating BA 1682, MA 1684, and DD 1700. He does not seem to have held a fellowship. After taking his MA he became schoolmaster of Bicester, Oxfordshire. Beginning in 1691 he was vice-principal of St Edmund Hall. According to an early biographer—whether or not his facts are correct, he may report a reputation that Swift was aware of—Kennett was at Oxford 'in the meanest Condition of those that were wholly maintain'd by their Parents, a Battler, or Semi-Commoner' ([William Newton], *The Life of the Right Reverend Dr. White Kennett* (London: Billingsley, 1730), 4). In 1701 he became chaplain to Bishop Gardiner and was named archdeacon of Huntingdon: Ehrenpreis contrasts Kennett's careerism at this stage with Swift's more principled quest for preferment (i. 253). He became a minister or curate at St Botolph Aldgate, London, where he preached twice on Sundays and was diligent in visiting the sick (*Life*, 16–17). Though early a Royalist, he came to be known as 'Weathercock Kennett' and was in 1704 accused of condoning the execution of Charles I (*White against Kennet: or, Dr. Kennet's Panegyrick upon the Late King James. . . By a Gentleman* (London: Nutt, 1704)). Visibly Latitudinarian, he was sympathetic toward Dissenters: 'And tho' he utterly dislik'd the Way of Separation, yet he express'd great Charity and Moderation towards those who are so unhappy as to differ from us' (*Life*, p. x). At the funeral of the Duke of Devonshire in 1707, he preached a sermon commonly regarded as excusing the sins of the titled while it condemned those of ordinary people and flattered the duke's successor (see TE i. 302–4, iv. 180–1). In 1708 he became rector of two city of London parishes and dean of Peterborough. His drive for promotion occasioned public ridicule: he 'is so exact in the Observation of the Rubricks and Cannons of our Church; . . . he takes so much pains, and makes such Courtship to the D[uke?] to be a Bishop', Isaac Sharpe railed in *The Wou'd Be Bishop: or, The Lying Dean. Being a Defence of the Curate of Stepney, against the Infamous Slanders of Dr. K—t, the (Pretended) Vindicator of the Church of England* (London: the booksellers of London and Westminster, 1709), 3. Thomas Hearne (hardly an unbiased source) classed him with 'Prickear'd, starch, sanctify'd Fellows yᵗ under a Pretence of Reformation . . . will cry up the greatest Villains for saints' (*Remarks and Collections*, ii (Oxford, 1886), 74). He was a chaplain-in-ordinary from 1710 to 1718, when he was elevated to the bishopric of Peterborough. He was active in the Society for the Promotion of Christian Knowledge, the Society for the Propagation of the Gospel, and the charity school movement. After becoming bishop, he used his influence to further his son's career in the Church, ordaining him deacon and priest and giving him a prebend in Peterborough cathedral, all within a month; the son got prebends in Lincoln cathedral and St Paul's cathedral during the next two years. The father did not quite reach 'the top of the Ladder Ecclesiastical': the bishop of Peterborough died in December 1728. (Most of my information about Kennett comes from G. V. Bennett, *White Kennett* (London, 1957).)

Swift may have encountered Kennett at Oxford in 1692. Kennett had known Swift, or at any rate had known who he was, at Queen Anne's court. Kennett recorded in his diary that he 'could not but despise' Swift, and recounted preaching before the queen at Windsor castle when Swift, who was present, 'drew the eyes of many upon him, when I happen'd to mention among other corruptions of the Age, the prevailing foolishness of Wit and Humour so called'. The diary entries, which portray Swift as officious and self-important, are reproduced in *Corresp.* v. 228–9.

If Kennett fits Corusodes in many such respects—and I have no information about his susceptibility to catarrh—there seems no evidence that he was a farmer's son, that any of his four sisters was a waiting woman, that he was chaplain to a nobleman who seduced his sister, or that he married a citizen's widow who schooled him in money-lending.

Other candidates, somewhat less plausible than Kennett, would include Lancelot Blackburne (archbishop of York), Samuel Bradford (bishop of Rochester and dean of Westminster), Edmund Gibson (bishop of London), and Richard Willis (bishop of Winchester), for each of whom see *DNB*.

NUMB. VII.

——Probitas laudatur & alget.

CORUSODES an *Oxford* Student, and a Farmers Son, was never absent from Prayers, or Lecture, nor once out of his College after *Tom* had tolld. He spent every Day ten hours in his Closet, in Reading his Courses, Dozing, clipping Papers, or darning his Stockings, which last he performed to Admiration. He could be soberly Drunk at the expence of others, with *College* Ale, and at those Seasons was always most Devout. He wore the same Gown five years, without dagling or tearing. He never once looked into a Play-book or a Poem. He Read *Virgil* and *Ramus* in the same Cadence, but with a very different Taste. He never understood a Jest, or had the least Conception of Wit.

For one saying he stands in Renown to this Day. Being with some other Students over a Pot of Ale; one of the Company said so many pleasant things, that the rest were much diverted, only *Corusodes* was silent and unmoved. When they parted, he called this merry Companion aside, and said; *Sir, I perceived by your often speaking, and our Friends laughing, that you spoke many jests, and you could not but observe my Silence. But Sir, this is my humour, I never make a jest myself, nor ever laugh at another Man's.*

Corusodes thus endowed, and got into Holy Orders, having by the most extreme Parsimoney, saved thirty four Pounds out of a very Beggarly Fellowship, went up to *London*, where his Sister was Waiting-woman to a Lady, and so good a Sollicitor, that by her means he was admitted to Read Prayers in the Family twice a Day, at fourteen shillings a Month. He had now acquired a low Obsequious awkward Bow, and a talent of gross flattery both in and out of season; he would shake the Butler by the Hand; He taught the Page his *Catechism*, and was sometimes admitted to Dine at the Stewards Table. In short he got the good Word of the whole Family, and was Recommended by my Lady for Chaplain to some other Noble House, by which his Revenue (beside Vales) amounted to about 30 *l.* a Year. His Sister procured him a Scarf from my Lord (who had a small design of Gallantry upon her) And by his Lordships Sollicitation he got a Lectureship in Town of 60 *l.* a Year; where he Preached constantly in Person, in a grave manner, with an Audible Voice, a Style

Ecclesiastick, and the matter (such as it was) well suited to the intellectuals of his Hearers. Some time after, a Country Living fell in my Lord's Disposal, and his Lordship who had now some encouragement given him of Success in his Amour, bestowed the
40 Living on *Corusodes*, who still kept his Lectureship and Residence in Town, where he was a constant Attendant at all Meetings relating to Charity, without ever contributing further than his frequent Pious Exhortations. If any Women of better fashion in the Parish happened to be absent from Church, they were sure of a Visit from him in a Day
45 or two, to Chide and to Dine with them.

He had a select number of Poor constantly attending at the Street Door of his Lodgings, for whom he was a common Sollicitor to his former Patroness, dropping in his own Half Crown among the Collections and taking it out when he disposed the money. At a Person
50 of Qualities House, he would never sit down till he was thrice bid, and then upon the corner of the most distant chair. His whole demeanor was formal and starched, which adhered so close, that he could never shake it off in his highest Promotion.

His Lord was now in high Employment at Court, and attended by
55 him with the most abject Assiduity, and his Sister being gone off with Child to a private Lodging, my Lord continued his Graces to *Corusodes*, got him to be a Chaplain in ordinary, and in due time a Parish in Town, and a *Dignity in the Church*.

He paid his *Curates* punctually, at the lowest Sallery, and partly out
60 of the communion money, but gave them good advice in abundance. He Marryed a Citizens Widow, who taught him to put out small sums at *ten per cent*, and brought him acquainted with Jobbers in *Change-Alley*. By her dexterity he sold the Clarkship of his Parish, when it became vacant.
65 He kept a miserable house, but the Blame was layed wholly upon *Madam*; For the good Doctor was always at his *Books*, or visiting the Sick, or doing other Offices of Charity and piety in his Parish.

He treated all his inferiors of the Clergy with a most sanctifyed pride; was rigorously and universally, censorious upon all his brethren
70 of the Gown, on their first appearance in the world, or while they continued meanly preferred; But gave large allowance to the Layity of high rank, or great riches, using neither Eyes nor Ears for their faults. He was never sensible of the least corruption in *Courts*, *Parliaments*, or *Ministries*, but made the most favourable constructions of all publick
75 proceedings; and Power, in whatever Hands, or whatever Party, was

always secure of his most charitable opinion. He had many wholsome maxims ready to excuse all miscarriages of State. *Men are but Men*. *Erunt vitia donec homines*; and *Quod Supra nos nihil ad nos*. with several others of equal weight.

It would lengthen my paper beyond measure to trace out the whole 80 System of his conduct: His dreadfull apprehensions of Popery; his great moderation towards Dissenters of all Denominations; with hearty wishes that by yielding somewhat on both sides, there might be a general Union among Protestants; his short inoffensive Sermons in his turns at Court, and the matter exactly suited to the present 85 juncture of prevailing Opinions. The arts he used to obtain a Mitre, by writing against Episcopacy, and the proofs he gave of his loyalty by palliating or defending the murder of a martyred Prince.

Endowed with all these accomplishments we leave him in the full Carrier of Success, mounting fast towards the top of the Ladder 90 Ecclesiastical, which he hath a fair probability to reach, without the merit of one single Virtue, moderately stocked with the least valuable parts of Erudition, utterly devoyd of all *Taste*, *Judgment* or *Genius*; and in his grandeur naturally chusing to hawl up others after him, whose accomplishments most resemble his own, except his beloved Sons, 95 Nephews, or other kindred be not in competition, or lastly except his inclinations be diverted by those who have power to mortify or further advance him.

Eugenio Set out from the same University, and about the same time with *Corusodes*; He had the reputation of an arch Lad at School, and 100 was unfortunately possessed with a *Talent* for *Poetry*, on which account he received many chiding Letters from his Father, and grave advice from his Tutor. He did not neglect his College Learning, but his chief Study was the Authors of Antiquity, with a perfect knowledge in the *Greek* and *Roman Tongues*; He could never Procure himself to be 105 chosen Fellow; for it was objected against him that he had written Verses, and particularly some wherein he glanced at a certain Reverend Doctor, famous for Dullness: That he had been seen bowing to Ladies, as he met them in the Streets; And it was proved that once he had been found dancing in a private family with half a 110 dozen of both Sexes.

He was the younger Son to a Gentleman of a good birth, but small fortune, and his Father Dying he was driven to *London*, to seek his fortune: he got into Orders, and became Reader in a Parish Church at twenty Pounds a Year; was carryed by an *Oxford* friend to *Wills Coffee-* 115

house, frequented in those Days by the Men of Wit; where in some
time he had the bad luck to be distinguished. His Scanty Sallery
compelled him to run deep in debt for a new Gown and Cassock,
and now and then forced him to Write some Paper of Wit or humour,
120 or Preach a Sermon for Ten shillings, to supply his Necessities.
He was a thousand times recommended by his Poetical Friends to
great Persons, as a young man of excellent parts, who deserved
encouragement and received a thousand Promises; But his modesty,
and a generous spirit which disdained the Slavery of continual
125 application, and attendance, always disappointed him, making room
for Vigilant Dunces, who were sure to be never out of sight.

He had an excellent faculty in preaching, if he were not sometimes a
little too refined, and apt to trust too much to his own way of thinking,
and reasoning.

130 When upon the vacancy of Preferment he was hardly drawn to
attend upon some promising Lord he received the usual Answer, that
he came too late, for it had been given to another the very day before.
And he had onely this comfort left, that every body said, it was a
thousand pities some thing could not be done for Poor Mr. *Eugenio*.

135 The Remainder of his Story will be dispatched in a few Words.
Wearied with weak hopes, and weaker pursuits he accepted a Curacy
in *Darby-Shire*, of thirty Pounds a Year, and when he was five and
forty, had the great felicity to be preferred by a friend of his Father to a
Vicaridge worth annually 60 pound, in the most desert parts of *Lincoln-*
140 *shire*, where his spirit quite sunk with those reflections, that solitude
and disappointments bring, he married a Farmers widow, and is
still alive, utterly undistinguished and forgotten, onely some of the
Neighbours have accidentally heard *that he had been a notable man in
his Youth.*

MOTTO. Juvenal, *Satires*, i. 74: 'Honesty is praised and left to shiver' (Loeb).

1. *Corusodes*: Sniveler, from κορυζώδης, 'suffering from catarrh'. The explanation was
   first offered by Jack G. Gilbert, *Jonathan Swift: Romantic and Cynic Moralist* (Austin,
   1966), 36.

3. *after Tom had tolld*: Great Tom, the largest bell of Christ Church, Oxford, rang the
   curfew for the Oxford colleges every evening at nine Oxford time. See Anthony à
   Wood, *Athenae Oxonienses*, new edn., ed. Philip Bliss (London, 1820), iv. 195; and
   Frederick Sharpe, *The Church Bells of Oxfordshire*, iii (Oxford, 1951), 248–50, 260, 271,
   273, 275, 277.

6. *College Ale*: 'So Academick dull Ale-drinkers | Pronounce all Men of Wit, Free-
   thinkers.' Swift, *To Dr. D—l—y*, in *Poems*, ii. 503.

9. *Ramus*: Peter Ramus, the 16th-century logician and rhetorician, described as a 'great

Dunce' in *Gulliver's Travels*, iii. 8. See Eugene Washington, 'Swift and Ramus', *Utah Academy Proc.* 53, pt. i (1976), 30–2.

20. *Corusodes thus endowed, and got*: An absolute construction: Corusodes, being thus endowed, and being got into holy orders.... The *29* editor, followed by all later editions, failed to understand this syntax and removed the *and*; see textual variants.

31. *Vales*: Or vails. Johnson, citing this passage, says simply 'Money given to servants'; *OED*, also citing this passage, speaks of 'a casual or occasional profit or emolument in addition to salary, stipend, wages, or other regular payment, esp. one accruing or attached to an office or position; a fee or offering of this nature'.

32. *a Scarf*: Vestment worn by the chaplain in a noble household.

49. *disposed*: To dispose is to 'bestow, make over, hand over; deal out, dispense, distribute' (*OED*, sense 4); the transitive sense was perhaps already old-fashioned; see textual variants.

57. *Chaplain in ordinary*: There were nominally 48 chaplains-in-ordinary to the monarch, each of them preaching once a year.

59–60. *partly out of the communion money*: The Communion rubrics in the Book of Common Prayer specify that 'the Money given at the Offertory shall be disposed of to ... pious and charitable uses'. Canon 47 of the Church of England provided that the incumbent 'shall maintain' the curate.

62. *at ten per cent*: Usurious; 6% was the highest legal interest in England before 1714 (Sidney Homer, *A History of Interest Rates*, 2nd edn. (New Brunswick, NJ, 1977), 163–5.

62–3. *Change-Alley*: 'Exchange Alley ... hath two Passages out of *Cornhil*: one into *Lombard Street*, and another bending East into *Birchin Lane*. [It] is a Place of a very considerable Concourse of Merchants, Seafaring Men and other Traders, occasioned by the great Coffee-houses (*Jonathans* and *Garways*) that stand there. Chiefly now Brokers, and such as deal in buying and selling of Stocks, frequent it.' John Stow, *A Survey of the Cities of London and Westminster ... Corrected, Improved and Very Much Enlarged ... by John Strype* (London: Churchill *et al.*, 1720), I. ii. 149.

77. *Men are but Men*: Proverbial; Tilley M541.

78. *Erunt vitia donec homines*: Correctly, 'Vitia erunt, donec homines': 'There will be vices so long as there are men' (Tacitus, *Histories*, iv. 74; Loeb tr.).

78. *Quod Supra nos nihil ad nos*: 'That which is above us does not concern us' (Tertullian and Minucius Felix, Loeb tr., 347). Swift mockingly quotes the adage in his letter to the 17-year-old Esther Johnson in 1698 (*Corresp.* i. 24; I agree with A. C. Elias, Jr, that Stella is the addressee: 'Stella's Writing-Master', *Scriblerian*, 9 (1977), 138–9 and n. 8). The proverb (Tilley T206) had been widely circulated by means of Erasmus's *Adagia* and derivative collections. Early sources attribute the saying to Socrates (Minucius Felix, Lactanius, Jerome) or to Epicurus (Tertullian); see Jean Beaujeu (ed.), Minucius Felix's *Octavius* (Paris, 1964), 93–4.

88. *palliating or defending the murder of a martyred Prince*: See notes to no. 6.

90. *Carrier*: Career.

95–6. *except his beloved Sons, Nephews, or other kindred be not in competition*: That is, his relations are those 'whose Accomplishments most resemble his own'. The *1730* edition plausibly emended this tortured passage by removing the 'not', leaving an easier sense but not exactly that of the original.

99. *Eugenio*: From Greek εὐγενής, well-born, noble-minded, generous. Swift uses the name to reflect on the low social caste of many bishops. See introductory note.

101. *unfortunately possessed with a Talent for Poetry*: See the introductory note to no. 5.

115–16. *Wills Coffee-house*: 'Will's Coffee-House, was formerly the Place where the Poets usually met, which tho it be yet fresh in memory, yet in some Years may be forgot, and want this Explanation.' Swift's note in the 1710 edition of *A Tale of a Tub*,

Introduction. According to *Letters of Wit, Politics and Morality* (London: Hartley, Turner, and Hodgson, 1701), possibly by Abel Boyer, among the meeting places of the 'most ingenious Persons' of England, no coffee house was more important than '*Will*'s Coffee-house in *Covent-Garden* . . . as being consecrated to the Honour of *Apollo*, by the first-rate Wits that flourish'd in King *Charles* II's Reign, such as the late Earl of *Rochester*, the Marquis of *Normanby*, the Earl of *Dorset*, Sir *Charles Sidley*, the Earl of *Roscommon*, Sir *George Etherege*, Mr. *Dryden*, Mr. *Wycherly*, and some few others. . . . The Company which now generally meets at *Will*'s [includes wits] of distinguish'd Merit and Abilities, such as Mr. *Wycherly*, Dr. *Garth*, Mr. *Congreve*, the Honourable Mr. *Boyle*, Colonel *Stanhope*, Mr. *Vanbruk*, Mr. *Cheek*, Mr. *Walsh*, Mr. *Burnaby*, Mr. *Rowe*, and some few others' (216). Bryant Lillywhite, *London Coffee Houses* (London, 1963), 655–8, finds that the wits frequented Will's until 1713.

probably 29 June–2 July 1728

Mullinix—'Captain' John Molyneux—was a Dublin street character known for his outspoken Tory politics, as may be surmised from an undated but clearly contemporary halfsheet, *Countrymen and Fellow-Citizens*. It is purportedly from one of his low-life cohorts, 'Doctor Anthony', who seeks election to Parliament from Dublin, 'having always acted contrary to the Politicks of Captain *John Molyneux*' (copy: BL 1890.e.5 (102)). Swift classes Molyneux with 'Ideots roaring to the Boys' and 'scow'r[ing] the Streets without a Shirt' (*Poems*, iii. 788), and another contemporary poem describes him as 'guz'ling Belch and Brandy in *Smock-Ally* | With *Bawds*, *Pimps*, *Bullies*, *Pickpockets*, and *Whores*': this from *An Elegy on Capt. Molineux, commonly call'd Wife and No Wife; who was suppos'd to have been most barb'rously strangled by an inhuman Strumpet, with his own Two-leg'd-wig in 1728*, printed in *Poems Written Occasionally by John Winstanley... Interspers'd with Many Others, by Several Ingenious Hands*, i (Dublin: Powell, 1742), 192–7. Finally, on 7 August 1733, the *Dublin Gazette* reported, 'Last Week Crazy Mollineux, who call'd himself Capt. Mollineux, dropt down dead of an Apoplexy in Capel street.'

Timothy—that is, Richard Tighe (?1678–1736), an Irish privy councillor—was by no means Swift's typical villain on the Irish scene: not a placeholder, a military officer, a government contractor, an absentee landlord, or an Englishman. He is presumably the same Richard Tighe to whom Farquhar dedicated *The Inconstant* (1702), praising him as 'a gay, splendid, generous, easie, fine young Gentleman'. Sir Walter Scott observed that in Farquhar's description 'there may be discerned . . . the outlines of a light mercurial character, capable of being represented as a coxcomb or fine gentleman, as should suit the purpose of the writer' (Scott (1824), xii. 418). But there is no reason to doubt Swift's remark to Pope that Tighe was 'a fellow we all hated', and for worse than being a mere coxcomb (Pope, *Corresp.* iii. 292, following a more complete copy-text than does Swift's *Corresp.* iv. 30). *Mad Mullinix and Timothy* is only the most ingenious of perhaps six verse lampoons Swift wrote against him (*Poems*, iii. 772–89; the authorship of some of them is uncertain).

In Tighe's earlier years on the public scene, he had been Swift's friend and seems to have played chess with Stella. We know neither what sustained this friendship nor why it reached an unpleasant end in 1710 (*Journal to Stella*, i. 71, 360). In 1724 he signed the proclamation against the Drapier, however (*Prose*, x. 205), and the antipathy was assuredly fuelled in 1725, after Lord Carteret gave a Dublin Castle chaplaincy and a church living to Sheridan on Swift's recommendation. On the anniversary of the Hanoverian Succession that year, Sheridan, forgetful of the date, preached on the text 'Sufficient unto the day is the evil thereof', and it was Tighe who informed on Sheridan, got him dismissed as chaplain, and blocked him from further advancement. Swift encouraged Sheridan to retaliate and added, 'You shall have Help.' Two verse attacks, not improbably by Sheridan, appeared in 1725 (Foxon T373–4); Swift attacked Tighe not only as Timothy in *Intelligencers* 8 and 10 but also as Pistorides (baker's descendant) in *A Vindication of Lord Carteret* (1730) and as Dick Fitz-Baker in *The Legion Club* (1736), Tighe's grandfather having supplied bread to Cromwell's army in Ireland. Tighe was moreover mentioned in assorted derogatory Latino-Anglicus exchanges between Swift and Sheridan. See *Corresp.* iii. 98–101, 296 (I accept the identification of T— as Tighe); iv. 30, 32, 363–4; *A Vindication of Lord Carteret*, in *Prose*, xii. 163; Forster MS 530; Swift, *Miscellanies*, x (1745), 155–8; Thomas Sheridan the younger's *Life* of Swift (London: Bathurst, 1784), 379–84; George Mayhew, 'Swift's Games with Language in Rylands English MS. 659', *BJRL* 36 (1953–4), 426, 436–8, 443–6; Mayhew, *Rage or Raillery*, 145–7; Leland D. Peterson, 'A Variant of the 1742–46 Swift–Pope *Miscellanies*', *Papers Bibl. Soc. America*, 66 (1972), 310n.; Ehrenpreis, iii. 252, 362–5, 579–80, 830–1; and the General Introduction, above.

Tighe had entered the Irish House of Commons in 1703, though before 1715 his name hardly appears in the journal. He seems to have had no connection with the government of the High Tory second Duke of Ormonde, Lord Lieutenant 1703–7 and 1710–13. But when George I came in, Tighe at once became a key figure and was appointed to many parliamentary committees. One of the most important acts of the 1715–16 session deprived the Duke of Ormonde, a Jacobite sympathizer, of his Irish honours and estates. This was Tighe's bill: the journal associates him with it at every stage from its initial drafting to its final passage. (I follow Sheila Lambert's suggestions for the interpretation of parliamentary journals in *House of Commons Sessional Papers of the Eighteenth Century* (Wilmington, Del., 1975), i. 10–11.) In the following session he was as intimately associated with a bill to disenfranchise Jacobites in Kilkenny. The campaign against Jacobites was supported by the fear of Protestant landowners like Tighe that their estates, gained through the confiscations of 1641 and 1691, would be lost if the Jacobites and Catholics ever regained power. (On Tighe as a beneficiary of the Williamite confiscations, see John O'Hart, *The Irish and Anglo-Irish Landed Gentry* (1884; reprinted New York, 1969), 517, 520.)

Presumably for his vigour in this crusade, Tighe was appointed to the Irish Privy Council in 1718. This body was disproportionately more important than its English counterpart, since its approval was required before any bill could be passed into law (McCracken, 51–61). Unlike most members of the council, Tighe was neither a peer nor an officer of state, and unlike most, he was active: his name appears regularly on the council's proclamations.

During the 1720s Tighe appears in the Commons journal less often and is associated with less important legislation. We may guess that as the Whig government and the House of Hanover became more clearly acknowledged as secure, Tighe's anti-Tory performance was of less significance. The serious issue it raised for Swift, as he later made clear in *A Vindication of Lord Carteret* (1730), was that many '*Whigs . . . of the old fashioned Stamp*' (and he considered himself one) could be of 'very good Use' to the kingdom if Tighe 'and his Gang' did not stigmatize them as Tories and Jacobites (*Prose*, xii. 156, 160). During the session immediately preceding *Mad Mullinix and Timothy*—the opening session of the parliament of George II—one might have looked for a weakening of the old power structure in Ireland. Instead, it was stronger than ever. There was unprecedented Whig success in Parliament, and the Whigs passed all their bills. There were, as Swift discovered, comic possibilities in the supposition that the Whig success betokened a utopian end to parties in Ireland and rendered Tighe's anti-Jacobitism pointless.

It was left to the *Intelligencer*'s readers to identify Tim as Tighe; at least some were equal to the challenge, if the contemporary manuscript annotation ('Mr. Tighe') in a copy at the Royal Irish Academy is a representative sample. For further information on Richard Tighe (not *Sir* Richard as some scholars have dubbed him) see *Burke's Landed Gentry of Ireland*, 4th edn. (London, 1958), 691; Somerset Lowry Corry, 4th Earl of Belmore, *Parliamentary Memoirs of Fermanagh and Tyrone, from 1613 to 1885* (Dublin, 1887), 276; Hore, 561; *Alumni Dublinenses*; Dublin Castle, Genealogical Office MS 178, pp. 369 ff.; McCracken, 376.

NUMB. VIII.

Par coeatque pari.

HAVING lately had an Account, that a certain Person of some Distinction swore in a publick Coffee-house, that Party should never Dye while he lived (although it has been the Endeavour of the best and wisest among us, to Abolish the Ridiculous Appellations of *Whig* and *Tory*, and entirely to turn our thoughts to the good of our *Prince* and *Constitution in Church and State*) I hope those, who are well-wishers to our Country, will think my Labour not ill bestowed in giving this Gentleman's Principles the proper Embellishments which they deserve, and since mad *Mullinix* is the only *Tory* now remaining, who dares own himself to be so, I desire I may not be Censured by those who are of his Party, for making him hold a Dialogue with one of less Consequence on 'tother side. I shall not venture so far, as to give the *Christian Nick-name* of the Person

15 chiefly concerned, lest I should give offence, for which reason, I shall call him *Timothy*, and leave the rest to the Conjecture of the World.

MAD MULLINIX and TIMOTHY.

M.　I Own 'tis not my Bread and Butter,
　　　But prithee *Tim*, why all this Clutter?
Why ever in these raging Fits,
Damning to Hell the *Jacobits*?
When, if you search the Kingdom round,　　　　5
There's hardly twenty to be found;
No, not among the *Priests* and *Fryers*.
　　T.　'Twixt you and me G—— Damn the Lyers.
　　M.　The *Tories* are gone ev'ry Man over
To our Illustrious House of *Hanover*.　　　　10
From all their Conduct this is plain,
And then—　*T.*　G—— Damn the Lyars again.
Did not an Earl but lately Vote
To bring in (I could Cut his Throat)
Our whole Accounts of publick Debts?　　　　15
　　M.　Lord, how this Frothy Coxcomb frets!　　(aside)
　　T.　Did not an able Statesman
This dang'rous horrid motion Dish up?
As *Popish* Craft? Did he not rail on't?
Shew Fire and Faggot in the Tail on't?　　　　20
Proving the *Earl* a grand Offender,
And in a Plot for the *Pretender*?
Whose Fleet, 'tis all our Friends Opinion,
Was then embarking at *Avignion*.
　　M.　In every A—— you run your Snout　　　25
To find this Damn'd *Pretender* out,
While all the silly Wretch can do
Is but to frisk about like you.
But *Tim* Convinc't by your Perswasion,
I yield there might be an Invasion,　　　　30
And you who ever F—— in vain,
Can F—— his Navy back again.
　　T.　Z——ds Sir.　*M.*　But to be short and serious;
For long disputes will only weary us.

These brangling jars of *Whig* and *Tory*, 35
Are Stale, and Worn as *Troy-Town Story*.
The Wrong, 'tis certain, you were both in,
And now you find you fought for nothing.
Your Faction, when their Game was new,
Might want such noisy Fools as you; 40
But you when all the Show is past
Resolve to stand it out the last;
Like *Martin Marrall*, gaping on,
Not minding when the Song was done.
When all the *Bees* are gone to settle, 45
You Clatter still your Brazen Kettle.
The Leaders whom you listed under,
Have dropt their Arms, and seiz'd the Plunder.
And when the War is past, you come
To rattle in their Ears your Drum. 50
And, as that hateful hideous *Grecian*
Thersites (he was your Relation)
Was more abhor'd, and scorn'd by those
With whom he serv'd, than by his Foes,
So thou art grown the Detestation 55
Of all thy Party through the Nation.
Thy peevish and perpetual teizing,
With Plots, and *Jacobites* and Treason;
Thy busy, never-meaning Face;
Thy Screw'd up front; thy State Grimace; 60
Thy formal Nods; important Sneres;
Thy Whisp'rings foisted in all Ears;
(Which are, whatever you may think,
But Nonsence wrapt up in a Stink)
Have made thy Presence, in a true Sence, 65
To thy own Side so Damn'd a Nuisance,
That when they have you in their Eye,
As if the *Devil* drove, they fly.
    T. My good Friend *Mullinix*, forbear.
I vow to G—— you're too severe. 70
If it could ever yet be known
I took Advice except my own,
It shou'd be yours. But D—— my Blood,
I must pursue the publick Good.

The Faction, (is it not Notorious?)   75
Keck at the Memory of *Glorious*.
'Tis true, nor need I to be told,
My quondam Friends are grown so Cold,
That scarce a Creature can be found,
To Prance with me the Statue round.   80
The publick Safety, I foresee,
Henceforth depends alone on me.
And while this Vital Breath I blow,
Or from above, or from below,
I'll Sputter, Swagger, Curse and Rail,   85
The *Tories* Terror, Scourge and Flail.
    M.   *Tim*, you mistake the matter quite,
The Tories! you are their Delight.
And should you act a diff'rent Part,
Be grave and wise, 'twou'd break their Heart.   90
Why, *Tim*, you have a Taste I know,
And often see a Puppet-show.
Observe, the Audience is in Pain,
While *Punch* is hid behind the Scene,
But when they hear his rusty Voice,   95
With what Impatience they rejoice.
And then they value not two Straws,
How *Solomon* decides the Cause,
Which the true Mother, which *Pretender*,
Nor listen to the Witch of *Endor*;   100
Shou'd *Faustus*, with the Devil behind him,
Enter the Stage they never mind him;
If *Punch*, to spur their fancy, shews
In at the door his monstrous Nose,
Then sudden draws it back again,   105
O what a pleasure mixt with pain!
You ev'ry moment think an Age,
Till he appears upon the Stage.
And first his Bum you see him clap
Upon the Queen of *Sheba's* lap.   110
The Duke of *Lorrain* drew his Sword,
Punch roaring ran, and running roar'd.
Reviles all People in his Jargon,
And sells the *King of Spain* a Bargain.

St. George himself he plays the wag on, 115
And mounts astride upon the *Dragon*.
He gets a thousand Thumps and Kicks,
Yet cannot leave his roguish Tricks;
In every Action thrusts his Nose,
The reason why, no Mortal knows. 120
In doleful Scenes, that break our heart,
Punch comes, like you, and lets a F——t.
There's not a Puppet made of Wood;
But what wou'd hang him if they cou'd.
While teizing all, by all he's teiz'd, 125
How well are the Spectators pleas'd!
Who in the motion have no share;
But purely come to hear, and stare;
Have no concern for *Sabra*'s sake,
Which gets the better, Saint, or Snake. 130
Provided *Punch* (for there's the Jest)
Be soundly mawl'd, and plagues the rest.
　Thus *Tim*, Philosophers suppose,
The World consists of Puppet-shows;
Where petulant, conceited Fellows 135
Perform the part of *Punchinelloes*;
So at this Booth, which we call *Dublin*,
Tim thou'rt the *Punch* to stir up trouble in;
You Wrigle, Fidge, and make a Rout,
Put all your Brother Puppets out, 140
Run on in a perpetual Round,
To Teize, Perplex, Disturb, Confound,
Intrude with Monkey grin, and clatter,
To interrupt all serious Matter,
Are grown the Nuissance of your *Clan*, 145
Who hate and scorn you, to a Man;
But then the Lookers on, the *Tories*
You still divert with merry Stories;
They wou'd Consent, that all the Crew
Were hanged, before they'd part with you. 150
　But tell me, *Tim*, upon the spot,
By all this Coyl what hast thou got?
If *Tories* must have all the sport,
I fear you'll be disgrac'd at *Court*.

  T. Got? D—— my Blood *I frank my Letters*,   155
Walk by my place, before my Betters,
And simple as I now stand here,
Expect in time, to be a P——
Got? D—— me, why I got my will!
Ne're hold my peace, and ne'er stand still.   160
I F——t with twenty Ladies by;
They call me Beast, and what Care I?
I bravely call the Tories Jacks,
And Sons of Whores—behind their Backs.
But cou'd you bring me once to think,   165
That when I strut, and stare, and stink,
Revile, and slander, fume and storm,
Betray, make Oath, impeach, inform,
With such a constant, Loyal Zeal,
To serve my self, and Common-weal,   170
And fret the *Tories* Souls to Death,
I did but lose my precious Breath,
And when I damn my Soul to plague 'em,
Am, as you tell me, but their may-game,
Consume my Vitals! they shall know,   175
I am not to be treated so;
I'd rather hang my self by half,
Than give those Rascals cause to laugh.
  But how, my Friend, can I endure
Once so renown'd to Live obscure?   180
No little Boys and Girls to cry
There's Nimble Tim a passing by.
No more my dear Delightful way tread,
Of keeping up *a party hatred.*
Will none the *Tory Dogs* pursue,   185
When thro' the streets I cry *holloo*?
Must all my D—mee's, Bl—s and W—ds
Pass only now for empty sounds?
Shall *Tory* Rascals be Elected,
Although I swear them Disaffected?   190
And when I roar a Plot, a *Plot*,
Will our own Party mind me not?
So qualify'd to Swear and Lye,
Will they not trust me for a Spy?

Dear *Mullinix*, your good Advice   195
I beg, you see the Case is nice.
O, were I equal in Renown,
Like thee, to please this thankless Town!
Or blest with such engaging Parts,
To win the Truant School-Boys Hearts!   200
Thy Vertues meet their just Reward,
Attended by the *Sable-guard*,
Charm'd by thy voice the 'Prentice drops
The Snow-ball destin'd at thy Chops;
Thy graceful Steps, and Coll'nell's Air   205
Allure the Cinder-picking Fair.
    M.   No more—In mark of true Affection
I take thee under my Protection.
Your Parts are good, 'tis not deny'd,
I wish they had been well apply'd.   210
But now observe my Counsel (*viz*)
Adapt your Habit to your Phiz.
You must no longer thus equip 'ye
As *Horace* says, *Optat ephippia.*
There's *Latin* too that you may see   215
How I improv'd by Dr. ——
I have a Coat at home, that you may try,
'Tis just like this, which hangs by Geometry.
My Hat has much the nicer air,
Your Block will fit it to a hair.   220
That Wig, I wou'd not for the world
Have it so formal, and so Curl'd,
'Twill be so oyly, and so sleek
When I have lain in it a Week!
You'll find it well prepar'd to take   225
The figure of *Toope* and *Snake.*
Thus drest alike from Top to Toe,
That which is which, 'tis hard to know.
When first in publick we appear,
I'll lead the Van, keep you the Rear.   230
Be careful, as you walk behind,
Use all the Talents of your mind.
Be studious well to imitate
My portly Motion, Mien, and Gate.

Mark my Address, and learn my Style,   235
When to look Scornful, when to Smile,
Nor sputter out your Oaths so fast,
But keep your Swearing to the last.
Then at our leisure we'll be witty,
And in the Streets divert the City: 240
The Ladies from the Windows gaping,
The Children all our motions Aping.
Your Conversation to refine,
I'll take you to some Friends of mine;
Choice Spirits, who employ their Parts,   245
To mend the World by useful Arts.
Some cleansing hollow Tubes, to spy
Direct the *Zenith* of the Sky;
Some have the City in their Care,
From noxious Steams to purge the Air;   250
Some teach us in these dang'rous Days,
How to walk upright in our ways;
Some whose reforming Hands engage,
To lash the Lewdness of the Age;
Some, for the publick Service go,   255
Perpetual Envoys to and fro;
Whose able Heads support the Weight,
Of twenty M——rs of State.
We scorn, for want of talk, to jabber
Of Parties o're our *Bonny-Clabber*.   260
Nor are we studious to enquire,
Who votes for Manners, who for Hire.
Our Care is to improve the mind,
With what concerns all human kind;
The various Scenes of mortal Life,   265
Who beats her Husband, who his Wife;
Or how the Bulley at a stroke
Knockt down the Boy, the Lanthorn broke;
One tells the Rise of Cheese, and Oat-meal,
Another when he got a hot Meal;   270
One gives Advice in Proverbs Old,
Instructs us how to tame a Scold;
One shows how bravely *Audoin* Dy'd,
And at the Gallows all deny'd;

How by the *Almanack* 'tis clear,   275
That Herrings will be cheap this Year.
T.   Dear *Mullinix*, I now lament
My precious Time, so long mispent,
By nature meant for nobler Ends,
O, introduce me to your Friends!   280
For whom, by Birth, I was design'd,
'Till Politicks debas'd my mind.
I give my self intire to you,
G—— d—— the *Whigs* and *Tories* too.

MOTTO. 'That like may meet with like', echoing Horace, *Epistles*, i. 5. 25–6: 'ut coeat par |
iungaturque pari'.

INTRODUCTION
13. *Nick-name*: Dick, i.e., Richard Tighe, for whom see introductory note.

POEM
2. *Clutter*: 'Noisy turmoil or disturbance, hubbub' (*OED*, sense 4; compare sense 3).
6. *hardly twenty*: In Ireland the extent of serious Jacobitism (as opposed to sentimental
Jacobitism or Jacobitism as a gesture of popular protest or as a formality of bardic
poetry) is very hard to gauge. Though it is true that Tories often minimized the
strength of the Jacobites, Swift's estimate may not be far wrong as to the number of
landed, politically serious Jacobites.
13. *Did not an Earl but lately Vote*: The Earl of Barrymore, according to a footnote in *35u*.
In the Irish House of Lords, a debate began 18 Dec. 1727 on a motion that 'the
publick Accounts of the Nation' be laid before the house. 'We had an attempt made
in our House to call for the accounts of the nation, which as it was new here, might
have occasioned a quarrel with the House of Commons, and probably was intended
so to do, but it was overruled by about 28 to 11' (Boulter, i. 165). Seven lords
recorded a protest: the Earls of Barrymore, Kildare, Meath, and Rosse, Viscounts
Massareene and Mayo, and Baron Howth (*Journals of the House of Lords of Ireland*, iii
(Dublin: Sleater, 1779), 18–19, 39). The Tory James Barry, 4th Earl of Barrymore
(1667–1748), a general, a privy councillor, and British MP, was perhaps the leader of
this group. Barrymore was in 1733 the dedicatee of Sheridan's edition of Sir John
Davi[e]s's *Historical Relations: or, A Discovery of the True Causes Why Ireland Was Never
Entirely Subdued* and later was an active Jacobite; see Eveline Cruickshanks's article
on him in Sedgwick, i. 440–2.
17. *an able Statesman [Bishop]*: Perhaps Archbishop Boulter. The unusual tacit blank
suggests that the reference is dangerous.
18. *Dish up*: i.e., dish, defeat completely.
20. *Fire and Faggot*: i.e., the Inquisition.
24. *Avignon*: As Swift conceivably had heard, James, the Pretender, had moved from
Bologna to the papal city of Avignon upon the accession of George II, but after the
British expressed their displeasure to the pope, James had returned to Bologna
early in 1728 (Martin Haile, *James Francis Edward* (London, 1907), 325–8; Sir Charles
Petrie, Bt., *The Jacobite Movement* (London, 1959), 326). Swift presumably considered it doubtful that the Pretender had a navy (he didn't), or if he had, that it
would have sailed from Avignon, 'a mid-land City in *France*', according to a note in
35u. Avignon is on the Rhône, a river not navigable for ships of any size.

43. *Martin Marrall*: See textual variants. Writers frequently alluded to the exquisite scene in Dryden's *Sir Martin Mar-all, or The Feign'd Innocence* (1668), v. 1.

45–6. *Bees . . . Brazen Kettle*: Supposedly to make bees swarm, it was customary to 'take a Brass *Bason*, *Pan, or Candlestick*, and make a tinkling noise there-upon, for they are so delighted with *Musick*, that by the sound thereof they will presently knit upon some branch or bow of a Tree' [Gervase Markham], *Cheap and Good Husbandry, for the Well-Ordering of All Beasts and Fowls*, 14th edn. (London: T. B., 1683), 140. Swift alludes to the custom in *Prometheus* (*Poems*, i. 345), as Rogers notes, 777.

52. *Thersites*: Since it is Mullinix who views Tighe as a Thersites-figure, one may surmise that the allusion is to a puppet play or some other popular medium for the Thersites story, deriving perhaps from plays such as (Udall's?) interlude *Thersites* or from rhetoric texts and collections of adages representing him as a type, foul-mouthed, hunchbacked, malicious, and blustering. To the modern reader Thersites is better known from the *Iliad*, ii. 211–77, or from Shakespeare's *Troilus and Cressida*. For the vernacular tradition, see Robert Kimbrough, *Shakespeare's* Troilus and Cressida *and Its Setting* (Cambridge, Mass., 1964), 37–9.

68. *As if the Devil drove*: Proverbially, 'He needs must go that the Devil drives' (Tilley D278).

76. *Keck at the Memory of Glorious*: Loyal toasts to the 'glorious memory' of William III were opposed as being a mockery of the Eucharist, notably by Peter Browne (1665?–1735), bishop of Cork and Ross; see A. R. Winnett, *Peter Browne* (London, 1974), 68–85. Williamites viewed such objection as Jacobite. Sheridan in no. 18 disapproves 'that *Bumper-Loyalty*, of getting Drunk to the Memory of the Dead'. In *The Legion Club*, Swift envisages Tighe as a lunatic 'Toast[ing] *old Glorious* in [his] Piss' (*Poems*, iii. 835).

80. *To Prance . . . the Statue round*: 'A Statue of King *William* in *College Green, Dublin*, round which his Adorers, every Year of his Birth, go on Foot, or in their Coaches: But the Number is much lessened' (*35u* note). Grinling Gibbons's equestrian statue, which had been in College Green since 1701, was the site of elaborate ceremonies annually on 4 Nov., the anniversary of William's landing in England and also his birthday. The ceremony included a procession of dignitaries around the statue three times. The statue was from time to time defaced by Jacobites and College pranksters. Swift's (?) note in *35u* can be confirmed by James Arbuckle's remark in the *Dublin Weekly J.* 26 Nov. 1726: 'The *Fourth of November*, which used to be celebrated with so much Joy by the Protestants of this Kingdom, in Memory of our Glorious Deliverer, King *WILLIAM*, has not lately been honoured with the same Solemnity and Acclamation as formerly.' See also *Dublin Intelligence*, 7 Nov. 1727; *Journal to Stella*, i. 129–30; Gilbert, *Dublin*, iii. 40–5; Mary Delany, *The Autobiography and Correspondence of Mary Granville, Mrs. Delany*, ed. Lady Llanover, iii (London, 1861), 54; and F. E. Dixon, 'Dublin Portrait Statues', *Dublin Historical Record*, 31 (1978), 67 and photograph facing p. 61.

98. *How Solomon decides the Cause*: This and the following allusions are to puppet shows that have not survived, the show in this case deriving from 1 Kings 3: 16–28. From *Strephon and Chloe* we know that Solomon, the Queen of Sheba, and the Duke of Lorraine were familiar figures in puppet shows (*Poems*, ii. 592). Further on Swift's interest in puppets, see his *Preface to the B—p of S—m's Introduction*, in *Prose*, iv. 58; John M. Bullitt, *Jonathan Swift and the Anatomy of Satire* (Cambridge, Mass., 1955), 170–81; and Aline Mackenzie Taylor, 'Sights and Monsters and Gulliver's *Voyage to Brobdingnag*', *Tulane Stud. in English*, 7 (1957), 61–2.

100. *the Witch of Endor*: A show deriving from 1 Sam. 28: 7–25.

101. *Faustus, with the Devil*: A show probably based not on Marlowe's play but on popular sources such as the chapbook apparently alluded to in *Tale*, 68.

110. *the Queen of Sheba*: A show deriving from 1 Kings 10 and 2 Chr. 9.

111. *Duke of Lorrain*: Probably a representation of Charles V, Duke of Lorraine (1643–90), who led imperial forces in defeating the Turks at the Siege of Vienna in 1683.

114. *sells . . . a bargain*: Gives 'an unexpected reply, tending to obscenity' (Johnson). 'The seller [names] his or her hinder parts, in answer to the question, What? which the buyer was artfully led to ask. As a specimen, take the following instance: A lady would come into a room full of company, apparently in a fright, crying out, It is white, and follows me! On any of the company asking, What? she sold him the bargain, by saying, Mine a—e.' [Francis Grose], *A Classical Dictionary of the Vulgar Tongue*, 3rd edn. (London: Hooper, 1796), under 'bargain'.

129. *Sabra*: Maiden of Silene in Libya whom St George rescued from the dragon. The character appeared in *The Golden Legend* and from there seems to have become part of popular lore about St George. See E. O. Gordon, *Saint George* (London, 1907), 16–18; David Scott Fox, *Saint George* (Windsor Forest, 1983), 152; *Oxford Companion to Eng. Lit.*, 4th edn.

133. *Philosophers*: Plato, in his allegory of the cave, *Republic*, vii. 514 B; and in *Laws*, i. 644 D–E.

139. *Fidge*: To fidget; compare no. 10, and this from Mrs Marwood in Congreve's *The Way of the World*, v: 'The good Judge . . . Simpers under a Grey beard, and fidges off and on his Cushion as if he had swallow'd *Cantharides*, or sat upon *Cow-Itch*.'

152. *Coyl*: The emendation to 'Toil' in *30* is conceivably authorial.

155. *I frank my Letters*: As a member of Parliament.

156. *Walk by my place*: As a privy councillor, Tighe was entitled to a prominent place in processions of state. He was one of very few commoners in the council.

163. *Jacks*: In *35u* (Swift's?) note offers this explanation in mock-seriousness: 'A Cant Word for *Jacobites*, or those who continued in the Interest of King *James II.* after King *William* got the Crown, and now are for his Son, commonly called the *Pretender*'.

174. *may-game*: B. E., *A New Dictionary of the Terms Ancient and Modern of the Canting Crew* (London: Hawes *et al.*, 1699): May-games were 'Frolicks, Plaies, Tricks, Pastimes, &c. Do you make a May-game of me? do you Abuse or Expose me?'

187. *D—mee's, Bl—s and W—ds*: Dammee's, bloods, and wounds—minced oaths.

202. *the Sable-guard*: Vagrant boys, shoeboys; blackguards literalized.

206. *the Cinder-picking Fair*: i.e., cinder wenches, 'female[s] whose occupation it is to rake cinders from among ashes' (*OED*).

214. *Optat ephippia*: Horace, *Epistles*, i. 14. 43: 'optat ephippia bos' ('the ox longs for the horse's trappings' (Loeb)); i.e., don't try to be something you're not. Proverbial since its inclusion in Erasmus's *Adagia*.

216. *How I improv'd by Dr. [Leigh]*: According to the note in *35u*, which fills the blank as 'Lee', 'A deceased Clergyman, whose Footman he was.' 'The famous TOM LEIGH' (*c.* 1681–Jan. 1727/8) was a punning acquaintance of Swift, Stella, Tisdall, Delany, and others of their circle; Swift viewed him as a 'Coxcomb', rude and conceited. He attended TCD, graduating BA in 1692, MA in 1695, and BD and DD in 1710. From 1696 until being deprived in 1700, he was a petty canon of St Patrick's, Dublin; subsequently he was chancellor of Dromore and held various livings in the diocese of Armagh. See *Poems*, i. 217, iii. 968; an amusing account of him in *Journal to Stella*, ii. 587; Hugh Jackson Lawlor, *The Fasti of St. Patrick's, Dublin* (Dundalk, 1930), 203; James B. Leslie, *Armagh Clergy and Parishes* (Dundalk, 1911), 309; and George Mayhew, 'Swift and the Tripos Tradition', *PQ* 45 (1966), 89. There was no other Church of Ireland clergyman named Lee, Lea, or Leigh, according to records compiled at the Representative Church Body Library, Dublin. The claim that John Molyneux had served Thomas Leigh as a footman is not now open to independent verification.

218. *hangs by Geometry*: Hangs straight down, without support; of clothing, the term is derogatory, implying bad fit or absence of proper underpinnings. Rogers, 778, notes other instances in *Prose*, iv. 159 and *Poems*, i. 99; see examples quoted in *OED* under *geometry*, sense 3, though I differ with the definition offered there.

226. *The figure of Toope and Snake*: The full-bottomed wig, 'so formal, and so Curl'd' (222), was beginning to go out of fashion, and though Swift continued to wear it, younger men adopted shorter bobbed wigs and tie-wigs. When the hair of these wigs was brushed straight back from the forehead and up over a pad, they were called *toupees*. The snake was an extreme variety of the pigtail tie-wig in which the queue was wrapped in ribbon and tied with a bow at the bottom; the monkey with which Swift compares Tighe in no. 10 is shown with such a snake (Fig. 2). See also *Poems*, ii. 426; various engravings by Hogarth; A. Racinet, *Le Costume historique* (Paris, 1888), vol. v; R. Turner Wilcox, *The Mode in Hats and Headdress* (New York, 1945), [162].

245. *Choice Spirits*: 'Thoughtless, laughing, singing, drunken fellow[s]'. [Francis Grose], *A Classical Dictionary of the Vulgar Tongue* (London: Hooper, 1785).

247. *Some cleansing hollow Tubes*: 'Chimney-Sweepers' (*35u* note).

249. *Some have the City in their Care*: 'Scavengers' (*35u* note).

251. *Some teach us*: 'Coblers' (*35u* note); 'walk upright' is a biblical echo; cf., among many other verses, Prov. 11: 20, Ps. 15: 2 and 84: 11.

253. *Some whose reforming Hands*: 'Keeper of *Bridewell*' (*35u* note). John Hawkins, keeper of Newgate Prison and the Black Dog Prison (the sheriff's marshalsea) in Dublin, practised extraordinary extortion and cruelty, and one of his victims was Audouin (line 273); see *Corresp*. iii. 327; Gilbert, *Dublin*, i. 265–9; and *Commons J. Ireland*, III. ii. appendix, pp. ccclxxxvi–cccxc.

255. *Some, for the publick Service go*: 'Porters' (*35u* note).

258. *M——rs*: Ministers.

259. *We scorn, for want of talk . . .*: As the footnote in *35u* points out with slight misquotation (see textual variants), the following passage parodies Horace's account of a rural banquet (*Satires*, ii. 6. 70–6): 'And so begins a chat, not about other men's homes and estates, nor whether Lepos dances well or ill; but we discuss matters which concern us more, and of which it is harmful to be in ignorance—whether wealth or virtue makes men happy, whether self-interest or uprightness leads us to friendship, what is the nature of the good and what is its highest form' (Loeb). For Sheridan's translation, see *Intelligencer* 4.

260. *Bonny-Clabber*: Clotted sour milk, the staple of native Irish diet most commonly mentioned by contemporary English writers; see A. T. Lucas, 'Irish Food before the Potato', *Gwerin*, 3, no. 2 (1960), 21–4; and Alan Bliss, *Spoken English in Ireland, 1600–1740* (Dublin, 1979), 271–3.

262. *Manners*: 'Mannors' in the Harding edition; changed to 'Manours' in *29*, followed by *30* and *32*; corrected by Swift in his own copy of *32* to 'Manners', the reading adopted in *35u*.

273. *how bravely Audoin Dy'd*: The Dublin surgeon John Audouin was on strong evidence sentenced to be hanged, drawn, and quartered 5 June 1728 for the barbarous murder of his servant Margaret Keif. Under the scaffold with the noose around his neck, Audouin pathetically protested his innocence. Then he jumped from the cart with sudden force, killing himself instantly and so avoiding disembowelment while still conscious. The crime and its aftermath occasioned a flood of sensational newspaper articles and halfsheets; James Carson's Dublin compilation, *A Chronology of Some Memorable Accidents*, first published in 1743 and listing the important events 'from the Creation of the World' to the present, includes Audouin's execution among them. See also J. Woolley, 'The *Intelligencer*: Its Dating and Contemporaneity', in H. J. Real and H. J. Vienken (eds.), *Proc. First Münster Symposium on Jonathan Swift* (Munich, 1985), 347–8.

The nobility interested Swift keenly. A few months after composing this *Intelligencer*, he drew up a list of forty-one lords and other famous friends of his, including several he discusses in this essay: Somers, Addison, Oxford, Harcourt, and Bolingbroke (*Corresp.* v. 271–2). In the *Examiner* and in *Gulliver's Travels* he had already complained about the corrupt education given to the sons of peers (*Swift vs. Mainwaring*, 419; *Prose*, xi. 256). And in his sermon 'On Mutual Subjection', he applies the complaint to princes as well: 'Princes are born with no more Advantages of Strength or Wisdom than other Men; and, by an unhappy Education, are usually more defective in both than thousands of their Subjects' (*Prose*, ix. 142–3; and see also 228–9).

But when he argues that decadent education results in 'noble Families' whose 'Titles and Priviledges out-live their Estates', and that that is 'dangerous to the Publick', he almost certainly alludes to the Irish Lords' heated debate only two months before, over a measure to limit the parliamentary privilege that shielded members from arrest for debt. The bill barely passed over the objections of the 'young indebted lords', who, Archbishop Boulter said, 'value[d] themselves upon paying nobody'. (The majority in the Lords was made up largely of bishops; see James, 142, quoting Boulter to Newcastle, 30 April 1728, PRO, SP 63/390, fo. 72; and William King to Edward Southwell, 27 April 1728, quoted in *A Great Archbishop of Dublin: William King, D.D.*, ed. Sir Charles S. King, Bt. (London, 1906), 263.) Swift did not disagree with the lord (the Earl of Abercorn?) who in the debate had argued that the Irish 'Peerage is grown less powerful, tho' much more Numerous; and consequently less considerable, then it Originally was' (*The Speech of a Noble Peer: Made in the House of Lords in Ireland, When the Priviledge-Bill Was in Debate There* (Dublin: Harding, 1728), 13).

During Queen Anne's reign Swift would have had a close look at how lack of wealth opened peers to financial manipulation: see Edward Gregg and Clyve Jones, 'Hanover, Pensions, and the "Poor Lords"', in C. Jones and D. Jones (eds.), *Peers, Politics and Power* (London, 1986), 177–84. *Intelligencer* 9 probably reflects that experience as well as the most recent full-scale political discussion of the dangers of a 'numerous' and 'decayed' nobility—namely, the pamphlet war in 1719 over the (British) Peerage Bill, an attempt to limit the creation of new peerages and to replace the Scottish representative peers with hereditary peers. The 1719 pamphleteers voiced these concerns among others: (1) that poor lords were ill qualified to act as judges of property matters in the court of last resort, since they had little property of their own to protect, or since they might be dependent and therefore subject to manipulation; (2) that they could not afford the expense of sitting in Parliament; (3) that by being insulated from arrest for debt, they hurt honest tradesmen; and (4) that they might be badly trained for their work as legislators. (These views are variously expressed in Addison's *Old Whig*, no. 1; *Some Considerations Humbly Offer'd, Relating to the Peerage of Great Britain*. By a gentleman (London: Creake *et al.*, 1719); *The Constitution Explain'd, in Relation to the Independency of the House of Lords* (London: Roberts, 1719); *A Supplement to the Papers, Writ in Defence of the Peerage Bill* (London: Boreham, 1719); and the *Patrician*, no. 3, perhaps by Lord Molesworth.)

How such problems pertained to education was clearly stated in *A Letter from a Nobleman of Scotland to a Gentleman of England*, quoted in Steele's *Plebian*, no. 4 (1719): 'As to the Peerage, if we look into their Assembly, and compare the many that sit there by Right of Descent, with the Characters of those who were first created to those Honours, and consider the modern Education by which they are usually form'd to their future Greatness, how much Looseness, Flattery and false Politeness they affect from their first entrance into Life; we shall be able to form some Notion of what sort of Genius's that Assembly will be compos'd 20 Years hence, in case this Bill should pass . . .' (10). Swift's idea in *Intelligencer* 9 that 'New-men' had degraded the peerage was shared by Harley, he claimed in *The History of the Four Last Years of the Queen*: Harley 'considered the House of Peers as a Body made up almost a Fourth Part of New Men within Twenty Years past; all Clients or Proselytes to the Leaders of the opposite Party, and consequently stocked with Principles little consistent with the old Constitution: That, this Infection had spread yet farther among the Bench of Bishops, and, that many of the younger Peers had been educated under the same Masters' (*Prose*, vii. 19).

On the other hand, a more radical criticism of the peerage was not difficult. Writing to Charles Ford about the Peerage Bill, Swift reported having changed his mind: 'I remember to have agreed many years ago with some very great men [Harley?], who thought a Bill for limiting the Prerogative in making Peers would mend the Constitution, but as much as I know of this it was wholly naught, and there is one invincible obvious Argument which Steel lightly touches [in *A Letter to the Earl of O——d, Concerning the Bill of Peerage* (1719)]; That the Lords degenerate by Luxury Idleness &c and the Crown is always forced to govern by new Men. I think Titles should fall with Estates' (8 Dec. 1719, *Corresp.* ii. 331). In the *Intelligencer*, however, Swift chooses a more hopeful position—one that, to be sure, does not envisage the wholesale creation of new peerages such as that of 1711, which he himself defended elsewhere (*Prose*, vii. 19–21). Rather he holds out the prospect that proper education of future lords could regenerate the nobility. This is not very different from his earlier stance in the *Examiner*.

When Swift seeks more and better education for princes and the scions of aristocracy, it is not primarily either for polish or for intellectual training. He believes that education inculcates morality, one of whose implications is that the Constitution in Church and State should be profoundly respected and cherished. Neither extraordinary intelligence nor even extraordinary education is necessary for administrative success:

> God . . . hath made the Science of Governing sufficiently obvious to common Capacityes, otherwise the World would be left in a desolate Condition if great Affairs did always require a great Genius, whereof the most fruitfull Age will hardly produce above three or four in a Nation, among which Princes, who of all other Mortals are the worst educated have twenty Millions to one against them that they shall not be of the Number; and proportionable Odds for the same Reasons are against every one of Noble Birth or great Estates: Accordingly we find that the Dullest Nations antient and Modern have not wanted good Rules of Policy, or Persons qualifyed for Administration. (*Enquiry*, 15–16.)

That virtue should be the goal of education was by no means a novel proposition; see George C. Brauer, Jr, *The Education of a Gentleman: Theories of Gentlemanly Education in England, 1660–1775* (New York, 1959). Further on Swift's view of the nobility, see F. P. Lock, *Swift's Tory Politics* (Newark, Del., 1983), 174–8. No. 9 has been usefully annotated by Louis A. Landa in *Gulliver's Travels and Other Writings* (Boston, 1960), 544–6.

NUMB. IX.

FROM frequently reflecting upon the Course and Method of Educating Youth in this and a Neighbouring Kingdom, with the general Success and consequence thereof; I am come to this Determination, That Education is always the worse in Proportion to the Wealth and Grandeur of the Parents. Nor do I doubt in the 5 least, that if the whole World were now under the Dominion of one Monarch (provided I might be allowed to chuse where he should fix the Seat of his Empire) the only Son and Heir of that Monarch, would be the worst Educated Mortal, that ever was born since the Creation: And, I doubt the same Proportion will hold through all Degrees and 10 Titles, from an Emperor downwards, to the common Gentry. I do not say that this hath been always the case: for in better times it was directly otherwise; and a Scholar may fill half his *Greek* and *Roman* Shelves with Authors of the Noblest Birth, as well as highest Virtue. Nor, do I tax all Nations at present with this defect, for I know there 15 are some to be excepted, and particularly *Scotland*, under all the Disadvantages of it's Clymate and Soyle, if that happiness be not rather owing even to those very dis-advantages. What is then to be

done, if this Reflection must fix on two Countries, which will be most
20 ready to take Offence, and which of all others it will be least prudent or
safe to offend?

But there is one Circumstance yet more Dangerous and
Lamentable. For if, according to the Postulatum already laid down,
the higher Quality any Youth is of, he is in greater likelyhood to be
25 worse Educated, it behooves me to dread, and keep far from the Verge
of *Scandalum Magnatum.*

Retracting therefore that hazardous Postulatum, I shall venture no
further at present than to say, that perhaps some Additional Care in
Educating the Sons of Nobility, and principal Gentry, might not be ill
30 employed. If this be not delivered with softness enough, I must for the
future be Silent.

In the mean time, let me ask only two Questions, which relate to
a Neighbouring Kingdom, from whence the Chief among us are
descended, and whose manners we most affect to follow. I ask first,
35 how it comes about, that for above 60 Years past, the Chief Conduct of
Affairs in that Kingdom hath been generally placed in the Hands of
New-men, with very few Exceptions. The Noblest Blood of *England*
having been shed in the grand Rebellion, many great Families became
extinct, or supported only by Minors: when the King was Restored,
40 very few of those Lords remained, who began, or at least had improved
their Education, under the happy Reign of King *James*, or King
Charles I, of which Lords the two principal were the Marquiss of
Ormonde, and the Earl of *Southampton*. The Minors had, during the
Rebellion and Usurpation, either received too much Tincture of bad
45 Principles from those Fanatick Times, or coming to Age at the
Restoration, fell into the Vices of that dissolute Reign.

I Date from this Æra, the Corrupt Method of Education among us,
and the consequence thereof, in the Necessity the Crown lay under of
Introducing *New-men* into the chief Conduct of publick Affairs, or
50 to the Office of what we now call Prime Ministers, Men of Art,
Knowledge, Application, and Insinuation, meerly for want of a supply
among the Nobility. They were generally (though not always) of
good Birth, sometimes Younger Brothers, at other times, such who
although inheriting good Estates, yet happened to be well Educated,
55 and provided with Learning; such under that King, were *Hyde*,
Bridgman, *Clifford*, *Coventry*, *Osborn*, *Godolphin*, *Ashley-Cooper*; Few or
none under the short Reign of King *James* II. Under King *William*;
Summers, *Montague*, *Churchil*, *Vernon*, *Harry Boyle*, and many others:

Under the Queen; *Harley*, *St. John*, *Harcourt*, *Trevers*, who indeed
were Persons of the best private Families, but unadorn'd with Titles. 60
So in the last Reign, Mr. *Robert Walpole*, was understood for many
Years, to be Prime Minister, in which Post he still happily continues;
His Brother *Horace* is Ambassador Extraordinary to *France*. Mr.
Addison, and Mr. *Craiggs*, without the least Allyance to support them,
have been Secretaries of State.   65

If the Facts have been thus for above 60 years past (whereof I could
with a little further Recollection produce many more Instances) I
would ask again, how it hath happened, that in a Nation plentifully
abounding with Nobility, so great share in the most important parts of
publick management, hath been for so long a Period chiefly entrusted 70
to Commonners; unless some Omissions, or Defects of the highest
Import, may be charged upon those to whom the care of Educating
our Noble Youth hath been committed. For, if there be any difference
between human Creatures in the point of natural Parts, as we usually
call them, it should seem, that the Advantage lyes on the side of 75
Children born from Noble and Wealthy Parents; the same Traditional
Sloth and Luxury which render their Body Weak and Effeminate,
perhaps refining and giving a freer motion to the Spirits, beyond what
can be expected from the gross robust Issue of meaner Mortals. Add to
this, the peculiar Advantages, which all young Noblemen possess, by 80
the Priviledges of their Birth; Such as a free access to Courts, and a
universal Deference pay'd to their Persons.

But as my Lord *Bacon* chargeth it for a fault on Princes, that they
are impatient to compass Ends without giving themselves the trouble
of consulting or executing the means. So perhaps it may be the 85
disposition of young Nobles, either from the Indulgence of Parents,
Tutors and Governors, or their own Inactivity, that they expect the
accomplishments of a good Education without the least expence of
Time or Study, to acquire them.

What I said last, I am ready to retract; For the case is infinitely 90
worse; and the very Maxims set up to direct modern Education, are
enough to destroy all the Seeds of Knowledge, Honour, Wisdom, and
Virtue among us. The current Opinion prevails that the study of *Greek*
and *Latin* is loss of Time; that publick Schools by mingling the Sons
of Noblemen, with those of the Vulgar, engage the former in bad 95
Company; That whipping breaks the Spirits of Lads well Born; That
Universities make young Men Pedants. That, to Dance, Fence, speak

French, and know how to behave your self among great Persons of both Sexes, comprehends *the whole duty of a Gentleman.*

100   I cannot but think this wise System of Education, hath been much cultivated among us by those Worthies of the Army, who during the last War returning from *Flanders* at the close of each Campaign, became the Dictators of Behaviour, Dress and Politeness to all those Youngsters, who frequent Chocolate-Coffee-Gaming-Houses,
105 Drawing-Rooms, Opera's, Levees, and Assemblies; where a Colonel by his Pay, Perquisites, and Plunder, was qualifyed to outshine many Peers of the Realm; and by the influence of an *exotick* Habit and Demeanor, added to other foreign Accomplishments, gave the Law to the whole Town, and were copyed as the Standard-Patterns
110 of whatever was refined in Dress, Equipage, Conversation, or Diversions.

I remember in those Times, an Admired Original of that Vocation, sitting in a Coffee-house near two Gentlemen, whereof one was of the Clergy, who were engaged in some discourse that savoured of
115 Learning; This Officer thought fit to interpose, and professing to deliver the Sentiments of his Fraternity as well as his own (and probably did so of too many among them) turning to the Clergyman, spoke in the following manner. *D—n me, Doctor, say what you will, the Army is the only School for Gentlemen. Do you think my Lord* Marlborough
120 *beat the* French, *with* Greek *and* Latin. *D—n me, a Scholar when he comes into good Company; what is he but an Ass? D—n me, I would be glad by G—d to see any of your Schollars with his Nouns, and his Verbs, and his Philosophy, and Trigonometry, what a figure he would make at a Siege or Blockado or reconoitring— D—n me* &c. After which he proceeded with a Volley of
125 Military Terms, less significant, sounding worse, and harder to be understood than any that were ever Coyned by the Commentators upon *Aristotle*. I would not here be thought to charge the Soldiery with Ignorance and contempt of Learning, without allowing Exceptions, of which I have known many, and some even in this Kingdom, but
130 however, the worse example, especially in a great Majority will certainly prevail.

I have heard that the late Earl of *Oxford* in the time of his Ministry, never past by *White*'s *Chocolate-house* (the common Rendezvous of infamous Sharpers, and noble Cullies) without bestowing a Curse
135 upon that famous Accademy, as the Bane of half the *English* Nobility. I have been likewise told another passage concerning that great Minister; which because it gives a humorous Idea of one principal

Ingredient in modern Education, take as followeth. *Le-Sac* the Famous *French* Dancing-master in great Admiration asked a friend, whether it were true that Mr. *Harley* was made an Earl, and Lord Treasurer: And finding it confirmed, said; *Well, I wonder what the Devil the Queen could see in him; for I attended him two Years, and he was the greatest Dunce that ever I taught.*

Another hindrance to good Education, and I think, the greatest of any, is that pernicious custom in Rich and Noble Families, of entertaining *French* Tutors in their Houses. These wretched *Pædagogues* are enjoyned by the Father, to take special care, that the Boy shall be perfect in his *French*; By the Mother, that *Master* must not walk till he is hot, nor be suffered to play with other Boys, nor be wet in his Feet, nor daub his Cloaths, and to see that the Dancing-master attends constantly, and does his Duty: she further insists that the Child be not kept too long poring on his Book, because he is subject to sore Eyes, and of a weakly Constitution.

By these methods the young Gentleman is in every Article as fully accomplished at 8 Years old as at eight and twenty (Age adding only to the growth of his Person and his Vice) so that if you should look at him in his Boyhood through the magnifying end of a Perspective, and in his Manhood through the other, it would be impossible to spy any difference: The same Airs, the same Strutt, the same Cock of his Hat, and posture of his Sword (as far as the change of fashions will allow) the same understanding, the same compass of knowledge, with the very same Absurdity, Impudence, and Impertinence of Tongue.

He is taught from the Nursery that he must inherit a great Estate, and hath no need to mind his Book, which is a Lesson he never forgets to the end of his life. His chief Solace is to steal down and play at Span-farthing with the Page, or young Black-a-moor, or little favorite Foot-boy, one of which is his principal Confident, and Bosom-friend.

There is one young Lord in this Town, who by an unexampled piece of good Fortune, was miraculously snatched out of the Gulph of Ignorance, confined to a publick School for a due Term of Years, well Whipped when he deserved it; clad no better than his Comrades, and always their Play-fellow on the same foot, had no Precedence in the School, but what was given him by his Merit, and lost it whenever he was Negligent. It is well known how many Mutinies were bred at this unpresidented Treatment, what complaints among his *Relations*, and other *Great ones* of both Sexes; that his Stockings with silver Clocks were ravished from him, that he wore his own Hair, that his dress was

undistinguished; that he was not fit to appear at a Ball or Assembly,
nor suffered to go to either. And it was with the utmost difficulty that
180 he became qualifyed for his present removal, where he may probably
be farther Persecuted, and possibly with Success, if the firmness of
a very Worthy Governor, and his own good Dispositions will not
preserve him. I confess, I cannot but wish he may go on in the way
he began, because I have a curiosity to know by so singular an
185 Experiment, whether Truth, Honour, Justice, Temperance, Courage
and good Sense acquired by a *School* and *College* Education, may not
produce a very tolerable Lad, although he should happen to fail in one
or two of those accomplishments, which in the general Vogue, are held
so important to the finishing of a Gentleman.

190   It is true, I have known an Accademical Education to have been
exploded in publick Assemblies; and have heard more than one or two
Persons of high Rank, declare they could learn nothing more at *Oxford*
and *Cambridge*, than to drink Ale and smoke Tobacco; wherein I
firmly believ'd them, and could have added some hundred Examples
195 from my own observation in one of those Universities, but they all
were of young Heirs sent thither, only for form, either from Schools
where they were not suffered by their careful Parents, to stay above
three Months in the Year, or from under the management of *French*
Family-Tutors, who yet often attended them to their *College*, to
200 prevent all possibility of their Improvement. But, I never yet knew any
one Person of Quality, who followed his Studies at the University, and
carryed away his just Proportion of Learning, that was not ready upon
all occasions to celebrate and defend that course of Education, and to
prove a Patron of Learned Men.

205   There is one circumstance in a learned Education, which ought to
have much weight, even with those who have no Learning at all. The
Books read at *Schools* and *Colleges*, are full of Incitements to Virtue,
and Discouragements from Vice, drawn from the wisest Reasons, the
strongest Motives, and the most influencing Examples. Thus, young
210 Minds are filled early with an inclination to Good, and an abhorrence
of Evil, both which encrease in them, according to the advances they
make in Literature: And, although they may be, and too often are,
drawn by the Temptations of Youth, and the Opportunities of a large
Fortune, into some Irregularities, when they come forward into the
215 great World, it is ever with Reluctance and Compunction of Mind,
because their Byas to Virtue still continues. They may stray sometimes
out of Infirmity or Complyance, but they will soon return to the right

Rode, and keep it always in view. I speak only of those Excesses, which are too much the Attendants of Youth and warmer Blood; for, as to the Points of Honour, Truth, Justice, and other noble Gifts of the Mind, 220 wherein the temperature of the Body hath no concern, they are seldom or never known to be misled.

I have engaged my self very unwarily in too copious a Subject for so short a Paper. The present Scope I would aim at is to prove, that some Proportion of human Knowledge appears requisite to those, who by 225 their Birth or Fortune, are called to the making of Laws, and in a subordinate way to the execution of them; and that such Knowledge is not to be obtained without a Miracle, under the frequent, corrupt, and sottish Methods, of educating those who are born to Wealth or Titles. For, I would have it remembred, that I do by no means confine these 230 Remarks to young Persons of Noble Birth; the same Errors running through all Families, where there is Wealth enough to afford, that their Sons (at least the Eldest) may be good for nothing. Why should my Son be a Scholar, when it is not intended that he should live by his Learning? By this Rule, if what is commonly said be true, that Money 235 answereth all Things, why should my Son be honest, temperate, just, or charitable, since he hath no intention to depend upon any of these Qualities for a Maintenance?

When all is done, perhaps upon the whole, the matter is not so bad as I would make it; and, God, who worketh good out of evil, acting 240 only by the ordinary Course and rule of Nature, permits this continual Circulation of human things, for his own unsearchable Ends. The Father grows rich by Avarice, Injustice, Oppression; he is a Tyrant in the Neighbourhood, over Slaves and Beggars, whom he calls his Tenants. Why should he desire to have qualities infused into his Son, 245 which himself never possessed, or knew, or found the want of in the acquisition of his Wealth? The Son bred in Sloth and Idleness, becomes a Spendthrift, a Cully, a Profligate, and goes out of the World a Beggar, as his Father came in: Thus, the former is punished for his own Sins, as well as for those of the latter. The Dunghil having raised 250 a huge Mushroom of short duration, is now spread to enrich other Mens Lands. It is indeed of worse consequence, where noble Families are gone to decay; because their Titles and Priviledges out-live their Estates: And, Politicians tell us, that nothing is more dangerous to the Publick, than a numerous Nobility without Merit or Fortune. But 255 even here, God hath likewise prescribed some Remedy in the order of Nature; so many great Families coming to an end by the Sloth,

Luxury, and abandoned Lusts, which enervated their Breed thorough every Succession, producing gradually a more effeminate Race,
260 wholly unfit for Propagation.

8. *the only Son and Heir of that Monarch*: Swift presumably found it at least mildly ironic that George II's heir Prince Frederick had been appointed chancellor of the University of Dublin the previous year (*Corresp.* iii. 220 n.).

26. *Scandalum Magnatum*: Malicious public statements about the great; prohibited in 1275 by 3 Edw. I (West.), c. 34 and the prohibition several times strengthened, notably in the Star Chamber case *de Libellis Famosis* (1606). Swift jokingly exaggerates; there were few prosecutions for *scandalum magnatum* in his time. See Francis Ludlow Hunt, *The Law of Libel* (London, 1812), 150–4; W. C. Holdsworth, *A History of English Law*, 3rd edn., iii (London, 1923), 409–10; Fredrick Seaton Siebert, *Freedom of the Press in England, 1476-1776* (1952; Urbana, 1965), 118–20; and cf. *Tale*, 53.

28. *some Additional Care*: By omitting 'Additional' *35* heightens the sarcasm; see textual variants.

37–8. *The Noblest Blood of England having been shed in the grand Rebellion*: A difficult claim to defend. Most members of the English House of Lords in 1640 survived until 1661; of the noble titles that became extinct in that interval, most were of recent creation.

[*In the following notes I ordinarily seek to do no more than specify the dates, parentage, education, noble titles, and offices of state held by those named.*]

43. *Ormonde*: James Butler, 12th Earl of Ormond in the Irish peerage (1610–88), was grandson of the 11th earl. He had been a royal ward and was educated by Archbishop Abbot at Lambeth. He was commander-in-chief under Charles I and created Marquess of Ormonde in 1642; he was appointed lord steward of the royal household in 1660 and became Duke of Ormonde in 1661. He served as Lord Lieutenant of Ireland 1643, 1649–50, 1662–8, and 1677–85; his dukedom was made English in 1682. GEC; *Hdbk Brit. Chron.*

43. *Southampton*: Thomas Wriothesley, 4th Earl of Southampton (1608–67), educated at Eton and Magdalen College, Oxford; adviser to Charles I; Lord High Treasurer 1660–7. GEC; *DNB*.

55. *Hyde*: Edward Hyde, first Earl of Clarendon (1609–74), the third son of a third son, was educated at home, at Magdalen Hall, Oxford, and at the Middle Temple. Chancellor of the Exchequer under Charles I and again, before the Restoration, under Charles II, he was created Baron Hyde in 1660 and Earl of Clarendon in 1661, continuing as Lord Chancellor until his removal and impeachment in 1667; wrote *The True Historical Narrative of the Rebellion and Civil Wars in England* (1702–4) and other historical works. His daughter, the Duchess of York, was the mother of Queen Mary and Queen Anne. Swift considered him an example of 'Men of exalted Abilities' who, 'when they are called to publick Affairs, are generally drawn into Inconveniencies and Misfortunes, which others of Ordinary Talents avoid' (*Prose*, viii. 138; see also *Corresp.* ii. 333), and said that his 'character ... might be a pattern for all ministers' (*Prose*, vol. vii, p. xxxvi). Sir Henry Craik, *The Life of Edward, Earl of Clarendon* (London, 1911), vol. i; Edward Foss, *The Judges of England*, vii (London, 1864), 122–30; *DNB*.

56. *Bridgman*: Sir Orlando Bridgeman (*c.* 1606–74), son of a bishop, was educated at home and at Magdalene College, Cambridge. He held various offices under Charles I, who knighted him; was made Chief Baron of the Exchequer and a baronet in 1660 and, in the same year, Chief Justice of the Common Pleas. From

1667 to 1672, when he was removed, he was Lord Keeper of the Great Seal. Foss, *Judges of England*, vii. 60–2; *DNB*.

56. *Clifford*: Thomas Clifford (1630–73), of obscure parentage, was educated at Exeter College, Oxford, and the Middle Temple. In 1672 he was appointed Lord High Treasurer and acting Secretary of State and was created first Baron Clifford of Chudleigh. Clifford was a member of the Cabal and worked to establish Roman Catholicism in England. Cyril Hughes Hartmann, *Clifford of the Cabal* (London, 1937); *DNB*.

56. *Coventry*: See textual variants. Sir Henry Coventry (1619–86), younger son of the first Lord Coventry and a fellow of All Souls College, Oxford, was Secretary of State 1672–80. *DNB*.

56. *Osborn*: Sir Thomas Osborne, Bt. (1632–1712), eldest surviving son of the first baronet, a Yorkshire merchant, had a 'seriously defective' education, according to his biographer Andrew Browning. In 1673 he received a Scottish peerage and was appointed Lord Treasurer, a post he held until 1679. In 1674 he was created Earl of Danby, the title by which he is best known, being further elevated as Marquess of Carmarthen (1689) and Duke of Leeds (1694). He was again, in effect, first minister under William and Mary (1690–3). He was twice impeached. Browning, *Thomas Osborne, Earl of Danby and Duke of Leeds* (Glasgow, 1951); *DNB*; see also introductory note to *Intelligencer* 12.

56. *Godolphin*: Sidney Godolphin (1645–1712), was, according to Swift's *History of the Four Last Years of the Queen*, 'originally intended for a Trade, before his Friends preferred him to be a Page at Court; which some very unjustly have objected as a Reproach' (*Prose*, vii. 8). Macky in his *Memoirs* said he was 'the second Son of a good Family in *Cornwal*' (1733), 23. He was First Lord of the Treasury, 1684–5, 1690–7; Secretary of State for the Northern Department, 1684; Lord High Treasurer, 1702–10. Created Baron Godolphin of Rialton in 1684 and Earl of Godolphin in 1706. *DNB*; GEC; *Hdbk Brit. Chron.*

56. *Ashley-Cooper*: Anthony Ashley Cooper (1621–83), the eldest son of a baronet, was orphaned by age 10. He briefly attended Exeter College, Oxford, and Lincoln's Inn. He was Field Marshal-General in the Parliamentary army. In 1660 he was pardoned and the next year appointed Chancellor of the Exchequer. In 1661 he was created Baron Ashley, and in 1672 Earl of Shaftesbury; he served as Lord Chancellor 1672–3. A leading proponent of the Exclusion Bill and of Monmouth as a successor to Charles II, he was charged with treason. Swift deemed Shaftesbury 'a great Vilain' and 'an early Rogue' (marginalia on Clarendon, *Prose*, v. 303). See further Foss, *Judges of England*, vii. 71–81; K. D. H. Haley, *The First Earl of Shaftesbury* (Oxford, 1968).

58. *Summers*: John Somers (1651–1716), second son of a Cromwellian attorney, was educated at public and private schools, at Trinity College, Oxford, and at the Middle Temple. He was made Lord Keeper of the Great Seal in 1693; in 1697 he was created Baron Somers of Evesham and was Lord Chancellor 1697–1700 and Lord President of the Council 1708–10. See further the notes to no. 5; and Geoffrey Holmes, *Augustan England: Professions, State and Society, 1680–1730* (London, 1982), 125. On Swift's complex attitude toward Somers's ancestry, see Ehrenpreis, *Acts of Implication* (Berkeley, 1980), 57. Swift glances at Somers's ancestry in dedicating *A Tale of a Tub* to him; see also *Swift vs. Mainwaring*, 215, and Swift's marginalia on Macky's *Characters*, where he calls Somers's family 'very mean', adding that 'his father was a noted Rogue' (*Prose*, v. 258). In *The History of the Four Last Years of the Queen*, Swift describes Somers as an 'extraordinary Genius' who 'hath raised himself . . . without the least Support from Birth or Fortune'. Swift charges that the political leaders in William's reign backed Somers because 'such Men [as he] were perfectly indifferent to any or no Religion; and . . . were not likely to inherit much

Loyalty [i.e., 'to the Established Church, and to the Rights of Monarchy'] from those to whom they owed their Birth' (*Prose*, vii. 5, 7; similar views are in *Corresp.* ii. 333).

58. *Montague*: Charles Montagu (1661–1715), educated at Westminster School and Trinity College, Cambridge, was First Lord of the Treasury 1697–9; Chancellor of the Exchequer 1694–9; created Baron Halifax of Halifax 1700; impeached 1701 (Swift defended him in *A Discourse*); First Lord of the Treasury 1714; created KG and Earl of Halifax 1714 (*DNB*). Halifax had promised Swift his patronage (*Prose*, viii. 119).

58. *Churchil*: John Churchill (1650–1722), son of a royalist politician, was educated at St Paul's School, then became an army officer and servant of the Duke of York. He was created Baron Churchill in the Scottish peerage 1682 and in the English peerage 1685; Earl of Marlborough 1689; Commander-in-Chief 1690–2; Captain-General during the war of the Spanish Succession, 1702–12; created Duke of Marlborough 1702. In his character of Marlborough, Swift wrote, 'He was bred in the height of what is called the Tory Principle; and continued with a strong Biass that way, untill the other Party had bid higher for him than his Friends could afford to give. His Want of Literature is in some sort supplyed by a good Understanding, a degree of natural Elocution, and that Knowledge of the World which is learned in Armies and Courts' (*Prose*, vii. 7). The rumour that Marlborough was descended from a black-smith may reverberate in this passage as well as in the end of Swift's *Satirical Elegy on the Death of a Late Famous General*; see *Swift vs. Mainwaring*, 215 n.; *POAS* vii. 660–1; Winston S. Churchill, *Marlborough: His Life and Times*, rev. edn. (1934; London, 1947), i. 33–4; *Poems*, i. 295–7. On Swift's writings against Marlborough generally, see Ehrenpreis, ii. 526–35.

58. *Vernon*: See textual variants. James Vernon (1646–1727), a second son, was educated at Oxford; he 'in no way distinguished himself as Secretary' of State, 1697–1702, in the view of Mark A. Thompson, *The Secretaries of State, 1681–1782* (Oxford, 1932), 8.

58. *Harry Boyle*: See textual variants. Hon. Henry Boyle (*c.* 1677–1725), youngest son of Lord Clifford of Lanesborough, was educated at Trinity College, Cambridge. He was Chancellor of the Exchequer 1701–8, Lord Treasurer of Ireland 1704–15, Secretary of State for the Northern Department 1708–10, and Lord President of the Privy Council 1721–5. He was created Baron Carleton of Carleton in 1714. Swift recalled that he 'had some very Scurvy Qualityes particularly avarice'. *DNB*; Basil Duke Henning, *The House of Commons, 1660–1690* (London, 1983), i. 701; *Prose*, v. 260.

59. *Harley*: Robert Harley (1661–1724), eldest son of Sir Edward Harley, attended dis-senting academies and the Inner Temple; was Speaker of the House of Commons 1701–5, Secretary of State for the Northern Department 1704–8, Chancellor of the Exchequer 1710–11; created Earl of Oxford and Mortimer 1711, Lord Treasurer 1711–14; impeached 1717. In *An Enquiry into the Behaviour of the Queen's Last Ministry*, Swift praised Oxford's intellect but noted that 'as his own Birth was illustrious, being descended from the Heirs generall of the Veres and the Mortimers, so he seemed to value that accidentall Advantage in himself and others more than it could pretend to deserve'. (*Enquiry*, Ehrenpreis edn., 10–14.) Harley's claim to illustrious birth was erroneous; did Swift know that? See Ehrenpreis's discussion in *Acts of Implication*, 55–8.

59. *St. John*: Henry St John (1678–1751), the son of 'a typical Restoration rake' of the same name, may have been educated in a dissenting academy (H. T. Dickinson, *Bolingbroke* (London, 1970), 1–4, correcting earlier views). He was Secretary at War 1704–8, Secretary of State 1710–14, created Viscount Bolingbroke 1712, attainted 1714, Secretary of State to the Pretender 1715–16, and pardoned 1723. Swift in his *Enquiry* wrote that Bolingbroke was 'Descended from the best Familyes in England

[and] Heir to a great patrimoniall Estate'; he went on to praise 'the Accomplishments of his Mind' (8).

59. *Harcourt*: Simon Harcourt (*c.* 1661–1727) was educated at Pembroke College, Oxford, and the Inner Temple; knighted in 1702, he was Solicitor-General 1702–7, Attorney-General 1707–8 and briefly in 1710, and Lord Keeper 1710–13; he was created Baron Harcourt in 1711 and was Lord Chancellor 1713–14. In 1721 he was created Viscount Harcourt. *DNB*.

59. *Trevers*: Thomas Trevor (*c.* 1658–1730, son of Sir John Trevor, Secretary of State under Charles II, was educated at the Inner Temple; knighted in 1692, he was named Solicitor-General in the same year, Attorney-General 1695, Chief Justice of the Common Pleas 1701–14; created Baron Trevor of Bromham 1712, one of the twelve so advanced by the Harley administration; Lord Privy Seal 1726–30; Lord President of the Council 1730. *DNB*; Foss, *Judges of England*, viii (London, 1864), 71–6.

61. *Robert Walpole*: A younger son, Walpole (1676–1745) was educated at Eton and King's College, Cambridge; was Lord High Admiral 1705, Secretary at War 1708–10, Treasurer of the Navy 1710–11, Chancellor of the Exchequer 1715–17, and Lord Treasurer—in effect prime minister—1721–42; created Earl of Orford 1742. Swift said he 'was of a family not contemptible', and added that 'he had some small smattering in books, but no manner of politeness; nor, in his whole life, was ever known to advance any one person, upon the score of wit, learning, or abilities for business' (*Prose*, v. 101–2). See also notes to nos. 3 and 12.

63. *Horace [Walpole]*: Robert's younger brother (1678–1757); educated at Eton, King's College, Cambridge, and Lincoln's Inn; Secretary to the Treasury 1715–17, 1721–30; diplomat; created Baron Walpole of Wolterton 1756. *DNB*; Sedgwick, ii. 509–10; see further the notes to no. 12.

64. *Addison*: Joseph Addison (1672–1719) was eldest son of the dean of Lichfield, from whom he inherited only £100. He was educated at Charterhouse and at Queen's College, Oxford. In 1716 he married the dowager Countess of Warwick, but he was by no means financially dependent on this alliance. Addison was Secretary of State 1717–18. Peter Smithers, *The Life of Joseph Addison*, 2nd edn. (Oxford, 1968).

64. *Craiggs*: James Craggs the younger (1686–1721), younger son of the Postmaster-General, who in a jaundiced obituary is said to have been 'born . . . of People of the meanest Rank' and later apprenticed 'to a Barber in a Country Town'. The son had 'a modish *French* Education in a Seminary at *Chelsea*' (*Pol. State*, 22 (1721), 442–3). He was Secretary at War 1717–18 and Secretary of State 1718–21.

64. *Allyance*: See textual variants.

69. *important*: See textual variants.

83. *Bacon*: In 'Of Empire': 'For it is the Soloecisme of Power, to thinke to Command the End, and yet not to endure the Meane.' *The Essayes or Counsels, Civill and Morall*, ed. Michael Kiernan (Cambridge, Mass., 1985), 60.

93–4. *the study of Greek and Latin is loss of Time*: 'Critics of contemporary education seldom called for the elimination of Greek and Latin; they deplored the excessive emphasis on these subjects. Particularly they were critical of the methods used in teaching them.' Landa, *Gulliver's Travels and Other Writings*, 545. See further a letter from *Brice's Weekly J.* in Appendix D.

94–6. *publick Schools . . . engage [students] in bad Company*: Locke in *Some Thoughts on Education* (1693) had argued against public education for this reason. 'On the whole, families of quality preferred the private to the public method' of education; critics of public schools frequently objected to corporal punishment (George C. Brauer, Jr, *The Education of a Gentleman*, 195, 203).

99. *the whole duty of a Gentleman*: An allusion to *The Whole Duty of Man*, a manual of spiritual and moral instruction usually attributed to Richard Allestree (but see

Prose, v. 282); first published in 1658, it had by 1728 gone through more than forty editions.

101–2. *the last War*: War of the Spanish Succession, 1702–13. Swift was of course in London during much of this period, and he is not improbably the clergyman referred to.

118. *D—n me, Doctor*: 'Swift has versified very near the whole of this passage in his poem on Hamilton's Bawn, where it is put in the mouth of the Captain of Dragoons.' Scott (1824), ix. 165 n.; compare i. 471 n., and Swift, *Works* (18° edn.: Dublin: Faulkner, 1762), i. 282 n. Scott refers to *The Grand Question Debated*, written in 1728 or 1729 (*Poems*, iii. 872–3). Further on the bad influence of the military on the contemporary vocabulary, see Swift's *Tatler* 230, *Prose*, ii. 176; and Addison's *Spectator* 165.

133. *White's Chocolate-house*: On the west side of St James's Street, below St James's Place; notorious for gambling for large stakes. See *The History of White's* (London, 1892), i. 8–16; Bryant Lillywhite, *London Coffee Houses* (London, 1963), 639–43.

138. *Le-Sac*: 'The Author's Friends have heard him tell this Passage as from the Earl himself.' *35* note. That young Harley learned dancing can be documented; the masters' names are not otherwise known (letter from his mother, 23 Feb. 1676/?7, BL MS Loan 29/139; letter to his father, 11 Sept. 1677, BL MS Loan 29/182, fo. 251; letter from his father to his mother, 6 July 1680, Hist. MSS Comm. 29, *Portland* iii (1894), 366). Mr Le Sac (or Lesac or L'Sac) is recorded as a theatre dancer in 1700 and again several times in 1710 (*London Stage*, i. 531; ii. 228–9); he presumably is the dancer Swift had in mind, even though there is little evidence that he was 'Famous' (dancers leave little documentation behind them). Some of Swift's editors have supposed that 'Le-Sac' was a mistake for Isaac, apparently because the name Le Sac was unknown to them and because there was a famous dancing master named Isaac. Since there were a number of Le Sacs among the French community in London, however, the conclusion that Le Sac was Isaac appears unwarranted, despite its adoption in *A Biographical Dictionary of Actors . . . 1660–1800*, viii (1982), under 'Mr Isaac'; compare the articles on various Le Sacs in ix (1984).

147. *Pædagogues*: Tutors to young boys (*OED*). Much the same complaint about French tutors, subservient to the mother's wishes, appears in a letter from 'Dublino-Oxoniensis' in Mist's *Weekly J. or Saturday's Post*, 14 Oct. 1721, reprinted in *A Collection of Miscellany Letters, Selected out of Mist's Weekly Journal*, iii (London: Warner, 1727), 1–7.

166. *Span-farthing*: 'A very simple game in which a player attempts to throw his farthings so close to those of his opponents that the distance between them can be spanned with one hand.' Landa, *Gulliver's Travels and Other Writings*, 545.

168. *one young Lord in this Town*: 'The Author is supposed to mean the Lord Viscount *Montcassel*, of *Ireland*.' *35* note. Edward Davys, 3rd Viscount Mountcashel (1711–36), Sheridan's former student, entered TCD 1 Dec. 1727. Sheridan, in dedicating his translation of Persius to Mountcashel in 1728, writes: 'I shall make You no *Complements* upon your *Birth* or *Title*, for which, *You* and your *School-fellows* will witness for me, That I never did once either distinguish or spare You, while You were under my Care.' (Dublin: Grierson, 1728), p. vi.

176. *silver Clocks*: These embroidered ornaments were 'mark[s] of great elegance in dress' (Katherine Morris Lester and Bess Viola Oerke, *Accessories of Dress* (Peoria, 1940), 296; see *Spectator*, iii. 163).

182. *a very Worthy Governor*: Mountcashel's tutor at Trinity was 'Mr. Clark', probably Henry Clarke (1701?–77), a future vice-provost who had been made a fellow in 1724 (TCD MUN V 27/3, p. 19); see *Corresp*. iv. 273–4. The words 'very Worthy' were deleted in *35*.

195. *my own observation in one of those Universities*: Swift visited Oxford briefly in December 1691 and was a member of Hart Hall, Oxford, for a few weeks in 1692, when he took his MA. In 1714 he was in Oxford on two short visits (Ehrenpreis, i. 108; ii. 733, 754). He later claimed that his Oxford residency had lasted 'some years': *Corresp.* iv. 274.

196. *young Heirs sent thither, only for form*: University statutes relaxed degree requirements for noblemen or noblemen's sons. [Nicholas Amhurst], writing in *Terrae-Filius: or, The Secret History of the University of Oxford*, 2nd edn. (London: Francklin, 1726), commented, 'The education of a person of distinction at OXFORD, instead of being, as it ought, the most strictly taken care of, is of all the most neglected; a nobleman may bring anything from college but learning' (i. 47).

212. *Literature*: Learning, erudition (A. Boyer, *The Royal Dictionary Abridged*, 5th edn. (London: Knapton *et al.*, 1728). Swift used the term in this sense in *A Proposal for Correcting the English Tongue* (*Prose*, iv. 10); see also the note on 'Churchil' above.

221. *temperature*: 'The combination of "humours" in the body' (*OED*).

222. *misled*: See textual variants.

235–6. *Money answereth all Things*: Proverbial, from Eccl. 10: 19 (Tilley M1052).

242. *human things*: i.e., *res humanae*, 'the activities and business of human life' (*Oxford Latin Dictionary*).

249–50. *the former . . . the latter*: Former=son, latter=father; an allusion to the Commandments' 'visiting the iniquity of the fathers upon the children' (Exod. 20: 5).

254. *Politicians tell us*: In addition to the more recent sources cited in the introductory note, see Bacon, 'Of Nobility', *Essays*: 'A Numerous *Nobility*, causeth Poverty, and Inconvenience in a State: For it is a Surcharge of Expence; And besides, it being of Necessity, that many of the Nobility, fall in time to be weake in Fortune, it maketh a kinde of Disproportion, betweene Honour and Meanes' (42; see also 201 n.).

258. *thorough*: Through.

No. 10: Swift, with Sheridan's Introduction

probably 13–16 July 1728

Swift claimed 'only the Verses, and of those not the four last slovenly lines'; thus the introduction and the final quatrain are Sheridan's (*Corresp.* iv. 30). Sheridan's role was presumably to stretch a short and incomplete or defective poem by Swift into an eight-page pamphlet. Sheridan's irony rehearses the Irish economic plight as Swift had presented it in *A Short View of the State of Ireland* (to be reprinted as no. 15) and as he himself had done in no. 6.

Swift and Sheridan allude to *The Monkey Who Had Seen the World*, Fable xiv of John Gay's *Fables* (London: Tonson and Watts, 1727), 46–9, and to the accompanying engraving (Fig. 2). Although Swift has inscribed his own copy of the *Fables* 'The gift of my friend the Author | 1730' (Rothschild 926; the description in *The Rothschild Library* is incorrect), he had surely seen the book in London in 1727. He met the artist, John Wooton, and in December 1727,

Fig. 2. The Monkey Who Had Seen the World. Engraving by Gerard van der Gucht from a design by John Wooton. *Fables. By Mr. Gay* (London: J. Tonson and J. Watts, 1727), 46.

writing to Motte about possible illustrations of *Gulliver's Travels*, he recommended that he get Gay to introduce him to Wooton (*Corresp.* iii. 258).

By referring to the Wooton engraving prefixed to the fable, Swift draws particular attention to Tighe as a 50-year-old beau, suggested in part by the traditional association of monkeys with *vanitas* and in part by the ape's foppish posture—'The Twist, the Squeeze, the Rump, the Fidge an' all'—and simpering face. As in *Mad Mullinix and Timothy*, Swift leaves the reader to discern that Tim is Tighe, in part, I presume, from the sheer physical resemblance between him and the Punch-jackanapes-Thersites figures of these poems. The engraving's ape, like Punch and Thersites, is hunchbacked; in *Verses on the Death of Dr. Swift*, Swift claimed that he 'spar'd a Hump or crooked Nose, | Whose Owners set not up for Beaux' (*Poems*, ii. 572). On Swift's use of ape imagery, see George Mayhew, 'Swift's Games with Language in Rylands English MS. 659', *BJRL* 36 (1953–4), 445–6; and Aline Mackenzie Taylor, 'Sights and Monsters and Gulliver's *Voyage to Brobdingnag*', *Tulane Studies in English*, 7 (1957), 32, 36, 42, 59–60. On the ape traditions generally, see H. W. Janson, *Apes and Ape Lore in the Middle Ages and the Renaissance* (London, 1952), 212–18, 239, 287–325.

NUMB. X.

Magnas Componere lites.

Lucass's Coffee-house, July 4th.

Mr. *Intelligencer*,

I Am desired to return you the Thanks of this House, for that Seasonable Dialogue between *Timothy* and *Mullinix*. You have intirely reconciled them both by it, and thereby given the 5 finishing stroke to a Party, which gives universal Joy and Satisfaction to all well-wishers of our Constitution. It was very much lamented, that Men of their extraordinary Talents, (and who might by their united Interest contribute very much to the good of our Country) should not have a better understanding between them; because the 10 perpetual Feuds and Animosities which they raised, had like to have proved of the most fatal ill Consequence to this unfortunate, poor, divided Nation. Now the Clouds which hung over us, are dispelled; Things begin to clear up; and we have the best reason to think, by this Union, that we shall be a Great and a Flourishing People. We are now 15 in a profound Peace, Trade flourishes.—Plenty, which fled from

hence to *Scotland*, is returned.—You see Joy and Fatness in every
Countenance, especially in those of the Natives.—The younger Sons
of Gentlemen, who languished, loitering at Home, for want of
20 Business, are now in a fair way of Employment. Arts and Sciences
begin to revive in our University; that great Nursery of the best
Education! which Annually supplies the Pulpit, Bench and Bar, and
every other useful Office. All our Nobility and Gentry, who fled to
Great-Brittain, to avoid the Civil Broils occasioned by *Tim Cæsar*, and
25 *Mullinix Pompey*, are now returning, to live quietly at Home, and to
bring a Blessing to their Native Soil, by residing in it; which will be a
means to keep our Money at Home; to encourage Agriculture,
especially Tillage; and then, *Sing O be Joyful*, we shall all wallow in
Wealth, because by this we shall have nine hundred thousand Pounds
30 a Year more in this Nation. These and numberless Advantages beside,
we owe to your excellent Paper, which *Tim* himself allows to be
written with a very good Intention, although it places him in a
ludicrous Light, but he is a Man of such excellent Taste and Temper,
that a Jest, when it is finely Couched, never gives him the least
35 Offence. This encourages me to let you know, he is very angry at Mr.
Gay; for he thinks the *Fable* of the *Monkey* which had seen the World
is levelled at him. If you have leisure to write something merry upon
the occasion, let us have it immediately, and answer this Letter
another time. For, you must know, we are very great Jokers in this
40 *Coffee-House*. There is a little dapper Lord, an Acquaintance of *Tim*'s,
will laugh and teize him into his Chair, and home again.

Tim and the *Fables*.

MY meaning will be best unravell'd,
     When I premise, that Tim *has Travell'd*.
In *Lucass*'s by chance there lay
The *Fables* writ by Mr. *Gay*,
Tim set the Volume on a Table,   5
Read over here and there a *Fable*,
And found, as he the pages twirl'd,
The *Monkey*, who had seen the World.
(For *Tonson* had, to help the Sale,
Prefixt a Cut to ev'ry Tale.)   10
The *Monkey* was compleatly drest,

The *Beau* in all his Ayrs exprest.
Tim with surprize and pleasure staring,
Ran to the Glass, and then comparing
His own sweet Figure with the Print,   15
Distinguish'd ev'ry Feature in't;
The Twist, the Squeeze, the Rump, the Fidge an' all,
Just as they lookt in the Original.
By ⸻ says *Tim* (and let a F⸻t)
This Graver understood his Art.   20
'Tis a true Copy, I'll say that for't,
I well remember when I sat for't.
My very Face, at first I knew it,
Just in this dress the Painter drew it.
Tim, with his likeness deeply smitten,   25
Wou'd read what underneath was written,
The merry Tale with moral Grave.
He now began to storm and rave;
The cursed Villain! now I see
This was a Libel meant at me;   30
These Scriblers grow so bold of late,
Against us Ministers of State!
Such Jacobites as he deserve, ⸻
Dammee, I say, they ought to starve.
Dear *Tim*, no more such angry Speeches,   35
Unbutton and let down your Breeches,
Tare out the Tale, and wipe your A⸻
I know you love to act a *Farce*.

MOTTO. To settle the great controversy; a misquotation of Virgil, *Eclogues*, iii. 108: 'Non nostrum inter vos tantas componere lites'.

INTRODUCTION

1. *Lucass's*: A fashionable Dublin coffee house; see further the notes to no. 4.

3–4. *that Seasonable Dialogue*: In no. 8.

14. *Things begin to clear up*: For the serious exposition of Ireland's plight which Sheridan here ironically echoes, see the notes to nos. 6 and 15 (the latter previously published as *A Short View of the State of Ireland*).

29–30. *nine hundred thousand Pounds a Year more*: A commonly accepted estimate was £600,000 a year; see notes to no. 15.

35–6. *Mr. Gay . . . the Fable*: See introductory note.

POEM

17. *the Fidge*: 'The action . . . of fidgeting' (*OED*, quoting this passage); see notes to no. 8.

20. *This Graver*: Gerard van der Gucht (1697–1776), working from a design by John Wooton (d. 1765), an animal painter. See Hanns Hammelmann, *Book Illustrators in Eighteenth-Century England*, ed. T. S. R. Boase (New Haven, 1975), 86–8, 102.

27. *merry Tale with moral Grave*: The entire fable should be consulted, but two passages are especially pertinent. The monkey speaks:

> Seek ye to thrive? In flatt'ry deal,
> Your scorn, your hate, with that conceal;
> Seem only to regard your friends,
> But use them for your private ends,
> Stint not to truth the flow of wit,
> Be prompt to lye, whene'er 'tis fit;
> Bend all your force to spatter merit;
> Scandal is conversation's spirit. . . .

And in the concluding 'moral Grave':

> Thus the dull lad, too tall for school,
> With travel finishes the fool,
> Studious of ev'ry coxcomb's airs,
> He drinks, games, dresses, whores and swears,
> O'erlooks with scorn all virtuous arts,
> For vice is fitted to his parts.

Gay, *Poetry and Prose*, ed. Vinton A. Dearing (Oxford, 1974), ii. 320–1.

32. *Ministers of State*: Tighe was not one.

Jonathan Smedley was born in Dublin *c.* 1672 and entered Trinity College in his eighteenth year, in 1689. After wartime delays, he took his BA in 1695 and his MA in 1698. In his later years he was one of Swift's most visible enemies. They differed profoundly in politics. In 1715 Sir Richard Steele and the other stewards of the Protestants of Ireland in London recommended Smedley to Lord Townshend as 'having signalized himself for adhering to the interest of the succession of the House of Hanover for several years last past, and having suffered in his fortune for the same' (Steele, *Correspondence*, ed. Rae Blanshard, rev. imp. (Oxford, 1968), 529–30). The nature of the suffering is not now known, but it may have heightened his differences with Swift. For their verse exchanges, see *Poems*, ii. 357–62, 369–73; also iii. 1100–1.

From 1709 to 1720 Smedley was rector and vicar of Rincurran, in Co. Cork, and during at least part of the same period was chaplain of Charles Fort, Kinsale, which was in his parish (James B. Leslie, *Clogher Clergy and Parishes* (Enniskillen, 1929), 33–4; Charles Dalton, *George the First's Army, 1714–1727*, ii (London, 1912), 154; Craig, p. xvii). In 1713 he wrote the verses 'Fix'd on a Church Door' ('To day, this Temple gets a *Dean*') on the occasion of Swift's installation as dean of St Patrick's. He was chaplain to the Earl of Sunderland, Lord Lieutenant of Ireland 1714–15 (Blenheim Papers, BL MS Add. 61639, fo. 167). In 1718, he used Swift's *A Letter . . . Concerning the Sacramental Test* (1708) against him in a vigorous argument against the Test Act, *A Rational and Historical Account of the Principles which Gave Birth to the Late Rebellion, and of the Present Controversies of the English Clergy* (London: Wilkins); see Edward Graham, 'Smedley and Swift—"Further Reasons for Their Enmity"', *PQ* 48 (1969), 416–20. From 1718 to 1724 he was dean of Killala, having been recommended by Lord Townshend; in 1720 he was briefly rector of Ringrone on the presentation of Lord Kinsale. He had collected some of his published and unpublished sermons, mostly partisan, as *Nine Sermons on Several Subjects* (London: Wilkins, 1719). He published his *Poems on Several Occasions* anonymously in 1721 (London: Printed by Samuel Richardson, for the Author); an expanded version was issued in 1723 and reissued in 1730 (Foxon, i. 735–6). According to Pope, in 1722–3 he wrote a government newspaper in London, *Baker's News; or, The Whitehall Journal* (later simply the *Whitehall Journal*), and he may also have written the *St. James's Journal* (TE v. 136). In 1724 he became vicar of Knockmark, Co. Meath. He was from 1717 to 1723 a ratepayer in Gerrard Street, Soho, and his poem *An Epistle to His Grace the Duke of Grafton* (1724) suggests that his wife preferred to be in London as much as possible (*Survey of London*, xxxiv (1966), 394; *Poems*, ii. 359).

From 1724 to 1727 he was dean of Clogher, almost immediately mortgaging the income to his patron Benjamin Hoadly, bishop of Salisbury (deed of 25

June 1725, Registry of Deeds, Dublin: Memorial 45-282-29251). In March 1727 came signs of further financial difficulty, as he applied to his debt to Hoadly some of the income of the rectory of Clogher, 'taken to be the corps of the Deanery of Clogher' (deed of 20 March 1726[/7], Registry of Deeds, Dublin: Memorial 52-365-34876). In 1727 he seems to have resigned his deanery and come to London, perhaps, as no. 20 suggests, to avoid arrest for debt. In London, he tried unsuccessfully to swap the deanery of Clogher for a London parish, according to an undated letter apparently written to Birch during compilation of the *Universal View* (BL MS Add. 4318, fo. 196).

Meanwhile, he engaged in two publishing ventures. *Gulliveriana*, a volume abusing Swift and Pope, appeared 13 August 1728 ('This Day is Published . . .', *Daily Journal*); Smedley had advertised it and solicited contributions on 13 April (ibid.), and it too was printed by Samuel Richardson (William M. Sale, Jr, *Samuel Richardson: Master Printer* (Ithaca, 1950), 205). It earned him a place in the *Dunciad* and presumably occasioned the *Intelligencer*'s retaliation in nos. 11 and 20. He also opened a subscription for *An Universal View of All the Eminent Writers on the Holy Scriptures*, to be a two-volume compilation of important commentary on selected passages of the Bible. His assistant in this project was the young Thomas Birch, to whom Smedley spoke of their work as a 'Search, after Fame' (Birch MSS, BL MS Add. 4318, fo. 195). He published a prospectus and a 66-page *Specimen* (see notes), but the *Universal View* itself never materialized. In October he laid plans for *Gulliveriana Secunda* and advertised it in the *Craftsman* of 9 November 1728, but this never appeared either (BL MS Add. 4318, fo. 192).

In early 1729 he managed to secure an East India Company chaplaincy at Fort St George, Madras. See further the introductory note to no. 20; on the earlier part of Smedley's career, see W. Maziere Brady, *Clerical and Parochial Records of Cork, Cloyne, and Ross* (London, 1864), i. 233, 242; J. B. Leslie, 'Killala. Biographical Succession List', 1938—a typescript in the Representative Church Body Library, Dublin; *DNB*.

NUMB. XI.

———*Ut dehinc Speciosa miracula promat.*

Hor.

Mr. *Intelligencer*,

HAVING but lately met with the following *Proposals* in a Letter to the Author of the *London-Journal*, bearing Date *March 30th*. 1728. And having the greatest Veneration and
5 Esteem for the *Writer* of it, as well as the best Opinion of his *vast Abilities* for the Undertaking; I hope, I do not come too late, in giving *a*

helping Hand to spread it abroad for the *Author*'s Advantage, and
Benefit of the *Learned World*, by giving it a *Poetick Dress*, which I think
would have been much better from *his own Pen*, had he been in a
humour of *versifying*; for he has the most *extraordinary Talents* that way 10
of any Man now living, except *A. P.* There is a turn and beauty of
Language, as well as Thought, carry'd on with the greatest Perspicuity
thro' the whole, much in the manner of *Voiture.* This I own has been of
singular Advantage to me; for the *easiness* and *politeness* of his *Prose*,
contributed much to the *smoothness* and *Musick* of my *Verses*, purely 15
owing to my Transferring as much of his Expression, as I possibly
could, into my Performance. From this elegant *Specimen* of his, the
World will see what they are to expect from him; at least a vast deal
of *Orthodox Divinity*, *Critical Remarks*, *Solid Argument*, *wholesome
Instruction*, *clear Information*, with an *entertaining beauty of Style*, peculiar 20
to the Great and Learned *S---d---l---y.* And now I have named him, I
need say no more to recommend the Work but what follows.

> Your great Admirer and Well-wisher,
> *A. B.*

To the Author of the LONDON JOURNAL.

SIR,

I have published the *Specimen* of a Book, entitled, *An Universal View
of all the eminent Writers on the Holy Scriptures; being a Collection of
the Dissertations, Explications, and Opinions, of learned Men in all Ages,* 30
*concerning the difficult Passages and obscure Texts of the Bible; and of
whatsoever is to be met with in Profane Authors, which may contribute towards
the better Understanding of Them.*

I beg the Favour of communicating to the World, by means of your
Paper, what I think at present necessary to say, towards the unfolding 35
my Design in this Work, and to answer the Objections which I have
heard made against it.

Most of the Articles whereof I treat, are, at one time or other, made
the Subject of common Discourse; and too many Persons, who debate
in private on these Points, are unfurnish'd with proper and rational 40
Materials for such Conversation.

These Observations occasion'd my forming a Design, to collect,

into *one View*, the chief Sentiments of the best Authors, in most Languages, on those Subjects, for the Benefit only of common
45 Discourse and Instruction: But when I came to reflect more closely on the Matter, I found, besides my obliging the Generality of Readers, and my enlarging the Fund of Scriptural Knowledge amongst the Unlearned, that I was in a fair way of doing Service to the Learned and more Intelligent Part of my Countrymen likewise; because, by means
50 of this Work, they wou'd save abundance of Time, which is now lost, in turning over from Book to Book, and from Page to Page, the numberless Authors, which I shall quote. And if any of them are inclin'd to consult the Originals, I promise to refer them faithfully to the Line and Page; and I began further to conceive, that I should
55 oblige many amongst the Learned, by saving them abundance of Cost and Expence in purchasing several Books, which it will be sufficient for them to see and hear of, in the Quotations of my *View*.

The Reader is desir'd to observe, that there is no *Bibliotheque*, no Collection of this kind, so compleat, now extant, in any Language, as I
60 shall shew in my general Preface to the Whole; and it must not be forgot, that the *English* want such a Collection, more than most other Christian Nations.

All the Objections, which I have heard, will be answer'd by what follows; whereby those Persons, particularly, will find themselves
65 mistaken, who imagine, that the *Immensity of the Work* ought both to terrifie them from encouraging, and me from undertaking it. For I shall not go thro' the whole Bible Verse by Verse, as in the *Specimen*. MOSES's first Chapter is an entire Piece, on the *Creation*, and I could not omit one Line of it; but my subsequent Articles will be taken from
70 Books, Chapters and Verses, very distant often from one another: Nay, I shall leave whole Books of the Bible untouch'd, viz. such as are Moral or Poetical only, or meerly Historical; and I shall take Notice of no Parts of those Books, but such as are very Curious and Intricate, and have occasion'd something extraordinary to be said on them.
75 Besides, it must be considered that I shall omit numberless Authors, on every Subject; and that, without any dread of displeasing, or hopes of pleasing any Sects or Parties of People; and I shall only collect from the most received Authors on every Article, and such as none shall except against for Learning or Abilities, whatever they may do for
80 Opinion.

The Sentiments of the *Fathers* and antient *Commentators* will be sufficiently answer'd for out of POOLE's *Synopsis*; for it wou'd be an endless, idle and dusty Work, to contract all their heavy and voluminous Writings; but whatever may be still thought wanting of these Antients, will be supplied even to Satiety, from PETAVIUS, 85 CALMET, and others. Further, nothing could be so disagreeable either to me or to the Reader, as to give a full Detail of all the Stuff that was published Abroad about the Time of, and a long while after the *Reformation*; and it wou'd be more nauseous still to revive what was writ at Home, from the Beginning of the last Century till towards the 90 End of it, and indeed for some part of the Century before it.

But, God be thanked, there wanted not great Genius's, who wrote in several Places at the same Times; and if I raise the Work to Two large Vols. in *Folio*, with what the learned and bright Part of Mankind alone have left us, I may reasonably expect Forgiveness for not 95 swelling my Labours into Four or more *Folio's*, by interspersing tedious Observations, and ridiculous, wild and low Expositions.

I shall print the Two Vols. within a reasonable time after my Subscriptions come in; for I have my *Additions and Amendments*, that are to compleat the *Specimen*, ready and prepared: which *Specimen* 100 being to be reprinted for the Body of the Work, will, together with what Collections I have by me for succeeding Articles, give me all imaginable Advantage of the Printer, who cannot work at the Press so fast as I can supply him with Copy; besides which I have procur'd the Assistance of some learned Persons to *collect* for me, and have got so 105 diligent and expert an *Amanuensis*, to transcribe for the Press, that it can never stand still.

I beg leave to remark, that besides the Benefit which every *English* Reader, of common Sense, will reap by this Undertaking, it will be of more special Service to *young Divines*, who may hereby at the same 110 time procure variety of Learning, and indulge a studious *Curiosity*, at a small Expence; and who, by means of this Collection, will be sufficiently furnish'd with *a Bibliotheca Sacra*; to which, if they add only POOLE's *English Annotations* on the *Old*, and HAMMOND's *Exposition* of the *New Testament*, they will need few other Books for 115 some Years, unless it be a Concordance to understand Scripture.

As to those who object, that such a Variety of Opinions on one Subject, as I shall always produce, will rather confound than satisfy People, I beg leave to disagree with them: because every intelligent Person can judge for himself; and because those of meaner Capacities 120 may consult others of better Understanding; every thing being laid before them in plain *English*.

And, in Truth, I cannot but esteem such a Work, to be, in justice, due to the Inhabitants of our Islands. Monsieur CALMET gives the
125 following reason for publishing Nine Volumes in Folio, containing, not only, his own Comments, but *Variety of Opinions*, concerning the difficult Parts of the Bible, *viz.* that his Countrymen might, now, read in their *own Language*, what has hitherto been conceal'd from them in *Hebrew*, *Greek*, *and Latin*.
130 *A noble Attempt in a Papist!* and his Work is so well executed, that I wish Encouragement were given to have it all translated into *English*.

However, tho' CALMET's Religion, and the Laws of his Country, would not permit him to quote so freely as he ought; yet, thank God, we have that Liberty here; and, I hope, the use I make of it won't want
135 Encouragement, since my Design is the same with CALMET's, *viz.* publick Information.

His Religion, indeed, has no way to subsist, but by the Benefit of *unknown Tongues*; but the *Truth of Holy Scripture*, and of the *Protestant Religion*, want no *learned Veils*, or *Foreign Couvertures*.
140 *English Popery is much more abominable, than the Romish!*

I wou'd now have it remembered, that I shall produce nothing but what has been publish'd already in some Language or other; unless, perhaps, some private Piece, very new and extremely curious, should fall in my way. And I would have those Persons who are too fearful of
145 my encouraging *Scepticism* by these Books, believe, that I shall insert no Opinions which give Offence either to *Natural*, or *Reveal'd Religion*; my intent being to establish *Truth*, which can only be done by comparing different Sentiments on the same Subject.

To let the Reader further into the Nature of my Design, I here
150 present him with the Titles of my Articles, from the *Creation*, to *the Deluge*; by which he may form a Judgment of the rest.

1. Of the *Creation*.
2. Of the *Sabbath*.
3. Of the *Paradisaical State*.
155 4. Of the *Fall*.
5. Of *Sacrifice*.
6. Of *Cain* and *Enoch*.
7. Of the *Depravity* of *Men*, before the *Flood*.
8. Of the *Deluge*.

160 I cannot make an End, without observing, that I shall neither oppose, nor interfere with the Proposals of Dr. INNES. The Doctor's

Work (as I am told) is wholly *Moral*; mine is wholly *Critical*: He designs to make Men Better; my Aim is to make them Wiser.

    The Doctor resolves, (as I hear) to pass by what ever has, hitherto, been written in the *Moral way*, on the Bible, and to moralize anew on it 165 himself. I am in a quite different Train: I shall publish little or nothing of my own, nor shall I produce any one Author in the Doctor's way of Proceeding.

I am, SIR,

Your humble Servant,   170

JONATHAN SMEDLEY.

Y OU *that would read the Bible turn all*
   To April 6 *the* London *Journal,*
And by a Letter there you'll see
How much the Text will owe to me.
Five thousand Years and more—'tis odd   5
None cou'd explain the Word of GOD!
Of all the Learned, *in all Ages,*
Thro' all their long, laborious Pages,
'Till I, the Top of IRISH DEANS,
Have made it out with Wond'rous pains.   10
I've Read the Dev'l and all of Books,
The World may Read 'em in my looks:
Above ten Waggon load at least,
Within my Skull in Order place't;
From thence to sally forth anew,   15
One Universal single View.
I've likewise ransack'd Books prophane,
Which I shall muster, to explain
Whate'er is hid obscure, perplext,
As plain as Pike-staff, ev'ry Text.   20
Most Articles, whereof I treat,
Have been the Subject of Debate,
Full often o'er a Pot of Ale,
When I was Rabby *at* Kinsale.
But then, for want of Antient Learning,   25
The Scripture Sense not well discerning,
Our Nights were past in great Confusion,
No mortal making one Conclusion.

To find a Remedy for this,
I hope it will not be amiss,   30
To furnish my Associates quondam,
(That they no more dispute at randome)
With choice Collected Dissertations,
Answers, Rejoinders, Replications,
That each may have enough to say,   35
And hold the Scripture his own way.
Profecto legi plus quam satis,
More Languages than Mithridates.
All which I Learn'd (as will appear
Since I left Ireland) in one Year;   40
Where such, as knew my stock, can tell,
I scarcely cou'd Read English well.
In this one Book I've done much more,
Than all the World has done before;
No Bibliotheque, that is now extant,   45
Has half so well explain'd a Text on't;
With so much ease I can Command it,
The greatest Dunce may understand it.
If any thinks the Work too long
For one Man's Head, I'll shew he's wrong;   50
Because the way, which I intend
Will bring it quickly to an end.
In Chapters here and there I'll dip,
Whole Books not worth the Reading Skip,
Whate'er's Poetical, or Moral,   55
To them I have a mortal Quarrel;
What meerly is Historical,
I shall not touch upon at all;
You'll see me such a Bible-trimmer,
That I'll reduce it to a Primmer.   60
As for the Fathers, they are all met,
In Pool, Petavius, and Calmet,
I've Read 'em Page by Page, and find
No gleaning Work for me behind.
And when I cut one Folio short,   65
Will not the Reader thank me for't?
For I have so much Antient Lore
I could have swell'd 'em into four.

We wait Subscriptions coming in,
We're just beginning to begin;   70
'Tis this the Printer's *sole pretence is,*
We've Paper, Types, Amanuensis;
And all, but what few Pence are owing,
To set the Press *and me a going.*
One thing I beg leave to remark——   75
For Young Divines, *who're in the dark;*
And English Readers, *who are straining*
In every Chapter *for a meaning;*
For Men *of* Letters, *and good Sense,*
Here's Learning at a small expence;   80
They'll find my Books, when well examin'd,
Will do by Help of Pool *and* Hammond;
And if the Parsons *can afford once*
A Bible *with a large* Concordance,
I know not any thing they lack   85
Except it be an Almanack.
In my Compilement they shall see
Opinions, great Variety!
That every Schismatick *with ease,*
May find a Gloss *himself to please.*   90
Now Monsieur Calmet *(like an* Olio)
Disht up nine Tracts of his in Folio.
To all his Country-Men reveal'd,
What Latin, Hebrew, Greek *conceal'd,*
So plain in French, *that every Peasant*   95
Breaks out with Rapture in the praise on't.
O what a Glorious learned heap is't!
A wond'rous Author for a Papist!
I wish in English *'twere Translated,*
And mine to wipe his Rev'rence fated.   100
To what Perfection had he brought
His Books, with Liberty of Thought!
But all along he's Crampt I find,
And therefore durst not speak his mind;
For had he said a Word 'gainst Popery,   105
The Laws wou'd turn his Neck with Rope a wry.
Thus Foreign Pop'ry *is a Curse,*
But English Popery *is worse.*

Remember all, before you're told,
That what I Write for New, is Old;   110
If any Man of Reading looks
He'll find it all in other Books;
As I'm an Orthodox Divine,
I've stol'n my Comments *ev'ry line.*
There's all the wrangling Tracts I know   115
Collected here both con *and* pro,
So well dispos'd of, ev'ry Man
May find the Truth out, if he can.
From the Creation to the Flood
(To shew you that my Work is good)   120
I've drawn a Sketch, as I thought best,
To form a Judgment of the rest.
A word or two before I close all,
One Doctor Innis *makes* Proposal,
A poor Insipid Moral *Tool,*   125
He'd have the World to walk by Rule.
He thinks I've nought to do, but nose him,
I'd see him hang'd e'er I oppose him.
He strives to make Men good, *but I Sir*
Resolve to make them worse, *and* Wiser.   130
It ever was my way to love
The Serpent, *rather than the* Dove.
The Doctor, by a vain Pretension,
Depends upon his own Invention;
But I, who always liv'd on loan,   135
Shan't Write a Sentence of my own.

SIR,

I Have inserted your *Poem*, and think you have done your self great Honour, by shewing so much Regard to a Person remarkably Eminent; besides a most laudable Zeal in recommending a Work,
5 which is likely to prove of the Greatest Advantage to our Church in general, in this degenerate Age of Prophaness and Infidelity.

I am with due Respect Your's, *&c.*

The *Intelligencer*.

MOTTO. *Ars Poetica*, 144: 'That then he may set forth striking and wonderful tales' (Loeb).

11. *A. P.*: Alexander Pope or, facetiously, Ambrose Philips, then in Dublin as secretary to Archbishop Boulter. For his verse the Dublin wits, possibly including Swift and Sheridan, had recently ridiculed Philips as Namby-Pamby; and in early 1728 Pope had labelled him 'the greatest Master' of the 'infantine'; see Foxon, ii. 269 (under 'Namby Pamby') and ii. 274 (under Philips); Philips, *Poems*, ed. M. G. Segar (Oxford, 1937), 181–2; Pope, *Peri Bathous*, in his *Prose Works*, ii. 214. Pope also mocked Philips in *The Dunciad*, which had appeared in May 1728 (TE, vol. v, pp. xvii, 188).

13. *in the manner of Voiture*: Vincent Voiture (1597–1648), admired for his epistolary elegance, both in French and in English translation. Swift was 'fond of' him, particularly for his skill at raillery: 'His Genius first found out the Rule | For an obliging Ridicule' (*Poems*, i. 216; *Corresp.* iii. 373; iv. 408). John Dennis, though conceding that Voiture's 'Expression was often defective', wrote that he 'was easie and unconstrain'd, and natural when he was most exalted, [and] that he seldom endeavoured to be witty at the expence of right Reason' (*Critical Works*, ii. 382). Pope too praised him (TE vi. 62).

21. *S---d---l---y*: See introductory note.

25. *Church-street*: Smedley lived in Church Street, now Romilly Street, from 1724 to 1728 (*Survey of London*, xxxiii (1966), 203).

28. *the Specimen*: i.e., *A Specimen of An Universal View ... by the Reverend Jonathan Smedley, Dean of Clogher* ([London]: Printed for the Author, 1728), a 66-page folio pamphlet. Smedley publicized his book not only through the *Specimen* and the *London Journal* letter but through an advertisement 28 Aug. (*Daily Journal*) and a proposal, mentioned in the letter of 28 Aug. and published 9 Nov. 1728 (see textual note). Though Smedley failed to publish the *Universal View*, it seems unlikely that the *Intelligencer* was a significant deterrent.

58. *Bibliotheque*: A collection of works by several authors, or a commentary: 'Any Book that speaks indifferently of all sorts of Authors, and Writings, composed upon different Occasions, may be called a *Bibliotheca*', according to Louis Ellies du Pin, *Bibliotheque des auteurs ecclesiastiques*; I quote the translation, *A New History of Ecclesiastical Writers* (Dublin: Grierson, 1722), vol. i, p. i; see also the following note on Poole's *Synopsis*. Smedley's most notable competition in bibliotheques would have been Samuel Parker's *Bibliotheca Biblica; Being a Commentary upon All the Books of the Old and New Testament*. Its fourth volume appeared in 1728, and it ceased publication with vol. v in 1735, not having got beyond the Pentateuch.

82. *Poole's Synopsis*: The puritan Matthew Poole's *Synopsis Criticorum Aliorumque S. Scripturae Interpretum*, 5 vols. (London: Flesher and Roycroft, 1669–76 and several later editions). Thomas Barlow, in *'ΑΥΤΟΣΧΕΔΙΑΣΜΑΤΑ, De Studio Theologiae: or, Directions for the Choice of Books in the Study of Divinity* (Oxford: Lichfield, 1699), recommended the *Synopsis*, 'the benefit of which Book is very great (I may call it *Bibliotheca*)' (9).

85. *Petavius*: Denis Petau (1583–1652), a French Jesuit. In his *Specimen*, which treats Genesis 1, Smedley uses Petau's *De Theologicis Dogmatibus* (1644–50), especially the volume *De Sex Primorum Mundi Dierum Opificiis*. Petau also wrote a widely circulated work on chronology, *Doctrina Temporum*, abridged as *Rationarium Temporum*. See *Specimen*, 34; F. X. Murphy's article on Petau in the *New Catholic Encyclopedia* (New York, 1967); and *Oxford Dictionary of the Christian Church*.

86. *Calmet*: Augustin Calmet (1672–1757), a Benedictine exegete, wrote *Commentaire littérale sur tous les livres de L'Ancien et du nouveau testament*, 9 vols. (Paris: Emery *et al.*, 1724; there were earlier editions).

105. *some learned Persons to collect for me*: Notably Thomas Birch (1705–66), the future

historian. He had assisted Smedley for 'near two Years', as appears from a letter of Smedley's among the Birch papers, BL MS Add. 4268, fo. 34; see also BL MS Add. 4318, fo. 191–6; Samuel Ayscough, *A Catalogue of the Manuscripts Preserved in the British Museum*, vol. i (London: Rivington, 1782), p. v; John Nichols, *Literary Anecdotes of the Eighteenth Century*, v (London, 1812), 282–3 n.; and *Intelligencer* 20.

114. *Poole's English Annotations*: Matthew Poole, *Annotations upon the Holy Bible. Wherein the Sacred Text Is Inserted and Various Readings Annex'd* (London: Parkhurst, 1683–5).

114–15. *Hammond's Exposition*: H[enry] Hammond, *A Paraphrase, and Annotations upon All the Books of the New Testament: Briefly Explaining All the Difficult Places Thereof* (London: Flesher, 1653; several later editions).

124–5. *Calmet gives the following reason*: 'Nous n'ignorions pas qu'on n'eût composé un très-grand nombre d'excellens Ouvrages sur l'Ecriture; c'est dans leur lecture même que nous avons conçû l'envie de faire celui-ci, en faveur de ceux qui aiment l'étude des Livres saints, & qui ne peuvent pas lire dans les sources tous les livres écrits en Latin, & remplis de citations & de passages Hébreux, Grecs, Latins & Arabes' (1724 edn., vol. i, part I, p. i).

133. *would not permit him to quote*: 'Nous avons quelquefois cité des Auteurs Protestans; mais seulement dans des choses de critique, & d'une litterature humaine & profane, & rarement en matiere de Théologie, si ce n'est dans les points où ils conviennent avec l'Eglise Romaine, ou dans ceux où nous avons jugé à propos de les refuter' (p. iii).

161. *the Proposals of Dr. Innes*: Alexander Innes's ἈΡΕΤΗ-ΛΟΓΙΑ, *or, An Enquiry into the Original of Moral Virtue* (Westminster, 1728) was published the day Smedley wrote his letter (advt. 'This Day is published', *Whitehall Evening-Post*, 30 Mar. 1728). Innes, a fellow-traveller of the hoaxer George Psalmanazar, stole the work from Archibald Campbell. See Boswell, *Life of Johnson*, under 1761; *DNB* under Archibald Campbell (1691–1756); and Bernard Mandeville, *The Fable of the Bees*, ed. F. B. Kaye (Oxford, 1924), ii. 25–6. I have not found evidence that Innes actually published proposals.

POEM

20. *As plain as Pike-staff*: Proverbial; Tilley P322.

24. *Rabby at Kinsale*: See introductory note.

37. *Profecto legi plus quam satis*: 'Truly I have collected more than enough'; an echo of Smedley's claim that ancient authorities 'will be supplied even to Satiety'.

38. *Mithridates*: Mithridates VI, king of Pontus (*c.* 131–63 BC) knew twenty-two languages; see Pliny, *Natural History*, VII. xxiv. 88; xxv. 2; Quintilian, XI. ii. 50; and Gellius, xvii. 17 (some texts of Gellius say twenty-five).

40. *Since I left Ireland) in one Year*: This seems to be the clearest surviving evidence for the date of Smedley's departure from Ireland.

71. *pretence*: 'Expressed aim, intention, purpose, or design' (*OED*).

132. *The Serpent, rather than the Dove*: Cf. Matt. 10: 16.

135. *always liv'd on loan*: See introductory note, as well as no. 20 and its introductory note.

Sheridan's role is merely to introduce this spritely anonymous poem, which, because of its reprinting in the *Intelligencer*, has several times been attributed to Swift. But Swift's denials to Pope and Ford are definitive: 'I have some confused notion of seeing a paper called *Sir Ralph the Patriot*, but am sure it was bad or indifferent' (6 March 1728/9, to Pope); 'As to what you say of writing, you are mistaken about Sr Ralph the Patriot, for I believe it was writ in England; I think I saw it, but do not remember it was printed here' (18 March 1728/9, to Ford); and 'I forgot to tell you [in specifying which *Intelligencers* were his] that the Tale of Sir Ralph was sent from England' (12 June 1732, to Pope; *Corresp.* iii. 314 and 322; iv. 31). As Sheridan says, the poem was first printed in *The Country Journal: or, The Craftsman* (then and subsequently known simply as *The Craftsman*), a powerful Opposition paper written chiefly by Lord Bolingbroke, William Pulteney, and Nicholas Amhurst. (See the textual note.)

As printed in the *Craftsman*, the poem follows a long essay by 'Old Whig', paralleling Walpole with Thomas Osborne, Earl of Danby, the Lord Treasurer impeached in 1678 for bribing members of the Pensionary Parliament (1661–78) with pensions and other payments out of secret service money. (In the 1731 reprint of the *Craftsman*, the essay is also signed 'C.D.'—Caleb D'Anvers, the nominal author of the *Craftsman*.) On Walpole's deft use of bribes, pensions, and other financial rewards to manage Parliament, see Plumb, ii. 103–6, 123, 128, 176–81; and E. A. Reitan, 'The Civil List in Eighteenth-Century Politics', *Historical Journal*, 9 (1966), esp. 321–3. The law prevented any holder of a pension from sitting in the British House of Commons (1 Geo. I, c. 56), but Walpole could circumvent this restriction by paying pensions out of the secret service money.

NUMB. XII.

SINCE our *English* Friends have done us the Honour to Publish to their Countrymen, some of the Pieces from this *Paper*; We think ourselves oblig'd in Justice to return the Favour, by making the following *Tale* from the *Country-Journal*, Dated the 3*d* of *Aug.* 1728, the Subject of this Day's Entertainment.

5

From my own Chambers.

WHEN I was a young Man, I was very curious in collecting all the occasional *State Tracts*, or Pieces of *Poetry*, which were publish'd at that Time; and, upon looking them over, I find some, which I believe my Readers will think not altogether *mal apropos* at present. The following *Verses* are of this kind, which appear plainly enough to be levell'd at some *Pensionary Parliament*; but as the Author of this little Piece hath not sufficiently distinguished the *Characters*, which He designed to expose, by any particular Marks; so my Memory will not enable me to explain the Sentiments of the Publick on that Occasion. However, as it seems to contain a *good*, *general Moral*, I have ventur'd to give it to my Readers; and if it should happen to meet with any Success, I may, perhaps, communicate others, which are not to be met with in any of the *publick Miscellanies* of those Times.

The Progress of PATRIOTISM. A TALE.

Vendidit HIC *Auro Patriam.*

SIR *RALPH*, a simple, rural Knight,
Could just distinguish Wrong from Right;
When He receiv'd a Quarter's Rent,
And almost half in *Taxes* went,
He rail'd at *Places*, *Bribes* and *Pensions*,   5
And *secret Service*, new *Inventions*;
Preach'd up the true, old *English* Spirit,
And mourn'd the great Neglect of *Merit*;
Lamented our forlorn Condition,
And wish'd the Country would *Petition*;   10
Said, He would first subscribe his Name,
And added, 'Twas a burning shame
That *some Men* large Estates should get,
And fatten on the *Publick Debt*;
Of his poor Country urg'd his Love,   15
And shook his Head at *Those above*.
    This Conduct, in a private Station,
Procur'd the *Knight* great Reputation;
The Neighbours all approv'd his Zeal,
(Though few Men *judge*, yet all Men *feel*)   20

And with a general Voice declar'd
Money was scarce, the Times were hard;
That what Sir *Ralph* observ'd was true,
And wish'd the *Gallows* had its Due.
    Thus blest in popular Affection, 25
Behold! there came on an *Election*,
And who more proper than Sir *Ralph*
To guard their Privileges safe?
So, in Return for Zeal and Beer,
They chose him for a *Knight o'th' Shire*. 30
    But mark how *Climates* change the Mind,
And *Virtue* chops about like Wind!
Duely the *Knight* came up to Town,
Resolv'd to pull *Corruption* down,
Frequented Clubs of the *same Party*, 35
And in the Cause continued hearty,
Broach'd his Opinions, wet and dry,
And gave some *honest* Votes awry.
    At length, in that *old*, *spacious Court*,
Where *Members* just at Noon resort, 40
Up to our *Knight* Sir *Bluestring* came,
And call'd him frankly by his Name,
Smil'd on Him, *shook Him by the Hand*,
And gave Him soon to understand,
That though his Person was a Stranger, 45
Yet that in Times of greatest Danger,
His faithful Services were known,
And all his Family's here in Town,
For whom He had a great Affection;
And wish'd Him Joy of his Election, 50
Assur'd him that his Country's Voice
Could not have made a better Choice.
    Sir *Ralph*, who, if not much bely'd,
Had always some Degrees of Pride,
Perceiv'd his Heart begin to swell, 55
And lik'd this Doctrine mighty well,
Took Notice of his Air and Look,
And how familiarly He spoke;
Such Condescensions, such Professions
Remov'd all former ill Impressions. 60

The *Statesman* (who, we must agree,
Can far into our *Foibles* see,
And knows exactly how to flatter
The *weak*, *blind* Sides of human Nature)
Saw the *vain Wretch* begin to yield,   65
And farther thus his Oil instill'd.
    Sir *Ralph*, said He, all Forms apart,
So dear I hold you at my Heart,
Have such a Value for your *Worth*,
Your *Sense* and *Honour* and so forth,   70
That in some Points, extremely nice,
I should be proud of your Advice;
Let me, good Sir, the Favour pray,
To eat a Bit with me to Day;
Nay, dear Sir *Ralph*, you must agree——   75
Your Honour's Hour?——exactly Three.
    These Points premis'd, they bow and part,
With Hands press'd hard to either Heart;
For now the publick Business calls
Each Patriot to St. *Stephen*'s Walls;   80
Whether the *present Debts* to State; ⎤
Or on some *new Supplies* debate, ⎬
Would here be needless to relate. ⎦
    From thence, at the appointed Hour,
The *Knight* attends the *Man of Power*,   85
Who, better to secure his Ends,
Had likewise bid some courtly Friends,
His Brother *Townly* and his *Grace*,
Great *Statesmen* both and both in Place;
Our *British Horace*, fam'd for Wit,   90
Alike for *Courts* and *Senates* fit;
Sir *William*, from his early Youth,
Renown'd for *Honour*, *Virtue*, *Truth*;
And *Bub-ble*, just restor'd to Favour,
On Pardon ask'd for *late Behaviour*.   95
    The *Statesman* met his *Convert-Guest*, ⎤
Saluted, clasp'd Him to his Breast, ⎬
Then introduc'd Him to the rest. ⎦
    Whilst He, with Wonder and Amaze,
The Splendour of the House surveys,   100

Huge China Jars and Piles of Plate,
And *modish Screens* and Beds of State,
Gilt Sconces, of stupendous Size,
And costly Paintings strike his Eyes,
From *Italy* and *Flanders* brought 105
At the Expence of Nations bought;
Yet doth not one of these relate
The tragick End of R——s of State,
Although such Pictures might supply
Fit Lessons to the *Great Man's* Eye; 110
But *o'ergrown Favourites* dread to think
From whence they rose, and how may sink.

    Dinner now waited on the Board,
Rich as this City would afford,
(For every Element supplies, 115
His Table with its Rarities)
The Guests promiscuous take their Place,
Pro more, without *Form* or *Grace*;
There might the *little Knight* be seen
With *Ribons blue* and *Ribons green*, 120
All complaisant and debonair,
As if the King Himself were there;
Obsequious each consults his Tast,
And, begging to be serv'd the last,
Points round by turns to every Dish; 125
Will you have Soop, *Sir* Ralph, *or* Fish?
This Fricasee *or that* Ragoust?
Pray, Sir, be free and let me know.

    The Cloth remov'd, the Glass goes round,
With loyal Healths and Wishes crown'd; 130
May King *and* Senate *long agree!*
Success attend the Ministry*!*
Let publick Faith *and* Stocks *increase!*
And grant us Heav'n! a speedy Peace*!*

    Discourse ensues on *homebred Rage*, 135
That rank Distemper of the Age,
And instantly they all agree,
They never were so *blest*, or *free*;
That all *Complaints* were nought but *Faction*,
And *Patriotism* meer *Distraction*, 140

Though full of *Reason*, void of *Grace*,
And only meant to *get in Place.*
   Sir *Ralph* in Approbation bow'd;
Yet own'd, that with the giddy Croud,
He formerly had gone astray,   145
And talk'd in quite another Way,
Possess'd with Jealousies and Fears,
Dispers'd by restless Pamphleteers,
In Libels *weekly* and *diurnal*,
Especially the * *Country Journal*;   150
But as he felt sincere Contrition,
He hop'd his Faults would find Remission.
   Dear Sir, reply'd the *Blue-string Knight*,
I'm glad you think Affairs go right,
All Errors past must be excus'd,   155
(Since the best Men may be abus'd)
What's in my Power you may command,
Then shook Him once more by the Hand,
Gave him great Hopes (at least his *Word*)
That He should be a *Treasury-Lord*,   160
And to confirm his good Intention,
At present order'd him a *Pension.*
   By these Degrees, Sir *Ralph* is grown
The stanchest Tool in all the Town,
At *Points* and *Job-work* never fails;   165
At all his old Acquaintance rails;
Holds every Doctrine now in Fashion;
That *Debts* are Blessings to a Nation;
That *Bribery*, under *Whig-Direction*,
Is needful to discourage Faction;   170
That *standing Armies* are most fitting
To guard the Liberties of *Britain*;
That *F——e* is her sincerest Friend,
On whom, she always should depend;
That *Ministers*, by *Kings* appointed,   175
Are, under them, the *Lord's anointed*;
Ergo, it is the self-same Thing,
T' oppose the *Minister* or *King*;

---

* From hence it appears that a Paper was published under *that Name*, long before *this*,
in which we are at present engaged.

Ergo, by Consequence of Reason,
To censure *Statesmen* is *High Treason*.   180
    In fine, his *standing Creed* is this;
That *right* or *wrong*, or *hit* or *miss*,
No Mischiefs can befal a Nation,
Under so *wise a Ministration*;
That *Britain* is Sir *Blue-string*'s Debtor,   185
And *Things did surely ne'er go better!*
    So the plain Country Girl, untainted,
Nor yet with wicked Man acquainted,
Starts at the first leud Application,
Though warm perhaps by Inclination,   190
And swears she would not, with the King,
For all the World do *such a Thing*;
But when, with long, assiduous Art,
Damon hath once seduc'd her Heart,
She learns her Lesson in a trice,   195
And justifies the pleasing Vice,
Calls it a natural, harmless Passion,
Implanted from our first Creation,
Holds there's no Sin between clean Sheets,
And lies with every Man she meets.   200

INTRODUCTION

2–3. *some of the Pieces from this Paper*: No. 3, reprinted in *Mist's Weekly J.*, 6 July 1728; no. 6 in *Mist's*, 27 July 1728; no. 9 in *Mist's*, 10 and 17 Aug. 1728.

4. *the Country-Journal*: See introductory note.

6. *From my own Chambers*: This introductory note is in the persona of Caleb D'Anvers.

12. *some Pensionary Parliament*: See introductory note.

POEM

MOTTO. *Vendidit HIC Auro Patriam*: Virgil, *Aeneid*, vi. 621. The context is relevant: 'vendidit hic auro patriam dominumque potentem | imposuit; fixit leges pretio atque refixit': 'This one sold his country for gold, and fastened on her a tyrant lord; he made and unmade laws for a bribe' (Loeb).

26. *an Election*: The most recent general election, in 1727, had brought 150 new members into the Commons (Plumb, ii. 183 n.).

39. *that old, spacious Court*: Almost certainly the twelfth-century Court of Requests: 'During the Session of Parliament it is filled with Lords, Commoners, and others, who meet here to converse about Business.' *London in Miniature* (London: Corbett, 1755), 122; see Clyve Jones and Geoffrey Holmes (eds.), *The London Diaries of William Nicolson, Bishop of Carlisle 1702–1718* (Oxford, 1985), 73–5.

40. *just at Noon resort*: i.e., before going into the House. Information on the Commons's daily schedule is scarce for the early eighteenth century, but P. D. G. Thomas estimates that 'the great majority of debates . . . began in the early afternoon, usually

between midday and 2 p.m.' (*The House of Commons in the Eighteenth Century* (Oxford, 1971), 156).

41. *Sir Bluestring*: Sir Robert Walpole so flaunted the blue ribbon of the Order of the Garter that 'Sir Blue-String became one of his most common nicknames' (Plumb, ii. 101).

80. *St. Stephen's Walls*: The Commons met in St Stephen's chapel in the then Palace of Westminster.

81. *the present Debts*: The new parliament had extensively debated the sinking fund (Walpole's own invention) and the national debt in Mar. and Apr. 1727/8; see *Pol. State*, 35 (1728), 276–82 and 365–87; William Coxe, *Memoirs of . . . Walpole* (London: Cadell and Davies, 1798), i. 294–9.

88. *His Brother Townly and his Grace*: Charles, 2nd Viscount Townshend, Secretary of State for the Northern Department, was the widower of Walpole's sister (Plumb, ii. 132). Thomas Pelham-Holles, 1st Duke of Newcastle, was Secretary of State for the Southern Department.

90. *British Horace*: Horace Walpole, Sir Robert's brother and the ambassador to Paris. His presence at dinner suggests that it occurred in early 1728, after the new parliament opened in January and before the opening in June of the Congress of Soissons, at which he was the British plenipotentiary. Horace was known as a graceless, 'often totally unintelligible' speaker. *DNB*; Hervey, i. 185; see also the notes to no. 9.

92. *Sir William*: Probably Sir William Yonge, Bt., formerly a lord of the Treasury. Hervey describes him as he was about 1727: 'Without having done anything that I know of remarkably profligate—anything out of the common track of a ductile courtier and a parliamentary tool—his name was proverbially used to express everything pitiful, corrupt, and contemptible. It is true he was a great liar, but rather a mean than a vicious one. . . . Sir Robert Walpole . . . caressed him without loving him, and employed him without trusting him; but the éclat even of this great minister's favour could neither whiten Sir William Yonge's character nor keep him in employment' (i. 36).

94. *Bub-ble*: George Bubb Dodington, one of the lords of the Treasury. At George II's accession in 1727, many had paid their court to Sir Spencer Compton, believing he would replace Walpole as first minister. 'Among these herds', Hervey reports, 'was Mr. Dodington . . ., whose early application and distinguished assiduity at this juncture to the supposed successor of his former patron and benefactor was never forgiven' (i. 29). The poem disagrees with the latter assessment.

100. *The Splendour of the House*: In Walpole's house on the grounds of the Royal Hospital, Chelsea, he was amassing the notable collection of paintings later at Houghton and now for the most part in the Hermitage, Leningrad. This passage appears to be one of the most detailed surviving records of the house's interior, but see Alfred Beaver, *Memorials of Old Chelsea* (London, 1892), 287–90, perhaps relying on Daniel Lysons, *Environs of London* (London: Cadell and Davies, 1795), ii. 90–1; see also *Survey of London*, ii (1909), 3–7; and Plumb, i. 206; ii. 87.

108. *R——s*: Rogues.

111. *o'ergrown Favourites*: An allusion to Walpole's corpulence.

118. *Pro more*: According to custom.

120. *Ribons blue and Ribons green*: Walpole, Townshend, and Newcastle were all Knights of the Garter; Yonge, a Knight of the Bath, was entitled to wear a red ribbon; *green* seems here only for the rhyme, since the green ribbon adorned members of the Order of the Thistle, none of whom—mainly Scottish nobility—is mentioned as present at Walpole's gathering.

134. *a speedy Peace*: With Spain; preliminaries had been agreed in Paris, May 1727, and they led eventually to the Congress of Soissons, which had opened in June 1728. A

London newsletter of 11 June reported, 'The Grand Discourse of all Conversations is upon the Congress at Soissons'. Newsletters to Lord Percival, later 1st Earl of Egmont, BL MS Add. 47081, fo. 137.

165. *Points*: Perhaps 'punctilio[s]; nicet[ies]' (Johnson).

171. *standing Armies*: Though standing armies were forbidden in peacetime by the Bill of Rights, there was nevertheless a large force in 1728, and in July it had been objected to, perhaps by Bolingbroke, in *Reasons Shewing the Necessity of Reducing the Army, and, Proving that the Navy of England is Her Only, and Natural Strength and Security* (London: A. Moore, 1728). See *Pol. State*, 36 (1728), 1–32.

173. *F——e*: France.

Swift and Sheridan's keen interest in good conversation and story-telling was shared with many essayists and courtesy-writers. Sheridan had written on conversation in *Ars Pun-ica*, and the 'short stories' assembled here are good examples of the anecdotes he collected. Swift's many discussions of good conversation include 'Hints toward an Essay on Conversation', 'Hints on Good-Manners', and the burlesque introduction to *A Compleat Collection of Genteel and Ingenious Conversation* (*Prose*, iv. 87–95, 99–124, 221–2).

In this essay, Sheridan sets up an exemplary figure nearly all his readers would have recognized as Swift. Swift himself remarked in *Verses on the Death of Dr. Swift* that he 'knew an hundred pleasant Stories', and Patrick Delany acknowledged his artistry as a raconteur (*Observations upon Lord Orrery's Remarks* (London: Reeve, 1754), 218). Moreover, according to John Lyon, Swift's caretaker in his last years, 'he often check'd dull circumstantial story-tellers from drawing out their Tales to too great a length, by pulling out his watch, or by giving some other Innuendo'—a punishment Sheridan threatens in his conclusion. (Lyon's annotated copy of John Hawkesworth, *The Life of the Revd. Jonathan Swift, D.D.* (Dublin: Cotter, 1755), 134; this is Forster MS 579.)

NUMB. XIII.

Sermo datur cunctis, animi sapientia paucis.

Cato.

THERE is one kind of Conversation, which every one Aims at, and every one almost fails in; It is that of *Story-telling*. I know not any thing which engages our Attention with more Delight, when a Person has a sufficient stock of Talents Necessary for it, such
5 as *Good Sense*, *True Humour*, *a clear Head*, *a ready Command of Language*, and *a Variety of proper Gesture*, to give Life and Spirit to what he says. If any of these be wanting, the Listners, instead of being diverted, are made very uneasy; but if the Person be utterly Void of them all, as it is very often the Case, he becomes a Nuissance to the Company, and
10 they are so long upon the Rack as he speaks. It has sometimes fallen to my Lot, that a Man whom I never offended, has laid me under the Persecution of a long Story, and Compelled me to hear, what neither concerned himself, nor me, nor indeed any Body else, and at the same time, he was as much in earnest, as if both our Lives and Fortunes, and

the Felicity of the whole Kingdom depended upon what he said. A 15
Humour very unaccountable! That a Man shall be letting off Words
for an hour or two, with a very innocent Intention, and after he has
done his best, only makes me uneasy, and himself Contemptible.

This natural Infirmity in Men, is not only confined to *Story-telling*,
but it appears likewise in every Essay whatsoever of their Intellectuals. 20
As for Instance; If one of these be a Preacher of GOD's Word, by
far fetched Criticisms, numerous Divisions, and Sub-divisions, in-
coherent Digressions, tedious Repetitions, useless Remarks, Weak
Answers to strong Objections, Inferences to no Premises, tedious
Exhortations, and many other Methods of Protraction, he shall draw 25
you out a Discourse for an hour and a quarter, unequally dispensing
Opium and Edification to his Flock, there being seven Sleepers for
one Hearer. If he be a Lawyer, he shall, by an uncommon Way of
Amusement, run away with a Subject, which might be explained in
two Minutes, and Dilate upon it two hours, with such a Volubility of 30
Tongue, such Affluence of Expression, with something so like a good
Style, and manner of Thinking, that the Judges and Jury, attend with
as much Gravity, as if there were a continued Chain of true Reasoning,
and solid Argument. If he be a Member of the Upper or Lower House,
he does not proceed four Sentences, before the Rest know where to 35
have him an hour hence; in the mean time they Divert one another, in
talking of matters indifferent, till the Gentleman has done. I could give
many more Instances, but that I think these sufficient for my present
purpose; beside, least I should incur the like Reproach my self, I must
in a few Words, divide the *Story-tellers*, into *the short*, *the long*, *the* 40
marvellous, *the Insipid*, and *the Delightful*.

The short Story-teller is he, who tells a great deal in few Words,
engages your Attention, pleases your Imagination, or quickly excites
your Laughter. Of this Rank were *Xenophon*, *Plutarch*, *Macrobius*,
among the Ancients. *Ex. gr.* 45

When the *Nephelai* of *Aristophanes*, a Satyr upon *Socrates* was Acting,
his Friends desired him to retire, and hide behind them. No said
Socrates, I will stand up here, where I may be seen; for now I think my
self like a good Feast, and that every one has share of me. *vid. Feast of*
Xenophon. 50

Brasidas the Famous *Lacedemonian* General caught a *Mouse*. It bit
him, and by that means made its escape. O *Jupiter*, said he, what
Creature so Contemptible, but may have it's Liberty if it will Contend
for it. *vid. Plutarch. de profect. virtut.*

55   *Diogenes* having sailed to *Chios*, while it was under the Dominion of
the *Persians*, said in a full Assembly, the Inhabitants were Fools for
Erecting a Colledge, and Building Temples, since the *Persians* would
not allow them the privilege of making their own *Priests*, but sent them
over the most Illiterate of their *Magi*.

60   *Augustus* while he was encamped with his Army, some where near
Mantua, was disturbed three Nights successively, by the hooting of an
Owl. Proclamation was made to the Soldiers, that whoever caught the
Offender, (so that he might be brought to Justice,) should have an
ample reward for his pains. Every one was Loyally engaged in the

65   pursuit of this *Bird*. At last, one more Vigilant than the rest, found him
in a Hollow-tree, so brought him in Triumph to the Emperor, who
saw him with the greatest Joy, but gave the Soldier a sum of Money, so
far below his Expectation, that he let the *Owl* fly away that Instant, so
true a Sense of Liberty, ran through the very meanest of the *Romans*.

70   *Macrob. Sat.*

The *long Story-teller* is one, who tells little or nothing in a great
number of Words; for this, many among the Moderns are famous,
particularly the *French*. And among our selves in this Kingdom we
have a vast Number of the better sort. As well as I can recollect there

75   are six Deans, four Judges, six and thirty Councellors at Law, sixty five
Attorneys, some few Fellows of the College, every Alderman through
the whole Nation, except one, all old Gentlemen, and Ladies, without
exception, five of the College of Physicians, three or four Lords, two
hundred Squires, and some few People of distinction beside.

80   I shall here insert a fragment of a long Story, by way of example,
containing 129 Words, which might have been said in these ten
following, *viz. Nine Years ago I was to Preach for a Friend.*

I remember once, I think it was about seven Years ago—No I lye—
It was about nine Years ago; for it was just when my Wife was Lying in

85   of *Dicky*, I remember particularly the Mid-wife would have had me
stay to keep her company, and it was the heaviest Day of Storm and
Rain, that I ever saw before, or since, but because I engaged to Preach
for a very Worthy Friend of mine, who lived about twenty Miles off,
and this being *Saturday*, I could not defer it to the next Morning,

90   though I had an excellent Nag, which could have Rid it in three hours,
I bought him of a Neighbour one Mr. *Masterson*, yet because I would
not put my Friend in a fright *&c.* Thus far he went in one Minute. The
Story lasted an Hour, so that upon a fair computation he Spoke 7740
Words, instead of 600, by which means he made use of 7140 more than

he had occasion for. If a right application were made of this hint, 95
which I have given, it would be of admirable Effect in the dispatch of
publick business, as well as private conversation, nay in the very
Writing of Books, for which I refer the reader to the *Fable of the Bees*,
and the two Elaborate Treatises, Written by the Learned Mr.
H———n.   100

The *marvellous*, is he, who is fond of telling such things as no Man
alive, who has the least use of his reason, can believe. This humour
prevails very much in Travellers, and the Vain glorious, but is very
pardonable, because no Man's Faith is imposed upon, or if it should
be so, no ill consequence attends it. And beside, there is some kind of 105
Amusement in seeing a Person seriously extravagant, expecting
another should give Credit to what he knows impossible for the
greatest Dunce to Swallow.

One of these, who had travelled to *Damascus*, told his Company,
that the *Bees* of that Country were as big as *Turkies*. Pray Sir, said a 110
Gentleman (begging pardon for the Question) How large were the
Hives? The same size with Ours, replied the Traveller. Very strange,
said the other. But how got they into their Hives? That is none of my
business, I Gad let them look to that.

Another, who had Travelled as far as *Persia*, spoke to his Man *John*, 115
as he was returning home, telling him, how Necessary it was, that a
Traveller should draw things beyond the Life, or else, he could not
hope for that respect from his Country-Men, which otherwise he
might have. But at the same time, *John*, said he, wheresoever I shall
Dine, or Sup, keep you close to my Chair, and if I do very much 120
exceed the bounds of Truth, Punch me behind, that I may correct my
self. It happened on a Day, that he Dined with a Certain Gentleman,
who shall be Nameless, where he affirmed, that he saw a *Monkey* in the
Island *Borneo*, which had a Tail three-score Yards long. *John* punched
him. I am certain it is fifty at least. *John* punched again. I believe to 125
speak within compass, for I did not measure it, it must have been forty.
John gave him tother Touch. I remember it lay over a Quick-set
hedge, and therefore could not be less than thirty. *John* at him again. I
could take my Oath it was twenty. This did not satisfy *John*. Upon
which the Master turned about in a Rage and said, Damn you for a 130
Puppy, would you have the *Monkey* without any Tail at all?

Did not the famous Dr. *Burnet*, whose History is much of the same
stamp with his Travels, affirm that he saw an *Elephant* play at Ball?
And that grave Gentleman *Ysbrant Ides*, in his Travels through

135 *Muscovy* to *China*, assures us, that he saw *Elephants*, which were taught
     to low like *Cows*, to yell like *Tigers*, and to mimick the sounding of a
     Trumpet; but their highest Perfection, as he relates it, was that of
     singing like Canary birds. However this is not so marvellous (for *Pliny*
     relates Wonderful things of their Docility) as what a Gentleman told a
140 full Company in my hearing within this fortnight. That he had seen a
     Show at *Bristol*, which was a *Hare*, taught to stand upon her hind-legs
     and bow to all the Company, to each Person in particular, with a very
     good Grace, and then proceed to beat several Marches on the Drum.
     After this a *Dog* was set upon the Table. His Master, the *Show-man*,
145 made many grievous Complaints against him, for High Crimes, and
     Misdemeanors. The *Hare* nits her Brows, kindles her Eyes like a
     Lady, falls in a Passion, attacks the *Dog* with all her Rage and Fury, as
     if she had been his Wife, Scratches, bites, and cuffs him round the
     Table, till the Spectators had enough for their Money.
150   There is a certain Gentleman, now in *Ireland*, most remarkably fond
     of the marvellous (but this through Vanity) who among an infinite
     Number of the like Rarities, affirms, that he has a *Carp*, in a Pond by it
     self, which has for twenty Years past, supplyed him and his Friends,
     with a very good Dish of Fish, when they either came to Dine, or Sup
155 with him. And the manner of it is thus. The Cook-maid goes with a
     large Kitchin-knife, which has a Whistle in its handle; she no sooner
     blows it, but the *Carp* comes to the Sluice and turns up its Belly, till
     she cuts out as much as she has occasion for, and then away it scuds.
     The Chasm is filled in a Day or two, and the *Carp* is as sound as a
160 *Roach*, ready for the Knife again. Now, if he and his Cook-maid took
     the most solemn Oath to the truth of this, or the most sanctifyed
     Quaker should say YEA to it, which is made equal to any Prelate's
     Oath, I would no more give Credit to them, than I would to the
     Collonel, who said he was at the Battle of *Landen*, where his Majesty
165 King *William*, of Glorious Memory, lost the Day. And this *Collonel*,
     being in the utmost Confusion, fled among the rest. He Swore he had
     Galloped above two miles, after his Horses Head was Shot off, by a
     Cannon-ball, which he should not have missed, if the poor Creature
     had not stooped at a River side to Drink.
170   I should be glad to spend an Evening with half a dozen Gentlemen
     of this uncommon Genius, for I am certain they would improve upon
     one another, and thereby I might have an Oportunity of observing how
     far the Marvellous could be carryed, or whether it has any bounds
     at all.

The insipid, who may not unfitly be called *Soporifick*, is one who goes 175
plodding on in a heavy dull Relation of unimportant Facts. You Shall
have an Account from such a Person of every Minute Circumstance,
which happened in the Company where he has been, what he did, and
what they did, what they said, and what he said, with a Million of trite
Phrases, with an *and so* beginning every Sentence. And *to make a long* 180
Story short. And *as I was saying*, with many more expletives of equal
Signification. It is a most dreadful thing, when Men have neither the
Talent of speaking, nor the Discretion of holding their Tongues, and
that, of all People, such as are least qualifyed, are commonly the most
earnest in this way of Conversation. 185

The Delightful Story-teller is one, who speaks not a Word too much,
or too little; who can, in a very careless manner, give a great deal of
pleasure to others, and desires rather to Divert, than be Applauded;
who shews good understanding, and a delicate turn of Wit in every
thing which comes from him; who can entertain his Company better 190
with the History of a Child and its *Hobby-horse*, than one of the
Soporificks can with an Account of *Alexander*, and *Bucephalus*. Such a
Person is not unlike a bad Reader who makes the most ingenious
Piece his own, that is, Dull and Detestable, by only coming through
his Mouth. But to return to the Delightful *Story-teller*, I cannot 195
describe him by any Words so well, as his own, and therefore take the
following Story to shew him in the most agreeable light.

A Mountebank in Leicester-Fields *had drawn a huge Assembly about*
him; among the rest a Fat unwieldy Fellow, half stifled in the Press, would be
every fit Crying out Lord! what a filthy Crowd is here! pray good People give Way 200
a litle! bless me! what a Devil has raked this Rable together? Zounds what
squeezing is this! Honest Friend remove your Elbow. At last a Weaver, that stood
next him, could hold no longer. A Plague confound you, said he, for an Over
grown Sloven; and who, in the Devil's Name, helps to make up the Crowd half so
much as your self? Don't you consider (with a Pox) that you take up more room 205
with that Carcass than any five here? Is not the Place as fit for us, as for you? bring
your own Guts to a reasonable Compass (and be Damnd) and then I'll engage we
shall have room enough for us all.

This I have transcribed from a most Celebrated Author, with great
pleasure, and do earnestly recommend it to my Country-men, as the 210
true standard of *Story-telling*, both as to Style, and Manner, and every
thing requisite not only to please the Hearer, but to gain his favour and
Affection. And for the Time to come, be it Enacted, that if any person,
of what Rank soever, shall presume to exceed Six Minutes in a Story,

215 to *hum* or *haw*, use *hyphens* between his Words, or Digressions, or
offers to engage the Company to hear another Story when he has done,
or speaks one Word more than is Necessary, or is a Stammerer in his
Speech, that then it shall, and may be lawful for any one of the said
Company, or the whole Company together, to pull out his, hers, or
220 their Watches to make use of broad hints, or inuendoes for him the
said *Story-teller*, to break off, although abruptly, otherwise he is to have
a Glove, or Handkerchief, crammed into his Mouth for the first
default, and for the second, to be kicked out of Company.

MOTTO. *Catonis Disticha*, i. 10: 'On all is speech bestowed: good sense on few' (*The Distichs of Cato*, tr. W. J. Chase, 1922).

49. *has share*: Though the Bowyer–Davis editions emend to 'has a share', *share* appears unmodified in Swift, *Poems*, i. 67 and ii. 449, and *Prose*, iv. 173.

49–50. *Feast of Xenophon*: The story is not in Xenophon; a similar anecdote, however, occurs in Plutarch, *Moralia*, 10C–E.

54. *Plutarch*: 'De profectibus in virtute', *Moralia*, 79E. In Sheridan's collection of *bons mots* he translates this anecdote twice, once adding: 'An excellent remark, if but rightly considered, the least Republick in the world would not be insulted.' (Gilbert MS 123, pp. 16–17; MS 125, fo. [8].)

55. *Diogenes*: Source unidentified. The story is so apposite to Sheridan's view of Ireland that he may be suspected of writing allegory.

70. *Macrob[ius] Sat[urnalia]*: II. iv. 26, freely translated; Sheridan gives a more literal version in Gilbert MS 124, p. 13.

76–7. *every Alderman . . . except one*: Perhaps the merchant Richard Grattan, a Dublin alderman since 22 July 1728 (*Dublin Weekly J.*, 27 July 1728). For the association of Swift (and Sheridan) with the Grattans, see *Corresp.* ii. 152, iv. 323, 397, and 503; and T. S. Smyth, 'Grattan Family Links with Cavan', *Breifne*, 2 (1965), 378–84.

98. *the Fable of the Bees*: By 1723 Bernard Mandeville's 433-line poem (as first published in 1705) had swelled to two volumes. Sheridan objected not only to its length but, as was common, to its doctrine. He sarcastically calls the *Fable* 'incomparable for Style and Argument' and groups Mandeville with the deists John Toland, Matthew Tindal, 'and others of that Tribe' (*A Poem on the Immortality of the Soul* (Dublin: Hyde and Dobson, 1733), sig. A3).

99. *two Elaborate Treatises*: Probably Francis Hutcheson's *An Inquiry into the Original of Our Ideas of Beauty and Virtue* (London: Darby, 1725) and *An Essay on the Nature and Conduct of the Passions and Affections* (London: Darby and Browne), just published in Jan. 1727/8. Laetitia Pilkington deemed the latter 'impenetrably obscure' and said that even the learned Edward Synge (bishop of Clonfert, etc.) could not understand it (*Memoirs*, iii (London: Griffiths, 1754), 132). In 1728 Hutcheson was a Dublin schoolmaster. See his *A System of Moral Philosophy* (Glasgow: Foulis, 1755), pp. vi–x; and *Illustrations on the Moral Sense* (Cambridge, Mass., 1971), 5–6.

132. *the famous Dr. Burnet*: Sheridan seems to imply that the account of an elephant occurs in Gilbert Burnet's travels, i.e., *Dr. Burnet's Travels* (Amsterdam: Savouret & Fenner, 1687), but no such description is there. (Both the *Travels* and *Bishop Burnet's History of His Own Time* (vol. i, 1724) had been roundly criticized for inaccuracies.) Whatever the source of the elephant story, Sheridan is probably judging it without himself ever having seen an elephant.

134. *Ysbrant Ides*: i.e., *The Three Years Land Travels of His Excellency E. Ysbrant Ides from*

Mosco to China (London, 1705, according to the engraved title-page; the printed title-page is dated '1706' and the title differs in several respects), 80.

138–9. *Pliny relates Wonderful things*: In *Natural History*, viii.

159–60. *sound as a Roach*: Proverbial; Tilley R143.

162–3. *made equal to any Prelate's Oath*: In the session just concluded, the Irish Parliament had permitted Quakers to affirm on any occasion legally requiring an oath (1 Geo. II, c. 5, Irish, more liberal than the earlier acts: 8 Anne, c. 3, Irish; and 6 Geo. I, c. 5–6, Irish). See also *The Ladies Opera* [Dublin, ?1728]. Swift ridiculed such permission (*Prose*, vii. 106–7).

164. *Landen*: The bloodiest battle of the War of the League of Augsburg, at Landen and Neerwinden in the Spanish Netherlands, now Belgium, 29 July 1693.

192. *Bucephalus*: Plutarch's life of Alexander the Great (vi) dramatically records his boyhood prowess in taming the warhorse Bucephalus.

209. *Celebrated Author*: The obliquity of this praise of Swift may owe something to his not having acknowledged authorship of *A Tale of a Tub*; the quotation is from its Preface.

215. *hyphens*: As meaning short pauses in speech, *OED* records no use earlier than 1868.

223. *default*: Offence (*OED*, sense 5).

Despite this essay's shaky logic, the preface to the Bowyer–Davis edition highlights its politics—and its outrageousness. To compare 'Upstart Scoundrels' with excrement, the preface suggests, 'may be thought a Reflection on one or other of *First Quality* and *Distinction*', that is, Walpole. (See Appendix I.)

Sheridan's view of women here, though conventional, would have been supported by his own unhappy marriage, for which see the General Introduction. With no. 14 may be compared no. 4 and Sheridan's *A New Simile for the Ladies, with Useful Annotations*, in *Poems*, ii. 612–16.

NUMB. XIV.

Naturam expellas furcâ licet usque recurret.

Hor.

THERE is an old Heathen Story, That *Prometheus*, who was a Potter in *Greece*, took a frolick to turn all the Clay in his Shop into Men and Women, separating the Fine from the Course, in order to distinguish the Sexes. The *Males* were formed of a mixture
5 *Blue* and *Red*, as being of the toughest Consistence, fitter for Creatures destin'd to Hardships, Labour, and difficult Enterprizes; the *Females* were molded out of the most refined Stuff, much of the like substance with *China-ware*, Transparent, and Brittle; designing them rather for Show and Beauty, than to be of any real use in Life, farther
10 than that of Generation. By the Transparency he intended the Men might see so plainly through them, that they should not be capable of *Hypocrisy*, *Falshood* or *Intrigue*; and by their britleness, he taught them, they were to be handled with a Tenderness suitable to their delicacy of Constitution.
15 It was pleasant enough, to see with what Contrivance and Order, he disposed of his Journey-men in their several Appartments, and how judiciously he assigned each of them his Work, according to his Natural Capacity, and Talents, so that every Member, and part of the Humane Frame, was finished with the utmost exactness and Beauty.
20 In one Chamber you might see a *Leg-shaper*; in another a *Skull-roller*; in a third an *Arm-stretcher*; in a fourth a *Gut-winder*; for each Workman was distinguished by a proper Term of Art, such as *Knuckle-turner*, *Tooth-grinder*, *Rib-cooper*, *Muscle-maker*, *Tendon-*

drawer, *Paunch-blower*, *Vein-brancher*, and such like; but *Prometheus* himself made the *Eyes*, the *Ears*, and the *Heart*, which, because of their 25 Nice and Intricate Structure, were chiefly the business of a *Master-Workman*. Beside this, he compleated the whole, by fitting and joyning the several parts together, according to the best Symetry and Proportion. The Statues are now upon their Legs. *Life* the chief ingredient is wanting, *Prometheus* takes a *Ferula* in his Hand, (a Reed 30 of the Island *Chios* having an Oily Pith) steals up the Back-stairs to *Apollo*'s Lodgings, lights it Clandestinely at the Chariot of the *Sun*, so down he creeps upon his Tip-toes to his Ware-house, and in a very few Minutes, by an Application of the Flame to the Nostrils of his *Clay Images*, sets them all a stalking and staring through one another, but 35 intirely insensible of what they were doing. They looked so like the latter end of a *Lord-Mayor*'s Feast, he could not bear the sight of them. He then saw it was absolutely Necessary to give them *Passions*, or Life would be an insipid thing, and so from the Super-abundance of them in other *Animals*, he culls out enough for his purpose, which he 40 Blended and Tempered so well, before Infusion, that his Men and Women became the most amiable Creatures, that thought can conceive.

Love was then like a pure Vestal-flame, not made up of sudden Joy, Transports, and Extasies, but Constant, Friendly and Benevolent. 45

Anger did not appear horrid, and frightful by Turbulent Emotions of the Breast, and Distortions of the Face, but preserved a Dignity of Resentment in the Countenance, commanding a Reverential awe in the Offender.

Fear did not in the least encroach upon the Bounds of Fortitude, by 50 a slavish Dejection of Spirits, nor was it ever seen upon any occasion, but as a Monitor, to prevent the doing of any Action, which might be attended with Disgrace, or Repentance.

In the same manner was every Passion and Appetite under the best Regulation and Dominion of reason. The World would have been a 55 most delightful Scene had People continued in this Situation, but alass! there can be no Happiness here without a mixture of misery.

Prometheus is apprehended for his Theft, and Presumption, bound fast in Chains to a Rock, with a *Vulture* to prey upon his Liver. His Journey-men get Drunk for joy, they were now their own Masters, 60 during which interval, they fall to Man and Woman making with excessive Precipitation and hurry. Now you might see a small Head set upon a pair of broad Shoulders; a Nose too long, too short, too

thick, too small, or awry on the Face; A large heavy Carcass reard
65 upon a small pair of Spindle Shanks, by which means they became
bandy; a long Chin to a short Face; One Arm longer than the other;
Eyes too big for their Sockets; Mouths three times too wide, or too
narrow; every Part and Limb almost chosen and put together at
random. But to conclude the Farce, when they came to the Passion-
70 work, instead of blending, and tempering them in true Proportion,
they took them from the worst of *Animals* simply, and by guess. To one
was given the Rage and Fury of a *Wolf*. Hence came a most Virulent,
Persecuting, Malicious Villain; from whom has descended those
boistrous and outragious Pests of Society, who are every Day
75 disturbing our Peace; the only blessing we can enjoy upon Earth. To
another the Poison and Rancour of a *Toad*, from whom sprang the
revengeful, who upon the least touch of Offence, are ever upon the
watch, to ruin the inadvertent. To another the Subtilty and Cunning of
a *Fox*, from whom we trace the *Politician*, who turns all the motions of
80 his Soul to *Seducing, Betraying, Surprizing, Fair-Promises with foul
Intentions, perpetual Stratagems to his own advantage, under the Specious
appearance of the publick Good.*

To another the Alertness of a Monkey. He begat a large family of
Jibers, Buffoons, and Mimicks; these are a numerous breed and
85 dispersed over the Face of the whole Earth. The chief business of their
Lives is to make People laugh at one another, and not to spare even
their nearest Friends; who while they are Copying the imperfections
of others, bring themselves to be *Originals.* You may distinguish this
happy Race by their Hawk-noses, One Eye less than t'other, and a
90 perpetual Sneer, which by repeated Habit, becomes inseparable from
their Faces. To another the Pride of a *Peacock*. He turns *Beau*, stiches
all the Tinsel about him, that he can; hangs a Tayl to his Head, and so
Walks through the World. To another the Gluttony, Laziness and
Luxury of a *Hog*. From him are descended your pamper'd Citizens,
95 and others, whose chief exercise consists in Eating and Drinking:
They are very easily distinguished by the Plumpness and Rotundity
of their *Dewlap*, the *Torosity* of their *Necks* and *Breasts*, and the
prominence of their *Abdomen.* Numberless are the Instances might be
given of the predominance of Brutes, thus occasioned in Men, but that
100 I hasten to give a Summary Account of the *Animals*, chiefly chosen by
these Journey-men, to give proper accomplishments to the other Sex,
viz. *Cats, Ferets, Weazels, Vipers, Magpies, Geese, Wagtails, Rats, Stoats,
Ratle-Sneaks, Wasps, Hornets*, and some few others. It is needless to

inform the Reader, what Qualities were infused from these, when he can behold them so plainly in one half or more of his Female 105 Acquaintance. And I dare venture to say, that you can hardly go into a Family, where you may not distinguish some one Lady eminently remarkable for a lively resemblance to one, or more of the aforesaid *Animals*. Upon the whole, I shall make this Remark, that the Handy-work of *Prometheus*, and their Progeny, are to be distinguished with the 110 greatest ease, from that of his Journey-men; his being all *Humane*, *Benevolent*, *Easy*, *Affable*, *Good-humoured*, *Charitable* and *Friendly*; whereas those of his Journey-men are *Cruel*, *Malicious*, *Turbulent*, *Morose*, *Ill-natured*, *Snarling*, *Quarrelsome*, *Pragmatical*, *Covetous*, and *Inhuman*, which we dayly experience among the *great Vulgar* and *the* 115 *Small*, nor can all the Power of Art, or Education, intirely Wash away the Dirt of the Journey-man's Palm, or quite Abolish, or restrain that Exuberance of wrong Passions which are owing to the cause already assigned. And I will say farther, that I know nothing else in Nature, but what may by *Cultivation*, or *Chymistry* change it's Nature, such 120 Persons only excepted, who have had a wrong Impression at first, and *Human Excrements*; But this being of too foul a Nature, to bear a Dissertation in *prose*, I shall Transcribe it, as it was Cooked up in *verse*, for the Taste of the Polite, being a very fit Emblem, to explain this Great, and useful Maxim, *That there is no method, as yet found out, to* 125 *change Natural Inclination.*

THE TALE
OF THE T—D.

A *Pastry-Cook* once molded up a T——
(You may beleive me when I give my Word)
With nice Ingredients of the fragrant kind,
And *Sugar* of the best, right Doubl' refin'd,
He blends them all; for he was fully bent 5
Quite to annihilate it's Taste, and Scent.
With Out-stretcht Arms, he twirls the Rolling-Pin,
And spreads the yielding *Ordure* smooth and Thin.
'Twas not to save his Flow'r, but shew his Art,
Of such foul *Dough* to make a sav'ry *Tart*. 10
He heats his Ov'n with care, and bak'd it well,
But still the Crust's offensive to the Smell;

The *Cook* was vext to see himself so foil'd,
So Works it to a *Dumpling*, which he boyl'd;
Now out it comes, and if it stunk before,   15
It stinks full twenty times as much, and more.
He breaks fresh *Eggs*, converts it into *Batter*,
Works them with *Spoon* about a Wooden-Platter,
To true consistence, such as *Cook-maids* make
At *Shrovetide*, when they toss the *pliant Cake*.   20
In vain he twirls the *Pan*, the more it fries,
The more the Nauseous, fetid Vapours rise.
Resolv'd to make it still a sav'ry bit,
He takes the *Pan-Cake*, rolls it round a *Spit*,
Winds up the *Jack*, and sets it to the fire,   25
But roasting rais'd it's pois'nous fumes the high'r.
Offended much (although it was his own,)
At length he throws it, where it shou'd be thrown,
And in a Passion, storming loud, he cry'd,
If neither bak'd, nor boyl'd, nor roast, nor fry'd,   30
Can thy offensive Hellish Taint reclaim,
Go to the filthy Jakes from whence you came.

THE
MORAL.

THIS *Tale* requires but one short Application,
It fits all Upstart Scoundrels in each *Nation*,
Minions of Fortune, Wise Men's jest in Pow'r,   35
Like Weeds on *Dunghils* Stinking, Rank, and Sour.

MOTTO. Horace, *Epistles*, I. x. 24: 'You may drive out Nature with a pitchfork, yet she will ever hurry back' (Loeb). A saying well known from Erasmus's *Adagia*; Swift quotes it as a cliché in 'A Tritical Essay' (*Prose*, i. 248).

INTRODUCTION

  1. *an old Heathen Story*: Well known from Apollodorus, i. 7, and other sources.
 30. *a Ferula*: Fire is best kept alight in a ferula, according to Pliny, *Natural History*, xiii. 126.
 37. *Lord-Mayor's Feast*: An annual event, proverbially gluttonous.
 92. *a Tayl to his Head*: The 'snake'; see notes to no. 8 and introductory note to no. 10.
 97. *Torosity*: 'Fatness, grossness', according to N. Bailey, *The Universal Etymological English Dictionary*, vol. 'ii' (London: Cox, 1727).
114. *Pragmatical*: 'Officious, meddlesome, interfering, obtrusive' (*OED*).

POEM

20. *At Shrovetide, when they toss the pliant Cake*: Various Shrove Tuesday contests involved tossing the traditional pancakes; see Christina Hole, *English Traditional Customs* (London, 1975), 29–30.

No. 15: Swift, with Sheridan's Introduction

probably 5–9 November 1728

Swift's *A Short View of the State of Ireland*, 'a particular Description of our present misery', is the most important single background source for the *Intelligencer* (*Prose*, xii. 66). It was published 19 March 1727/8, and Sheridan reprinted it in *Intelligencer* 15, Swift said, 'merely for laziness not to disappoint the town' (*Corresp.* iv. 30). Perhaps so, but it was an apt choice, illuminating no. 6, already published, and nos. 16–19 to come. *A Short View* refutes the contention that Ireland was a flourishing kingdom. In so doing, it summarizes Swift's political analysis of Ireland's economic plight, since 1726 exacerbated by crop failures and famine. This analysis rests firmly on the familiar principles of mercantile economics (minimize imports, maximize exports, export manufactured rather than raw goods). The analysis had been adumbrated in his pamphlets of 1720, in the Drapier's Letters of 1724–5 (particularly the then unpublished 'Humble Address to Both Houses of Parliament'), and in his letter to Lord Peterborough, 28 April 1726 (*Corresp.* iii. 131–5)—a letter Swift had hoped Peterborough would pass on to Walpole.

In *Jonathan Swift and Ireland* (146, 189–90), Oliver W. Ferguson has argued that *A Short View* appeared as an immediate response to *Seasonable Remarks on Trade* (Dublin: Powell, 1728), a pamphlet by the Drapier's former enemy John Browne of the Neale, perhaps erroneously referred to as Sir John Browne. *Seasonable Remarks*, probably published in March 1727/8, exaggerated Ireland's wealth and maintained that 'the People are incumbred with very few Taxes' (37). Speaking as an Englishman to the English, Browne argued that Britain would benefit from keeping Ireland wealthy: '*Ireland* is to *England* . . . a milch Cow, if we let it run into good Pasture it will overflow our Pails' (53). However, Bryan Coleborne's study of Browne and contemporary Dublin writers points out that Ferguson's evidence is not conclusive: Swift may, but need not, have had the *Seasonable Remarks* in mind. He may indeed have written *A Short View* before seeing *Seasonable Remarks*, to which he makes no explicit reference ('Jonathan Swift and the Dunces of Dublin', Ph.D. thesis (National Univ. Ireland, 1982), 111–18). Moreover, Archbishop King seems for several years to have been opposing the view that Ireland was flourishing (Appendix A). That is, in embracing that view, Browne was not alone. Though Browne's pamphlet *may* have been his immediate impetus, Swift seems to have been responding to what he considered a common error.

Particularly on the question of whether Ireland was a flourishing kingdom, *A Short View* provoked further discussion, much of which was in the background by the time Sheridan reprinted the pamphlet as *Intelligencer* 15. One pamphlet, *To the R——d Dr. J——n S——t. The Memorial of the Poor Inhabitants, Tradesmen, and Labourers of the Kingdom of Ireland* (Dublin: Walsh, [1728]), stated, 'It may be considered how strange and suprizing it would be in foreign Parts to hear that the Poor was Starving in a rich Country, where such immence Sums were daily laid out' (*Prose*, xii. 305). This was probably not by Browne, though Swift may have thought it was (Coleborne, 344–6). Swift hit back in *An Answer to a Paper, Called A Memorial*, dated 25 March 1728: 'Are you in earnest? Is *Ireland* the *rich Country* you mean? Or are you insulting our *Poverty*? Were you ever out of *Ireland*? Or were you ever in it till of late?' (*Prose*, xii. 21). There was a rejoinder, apparently by the author of the original *Memorial.* This was *To the R——d D—n S—t. A Reply, to The Answer Given to the Memorial of the Poor Inhabitants, Tradesmen, and Labourers, of the Kingdom of Ireland* (Dublin: Walsh, 1728; copy: Bodleian):

> The Author of the Memorial is convinced, Ireland is not a Rich Country in Comparison of other Countrys; but Veiwing the Quays almost cover'd wi[t]h Hogsheads of Wine, the Number of Coaches, the fine Apparrell and Sumptuous Equipages on State Days, and Observing the dearness of Lands, and great Sums laid out about Elections, he thought the Country was very Rich, for he had not then Read the Short View of the State of IRELAND; however, he did [?not] Vindicate the Tartarian Custom, of over running the Fertil Arable Fields, with Flocks of Cattle, nor the Oppression of the People with Rack Rents, or short Leases, by Country Squires; he likes a little Mutton, and wonders why it is so dear when none is exported. He is sorry to observe a decay already in the Revenue, and fears his Majesty's Army may, too soon, become fellow Sufferers with others. (6–7)

An anti-Browne pamphlet sometimes attributed to Swift is *Considerations on Two Papers Lately Published. The First, Called, Seasonable Remarks, &c. And the Other, An Essay on Trade in General, and on That of Ireland, in Particular* (Dublin, 1728). *Considerations on Two Papers* makes plain the fundamental objection to claims that Ireland flourishes: 'If what my Author says, of the Encrease of the Wealth of *Ireland*, were true . . ., does it not follow, that our Taxes ought to be proportionably encreased? which, I hope, is not the Conclusion [he] aims at' (6–7).

Swift's reference in *A Short View* to 'L[ord] C[hief] J[ustice] *W[hitshed]*'s Ghost' evoked a wittily sympathetic half-sheet reply, *W—tt's Ghost Appears to the R——d D—n S—t* ([Dublin, 1728]; copy: TCD). Others, however, objected to Swift's attack on the recently deceased judge, leading to Swift's quotable retort in *An Answer to a Paper, Called A Memorial*: 'Such Creatures are not to be reformed; neither is it Prudence, or Safety to attempt a Reformation. Yet, although their Memories will *rot*, there may be some Benefit for their Survivers, to smell it while it is *rotting*' (*Prose*, xii. 25). Browne wrote other pamphlets, including *A Letter to the Author of the Short View* (Dublin: Powell, 1728); and such pamphlets by Thomas Prior, Arthur Dobbs, and others are part of a rich lode of controversial writing on Irish economics in the late 1720s.

The pamphleteers frequently debated the shortage of gold and silver coins. It was not a new problem when Swift brought it up in *A Short View*. In 1725 he had mentioned it in his 'Humble Address to Both Houses of Parliament' (*Drapier's Letters*, 152; and compare 9); in 1725 he had written *A Simile, on Our Want of Silver* (*Poems*, i. 353–4). In his *Scheme of the Money-Matters of Ireland* (Dublin: Powell, 1729), John Browne estimated that there was £500,000 in gold coin circulating in Ireland, compared with £10,000 of silver and £4,000 of copper (17). Thomas Prior supposed a total of £400,000 cash in circulation, £40,000 of it silver (*Observations on Coin in General* (Dublin: Rhames, 1729), 44).

Bankers and others profited from exporting silver and, to a lesser extent, gold coin. Ireland had no silver and gold coins of its own, though it had a notional system of pounds, shillings, and pence. The English shilling was worth 1*s.* 1*d.* Irish, which complicates the explanation slightly. In Ireland the value of gold relative to silver differed from the ratio established in England. The guinea was worth 21*s.* in England, but its value in Ireland was 21*s.* 3*d.* English (or 23*s.* Irish). There was thus a profit of threepence for every guinea brought to Ireland from England and exchanged for shillings. Over the years the silver circulating in Ireland was depleted, as Archbishop King explained to Lord King, the English Lord Chancellor:

> As to Coin we have hardly any Silver left, for the proportion between Gold and Silver being wrong stated and the advantage given to the former, it is worth the Banquers while to carry away the Silver and Exchange it for Gold. (6 Dec. 1726, TCD MS 750/8, fo. 163.)

A further complication was that the various pieces of foreign gold did not each bear the same proportional value to silver, and that both silver and gold were gradually being drained from Ireland because it was more profitable to deal in cash than in credit. Silver, being undervalued, went first, followed by the less-overvalued gold coins such as the guinea and the louis d'or, leaving Ireland's circulating cash with a preponderance of the more overvalued gold coins such as the moidore. But—as the archbishop wrote to Samuel Molyneux—even the moidore could be profitably shipped to England:

> The species in which there is the greatest loss, when Transported is that of Moydores, they pass here for 30 Shillings and 27 in England as I am inform'd, if so there is £15 loss in an 100 Moydores, that is Ten percent: But if a man take a bill of Exchange he pays 13 or 14 and some times 15 percent: therefore by carrying Moydores he saves 3, 4, or 5 percent: it is easy to see what must be the consequence of this, that Gent. going into England will carry even Moydores rather than Bills of Exchange, there is less loss in Guineys & Louidore and therefore we have hardly any left. (30 May 1727, TCD MS 750/8, fos. 200–1; abbreviations expanded.)

See [Thomas Prior], in *Observations on Coin in General* (Dublin: Rhames, 1729); and Boulter, i. 91, 201–2, 204–6.

For further commentary on *A Short View* see Swift, *An Answer to a Paper, Called A Memorial*, in *Prose*, xii. 17–25; Henry Craik (ed.), *Swift: Selections*, ii (Oxford, 1893), 438–40; Louis A. Landa, 'Swift's Economic Views and Mercantilism', *ELH* 10 (1943), 310–35; Ferguson, chs. 1 and 5; Cullen, *Econ. Hist.* chs. 1–4; and Ehrenpreis, iii. 572–4. On Browne, one of the villains in the Wood's halfpence controversy, see Coleborne's thesis and also his essay in *Swift Studies*, 2 (1987), 15–24.

Swift returned to many of *A Short View*'s topics in various papers written in 1729 though published only posthumously: 'A Letter Concerning the Weavers', 'Answer to Several Letters from Unknown Persons', 'An Answer to Several Letters Sent Me from Unknown Hands', 'A Letter on Maculla's Project about Halfpence', 'A Proposal that All the Ladies and Women of Ireland Should Appear Constantly in Irish Manufactures', and 'Maxims Controlled in Ireland' (*Prose*, xii). He had more to say about the cash shortage in *Intelligencer* 19. The argument against absentees in *A Short View* and 'A Letter to Lord Chancellor Middleton' seems directly to have influenced Thomas Prior's famous *List of the Absentees of Ireland* (Dublin: Gunne, 1729).

NUMB. XV.

Lamentations, Chap. 2. v. 19.

Arise, cry out in the Night: in the beginning of the Watches, pour out thine Heart like Water, before the Face of the Lord: lift up thy Hands towards him, for the Life of thy Young Children that faint for Hungar, in the Top of every Street.

I Do remember to have Read an Account, that an Ode which *Pindar* Writ, in honour to the Island *Delos*, was Inscribed in the Temple of *Minerva*, at *Athens*, in large Letters of Gold; A publick and very laudable acknowledgment for the Poet's Ingenuity, and for no more than a bare Compliment! Such was the encouragement given 5 by the great, and publick Spirited *Athenians*. Had the same Poet, inspired by a Noble and Heroick Ardor, by another Ode, awakened and rouzed their whole State against an invading Enemy; or opened their Eyes against any Secret and Wicked Contrivers of their Destruction, they would have erected him a Statue at least. But Alass 10 that Spirit is fled from the World! and, long since neglected. Virtue is become her own Pay-master. My *Country-men*, I hope, will forgive me, if I complain there has been so little Notice taken of a small, but most

excellent *Pamphlet*, Written by the DRAPIER. It is Intitled, *A SHORT*
15 *VIEW OF THE STATE OF IRELAND.* There never was any Treatise
yet published, with a Zeal more generous for the Universal good of
a Nation, or a design more seasonable, considering our present
lamentable Condition, yet we listen not to the Voice of the Charmer.
Whereas it should have been Inscribed in Capital Letters (as Glorious
20 as those of the Poet) in the most publick part of every *Corporation-*
town, through this whole *Kingdom*, that People might behold the
several unprovoked causes of their Poverty, our Offences towards
Heaven excepted. Nay, I will proceed farther, and say, that every
Head of every Family, ought to instruct the Children so far in this
25 most *incomparable Pamphlet*, that they should not only understand, but
be able, to repeat by Heart every single *Paragraph*, through the Whole.
This was the Method laid down by the wisest Law-giver, that ever the
World produced; To gain the Hearts of the People, by working upon
their Memories.
30 Deut. chap. 6. v. 7. *And thou shalt Teach them diligently unto thy*
Children, and shalt talk of them, when thou sittest in thine House, and when thou
walkest by the Way, and when thou liest down, and when thou risest up.
    8. *And thou shalt bind them for a Sign upon thine Hand, and they shall be as*
frontlets between thine Eyes.
35 9. *And thou shalt Write them upon the Posts of thy House, and on thy Gates.*
    And, where would be the great Trouble, since we have little else to
do, if every Man would read a Lecture of the *Short View* every Day in
his Family, after Reading Prayers? Nor do I think the expence would
be extravagant, if he should have every Page of it Re-printed, to be
40 hung up in Frames, in every Chamber of his House. That it might be
as evident, as, the *Hand Writing on the Wall.*
    And, since I have ventured thus far, to praise and recommend this
most inimitable Piece, let me Speak a few Words in favour of it's
AUTHOR.
45 I would propose to *My Country-men*, before all their MONY goes
off, (it is going as fast as possible) to convert it into a few Statues to the
DRAPIER, in those Memorable parts of this Kingdom, where our
Heroes have shone with the greatest Lustre, in Defence of our *Liberty*,
and the PROTESTANT RELIGION over all *Europe.* At *DERRY*, at
50 *ENNISKILLEN*, at *BOYN*, at *AUGHRIM.* Nor would it be amiss, to
set up a few more about our *Metropolis*, with that Glorious Inscription
Libertas et Natale Solum.
    If our MONY were metamorphosed upon such a good occasion, as

this, it would not be in the Power of any * *Cypselus*, to get it into his own Coffers, and it would be the only method, to prevent it's being 55 carry'd off, except our *Vice-roys* should Act like the *Roman Prefects*, and Run away with our very Statues.

Courteous READER, Mark well what follows.

I Am assured that it hath for some time been practised as a method of making Men's Court, when they are asked about the Rate of 60 Lands, the Abilities of Tenants, the State of Trade and Manufacture in this Kingdom, and how their Rents are payed; to Answer, That in their Neighbourhood all things are in a flourishing Condition, the Rent and Purchase of Land every Day encreasing. And if a Gentleman happens to be a little more sincere in his Representations, besides 65 being looked on as not well affected, he is sure to have a Dozen Contradictors at his Elbow. I think it is no manner of Secret why these Questions are so cordially asked, or so obligingly Answered.

But since with Regard to the Affairs of this Kingdom, I have been using all Endeavours to subdue my Indignation, to which indeed I am 70 not provoked by any Personal Interest, being not the Owner of one Spot of Ground in the whole *Island*, I shall only enumerate by Rules generally known, and never Contradicted, what are the true Causes of any Countries flourishing and growing Rich, and then examine what Effects arise from those Causes in the Kingdom of *Ireland*. 75

The first Cause of a Kingdom's thriving is the Fruitfulness of the Soyl, to produce the Necessaries and Conveniencies of Life, not only sufficient for the Inhabitants, but for Exportation into other Countries.

The Second, is the Industry of the People in Working up all their 80 Native Commodities to the last degree of Manufacture.

The Third, is the Conveniency of safe Ports and Havens, to Carry out their own Goods, as much manufactured, and bring in those of others, as little manufactured, as the Nature of mutual Commerce will allow. 85

The Fourth, is, That the Natives should as much as possible, Export and Import their Goods in Vessels of their own Timber, made in their own Country.

The Fifth, is the Liberty of a free Trade in all Foreign Countries

---

* Cypselus, *A Governor of* Corinth, *who Contrived a Tax, which brought all the Mony of that State to himself in ten Years Time.* vid. Aristot. polit.

90 which will permit them, except to those who are in War with their own Prince or State.

The Sixth, is, by being Governed only by Laws made with their own Consent, for otherwise they are not a free People. And therefore all Appeals for Justice, or Applications for Favour or Preferment to
95 another Country, are so many grievous Impoverishments.

The Seventh, is, by Improvement of Land, encouragement of Agriculture, and thereby encreasing the Number of their People, without which any Country, however Blessed by Nature, must continue Poor.

100 The Eighth, is the Residence of the Prince, or Chief Administrator of the Civil Power.

The Ninth, is the Concourse of Foreigners for Education, Curiosity or Pleasure, or as to a general Mart of Trade.

The Tenth, is by disposing all Offices of Honour, Profit or Trust,
105 only to the Natives, or at least with very few Exceptions, where Strangers have long Inhabited the Country, and are supposed to Understand, and regard the Interest of it as their own.

The Eleventh is, when the Rents of Lands, and Profits of Employments, are spent in the Country which produced them, and
110 not in another, the former of which will certainly happen, where the Love of our Native Country prevails.

The Twelfth, is by the publick Revenues being all Spent and Employed at Home, except on the Occasions of a Foreign War.

The Thirteenth, is, where the People are not obliged, unless they
115 find it for their own Interest, or Conveniency, to receive any Monies, except of their own Coynage by a publick Mint, after the manner of all Civilized Nations.

The Fourteenth, is a Disposition of the People of a Country to wear their own Manufactures, and Import as few Incitements to Luxury,
120 either in Cloaths, Furniture, Food or Drink, as they possibly can live conveniently without.

There are many other Causes of a Nation's thriving, which I cannot at present recollect; but without Advantage from at least some of these, after turning my Thoughts a long time, I am not able to discover
125 from whence our Wealth proceeds, and therefore would gladly be better informed. In the mean time, I will here examine what share falls to *Ireland* of these Causes, or of the Effects and Consequences.

It is not my Intention to complain, but barely to relate Facts, and the matter is not of small Importance. For it is allowed, that a Man who

lives in a Solitary House far from help, is not Wise in endeavouring to 130
acquire in the Neighbourhood, the Reputation of being Rich, because
those who come for Gold, will go off with Pewter and Brass, rather
than return empty; and in the common Practice of the World, those
who possess most Wealth, make the least Parade, which they leave to
others, who have nothing else to bear them out, in shewing their Faces 135
on the *Exchange*.

As to the first Cause of a Nation's Riches, being the Fertility of the
Soyl, as well as Temperature of Clymate, we have no Reason to
complain; for although the Quantity of unprofitable Land in this
Kingdom, reckoning Bog, and Rock, and barren Mountain, be double 140
in Proportion to what it is in *England*, yet the Native Productions
which both Kingdoms deal in, are very near on equality in point of
Goodness, and might with the same Encouragement be as well
manufactured. I except Mines and Minerals, in some of which
however we are only defective in point of Skill and Industry. 145

In the Second, which is the Industry of the People, our misfortune
is not altogether owing to our own Fault, but to a million of
Discouragements.

The conveniency of Ports and Havens which Nature bestowed us so
liberally is of no more use to us, than a beautiful Prospect to a Man 150
shut up in a Dungeon.

As to Shipping of it's own, this Kingdom is so utterly unprovided,
that of all the excellent Timber cut down within these fifty or sixty
Years, it can hardly be said that the Nation hath received the Benefit
of one valuable House to dwell in, or one Ship to Trade with. 155

Ireland is the only Kingdom I ever heard or read of, either in ancient
or modern Story, which was denied the Liberty of exporting their
native Commodities and Manufactures wherever they pleased, except
to Countries at War with their own Prince or State, yet this by the
Superiority of meer Power is refused us in the most momentous parts 160
of Commerce, besides an Act of Navigation to which we never
consented, pinned down upon us, and rigorously executed, and a
thousand other unexampled Circumstances as grievous as they are
invidious to mention. To go unto the Rest.

It is too well known that we are forced to obey some Laws we never 165
consented to, which is a Condition I must not call by it's true
uncontroverted Name, for fear of my L— C— J— W—'s Ghost with
his *LIBERTAS ET NATALE SOLUM*, written as a Motto on his
Coach, as it stood at the Door of the Court, while he was Perjuring

170 himself to betray both. Thus, we are in the Condition of Patients who
have Physick sent them by Doctors at a Distance, Strangers to their
Constitution, and the nature of their Disease: And thus, we are forced
to pay five hundred *per Cent* to decide our Properties, in all which we
have likewise the Honour to be distinguished from the whole Race of
175 Mankind.

As to improvement of Land, those few who attempt that or Planting,
through Covetousness or want of Skill, generally leave things worse
than they were, neither succeeding in Trees nor Hedges, and by
running into the fancy of Grazing after the manner of the *Scythians*, are
180 every Day depopulating the Country.

We are so far from having a King to reside among us, that even the
Viceroy is generally absent four Fifths of his time in the Government.

No Strangers from other Countries make this a part of their
Travels, where they can expect to see nothing but Scenes of Misery
185 and Desolation.

Those who have the Misfortune to be born here, have the least Title
to any considerable Employment, to which they are seldom preferred,
but upon a Political Consideration.

One third part of the Rents of *Ireland* is spent in *England*, which
190 with the Profit of Employments, Pensions, Appeals, Journeys of
Pleasure or Health, Education at the *Inns* of Court, and both
Universities, Remittances at Pleasure, the Pay of all Superior Officers
in the Army and other Incidents, will amount to a full half of the
Income of the whole Kingdom, all clear profit to *England.*

195 We are denyed the Liberty of Coining Gold, Silver, or even Copper.
In the Isle of *Man*, they Coin their own Silver; every petty Prince,
Vassal to the *Emperor* can Coin what Money he pleaseth. And in this
as in most of the Articles already mentioned, we are an exception to all
other States or Monarchies that were ever known in the World.

200 As to the last, or Fourteenth Article, we take special Care to Act
diametrically contrary to it in the whole Course of our Lives. Both
Sexes, but especially the Women despise and abhor to wear any of
their own Manufactures, even those which are better made than in
other Countries, particularly a sort of Silk Plad, through which the
205 Workmen are forced to run a sort of Gold-thread that it may pass for
Indian. Even Ale and Potatoes in great quantity are imported from
England as well as Corn, and our foreign Trade is little more than
Importation of *French* Wine, for which I am told we pay ready Money.

Now if all this be true, upon which I could easily enlarge, I would

be glad to know by what secret method it is that we grow a Rich 210
and Flourishing People, without Liberty, Trade, Manufactures,
Inhabitants, Money, or the privilege of Coining; without Industry,
Labour or Improvement of Lands, and with more than half of the Rent
and Profits of the whole *Kingdom*, Annually exported, for which we
receive not a single Farthing: And to make up all this, nothing worth 215
mentioning, except the Linnen of the *North*, a Trade casual, corrupted
and at Mercy, and some Butter from *Cork*. If we do flourish, it must
be against every Law of Nature and Reason, like the Thorn at
Glassenbury, that blossoms in the midst of Winter.

Let the worthy *C———rs* who come from *England* ride round the 220
Kingdom, and observe the face of Nature, or the faces of the Natives,
the Improvement of the Land, the thriving numerous Plantations, the
noble Woods, the abundance and vicinity of Country-Seats, the
commodious Farmers-Houses and Barns, the Towns and Villages,
where every body is busy and thriving with all kind of Manufactures, 225
the Shops full of Goods wrought to Perfection, and filled with
Customers, the comfortable Dyet and Dress, and Dwellings of the
People, the vast Numbers of Ships in our Harbours and Docks, and
Shipwrights in our Seaport-Towns, the Roads crouded with Carryers
laden with rich Manufactures, the perpetual Concourse to and fro of 230
pompous Equipages.

With what Envy and Admiration would these Gentlemen return
from so delightful a Progress? What glorious Reports would they make
when they went back to *England*?

But my Heart is too heavy to continue this Irony longer, for it is 235
manifest that whatever Stranger took such a Journey, would be apt to
think himself travelling in *Lapland* or *Ysland*, rather than in a Country
so favoured by Nature as Ours, both in Fruitfulness of Soyl, and
Temperature of Climate. The miserable Dress, and Dyet, and
Dwelling of the People. The general Desolation in most parts of the 240
Kingdom. The old Seats of the Nobility and Gentry all in Ruins, and
no new Ones in their stead. The Families of Farmers who pay great
Rents, living in Filth and Nastiness upon Butter-milk and Potatoes,
without a Shoe or Stocking to their Feet, or a House so convenient as
an *English* Hog-sty to receive them. These indeed may be comfortable 245
sights to an *English* Spectator, who comes for a short time only *to learn
the Language*, and returns back to his own Country, whither he finds all
our Wealth transmitted.

Nostrâ miseriâ magnus es.

250 There is not one Argument used to prove the Riches of *Ireland*, which is not a logical Demonstration of it's Poverty. The Rise of our Rents is squeesed out of the very Blood and Vitals, and Cloaths, and Dwellings of the Tenants, who live worse than *English* Beggars. The lowness of Interest, in all other Countries a sign of Wealth, is in us a 255 proof of misery, there being no Trade to employ any Borrower. Hence alone comes the Dearness of Land, since the Savers have no other way to lay out their Money. Hence the Dearness of Necessaries for Life, because the Tenants cannot afford to pay such extravagant Rates for Land (which they must take, or go a begging) without raising the Price 260 of Cattle, and of Corn, although themselves should live upon Chaff. Hence our encrease of Buildings in this City, because Workmen have nothing to do but employ one another, and one half of them are infallibly undone. Hence the daily encrease of *Bankers*, who may be a necessary Evil in a Trading-Country, but so ruinous in Ours, who for 265 their private Advantage have sent away all our Silver, and one third of our Gold; so that within three Years past, the running Cash of the Nation, which was about Five hundred thousand Pounds, is now less than two, and must daily diminish unless we have Liberty to Coin, as well as that important Kingdom the Isle of *Man*, and the meanest 270 Prince in the *German Empire*, as I before observed.

I have sometimes thought, that this Paradox of the Kingdom growing Rich, is chiefly owing to those worthy Gentlemen the BANKERS, who, except some Custom-house Officers, Birds of Passage, oppressive thrifty 'Squires, and a few others that shall be 275 Nameless, are the only thriving People among us: And I have often wished that a Law were enacted to hang up half a Dozen *Bankers* every Year, and thereby interpose at least some short Delay, to the further Ruin of *Ireland*.

Ye are idle, ye are idle, answered *Pharoah* to the *Israelites*, when they 280 complained to his MAJESTY, that they were forced to make Bricks without Straw.

England enjoys every one of these Advantages for enriching a Nation, which I have above enumerated, and into the Bargain, a good Million returned to them every Year without Labour or Hazard, or 285 one Farthing value received on our side. But how long we shall be able to continue the payment, I am not under the least Concern. One thing I know, that *when the Hen is starved to Death, there will be no more Golden Eggs.*

I think it a little unhospitable, and others may call it a subtil piece of

Malice, that, because there may be a Dozen Families in this Town 290
able to entertain their *English* Friends in a generous manner at their
Tables, their Guests upon their Return to *England*, shall report that
we wallow in Riches and Luxury.

Yet I confess I have known an Hospital, where all the Household-
Officers grew Rich, while the Poor for whose sake it was built, were 295
almost starving for want of Food and Raiment.

To Conclude. If *Ireland* be a rich and flourishing Kingdom, it's
Wealth and Prosperity must be owing to certain Causes, that are yet
concealed from the whole Race of Mankind, and the Effects are
equally Invisible. We need not wonder at Strangers when they deliver 300
such Paradoxes, but a Native and Inhabitant of this Kingdom, who
gives the same Verdict, must be either ignorant to Stupidity, or a Man-
pleaser at the Expence of all Honour, Conscience and Truth.

1. *I do remember*: It was the Rhodians of Lindus who inscribed Pindar's seventh Olym-
pian ode in golden letters in their temple of Athena (Minerva). Sheridan could have
read of the inscription in Sudorius's Pindar (Oxford: Sheldonian Theatre, 1697),
which he owned (p. 88n.; Sheridan, *Library*, 468). Presumably he recalls Pindar's
famous fragmentary *prosodion* in honour of Delos and mistakenly associates it with
the Rhodian inscription. I have found no evidence that any of Pindar's odes was
inscribed in the Parthenon. Yet Sheridan was sufficiently fond of this golden
inscription (as he remembered it) to cite it again in his letter to J. Oughton, 26 Mar.
1737 (Osborn Collection MSS, Yale Univ. Library).

10. *they would have erected him a Statue*: Sheridan forgets Pausanias's testimony that the
Athenians did erect a statue of Pindar on the Acropolis (I. viii. 4).

12. *her own Pay-master*: Proverbially, virtue is its own reward (Tilley V81).

18. *Voice of the Charmer*: The ungodly are 'like the deaf adder, that stoppeth her ears;
Which refuseth to hear the voice of the charmer: charm he never so wisely' (Ps.
58: 3–5, Book of Common Prayer translation). Swift quotes the passage in the
Drapier's Letters, 28.

49–50. *Derry . . . Enniskillen . . . Boyn . . . Aughrim*: The Jacobite forces' seige of Derry, a
Protestant garrison, failed 31 July 1689 after three months; Enniskillen was the
headquarters of Protestant raiders whose important successes against the Jacobites
in 1689 included the Battle of Newtownbutler, 31 July; William defeated James at
the Battle of the Boyne, 1 July 1690; at Aughrim the Williamites resoundingly
defeated the Jacobites, 12 July 1691. See J. G. Simms, *Jacobite Ireland, 1685–91*
(London, 1969), 95–119, 136–57, 216–29.

52. *Libertas et Natale Solum*: 'Liberty and my native Country' (Faulkner's translation; see
also *Poems*, i. 347). The motto was in 1705 registered to the future Lord Chief Justice
of the King's Bench in Ireland, William Whitshed; see *Prose*, vol. x, pp. xxii–xxiii,
101; and *Poems*, i. 236; Sir Bernard Burke, *The General Armory of England, Scotland, Ireland and Wales* (London, 1884), 1106; and below. Sheridan's willingness to claim the
motto for Swift himself may give special point to Swift's lines in *Whitshed's Motto on
His Coach*: '*Libertas & Natale Solum*; | Fine words; I wonder where you stole 'um'
(*Poems*, i. 348). Yet 'as a motto is not as a general rule an integral part of a Grant of
Arms, it can be adopted or changed at will'; and Swift's own motto is said to have

been 'Cum magnis vixisse'—'To have lived with the great' (R. Pinches, *Elvin's Handbook of Mottos Revised* (London, 1971), preface and pp. 36, 109).

54. *Cypselus*: Aristotle's *Politics* (1313ᵇ), after referring to Cypselus, refers to such taxation, but in Syracuse.

56. *Roman Prefects*: When Rome sacked Corinth in 149 BC, the consul Mummius and others destroyed pictures and carried off statues (Pausanias, VII. xvi. 8; Livy, liii; Velleius Paterculus, I. xiii. 4; Florus, *Epitome*, I. xxxii. 6). The Romans had also taken statues at the capture of Syracuse in 212 BC (Livy, xxv. 40).

63. *all things are in a flourishing Condition*: That Ireland was being exploited by such claims had earlier been asserted by Archbishop King in a seemingly influential unpublished essay (Appendix A). Most recently Swift seems to have believed that John Browne, who had given offence in the Wood's halfpence controversy, was guilty of this exploitation in his *Seasonable Remarks on Trade*, to which *A Short View* was possibly, among other things, a reply; see introductory note.

71. *any Personal Interest*: A disingenuous remark if spoken by Swift *in propria persona*. His ecclesiastical income was tied to Irish land (*Account Books*, pp. xcv–ci); and in *To the R—d D—n S—t. A Reply, to the Answer Given to the Memorial of the Poor Inhabitants, Tradesmen, and Labourers, of the Kingdom of Ireland* (Dublin: Walsh, 1728), it is claimed that 'most of the Reverend Clergy' find that 'the Value of their Country Tiths, encrease very much by the dearness of the Corn' (p. 7). In 1726 Archbishop King had claimed the reverse (TCD MS 750/8, fo. 153).

93. *not a free People*: A doctrine deriving from the second of Locke's *Two Treatises of Government*, ch. 4, 'Of Slavery'; and Molyneux, 116.

96–7. *encouragement of Agriculture*: On the idea that tillage fosters populousness, see Clayton D. Lein, 'Jonathan Swift and the Population of Ireland', *Eighteenth-Cent. Stud.* 8 (1975), 445–6.

138. *Temperature*: Temperateness. Swift 'loved Irelᵈ & often spoke with pleasure of its excellent Soil, fine Climate[,] Harbours & many other natural Advantages', according to John Lyon, who cared for him in his old age. Lyon's annotated copy of John Hawkesworth, *The Life of the Revd. Jonathan Swift, D.D.* (Dublin: Cotter, 1755), preliminary leaves; this is Forster MS 579.

157. *denyed the Liberty of exporting*: The Cattle Act of 1666 (18 Chas. II, c. 2; confirmed in 32 Chas. II, c. 2, 1680) prohibited Ireland from sending livestock into England. The Woollen Act of 1699 (10 & 11 Will. III, c. 10) effectively prohibited Ireland from exporting wool or woollen cloth. See [John Browne], *An Essay on Trade in General* (Dublin: Powell, 1728), 74–90. L. M. Cullen has argued that these and the navigation acts, though much resented, did little practical damage to the Irish economy (see his 'Problems in the Interpretation and Revision of Eighteenth-Century Irish Economic History', *Trans. Royal Hist. Soc.*, 5th ser., 17 (1967), 2–5; and his *Econ. Hist.* 36–42); for a contrary view, see Rosalind Mitchison, 'Ireland and Scotland: The Seventeenth-Century Legacies Compared', in *Ireland and Scotland 1600–1850*, ed. T. M. Devine and David Dickson (Edinburgh, 1983), 8–9.

161. *an Act of Navigation*: In 1696, William Molyneux argued influentially that the Navigation Act (1663), the Cattle Acts, and the Woollen Act did not 'Rightfully' bind Ireland, because they were passed 'without and against' Irish consent, that is, 'against Reason, and the Common Rights of all Mankind' (Molyneux, esp. 87–8, 116). 'The original Navigation Act treated Ireland on an equal footing with England. The act, however, was succeeded in 1663 by that of 15 Charles II c. 7, in which it was declared that no European articles, with few exceptions, could be imported into the colonies unless they had been loaded in English-built vessels at English ports. Nor could goods be brought from English colonies except to English ports. By the Acts 22 and 23 of Charles II. c. 26 the exclusion of Ireland was confirmed, and the Acts 7 and 8 of Will. III c. 22, passed in 1696, actually pro-

hibited any goods whatever from being imported to Ireland direct from the English colonies. These are the reasons for Swift's remark that Ireland's ports were of no more use to Ireland's people "than a beautiful prospect to a man shut up in a dungeon".' (Temple Scott, vii. 86; see also *Prose*, xii. 66.)

166–7. *true uncontroverted Name*: Slavery.

167. *my L[ord] C[hief] J[ustice] W[hitshed]'s Ghost*: William Whitshed, Chief Justice of the Common Pleas in Ireland, had died 26 Aug. 1727. In 1720, as Chief Justice of the King's Bench, he had presided over the trial of Edward Waters for printing Swift's *Proposal for the Universal Use of Irish Manufacture*; in the same capacity he failed to persuade the grand jury to indict John Harding for printing *Seasonable Advice* in 1724. Swift considered Whitshed an 'infamous Wretch' (*Prose*, x. 211), though others, notably Archbishop William King, viewed him with affectionate respect (King to Lord Lieutenant Carteret, 12 Sept. 1727, TCD MS 750/9, fos. 20–2). For a sketch of him, see Ferguson, 196–7; see also F. Elrington Ball, *The Judges in Ireland, 1221–1921* (London, 1926), ii. 80–1, 96–7, 99–100, 103–5, 116–18, 189–90. For subsequent controversy about this passage, see the introductory note.

168–9. *as a Motto on his Coach*: Swift recalls seeing Whitshed's coach outside the Court of King's Bench at Christ Church cathedral, Dublin, in 1720, during the trial of Edward Waters: 'I observed, and I shall never forget upon what Occasion, the Device upon his Coach to be *Libertas & natale Solum*; at the very Point of Time when he was sitting in his Court, and perjuring himself to betray both' (*Drapier's Letters*, 125). Swift explained the perjury in 'An Humble Address to Both Houses of Parliament': Whitshed 'on the Bench *invoking God for his Witness* . . . asserted, that the Author's Design was to bring in the *Pretender*' (1725; *Drapier's Letters*, 167). Swift similarly describes Waters's trial in his 'Letter to Mr. Pope' (1721; *Prose*, ix. 27) and in 'A Proposal that All the Ladies and Women of Ireland Should Appear Constantly in Irish Manufactures' (1729; *Prose*, xii. 121). From the fact that Swift's lampoon *Libertas et Natale Solum* (*Poems*, i. 347–9) is occasioned by Whitshed's supervision of the grand jury proceedings concerning Harding in 1724, Herbert Davis has concluded, erroneously I believe, that Swift's allusions to the motto elsewhere refer to Whitshed's dismissal of the grand jury 21 Nov. 1724; Davis even thinks, on this basis, that Swift may have been in Whitshed's court at the time (*Prose*, vol. x, p. xxii). Given Swift's clear association of the perjury charge with 1720, a more plausible supposition is that Swift took umbrage at the motto in 1720 and remembered it when lampooning Whitshed in 1724. The 1724 poem deals with current matters and does not mention perjury.

172–3. *forced to pay five hundred per Cent to decide our Properties*: Swift refers to the expense of carrying an appeal to London, 'a Mark of *Servitude* without Example' (*Drapier's Letters*, 156, 159). The Declaratory Act of 1719 (6 Geo. I, c. 5 British) had effectively established the British House of Lords as the court of last resort for Irish cases. Irish appeals had sometimes previously been carried to England, however (F. H. Newark, *Notes on Irish Legal History*, 2nd edn. (Belfast, 1960), 16–17).

176. *improvement*: '*Improvements* is yᵉ fashionable word for Plantations of Trees, even in Hedge-Rows.' Loveday, 59.

179. *Grazing after the manner of the Scythians*: Spenser's *View of the State of Ireland* (Dublin: Society of Stationers, 1633), 27, and various chronicles maintained that the Irish were descended from the barbaric Scythians, in part because both were nomadic herders (see Herodotus, iv. 19, 46). Sir William Petty denied the Scythian descent in *The Political Anatomy of Ireland* (1691): Petty, *Economic Writings*, ed. C. H. Hull (reprinted New York, 1964), i. 204. Nevertheless, Swift refers to the Scythian ancestry of the Irish in *An Answer to a Paper, Called A Memorial* (1728) and 'The Answer to the Craftsman' (1731) and elsewhere (*Prose*, xii. 19, 178). See Claude

Rawson's analysis of these Scythian references in 'A Reading of *A Modest Proposal*' (1978), reprinted in his *Order from Confusion Sprung* (London, 1985), 131–2, 142–3.

181–2. *the Viceroy is generally absent*: Lord Lieutenants were ordinarily resident only during the biennial session of Parliament. Among recent viceroys, Bolton was in Dublin 7 Aug. 1717–9 Jan. 1717/18 and 31 May–20 Nov. 1719; Grafton 28 Aug. 1721–24 Feb. 1721/2 and 13 Aug. 1723–9 May 1724; Carteret 22 Oct. 1724–2 Apr. 1726 and 19 Nov. 1727–15 May 1728 (*New Hist. Ire.* ix. 492–3, 606; newspaper accounts of Carteret's departure in 1728).

186–7. *the least Title to any considerable Employment*: On Archbishop Boulter's efforts, only partially counterbalanced by Carteret, to give the more important Irish preferments to the English, see James, 129–31.

189. *One third part of the Rents . . . spent in England*: 'The rents of *Ireland* are computed to be about a million and a half, whereof one half million at least is spent by lords and gentlemen residing in *England*, and by some other articles too long to mention.' Swift to Peterborough, 28 Apr. 1726, *Corresp.* iii. 133. In 'An Humble Address to Both Houses of Parliament' (1725), Swift had estimated the annual rents of Ireland at two million pounds, 'whereof one third Part, at least, is directly transmitted to those, who are perpetual Absentees in *England*' (*Drapier's Letters*, 156). In no. 10, Sheridan puts payments to absentees at £900,000 a year, a patent exaggeration. The estimate of £600,000 a year appears in Thomas Prior's *List of the Absentees* and *Observations on Coin in General* (Dublin: Rhames, 1729), 56; John Browne's *A Scheme of the Money Matters of Ireland* (Dublin: Powell, 1729), 50; and in other Dublin economic pamphlets of the period. Cullen more soberly estimates the amount as 'probably in excess of £300,000' a year (*Econ. Hist.* 45). Swift and his contemporaries may have overstated the absentees' harm to the economy; see T. M. Devine, 'The English Connection and Irish and Scottish Development in the Eighteenth Century', in Devine and D. Dickson (eds.), *Ireland and Scotland, 1600–1850* (Edinburgh, 1983), 17.

191. *Education at the Inns of Court*: Lawyers practising in Irish courts were required by 33 Hen. VIII, sess. 2, c. 3 (Ir.) (1542) to have spent at least six terms in one of the English Inns of Court; in 1728, one out of three students admitted to the Middle Temple was Irish (V. T. H. Delany, 'The History of Legal Education in Ireland', *J. of Legal Education*, 12 (1960), 397–8; *Register of Admissions to the Honourable Society of the Middle Temple*, comp. H. A. C. Sturgess (London, 1949), vol. i).

193. *Incidents*: Incidental charges or expenses (*OED*).

195. *the Liberty of Coining*: In the second Drapier's Letter, Swift had complained that Ireland lacked its own mint (*Drapier's Letters*, 20, 203–4). James Maculla had raised the issue again, in late 1727, in *Proposals for a Publick Coinage of Copper Half-Pence and Farthings in the Kingdom of Ireland* (Dublin: Gowan, 1727; copy: Goldsmiths'). Maculla's undated proposal to the Irish Parliament, 'shewing the Nation's Annual loss of 1,200,000 Sterl. and Grievance of 1,360,000 Sterl. drawn off, and proposing to redress the same, and to Manufacture 40 or 50,000 l Sterl. worth of lawful and valuable copper change for Ireland' may also antedate *A Short View* (see L. W. Hansen, *Contemp. Printed Sources for British and Irish Econ. Hist., 1701–1750* (Cambridge, 1963), 3872). He followed it, probably about Apr. 1728, with *The Lamentable Cry of the People of Ireland to Parliament. A Coinage, or Mint, Proposed* (Dublin: Waters, 1728; copy: RIA).

196. *In the Isle of Man*: Owned by the Earls of Derby, the Isle of Man issued only copper coins, and they do not appear to have been minted on the island. Charles Clay, *Currency of the Isle of Man*, Manx Soc. Pub. xvii (Douglas, 1869), 49–65; James Atkins, *The Coins and Tokens of the Possessions and Colonies of the British Empire* (London, 1889), 8–9.

201–3. *Both Sexes . . . abhor to wear any of their own Manufactures*: See Swift's *Proposal for the*

Universal Use of Irish Manufacture, in Cloaths and Furniture of Houses, &c. Utterly Rejecting and Renouncing Every Thing Wearable That Comes from England (1720), in *Prose*, ix. 13–22; and his posthumously published 'Humble Address to Both Houses of Parliament' (1725), in *Drapier's Letters*, 164–5, 169. He makes a similar point in his sermon 'Causes of the Wretched Condition of Ireland', *Prose*, ix. 200.

204. *a sort of Silk Plad*: Poplin, such as Swift had given as presents to Mrs Howard and Queen Caroline, then Princess of Wales, in the winter of 1726–7 (*Corresp.* iii. 176–7, 181, 184–5, 188, 192, 195, 392; *Poems*, ii. 559 n.).

218–19. *the Thorn at Glassenbury*: At Glastonbury, Somerset, a thorn tree that according to legend had sprouted from the staff of Joseph of Aramathea. It bloomed every year at Christmas; Defoe in *A Tour through the Whole Island of Great Britain*, Letter 4, says its Christmas blooming is 'universally attested'. See commentary by Claude Rawson, in 'The Injured Lady and the Drapier: A Reading of Swift's Irish Tracts', *Prose Studies*, 3 (1980), 20–1.

220. *the worthy C[ommissione]rs*: There were seven Revenue Commissioners: five Commissioners of Excise and two Commissioners of Customs, each paid £1000 a year; together they constituted probably the most extensive employer of government functionaries, thereby manipulating an extensive patronage system. Swift in his fourth Drapier's Letter (1724) said that 'Four of [the Commissioners] generally live in *England*'. In his unpublished 'Humble Address to Both Houses of Parliament' (1725) he said that the four were 'always absent'; Thomas Prior, who seems to have seen Swift's manuscript, repeated the claim in his influential *List of the Absentees of Ireland* (Dublin: Gunne, 1729), 10, changing 'always' to 'generally' in his second edition. In early 1728, when Swift wrote *A Short View*, the seven commissioners were William Conolly, speaker of the Irish House of Commons, Thomas Wylde, William Harrison, an Irish MP, Sir Thomas Frankland, Bt. (resigned in 1728 to become Commissioner of Trade in England), Edward Thompson, Anthony Lowther, and Robert Sawyer Herbert. Seán Réamonn, *History of the Revenue Commissioners* (Dublin, 1981), 5–6, 9–21; *Drapier's Letters*, 74, 156; *Lib. Mun. Pub. Hib.* i. ii. 134; McCracken, 68–9.

235. *this Irony*: See textual notes.

237. *Ysland*: Iceland.

241. *old Seats of the Nobility and Gentry all in Ruins*: See *Drapier's Letters*, 159, and the introductory note to *Intelligencer* 6.

249. *Nostrâ miseriâ magnus es*: 'Because of our misery you are great' (Cicero, *Epist. ad Atticum*, ii. 19). 'I confess I am at a Loss to understand to whom this last Expression is to be address'd', *Mist's* commentator dryly remarked (20 Apr. 1728). Faulkner's 1735 edn. emends 'magnus' to 'magna', perhaps to make it agree with *Britannia*.

254. *lowness of Interest*: Swift made the same claim in 'Maxims Controlled in Ireland': *Prose*, xii. 133–4 (and 310). The going Irish interest rate, about 6 per cent, seems in fact to have been slightly higher than that in England; Cullen, *Anglo-Irish Trade*, 20, 184; Sidney Homer, *A History of Interest Rates*, 2nd edn. (New Brunswick, 1977), 156–65. One indication of a recent decline in Irish interest rates, however, is *Tables of Interest, at Six, Seven, and Eight, Per Cent* (Dublin: Wilmot, 1727); appended, apparently as an afterthought, is 'Tables of Interest at Five per Cent'.

256. *the Dearness of Land*: Cullen, *Econ. Hist.* 44–5; Ehrenpreis, iii. 175–86; *Drapier's Letters*, 156; *Prose*, xii. 134, 210, 309–10.

261. *our encrease of Buildings in this City*: See Appendix F.

263. *the daily encrease of Bankers*: Cullen, *Anglo-Irish Trade*, 169, 191–2. See also no. 17.

265–6. *all our Silver, and one third of our Gold*: See introductory note.

266–7. *the running Cash of the Nation*: Swift had estimated it at 'under' £500,000 in his 'Letter to the Lord Chancellor Middleton' of 1724 (*Drapier's Letters*, 138; compare his letter to Peterborough, 28 Apr. 1726, *Corresp.* iii. 131–5; and his *Answer to a*

Paper, Called A Memorial (1728), where he estimates it at less than £110,000 (*Prose*, xii. 20)). In his essay 'Of the Balance of Trade' (1752), David Hume ridicules Swift's reasoning.

279. *Ye are idle . . . answered Pharoah*: Exod. 5: 17; compare a similar allusion in 'Causes of the Wretched Condition of Ireland', *Prose*, ix. 201.

283–4. *a good Million*: The total of all remittances, not just payments to absentees.

287. *when the Hen is starved*: The story is given among the fables of Anianus in L'Estrange's Aesop.

294. *I have known an Hospital*: Possibly the Foundling Hospital, Dublin, of which Swift was a governor. He had been a governor of Bethlehem Hospital, London, since 1714; but it is doubtful that he 'knew' the institution very well. William Dudley Wodsworth (ed.), *A Brief History of the Ancient Foundling Hospital of Dublin, from the Year 1702* (Dublin, 1876), 5; Edward G. O'Donoghue, *The Story of Bethlehem Hospital* (London, 1914), 249. On the daring of Swift's anecdote, see Appendix D.

301. *a Native and Inhabitant of this Kingdom*: John Browne, if Ferguson's conclusions about the essay's occasion are accepted; see introductory note.

302–3. *a Man-pleaser*: Cf. Gal. 1: 10; Eph. 6: 6; Col. 3: 22; and see Richard Baxter, *A Christian Directory*, ch. 4, pt. 4, 'Directions against Inordinate Man-pleasing', in his *Practical Works* (London: Parkurst *et al.*, 1707), i. 173–82.

Sheridan's allegory of the three brothers is (to say nothing of *A Tale of a Tub*) in some respects reminiscent of Swift's then unpublished *Story of the Injured Lady*, which he probably knew (*Prose*, ix. 3–12). Because to be for Ireland was in England a way of opposing Walpole, Sheridan's essay, when it was reprinted in London, evoked energetic replies. These are reproduced in Appendix G.

NUMB. XVI.

Sed virum verâ virtute vivere animatum addecet,
Fortiterq; innoxium vacare adversum adversarios.

Enn:

Mr. *Intelligencer*.

I T may appear to you perhaps a thing very unnatural, to receive a Complaint from a *Son* against his *Father*, but the treatment, which I meet with from mine, is of such a Nature, that it is impossible for me not to complain.   5

You must know there are three Brethren of us, *George*, *Patrick*, and *Andrew*; I am the second, but the last in Affection with my *Father*, for which I call Heaven and Earth to Witness, I never committed any Fault to incur his displeasure, or to deserve his neglect. But so it is, that the best of Men have oftentimes been misled in the choice of their   10 Minions, and very undiscerning in conferring their favours where they ought.

If Parents could but once bring themselves to be impartial, it would beyond all doubt, produce a delightful Union in their Children, and be the most binding Cement, that could be thought of, to preserve   15 their Affections, because an equal Dispensation of favours would entirely remove all cause of murmuring, repining, or envy. And, what is of the greatest Consequence, would secure the love and esteem of their Children; whereas a partial behaviour in Parents, must necessarily produce the contrary.   20

But to State my Case, in the best manner I can, and with an unbiassed regard to Truth, I think it first necessary to give you our Characters, with an Account of my *Father's* behaviour, that you may be the better able to give me your *Advice*.

25 First then, to begin with my Brother *George*. He was ever a great
lover of his Belly, and formerly used to Cram himself with *Beef*,
Pudding, and *White-pot*, but for some time past, he has taken more
delight in New-fangled *Toss-ups*, and *French Kick-shaws*. This high
Feeding does naturally dispose him to be Haughty, Stuborn,
30 Cholerick and Rebellious, insomuch, that beside his insults towards
others, he is ready, upon all occasions, to fly in his own *Father's* Face,
and apt to despise every Body, but himself.

He is so various in his Opinions, that he is of as many *Religions*, as
there are and have been *Sects*, since the beginning of *Christianity*; but
35 the *True* and *Reformed Church*, *as by Law Established*, is what he chiefly
frequents. He was once a great Admirer of Ancient Learning, but he
has long since quitted this, for the Reading of *News-Papers*, *Pamphlets*,
and *Modern Languages*. In his younger Years, he was fond of Manly
Exercises, such as *Fencing*, *Leaping*, *Boxing*, *Pitching the Bar*, *Wrestling*,
40 *Hurling*, *Foot-ball*, *Hunting*, &c. But of late he has faln into a strange
and unaccountable Effeminacy, and seems to take delight in nothing,
but *Masquerades*, *Plays*, and *Italian Operas*. He is very fond of *Italian*
Magnificent Buildings, although entirely inconsistent with our
Climate, extravagant in the highest degree, in purchasing fine
45 Paintings, and Statues, and no less expensive in vast extensive Parks
and Gardens, by which means, he has almost run out all his Fortune.

My youngest Brother *Andrew*, who has cunning enough to outwit
the *Devil*, joyned with Brother *George* some Years ago, and they
manage so dextrously together, that whatever they say is a *Law* with
50 my *Father*; however, they are not without their Quarrels now and then,
but Brother *Andrew* still comes by the worst, although he is cautious
enough, to go always armed; for Brother *George* wears a longer Sword.
Brother *Andrew* is not very nice in his Food, but loves fine Cloaths.
This I suppose he has learned abroad; for he is a great Traveller. His
55 chief Studies are *Mathematicks*, and the *Civil-law*, in both which he has
made a considerable Progress. As for his *Religion*, although he openly
professes himself a most Rigid *Fanatick of the Kirk*, yet he is shrewdly
suspected, to have a hankering after *Popery*. He has one eminent bad
Quality, which is, that he cannot easily forgive and forget. I remember
60 I was once so unfortunate, as to tell a fair Lady, (a Mistress of mine)
before his Face, that I would stand by her against him, and all her
other Adversaries, which he took hainously ill, and has not forgiven
me to this hour, but lies upon the Watch, to do me all the ill Offices he
can.

I come now to my own Character, in which I shall not Conceal, nor 65
Gloss over my Vices, Errors, or Failings, but at the same time, I shall
not think it inconsistent with Modesty, to tell you my Virtues.

I have but a small Fortune, can hardly keep Soul and Body together,
yet out of a regard to my Family, which is very Ancient, I love to make
what they call a Figure, upon extraordinary occasions. And now and 70
then I furnish my Table with Victuals, and Liquors of the best kinds,
which makes my *Father*, and Brother *George*, think I have got the World
in a String. I am kind and hospitable to Strangers, although they
frequently Rob my House, and turn my Children to ly in the Barn.

I am so fond of Learning, that I put them to the best School in the 75
Kingdom, and I plainly see they will be only the wiser, but never the
richer for it, because my *Father* uses all his Interest for brother *Georges*
Sons, and the greatest *Dunce* among them shall be better provided for,
than the most Ingenious of mine. And I must say I have some who are
equal in Learning to the best of his. I had a designe once, to follow 80
Merchandise; that I might be the better able to Provide for my Poor
Children, but Brother *George* having a mind to make a *Monopoly*,
prevailed upon my *Father*, to join against me, and so at last they
contrived it, that I should sell nothing but a few of my Catle, and some
Linnen Cloath, which is all the Support I have; Whereas brother 85
George can Sell every thing he has, all the World over. And so cruel is
he to me, that he will not let me have even a bit of his dirt, if he thinks it
will be of any advantage to me. My *Religion* is of three Sorts, The
Established, *Popish* and *Presbyterian*, but I have a greater Share of the
First in me. I think it is best, because it encourages obedience to my 90
Father, more than either of the other two. It is not long since Brother
George, and *Andrew*, were in a confederacy against my Father, with an
Intent to turn him out of his House, and give another the Possession,
at which critical Juncture, I mustered up a great Number of my Sons,
and Servants, to his Assistance, and for ought I know saved both his 95
Life, and Fortune.

Soon after this, I had like to have been ruined by a Project; for one
of my Brother *George's* Family endeavoured to perswade my *Father*,
that *Gold*, and *Silver*, were of no use to me, and desired leave to
furnish me with a few *Counters*, in lieu thereof, and I fear I should have 100
been so Weak, as to accept of them, had it not been for the Seasonable
Remonstrances, made by Some of my own *House*.

These are a fewe of the many Hardships I have suffered, not
withstanding all which, I am willing to continue a *Passive Obedience*,

105 to my Dear *Father*; for I have Reason to believe, that his unkindness to
me is owing to ill Advisers, who have prejudiced him against me, and
my Children; but I Hope, before long, he will be able to distinguish his
most faithful Son. In the mean time, I do humbly entreat the Favour of
you to Write a Letter to my *Father*, which he may See in Print, for I
110 Fear all my Letters to him hitherto have been Intercepted.

SIR,

Y OU have not told me your *Father's* Name, nor his Quality, and
therefore I am at a loss in what manner I should Address him. But
in common Humanity (because I think your case deplorable) I will
115 give you what Comfort I am able, together with my best Advice.

You are not the only Instance of *Suffering Innocence*, and therefore it
ought not to Surprize you that *Providence* (for reasons unaccountable
to us) has laid two great Tryals in your way, *Oppression* from your
Brethern, and *Unkindness* from your *Father*, this too without any Fault
120 on your Side. If you did not meet with these Afflictions, you would
want an Opportunity of shewing your Humility, and Resignation, as I
understand you do not by your Letter.

Let me Advise you, to consider that your Condition is not quite so
Lamentable, as that of *Joseph*, who triumphed in GOD's own time
125 over all his Misfortunes, and sufferings, and at last had the pleasure of
doing good, even to his Persecutors; but indeed there is this
Difference, that his grievance was chiefly from his *Brethern*; for had his
Father joined in the Cruelty, the Wounds would have Pierced nearer
to his Heart.

130 I do not in the least doubt, but there are some about your Father,
who do you ill Offices, (I hope some time or other they will be
detected). You may find a convenient Oportunity of getting fairly at
him. State your Case and expostulate with him concerning your own
and your Children's Sufferings. When he hears your Story, and
135 beholds your Sincerity, you may be sure of his Compassion, and a
Redress; for there is no Heart so hard as not to Sympathize with real
Woe, no Advocate so Powerful, as Innocence. In the mean time, let me
Conjure you, not to turn aside to the Right or to the Left, from that
indispensable Duty, which the express Laws of GOD enjoin you, for
140 let me assure you, that Ingratitude to a Parent is, no less than
Rebellion, like the Sin of Witchcraft.

I Commit you to his Care and Direction, who is best able to Govern
the unruly affections of Men, to turn the Hearts of the Malicious,

and to Relieve and Support those who suffer for the Sake of
Righteousness. 145

> I am your faithful Friend;
> The *Intelligencer*.

MOTTO. A fragment from Ennius's *Phoenix*, quoted by Gellius, VI. xvii. 10: 'But it
behoves a man to live animated by true virtue, courageously blameless in the face of
his enemies.' In 1729, Bowyer, in accordance with many editions of Gellius,
emended Sheridan's *vacare* to *vocare*, but *vacare* is found in *Auli Gellii Noctium
Atticarum Libri XX*, ed. Jacobus Gronovius (Leyden: Boutesteyn and Du Vivié,
1706), 412, which Sheridan owned (Sheridan, *Library*, 450).

7. *I am the second*: Ireland was united to the English crown in 1541, Scotland in 1603.
27. *White-pot*: 'A dish made (chiefly in Devonshire) of milk or cream boiled with various
ingredients, as eggs, flour, raisins, sugar, spices, etc.; a kind of custard or milk-
pudding' (*OED*).
28. *Toss-ups*: Presumably a quickly-assembled dish; not in *OED*, but compare *OED*
under *toss*, *v.*, 14. c., and *tossing-pan*, *vbl. sb.*, b.
28. *Kick-shaws*: i.e., *quelque chose*; 'a fancy dish in cookery. (Chiefly with contemptuous
force: A "something" French, not one of the known "substantial English" dishes)'
(*OED*); see also *The Stanford Dictionary of Anglicised Words and Phrases*, ed. C. A. M.
Fennell (1892; Cambridge, 1964). Hannah Glasse describes kickshaws as fruit-filled
puff pastries: *The Art of Cookery* (London: for the Author, 1747), 84.
39–40. *Fencing . . .*: 'Foot-ball . . ., Leaping, Wrestling, [and] Pitching of the Bar' were
recreations for 'the Citizens and Peasants', while hunting and fencing were for 'the
Nobility and Gentry', as were balls, plays, operas, and masquerades, according to
John Chamberlayne, *Magnae Britanniae Notitia*, 29th edn. (London: Midwinter,
1728), i. 188. Compare [Thomas Baker], *Tunbridge-Walks: or, The Yeoman of Kent*
(London: Lintott, 1703), 41: 'Then your *Kentish* Men here are for leaping; and
throwing a great Iron-Bar, as if the Slavish Exercises of a Porter, cou'd heighten the
Character of a Gentleman.' 'Hurling' is apparently not Irish hurling, which
Sheridan would have known. See *OED*; and Liam Canny, 'The Irish Game of
Hurling', *Folk Life*, 19 (1981), 95–103.
42. *Plays . . . Italian Operas*: Sheridan, a great lover of the theatre, would not ordinarily
have considered delight in plays decadent; compare the reply, reprinted from the
British Gazetteer (Appendix G). The association of Italian opera with effeminacy
echoes Swift's *Intelligencer* 3.
42–3. *Italian Magnificent Buildings*: Sheridan appears to adopt the stance of the rising
neo-Palladians, who prided themselves on being both 'ancient' and (through
descent from Inigo Jones) English, in opposition to the foreign—Sheridan facilely
says 'Italian'—Baroque practised by Wren, Vanbrugh, and Hawksmoor in such
'magnificent' buildings as St Paul's cathedral, Castle Howard, and Blenheim
palace. In general this is the position taken by Colen Campbell in his influential
Vitruvius Britannicus (1715). See Rudolf Wittkower, *Palladio and Palladianism* (New
York, 1974), 178; and John Summerson, *Architecture in Britain, 1530 to 1830*
(Baltimore, 1954), 197–9.
48. *joyned with Brother George*: In the Act of Union, 1707.
52. *always armed*: Sheridan, arguing that a Jacobite threat to the Crown is much greater
in Scotland than in Ireland, agrees with Parliament that the Highland custom of
bearing arms 'has in a peculiar Manner been one of the fatal Causes of the late
unnatural Rebellion [of 1715], and may occasion the like or greater Calamity in

Time to come' (Disarming Act of 1715, 1 Geo. I, Stat. 2, c. 54; later Disarming Acts, 11 Geo. I, c. 26 (1724) and 19 Geo. II, c. 39 (1746) testify to continued arms-bearing in Scotland).

53. *not very nice in his Food*: 'The [Scots] Tradesmen, Farmers and common People are not successive devourers of *Flesh* as Men of the same Rank are in England. Milk-meats and Oatmeal several ways prepar'd, and *Cale* and *Roots* dressed in several manners, is the constant Diet of the poor People.' *Magnae Britanniae Notitia* (1728 edn.), i. 428.

54. *great Traveller*: The Scots are 'zealous Lovers of their Country, tho' very willing to settle abroad when they have any Opportunity of doing so', according to *Magnae Britanniae Notitia* (1728 edn.), i. 346.

55. *Mathematicks, and the Civil-law*: Alluding, probably, to the achievements of John Napier (1550–1617), who invented logarithms and wrote *Mirifici Logarithmorum Canonis Descriptio* (Edinburgh: Hart, 1614); and of Sir James Dalrymple, 1st Viscount Stair, who wrote the famous treatise *The Institutions of the Law of Scotland* (Edinburgh: Anderson, 1681).

58. *a hankering after Popery*: Primarily an allusion to Scotland's Jacobite sympathies, but compare John Arbuthnot, *The History of John Bull*, ed. Alan W. Bower and Robert A. Erickson (Oxford, 1976), 51 and n.

60. *Lady*: Probably Queen Anne. The Irish Commons, appealing for a union with England, vowed to defend her and her heirs 'even to the last drop of our blood'—this in Oct. 1703, only months after the Scottish Parliament had abridged the right of future monarchs to declare war for Scotland and had threatened to separate the Scottish and English crowns upon Anne's demise. James, 59; William Ferguson, *Scotland's Relations with England: A Survey to 1707* (Edinburgh, 1977), 210–12; *English Historical Documents*, viii (London, 1953), 677, 780–1.

73. *Strangers*: Englishmen.

75–6. *the best School in the Kingdom*: A reference to Sheridan's own school; see 'Sheridan's Life' in the General Introduction.

83–4. *they contrived it*: In the Cattle Act of 1666, 18 Charles II, c. 2, and the Woollen Act of 1696, 7 and 8 William III, c. 22, discussed in the notes to no. 15.

92. *confederacy*: The Jacobite rising of 1715 in Scotland, quelled, as Sheridan and others liked to observe, with the aid of Irish forces. See W. E. H. Lecky, *A History of England in the Eighteenth Century* (1891; London, 1925), i. 266; *Drapier's Letters*, 45, 79; *Pol. State*, 10 (1715), 375, 415, 479; Charles Dalton, *George the First's Army, 1714–1727*, ii (London, 1912), 129–47.

97–8. *one of my Brother George's Family*: William Wood; for an account of his halfpence, and the 'Seasonable Remonstrances' against them by Swift, Sheridan, and others, see Ehrenpreis, iii. 187–318.

104. *Passive Obedience*: According to the Whigs, this was the Tory doctrine that the subject owed absolute submission to the sovereign. Sacheverell's trial in 1710 had emphasized this sense of the term. Sheridan here uses the phrase to exaggerate Irish loyalty to the Hanoverians, working as always to distance himself from the imputation of Jacobite sympathies.

124. *Joseph*: Gen., chs. 37 and 39–45.

138. *not to turn aside*: Deut. 5: 16, 32.

141. *Rebellion*: 1 Sam. 15: 23.

143. *turn the Hearts*: Cf. Luke 1: 17.

144–5. *suffer for the Sake of Righteousness*: Matt. 5: 10; 1 Pet. 3: 14.

In the guise of a correspondent, Sheridan adopts the premiss ridiculed in nos.
6 and 15: that Ireland is a rich and flourishing nation.

NUMB. XVII.

*Quantum stagna Tagi rudibus stillantia venis
Effluxere decus! quanto pretiosa metallo
Hermi ripa micat; quantas per Lydia culta
Despumat rutilas dives Pactolus arenas.*

Claudian.

Mr. *Intelligencer,*

HAVING lately, with great Candor, and Impartiality,
perused some of your *Papers*, upon the Distress and Poverty
of this *Island*, which you take care to describe in the most
Pathetick manner, you must forgive me if I differ from you, and think it 5
one of the most Flourishing and Wealthy Kingdoms in the whole
world, and to support my Opinion, I will venture to affirm, that there
never was such Affluence of ready Cash, as at this present juncture;
For have we not more *Bankers* than ever were known among us? And
whether the *Money* Circulates in *Specie*, or *Paper*, it is the same thing 10
to us, since those, who would rather have *Cash* than *Paper*, can (as is
well known) have their choice, whenever they please. It is to be
presumed that no *Banker* gives a NOTE before the *Money* is first laid
down on his *Counter*; then of Consequence there is as much *Money*, as
there is *Paper*, and that we have a great deal of *Paper* is most certain, 15
therefore a great deal of *Money*. But I will proceed farther, and prove
that we have much more *Money* than *Paper*, because there are
Multitudes who keep their own *Money*. This appears from the great
number of *Iron-chests* imported from *Holland*, within these last *seven*
Years; For what use can they be of, but to lodge *Money*. They are at 20
least two hundred. We will suppose, that these, one with another, may
contain *two thousand pounds* a piece, then the Sum total, amounts to
Four hundred thousand pounds, which is so much Superfluous, and
unnecessary *Cash.*

If this *Island* were not very Wealthy, it is strongly to be presumed, 25
That so many Wise and Able Heads, Men of great Learning and

superior Talents, whose Reputations reacht us from distant Regions, long before they came among us, so well distinguished in their own *Countries* for their great Knowledge, in their several professions, and
30 here more especially; remarkable for their speaking in publick, and their profound Skill in Religion, Politicks, and Law; I say that Men of such Accomplishments would never quit their own Native Soil, where so many great Estates are daily made, if they were not sure that this *Island* must, on Account of its greater Wealth, Afford them
35 Opportunities of making larger Acquisitions, than they could at home.

Have not almost all the Gentlemen through this *Kingdom*, for some years past, declined all profitable Employments, and left them to be filled by others. Can there be a stronger Argument of their Wealth, than their choosing to live at their ease, out of Office, rather than be at
40 the small trouble, which attends the discharge of a beneficial Employment?

Could so many Estated Gentlemen, through the *North* of *Ireland*, afford to keep so much of their Lands waste, and untenanted, if they had not *Money* enough by them, to live without Tenants, and would
45 not the Tenants likewise be glad, to take this Waste Land to Plow, and Sow, but that they have ready money enough to buy *Bread Corn*, and other Necessaries, from all the World beside.

As another signal mark of our Riches, there is Scarce a Gentleman, who does not educate his Sons at our UNIVERSITY (*which as the*
50 *World sees, wants not it's due Encouragement*) where they live at vast Expences, take Degrees, return to their Fathers, who without ever troubling *Law*, or *Gospel*, maintain them afterwards at Home, like Gentlemen.

Do not many of our Nobility through Wantonness, and superfluity,
55 reside constantly in another *Kingdom*, where, it is well known, they make a better Figure, as to *Houses*, *Coaches*, and *Equipages*, than their Neighbours? And do not our young *Peers*, and *Gentry*, who go thither *to see the World*, *Game*, *Race*, *Drink*, &c. beyond any in *Great-Brittain*, of the same Age, and Quality, which they could not Possibly do, if
60 their Agents here had not an *undrainable fund*, *to suply them*? for as the *Philosopher* says, *Nemo dat quod non habet.* Or as the *Jugler* very Elegantly expresses it, *Where nothing is, there nothing can come out.*

If it be true, (I know it is confidently Reported) that a great Number of *English Robbers* are come over, that likewise is a very strong
65 Argument of our Wealth; for they would never quit the *English Streets*, and *Roads*, for ours, unless they were sure to find an Advantage by the

Change. It is most certain we never had such a Number of *Robbers*, as
at this very juncture; from whence we may conclude, that they could
not Possibly Multiply thus, if they did not find Houses, and People
enough to Rob, for all Professions and Trades encrease, according to 70
the Encouragement they meet with.

Are not whole Streets adding every Day to our *Metropolis*, when one
would think it Large enough already? Some entire Streets and many
Houses, I must confess, are waste, and unhabited. But does not this
shew the Wealth and Wantonness of the Inhabitants, who not content 75
with their present Dwellings, change them for others, more costly and
expensive?

Do not great Numbers of our Inhabitants, daily go off to *America*?
Will any Man say this can be done with empty Pockets? Can any Man
think otherwise, but that it must be the effect of vast superfluity, when 80
People wantonly take such long Voyages, and Journeys, to go where
they have no business?

The last Argument I shall offer for the Wealth of this Kingdom, is
the great Number of Beggars, in which it abounds; for it is a common
Observation, that Riches are the parent of Idleness, Sloth, and 85
Luxury, and are not these Naturally productive of Want and Beggary?

I could offer many more Arguments, but that I hope you and your
Country Men, are sufficiently convinced, by what I have said, that
Ireland is a place of great Wealth, affluence, and Plenty. Therefore let
me advise you, the next time you put Pen to Paper, not to dress up 90
Hibernia in Rags, and Dirt, but cloath her in *Scarlet*, and *fine Linen*; for
she can very well afford them. Draw the *God* of Riches, hovering over
your *Island*, shaking Ten Thousands of Golden Feathers from his
Wings, much more than the Inhabitants can gather, and thus will your
Country Men, who have retrenched upon your last groundless Alarm, 95
return to their former Hospitality, and we shall see *Halcyon*, that is,
Irish Days once more.

SIR,

I Have perused your Arguments, and thus I Answer them. You were certainly
fast asleep, and Writ them all in your Dream, nor do I in the least doubt, when 100
you awake from your Golden Slumber, but you will find your self as much
mistaken, as the Man in Æsop, who Dreamed the Devil shewed him a
Treasure. I wish you may not Likewise, be in the same pickle, and prove a Gold-
Finder, between your own Sheets.

Your's,   105
The *Intelligencer*.

MOTTO. Cl. Claudianus, 'Panegyricus Dictus Probino et Olybrio Consulibus', 51–4: [Probus 'scatter[ed] gifts of gold' everywhere,] 'exceeding all the gold dust carried down by Tagus' water trickling from unsmelted lodes, the glittering ore that enriches Hermus' banks, the golden sand that rich Pactolus in flood deposits over the plains of Lydia' (Loeb).

3. *your Papers*: Nos. 6, 15, and 16.

9. *more Bankers than ever were known*: On the influx of bankers, see no. 15. The Dublin bankers Mead & Curtis had suspended payments 14 June 1727 (*New Hist. Ire.* viii. 264).

10. *whether the Money Circulates in Specie, or Paper*: 'And were it not for Bankers Notes, which we have passing in good Plenty, it would be impossible to manage our Domestick Traffick half so well as we do.' [Thomas Prior], *Observations on Coin in General* (Dublin: Rhames, 1729), 45; see L. M. Cullen's comment on this passage in 'Landlords, Bankers, and Merchants', *Hermathena*, 135 (1983), 29. John Browne, in *A Scheme of the Money-Matters of Ireland* (Dublin: Powell, 1729), assumed a circulation of about £500,000 in specie and £400,000 in banker's notes (17).

43. *Lands waste, and untenanted*: See no. 19 and notes.

61. *Nemo dat quod non habet*: Nobody gives what he doesn't have; a parody of Aristotle, *Physics*, i. 4. 187ᵃ: 'The dogma, common to all the Physicists, [is] that "nothing can come out of what does not exist"' (Loeb).

61. *Jugler*: Sleight-of-hand artist.

62. *Where nothing is, there nothing can come out*: Proverbial; see Persius, iii. 84; Lucretius, *De Rerum Natura*, i. 155; *King Lear*, I. i. 92; *The Oxford Dictionary of English Proverbs*, 3rd edn. (Oxford, 1970), under 'nothing'; Tilley N285.

72. *whole Streets adding every Day to our Metropolis*: See Appendix F.

78. *great Numbers of our Inhabitants, daily go off to America*: See the introductory note to no. 19.

84. *the great Number of Beggars*: 'Yesterday the High Constable of the City, with his Assistants, began to clear our Streets of idle Vagrants and Vagabonds, with such Success, that many People who have been insulted at times by these Strollers, received great Satisfaction thereby. They were sent to the Poor-House, which is again on Foot, where extraordinary Provision is made for their Maintenance.' Dublin news of 19 Sept. 1728 reported in the London *Daily J.* 1 Oct. 1728. See also *Intelligencer 6*.

92. *the God of Riches*: Plutus was 'painted with Wings, to signify the Swiftness of his Retreat, when he is departing from any Person', according to [William] King's schoolbook, *An Historical Account of the Heathen Gods and Heroes* (4th edn.; London: Lintot, 1727), 55–6.

102. *the Man in Æsop*: In 'A Man Dreamt He Found Gold', Fable 359 in L'Estrange's Aesop, where it is in fact attributed to Poggius. A man dreams that the devil leads him to buried treasure, advising him to leave it there but mark the spot with his excrement. The man awakes to discover that he has befouled himself.

103–4. *Gold-Finder*: 'One who empties Privies or Houses of Easement' (N. Bailey, *The Universal Etymological English Dictionary*, vol. 'ii' (London: Cox, 1727)).

Sheridan wrote this brief piece to instigate a celebration of Swift's birthday 30 November and to seek Christmas presents for Sarah Harding. Sheridan's praise of Swift as the Drapier incorporates a historical account of Irish cannibalism which may have influenced *A Modest Proposal*. See George Wittowsky, 'Swift's *Modest Proposal*: The Biography of an Early Georgian Pamphlet', *JHI* 4 (1943), 92–3; and Thomas B. Gilmore, Jr, '*A Modest Proposal* and *Intelligencer* Number XVIII', *Scriblerian*, 2 (1969), 28–9.

The Dublin newspaper reports must have gratified Sheridan:

> Saturday last being the Festival of St. Andrew, and the Birth-day of that memorable Patriot M. *B. Drapier*, the great Deliverer of this Kingdom from Wood's base Coin, it was usher'd in with ringing the Bells of St. Patrick's Church, which continued the greatest Part of the Day, and at Night there were Illuminations and Bonfires, at many of which Healths were drunk by the Populace, to his Long Life and Prosperity, with loud Acclamations of Joy for his present Welfare.

The *Weekly Journal: or, The British Gazetteer* (London), 28 December 1728, quoting Dublin reports of 14 December; 'Saturday last' is of course an error, suggesting that the report made a delayed appearance in Dublin. The Dublin papers themselves do not survive.

NUMB. XVIII.

Hic dies anno redeunte festus.
Hor:

My Dear Country-Men,

IT has been the Custom of all wise Nations, not only to confer immediate honours upon their Benefactors, but likewise to distinguish their *Birth-Days*, by Anniversary rejoycings. This was a most generous Institution, to transmit those Heroes to posterity, 5 who gloriously signalized themselves, in the Defence of their Country, that others, being Spirited up by their Example, might endeavour to deserve the same Encouragement. It is for this reason, that I recommend *Saint Andrew*'s-*Day* unto you, to be Celebrated in a most Particular manner, being (as I am very well informed) the DRAPIER's 10 Birth-Day. But before I shall make out the great Obligations, we have to him, I think it first necessary, to relate unto you a passage, untoucht

upon before, by those who Writ against *Wood*'s Half-pence, which I
have read in an *English* Historian of great probity, and Truth.

15 His Name is *Fines Morrison*. He was Secretary of State to the Lord
Monjoy, our chief Governour, in the Reign of *Queen Elizabeth*, and
therefore had the best oportunity, of knowing the State of this Nation
at that time. He tells you that the Queen, had received an Account of
the *Irish* being up in Arms (though to speak the truth it was the
20 *English*, rather; for the *Giraldies*, the *Tools*, the *Cavanaghs*, and the
Byrns who were the Ring-leaders, were all of *English* Extraction.) She
called a Council, where after several Schemes had been proposed, for
reducing the Rebels, it was at last agreed upon, as the best expedient,
to make a base Coin current among them; for this it was thought would
25 quickly Subdue their stuborn Spirits, by introducing Poverty, the
great humbler of Families and Nations.

Accordingly this expedient was set on Foot, and it had the intended
Effect; for the Merchants, who generally Speaking, consider nothing
but their own private advantage, imported vast Sums of this base Coin,
30 every hundred Pounds of which stood them not in above Forty, for so
they bought it from the *Dutch*, who thrust their cloven Foot into all
affairs. This being discovered, the Rates of things were raised to Ten
times their value, the middle Rank of People were all ruined by it, and
the Poor, through this whole Kingdom, reduced to Famine, in so
35 much, that all the publick Roads were strowed with Dead Carcases
of miserable Wretches, whose Mouths were Green (as the Author
expresses it) with their last meal of Grass.

He likewise gives a Relation, of a very horrible Fact; too horrible
indeed to mention! That a poor Widow of *Newry*, having six small
40 Children, and no food to support them, shut up her Doors, Died
through despair, and in about three or four Days after, her Children
were found Eating her Flesh. He says farther, That at the same time, a
discovery being made of Twelve Women, who made a practice of
stealing Children, to Eat them, they were all burned, by order of Sir
45 *Arthur Chichester*, then Governour of the *North* of *Ireland*. He likewise
tells us, that the poor Butchers, and other Trades-men, who could not
afford to part with their goods, at such Rates as the Army would have
them, were daily Dragooned by them. That the poor Soldiers were
also ruined, for not being able to Buy their Cloathing here, they were
50 obliged to be supplyed from *England*, at double Rates.

After many more Evils enumerated, the good Natured, and
Compassionate *Author*, who all along deplores the miserable

Condition of the poor Natives, tells us, their Case was Represented
in such deplorable Circumstances, that the *Queen* quickly recalled
her Grant, and put a stop to the base *Coin*. And he concludes one 55
Paragraph thus (as well as I can remember.)

We her Majesty's Officers, who thought to make our Fortunes by our
Employments, lost what we had, and we lost our Hearts therewith.

I have now finished my Melancholy extract, from whence I shall
infer, that as like Causes ever have, and ever must produce like Effects, 60
that Villainous Project of *William Wood*, might have intirely ruined this
Kingdom, and have Converted it, into one large Poor House, had not
the DRAPIER (whom I shall honour while I live) prevented that by his
PEN, which perhaps *Twenty thousand* Swords, could not have done.
Some very great Men, whose Names I am loath to Mention, were so 65
Angry with the DRAPIER, for saving his *Country*, and disobliging
their Friend *William Wood*, that they orderd a good Sum of *Mony*,
as a reward to any one, who should discover which of the Town
DRAPIER's, it was, that durst be so Impudent, and had it been found
out, it is highly probable, they would have Seized all the *Goods* in his 70
Shop, and have *Imprisoned*, and *Pillored* him into the Bargain, to make
him an example to all PATRIOTS.

Consider then my dear *Country Men*, the hazard, which this Noble
Spirited DRAPIER did run for your Sakes. How like the old Heroe
Camillus, he flew in suddainly to our Rescue, when *Wood's* Half- 75
pence were like the Brazen Bucklers, thrown into the opposite Scale,
by our Enemies, to fill their Pockets more plentifully, with our *Gold*,
and *Silver*. That he has done his best endeavour, to save us from
Poverty and Slavery, and consequently has the strongest Title, to our
Gratitude. 80

Let us not Act then, in a Christian Country, like the Barbarous
Heathens, who frequently, when their greatest Deliverances were
wrought, either Slighted, or banished, or Poisoned, or Murthered the
Benefactors, or the *Heroes*, or reduced them to the Necessity, of Dying
by their own Hands. 85

So fell the great *Patriots Demosthenes*, *Cicero*, *Socrates*, *Phocion*,
Themistocles; And *Dion* of *Syracuse*, who was most inhumanly given up,
to be Butchered by some *Zacynthian Ruffians*, after he had recovered
the ungrateful *Sicilians* their freedom.

We ought likewise to consider, that we may possibly stand in need 90
of a DRAPIER's Assistance another Time.

And it must be an uncommon strain of Virtue in any Man, to serve those People, who will not at least offer him their thanks, or own their Obligation to him.

95 What makes the *Soldier*, and Consecrates the *Heroe*, but Rewards, and *Honours*!

Let a Prince be ever so great a *Soldier* himself, if he fails in this single point, of giving Valour its due Encouragement, he will find his *Soldiers* but very slack in their Duty, and full as loose in their Loyalty.

100 It is even so in all other Professions; let Men pretend what they will, as to Conscience, and Duty, they are but *Hypocrites*, when they say, they Act with a View to these alone. Proper Encouragements have ever been expected, by the best of Men, and it is very just, they should have their due, as well as *Cæsar*.

105 I dare venture to engage for the DRAPIER, that he expects no more, for his great Services, but that Love, and Regard, that Respect and Esteem, which every *Irish Man*, who has any Virtue left, ought to have, for so great a Benefactor. I have my self, one way, or other, *five hundred Pounds a Year*, and I am certain, I make the Computation in my

110 own Favour, when I say, that I owe him four hundred and fifty pounds *per Annum.* Let others in Proportion to their Fortune, make Use of the same *Arithmetick*, how much will the Nation owe him!

And can any one, after this, refuse a few Complements to his BIRTH-DAY, when *Furze*, and *Candles*, are so cheap, and

115 considering that our Houses can never be better adorned, than by Illuminations, in respect to those, who enable us to keep them?

I wish, my dear *Country-Men*, I could cast a Veil over one piece of Ingratitude, which you have been Guilty of, to one of your Deliverers; I mean to the Great and Glorious *King William*, that for two Years

120 past, you have laid aside his Anniversary-Dinner at the *Tholsel*, forgetting that he did not only, save us from *Popery* and *Slavery*, but did in a very Particular manner, Distinguish, and Reward the Gentlemen of this Kingdom, both of the *Gown* and the *Sword*, and made the People in general, so much his peculiar Care, that there was

125 *no complaining in our Streets.*

I would not here be understood, to approve of that *Bumper-Loyalty*, of getting Drunk to the Memory of the Dead, but to have an Annual meeting, to shew a decent Respect for those, who have been our True Friends, and Benefactors, either Living, or Dead, and to exclude all

130 others, who are not so, even from our flattery.

POSTSCRIPT.

I do make it my Request, that the Widdow, the PRINTER of these *Papers*, who did likewise *Print* the DRAPIER's Letters, may be enabled by Charitable Encouragements to keep *a merry Christmass*; for She, and her Family, were ruined by Iniquitous *Imprisonments*, and 135 *hardships*, for *Printing* those *Papers*, which were to the Advantage of this Kingdom in General.

MOTTO. *Odes*, III. viii. 9: 'This festal day, each time the year revolves' (Loeb).

9. *Saint Andrew's-Day*: 30 Nov., Swift's birthday.

15. *Fines Morrison*: Fynes Moryson, *An Itinerary . . . Containing His Ten Yeeres Travel through the Twelve Dominions of Germany, Bohmerland, Sweitzerland, Netherland, Denmarke, Poland, Italy, Turky, France, England, Scotland and Ireland* (London: Beale, 1617). Writing from memory (the book is not in the catalogue of his library), Sheridan forgets that Moryson's account had been 'touched upon' in *A Defence of the Conduct of the People of Ireland in Their Unanimous Refusal of Mr. Wood's Copper-Money* (Dublin: Ewing, 1724), 20, 28; see *Drapier's Letters*, 231–2.

16. *Monjoy*: Charles Blount, 8th Baron Mountjoy (1562–1606), Lord Deputy of Ireland from 1600 to 1603.

20–1. *the Giraldies, the Tools, the Cavanaghs, and the Byrns*: The leaders in Tyrone's Rebellion certainly included Cavanaghs, O'Tooles, and O'Byrnes, as well as some but by no means all Fitzgeralds (see Moryson, ii. 17 ff.). That the Fitzgeralds had come to Ireland by way of England was generally agreed (e.g., Aaron Crossly, *The Peerage of Ireland* (Dublin: Hume, 1725), 22). Sheridan follows Edmund Spenser's erroneous argument that the Tooles, Cavanaghs, and Byrnes were also originally English (Spenser, *A View of the State of Ireland*, part iii of *The Historie of Ireland* (Dublin: Societie of Stationers, 1633), 33, 81).

24. *to make a base Coin current among them*: Moryson, i. 283, ii. 90–1, 102. Moryson does not mention any discussion in Council; that it took place could be inferred, however, from William Camden's account, which Sheridan probably knew: [*Annales*]. *Tomus Alter, & Idem: or The Historie of the Life and Reigne of that Famous Princesse, Elizabeth*, tr. [Thomas Browne] (London: Harper, 1629), 347–8. See also *Drapier's Letters*, 13, 50, 69, 200, 231–2.

30. *stood them not in*: Did not cost them (*OED*, 'stand', sense 44. c). On the merchants' profits, see C. E. Challis, *The Tudor Coinage* (Manchester, 1978), 272.

32–3. *raised to Ten times their value*: 'double', says Moryson, ii. 154 [='150'].

35. *Dead Carcases*: Not redundant; *carcase* formerly meant simply 'body' (dead or alive).

36. *whose Mouths were Green*: 'And no spectacle was more frequent in the Ditches of Townes, and especiallie in wasted Countries, then to see multitudes of these poore people dead with their mouthes all coloured greene by eating nettles, docks, and all things they could rend up above ground' (Moryson, ii. 271–2).

38. *a very horrible Fact*: Again Sheridan distorts Moryson's account in some details: Moryson describes 'a most horrible spectacle of three children (whereof the eldest was not above ten yeeres old), all eating and knawing with their teeth the entrals of their dead mother, upon whose flesh they had fed twenty dayes past, and having eaten all from the feete upward to the bare bones, rosting it continually by a slow fire, were now come to the eating of her said entralls in like sort roasted, yet not divided from the body, being as yet raw. . . . Captaine *Trevor* & many honest Gentlemen lying in the *Newry* can witnes, that some old women of those parts, used to make a fier in the fields, and divers little children driving out the cattel in the cold

mornings, and comming thither to warme them, were by them surprised, killed and eaten, which at last was discovered by a great girle breaking from them by strength of her body, and Captaine *Trevor* sending out souldiers to know the truth, they found the childrens skulles and bones, and apprehended the old women, who were executed for the fact' (ii. 271).

54–5. *the Queen quickly recalled her Grant*: Rather she moderated it only slightly; Sheridan's memory is at fault.

57. *We her Majesty's Officers*: Moryson writes that 'the Queene's servants' were to be able to exchange the base Irish coin for English money, but 'this exchange soone failed, and our hearts therewith: for we served there in discomfort, and came home beggars' (ii. 90–1). See also Challis, p. 272.

65. *Some very great Men*: Carteret, acting presumably at Walpole's behest, issued a proclamation 27 Oct. 1724 offering a reward for information leading to the conviction of the Drapier, whose identity Sheridan is being playfully coy about acknowledging (*Prose*, x. 205; Plumb, ii. 103–4).

71. *Pillored*: Pilloried.

75. *Camillus*: Having agreed to pay the Gauls a certain weight of gold, the Romans objected to the Gauls' tampering with the scales. Thereupon the Gaul Brennus defiantly added his sword and belt (not 'brazen buckler') to the weights. In reply, Marcus Furius Camillus led the Romans in refusing any payment whatever to the Gauls (Plutarch, *Camillus*, xxviii).

86. *Demosthenes*: Demosthenes, the great orator, defended Athens against Philip and Alexander of Macedon. In the end he poisoned himself in a temple to avoid capture.

86. *Cicero*: Cicero, who had rescued Rome from the Catilinarian conspiracy and been given the title 'pater patriae', acted as head of state after Caesar's assassination but was executed by the triumvirate of Mark Antony, Octavian, and Lepidus.

86. *Socrates*: Socrates, who asserted at his trial that he was a public benefactor, was executed by poison (Plato, *Apology*, 30 c–32 e, 36 d–e; *Phaedo*, 117–18).

86. *Phocion*: Phocion, distinguished Athenian statesman and general, 4th cent. BC. He trusted Cassander's general Nicanor too far and thus lost Piraeus. The Athenians condemned him to be poisoned, though Plutarch records that they soon regretted having done so (*Phocion*, xxxiv–xxxviii).

87. *Themistocles*: Themistocles, architect of Athenian naval power, was accused of treason, fled to Persia and elsewhere, and according to Plutarch and others, committed suicide, either by drinking bull's blood or by taking poison (*Themistocles*, xxxi).

87. *Dion of Syracuse*: Dion liberated Syracuse in 357, but having assassinated his lieutenant and rival Heraclides, he was himself assassinated by Zacynthian agents of Callippus, subsequently tyrant of Syracuse (Plutarch, *Dion*, lvii).

103–4. *they should have their due, as well as Cæsar*: Cf. Matt. 22: 21; Romans 13: 7; Tilley C9, D634.

108–9. *five hundred Pounds a Year*: For Sheridan's income, see the General Introduction.

120. *Anniversary-Dinner at the Tholsel*: Since 1690, Dublin had elaborately celebrated William's birthday, 4 Nov., which fell only shortly before the appearance of this *Intelligencer*. Swift had noted a recent decline in the fervour of these observances (*Intelligencer* 8, line 80 and n.). The Tholsel, Dublin's city hall, was in Skinner's Row, since renamed Christchurch Place. See Gilbert, *Dublin*, i. 168–70; iii. 42; and J. G. Simms, 'Remembering 1690', *Studies*, 63 (1974), 231–42.

125. *no complaining in our Streets*: Ps. 144: 14 prays for deliverance, 'that there be no complaining in our streets'. Swift takes this passage as the text for his sermon, 'Causes of the Wretched Condition of Ireland', *Prose*, ix. 199.

126. *Bumper-Loyalty*: Drinking to the memory of the dead had been condemned by

Peter Browne (1665?–1735), bishop of Cork and Ross, in whose see Sheridan was at this time beneficed as rector of Rincurran. Browne's controversial campaign affected primarily the Williamite custom of drinking 'to the glorious, pious, and immortal memory of King William, who delivered us from Popery, slavery, and arbitrary power'. The Williamites in return derided Browne, perhaps unfairly, as a Jacobite; and to their toasts to 'the glorious memory' they added 'and a fig [or 'a fart'] for the Bishop of Cork'. A. R. Winnett, *Peter Browne* (London, 1974), 68–85.

131. *POSTSCRIPT*: For Sarah Harding, see Textual Introduction. She did not actually print the Drapier's Letters, but she and her husband John, who did, were imprisoned for printing them.

Editors have often erroneously stated that no. 19 was a reprint of an earlier pamphlet. This conclusion rests on a pardonable misreading of Swift's letter to Pope, 12 June 1732, where he explains which *Intelligencers* he had written: 'The 15th is a Pamphlet of mine printed before with Dr. Sh—n's Preface, merely for laziness not to disappoint the town; and so was the 19th' (*Corresp.* iv. 30–1). Swift means merely that no. 19 is his, not that it was 'a Pamphlet . . . printed before'.

No. 19 was, Swift continued, 'only a parcel of facts relating purely to the miseries of Ireland, and wholly useless and unentertaining'. This self-deprecatingly doleful estimate nevertheless points usefully to his subject—the miseries he had already discussed in such papers as *A Short View of the State of Ireland*, reprinted as no. 15. For the *Intelligencer*'s original audience, the 'entertaining' qualities of no. 19 would have been substantially accounted for by its political aggressiveness—as Marmaduke Coghill suggests to Edward Southwell, probably referring to no. 19: 'I have herewith sent a paper which we think to be Swifts, in which you will see the genius & spirit of the man with his usuall indiscretion' (Appendix B).

The 'miseries of Ireland' were not new; the continuing famine had begun in the 1725–6 season. Archbishop King wrote, 'The condition of Dublin and in truth of all Ireland is most miserable, alle necessaries of life being excessive dear and no mony stirring, in so much y^t many of ye poor have alredy starved, and many more are like to perish' (to the dowager Lady Southwell, 10 April 1728, TCD MS 750/9, fo. 52).

On 16 July 1728, Archbishop Hugh Boulter, one of the Lords Justices of Ireland, wrote to the Duke of Newcastle, British Secretary of State, stressing, as would Swift, the shortage of cash:

> Our want of silver here is such, that it is common to give six-pence for the change of a moidore, and to take a guinea or pistole for part of the change. And I know some in *Dublin*, who have occasion to pay workmen every *Saturday* night, that are obliged to pay four-pence for every twenty shillings in silver they procure.
>
> We have hundreds of families (all protestants) removing out of the north to *America*; and the least obstruction in the linen-manufacture, by which the north subsists, must occasion greater numbers following, and the want of silver increasing, will prove a terrible blow to that manufacture, as there will not be money to pay the poor for their small parcels of yarn. (Boulter, i. 201–2.)

A similar perspective is that of Captain Thomas Whitney, writing to Newcastle from Lough Larne, 27 July 1728:

here are a vast number of people shiping of for Pensilveana, and Boston, here are three ships at Learne 5 at Derry two at Coleraine 3 at Belfast and 4 at Sligo, Ime assured within these eight years there are gon above fourty thousand people out of Ulstor and ye Low part of Connaught, so y^t if they go on them Collonys will be very strong, ye Land Lords here has raised theyr land, to have ye name of a great Estate[.] ye Tennant cant pay it and they have nothing but a Long rent Roole to show and dont receive have ye money.

(State Papers, Ireland, PRO SP 63/390, fo. 121–2. See also R. J. Dickson's comments on this letter in his *Ulster Emigration to Colonial America, 1718–1775* (London, 1966), 33.)

By late October the realization was growing that Ireland's economy was in desperate straits. The emigration to America was primarily to the province of Pennsylvania, including what later became the state of Delaware; and though most who emigrated were Dissenters, it seems clear that their motivation was primarily economic, not religious. Alarmed at the drain of labour and cash and at the resultant decrease in the Protestant population, the Lords Justices looked for some action they could take. According to one report of Dublin news from 26 October,

Ye Lords Justices upon Information yt a great many Persons here have Transported ymselves & y^r Effects to ye Plantations abroad & yt Consid^ble Numbers of others were prepareing to do ye same have given Directions for putting ye Laws in Execution agst ye said Practice both to prevent yr going off & y^r. takeing y^r. mony & other Effects with them and tis added yt speedy & effectuall methods will be taken to punish those persons who go about to seduce ye Ignorant to Transgress ye Laws of ye Land (London newsletter to Lord Percival, later 1st Earl of Egmont, 2 Nov. 1728, BL MS Add. 48701, fo. 248).

On 29 October it was reported in Dublin that more than 1900 families had left Ulster for New England (*Daily J.*, London, 7 Nov. 1728). On 23 November the Irish Lords Justices asked the English Privy Council to forbid emigration and to take other emergency measures; the request was on the whole rejected. (*Acts of the Privy Council of England. Colonial Series*, iii (Hereford, 1910), 205–6; and Dickson, 33, 184–5.)

Writing to Newcastle the same day, Boulter gave a 'melancholy' report of conditions in Ulster:

. . . we have had three bad harvests together there, which has made oatmeal, which is their great subsistance, much dearer than ordinary, and as our farmers here are very poor, and obliged as soon as they have their corn, to sell it for ready money to pay their rents, it is more in the power of those who have a little money to engross corn here, and make advantage of its scarceness, than in *England.*

> We have had for several years some agents from the colonies in
> *America*, and several masters of ships that have gone about the country,
> and deluded the people with stories of great plenty and estates to be had
> for going for in those parts of the world: and they have been the better
> able to seduce people, by reason of the necessities of the poor of late
> (Boulter, i. 209).

Swift shared this view. He probably also heard rumours like the report in *Fog's
Weekly Journal* (16 November) that the master of a ship carrying 130 emigrants
to Philadelphia had sailed without provisions, intending to wreck the ship,
drown the passengers, save himself, and keep the fares.

In June 1728, Swift had gone to Market Hill, County Armagh, as the guest of
Sir Arthur and Lady Acheson. In this rural setting his first-hand view of the
country's hardship had reminded him of the *Intelligencer*. On 18 September he
had written to Sheridan, 'I think the Sufferings of the Country, for want of
Silver, deserves a Paper, since the Remedy is so easy, and those in Power so
negligent' (*Corresp.* iii. 297).

Although Swift probably finished no. 19 not long before publication, the
idea had, then, germinated considerably sooner.

The headnote casts *Intelligencer* 19 as a reply to a letter of 12 October from
Andrew Dealer and Patrick Pennyless. Oliver W. Ferguson has interestingly
suggested that Swift is responding to an actual letter written under these
pseudonyms, and that it was the same author who wrote to him in April or
May of 1729, signing himself Andrew Trueman and Patrick Layfield. Swift
replied to this second letter in his posthumously published essay, 'Answer to
Several Letters from Unknown Persons', writing that he had received the
previous letter 'last summer [*sic*], directed to Dublin, while I was in the
Country, whither it was sent me; and I ordered an answer to it to be printed,
but It seems it had little effect' (*Prose*, xii. 75). See Ferguson, 161–2, 191–5.

Intelligencer 19 was one of the first published discussions of a subject that
engaged a number of essayists during the following year—including Swift
himself in 'A Letter to the Archbishop of Dublin, Concerning the Weavers':

> I am weary . . . of so many contradictory Speculations about the raising or
> sinking the value of gold and silver. I am not in the least sorry to hear of
> the great Numbers going to America, though very much so for the Causes
> that drive them from us, since the uncontrolled Maxim that People are
> the Riches of a Nation is no maxim here under our Circumstances.
> (*Prose*, xii. 66, 358.)

Swift's persona in no. 19, A. North, and the 'Person of Quality' he mentions
are both modelled on Sir Arthur Acheson, Swift's host at the time of composition, as J. G. Simms first suggested. Acheson, like A. North, was a member of
Parliament; both were northern landlords of about the same income. The
person of quality, another northern landlord, was about the same age as

Acheson. Irvin Ehrenpreis adds that the descriptions closely match Swift's description, probably of Acheson, in 'Answer to Several Letters from Unknown Persons' a few months later (*Prose*, xii. 79). See Simms, 'Dean Swift and County Armagh', *Seanchas Ard Mhacha*, 6 (1971), 135; Ehrenpreis, iii. 609 and n.

On the emigration from Ulster to America in 1728, see Henry Jones Ford, *The Scotch-Irish in America* (Princeton, 1915), 270–1; Guy Soulliard Klett, *Presbyterians in Colonial Pennsylvania* (Philadelphia, 1937), 10–32; Wayland F. Dunaway, *The Scotch-Irish of Colonial Pennsylvania* (Chapel Hill, 1944), 29–61; J. C. Beckett, *Protestant Dissent in Ireland, 1687–1780* (London, 1948), 87–90; James G. Leyburn, *The Scotch-Irish: A Social History* (Chapel Hill, 1962), 170–86; Dickson; and Clayton D. Lein, 'Swift and the Population of Ireland', *Eighteenth-Cent. Stud.* 8 (1975), 443–5.

For general commentary on no. 19, see Ehrenpreis, iii. 583–6.

NUMB. XIX.

Having on the 12th *of* October *last, receiv'd a LETTER Sign'd* Andrew Dealer, *and* Patrick Pennyless*; I believe the following* PAPER, *just come to my Hands, will be a sufficient Answer to it.*

Sic vos non vobis vellera fertis oves.

Virg.

SIR,

I Am a Country Gentleman, and a Member of *Parliament*, with an Estate of about 1400 *l.* a Year, which as a *Northern* Landlord, I receive from above two Hundred Tenants, and my Lands having been Let, near twenty Years ago, the Rents, till very lately, were 5 esteemed to be not above half Value; yet by the intolerable Scarcity of *Silver*, I lye under the greatest Difficulties in receiving them, as well as in paying my Labourers, or buying any thing necessary for my Family from *Tradesmen*, who are not able to be long out of their *Money*. But the sufferings of me, and those of my Rank, are Trifles in Comparison, 10 of what the meaner sort undergo; such as the *Buyers* and *Sellers*, at *Fairs*, and *Markets*; The *Shop-keepers* in every *Town*, the *Farmers* in general. All those who Travel with *Fish*, *Poultry*, *Pedlary-Ware*, and other Conveniencies to sell: But more especially *Handy-crafts-men*, who Work for us by the Day, and common Labourers, whom I have 15

already mentioned. Both these kinds of People, I am forced to employ,
till their Wages amount to a *Double Pistole*, or a *Moydore*, (for we hardly
have any *Gold* of lower Value left among us) to divide it among
themselves as they can; and this is generally done at an *Ale-house* or
20 *Brandy shop*; where, besides the cost of getting *Drunk*, (which is usually
the Case) they must pay *ten pence* or a *Shilling*, for changing their *Piece*
into *Silver*, to some *Huckstering-fellow*, who follows that *Trade*. But
what is infinitely worse, those Poor Men for want of due Payment, are
forced to take up their *Oat-meal*, and other Necessaries of Life, at
25 almost double Value, and consequently are not able, to discharge half
their score, especially under the scarceness of *Corn*, for two Years
past, and the Melancholy disappointment of the present *Crop*.

The Causes of this, and a thousand other Evils, are clear and
manifest to you and all other Thinking Men, though hidden from the
30 Vulgar: These indeed complain of hard Times, the Dearth of Corn,
the want of Money, the badness of Seasons; that their Goods bear no
Price, and the poor cannot find Work; but their weak reasonings never
carry them to the Hatred, and Contempt, born us by our Neighbours,
and Brethren, without the least grounds of Provocation, who rejoice at
35 our Sufferings, although sometimes to their own Disadvantage; of the
dead Weight upon every beneficial Branch of our Trade; of half our
Revenues sent annually to *England*, and many other Grievances
peculiar to this unhappy Kingdom, excepted for our Sins, which keeps
us from enjoying the common Benefits of Mankind, as you and some
40 other Lovers of their Country, have so often observed, with such good
Inclinations, and so little Effect.

It is true indeed, that under our Circumstances in general, this
Complaint for the want of *Silver*, may appear as Ridiculous, as for a
Man to be impatient, about a *Cut Finger*, when he is struck with the
45 *Plague*, and yet a poor Fellow going to the *Gallows*, may be allow'd to
feel the smart of *Wasps*, while he is upon *Tyburn* Road. This
misfortune is too urging, and vexatious in every kind of small Traffick,
and so hourly pressing upon all Persons in the Country whatsoever,
that a hundred inconveniences, of perhaps greater Moment in
50 themselves, have been timely submitted to, with far less disquietude
and murmurs. And the Case seems yet the harder, if it be true, what
many skilfull Men assert, that nothing is more easy, than a Remedy;
and, that the Want of *Silver*, in proportion to the little *Gold* remaining
among us, is altogether as unnecessary, as it is inconvenient. A Person
55 of Distinction assured me very lately, that, in discoursing with the *Lord*

Lieutenant, before his last Return to *England*, His *Excellency* said, *He had pressed the matter often, in proper Time and Place, and to proper Persons; and could not see any difficulty of the least Moment, that could prevent us from being easy upon that Article.*

Whoever carrys to *England*, twenty seven *English* Shillings, and 60 brings back one *Moydore*, of full Weight, is a gainer of nine pence *Irish*; In a *Guinea*, the Advantage is three pence, and two pence in a *Pistole*. The BANKERS, who are generally Masters of all our *Gold*, and *Silver*, with this Advantage, have sent over as much of the latter, as came into their Hands. The Value of one thousand *Moydores* in *Silver*, would 65 thus amount in clear profit, to 37 *l.* 10 *s.* The *Shop-keepers*, and other *Traders*, who go to *London* to buy Goods, followed the same Practice, by which we have been driven into this insupportable Distress.

To a common Thinker, it should seem, that nothing would be more easy, than for the *Government* to Redress this Evil, at any time they 70 shall please. When the value of *Guineas* was lowred in *England*, from 21 *s.* 6 *d.* to only 21 *s.* the Consequences to this Kingdom, were obvious, and manifest to us all; and a sober Man, may be allowed at least to wonder, though he dare not complain, why a new Regulation of *Coin* among us, was not then made; much more, why it hath never 75 been since. It would surely require no very profound skill in *Algebra*, to reduce the difference of *nine Pence* in *thirty Shillings*, or *three Pence* in a *Guinea*, to less than a *Farthing*; And so small a Fraction could be no Temptation, either to *Bankers*, to hazard their *Silver* at Sea, or Tradesmen to load themselves with it, in their Journeys to *England.* In 80 my humble Opinion, it would be no unseasonable Condescension, if the *Government* would Graciously please, to signify to the *poor loyal Protestant Subjects* of *Ireland*, either that this miserable want of *Silver*, is not possible to be remedy'd in any degree, by the nicest skill in *Arithmetick*; or else, that it doth not stand with the good pleasure of 85 *England*, to suffer any *Silver* at all among us. In the former Case, it would be madness, to expect Impossibilities: And in the other, we must submit: For, Lives, and Fortunes are, always at the Mercy of the CONQUEROR.

The Question hath been often put in *printed Papers*, by the 90 *DRAPIER*, and others, or perhaps by the same *WRITER*, under different Styles, why this Kingdom should not be permitted to have a *Mint* of its own for the *Coinage* of *Gold*, *Silver*, and *Copper*, which is a Power exercised by many *Bishops*, and every petty *Prince* in *Germany.* But this Question hath never been answered, nor the least Application 95

that I have heard of, made to the *Crown* from hence, for the grant of a
Publick Mint, although it stands upon Record, that several Cities, and
Corporations here, had the Liberty of *Coining Silver*. I can see no
Reasons, why we alone of all Nations, are thus restrained, but such as I
100 dare not mention; only thus far, I may venture, that *Ireland* is the first
Imperial Kingdom, since *Nimrod*, which ever wanted Power, to *Coin*
their own *Money*.

I know very well, that in *England* it is lawful for any Subject, to
Petition either the *Prince*, or the *Parliament*, provided it be done in a
105 dutiful, and regular Manner; But what is lawful for a Subject of
Ireland, I profess I cannot determine; nor will undertake, that your
Printer shall not be prosecuted, in a *Court of Justice*, for publishing my
Wishes, that a poor Shop-keeper might be able to change a *Guinea*, or
a *Moydore*, when a Customer comes for a *Crown's* worth of Goods. I
110 have known less Crimes punished with the utmost Severity, under the
Title of *Disaffection*: And, I cannot but approve the Wisdom of the
Antients, who, after *Astrea* had fled from the Earth, at least took care to
provide *three upright Judges for Hell*. Men's Ears among us, are indeed
grown so nice, that whoever happens to think out of Fashion, in what
115 relates to the Welfare of this Kingdom, dare not so much as complain
of the *Tooth-ach*, lest our weak and busy Dablers in politick should be
ready to swear against him for *Disaffection*.

There was a Method practiced by Sir *Ambrose Crowley*, the great
Dealer in *Iron-works*, which I wonder the Gentlemen of our Country,
120 under this great Exigence, have not thought fit to imitate. In the
several Towns, and Villages, where he dealt, and many Miles round,
he gave *Notes*, instead of *Money*, from *two Pence*, to *twenty Shillings*,
which passed currant in all Shops, and Markets, as well as in Houses,
where Meat, or Drink was Sold. I see no Reason, why the like
125 Practice, may not be introduced among us, with some degree of
Success, or at least may not serve, as a poor Expedient, in this, our
blessed age of Paper, which, as it Dischargeth all our greatest Payments,
may be equally useful in the Smaller, and may just keep us alive, till an
English Act of Parliament shall forbid it.

130 I have been told, that among some of our poorest *American*
Colonies, upon the Continent, the People enjoy the Liberty of
cutting the little *Money* among them into halves, and quarters, for
the conveniences of small Traffick. How happy should we be in
Comparison of our present Condition, if the like Priviledge, were
135 granted to us, of employing the Sheers, for want of a *Mint*, upon our

foreign Gold; by clipping it into *half Crowns*, and *shillings*, and even lower Denominations; For Beggars must be content to live upon scraps; And it would be our Felicity, that these scraps would never be exported to other Countries, while any thing better was left.

If neither of these Projects will avail, I see nothing left us, but to truck and barter our Goods, like the *wild Indians*, with each other, or with our too powerful Neighbours; only with this disadvantage on our side, that the *Indians* enjoy the Product of their own Land, whereas the better half of ours is sent away without so much as a recompence in *Bugles*, or *Glass*, in return.

It must needs be a very comfortable Circumstance, in the present juncture, that some thousand Families are gone, or going, or preparing to go, from hence, and settle themselves in *America.* The poorer Sort, for want of Work, the Farmers, whose beneficial Bargains are now become a Rack-rent, too hard to be born. And those who have any *ready Money*, or can purchase any, by the Sale of their Goods, or Leases; because they find their Fortunes hourly decaying; that their Goods will bear no Price, and that few or none, have any *Money* to buy the very necessaries of Life, are hastening to follow their departed Neighbours. It is true, *Corn* among us, carries a very high price; but it is for the same reason, that *Rats*, and *Cats*, and Dead *Horses*, have been often bought for *Gold*, in a Town besieged.

There is a Person of Quality in my Neighbourhood, who twenty Years ago, when he was just come to age, being unexperienced, and of a generous Temper, let his lands, even as times went then, at a low Rate, to able Tenants, and consequently by the rise of Land since that time, looked upon his Estate, to be set at half value. But Numbers of these Tenants, or their Descendants are now Offering to sell their Leases by Cant, even those which were for Lives, some of them renewable for ever, and some Fee-farms, which the Landlord himself, hath bought in, at half the Price they would have yielded seven Years ago. And some Leases Let at the same time, for Lives, have been given up to him, without any Consideration at all.

This is the most favourable face of things at present among us, I say, among us of the *North*, who are esteemed the onely thriving people of the Kingdom: And how far, and how soon, this Misery, and Desolation may spread, is easy to foresee.

The vast Sums of *Money* daily carryed off, by our numerous Adventurers to *America*, have deprived us of our *Gold* in these Parts, almost as much as of our *Silver*.

And the good Wives who come to our Houses, offer us their Pieces of Linnen, upon which their whole Dependence lyes, for so little profit, that it can neither half pay their Rents, nor half support their Families.

180 It is remarkable, that this Enthusiasm spread among our *Northern* People, of sheltring them selves in the Continent of *America*, hath no other foundation, than their present insupportable Condition at home. I have made all possible inquiries, to learn what Encouragement our People have met with, by any Intelligence from 185 those Plantations, sufficient to make them undertake, so tedious, and hazardous a Voyage, in all seasons of the Year; and so ill accommodated in their Ships, that many of them have Dyed miserably in their Passage; But, could never get one satisfactory Answer. Some body, they know not who, had Written a Letter to his Friend, or 190 Cousin, from thence, inviting him by all means, to come over; that it was a fine fruitfull Country, and to be held for ever, at a *Penny* an Acre. But the Truth of the Fact is this, The *English* established in those Colonies, are in great want of Men to inhabit that Tract of Ground, which lyes between them, and the *Wild Indians*, who are not reduced 195 under their Dominion. We Read of some barbarous People, whom the *Romans* placed in their Armies, for no other service, than to blunt their Enemies Swords, and afterwards to fill up Trenches with their dead Bodies. And thus our People who Transport themselves, are settled in those interjacent Tracts, as a screen against the Insults of the *Savages* 200 and may have as much Land, as they can clear from the Woods, at a very reasonable Rate, if they can afford to pay about a *hundred* years Purchase by their Labour. Now besides the *Fox*'s reasons, which inclines all those, who have already ventured thither, to represent every thing, in a false light, as well for justifying their own Conduct, as 205 for getting Companions, in their misery; so, the Governing People in those Plantations, have Wisely provided, that no Letters shall be suffered to pass from thence hither, without being first viewed by the Council, by which our People here, are wholly deceived in the Opinions, they have of the happy condition of their Friends, gone 210 before them. This was accidentally discovered some months ago, by an honest Man who having transported himself, and family thither, and finding all things directly contrary to his hope, had the luck to convey a private Note, by a faithful hand, to his Relation here, entreating him, not to think of such a Voyage, and to discourage all his 215 friends from attempting it. Yet this, although it be a Truth well known,

hath produced very little effects; which is no manner of wonder; For as it is natural to a Man in a *Fever* to turn often, although without any hope of Ease, or when he is pursued to leap down a Precipice, to avoid an Enemy just at his back; so, Men in the extremest degree of Misery, and Want, will naturally fly to the first apperance of Relief, let it be ever so vain, or visionary. 220

You may observe, that I have very superficially touched the subject I began with, and with the utmost Caution: For I know how Criminal the least Complaint hath been thought, however seasonable or just, or honestly intended, which hath forced me to offer up my Daily Prayers, 225 that it may never, at least in my time, be Interpreted by innuendo's as a false, scandalous, seditious, and disaffected action, for a Man to roar under an acute fit of the *Gout*, which beside the loss, and the danger, would be very inconvenient to one of my Age, so severely Afflicted with that Distemper. 230

I wish you good success, but I can promise you little, in an ungrateful Office you have taken up, without the least view, either to Reputation, or Profit. Perhaps your Comfort is, that none but *Villians*, and *Betrayers* of their Country, can be your *Enemies*. Upon which, I have little to say, having not the honour, to be acquainted with many of 235 that sort, and therefore, as you easily may believe, am compelled to lead a very retired Life.

> I am Sir,
> Your most Obedient,
> Humble Servant, 240
> A. *NORTH.*

County of *Down.* }
  Dec. 2*d.* 1728. }

HEADING. *a Letter Sign'd Andrew Dealer, and Patrick Pennyless*: See introductory note.

MOTTO. *Sic vos non vobis*: 'Thus you [sheep bear fleeces] but not for yourselves'; part of a spurious anecdote, widely alluded to, in which Virgil blames the poetaster Bathyllus for having stolen one of his epigrams. The anecdote is from the life of Virgil formerly attributed to Tiberius Claudius Donatus; it stood at the head of many if not most 15th–18th-cent. edns. of Virgil. See H. Nettleship, preface to *Ancient Lives of Vergil* (Oxford, 1879); Franciscus Buecheler and Alexander Riese (eds.), *Anthologia Latina* (Leipzig, 1894), I. i. 212; Jacobus Brummer, *Vitae Vergilianae* (Leipzig, 1912), 31.

3. *as a Northern Landlord*: Tenant farms were much smaller in Ulster than in the rest of Ireland; thus a northern landlord could speak from direct experience about the plight of the poorer farmers who elsewhere would have been only subtenants. (I am grateful to W. H. Crawford for this information from his research in Ulster estate archives.)

5. *the Rents, till very lately. . .*: 'Rents were already rising sharply after the first decade of

the century. About 1717 and 1718 in particular the leases for much land which had been let for low rents while the country lay waste after the Williamite Wars began to fall in and the rents were doubled and trebled.' L. M. Cullen, *Anglo-Irish Trade*, 24–5. The fall 'very lately' was due to the famine.

6–7. *the intolerable Scarcity of Silver*: See introductory note to no. 15.

17. *a Double Pistole, or a Moydore*: The double pistole was a French or Spanish gold coin worth £1 17s. Irish; the Portuguese moidore was a gold coin worth £1 10s. Irish. '*Gold* of lower Value' would have included the French louis d'or (£1 2s.) as well as the half and quarter louis d'or, the pistole and the half and quarter pistoles (the latter worth only 4s. 7½d. Irish), and the half and quarter moidores, as well as the guinea. James Simon, *Simon's Essay of Irish Coins . . . with Mr. Snelling's Supplement* (1810; reprinted London, 1975), 68–9.

26. *the scarceness of Corn*: See introductory note.

33–4. *our Neighbours, and Brethren*: The English.

35. *sometimes to their own Disadvantage*: Swift seems here to accept one of John Browne's arguments; see introductory note to no. 15.

36–7. *half our Revenues sent annually to England*: Cf. the estimates in no. 15 and notes.

38. *excepted for our Sins*: The sense is that Ireland 'for our Sins' is excepted from the happiness elsewhere, which exception 'keeps us from enjoying the common benefits . . .'; cf. textual variants. Swift alludes to the observation, already made in *A Short View* (no. 15), that Ireland did not obey the accepted maxims of mercantile economics; see 'Maxims Controlled in Ireland', *Prose*, xii. 131–7.

39–40. *as you . . . have so often observed*: Perhaps an allusion to the Drapier's Letters. According to Faulkner's headnote in *35*, 'this Letter is supposed as directed to the *Drapier*'. It could more probably be 'supposed as directed to' Mr Intelligencer, however, and as referring to nos. 6, 15, 16, 17, and 18.

47. *urging*: Inciting, stimulating (see *OED*).

50. *timely*: In good time; quickly (*OED*); changed to 'tamely' in *35*.

55–6. *the Lord Lieutenant, before his last Return to England*: Carteret sailed for England about 15 May 1728. W. Maple makes a similar point about Carteret's unsuccessful efforts to raise the Irish value of silver in 1726 and 1728: *A Vindication of the Intended Alterations of the Value of the Several Coins Now Currant in the Kingdom* (Dublin: Rhames, 1729), 4. Archbishop Boulter's letters of 1728 and 1729 show him energetically encouraging such a revaluation.

61. *a gainer of nine pence Irish*: 'A moidore, which is worth about 27 s. in *England*, passes here for 30 s. *Irish*, or 27 s. *English*, and 9 d.' Boulter, ii. 122.

66. *37 l. 10 s.*: In Irish money.

71. *When the value of Guineas was lowred in England*: 22 Dec. 1717. In 1718 the Irish Privy Council unsuccessfully requested the Lord Lieutenant (the Duke of Bolton) to proclaim a reduction in the guinea from £1 3s. Irish to £1 2s. 9d. BL MS Add. 61640, fo. 160.

88–9. *at the Mercy of the CONQUEROR*: Swift cherished the notion that Ireland was a sovereign kingdom, in accordance with Molyneux's elaborate denial that Ireland was a conquered kingdom (30–9); proponents of the British Declaratory Act had argued that it was (*Several Speeches in the House of Commons in England, for and against the Bill for the Better Securing the Dependency of the Kingdom of Ireland, on the Crown of Gt. Britain* ([Dublin], 1720), 9, 12). Cf. Swift to Peterborough, 26 Apr. 1726, *Corresp.* iii. 132.

90–1. *by the DRAPIER, and others*: See no. 15 and notes.

97–8. *several Cities, and Corporations here*: See *Corresp.* iii. 112, 287; *Prose*, xii. 105.

99–100. *such as I dare not mention*: i.e., that Ireland's Parliament, being composed of slaves, has failed to exert itself.

101. *Nimrod*: Gen. 10: 8–10. Traditionally considered the first king (*Prose*, ix. 264); on

Swift's view of him as 'an archetype of tyrannical monarchy' see Daniel Eilon, 'Swift Burning the Library of Babel', *Mod. Lang. Rev.* 80 (1985), esp. 272–4, where by a slip *Intelligencer* 19 is cited as one of the Drapier's Letters.

103–4. *in England it is lawful . . . to Petition*: The ancient English right of petition is implicit in Magna Charta (though this was debated in 1689) and was formally guaranteed in the Bill of Rights, 1689: 'It is the right of the subjects to petition the king, and all commitments and prosecutions for such petitioning are illegal.' In 1701, Lord Somers defended the right to petition without relying on the Bill of Rights, saying that the right was 'as large and ample a one, and what will as little bear controverting, as any thing that we can think of, since 'tis justified by the Law of Nature [and] the Practice of all States in the World' (Somers, *Jura Populi Anglicani: or, The Subject's Right of Petitioning Set Forth* (London, 1701, the 64-page edn.), 30). There was no Irish bill of rights, nor did the Irish statutes treat petitioning, leaving it seemingly in constitutional limbo in Ireland; but the English Bill of Rights was generally considered in force in Ireland. N. Robbins, in the preface to his *Exact Abridgment of All Irish Statutes . . . with an Abridgment of All the English Statutes, in Force in Ireland* (Dublin: Grierson, 1736), describes it as 'of the highest Authority in Law'. See Lois G. Schwoerer, *The Declaration of Rights, 1689* (Baltimore, 1981), 69–71.

109. *a Crown's worth*: 5s. 5d. Irish.

112. *Astrea*: Justice, the last of the immortals to leave the earth in the Iron Age (Aratus of Soli, *Phaenomena*, 96–136; Ovid, *Metamorphoses*, i. 150; Hyginus, *Poetica Astronomia*, ii. 25); compare *Tale*, 52; *Prose*, i. 248.

113. *three upright Judges*: Minos, Rhadamanthus, and Aeacus, sons of Jupiter (Plato, *Gorgias*, 523 E–524 A; Diodorus Siculus, v. 79. 1–2; *Aeneid*, vi. 432, 566; Ovid, *Metamorphoses*, xiii. 25–6). To paraphrase, 'Ireland has not got three upright judges' (Ehrenpreis, iii. 585).

116. *politick*: Policy, politics (*OED*, sense B. 2).

118. *Sir Ambrose Crowley*: Creator of 'probably the greatest industrial organization of his age', Crowley (1635–1713) issued what he called 'current bills' beginning about 1699. They were bills of exchange, payable to the bearer for specific amounts (not issued only in round figures and not limited to 20s.) and to be cashed at company offices in County Durham or in London. See M. W. Flinn, *Men of Iron: The Crowleys in the Early Iron Industry* (Edinburgh, 1962), 55, 180–2; and Flinn (ed.), *The Law Book of the Crowley Ironworks*, Surtees Soc. Pub. CLXVII (1952 [1957]), 54–8; *Drapier's Letters*, 49.

125. *may not be introduced among us*: It is unclear whether Swift was aware this early of James Maculla's plans to issue copper halfpence—promissory notes on copper. Maculla announced his scheme in Feb. 1728/9 (*Daily J.* (London), 17 Feb. 1728/9, reprinting Dublin news of 8 Feb.), and Swift drafted a critique, 'A Letter on Maculla's Project about Halfpence' (*Prose*, xii. 93–105). That Maculla's plans had taken shape earlier is suggested by specimens dated 1728 (Simon, supplement, 6–7; Aquilla Smith, 'On the Copper Tokens Issued in Ireland from 1728 to 1761', *J. Hist. and Archaeol. Assn. of Ireland*, 3rd ser., 1 (1869), 418, 424–5; W. J. Davis, *The Nineteenth-Century Token Coinage* (London, 1904), 237–8).

127. *blessed age of Paper*: See notes to no. 17.

128–9. *an English Act of Parliament*: An allusion to the Declaratory Act of 1719, 6 Geo. I, c. 5 (British).

130–1. *our poorest American Colonies*: Not a claim easily documented for this period, but a Maryland statute of 1729 says that 'the Cutting or Clipping of Foreign Coins is now in some Measure necessary for the making of Change' (*Laws of Maryland, Enacted . . . 1729* (Annapolis: Parks, 1729), 1). Other colonial statutes, setting rates of exchange for various foreign coins, provide that halves, quarters, and eighths be valued proportionately: Massachusetts Statutes, 6 Anne, c. 95 (1707), in *The Charters and*

General Laws of the Colony and Province of Massachusetts Bay (Boston, 1814), 383–5, also 744; a Virginia proclamation of 1683, in *Executive Journals of the Council of Colonial Virginia* (Richmond, 1925), i. 35–8; and a Maryland act of 1708, in *A Compleat Collection of the Laws of Maryland* (Annapolis: Parks, 1727), 54–5.

134–5. *if the like Priviledge, were granted to us*: See the section on dating the *Intelligencers* in the General Introduction.

147. *some thousand Families are gone, or going*: See introductory note.

164. *Cant*: Auction.

165. *Fee-farms*: Land holdings 'in fee-simple subject to a perpetual fixed rent' (*OED*).

168. *without any Consideration*: Gratis.

188–9. *Some body . . . had Written a Letter*: e.g., William Bull, a Philadelphia justice of the peace, to his sister, 30 Aug. 1728, begging her to leave Ireland for Philadelphia. He praises the great style in which many formerly poor Irishmen live there, offering as an example 'Mͬ Edward Verner who Lived in Armagh . . . is accounted here to great Degree—he has Two Negroes waiting on him.' The letter was somehow passed along to Edward Southwell with the note, 'Mͬ. Verner yͭ is mentioned in this letter to be so great was a shoemaker in this Town & ran away above 2 or 3 yrs agow. his wife & Children here in a poor way.' Southwell Papers, BL MS Egerton 917, fo. 241. See also Marmaduke Coghill to Edward Southwell, 5 Nov. 1728, Huntington MS HM 28678.

195. *We Read of some barbarous People*: Tacitus, *Agricola*, 35, reports the use of such *auxilia* in the Roman conquest of Britain; cf. Appendix K.

198–9. *settled . . . as a screen*: Swift makes a similar charge in *An Answer to the Craftsman* (1731), *Prose*, xii. 176. The charge can be independently confirmed: James F. Watson, *Annals of Philadelphia* (Philadelphia, 1830), ii. 477.

199. *Insults*: i.e., assaults.

202. *the Fox's reasons*: Aesop's fox, having lost his tail, tries to persuade the other foxes to cut off theirs. Swift also alludes to this fable in *Tale*, 141.

206–7. *no Letters shall be suffered to pass from thence hither*: A highly implausible assertion, since most transatlantic mail was carried privately and not subject to governmental regulation. Swift aroused a colonial protest; see Appendix K. Yet there is evidence that Swift did not fabricate his claim out of whole cloth. A Quaker, Robert Parke of Chester Township, Pennsylvania, wrote to his sister Mary Valentine in Bally-brumhill, Co. Carlow, 10th Month, 1725: 'As to what thee writt about the Governours Opening Letters it is Utterly false & nothing but a Lye & any one Except bound Servants may go out of the Country when they will & Servants when they Serve their time may Come away If they please but it is Rare any are such fools to leave the Country Except mens business require it, they pay 9 Pounds for their Passage (of this money) to go to Ireland.' Albert Cook Myers, *Immigration of the Irish Quakers into Pennsylvania, 1682–1750* (Swarthmore, 1902), 74–5.

226. *innuendo's*: In a libel case, parenthetical explanations inserted by the prosecution to make a text's libellous intent obvious.

No. 20 appeared too late for inclusion in *29*, probably the volume Swift consulted when listing his *Intelligencers* for Pope (*Corresp.* iv. 30–1). Similarly, Faulkner seems to have used *29* (and not *30* or the original Harding numbers) in preparing his edition of Swift's *Works*, so the fact that both Swift's letter and his *Works* pass over no. 20 cannot properly be construed as providing any information whatever about its authorship. Entirely forgotten by the first generation of Swift's editors, the poem was first admitted to Swift's canon in 1779, in John Nichols's *Supplement* to Swift's *Works*, and so it has remained, with little if any discussion of the attribution. (See textual note.)

The attribution to Swift is, it must be conceded, conjectural. On behalf of an attribution to Sheridan, it could be said that in no. 11 he uses a similar technique on a similar occasion, and that in *Gulliveriana* Smedley had given Sheridan some reason to retaliate. As a classicist, Sheridan might have taken a particular interest in burlesquing Smedley's Latin. Yet Swift's Latin was certainly adequate to the task, and he had far greater reason to attack Smedley. Moreover, *Dean Smedley Gone to Seek His Fortune* uses some characteristic Swiftian diction and techniques. The forty-four/score rhyme also appears in *Cadenus and Vanessa* (*Poems*, ii. 703). In line 32, 'swell'd like any *porpus*' is echoed by the cliché 'fat as a Porpoise' in *A Compleat Collection of Genteel and Ingenious Conversation* (*Prose*, iv. 187, 194; the spelling *porpus* occurs in the London edition). Swift enjoyed putting improper language in the mouths of his victims: *phiz* (=physiognomy, face; line 21) recurs in *Genteel and Ingenious Conversation* (*Prose*, iv. 113, 120, 161), and similar instances from this very period are in *Mad Mullinix and Timothy* (=no. 8), line 202; and in *Poems*, iii. 786, 905. With the line 'He hated *Bailiffs* at his shoulder' may be compared, as to image, Swift's line from *The Dean and Duke*, 'From Bayliffs claws thou scarce cou'd keep thy Bum free' (*Poems*, ii. 678). The italicizing for emphasis, which Swift usually does better than Sheridan, is well carried out here. Swift had earlier parodied Smedley's productions, if *His Grace's Answer to Jonathan* and *A Letter from D. S—t to D. S—y* are his (for doubts about the latter, see Rogers, 746–7; *Poems*, ii. 361–2, 371–3). More significantly, *Dean Smedley Gone to Seek His Fortune*, in sending up its victim's text, demonstrates Swift's characteristic terrier-like tenacity, a quality Sheridan's no. 11 lacks. Sheridan's prose introduction to no. 11, moreover, is flaccid, whereas the prose in no. 20 is tight and the humour wry—in short, Swiftian.

As to authorship, then, the evidence on balance favours Swift. As to the Smedleian occasion, however, much greater precision is possible.

According to Thomas Birch, Smedley vowed in 1728 to go to India should his project to publish *A Universal View* fail (see introductory note to no. 11; and A. E. Gunther, *An Introduction to the Life of the Rev. Thomas Birch* (Halesworth,

1984), 10). In 1729 he sailed for Fort St George, Madras, as an East India Company chaplain. Some chaplains got rich in India from private enterprise and burial fees, and Smedley clearly went there to make money. (See M. E. Gibbs, *The Anglican Church in India, 1600–1970* (Delhi, 1970), 10.)

What seems to have happened was a three-way exchange: Paschal Ducasse, who had resigned as Dean of Ferns in ?1727, became Dean of Clogher in early 1728/9 (*Dublin Gazette*, 28 Jan. 1728/9; *Lib. Mun. Pub. Hib.* II. v. 125). Ferns had been offered to Smedley in early 1728, but he had declined (Carteret to Newcastle, 17 Dec. 1728, in State Papers, Ireland, PRO SP 63/390, fo. 189). Thomas Sawbridge, chaplain at Fort St George, left India in September 1727 and became dean of Ferns in January 1728/9, the deanery having in effect been vacant for a year. He shortly became notorious as—in Swift's phrase—'the true *En[gli]sh* D[ea]n to be hang'd for a R[a]pe' (*Poems*, ii. 516; on Sawbridge's career see *Records of Fort St. George. Diary and Consultation Book of 1727* (Madras, 1930), 93–4, 124, 128, 130; *Whitehall Evening-Post*, 21 Dec. 1728; James B. Leslie, *Ferns Clergy and Parishes* (Dublin, 1936), 25). Smedley, without a deanship though he continued to describe himself as dean of Clogher, was appointed by the United East India Company's court of directors as chaplain at Fort St George, Madras, on 8 January 1728/9. He sailed for Madras in February 1728/9, carrying clothing, '1 Box Prints', and 432 bottles of wine (East India Company court book, India Office Records B/60, p. 168; *Records of Fort St. George. Despatches from England 1728–1729* (Madras, 1929), 29, 53).

His activities thereafter have been the subject of speculation or misstatement. But the ship's log recounts his demise. The *Eyles* left Gravesend 14 February 1728/9 and passed Eddystone Light 11 March 1728/9. On Sunday, 30 March, 'att 6 in the Evening the Reverend … Dean Jonathan Smedley Departed this Life of a Feavour and Mortification in one of his Leggs after 8 Days Illness[;] the same Night we Committed his Body to the Deep and fired 11 halph Minute Guns' (Log of the *Eyles*, 1729–30, India Office Records L/MAR/661/D).

By this time the *Dunciad Variorum* had already begun to be distributed privately in London. In revenge for *Gulliveriana*, Pope had written Smedley into the mud-diving games of Book II:

> Next Smedley div'd; slow circles dimpled o'er
> The quaking mud, that clos'd, and ope'd no more.
> All look, all sigh, and call on Smedley lost;
> Smedley in vain resounds thro' all the coast.

Smedley eventually 'rose, in majesty of mud' (TE v. xxviii, 135–6). Pope could not have been aware, nor could Swift and Sheridan, that Smedley had already dived beyond the reach of punishment; word of his death did not reach London until May 1730 (*Records of Fort St. George. Despatches to England 1727–*

1733, p. 61). Thus the *Intelligencer* in May of 1729 cheerfully devoted the first (and only) issue of its third series to demolishing the lapidary panegyric of Smedley first published in the *Daily Post* 13 February. The survival of a revised draft of the inscription in Birch's hand dated 15 February (see textual notes) raises the possibility that Birch was the author and not Smedley, as the *Daily Post* claimed and Swift assumed. (If so, the character becomes significantly less fatuous and less interesting.) Though Smedley may actually have boarded the *Eyles* 13 February, as the published version claims, he and Birch were in communication thereafter: the Birch manuscripts include a copy of a letter of recommendation Smedley wrote for Birch from Deal 26 February, and the ship was in the Downs until at least 6 March (BL MS Add. 4268, fo. 34; East India Company Miscellanies, India Office Records E/1/202, p. 398). It may be surmised that after the *Daily Post* had smirked at the original ill-advised inscription, Birch or Smedley (or both) attempted to remove some of its excesses. When at the beginning of March the *Political State* reprinted the *Daily Post* article, Birch not improbably deemed the situation hopeless and cancelled the engraving altogether. No copy exists in such comprehensive collections of engraved portraits as those of the National Portrait Gallery and the British Museum, suggesting that it was never published.

NUMB. XX.

DEAN SMEDLEY
Gone to seek his
FORTUNE.

Per varios casus per tot discrimina rare Rum.

A short HISTORY *of the DEAN,*
by way of illustration.

HIS first rise in the *Church* was a small living in the Diocese of *Cork*, given him by the GOVERNMENT, to the Surprize of the whole World. This Living he swapped soon after for a Chaplain's Post to a Regiment, which he Sold for five Hundred Pounds. He turned his Hand with this Money, and in a very litle time, got a *DEANERY*, this he swapped likewise for another Living. After this again he got another *DEANERY*, by some unacountable methods, but being much in Debt, he was forced to fly his *Country*, and disposed of it, in what manner no Body can tell, but himself and another. He has left one

10 living behind him, which he could not avoid doing, because it was
sequestred for his Debts. When he went for *England*, in order to turn
the Penny, he received Subscripsions from Numbers of Gentlemen, to
carry on a Work, which would have taken ten years to accomplish, if
the most Ingenious and Learned Person had undertaken it, and which
15 he himself could not have done in ten Thousand Years. After all this,
he run off to *FortSt. George*, and left the following Character of himself.

From the Political State for the Month of *February* 1729 pag. 209.

ABOUT the same time it was published (in the *Dayly Post* of
February 13*th*) that a *Mezzotinto* is engraving from an Original
20 Picture of *Dean Smedley*, with this remarkable Inscription, Written by
Himself.

REVERENDUS *Decanus, Jonathan Smedley: Theologia instructus; in
Poesi exercitatus; Politioribus excultus Literis: Parce Pius, Impius minime:
Veritatis Indagator; Libertatis Assertor: Subsannatus multis; Fastiditus
25 Quibusdam; Exoptatus plurimis; Omnibus Amicus; Author hujus Sententiæ,*

PATRES SUNT VETULÆ.

*Domata Invidia; Superato Odio; per Laudem et Vituperium; per Famam atq;
Infamiam: Utramque Fortunam, Variosq; expertus Casus; Mente Sana; Sano
Corpore; Volens, Lætusq; Lustris plus quam* XI *numeratis; ad Rem Familiarem
30 Restaurandam, augendamq; et ad Evangelium, Indos inter Orientales,
prædicandum; Grevæ, Idibus Februarii, Navem ascendens, Arcemq; Sancti
petens Georgii, Vernale per Æquinoxium; Anno Æræ Christianæ, Millesimo
Septingentesimo Vicesimo Octavo TRANSFRETAVIT.*
—Fata vocant—Revocentq; precamur.

Thus translated.

THE very Reverend *Dean Smedley*,
Of *Dullness*, *Pride*, *Conceit*, a medley,
Was equally allow'd to shine,
As *Poet*, *Scholar* and *Divine*.
With *Godliness* cou'd well dispense,   5
Wou'd be a *Rake*, but wanted Sense.
Wou'd strictly after *Truth* enquire
Because he dreaded to come nigh'r.

For *Liberty* no Champion bolder,
He hated *Bailiffs* at his shoulder.   10
To half the world a standing jest,
A perfect *Nuissance* to the rest.
From many (and we may believe him)
Had the best wishes they cou'd give him.
To all mankind a constant friend,   15
Provided they had *Cash* to lend.
One thing he did before he went hence,
He left us a *Laconick* Sentence,
By cutting of his Phrase, and trimming,
To prove that *Bishops* were old Women.   20
Poor Envy durst not shew her Phiz,
She was so terrify'd at his.
He waded without any shame,
Thro' thick and thin, to get a name.
Try'd ev'ry sharping Trick for Bread,   25
And after all he seldom Sped.
When *fortune* favour'd, he was nice,
He never once wou'd cog the *Dice*,
But if she turn'd against his play,
He knew to stop *a quater trois*.   30
Now sound in mind, and sound in *corpus*,
(Says he) tho' swell'd like any *porpus*,
He heys from hence at forty four,
(*But by his Leave he sinks a Score*,)
To the *East Indies*, there to cheat,   35
'Till he can purchase an Estate;
Where after he has fill'd his chest,
He'll mount his *Tub*, and preach his best,
And plainly prove by dint of Text,
This World is his, and theirs the next.   40
    Lest that the reader shou'd not know,
The Bank where last he set his Toe,
'Twas *Greenwich*. There he took a Ship,
And gave his Creditors the Slip.
But lest *Chronology* should vary,   45
Upon the *Ides* of *February*,
In seventeen hundred eight and twenty,
To *Fort St. George* a *Pedlar* went he.

Ye *Fates*, when all he gets is Spent,
RETURN HIM BEGGAR AS HE WENT.　　　　50

ALL Gentlemen, who are any ways attacked by Dunces, are desired
to send a formal Complaint to the *Intelligencer*, with the Names of
the Delinquents, there shall be ample Satisfaction given, by Printing
the Dunces Names at length, with Animadversions, suitable to their
5 Crimes and Qualities. By which means, we shall in time be enabled to
accomplish an *Irish* Dunciad, in imitation of that incomparable
Duncepick Poem, Written and Published, by the most Ingenious Mr.
Pope against the *Grub-street Scriblers* of *Great-Brittain*. The *Intelligencer*
does likewise for the Ease of the Publick, give Warning to all Dunces,
10 of what Rank soever, forthwith to lay aside their *Crambo*, or he does in
a most solemn manner declare he will Couple them together in their
own Rhymes. He does farther assure them, that if, after this his
Proclamation, any Dunce within this Realm of *Ireland*, shall presume
to touch Pen, Ink, or Paper, after the twentieth Day of this Instant,
15 before which time it is to be presumed he may hear this Read, that
then, *ipso facto*, he pronounces him an Out-law, and of Consequence
every Man has a right to his Head. And for every such Head, brought
in, the Reward shall be the current Price of a *Sheep's* Head, be the Rate
ever so High.

20　　　　　　　　　　　　　　Dated at our *Chambers*.
　　　　　　　　　　　　　　May, the 7*th* 1729.

MOTTO. Wordplay on *Aeneid*, i. 204: 'Per varios casus, per tot discrimina rerum':
'Through divers mishaps, through so many perilous chances, [we fare towards
Latium, where the fates point out a home of rest]' (Loeb). Literally *discrimina
rerum*=crises of things; *rum*, often modified by *rusty*, was, as Swift said in the same
year, 'a cant word in *Ireland* for a poor country Clergyman' (Swift's MS of *The Grand
Question Debated*, Rothschild 2271, p. 2). Chosen to echo 'Variosque expertus Casus'
in Smedley's inscription, the motto not only mocks Smedley as Aeneas but looks
forward to his voyage through all the mishaps and crises of an ironically 'rare'
(praiseworthy) poor country parson; so begins the attack on his financial irre-
sponsibility. Other such characteristic puns on *rum* occur in Swift and Sheridan's
Anglo-Latin word games; see Mayhew, *Rage or Raillery*, 132. The Bowyer–Davis
edition, followed by recent authorities, solemnly emends *rare Rum* to *rerum*.

INTRODUCTION

1–2. *a small living in the Diocese of Cork*: Rincurran.
3. *a Chaplain's Post*: See introductory note to no. 11. He apparently held Rincurran and
the chaplaincy simultaneously.
5. *a Deanery*: Killala.

6. *another Living*: Unidentified.

7. *another Deanery*: Clogher.

9. *no Body can tell, but . . . another*: Presumably Paschal Ducasse; see introductory note.

9–11. *one living . . . was sequestred*: Either Kilcommon Erris, in the diocese of Killala, or Knockmark, which Smedley was reported to have resigned, leaving it 'in his Majesty's disposal' (*London Evening-Post*, 23 Dec. 1729).

12–13. *Subscripsions . . . to carry on a Work*: See no. 11 and its introductory note.

19. *a Mezzotinto*: See introductory note.

22–34. *Reverendus Decanus . . .*: 'The Reverend Dean Jonathan Smedley, learned in theology, proficient in poetry, a cultivator of the politer letters, sparingly pious yet not at all impious, a seeker after truth, a champion of liberty, mocked by many, disdained by certain persons but longed for by most, a friend to all, and the author of the following aphorism: "The Fathers are little old women." Having conquered envy and overcome hatred, through praise and blame, through fame and infamy having experienced both fortune and various misfortunes, sound of mind and body, willing and cheerful, past his 55th year, needing to restore and increase the family fortune and to preach the gospel in India, he embarked at Gravesend 13 February and sailed to Fort St George during the Spring equinox, AD 1728.—The fates call; and we pray that they may recall.'

28–9. *Mente Sana; Sano Corpore*: Proverbial, from Juvenal, *Satires*, x. 356.

POEM

26. *Sped*: Succeeded.

28. *cog*: Load.

30. *a quater trois*: In English, at cater-trey—at the four and the three, implying loaded dice.

33. *at forty four*: In translating *Lustris plus quam* XI *numeratis*, the parodist disregards the usual meaning of *lustrum* (a five-year period), choosing to define it as a four-year period, as under the Julian calendar. Smedley was about 57.

38. *Tub*: Pulpit.

39. *Text*: e.g., the Beatitudes, Matt. 5: 3, 8.

43. *'Twas Greenwich*: An error; *Greva* is the Latin for Gravesend (C. T. Martin, *The Record Interpreter* (2nd edn.; London, 1910), 378).

CONCLUSION

6. *Dunciad*: The reference to the *Dunciad* replies to Pope's Letter to Sheridan, 12 Oct. 1728 (see Appendix B). Smedley, the dunce chiefly in question, first entered the *Dunciad* in the *Dunciad Variorum* version, published 8 Apr. 1729 but privately distributed during the preceding month (Foxon P771–3). Whether his inclusion owed anything to his mode of departure from England, or whether no. 20 owed anything to the *Dunciad Variorum*, is hard to say. The original *Dunciad* (1728) had been reprinted in Dublin; Swift read it 'twenty times' (*Corresp.* iii. 293).

10. *Crambo*: Doggerel; from a verse-game whose object was to use the same rhyme as many times as possible without repeating a word.

APPENDICES

APPENDIX A
Archbishop King on the Taxation of Ireland

Excerpt from Archbishop William King, 'Some observations on the Taxes Pay'd by Ireland to support the Government' (1721), TCD MS 1488, fos. 1, 40–3, 45, here printed with abbreviations expanded. An earlier version, dated 1716 (TCD MS 1995-2008/1806b), was printed in Hist. MSS Comm. *Report 2*, Appendix (1874), 256–7. The piece has been discussed by R. Dudley Edwards in 'The King Manuscripts in the Clarke Collection, T.C.D.', *Analecta Hibernica*, 8 (1938), 6–7; Ferguson, 141, 145–6, 187–8; Andrew Carpenter, 'Two Possible Sources for Swift's A Modest Proposal', *Irish Booklore*, 2 (1972), 147–8; and Bryan Coleborne, '"We flea the people & Sell their Skins": A Source for *A Modest Proposal?*', *Scriblerian*, 15 (1983), 132–3.

Tis a General opinion in Great Brittain, and passes Current without contradiction; that Ireland is in a flourishing condition; that Whilst England has been oppressed and Deeply sunk in Debt by Excessive Taxes, Ireland has been at Ease; contributed nothing to the Support of the Government, and is not one Shilling in Debt; This, I take to be the Inducement that prevailed with many to Say and Doe several things, which the People of Ireland look on as very hard upon them.

．　　　．　　　．　　　．　　　．

Perhaps some will Doubt of the truth of this representation of the miserable Estate of the common people of Ireland; but who Ever has been in their Cabbins have seen the Matter of fact to be so, and Can vouch the truth of it.

There are two sorts of men that I Except against as incompetent witnesses in this Case, first such English Gentlemen as come over into Ireland on Visits or Business, and secondly such Gentlemen of Ireland as live in England, or who although they Live Generally in Ireland, Yet are as much strangers to the Common people, and their way of Liveing as if they were Bred in Turkey; I Know these two represent Ireland as the Most plentifull Luxurious Country in Europe, and magnify the Excessive eating and Drinking in it:

To unfold the Mysterie of this; it must be observed that there are perhaps a Thousand Gentlemens familys in Ireland, who live tolerably well, keep good tables especialy to wellcome their friends and strangers, when therefore a Stranger Comes to them, they hospitably invite him, liberally entertain him and do the Best they Can to make him welcome, thus he is feasted from house to house whilst he stays, and he returns into England full of the plenty and Luxurie of Ireland: but he doth not Consider, that there are three hundred thousand families in Ireland, and among all these hardly a thousand Live in that condition, in which these Gentlemen Live who Intertained him, and for the Good Dinner he met there, three hundred Neighbours or tennants Dined on a potatoe without Salt; Nay perhaps the Gentleman who entertained him after that plentifull Manner is obliged to pinch himself and familie for many Days after, to make a mends for this profuseness in that one Dinner[.]

This and the plenty in the good houses in Dublin, by which many Citizens and Gentlemen undo themselves, deceive most Strangers, and give them Conceptions of Ireland very Distant from truth[.] Most Strangers that Come to Ireland go no farther than that City, and only Converse with Gentlemen or the richer sort there, and never are acquainted with the povertie of the Rest, which is so very Great, that perhaps a third part of that City it self needs Charity: as a proof hereof this Year 1721 above 5000 of one Trade were so miserable, that they must have starved if they had Not Been Relieved by Generall and Seasonable Charitys, the Names and Numbers of the familys were returned by the Ministers and Church wardens, and many Complained that they were omitted;

As to the Irish Gentlemen, who go to England or live there, they often Know little more then their fathers house or the City of Dublin, and are in truth Strangers to the Common way of Living in this Kingdom, or if they do Know it, either shame or vanity makes them conceal it as much as they Can; which I take to be Source of infinite Mischiefs to the Country, and provokes envy instead of pity in our Neighbours of Great Britain, and perhaps many of the Laws Complained of in Ireland owe their being to this Mistake;

.   .   .   .   .

I do not see, how Ireland Can on the present foot pay greater Taxes then it do's, without starveing the Inhabitants, and Leaveing them Intirely without Meat or Cloaths.

They have already given their bread, their ffish, their Butter, their

Shoes, their Stockings, their Beds, their furniture, and houses to pay their Landlords and Taxes, I Cannot see how any More Can be got from them, except we take a way their potatoes and Buttermilk, or flay them and Sell their Skins[.]

APPENDIX B

Unpublished Contemporary Comment

These comments were made in private letters. For published reaction to the *Intelligencer*, see Appendices D, E, G, I, and K.

[20 May 1728]
What makes Swift's little pamphlets so scarce; surely he will send your Lordship a copy of them? It will be said now that he writes out of pique and revenge. It is given out that he was much disappointed when he was last here; that he was in hopes, by the interest he had in a certain lady, to have exchanged his preferment in Ireland for as good in England. Nay, that at last he would have quitted all he had in Ireland, for 400*l. per annum* here, but could not get it.

[William Stratford to 2nd Earl of Oxford, from Oxford. Hist. MSS Comm. 29, *Portland* vii (1901), 463. The reference may be to *Intelligencer* 1 as well as *A Short View of the State of Ireland* and *An Answer to a Paper, Called A Memorial.*]

[18 June 1728]

[Marmaduke Coghill to Edward Southwell, Secretary of State for Ireland, referring probably to no. 6; quoted in the 'Dates of the *Intelligencers*' section of the General Introduction.]

[12 October 1728]
I am much pleas'd with most of the Intelligencers, but I am a little piqued at the Author of 'em for not once doing me the Honour of a Mention upon so honourable an Occasion as being slandered by the Dunces, together with my Friend the Dean. . . .

[Pope to Sheridan, Pope, *Corresp.* ii. 523. Pope responds to a letter in which Sheridan had presumably enclosed the *Intelligencers* thus far published. The reference is to Smedley's *Gulliveriana.*]

[5 November 1728]
Swift & his underlins publishe these Intelligencers, one of which I have sent you.

[Marmaduke Coghill in Dublin to Edward Southwell in London, apparently enclosing one or more *Intelligencers*. Huntington Library MS HM 28678.]

[14 December 1728]
I have herewith sent a paper which we think to be Swifts, in which you will see the genius & spirit of the man with his usuall indiscretion.

[Marmaduke Coghill in Dublin to Edward Southwell, probably enclosing *Intelligencer* 19. BL MS Add. 21122, fo. 62ᵛ.]

[21 December 1728]
. . . as for Poetrry & prose I see none butt what is in print, & here goes one to you; the Craftsman publishes scandal enough; I have your Intelligencers from Ireland, are not you the Squire and Militia Coll. in one of the first of them. . . .

[Henry Temple, 1st Viscount Palmerston, to his nephew William Flower in Dublin, alluding to no. 2. Osborn Collection MSS, Yale University.]

[14 February 1728/9]
I beg your pardon for not sending you the papers I promised you but they were not in my own power till two days since. I have sent you Ballads Two, epigrams Two, intelligencers five.—these last I must desire you will restore to me.

[Edward Harley, 2nd Earl of Oxford, to Pope. Pope, *Corresp.* iii. 17.]

[20 February 1728/9]
I return the Intelligencers, with that one which may well be calld An Intelligencer Extraordinary (in the modern style:) writ no doubt by some Wagg, & printed surreptitiously.

[Pope to the 2nd Earl of Oxford. Pope, *Corresp.* iii. 19. For the spurious no. 20 to which Pope refers, see Appendix H.]

[About February 1728/9]
[Both Charles Ford and Pope wrote assuming that Swift wrote *Intelligencer* 12; see introductory note to no. 12.]

[10 March 1728/9]
You will, I hope, excuse this liberty in one, who, to resent the indignity offered to you by *Ram*'s coachman, made him drunk soon after at *Gory*, which so much incensed the aforesaid *Ram*, that he discharged him his service, and he is now so reduced, that he has no other way of getting his bread but by crying in this city, *Ha' you any dirt to carry out?*

[Francis Geoghegan to Swift, alluding to no. 2. *Corresp.* iii. 316–17.]

[18 March 1728/9]

A friend from *Dublin* lately obliged me with a very entertaining paper, entitled *The Intelligencer*, it is number 20, a posthumous work of *Nestor Ironside*; a correspondent mentioning these papers in a letter raised my curiosity, with the specimen I had of them, to read the rest. For my part, I have buried myself in the country, and know little of the world, but what I learn from news-papers; you, who live so much in it, and from other more convincing proofs, I am satisfied are acquainted with the *Intelligencer*. I wish his zeal could promote the welfare of his poor country, but I fear his labour is in vain.

The miseries of the North, as represented [in no. 19], demand the utmost compassion, and must soften the malice of the most bitter enemy; I hope they, whose interest it is, if they rightly considered it, to relieve those miserable wretches, will redress so publick a calamity; to which, if, as I have heard, some of the clergy, by exacting of tithes, have contributed; they deserve as great censure, as a certain dean, who lends several sums without interest to his poor parishioners, has gained credit and honour by his charitable benificence. Bad men, to be sure, have crept in, and are of that sacred and learned order; the blackest of crimes, forgery, treason and blasphemy recently prove this: such should be spued out of it with utmost contempt, and punished according to their demerit with severe justice. If this allegation be true, I hope to see them censured by the *Intelligencer*, and recommend to him the words of *Jeremiah* to expatiate upon, c. x. ver. 21. c. xii. ver. 10, 11. I imagine the poor widow, his printer, is in danger of punishment. She suffered very cruelly for the *Drapier*'s works. I hope several contributed to ease her misfortunes on that occasion; I confess I am sorry I did not, but if you will give her a piece of gold, not in my name I beg, being unwilling to vaunt of charity, but as from a friend of yours, I shall by the first safe hand send one; in return I expect the *Drapier*'s Works entire.

I am sorry that, for the benefit of the ladies, the author has not given us the *English* of

> *Motus doceri gaudet* Ionicos
> *Matura virgo.*

Not having *Creech*'s *Horace*, a gentleman prevailed on me to attempt translating it in a couple of distichs; the science, which the compound *English* and *Greek* word signifies, little concerns a widower, but I should be glad to see it improved by good proficients in the *Ionick* jig.

[William Flower to Swift, from Castledurrow, Co. Kilkenny, alluding to nos. 18 and 19 and to the spurious no. 20 (Appendix H). The 'certain dean' is Swift himself. *Corresp.* iii. 318–20.]

William Duncombe's Essay on
The Beggar's Opera

This letter, originally published in the *London Journal*, 20 April 1728, was reprinted without acknowledgement by the *Dublin Weekly Journal*, 4 May 1728. It is attributed to Duncombe in the table of contents of *Letters from . . . Thomas Herring . . . to William Duncombe* (London: Johnson, 1777). Duncombe's erroneous insinuation that Gay had been patronized by the Spectator (Addison or Steele) was removed from later printings of the letter. For a related piece by Duncombe, see Ehrenpreis, iii. 559.

To the Author of the LONDON JOURNAL.

———*Non, si quid turbida Roma*
Elevet, accedas.———

PERSIUS.

SIR,

IT has been remark'd by an Author of distinguish'd Merit, 'That great part of the Writings which once prevailed among us under the Notion of Humour, are such as wou'd tempt one to think there had been an Association among the Wits of those Times, to rally Legitimacy out of our Island.' *Spectator*, N° 525.—It is matter of just Grief to Persons of sober Reflection, to find the same petulant Temper revived among us at present; and to observe, that some Writers, who were first produced to the World and recommended by that Noble Author, ungratefully spurn his Ashes, and endeavour with restless Pains to render his generous Labours useless to Mankind. These Gentlemen trace out new Paths to Fame, unknown to their pious Predecessors who flourish'd in the Reign of *Charles* the Second. Marriage indeed was then ridiculed, and the Clergy placed in a contemptible Light: But to chuse a Highwayman for the hero of the *Drama*, and to raise, not Indignation or Compassion, but Mirth and Laughter, by representing him on the Stage intoxicating himself with strong Liquors in order to *die hard*, as the Felons phrase it: This is a new Improvement, reserv'd to crown with Bays a living Bard! It were to be wish'd, for the Honour of the *British* Taste, that we cou'd conceal from our polite Neighbours abroad, the Success this Piece has met with. But (since That is impossible,) let it be known at the same Time, there are some among us, who (though they allow its Claim to low Humour) have so much Courage and Honesty, as to protest against the plan or Ground-work of it as absurd, and of dangerous Consequence. If it be granted, that *Dramatick* Performances have any Influence at all on the Minds of the People, (which, I believe, was never yet doubted,) it will follow, that an Entertainment of this Kind, where almost all the Characters are vicious and criminal, and yet, by the Poignancy of Raillery and Satyr joined to the Charms of Musick, pleasing and delightful; and where the vilest Principles are propagated in the most alluring manner; I say, such an Entertainment must highly tend to corrupt and debauch the Morals of the Nation.—I beg leave to conclude with a memorable Passage from the fore-cited Author, which I wish all who are concerned, would seriously lay to Heart; and especially those whose Fame or Fortune has been advanced by his powerful Recommendation: 'An Author may write (says he) as if he thought there was not one Man of Honour, or Woman of Chastity in the House, and come off with Applause: For an Insult upon all the Ten Commandments, with the little Criticks, is not so bad as the Breach of an Unity of Time or Place. Half Wits do not apprehend the Miseries that must necessarily flow from Degeneracy of Manners; nor do they know that order is the Support of Society.—Sallies of Imagination are to be over-looked, when they are committed out of Warmth, in the Recommendation of what is Praise-worthy; but a deliberate advancing of Vice with all the Wit in the World, is as ill an Action as any that comes before the Magistrate, and ought to be received as such by the People.' *Spectator*, Nº. 270.

> *I am,* SIR,
> *Your very humble Servant,*
> BENEVOLUS.

MOTTO: Persius, *Satires*, i. 5–6: 'And if thick-headed Rome does disparage anything, don't you go [and put right the tongue in that false balance of theirs]' (Loeb). In this fragmentary form, the epigraph may seem inappropriate to the essay, but it calls to mind the general theme of Persius' first satire, that Rome is decadent and all Romans are asses.

Commentary in *Mist's* and *Fog's*

Through London newspaper reprints the *Intelligencer* reached a far larger audience than through either the original Harding pamphlets or the Bowyer–Davis reprints of 1729 and 1730. The most important of the reprinting newspapers was *Mist's Weekly Journal*, an anti-ministerial paper with Jacobite leanings and an estimated circulation of 8,000–10,000.[1] One indication of these reprints' influence came in Anthony Collins's anonymous *Discourse Concerning Ridicule and Irony in Writing* (1729), where he charged,

> High-Church receives daily most signal Services from [Swift's] drolling Capacity, which has of late exerted itself on the Jacobite Stage of *Mist's* and *Fogg's* Journal, and in other little Papers publish'd in *Ireland*; in which he endeavours to expose the present Administration of publick Affairs to contempt, to inflame the *Irish* Nation against the *English*, and to make them throw off all Subjection to the *English* Government, to satirize Bishop *Burnet* and other *Whig* Bishops; and, in fine, to pave the way for a new or Popish Revolution, as far as choosing the most proper Topicks of Invective, and treating of them in the way of *Drollery*, can do.[2]

Fog's Weekly Journal, to which Collins alludes, appeared in September 1728 to replace *Mist's* after the government forced its cessation. Swift wrongly believed that the prosecutions were for *Mist's* abridgement of *A Short View*. The main prosecutions were in fact for an infamous Persian Letter by 'Amos Dudge' (perhaps the Duke of Wharton) published 24 August 1728, allegorically claiming that George II had been an illegitimate son.[3] However, *Mist's* printer was arrested for printing Sheridan's no. 6 in his paper of 27 July 1728.[4]

Mist's and *Fog's* usually prefaced the reprinted *Intelligencers* with a hint at Swift's authorship (even though most of the reprinted papers were Sheridan's). The tone of these preambles is frequently ironic and coy, as if to avoid

---

[1] For the circulation figure, see Arthur S. Limouze, 'A Study of Nathaniel Mist's Weekly Journals', Ph.D. thesis (Duke Univ., 1947), 13; see also Jeremy Black, 'An Underrated Journalist: Nathaniel Mist and the Opposition Press during the Whig Ascendency', *Brit. J. for Eighteenth-Cent. Stud.* 10 (1987), 38.

[2] (London: Brotherton, 1729), 39–40.

[3] *Prose*, xii. 122; the attribution to Wharton appears in an early marginal note in the BL copy.

[4] My information about the prosecutions comes from Limouze, 94–6, 119–20; Michael Harris, 'The London Newspaper Press ca. 1725–1746', Ph.D. thesis (London, 1973), 244–54; Harris, *London Newspapers in the Age of Walpole* (Rutherford, NJ, 1987), 144–6, 223; and the *Weekly J.: or, The British Gazetteer*, 10 Aug. 1728, reporting that Wolfe, *Mist's* printer, had been arrested because of a letter about Ireland published in *Mist's* 26 [rightly 27] July 1728.

responsibility for anything seditious. Since these notes significantly mediated between the *Intelligencer* and its largest audience, they are reprinted here, along with *Mist's* important comments on *A Short View* and related pieces.

Nathaniel Mist had run *Mist's Weekly Journal* until he voluntarily exiled himself to France, a few months before the *Intelligencer* began publication. Responsibility for reprinting the *Intelligencers* and writing the prefatory notes would seem to rest, then, with the person in charge of the newspaper during Mist's absence. This is likely to have been the Irish journalist Charles Molloy, as Limouze has argued.[5] Molloy, a minor dramatist and a legatee of John Barber, was the 'kinsman, and dear friend' of Neale Molloy, and through them the transcript of Swift's remarks on Gibbs's *Psalms* has come down to us.[6] Under Charles Molloy's supervision during 1728, *Mist's* took an even stronger interest in Swift's writings than before, using them, and Irish discontent generally, as a means of attacking Walpole. It is clear that *Mist's*, perhaps through Molloy, had an excellent supplier of Dublin materials.[7] That Swift or Sheridan had any active role in the London newspaper reprints of the *Intelligencer* seems doubtful, however.

Mist's, 30 March 1728, reported the Dublin publication of *A Short View*, quoting a Dublin dispatch of 20 March:

Yesterday . . . came out a small Pamphlet, Entitled, *A short View of the State of* Ireland, the Author of which every Body pretends to know by the bold Strokes in it. He likens the Publick 'to *an Hospital*, where the Governors and Officers grow rich, while the Poor, for whose Sake it was erected, being stinted both in Diet and Cloaths, are in a starving Condition.' 'Tis said the Printer will be taken up.

Mist's, 20 April 1728, published an abstract of *A Short View*, following these introductory paragraphs:

It is observ'd, that some Years past, several of the best Productions of Wit have come to us from *Ireland*; perhaps, Wit may, in some

---

[5] It could also have been Edward Bingley, who managed *Mist's* early in 1728 (Limouze, 89–90, 121, 237; and Black, 28–9; but see Harris's thesis, 166, 252, and his *London Newspapers*, 148, 223).

[6] *An Impartial History of the Life, Character, Amours, Travels, and Transactions of Mr. John Barber* (London: Curll, 1741; reprinted New York, 1974), p. xxv; Scott (1824), xii. 262. For these references I am indebted to Limouze, 232–3. Further on Molloy, see *DNB* and George H. Jones, 'The Jacobites, Charles Molloy, and *Common Sense*', *RES*, NS 4 (1953), 144–7. The Gibbs's *Psalms* transcript is now Forster MS 529.

[7] On the paper's interest in Swift, see Limouze, 232–44; and Paul Sawyer, 'Swift, Mist, and a Lincoln's Inn Fields Benefit', *Notes and Queries*, 222 (1977), 225–8. (I do not, however, accept Sawyer's inference that Swift, costumed as Gulliver, attended a theatrical benefit for Mist.)

Respects, be like Trade, of which they say, when it sinks in one Country, it certainly rises in another; besides, as it is a receiv'd Maxim, that Necessity is the Mother of Invention, it is likely that the *Irish* may be better intitled to it than we: For it is very natural to suppose, that the great *Frugality in our Fina[n]ces*, the *Decrease* of *Publick Debts*, and the vast *Increase of Trade*, may make us very easy and very dull; however, if Wit be a Commodity we can't work our selves, I am very glad we can have it by Importation; and as for my Part, I shall encourage the Use on't as much as I can, let it come from where it will, unless it be prohibited by Act of Parliament; nay, I can't help saying, I almost wish it was contraband, that People of fashion might grow fond of it.

But to speak more seriously, this Talent never comes so strongly recommended to me, as when it aims at propagating some publick Good; if a *Frenchman* or a *Spaniard* should endeavour to animate his Countrymen to something great and for the Honour of his Country, I should admire the Man, tho', perhaps, as an *Englishman*, I would do my utmost to oppose his Design.—There is a Pamphlet lately come from *Ireland*, Part of which perhaps I may dislike as an *Englishman*, yet I am sure the Author had the Good of his Country much at Heart.— He seems to apprehend that there is a Design of wheedling some Persons there to consent to a new Burthen which he thinks his Country is in no Condition to bear, (no doubt he is mistaken, for the Persons at present in the Administration can have no Views of that Kind, especially in Money Affairs) however, he draws up a short State of the Condition of his Country, which being a Thing curious, and very little understood here, we shall present our Readers with all the material Heads of the said Pamphlet.

The excerpts are concluded with these remarks:

The Author of this Pamphlet is not known, but the Publick, by Consent, has given it to a Gentleman in Orders, for no other Reason that I can understand, but because they like it; for they are willing to believe, that every Thing that's good must come from him.

I need only observe, that he is a Person who has made some Noise in the World, against whose Morals his Enemies have been able to say nothing, but that he is a Man of Wit, and against his Wit nothing but that it is generally grounded upon Truth.

I have only done the Part of a Transcriber, but as there were some Things in the Original, which seem'd to bear a little hard upon my *dear*

Country; I can't help owning, that I have purposely omitted them, as will be plain when the Thing is publish'd at length.—When that appears, if any ingenious Gentleman will furnish me with an Answer to it, I shall be very willing to insert it, provided it be such as shall be fit for Men of Sense to read.

The *Flying-Post; or, Post-Master*, 27 April 1728, in reply to Mist's abstract of *A Short View*:

In last *Saturday*'s *Mist*'s *Journal*, there's such an odd Representation of the State of *Ireland*, as I believe is hardly to be parallel'd, and I wonder you shou'd overlook it. It contains an Extract from a Pamphlet which the Publick have attributed to a certain Gentleman in Orders, who magnifies the Poverty and Misery of *Ireland*. The *Journalist* introduces this doughty Piece, with an Observation, That several of the best Productions of *Wit*, have lately come to us from *Ireland*, which he ascribes to the *Necessity* of that Kingdom, the Mother of Invention. But 'tis remarkable, that the *Journalist* in the very same Paper acquaints his Readers, that in Exchange for their exported *Wit*, the *Irish* have imported a great Quantity of *Wheat* and the *Beggars Opera*; and that they have another *Polly Peachum* at *Dublin*, which has had a Benefit of 150 *l. Sterling*, tho' at a late Sermon preach'd at St. *Patrick*'s, for all the Charity Children of *Dublin*, only 55 *l.* was collected: Your Reflections on this Subject will be very obliging to the Publick. . . .

The *Flying-Post* goes on to quote a piece from the *Dublin Weekly Journal* denying that the balance of trade is the problem and denying that Ireland needs its own mint.

Mist's, 4 May 1728, reported Dublin news of 23 April:

Soon after the Pamphlet call'd, *The short View of the present State of* Ireland was publish'd, came out another intitled, *A Memorial address'd to the Reverend Dean* S——. The Author of this Memorial taking Notice of the present Scarcity of Corn in that Kingdom, is of Opinion, that it would be for the publick Good that a Premium should be allow'd for the Importation of Corn; and as the Gentleman to whom he addresses [*sic*] is very much listen'd to by the People, the Memorialist would have the Proposal come from him.—In a few Days after, a third Pamphlet was publish'd, being an Answer to the said *Memorial*.

N.B. *This Pamphlet having been very popular in Ireland, we shall, in our next, present the Publick with an Abstract, if we have not Room for the Whole.*

Mist's, 11 May 1728, excerpted Swift's *Answer to a Paper, Call'd A Memorial*, with this introductory note:

In our last we took Notice of a Pamphlet printed in *Dublin*, intitled, *A Memorial address'd to the Reverend Dean* S——t, and also of its Answer.

As the latter contains some Observations which may suit other Countries as well as *Ireland*, we have, for that Reason, made Choice of it for this Day's Entertainment; and, we conceive, the great Reputation of its Author, as well as the good Sense which runs through it, will make any Apology for our inserting it altogether unnecessary.

The Dean begins with tracing the Causes of the present low condition of that Country, which he attributes partly to the Avarice of the top Farmers, and partly to the Cruelty of the Landlords to the Poor.—The first not improving their Ground, and the latter letting their Lands to Graziers, the Mistakes of which Conduct he goes on to explain as follows.

No. 3 was reprinted in *Mist's* for 6 July 1728 with this introductory note:

Our Correspondents in *Dublin* have lately transmitted to us several Tracts lately publish'd by the Wits of that City; among the rest is, an Essay upon *Humour*, of which Species of Writing the Author takes the *Beggars Opera* to be an Example.—I will not enter into a Critique here, upon the Justness of his Opinion in Relation to that Piece, the Subject itself is entertaining, and being treated in a Manner new and ingenious, I make no Doubt but our Readers will be pleas'd with it, and therefore I shall insert it as I find it.

Mist's, 27 July 1728, reprinted no. 6 with this introduction:

The following Piece comes to us from *Dublin*,—we may call it a Picture of that Country, but we shall leave it to the impartial Readers to judge how far the Painter has succeeded in the Likeness, we shall only say, that there are certain Strokes in it which shew the Master.

I only desire that what is here said of *Ireland* may not be imputed to us, as meant of any other Country, which some Men may be apt to do, because it has been reported, that the Poor in several Counties in *England* have lately been reduced to eat Grains, for my Part I don't believe it, for it is Plain, that there is Provision enough for *those that have Money enough to buy it.*—And sure no Body will be so bold to maintain, that the Poor, either for Want of Trade, or Weight of Taxes, are in a worse Condition than in former Times.

Mist's, 10 August 1728, reprinted the first part of no. 9 with this introduction:

We have lately given the Publick one or two Discourses which came to us from *Dublin*, with which we find they have been extremely satisfied: We shall now present them with another from the same Place, written upon a Subject upon which the Good of Society depends more than upon any Thing else in the Conduct of human Life.

We conceive it would be an unpardonable Vanity in us to reject any Thing that is excellent in its Way, and tending to the Instruction of Mankind, only for the Sake of inserting something of our own.— In this Case our Readers would have just Reason to complain of us, especially when they should come to know that the generous Principles which are the Aim of these Discourses, are such that (considering the Baseness and Flattery, which, at present, influences the Minds of most Writers) we may venture to say, the Publick here would never see them, except by Means of this Paper.

The Flying Post; or, Post-Master, 13 Aug. 1728, introduced an essay on education:

In *Mist's Journal* of *Saturday* last, a Lecture is begun upon the *Education of Children*, said to be written at *Dublin*. This being a Subject of such Importance to the Good of Society, we shall in this and some following Papers, present the Publick with a Discourse upon the same Subject, which we have receiv'd from *another* Hand in that City, in order to obviate the base Detraction and Falshood which at present influences the Minds of some Writers.

Mist's, 17 August 1728, concluded no. 9, following this note:

The following is a Continuation of our last.—It may be remembred, that the last concluded with the Sentiments of a Military Officer upon this Subject, in describing which the Author goes on in the following Manner.

A letter from a teacher of modern languages, in *Brice's Weekly Journal* (Exeter), 30 August 1728:

Since the Learning of *Modern Languages* has been recommended by our Sovereign, and encourag'd in our Universities by the Royal

Bounty, as Attainments necessary to the Gentleman and Man of Business, they seem to need no Recommendation from a Private Pen; but as the Author of a Discourse lately publish'd in *Mist*'s Journal on *Education* has (to advance an *antiquated Scheme*) cast a Fleer on this Part of Literature, I shall desire you in some future Paper to give Room to some Observations I have made on that *Hibernian* Rhapsody.[8]

On 31 August 1728, a week after the infamous Persian Letter for which *Mist's* was prosecuted, the paper led with an unsigned letter on partisan journalism, which included these remarks:

And thus a truly Reverend Dean has been traduced for no other Reason than having more Wit and Learning than his Slanderers; or what is to them yet more provoking, because he has so nobly and seasonably interposed and served his Country. An Action never to be forgotten, and a Disposition which a *certain Sett of Men* would by all Means suppress.

But notwithstanding their Calumnies, the Love of our Country is so amiable and beneficial a Quality, that whoever possesses and practices it ought to be esteem'd and honour'd, were he *Turk*, *Arab*, or wild *Tartar*.—The People of his (the Dean's) Country are said to be generally hospitable and good-natur'd, and therefore, it is to be hoped, they will demonstrate their Gratitude to a Gentleman who daily accumulates Benefits on them, whose Friends see and admire his Vertues, and even his Enemies acknowledge to be a Man of the finest Genius the Age has produced.—It will be a Demonstration of this Truth, to observe that no one will peruse this Paper but will immediately name the Person who is meant.

Fog's, 26 October 1728, reprinted no. 7 with this introduction:

The News of my late Kinsman's [Mist's] Death not having reach'd all his Correspondents, several Packets of Letters directed to him, have fallen into my Hands, since his Decease; amongst the rest, one from *Dublin*, in which was inclos'd the following Discourse, which is of the same Hand with some others, my late Kinsman gave the Publick last Summer, (as I understand by the Letter which accompany'd it.)—I need not name what Hand it is, the World will easily find it out.—It

---

[8] I have been unable to examine a complete file of *Brice's* and do not know whether the proffered Observations were ever published.

shews under feign'd Names, the Qualifications which are sometimes necessary towards *rising*, not towards *shining*, in the Church, and such young Clergymen, who have placed their Kingdoms altogether in this World, may be able to draw some useful Hints from it.

Fog's, 16 November 1728, reprinted no. 13 with this note:

The following Piece was sent us from *Dublin*; we shall say no more, but leave it to recommend itself.

Fog's, 23 November 1728, reprinted no. 14 with this note:

In our last, we gave our Readers a Discourse which a Correspondent sent us from *Dublin*; and as we find it had the Effect we propos'd, of diverting the Publick, it has encouraged us to give them another which came in the same Parcel, which we hope will not be less acceptable than the former.

Fog's, 11 January 1728/9, reprinted no. 16 with this note:

The following Discourse was sent us from *Dublin*; we have no Authority to name the Author, nor indeed can we do it any otherwise than by Guess, and that will be unnecessary; for it is probable, the Generality of Readers may have as good a Knack at guessing as we.

Fog's, 1 March 1728/9, reprinted no. 19 with this note:

Our News-Papers lately, have frequently given us Accounts from *Ireland*, of the unhappy Condition of the Protestants of the Northern Parts of that Kingdom.—The following Discourse sent us from thence, and first Printed there, will let the World into the Reasons of their present Miseries.

APPENDIX E

The True Character and *On Paddy's Character*

The poem *On Paddy's Character of the Intelligencer*—attributed to Swift—was not written to reprimand Patrick Delany for his attacks on the *Intelligencer*, contrary to John Nichols's mistaken assertion. Delany in fact commended the *Intelligencers* as 'papers of uncommon spirit'.[1] What is evident is that *On Paddy's Character* responds to *The True Character of the Intelligencer. Written by Pady Drogheda*, a Dublin halfsheet of 1728. *The True Character* is, in turn, an abridged halfsheet republication of William Tisdall's lampoon on Sheridan, *Tom Pun-sibi Metamorphosed; or, The Giber Gibb'd* (Dublin, 1724), as D. F. Foxon noted in 1975 (Foxon T318–19).[2] The latter poem, which is of some importance in fixing the canon of Sheridan's writings, was edited by Smedley in *Gulliveriana*, from which some notes are here taken.[3] Sheridan himself, I believe, replied to the poem point by point in *Letter from a Dissenting Teacher to Jet Black* (Dublin, 1724; copy: RIA). Orrery transcribes *Tom Pun-sibi Metamorphosed* in one of the interleaved copies of his *Remarks* (Harvard MS Eng. 218.14, pp. 84–7); his comments have been misunderstood as evidence for attributing the poem to Dean Ward (Harold Williams, review of *The Rothschild Library*, in the *Library*, 10 (1955), 287). The poem is attributed to Swift in *European Magazine*, 26 (1794), 365, and elsewhere.

In the guise of *The True Character*, the poem may have been issued in retaliation for no. 8, *Mad Mullinix and Timothy*, since Paddy Drogheda was a Dublin street character like Mullinix. Drogheda was a shoeboy, according to his facetious obituary in the *Dublin Intelligence*: 'Yesterday [29 June 1744] died of

---

[1] Walter Scott compounded Nichols's error. See Nichols's *Supplement* to Swift's *Works* (4° edn., T–S 87), xiv (London: Nichols, 1779), 711; Scott (1814), i. 376–7; *Poems*, ii. 457. Nichols was accepting F. Cogan's claim, voiced when the poem was first anthologized in 1746: 'Dr. *Thomas Sheridan* of *Dublin* published a weekly paper, called *The Intelligencer*, for the greatest part written by himself; but his Friend, the Dean of St. *Patrick*'s, sometimes supplied him with a Paper. Dr. *Patrick Delany* (who preferred his own Abilities, as a Writer, abundantly before *Sheridan*'s could not bear the Approbation which the Town afforded the *Intelligencer*; and therefore he attacks it Tooth and Nail, both in Conversation and in Print, but unfortunately stumbles on some of the Numbers which the Dean had written, and all the World admired; to which we owe the following Poem.' *The Entertainer. Consisting of Pieces in Prose and Verse, Witty, Humorous, or Curious* (London: F. Cogan, 1746), 4 (copy: Cornell). For Delany's views, see his periodical the *Humanist*, no. 1 (26 Mar. 1757).

[2] Although Foxon tended to accept the old supposition that *On Paddy's Character* was addressed to Delany, the only evidence for it seems to have been the nickname 'Paddy'; earlier scholars were not aware of *The True Character of the Intelligencer* or its supposed author.

[3] *Gulliveriana: or, A Fourth Volume of Miscellanies* (London: Roberts, 1728; reprinted New York, 1974), 260–4.

Decay, Paddy Drogheda, a very celebrated News-Hawker, much admired by Persons of the Greatest Distinction for his Wit and Humour. His Remains will be interred this Evening at Drumcondra. Great Interest is making to succeed him as Laureat to the Flying Stationers; but it is thought that little Bandy Reily will be unanimously elected' (quoted by Robert Munter, *The History of the Irish Newspaper 1685–1760* (Cambridge, 1967), 80). Drogheda has been otherwise associated with Swift. One of the original anecdotes in *Memoirs of the Life and Writings of Jonathan Swift, D.D.* (London [Dublin], 1752), largely a piracy of Orrery's *Remarks*, is as follows: 'PADDY DROGHEDA, a news-boy in *Dublin*, noted for a turn of low humour, pursued the Dean, with a paper in his hand, crying out, "ELOISA to ABELAIRD;" The Dean bid him desist; but, PADDY, still continued his vociferation; and, upon the Dean's offering to strike him, cryed out,

> Get away raw head and bloody bones,
> Here is a boy that does not fear you.

This was such a turn of humour, (the Dean being the reputed author of that song,) that it did not pass unrewarded' (117). See also a poem praising Swift, 'An Answer to the Verses in Last Saturday's Journal, on Mr. Bindon's Painting the Picture of the Rev. Dr. SWIFT. . . . By PATRICK DROGHEDA, I.S.T.', *Dublin Journal*, 17 Nov. 1739.[4]

THE TRUE CHARACTER OF
THE INTELLIGENCER.

Written by Pady Drogheda.

> *Our Black's apply'd to different Use;*
> *You blacken Men, I blacken Shoes.*

T OM was a little merry Grigg,
  Fiddl'd, and danc'd to his own Jigg,
Good Natur'd but a little silly,
Irresolute, and shally shilly:
What he shou'd do, he cou'd not guess,
They mov'd him like a Man at Chess.

---

[4] Paddy Drogheda was first identified by Mackie L. Jarrell, '"Ode to the King"', *Texas Stud. in Lit. and Lang.* 7 (1965), 157. On the Paddy Drogheda anecdote and the pirated *Memoirs*, see A. C. Elias, Jr, 'Lord Orrery's Copy of *Memoirs of the Life and Writings of Swift* (1751)', *Eighteenth-Century Ireland*, 1 (1986), 111–25. Another reference to Paddy Drogheda occurs in *The Funeral Procession of the Chevalier de St. Patrick* ([Dublin, 1734]), a lampoon on William Dunkin (copy: NLI).

S——t told him once, that he had Wit;
S——t was in jest, poor *Tom* was bit,
Thought himself second Son of *Phœbus*,
For Ballad, Pun, Lampoon, and Rebus:
He took a Draught of *Hellicon*,
But swallow'd so much Water down,
He got a Dropsie now they say 'tis
Turn'd to Poetick *Diabetis*;
And all the Liquor he has past,
Is without Spirit, Salt, or Taste;
But since it pass'd, *Tom* thought it Wit,
And therefore writ, and writ, and writ:
He writ the famous punning Art,[5]
The Benefit of Piss and Fart,[6]
He writ the Wonder of all Wonders,[7]
He writ the Blunder of all Blunders,[8]
He writ a merry Farce for Puppet,[9]
Taught Actors how to squeek and hop it,
A Treatise on the wooden Man,[10]
A Ballad on the Nose of *Dan*,[11]
The Art of making *April* Fools,[12]
And four and twenty quibbling Rules;[13]
The Learned say that *Tom* went Snacks
With *Philomaths* for Almanacks.
Tho' they divided are, for some say,
He writ for *Whaley* some for *Compsty*;[14]

[5] *Ars Pun-ica.*

[6] *The Benefit of Farting*, which Sheridan, however, 'utterly disclaims' in *A Letter from a Dissenting Teacher*, 6. Swift attributed it to 'one Dobbs a surgeon' (*Corresp.* ii. 421); similarly it is given to 'D—bs' in Laurence Whyte, 'Some Critical Annotations', *Poems on Various Occasions* (Dublin: Powell, 1740), 152. This may be the William Dobbs who was surgeon to an Irish regiment (Charles Dalton, *George the First's Army*, ii (London, 1912), 142).

[7] Claimed for Swift by Faulkner; see *Prose*, vol. ix, pp. xvii, 285–7, 378.

[8] Not the same *Blunder of All Blunders* listed as T–S 1217, p. 245, for it refers to contemporary reaction to the publication of *Gulliver's Travels* (1726), whereas *Tom Pun-sibi Metamorphosed* was first published in 1724.

[9] See *Punch Turn'd Schoolmaster*; see also *Poems*, iii. 1102–5.

[10] I have not identified the treatise, but the wooden man was 'a fam'd *Door-Post*' in Essex Street, Dublin, as Smedley and Orrery note.

[11] See *Poems*, iii. 990 ff.   [12] Not identified.

[13] 'Four and twenty' is an error in this edition for 'four and thirty'; there are thirty-four rules in *Ars Pun-ica*.

[14] 'Two famous *Irish Almanack makers*' (Smedley).

Hundreds there are that will make Oath,
Nay I will swear, he writ, for both,
And tho' they made the Calculations,
Tom writ the monthly Observations.[15]
Such were his Writings; but his Chatter
Was one continu'd Clitter-clatter;
S——t slit his Tongue and made it talk,
Cry Cup of Sack, and walk Knaves walk,
And fitted little prating Poll,
For Wier Cage in Common-Hall.
Made him expert at Quibble Jargon,
And quaint at selling of a Bargain.
Poll he cou'd talk in different Linguo's,
But he cou'd not be taught Distinguo's;[16]
S——t try'd in vain, and angry there at
Into a Spaniel turn'd his Parrot,
Made him to walk on the hind Legs,
He dances, paws, and fawns, and begs,
Then cuts a [c]aper o'er a Stick,[17]
Lies close, does whine and creep, and lick;
S——t puts a Bit upon his Snout,
Poor *Tom* he daren't look about;
But when that *S——t* does give the Word,
He snaps it up tho' t'were a T——d.

To this poem there was a halfsheet reply, *On Paddy's Character of the Intelli-gencer*, published in Dublin in 1728.[18] The poem was first attributed to Swift in Cogan's *Supplement to the Works of the Most Celebrated Minor Poets* (London: Cogan, 1750), iii. 78–9, a work of no reliability where attributions are

[15] Sheridan concedes authorship of them in *Letter from a Dissenting Teacher*, 7.

[16] *Distinguo's*: Distinctions; a term of scholastic logic. See Paul Robert, *Dictionnaire alphabétique et analogique de la langue française* (Paris, 1961); compare *OED Suppl.*

[17] 'This is, *literally*, true, between *Sw——t* and *Sheridan*' (Smedley).

[18] In reprinting the poem in 1746, Cogan's *Entertainer* hinted that the poem was by Swift, prefixing the discussion quoted in note 1 above with the observation that 'several Pieces of the late Dean *Swift* have been omitted in his *Dublin* edition' (3). The original halfsheet survives in a single copy, BL C.121.g.8. (173), whose imprint is cropped; only the rule above it is still visible. *The Entertainer*, however, in reprinting the halfsheet seems also to reprint its imprint: 'Printed in the Year 1728.' Though Williams dates the poem 1729, the *Intelligencer* was hardly an issue in Dublin in 1729. It seems likely, there-fore, that *On Paddy's Character* was published in 1728, even though it is bound with 1729 Dublin halfsheets in the BL collection. (The binding order appears to account for Wil-liams's dating.)

concerned, and thence in *A Supplement to the Works of Dr. Swift* (London: Cogan, 1752), 126–7. From one of these sources, apparently, John Nichols gathered the poem into Swift's canon (see *Poems*, ii. 457). Pat Rogers expresses doubt that the poem is Swift's; 'it could easily be Sheridan's' (790). If Swift wrote the poem, the earnest comparison of Swift to Jove in the final lines must be considered an outrageous display of vanity. Though Swift *may* have written those lines, with equal likelihood and much greater decorum they could have been written by someone else—Delany or one of the other Dublin wits such as Dunkin, if not Sheridan himself. One small point against Sheridan is that the poem was not published in the *Intelligencer*, nor, on typographical evidence, does it seem to have come from Sarah Harding's shop.

Once the intended victim of the poem is understood not to be Delany, its thrust requires reassessment. Clearly *On Paddy's Character* is not attacking the real Paddy Drogheda; that is, its author sees 'Pady Drogheda' as a pseudonym and means to attack the actual author. This victim seems possibly to have been William Tisdall, whether or not he was remembered as the author of *Tom Pun-sibi Metamorphosed* four years earlier. He fits the poem's description of a would-be poet envious of Sheridan's poetic success. In 1722 Swift wrote to Charles Ford, 'Tisdal lives but 7 miles off [from Loughgall], we meet him once a week at a Club. He is fifty times less agreeable than ever, but a great Poet, Writer and Divine, and we fall out every time we meet.' And in 1724, he told Ford, 'Sheridan pursues Tisdal with Ballads and Verses, and there is one very good, called the Cobler to Jet Black.'[19] Writing to Henry Jenney in 1732, Swift said that Tisdall had long been 'engaged in a kind of flirting war of satiric burlesque verse with certain wags both in town and country.... Whatever was writ to ridicule him, was laid at my door, and only by himself....' Swift claimed that he 'had never one single moment in my life the least inclination to enter the lists with' Tisdall; and while Swift is here painting with the same broad brush he uses in the public self-praise of *Verses on the Death of Dr. Swift*, his claim might seem to rule out *On Paddy's Character of the Intelligencer*.[20]

In short, however, neither the author nor the intended victim of *On Paddy's Character* can be fixed with certainty.

[19] *Corresp.* ii. 431; iii. 15; iv. 28n.
[20] *Corresp.* iv. 27–8. See also *Poems*, ii. 428; iii. 942; and iii. 1123.

Building in Dublin *c.* 1728

Both nos. 15 and 17 mention increased house-building in Dublin. Swift is frustrated both by the desertion of older houses in the centre of Dublin and by speculative builders' financial ruin. The problem is outlined in a Dublin half-sheet of 1728, *The Distress'd State of the Poor of Ireland, and Their Reasons for Leaving the Kingdom, Explained to Their Landlords* (copy: Yale):

> . . . the [rural] Tenants in Possession were forced to submit to what the Landlords pleas'd to charge; the Poor struggled to pay till they were ruined, and when they fail'd paying their Rent, they were obliged to shift and give up their Farms to the Landlords, who either set them to Stock-Masters, or stock'd the Land themselves. By this means, the Poor crowded to all Cities, Boroughs and Seaport-Towns to strive for a Livelihood, took Houses at any Rate, and consequently inspir'd the Tradesmen and Projectors with a *Spirit* of Building, by trucking and changing each Trade with the other the Materials of Work. This is the Way our Cities and Towns are over built for the Kingdom. And when these poor, broken Country Farmers spent their Substance, got as far as possible in Debt to the Brewers and Landlords of Houses, they were forc'd to go to the several Plantations abroad and leave the Country waste, without either Distress for Rent or Payment to the Brewers, or other Creditors.

Swift's most comprehensive discussion is in 'Maxims Controlled in Ireland', written in 1727 or 1728 and referring to the increase in Dublin's population:

> These and some other motives better let pass, have drawn such a concourse to this beggarly city, that the dealers of the several branches of building have found out all the commodious and inviting places for erecting new houses, while fifteen hundred of the old ones, which is a seventh part of the whole city, are said to be left uninhabited, and falling to ruin. Their method is the same with that which was first introduced by Doctor Barebone at London, who died a bankrupt. The mason, the bricklayer, the carpenter, the slater, and the glazier, take a lot of ground, club to build one or more houses, unite their credit, their stock, and their money, and when their work is finished, sell it to the best advantage they can. But, as it often happens, and more every day, that their fund will not answer half their design, they are forced to undersell it at the first story, and are all reduced to beggary. Insomuch, that I know a certain fanatic brewer, who is reported to have some hundreds of houses in this town, is said to have purchased the greater part of them at half value from

ruined undertakers, hath intelligence of all new houses where the finishing is at a stand, takes advantage of the builder's distress, and, by the advantage of ready money, gets fifty *per cent*. at least for his bargain.[1]

Swift's estimate, based evidently on some external source, that there were 9,000 inhabited houses in Dublin (1,500 × 6), is significantly less than the 11,718 inhabited houses reported in the Dublin hearth-money returns of 1733.[2] How this discrepancy is best explained is uncertain.

According to a note in Deane Swift's 1765 edition, the 'fanatic brewer' was Joseph Leeson (d. 1741), a speculative builder, for whom see Craig, 109–10, 191, 323. Swift's allusion appears to be the earliest extant evidence of Leeson's activities as a speculative builder. See Swift, *Works*, viii, part 1 (London: Johnson, 1765), 140 (T–S 87, p. 86).

In no. 17 Sheridan refers to new streets and uninhabited streets. The new streets were probably Henrietta Street and the adjoining Bolton Street north of the Liffey, and Dawson Street and probably also Grafton Street to the south. On Charles Brooking's map (1728), Henrietta and Molesworth Streets both appear, unnamed though laid out, and it may be that Sheridan is also apprehensive about other streets laid out but not yet built upon, e.g., Kildare Street; a number of such streets may be found by comparing Brooking's map of Dublin with that of John Rocque (1756).[3] For much of this information I am indebted to Maurice Craig and to his *Dublin 1660–1860*, 83, 102–3, 106–10. It should be noted that Brooking mapped some features not built but only planned.[4]

Dr Craig has suggested to me that the abandonment of city-centre houses must have been especially evident in the 1720s, when the largeness of the new houses on the periphery contrasted markedly with the cramped sites in the centre. One may speculate that the streets being abandoned in the 1720s were those which, though old, had new houses in the 1730s, 1740s, or 1750s (see Craig's Appendix i). These included Abbey Street and Bachelor's Walk north of the Liffey and Anglesea, Aungier, Clarendon, South William, and York Streets to the south. All these streets are in the oldest part of Dublin, near the Castle, and probably this rather small area was the primary site of abandonment, as the Molesworth Fields development flourished to the east. See also Nuala T. Burke, 'Dublin 1660–1800: A Study in Urban Morphogenesis', Ph.D. thesis (TCD, 1972), ch. 9.

---

[1] *Prose*, xii. 135.

[2] Gilbert MS 68, pp. 151 ff., is a transcript of the hearth-money returns.

[3] Brooking, *A Map of the City and Suburbs of Dublin* (London: Bowles, 1728); Rocque, *An Exact Survey of the City and Suburbs of Dublin* (1756; reprinted Lympne Castle, Kent, *c.* 1978).

[4] See J. H. Andrews, '"Mean Pyratical Practices": The Case of Charles Brooking', *Quarterly Bull. Irish Georgian Soc.* 23 (1980), 33–43.

Published Replies to No. 16

(*a*)

This essay, probably written by one of Sheridan's schoolboys, responds to *Intelligencer* 16 by protesting the law of primogeniture. His argument, though adolescent, shares the *Intelligencer*'s insistence that maxims and principles applicable to other civilized nations do not work in Ireland.

A LETTER TO THE INTELLIGENCER

Honos alit artes.

Written by a Young Gentleman, of Fourteen Years Old.

Mr. *Intelligencer*,

I Am a Boy about Fourteen, who have for some Years past, vigourously pursued my Studies, in one of the most Noted Schools in this Kingdom. My Master (whether it be his real thoughts or no) often tells me, that for my time, I have made no inconsiderable Progress. From this encouragement therefore, and my own Natural Inclinations, to be (what is so much Cryed up in the World) a Scholar, I shou'd, I fear, have still persisted in my Error, had not a late Excellent Paper of yours, *Numb.* xvi. seasonably interrupted me, and opened my Eyes e'er it was too late to see, where I was convinced of the Absurdity, and Barrenness of my pursuit; and upon a more serious Consideration, I found the greatest return I could reasonably expect from my Studies would hardly quit Costs, and make up for the expence of Books and Schoolling.

I may indeed Blind my self over *Greek* and *Latin*, yet I have no reason to hope, if I judge from what my Fellow Countrymen meet with, that all my Pains and Labour will procure me that Golden Antidote, which they call, *The Cure for sore Eyes.*

My Master since that, perceived a Considerable Alteration in me; And in short to deal ingeniously with him, I am not one of those, that is for a well stocked Brain, with an Empty Pocket; and that Learning and Wealth should go together, my innocent Country hath taken Care to prevent (it being my Misfortune, to have been Born an *Irish Man.*)

₂₅ I must not forget to let you know, that my Father is one of those happy Men, that lived in the Golden Age, when Riches stood within the reach of Industry, at which he hath stretched to good purpose, having gathered a considerable Fortune, sufficient to make both my Brother and I happy in the World; but my being the Younger Born, has ₃₀ effectually cut me off from all Claim and Title, as being a Son of *Ireland*, from all hopes of Preferment. Father's now a Days imagine, that the Name of Younger Child is enough to live upon; at least since the Publick will do nothing for them, they are resolv'd to be even with it, and neglect them as much. If the Kingdom won't dispose of their ₃₅ Son's to Advantage, they are resolved they shall lye upon it's Hands.

If you go to reason with them, and debate seriously upon the Matter, their strongest and most weighty Argument will be; let the *Varlet* get it, as his Father before him; never considering that the inconveniences with which we begin the World, are as Numerous as ₄₀ were their Advantages, every thing equally conspiring to enrich them, as now to keep us Poor.

But deaf to all reason, they must forsooth give their child (what they call) Gentleman's Education, and so think that they have discharged their duty, by leaving him and his Learning to beg after their Death.

₄₅ I wish these Men wou'd consider that our Climate is much altered, since their time; that 'tis now grown so Perverse, that 'twill suffer no Native Schollar to thrive in it; and from hence might give their Children an other turn, and by setting them to Mechanick Arts, of which I think our *Irish genius* is allowed capable, they might have put ₅₀ them in a Comfortable way of Living, at the same time they made them usefull to the Publick, which is now the summet of my Ambition. I am willing to serve my Country any way, and this, it seems, is the onely capacity we can do it in.

You cannot therefore but be sensible of the deplorable Condition of ₅₅ us *Younger Brothers*, having neither Friend in Father or Country, the time and Place of our Birth equally conspiring against us. Since then the Zealous Efforts you have repeated on all Occasions to the promoting the happiness of your Country, and Relieving it from the present State of Oppression (I am sorry to use the expression) have ₆₀ prov'd unsuccessful, we have nothing left, but to implore your kind Assistance, that you wou'd once more take up your pen, in almost as general a Cause, that you wou'd endeavour (since our Country is determind to do nothing for us) to convince Fathers, if possible, that the desires and tendencies of our Nature are the same, that we

demand the same necessary supports of Life with any of our *Eldest* 65
Brethren, from nothing else, but some such gross Ignorance, being able
to account for their irrational, and Inhumane proceedings towards us.

I am Sir, Your most Obedient
Humble Servant.

(*b*)

From the *Weekly Journal: or, The British Gazetteer* (London), 18 January 1728/9,
replying to the reprint of no. 16 in *Fog's Weekly Journal*.

To the Author of the BRITISH GAZETTEER.   70

SIR,

MR. *FOG* lately communicated to the Publick the Grievances
of my Brother *Patrick*, which were set forth to him in a
Letter from that brazen-fac'd Varlet; every Word of which,
relating to himself, I shall demonstrate to be false, notwithstanding his 75
unlimitted Assurance to out-front me. First I must inform you, that the
People among which he was educated are notorious for their
Impudence, and for standing in a Lie which they have once told; by
which Means they are become a Proverb among their Neighbours;
now I assure you my Brother so excels in the Virtue, for such they 80
esteem it, which I have mentioned, that he is, by many, called *the Man
of Brass*; judge therefore what Credit you ought to give to what he says.
My Name is *David*, and for my Honesty and Simplicity of Manners
the ill-natur'd Part of our Family have nick-nam'd me *Taffy*, thro'
Derision.   85

Patrick begun, and ended his Epistle, as is his Custom, with a Lie;
that he may be said to be of a Piece from the Beginning to the End.
First, says he, *there are three Brethren of us*, GEORGE, PATRICK, *and*
ANDREW; *and I am the Second.* This is so apparent a Falshood that I need
take but little Trouble to contradict him; for our Family is not so 90
obscure but every body knows our Father has four Sons, and that
DAVID, meaning myself, is the Second. What could induce him to tell
so unprofitable a Lie as this, I shall not enter into; for tho' I, and my
Children, are noted for being soon in a Passion, PATRICK shall see that
my Contempt for him shall turn even the Biass of my Nature; for my 95
Design is only to speak the direct Truth, without being fired with any
Spirit of Resentment; but I must take the Liberty to tell my Brother

Patrick this, that tho' we are all too honest to disown him, we are very
much ashamed of him, and his.

100   I shall now proceed in my Detection of the ill Grounds for his
Complaint, and his false Representations of Things. He complains of
the Partiality of our Father, when every body knows there never was a
more indulgent Parent; and was it not for his paternal Care, in sending
the best Governors to the Children of his Son *Patrick*, (witness the
105 present whom they all love as well as they do their Father,) they would
be like so many Brutes which delight in basking in Laziness, and often
prey on each other. He stomachs what he calls the Injustice of Brother
George's Sons possessing the best Places in his Territories, whereas he
ought to esteem this as a Blessing, for their Affairs would be turned
110 topsy-turvy under the Management of such wrong-headed Creatures
as his Sons; and they would want Examples of Humanity, and return
to their former, I may say native, Wildness; for poor *Patrick*, whether
he knows it or no, has from his Birth been called the wild Man.

    I declare, and I dare say you will read it, with Wonder, that *Patrick*
115 has once almost deviated into Truth. He says, GEORGE *was once a great
Admirer of ancient Learning, but he has long since quitted this, for the reading of*
News-Papers, Pamphlets, *and* Modern Languages. *Of late*, continues
he, *he has fallen into strange and unaccountable Effeminacy, and seems to take
Delight in nothing, but* Masquerades, Plays, *and* Italian Operas. Brother
120 *Patrick* has almost hit the Nail on the Head; but even where he says
a good Thing he cannot help discovering himself, for *Patrick* is very
apt to make Bulls; nay so apt, that when any Man makes a Blunder,
the Company cry out, there spoke *Patrick*. I must inform my Brother,
that those who encourage Masquerades, and *Italian* Operas, are no
125 Friends to Plays; nor is it possible they should; for Dramatick Poetry,
which I suppose my Brother means by Plays, differs as much from
Masquerades and Operas, as Sense from Nonsense; therefore he that
Admires the first can never be a Friend to the other: Besides, his
Slander on our Father is not just, for he is not of that vitiated Taste
130 which he would make him; indeed the Majority of his Family are too
much prone to Follies of that Nature which *Patrick* lays to his Charge;
but many of his Children are shining Ornaments in polite Literature
of all Kinds, and are daily using their Efforts to reclaim such of their
Brothers and Sisters as are degenerating. I think Gratitude to the
135 Governor of his own Family ought to have forced him to have
exempted that Nephew from the Censure cast on his Father *George*;
for *Patrick* knows, if Envy would let him confess it, that his Nephew

C——— is not only among the most learned and polite himself, but a
Patron to such of his Brothers as want his Assistance and have Merit
enough to entitle them to it.   140

What *Patrick* says of Brother *Andrew* I shall pass over in Silence, for
tho' some few Bickerings have been betwixt him and Brother *George*, I
hope the Malice of *Patrick* will never raise any ill Blood among us, to
break the Harmony of our House; for you must know *George*, *Myself*,
and *Andrew*, live in one large and magnificent Mansion House; and,   145
from the Consequence of former Discords, we too well know the
Sweets of brotherly Love to let *Patrick* set us together by the Ears. I
must, on this Occasion, inform you, that many of *Patrick*'s Sons have
forsook their Habitation, deny'd their Father, and thrust themselves
into their Uncle *George*'s House, and impudently asserted themselves   150
to be his Sons; and indeed *George*'s Family is so numerous, that this
Imposture would succeed oftener than it does, was it not for the
different Dialect which *Patrick*'s Sons have in their Speech, and a
disagreeable Brouge in the Throat, a Misfortune hereditary to them,
and which few of them ever get rid of. When Brother *Patrick* comes to   155
his own Character, he says, he *shall not conceal*, *nor gloss over*, his *Vices*,
Errors, *or Failings*; what Truth is in this Assertion I have already
detected, by setting forth such of his *Vices*, *Errors*, *or Failings*, as he and
his Sons furnish us with daily Instances of.

The Insinuations which *Patrick* makes against some of our Father's   160
Servants are on such a frivolous Foundation, that they scarcely deserve
our Notice; but I would have him assure himself that our Father's
Steward will discharge his Trust with Fidelity to his Master; and
continue a Friend even to *Patrick* and his Children, notwithstanding
their Ingratitude; for he takes as much Pleasure in doing good Offices,   165
as they in disowning them.

Since I have been so free with the Character of my Brother, I shall
conclude with some Account of Myself, and my Children. I must own
we are too liable to sudden Choler, but if we find our Anger was too
precipitate, we are as ready to acknowledge our Faults, as to exert a   170
Spirit of just Resentment. I have been the Subject of Ridicule to some
for training up my Sons in the Study of Heraldry. This is a Reflection
of which I am not ashamed; for would these refined Persons consider,
that Heraldry does not consist only in the Knowledge of Arms, and the
Blazoning Coats, but in the History of both Persons and Actions, they   175
would not be so rash in their Censures. In short, our Enemies miss
their Aim, if they think to ruffle us with any Witticisms of this abusive

Kind; for what I value myself most upon, is my unshaken Duty to my
Father; against whom, as I have no Reason for Complaint, I shall be
180 studious of preserving nothing more than his good Opinion of me.

Sir, If you think fit, by giving this a Place in your Paper, to do Justice
to an injured Family, as mine is from the Malevolence of Brother
Patrick, you may secure the Correspondence of

Your constant Reader,
185   *And humble Servant,*
DAVID, &c.

(*c*)

From the *Daily Journal* (London), 8 February 1728/9.

To the Author of the DAILY JOURNAL.

SIR,

MR. Fog having inserted in his Weekly Journal of the 11th of
190   last Month, a Letter of Complaint from PATRICK, against
GEORGE and ANDREW, whom he styles his Brothers, in
which he very partially represents his pretended Hardships from
GEORGE, and magnifies his own Duty to his *Father*, and his great
Merits; I beg you'll give a Place in your Paper to the following Letter
195 to Mr. FOGG, which sets all Matters in Dispute between GEORGE and
PATRICK in a clear and just Light, and shews the Groundlessness of the
Complaints of the latter, who, being blinded by Ambition and
Arrogance, has entirely mistaken his own Case.

To Mr. FOGG.

200   SIR,

I Have taken Notice of the Letter from your Dublin Correspondent,
in your Journal of the 11th past; but I guess by your Answer, that
you did not perfectly understand his Cant; otherwise, as I take you to
be a true Friend to the Gentleman he calls his Brother GEORGE, I
205 believe you would not have handled him so gently; and therefore, that
you may be the better aware of him for the future, and avoid giving
Offence to your Friend, I was willing to set you right in the Story, and
to shew you that PATRICK's grievous Complaint of *ill Usage* and
Hardships put upon him by his *Father*, is without any just Cause given
210 him on the Part of GEORGE, and that it proceeds only from his own
ambitious encroaching Humour.

You must know then that old SUPREMUS has had *two Wives*, each of which brought him a *Noble Estate*, which was *entailed* upon their *Posterity*, and he was obliged by the *Marriage Settlement* to take the *Advice* and *Consent* of his *Sons* (when they came of Age) in the *principal* 215 *Management* of the respective Estates. Now GEORGE is his *eldest Son* by the *first Wife*, and ANDREW by the *second*; but PATRICK is really the *Son* of GEORGE; so that you may see the *young Man*'s Brain is turn'd so far as to forget *who he is*, and *from whence* he came; how else could he have the Arrogance to stile himself *Brother* to his own *Father* and his *Uncle*? 220 Besides, he has had the Insolence and Folly to characterize GEORGE as 'a great Lover of his Belly, and that his high Feeding disposes him to be haughty, stubborn, choleric, and ready upon all Occasions to fly in his *own Father*'s Face,' which every one who knows him, will agree to be literally true of *himself*, and much more *his own* than GEORGE's 225 Character. But I must not take up your Time with making Remarks upon all his *unmannerly Sarcasms* upon both his *Father* and his *Uncle*; nor upon his own vain Boast of his *great Accomplishments* and *Merits*; and shall therefore confine myself to the principal Point only. To go on then with my Story: 230

SUPREMUS had also acquir'd *another* considerable Estate, by the Assistance of his Son GEORGE, who was thereby intitled to have a *Part* in the *Disposal* and *Management* of it, (tho' ANDREW had none) and so they agreed to settle GEORGE's eldest Son, this PATRICK, upon it; but under the Obligation always to pay a *dutiful Respect* to his *Grandfather* 235 and *Father*, and to obey such *superior Orders* as they should think fit to send him from Time to Time. However, as this Estate lay at a Distance from the others, they impower'd him to make such *Orders* as might be requisite for the *well managing* the Affairs of his *own Tenants* among *themselves*; but with this *Restriction*, that *none* of them should be 240 of *Force* till they had been approved by SUPREMUS and GEORGE. And thus PATRICK was well provided for, in a *good Country*, abounding with all the *Conveniencies of Life*: And tho' the *old Tenants* (whether from their not being *well-us'd*, or from their own *unciviliz'd* or *capricious Temper*) were sometimes *mutinous* and *troublesome* to him, yet GEORGE 245 always supported him against them, and *compel'd* them to submit; till at length the Quarrel about their *Difference in Religion* grew so high, that they made a *general Insurrection*, murder'd abundance of PATRICK's People, and had well nigh driven him and all the rest of them out of the Country. But GEORGE sent a *strong Army*, took a *severe Revenge* upon 250

the *Rebels*, intirely *subdued* them, and *secured* PATRICK in his *Possession*
by a *better Establishment* than ever he had *before*.

   I must now observe to you, that GEORGE had a very *numerous* and
chargeable Family at *home*, beside that he had also placed several *other*
255 of his *Sons* in *good Estates* (tho' *much inferior* to PATRICK's) *abroad*, and
found himself engag'd in very *great* and *continual* Expences to *protect*
and *defend* them all against any *Insults* or *Injuries* offered by their
Neighbours; but he was so tender of burdening his *Sons* Estates, that he
always rais'd the *whole Charge* upon his *own Tenants*: 'Tis true they
260 were *rich*, and *able* to bear it; but then as they gained their *Wealth*
principally by sending their *Woollen Manufactures* to all Markets *far*
and *near* that would take them off, it behoved GEORGE above all things
to secure his *own Tenants* in the *fullest Enjoyment* of this *Commerce*,
otherwise they must grow *poor*, and become unable to pay their *Rent*,
265 and consequently GEORGE himself would be put out of a *Capacity* to
maintain his *Family*, and *support* his *Sons* in the Enjoyment of the
Estates he had given them; and 'twas for this Reason (which you must
allow to be a very good one) that when it was found that PATRICK's
Estate produced abundance of *Wool*, GEORGE sent him a strict Order
270 not to suffer any of his Tenants to sell their *Wool*, but to his (GEORGE's)
Tenants) who should always buy it of them, and therefore they would
have no *good Reason* to complain, because they might keep as much as
they pleased for their *own Use*, and would have a *good Price* for the rest,
and this was no more than what he required of his *other Sons*, that they
275 should sell what their Lands produced more than for their *own Use*,
to none but to *his Tenants*. Again, When PATRICK sent such great
Quantities of *Cattel* to GEORGE's Market, that such of his *Tenants* who
lived by breeding of *Cattel* told him they must throw up their *Farms* if a
Stop were not put to it, GEORGE was *necessitated* to forbid PATRICK's
280 sending any more, which he took very heinously.

   After this, PATRICK's *old Tenants* made another *general Insurrection*,
and forced him and his People to quit their Farms, and betake
themselves to GEORGE for *Refuge* and *Help*; who received them very
kindly, fed many of them at his *own Table*, raised a *good Army*, made an
285 *intire Conquest* of the *rebellious Tenants*, and *reinstated* PATRICK and
all *his People* in their *Lands*; and this at a *vast Expence*, all raised
upon GEORGE's *Tenants*, without putting him to a *Penny Charge*, or
demanding any *Reimbursement* from him to *this Day*.

   But, see the *Gratitude* of this *selfish* Wretch! no sooner was he warm
290 in his *regain'd Habitation*, but he sets his People to work to make the

same sort of *Woollen Manufactures*, and send them to the *same Markets* with GEORGE's *Tenants*, where they *undersold* them so much, as that, if they had been suffer'd to go on, they would have beaten the *Tenants* out of their *Trade*, and so by Degrees have *impoverish'd* GEORGE to *enrich* PATRICK. GEORGE, therefore, to prevent so fatal a Consequence, 295 and well-knowing that PATRICK's Estate was capable of *many other* Improvements, (and particularly that of the *Linen Manufactury*, which he himself mentions) wherein he might employ the *Industry* of his own People, sufficiently to their Advantage, without *interfering* with *his Tenants*, made an *Order*, forbidding PATRICK's People to send *any more* 300 such *Woollen Manufactures* to the *Markets* where his *own Tenants* traded: But PATRICK was so angry at this, that he countenanc'd one of his *Sons* to publish a Book, wherein he pretended to prove that *their Estate* had *no Dependance* upon GEORGE; and that as they had *Power* (tho' 'twas only in the Manner before-mention'd) to make *Orders* by 305 *themselves*, he had no *Right* to make *any Orders* that should be *binding* upon *them*: But this Insolence was so much resented by GEORGE's Tenants, as that they *presented* the Book at the next *Quarter-Sessions*, when it was condemn'd to be *burnt* by the *common Hangman*, and PATRICK has been obliged to pay *Obedience* to *this Order* ever since. 310 *Hinc Illæ Lacrymæ!*

You will now be able to form your Judgment upon the *whole Matter*. You see on the one Hand a *careful* and *indulgent Father*, studious to *advance* and *prefer* his *Children* in the World, but *provident* and *prudent* withal to keep the *Staff in his own Hand*, and not to suffer *any of them* to 315 *usurp* upon his *paternal Authority*, or to *encroach* upon *him* in his *peculiar Way* of gaining his *Wealth* (since, as has been said, he has plac'd them in a Way of living well of themselves) for that would soon put him out of a Condition to *maintain himself, support* his *numerous Family* at *Home*, and *protect* his *Children Abroad*. You see, on the other 320 Hand, an *ambitious Son*, forgetting the *Duty* of his *Relation*, and his *just Subordination*, *repining* and *murmuring* against a *tender Father*, to whose *Bounty* he owes *all* that he *enjoys*, and who has always effectually *help'd* him in his *Distresses*, when he was no Way able to *help himself*, and given him all the *Liberty* that was proper for the *Station* he is in, 325 without ever laying any *Restraint* upon him but what was *absolutely requisite* for his *own Self-Preservation*, as I think I have sufficiently demonstrated.

You may do well then to advise PATRICK to cease his *grumbling*, content himself with his *Condition*, remember his *great Obligations*, and 330

retain a *dutiful Respect* to his *Father*, and then he may go on to *employ*
his *People* in all *such Ways* of *Industry* and *Commerce*, which do not
interfere with those Particulars which GEORGE has reserved to *his own
Tenants*; and so he will be always sure to find all the *Encouragement*,
335 *Assistance*, and *Protection* which GEORGE can give him, in every Thing
that is not *incompatible* with *his own Well-being*. I have now done with
your *Irish Correspondent*, and have only to note to you, that though I
have carried on the Relation of these Transactions in GEORGE's *Name*,
without mentioning SUPREMUS, 'twas because the *Management* was
340 chiefly left to GEORGE, yet nothing was ordered without the *Approbation*
and *Confirmation* of SUPREMUS.

> *I am, SIR,*
> *Your Humble Servant,*
> *Philo-Britannus.*

ITEM A

MOTTO. *Honos alit artes*: Honours nourish the arts (Cicero, *Tusculan Disputations*, I. ii. 4);
a tag well known from the *Adagia* of Erasmus.

ITEM B

73–4. *a Letter from that brazen-fac'd Varlet*: i.e., *Intelligencer* 16, reprinted in *Fog's Weekly
J.*, 11 Jan. 1728/9.
76. *First I must inform you*: On the view of the Irish and the Welsh expressed here, see
David Hayton, 'From Barbarian to Burlesque: English Images of the Irish c. 1660–
1750', *Irish Economic and Social History*, 15 (1988), 5–31.
92. *David . . . is the Second*: Wales was united with England in 1536.
137–8. *his Nephew C———*: John, Baron Carteret, Lord Lieutenant of Ireland since 1724.
163. *Steward*: Perhaps the prime minister, Sir Robert Walpole.
172. *Heraldry*: On the traditional Welsh pride of pedigree, see Francis Jones, 'The Old
Families of Wales', in Donald Moore (ed.), *Wales in the Eighteenth Century* (Swan-
sea, 1976), 27–32; and Glanmor Williams, *Religion, Language, and Nationality in Wales*
(Cardiff, 1979), 149–51.

ITEM C

202. *I guess by your Answer*: The writer erroneously assumes the reply to have been Fog's.
The presumption of Fog's ignorance and his friendship to George is ironic.
238. *they impower'd him to make such Orders*: Poynings's Law (1494).
248. *a general Insurrection*: Tyrone's rebellion in the 1590s.
302–3. *one of his Sons to publish a Book*: William Molyneux, *The Case of Ireland Stated*
(Dublin: Ray, 1698).
311. *Hinc Illæ Lacrymæ*: Hence those tears! i.e., That explains everything! Proverbial,
from Horace, *Epistles*, I. xix. 41, and other classical sources.

APPENDIX H
The Spurious No. 20

This paper gained a certain notoriety in Dublin. At least some of Swift's acquaintances believed him capable of writing it, but Pope was not deceived. For his and other contemporary comments, see Appendix B. For information about the publication and prosecution of this paper, see the textual notes to the appendices.

The *Intelligencer*.
NUMB. XX.
A *Posthumus* Worke Communicated.

Omne tulit punctum qui miscuit utile Dulci.

Hor.

I Think my self obliged (in the best Numbers I am Master of) to testifie my acknowledgments to my Correspondent, and at the same time declare to the World how much I think it is Obliged to him for the following Instructive piece.

Virtue Describ'd by Zeno *doth appear,*	5
A Dreadful Monster Rigidly severe.	
Her Ghastly form in Savage Garb Array'd,	
Seems more a Fury than a Heav'n born Maid.	
On pointed Clifts he places her Aboad,	
And hissing Serpents Guard the Arduous Road,	10
Impregnable to Man and E'en a task for God.	
In Sullen Majesty the Tyrant Reigns,	
O'er Dreary Mountains, and o'er Desart plains.	
Not so great Sage you shew the Beauteous Maid,	
In all the pride of Heavenly Charms Arrayed.	15
So tempting is the prize, so smooth the Way,	
Our very passions force us to obey.	
The Wife no more the Harlots Arts shall Dread,	
No tainted Joys shall stain the Marriage Bed.	
No Maids once fair in Poverty grown Old,	20
Shall Curse the Rival Charms of shineing Gold.	

> No Nymph Deform'd shall pine; your Arts supply,
> What Niggard fate or Nature can Deny.
> Each Day shall add new Glories to your Fame,
25   And Ages yet unborn shall Hail your sacred Name.

To the Intelligencer.

SIR.

THE Exact Similitude you bear to my dear old Uncle *Nestor Ironside* (of Reverend memory) in your Repeated Labours to Rescue your
30 Country from Vice and Folly, by shameing the Men out of the former, and Instructing the Ladies out of the Latter, points you out (alas since he is gone) the best Qualified Person Living for the Guardianship of young Ladies, to whom then but to you shou'd any of the unpublish'd Works of *Ironside* flie for protection. At the Death of that Venerable
35 Man, as next Heir, with his Estate I Inherited his Papers, in the peruseing of which the other Day I found, written by his own Hand, the tract I here present you with, which I believe you will find of too great Import to the World, not to give it a place in your next Paper. I have faithfully transcrib'd it from the sacred Original as it here follows.

40   *Fæcunda culpæ Sæcula.*

OF all the Crimes that Deform this Age, the perfidious Disloyalty of Men in the Marryed State, shou'd Engage every virtuous Pen to stop the progress of a Vice so Derogatory from the title of Rational and Human, that it seems to be a compound of the Vices contrarie's to all the
45 Virtues. When a Man is said to be an *Adulterer*, he is at the same time understood to be a *Sacrilegious*, *Perjur'd*, *Hard-hearted*, *Incontinent*, *Ungrateful*, and Inconstant *Villian*; who can be Insensible of the obligations imposed on him by the Laws Human and Divine, towards a Person who has made all his Interests hers, has deliver'd her self
50 absolutely into the Hands of a Man on whom she looks as the Guardian of her Honour, the partner of all her Joys or Afflictions, obliged by his Vows to Cherish and Comfort her in all her Necessities, with an Inviolable Fidelity. But what shou'd make Transgressions of this kind appear more Odious to a Man of Honour is, that the poor Injured Party
55 has no means left of Redress. I am Confident that every Man who is not an abandon'd Proselite to this fashionable Crime, will be Sensible of the Truth of this, on a fair and unprejudic'd stateing the Case, 'tis no

Excuse that after some time the Wife loosses her Charms, grows
Disagreeable and troublesome; then truly the fine Gentleman must
have variety, it being Inconsistent with the Character of a polite Man 60
to be long pleas'd with the same object, he squanders his own
Constitution and the neglected Gentlewoman's Fortune in a Giddy
pursuit of Pleasure and Infamy. And if he condescends to bestow an
odd Embrace on his Lady, 'tis still to gratifie his desire of Variety, the
Consequence of which is a dwindl'd, sickly, & halfbegotten Offspring, 65
a Truth too visible in this Age. But as a great deal may depend on the
Conduct of a well Educated Wife in rendering the conjugal State
Reciprocally happy, I wou'd recommend to all Mothers the utmost
Care and Diligence in the Instruction of their Daughters, for I am
convinc'd that a neglect or bad method in this has been frequently the 70
Cause of unspeakable Misfortunes and numberless Disquiets in many
Families. Therefore let Miss be taken out of the Nursery much Earlier
than usual, & made her Mother's Companion, bred up in such
Familiarity with her, that she shou'd not have the least restraint on her
words or Actions, by which she may sooner discover her natural bent 75
and Inclinations and the more Easily get the better of her Passions, as
yet Young and Unfix'd. All her Admonitions shou'd be convey'd in the
most free and easie manner, without the least simptom of Severity; the
Child shou'd rather be stolen than driven into the Paths of Virtue,
every the least good Quality she discover'd ought to be so Cherish'd 80
and Encourag'd, that she shou'd rather desire to please out of an
expectation of Reward than the fear of Punishment.—The first and
cheif Care shou'd be the cultivateing of the Mind, a Work so
necessary, that where it is happily perform'd, it produces Infinitely
more estimable Qualifications than Fortune, or the Beauties of the 85
Body. These will soon grow familiar, fade, and pass away. But they
will discover new Beauties every Day, look Green in old Age, bless her
partner or her Friend, and gently waft her through the vicissitudes of
Life, to Immortal Joys. There has been already so much very well said
on this subject, that I shall pursue it here no farther, but pass to the 90
necessary Qualifications of the Body, and lay down such Rules for
them as I don't doubt will, when fortunately join'd with those of the
Mind, put an effectual stop to *Adultery*, and make it the Interest of
every Man of pleasure to be a good Husband.

As Marriage is an Union of Bodies as well as Spirits, the perfections 95
of the former shou'd be so much regarded that Art ought not only
assist Nature but supply her Defects, so that the Improvement of one

Talent may make up for the want of many others. Thus the singing
Master's Art has often so Inchanted the Ear, that the bunch on the
100 Back has past unregarded, and a genteel easie Air has frequently
Charm'd with a disagreeable Voice and deformed Face. We first get
acquainted with the Body, by which our Judgment of the Mind is
frequently Influenc'd, and as the first Impressions are generaly
strongest, it is the Interest of every Lady to be Qualified in such a
105 manner as to secure them in her Favour. 'Tis true there is a certain
Jenesgai quoi (the sole Gift of Nature) we term Agreeable, which all
feel, but none can define. This has often Inspired a strong and lasting
Passion, but can never fail of success when assisted by Education. I
have known a Gentleman passionately in Love with a certain Nod of a
110 young Ladies Head; since so Inconsiderable a motion has so much
Power, how can we be surprized at the great Pleasure we find in
beholding a Person Walk or Dance gracefully, when so many distinct
Motions agree in a perfect Harmony, nor yet is Musick one of the least
Charming Qualifications of a Young Lady, and truly one should think
115 that a Person possess'd of these Advantages could not fail of fixing the
most Inconstant Heart, yet such is the depravity of this Age, that I have
known some possess'd of them, and many others in the highest degree
of perfection, after a few Months dispis'd and abandon'd for a sluggish
Indolence of their *Buttocks*, (as their faithless Husbands term'd it) and
120 others that have met the same ungenerous Usage for a Frigidity, or too
great Capacity in a part which Modesty did not hinder their hardn'd
Villians to Name, when they publickly compar'd them to old slippers
and draw Wells; but what surprized me more was to see them
succeeded by common Prostitutes, the Gleanings of the Stews, and
125 put me upon Examining the Causes of so detestable a Practice, which
by an indefatigable Application to the study of Men, Women and
Books; I have at length most happily found, as also an Infalliable
Scheme for the Effectual prevention of all such Disorders for the
future. I must here acknowledge my Obligations to *Anacreon*, *Horace*,
130 *Tibullus*, *Cicero*, and another Antient Author who shall be Nameless,
for the first hints, which have been much Improv'd by Reading
Smigliwhishey's, *Backsterus's* and *Pricknellius's* Historicrittical Notes on
the forgoing Authors, from whom & many others of the Antients, it is
most Evident that the *Roman* and *Grecian* Mothers were very Careful
135 in having their Daughters perfectly Instructed in the most agreeable
Art of *Heaveing* and *Setting*, for which purpose they had at a great
Expence Mistresses from *Ionia*.

Motus Doceri gaudet Ionicos
Matura Virgo, et fingitur artibus.
—————————————*Amores*   140
Detenero meditatur ungui.   Hor.

I could Site many other passages to prove how Necessary this
Qualification was Esteem'd among the Ancients to Secure the Wives
the fidelity of their Husbands. Every Roman Lady was perfect
Mistress of the *Muscles* of her *Backside*, and as they begun those 145
Exercises very Early, they could by a proper Behaviour of the upper
parts of their *Thiges*, with great facillity so contract or Dilate the
Orifice as to suit it to any Size. During the Celebration of *Hymen's*
rights no Limb lay Idle, Each was Employ'd in it's respective Office;
The lower *Muscles* of the *Belly* too were Extraordinary alert in a very 150
Titulateing motion which never failed to Communicate a Thrilling
Warmth to the main Scene of Action, and I am perswaded it was
Intirely Due to this Accomplishment that the *Grecian* and *Roman*
were so Generally more Fortunate in the Marry'd state than our
Ladies, for in all my Reading I have not met with one Instance of a 155
Grecian or *Roman* Lady's being slighted or reproach'd for Frigidity
or too great Capacity, and upon a strict Enquiery I have Discovered
that the Variety so much desired and sought after by our Modern
Husbands is occasion'd by a very few simptoms of this Bewitching
art which they find in the Prostitute, from Whence it is plain that if 160
our Women were well Instructed in Cuntinometry, the Husband
would no more Stray; but be sure of finding all his Desires at Home.
This was a Science in great Esteem among the Ancients, but with
many other of their Treasures Lost to Us, but as we Excell them in
Geometry and *Staticks* I don't Despair, through the great Love I bear 165
my Country, of restoring it in greater Perfection than Ever they had
it, and will lay down in the following Scheme, such Rules as shall be
Intirely Consistent with the utmost Decency and Decorum. I shall
also Explain how *Bunches* on the *Back*, and other Deformities in the
Shape may become Advantagious in the practice of this Excellent 170
Art.

Sir, I will here make bold to break off my Uncle's Discourse,
having alredy (I fear) transgress'd the Bounds of your Paper and will,
if this meets a Due Reception, send you the remaining Part, before
you Publish your Next. Sir. I am with Profound Respect *Roger* 175
Ironside.

May the presumption be forgiven, if I here Offer what I think would be a great assistance to the Laudable undertaking of Mr. Ironside, *I think it would much conduce to his End if the Fathers on their part would Endeavour to*
180 *habituate their Sons to Constancy from their Youth by making them Serve an Apprenticeship to Matrimony, which might be pretty easily Effected by keeping for each a Young Woman not very Hansom, with whome they shou'd Converse, as in the Maried state, from the Age of Fourteen or Fifteen, untill they realy became Husbands.*

MOTTO. Horace, *Ars Poetica*, 343: 'He has won every vote who has blended profit and pleasure' (Loeb).

  5. *Zeno*: Zeno of Citium, founder of the Stoic school.

  28. *Nestor Ironside*: Putative author of the *Guardian*, written primarily by Addison and Steele and published daily for more than six months in 1713. Ironside's supposed nephew feels thus qualified to stress the Intelligencer's capacity for the guardianship of young ladies.

  40. *Fœcunda culpæ Sæcula*: Horace, *Odes*, III. vi. 17: 'The age, teeming with sin'. Here as below, the writer perverts Horace's morality by recommending rather than reproving passion.

86–7. *they will discover*: 'they' refers to the qualifications produced in the young woman by the cultivation of her mind.

  99. *bunch*: Hump (*OED*).

106. *Jenesgai quoi*: i.e., *je ne sais quoi*, something indescribable.

117. *others*: i.e., other advantages.

136. *Heaveing and Setting*: Rising and falling, as waves in a heavy sea (*OED*, under *heave*, *v.*, B. 13. b; under *set*, *v.*, B. 10).

138. *Motus Doceri gaudet . . .*: Horace, *Odes*, III. vi. 21–4: 'The maiden early takes delight in learning Grecian dances, and trains herself in coquetry . . . and plans . . . amours with passion unrestrained' (Loeb). The ellipsis conceals Horace's disapproval of this behaviour.

APPENDIX I

The Bowyer–Davis Preface

To their London collected editions of 1729 and 1730, Bowyer and Davis added an epigraph—

> *Omne vafer vitium ridenti Flaccus amico*
> *Tangit, & admissus circum præcordia ludit.*
>
> Pers.

—a preface, and a table of contents which assigned titles to the nineteen numbers. These titles have been given in Appendix L, since, though lacking authority, they have been cited by later writers. According to George Faulkner, Bowyer was 'famous for writing prefaces', and it is a plausible supposition that this one is his (*Corresp.* ed. Ball, vi. 224).

TO THE READER.

THE following Productions I met straggling in a mean Condition, representing the Poverty of their Countrey by their outward Appearance; but by their Discourse they soon betrayed their good Birth and Education.

I had the same eager Desire of communicating them to the Publick, that most of us have of introducing a Man of Wit into Company, or of the second hand Merit of telling a Joke, when we have not the Sense to make one.

As they wanted nothing but a more genteel Dress to enable them to make their Fortune in *England*, I have given them the Cloathing of our own Countrey. And now, I doubt not, they will have the good Luck of being admitted to a Lady's Toilet, or the ill one of being closetted by a Prime Minister: I say the ill one, for they describe an unalterable Something, with the Abbreviations of T—D, and that perhaps may be thought a Reflection on one or other of *First Quality* and *Distinction*.

Having thus given these Essays new Birth, as it were, in a foreign Countrey, I may claim the Right over them of a secondary Parent: The real Parent will confirm it, I don't question, with the Honour of his own Donation: So the Pope made a Gift of *Ireland* to *Henry VIII.* after the King had annex'd it to his own Imperial Title.

MOTTO. Persius, *Satires*, i. 116–17: 'Horace, sly dog, worming his way playfully into the vitals of his laughing friend, touches up every fault' (Loeb). Bowyer's conventional use of this passage to label the *Intelligencer*'s satire Horatian was evidently meant to be recognized as mere camouflage, thrown up in the manner described by William Kupersmith, 'Vice and Folly in Neoclassical Satire', *Genre*, 11 (1978), 45–58.

Intended Papers: Swift's Manuscript Hints
(*a*) Hints: Education of Ladies
(*b*) Intelligencer [Miscellaneous Hints]

A glimpse at planning for the *Intelligencer* is afforded by Swift's letter to Sheridan from Market Hill, 18 September 1728: 'I think the Sufferings of the Country, for want of Silver, deserves a Paper, since the Remedy is so easy, and those in Power so negligent.... I think Lady *Dun*'s burning would be an admirable Subject to shew how hateful an Animal a human Creature is, that is known to have never done any good. The Rabble all rejoicing, &c. which they would not have done at any Misfortune to a Man known to be Charitable.'[1] The first of these topics came to fruition in no. 19. As for Lady Dun, the widow of the Dublin physician Sir Patrick Dun, the burning of her house had attracted the notice Swift mentions. He perhaps alludes to her energetic efforts to subvert her husband's public-spirited bequest of his house and medical library to the College of Physicians.[2] Sheridan did not take up this second topic, possibly because the morality of the matter seemed less clear in Dublin than at a distance.

Beyond these intended *Intelligencers*, some of Swift's 'hints' for possible papers are preserved in the John Rylands University Library, Manchester (English MS 659, items 9–10).[3] There are notes for an essay on the education of women as well as a collection of miscellaneous notes. None of these hints was actually used in the *Intelligencer*, bearing out Swift's remark to Pope that the periodical 'might have continued longer, for there were hints enough.' Some of them found their way into other essays, however: the 'Letter to the Archbishop of Dublin, Concerning the Weavers', the 'Answer to Several Letters from Unknown Persons', and the 'Answer to Several Letters Sent Me from Unknown Hands', all written in 1729, as well as some other pieces.[4] The note on 'stuff gowns' in the miscellaneous hints evidently refers to an event which occurred in March 1728/9, when, according to the 'Letter to the Archbishop', a delegation of weavers solicited Swift's help in promoting the

---

[1] *Corresp.* iii. 297–8.
[2] *Corresp.* ed. Ball, iv. 44 n.; J. D. H. Widdess, *A History of the Royal College of Physicians of Ireland, 1654–1963* (Edinburgh, 1963), 60–1.
[3] The hints, part of the Thrale–Piozzi manuscripts discovered by James Clifford, were privately printed by Herbert Davis's bibliography class at Oxford in 1954 and twice published in 1955: by Herbert Davis, in *Prose*, xii. 306–8; and by Clifford and Irvin Ehrenpreis in 'Swiftiana in Rylands English MS. 659 and Related Documents', *BJRL* 37 (1955), 375–8, an important discussion.
[4] These essays will be found in *Prose*, xii.

wearing of gowns of Irish stuff (woollen) by the clergy; Swift agreed, and then they failed to co-operate with Swift's plan. From this evidence it appears that in the spring of 1729 Swift still meant to continue the *Intelligencer*, as further appears from the note at the end of *Intelligencer* 20, published in May 1729. Perhaps the episode with the weavers led Swift to revive the *Intelligencer*, since he had reported to Pope 6 March that it had been 'dropt'.[5]

Swift's willingness to use these hints in other writings is not entirely consistent with his assertion to Pope in 1732 that the *Intelligencer* ceased because he and Sheridan could not do the writing themselves: 'If we could have got some ingenious young man to have been the manager, who should have published all that might be sent to him, it might have continued longer, for there were hints enough. But the Printer here could not afford such a young man one farthing for his trouble, the Sale being so small, and the price one half-penny; and so it dropt' (*Corresp.* iv. 30). Still, the implication that Swift and Sheridan simply tired of the routine is probably the best explanation for the *Intelligencer*'s unceremonious cessation at the very moment when it had been honoured by a handsome reprinting in London.

It is possible that 'Maxims Controlled in Ireland' was originally designed for the *Intelligencer*: the draft notes for it were found with the 'hints'. Both the notes and the essay are edited in *Prose*, xii, and a photograph of the notes is reproduced there, facing p. 131. It is also possible that some of the posthumously published essays that derive from the hints were designed for the *Intelligencer*, as well as 'A Letter on Maculla's Project about Halfpence and a New One Proposed' and 'A Proposal that All the Ladies and Women of Ireland Should Appear Constantly in Irish Manufactures' (*Prose*, xii. 93–105, 121–7). Other pieces that Swift may have written for the *Intelligencer* include 'A Discourse, to Prove the Antiquity of the English Tongue', proposed by Herbert Davis (*Prose*, vol. iv, p. xxxviii); 'Hints on Good Manners', Deane Swift's text of notes Swift had made for an essay, in a format probably very similar to that of the Rylands MSS (*Prose*, iv. 221–2) and on internal evidence later than Sept. 1727; and 'On Good-Manners and Good-Breeding' (*Prose*, iv. 213–18), proposed by Colin J. Horne, *Swift on His Age* (London, 1953), 230, but on grounds rejected by Herbert Davis: that the essay derives from 'Hints on Good Manners' (*Prose*, vol. iv, pp. xxxvi–xxxvii). Davis also maintains (ibid.) that 'Of the Education of Ladies' has nothing to do with the Rylands MS 'hints' reproduced below; Clifford and Ehrenpreis think otherwise (376). In *Prose*, vol. xiv, p. xiii, Davis and Ehrenpreis suggest that the notes headed 'Proposal for Virtue' were written about 1728 and perhaps intended for an *Intelligencer*. The suggestion is not repeated in Ehrenpreis, *Swift*, iii. 529, in

---

[5] In 'A Letter to the Archbishop', Swift says this event occurred 'about a Month ago'; the 'Letter' is said to have been written in Apr. 1729 (*Prose*, xii. 68, 329). For the remark to Pope, see *Corresp.* iii. 314. To be precise, Swift said that *Sheridan* had 'dropt it'; did he then think of carrying on without Sheridan?

part owing, no doubt, to George Mayhew's evidence that the manuscript dates from 1727.[6]

Most of these pieces were first published by Deane Swift in 1765.[7]

In January 1728/9, Swift sent Worrall *The Journal of a Dublin [Modern] Lady* for the *Intelligencer*, thinking it was still being published.[8] Scott believed that *The Grand Question Debated* was intended for the *Intelligencer*, and while that is possible (Swift dated the draft of the poem 2 Sept. 1728), Scott probably mis-identified as *The Grand Question Debated* the poem *Journal of a Dublin Lady*, to which Swift refers in the letter to Worrall cited earlier (Scott (1824), i. 389n.).

---

[6] Review of *Prose*, xiv, in *PQ* 48 (1969), 399; see also Mayhew's discussion of this MS in *Rage or Raillery*, 11, 18, 78, and 164.

[7] Swift, *Works*, viii (London: Johnson, 1765; T–S 87, p. 86).

[8] *Corresp.* iii. 308.

(a)

Hints   Education of Ldyes

No great matter for the bulk of women, since the men are as foolish & ignorant.

Begin. A person of Quality a little absolute, a man of tast and letters
5 who well knew how to support his opinions, which were gen[er]ally right, fell into one, which I thought he held in a sense not sufficiently limited, although he had many old proverbs and maxims on his side. which carry the authority of ages with him that women shoud only regard their Children & family &c.

10 My practice of advising Ldys to read, and what; and my way of instructing young Misses.

I used to stay a month or two. the Count[r]y desolate. the Neighborhood scarce and not very inviting.

A Companion for life to a man of Sense especially without
15 Employm^t, and violent lover of the Country. should have a reasonable companion, who could distinguish a man of Sense &c, and relish good conversation with out being talkative, positive or assuming

It would make the women love home better, and able to teach their Daughters.

20 The Lady was a considerable heiress used too fondly, lives in Town— had that kind of Education which is called the best. learning Italian, French, Musick and singing, all wch she forgot &c. fell into play, visits, assemblees &c.

No French Romances, and few plays. for young Ladyes

25 How hard for a woman to live solitary and not read;

A generall inspection into family affairs right: but not to be a Hous keeper &c. any more than an Architect should have his hands in mortar.

I have often thanked God that custom has made it detestable otherwise.
30 otherwise they have a good plea to keep a Gallant rathr than marry, I mean a great heiress, who when she is marryd can call nothing her own, & may want common necessaryes, by the churlishness of a husband &c. therefore I was never a against what they call pin-money. nor see the reason why people should not part when all agreem^t is desperate.

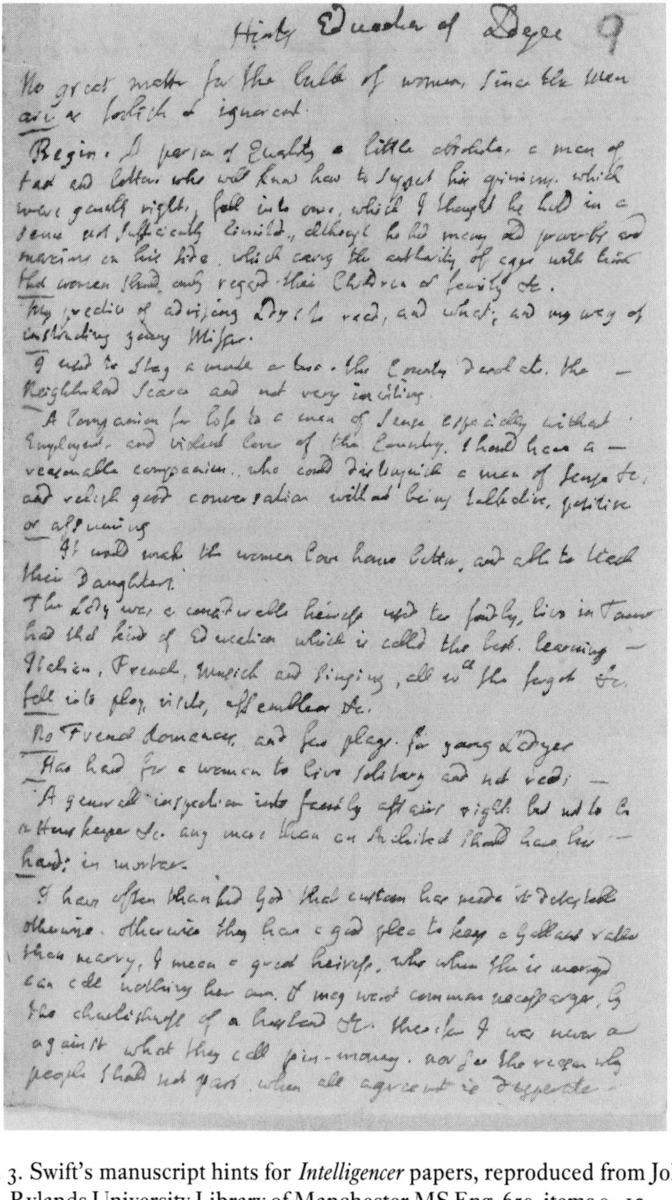

Fig. 3. Swift's manuscript hints for *Intelligencer* papers, reproduced from John Rylands University Library of Manchester MS Eng. 659, items 9–10.

Women I am to often want ballast &c. but it is
often through ignorance or half knowledge.
A sham that not one woman in a million can properly
be said to read or write, or understand.

Intelligencer

Beau's Dresser.

Clergy preaching. Led English &c

Endowed Knavery of all handicrafts &
Shopkeepers, and in the County of all farmers
Cottagers, &c. Scold once then finds, but
word when partake of public actions
Buildings, and praise of Peace
Improvements, penal clause, as to time &c,
for improved. & preservation of ways &
their kind — chuse Squire on this head

Knavery the effect of poverty and oppression; they
steal or cheat, as the quickest way to live, when industry
is not encouraged; therefore they do not stand on credit
or your buying and I time. Sacrifice your custom for
cheating you half a Crown.
That great rogue Badger
Shall guess what I do, and how the weaver acted.
Peter Walters —

Women I own do often want balast &c. but it is often through 35
ignorance or half knoledge.

A shame that not one woman in a million can properly be said to read
or write, or understand.

(*b*)

Intelligencer

Beau's dresses. 40

Clergy preaching. bad Engl—&c

Universal Knavery of all handicrafts & Shopkeepers, and in the
Count[r]y of all farmers Cottagers, &c. Scotch worse than Irish, but
worst when partake of both nations

Building, and praise of Pearce 45

Improvem^{ts}, penal clause, as to time &c for improvmt. & preservation
of trees, & their kinds—abuse Squires on this head

Knavery the effect of poverty and oppression: they steal or cheat, as
the quickest way to live, when industry is not encouraged: therefore
they do not stand on credit or y^r buying anoth^r time. Sacrifice your 50
custom for cheating you half a Crown.

That great rogue Badgers

Stuff gowns   what I did, and how the weavers acted.

Peter Walters—

23. *assemblees*: See notes to no. 1.
33. *pin-money*: See notes to no. 4.
45. *Pearce*: Sir Edward Lovett Pearce, the architect then beginning work on the new
Irish parliament house in Dublin (see Maurice Craig, 'Sir Edward Lovett Pearce',
Quart. Bull. Irish Georgian Soc. 17 (1974), 10–17). Why Swift wished to praise him is
unclear; compare the fault found with Dublin building in nos. 15 and 17, and see
Appendix F. Delany praised Pearce in 1730 (*Poems*, ii. 508), and in the same year
Pearce gave Swift at least four books (Clifford and Ehrenpreis, 378; Rothschild
2308 and 2315; Sotheby (London) sale catalogue, 23 June 1988, lot 101).
46. *Improvem^{ts}*: See notes to no. 15.
52. *Badgers*: Unidentified. I have examined this word using a macro-photographic
colour transparency and am satisfied that it is the correct reading, though queried
by Clifford and Ehrenpreis.
53. *Stuff gowns*: See discussion above.
54. *Peter Walters*: Peter Walter was an avaricious attorney and land-steward to wealthy
members of the English nobility, at whose expense he by industry and sharp practice became rich. Swift attacks him in 'The Answer of William Pulteney to Sir
Robert Walpole' (1730; *Prose*, v. 117); and in *To Mr. Gay* (1731; *Poems*, ii. 534–5); and
see Swift to Pope, 12 Oct. 1727, *Corresp.* iii. 243. See also Howard Erskine-Hill, *The
Social Milieu of Alexander Pope* (New Haven, 1975), ch. 4.

APPENDIX K

To the Author of Those Intelligencers (1733)

The most hostile contemporary reaction to the *Intelligencer*, albeit a delayed one, came from New York. This anonymous pamphlet defends both Ireland and the American colonies against the aspersions of nos. 6 and 19, and it incidentally reveals that both the original Harding pamphlets and the Bowyer–Davis octavo of 1729 circulated in the New World. The pamphlet was issued by the famous printer John Peter Zenger; it appears to survive in only one copy. As reprinted here, it is considerably abridged, omitting most references to New York political controversy and most praise of the king and government. The complete pamphlet is (barely legible) in the Readex Micro-card series *Early American Imprints*. Evans, *American Bibliography* (3722), and others wrongly attribute the pamphlet to 'Roscommon, *pseud.*' It ends with a quotation from the poet Roscommon, and the acknowledgement has been misinterpreted as a signature to the pamphlet as a whole.

To the Author of those Intelligencers printed at *Dublin*, to which is prefix'd the following Motto,

Omne vafer vitium ridenti Flaccus *amico*
Tangit, & admissus circum præcordia ludit.
5   *Persius.*

Being a Defence of the Plantations against the virulent Aspersions of that Writer, and such as copy after him.

·   ·   ·   ·   ·

I shall make no Apology for so late an Answer, because it was promised that the Cause of the Plantations should have been
10 undertaken by a more able Pen; but that Promise is not perform'd as yet: And moreover you will please to observe, that this Letter is from North *America*, where we receive all the Productions of *Europe* from the last Hand; and the Fame of your *Intelligencers* had reach'd me long before I could obtain a Sight of them.
15   Your 6*th* and 19*th* Numbers contain a melancholy Description of *Ireland* and its Inhabitants; but upon this Subject, and without one just Cause assign'd, His Majesty, the Ministry, and the People of *England* appear to be the principal Objects of your Wrath and Indignation, and when you have wearied your self and your Readers with those

offensive Ideas, which Rags, Filth, and the most abject Poverty is wont 20
to infuse, you rake all together into one Dunghill, mount the dirty
Eminence, and bespatter the Crown and its best Friends.

To so much of your Works you have had your Answer already (as I
am inform'd:) But as I am an Inhabitant of the Plantations, which are
seldom considered at home any otherwise than as one large Tract of 25
Infant Countries, some whereof are often wanting, and in their Turns
as frequently receiving the most tender Marks of Goodness and
Compassion, from the Hand of their immediate Lord and Royal
Master; and as we well know that we shall never want his Protection,
so long as we take Care to deserve it, we ought to be very much in 30
Earnest in order to obviate those vile and scandalous Aspersions,
which your 19*th Intelligencer* endeavours to fix upon this Continent:
For while you spread the grossest Misrepresentations, and wickedly
toil to make the World believe, that we are a Clan of *Kidnappers*,
Pickpockets, *Knaves*, and *Villains*, you give (as far as in you lyes) the 35
worst Impressions of us to those whose Patronage is no otherways to
be obtain'd than by Virtue and Integrity.

.   .   .   .   .

To shew you thus, (I say) and as in Truth you are, I must first expose
that untrue, that ugly, deform'd Picture which you give of your own
Country, and to do this I take your 6*th* and 19*th Intelligencers* together, 40
as of one Thread and one Piece, that like Figures in old Hangings
explain great Designs wretchedly executed.

In your 6*th Intelligencer, fol.* 36 you tell us, *That the Natives of* Ireland
*are sunk to the lowest Degree of Misery and Poverty, their Houses are Dunghills,
their Victuals the Blood of their Cattle, or the Herbs of the Field, and their* 45
*CLOATHING (to the Dishonour of God and Man) NAKEDNESS: That in
your late Journey from* Dublin *to* Dundalk *you went into the House of a
principal Farmer, where you took an Inventory of his Goods and Chattels; and
his whole Stock within Doors,* you describe in the following Manner,
instead of Glass, the Panes of the Windows were of brown Paper, because the 50
*Owner could not afford White; by the Hearth lay a Log of Wood, which supply'd
the Place of Chairs; there was one black Jug, one greasy Bowl, three horn Spoons,
one split Stick for a Candlestick, one rotten Bedstead, three Blankets, one for the
Farmer and his Wife, one for the Children, and one for the Man and the Maid:
That the Families of Farmers who pay great Rents, live in Filth and Nastiness,* 55
*upon Butter-Milk and Potatoes, without a Shoe or Stocking to their Feet, and in
Houses not so convenient as* English *Hogsties: That upon this Road the Signs of*

Inns are all taken from the Posts, lest the Wind should shake them down, and the
Houses with them, which are now distinguish'd by a Rag or a Wisp of Straw,
60 *stuck upon a Pole in some adjoyning Heap of Dung. Then in this Journey you saw*
    Twenty Jockies going to Fair with eight Horses, the Men had no Boots, and their
    Garrons no Shoes, amongst them all no more than four Saddles and those of
    Straw, and bridles of Wythys: Two Families driving one Cow and a Calf; and a
    Deal more of such lamentable Description, as a great Multitude of Poor People
65 *going to Dublin, in a tatter'd ragged Condition, without Cloths, Money or*
    Sustenance, who had no other Dependance upon Earth, but the Charity of the
    good People of the City; and here you conclude with a wicked Irony, *That*
    these wretched People are the Riches of a Country which the English *Plunderers*
    have reduced to so distress'd a Condition. But when you arrive at *Drogheda*,
70 there your pious Compassion overflows all Bounds; for, *after you had*
    travell'd through a Country, esteem'd (as you say) *the most fruitful Part of the*
    Kingdom, and so by Nature intended to be, no Ornaments or Improvements of
    such a Scene were visible, no Habitations fit for Gentlemen, no Farmers Houses,
    few Fields of Corn, and almost a bare Face of Nature, without new Plantations
75 *of any Kind, only a few miserable Cottages:* But this passed over, it was
    at *Drogheda you were mortifyed, and your Heart pierc'd with the sad*
    Contemplation of a most deplorable, most melancholly Scene of Woe and
    Horrour, rising from the Destruction of Churches, made by that Usurper
    Cromwell and his phanatick Zeal.
80   As *Cromwell's Zeal* is not propos'd to be the Subject of this Paper, I
    shall drop it with a short Digression, and then return to my first
    purpose; you know that Seventy and more Years have pass'd, since
    that Restoration which introduced again the Modes and Ceremonies
    of a Primitive Apostolical Church, and strange it is, that the pious Zeal
85 of *Charles* the second, a Prince of a most primitive Constitution too,
    should have done nothing towards re-edifying those his beloved
    religious Structures, which had sunk in the Defence of his Father's,
    and his own Cause: To him succeeded a Brother of less publick Spirit
    indeed, yet a Bigot to that Religion whose Votaries had ever enjoyd the
90 Offices exercised in, and the Benefices apply'd to these Structures,
    but nothing is done for them yet; the next was a most glorious Reign,
    but it was burthen'd with foreign War and homebred division, and
    therefore the Amount of all publick Expence was requir'd for the
    Support of one, and Reconciling the other; next came that immortal
95 Queen to the Throne, whose Virtue, Wisdom and Piety, have erected
    Monuments of everlasting Honour to her Memory. To Her succeeded
    King GEORGE the first, renown'd for Arms and Councils which

govern'd and preserv'd the Peace of Europe, so happily, and amidst the greatest Struggles so wisely maintain'd and continued to us by His present most illustrious, most sacred Majesty; yet the Roads from 100 *Dublin* to *Dundalk* afford, you tell us (and so does *Drogheda*) as pityfull a Prospect as ever? but he must read you with little Observation who does not remark, that here, all the intermediate time between *Cromwell* a Tyrant Usurper, and the Reign of our lawfull sovereign Lord King *GEORGE* the second is forgotten, or to speak the Truth, 105 willfully and maliciously omitted, and so much Shade, so little Light do you throw into this and the following part of your Work, that ignorant People are insensibly led to believe, that their Excellencies the late and present Lord Lieutenant of *Ireland* had carried off the Rubbish of their Ruins, and built Palaces out of their remains; or that 110 at least the present Ministry of *Great Brittain*, had so influenc'd the Councils of that Kingdom, as to have it enacted, that no Churches in *Ireland* should be built, rebuilt, or repair'd for the future; and as your Papers at first came hither in single Pieces to be scatter'd and retail'd as best serv'd a Faction, I should have found it the other Day a very 115 hard Task, to convince an honest plain Neighbour, who brought your Number 6 in his Pocket to my House, of the Falshood of your Remarks upon *Ireland*, and the malignant Design of them, if from Number 19 of the stitch'd Volume, and from his own Knowledge and Experience of this Country, by you so lately traduc'd, I could not have 120 demonstrated, that the Truth is not in you, and that your Writings have no Tendency to the Relief of those Poor, or the restoring those Churches whose Decay you would be thought to mourn, but are calculated for Raising groundless and unreasonable Discontents, in order to disturb the Peace of that Government, in the Administration 125 of which it is the Prayer of every good Man, that such turbulent and seditious Spirits as your Papers declare you to possess, may never have the least Share or Shadow of Power.

I now return to my first and principal Motive for thus appearing against you in the most publick Manner I am able; in the last 130 mentioned Intelligencer you tell the World, *That notwithstanding the Misery of your own Country*, which by the way, you most falsly exaggerate, *you cannot account for that Enthusiasm which has of late prevail'd upon so many Thousand Irish to flock over to the Plantations, for that all who go thither are immediately sent up to the Frontiers, there to remain as a Barrier* 135 *between the Planters and wild* Indians, *in order to be first devour'd; a Cruelty, say you, taken from the like Practice amongst the Romans, who were wont to place*

certain barbarous Nations, Prisoners of War in the Front of the Battle, in order to
take off the Fury of the first Onset, or to blunt the Edge of the Enemy's Sword.

140 This Story, or one like it, you found some where, but if you find it in
the Roman History between the first Year of *Romulus*, and the first
Year of the first Christian Emperour, I confess it will be a new
Discovery to me, unless this Station was assign'd by the *Lex Talionis*,
or for the Punishment of notorious Malefactors, but I am not farther

145 concern'd in this Point than to let you know, *That it is a scandalous and*
intolerable Abuse upon the Sense of Mankind, to impose one Lye upon them by
the Authority of another, it is no Entertainment to a generous Mind, to
see the greatest Infamy cast upon the greatest, wisest, and most human
People, that the World ever saw, nor is it easily to be born, that a living

150 People, who have a great Share of the Roman Spirit, who are as fond of
their Mother Country, and of the Laws, Liberties and Priviledges
which they inherit from her Bounty as the *Romans* themselves were of
Rome, and the Advantage of that most honourable Birth-right
insulted, for no better Reason than for the Resemblance they bear to a

155 Nation, which not only civilizd *Great Brittain*, but all Europe beside; it
is not improper in this Place to let you see, that Animosity and party
Rage have carried you to a Length, which lays your unhappy Talent
naked and exposed to one who is resolv'd not to spare you, upon a
Point of such Importance to the Honour and Wellfare of *America*; I am

160 therefore going to relate to you a known Truth (and I appeal to every
Native of *Ireland* upon this Continent whether it be not so) *viz.* That
some of the Colonies have laid a Tax of Twenty-Shillings per Head
upon every Irish Servant imported, so far are they from wanting any
Guards upon their Frontiers, or endeavouring to expose their fellow

165 Subjects for their own Preservation, and you know, I hope you have
Ingenuity enough to acknowledge it, that such as are not Servants,
whether *Irish*, *Scotch* or *English*, have Priviledges here equal to any
which they enjoy in their native Countries respectively;

. . . . .

But no Man whatsoever, unless he voluntarily lists himself in His

170 Majesty's Troops, is sent to the Frontiers, nor doe we want in Time of
Peace any other Forces, than what are maintain'd here by the Bounty
of His Majesty. . . .

. . . . .

And now I have gone thus far, it is absolutely necessary that I

should refute that Obloquy and Scandle with which you falsely
and audaciously charge the Government here, for in that one 175
comprehensive Word you sum up the King, the Ministry, the
Governour, and the whole Legislature of both Colonies, at this Mark
all your envenom'd Arrows are shot, and neither *Jersey* or *York*, had
been the Subject of your Papers, if tired with many impotent Efforts to
blacken the Administration at Home, you had not thereby lost all 180
Credit in the three Kingdoms, and were compell'd to shift the Scene
to a Country where perhaps your Works might not appear to admit of
Contradiction, till the intended Mischief had taken Effect; therefore
you affirm, *That altho' the Miseries of* Ireland (which are in Reality the
Forgeries of your own Brain) *are insuportable, yet such of its Natives as have* 185
exchang'd that Country for the Plantations, would be glad to return, if they were
not condemn'd and chain'd to the Frontiers; and no more would now embark for
those Northern Colonies, if the GOVERNMENT had not wisely taken Care,
That no Letters whatsoever should be suffered to be put on Board any Ship or
other Vessel, bound for Ireland, *before they were read and examined by the* 190
Boards of Council of the several Provinces.

I verily believe when this Assertion took hold of you, the foul Fiend
had deserted your Elbow, and that you were left entirely to the
Conduct of your own evil Genius; for it is so gross a Blunder, so
apparent a Falshood, as the reputed Subtilty of the Divil could not 195
have committed; yet I am willing to allow you as great a Share of
Probability in this Case as I possibly can. Let us suppose then that the
Sea-Coast extends no farther along the Inhabited Part of the
Continent than seven Hundred Miles, from *North* to *South*, and that
such *Irish* as came over Free-men, or have been emancipated within 200
these Twenty Years, are admitted to the free Use of Pen, Ink and
Paper, that no more than one Hundred Ships are constantly passing
between this Continent and *England*, *Scotland* and *Ireland*, and that
amongst all those who navigate them, there are no more than two
Hundred *Irish* Sailors, and that not above Fifty Thousand Men are 205
kept in constant Pay, for no other purpose but to seize all Letters and
Pacquets which have not the Pasport of the several Governours and
Council, for they must secure all Letters, at least open all for every
Part of *Europe*, there being a considerable Correspondence held with
Ireland by *Italy*, *Spain*, *Portugal*, *France* and *Germany*; yet so worthy 210
and so wise a Project could have no Effect, and in so many Years, at
least a Dozen or more Letters, besides that single one which a poor
old Man, with so great Care and Caution, at the Peril of his Life

transmitted to *Dublin*, would have escaped this Search either by Day
215 or Night:

·   ·   ·   ·   ·

But the Truth is, that the Rancour of your Heart has corrupted your
Head, and while you are charging the Ministry with *an Intent to destroy
Ireland*, you forget your self, and lay the Charge at the Doors of its own
Natives; you tell us, *That they are gone to* America *in great Numbers, and*
220 *we know that they were not sent for*, and now for the *Fox's Reason*, you tell
us, (*for a certain Fox it seems had lost his Tail, and would have perswaded all of
his Kind to take off theirs too, for Tails were out of Fashion, and very
Troublesome beside,) they tell fine Stories of their New World, and draw their old
Neighbours, Friends and Relations in the same Snare with themselves.* Thus
225 after all, and upon second Thoughts, Letters do pass from hence to
Ireland, and the *Irish* are their own Butchers: But this is one of those
general Accusations, which shew *That one Man may be found so depraved
in his own Nature, so abandon'd by all Goodness, as to believe that there is
neither Honour, Honesty, Love, Friendship or Affection to be found in the
230 Universe.* I shall always believe, thank God I know, *That these are not
Words of art, but are the greatest and best Gifts which Heaven bestows in this
Life.* The *Sinon* of *Virgil* was a Knave, and what he said of himself is a
fine Image of a deceitful Heart, yet the same Thing in Words less
elegant, may be truly spoken in another Case,

235   —— *Miseram si tristis Iernem,
Non etiam Vanum, mendacemque improba finxit,
Fortuna.* ——

43. *6th Intelligencer, fol. 36*: 'Folio' in the old sense of 'page'; '36' is an error for '46': the
    passage is on p. 46 of *29*.
143. *Lex Talionis*: Talion law; the exaction of an eye for an eye, etc.
235–7. *Miseram si tristis Iernem*: An adaptation of *Aeneid*, ii. 79–80: 'Though cruel For-
    tune has made sad Ireland miserable, she has not also made her false and lying.'

APPENDIX L

Unauthorized Titles of the *Intelligencers*

The italicized titles, though without authority, may be familiar, even though most *Intelligencers* appeared untitled in 1728. Some of these titles were first used in Bowyer and Davis's London editions of the *Intelligencer* (*29–30*). The rest first appeared in the 'third' volume of the Pope–Swift *Miscellanies* (*32*).

1. *Introduction* 29–30
2. *The Inhospitable Temper of 'Squire Wether* 29–30
3. *A Vindication of Mr. Gay, and the Beggars Opera* 29–30
4. *The Folly of Gaming* 29–30
5. *A Description of What the World Calls Discretion* 29–30
   An Essay on the Fates of Clergymen (with no. 7) 32
6. *A Representation of the Present Condition of Ireland* 29–30
7. *The Characters of Corusodes and Eugenio* 29–30
   An Essay on the Fates of Clergymen (with no. 5) 32
8. Mad Mullinix and Timothy
   A Dialogue between Mullinix and Timothy 29–30
   A Dialogue between Mad Mullinix and Timothy 32–35u
9. *The Foolish Methods of Education among the Nobility* 29–30
   An Essay on Modern Education 32
10. Tim and the Fables
    Tim and Gay's Fables 29–30
11. *Proposals in Prose and Verse for*, An Universal View of All the Eminent Writers on the Holy Scriptures, *&c.* 29–30
12. The Progress of Patriotism. A Tale.
    Sir Ralph the Patriot Turned Courtier 29–30
13. *The Art of Story-Telling* 29–30
14. *Prometheus's Art of Man-Making: And the Tale of the T—d* 29–30
15. [A Short View of the State of Ireland]
    The Services the Drapier Has Done His Country, and the Steps Taken to Ruin It 29–30
16. *The Adventures of the Three Brothers, George, Patrick, and Andrew* 29–30
    A Letter to the Intelligencer 32
17. *The Marks of Ireland's Poverty, Shewn to Be Evident Proofs of Its Riches* 29–30
    A Second Letter to the Intelligencer 32
18. *St. Andrew's Day, and the Drapier's Birth-Day* 29–30
19. *The Hardships of the Irish Being Deprived of Their Silver, and Decoyed into America* 29–30
20. Dean Smedley Gone to Seek His Fortune 28, 30

TEXTUAL NOTES

Conventions

In bibliographical descriptions

⌐ ¬ (e.g., ⌐ffl¬) indicates that the enclosed letters are a ligature.
Abbreviations of libraries: see Abbreviations and Short Titles, pp. xii–xv.

In lists of variants

~ stands for the corresponding word to the left of the square bracket.
∧ indicates punctuation absent here.

Sigla: see the General Bibliographical Note and textual notes to individual numbers, below.

Variants are listed by line number. The lemma—to the left of the right square bracket—is the reading of the present edition. It agrees literally with the copy-text except where an emendation is signalled by an *italicized* line number—and also by the position of the copy-text's siglum: to the right of the square bracket. Sigla and editorial notes appear in italics. For each number of the *Intelligencer*, sigla of texts whose variant readings are recorded appear in order, immediately preceding the list of variants, e.g.,

$$28a–28b–28c–29–30–35^8–35^{12}$$

In this case, if *28a* is the copy-text, the variant listing

226 new] old *28c*; older *30*

means that where line 226 reads 'new', the copy-text (*28a*) reads 'new', as do *28b*, *29*, *35⁸*, and *35¹²*; *28c* reads 'old' and *30* reads 'older'. Similarly

226 new] old *35*

means that both *35⁸* and *35¹²* read 'old', while the other listed texts agree with the copy-text in reading 'new'. Similarly,

226 new] old *28b–30*

means that *28b*, *28c*, *29*, and *30* all read 'old', while *28a*, *35⁸*, and *35¹²* all read 'new'. More precisely, since variants in accidentals are not ordinarily recorded except for the Harding printings, the last example means that *28a* reads 'new' and *35⁸* and *35¹²* read either 'new' *or some non-substantive variant such as* 'New'.

Ambiguous end-line hyphenation in the copy-text is listed among the variants and marked as an emendation; e.g.,

98 oftentimes] often-|times *28a*

or

98 often-times] often-|times *28a*

depending on whether or not the hyphen has been preserved in the present edition.

General Bibliographical Note

Because no adequate bibliographical account of the *Intelligencer* has previously been given, it has been necessary to undertake a full investigation, leading to the discovery of an unexpectedly complex history.[1]

BIBLIOGRAPHICAL DESCRIPTIONS

28 *The Harding editions* (T–S 666)

The *Intelligencer* originally appeared as small eight- or sixteen-page pamphlets, printed by Sarah Harding in Dublin, nos. 1–19 in 1728 and no. 20 in 1729. Bibliographical descriptions accompany the textual notes to each number. The various impressions and editions of these pamphlets can generally be distinguished according to the following points:

(*a*) On the title-page, the ornament and its placement. Punctuation following the black-letter word '𝕴𝖓𝖙𝖊𝖑𝖑𝖎𝖌𝖊𝖓𝖈𝖊𝖗'. In 'NUMB.' whether the period is raised or on the line.

(*b*) On inner pages, the ornaments, if any, and their placement. The location of running heads and page numbers, if present.

(*c*) Deterioration of the type page, particularly around its edges, where it would have been tied up between impressions. (Mrs Harding does not often appear to have read proof when reimposing type.)

The Harding ornaments, to which one must refer in differentiating editions and impressions, are shown in Fig. 4, which is keyed to this list:

(*a*) Basket.

(*b*) Cherub's head with wings.

(*c*) Cock: to be distinguished from a very similar ornament; see John Dillon, *The Pleasures of a Single Life* (Dublin: Printed and Sold at the Rein Deer in Montrath-Street, n.d.; copy: Forster); this is Foxon P503.

(*d*) Cupid.

(*e*) Arms of France (three fleurs-de-lis).

(*f*) Fountain with dolphins: a crudely carved imitation of a design used by J. Hyde and E. Dobson; see Sheridan's *Philoctetes* (Dublin: Hyde and Dobson, 1725), title-page.

(*g*) Five Shil.: headpiece evidently once part of a larger design.

(*h*) Globe: headpiece.

(*i*) Thistle-crown-rose: headpiece.

---

[1] For previous bibliographical comments see W. Spencer Jackson, 'Bibliography of the Writings of Jonathan Swift', in Temple Scott, xii. 149–51; H. Teerink, *A Bibliography of the Writings in Prose and Verse of Jonathan Swift, D.D.* (The Hague, 1937), item 666; *The Rothschild Library* (Cambridge, 1954), items 2110, 2113–15; *Prose*, xii. 323–9; T–S, pp. 329–33.

It is sometimes necessary to describe the size of the text type. There are two sizes in nos. 1–19: 63 mm. per 20 lines and 77.5 mm. per 20 lines. These are not standard sizes and are referred to simply as 'smaller' and 'larger'. See Philip Gaskell, *A New Introduction to Bibliography* (Oxford, 1974), 13–15. For further details on production, see the Textual Introduction, above.

Publication. As to dates of publication, see the section 'Dates of the Intelligencers' in the General Introduction, above. The price per copy was a halfpenny, according to Swift, *Corresp.* iv. 30.

Census of copies. Forster: nos. 1–20 (W. Monck Mason's set); Gilbert: no. 5; Harvard: no. 5; Huntington: nos. 8, 17, 20; Illinois: nos. 1–19; NLI: nos. 1–2 (2 copies), 3–4 (3 copies), 5 (2 copies), 6–8, 9 (3 copies), 10 (2 copies), 11 (4 copies), 12 (2 copies), 13–14, 15 (2 copies), 17, 19–20 (2 copies); RIA: nos. 1–13 (2 copies), 14–15, 17–18, 20; Rothschild: nos. 1–8 (2 copies), 9–11, 13–15, 20; Taylor: nos. 1–9, 10 (2 copies), 11–14, 16–19; TCD: nos. 1–6 (2 copies), 7–20; ULC: nos. 1–6; Yale: nos. 1–10, 11 (2 copies), 13–16. The Gilbert catalogue (*Catalogue of the Books & Manuscripts Comprising the Library of the Late Sir John T. Gilbert*, comp. Douglas Hyde and D. J. O'Donoghue (Dublin, 1918), 239) also lists nos. 1–15, but these have been missing for many years. Harold Williams's notes say that the Gilbert set lacked no. 12 (ULC MS Add. 7788, box 21).

Microfilm. The complete run of nos. 1–20 at TCD was issued as Reel 867 of the Xerox University Microfilms series English Literary Periodicals in 1973.

THE BOWYER–DAVIS EDITIONS

29 *The first Bowyer–Davis edition* (T–S 34)
THE | INTELLIGENCER. | [rule] | *Omne vafer vitium ridenti Flaccus amico* | *Tangit, & admiˢſˢus circum prˡæˡcordia ludit.* | Perf. | [rule] | [ornament] | [rule] | Printed at *DUBLIN.* | *LONDON* | Reprinted, and fold by *A. Moor* in St. *Paul*'s | Church-yard, and the Bookfellers of | *London* and *Weˢſtˡminˢſtˡer.* MDCCXXIX.

Demy 8°: A⁴ (− A4) B–O⁸ P⁴ (P4 + χ1 [= A4]); $4 signed (− A1, 3, K3, P3, 4; M4 signed 'M3'); pp. *i–vi* 1–217 *218*. *Contents*: *i* title, *ii* blank, *iii–iv* To the Reader, *v–vi* The Contents, 1–217 The Intelligencer [nos. 1–19], 217 Finis., *218* blank. From offsetting and the position of watermarks it can be confirmed that halfsheets A and P were part of the same sheet, and that A4 became χ1.

Production. Printed by W. Bowyer. Entered in the Bowyer paper stock ledger under the heading 'Intelligencer for W Bowyer & Mr. Davis'. Bowyer used 28 reams of second Gen[oa] demy to print 1000 copies of 14 sheets set in English type. The work was charged in the Bowyer customer account book 17 May 1729 and delivered 19–21 May in seven uneven batches.[2]

Publication. Charles Davis and William Bowyer, jun., entered their edition in the Stationers' Company register 20 May 1729 and deposited the nine required copies.[3] The volume was published 21 May at 3s. 6d. bound, with a

---

[2] For this and other information from his forthcoming edition of the Bowyer ledgers, I am indebted to K. I. D. Maslen.

[3] BL Dept. of MSS film M455/19.

a

b

c

d

e

f

g

h

i

Fig. 4. Printer's ornaments used in the Harding editions. Items a, d, e, h, and i are reproduced from the Rothschild copies of no. 3 (*28d*), no. 5 (*28a*), no. 2 (*28d*), no. 1 (*28d*), and no. 10 (*28a*), respectively. Items b, c, and g are reproduced from the Huntington copy of no. 20. Item f is reproduced from the Cambridge University Library copy of no. 1 (*28d*).

wide advertising campaign that had begun 13 May: '*Next Week will be published, Beautifully printed in 8vo. from the Irish Edition*, THE INTELLIGENCER. Printed and Sold by the Booksellers of London and Westminster. Price bound 3s. 6d.' Beginning 17 May, many advertisements added the phrase '*By the Author of the Tale of a Tub*' (*London Evening-Post*, 13, 15, 17, 20, 22 May; *Daily Post*, 19, 20, 21, 23 May; *Daily Post-Boy*, 27, 29 May; *Daily Journal*, 21, 22 May; *Whitehall Evening-Post*, 22, 27, 29 May; *Fog's Weekly Journal* and the *Country Journal*, 24, 31 May). It was sold by, among others, T. Warner, who advertises it in his reprint of the *Tribune* (London, 1729), and in Dublin by George Faulkner and his then partner James Hoey, who advertise it in the *Dublin Journal* 24 March 1729/30.[4] The actual imprint of 29 names the bookseller as 'A. Moor', widely used as a fictitious imprint for dangerous or pirated books.[5] The advertisements' phrase, 'sold by the booksellers of London and Westminster', was commonly used for the same purpose. Both these facts and the book's preface bespeak Bowyer and Davis's awareness that 29 might be violating copyright claimed by someone else; and indeed Swift himself thought of the *Intelligencer* as Sheridan's property.[6] More specifically, all these circumstances indicate that 29 was not undertaken at the instance of Sheridan but was simply a project to benefit Bowyer and Davis.

Copies collated. BL, Forster, OEFL (2), Rothschild, Teerink.

Variant state. An uncorrected state of the outer forme of sheet M, with 'pub-|Mint' rather than 'pub-|lick Mint' on pp. 163–4. *Copy collated*: Chicago.

29a *Reissue*
The original impression of 29, to which is added a rare unsigned 8° gathering of eight leaves (pp. 219–25 226). The new leaves contain *Intelligencer* 20, printed from the Harding edition. The reissue was perhaps assembled by a Dublin bookseller handling 29, which had been published in London only about two weeks after no. 20 had been circulated in Dublin. Dublin customers would thus be especially aware that the Bowyer–Davis edition was not up to date. The location of the only known copy suggests a Dublin origin as well. In any case, the additional gathering does not appear in the Bowyer ledgers.

Copy collated. RIA.

30 *The second Bowyer–Davis edition* (T–S 35)
THE | INTELLIGENCER. | [rule] | *Omne vafer vitium ridenti Flaccus amico* | *Tangit, & admiˉſſ⁻us circum prˉæˉcordia ludit.* | Perf. | [rule] | *By the Author of a* TALE *of a* TUB. | [rule] | *The* SECOND EDITION. | [rule] | [ornament] | [rule] |

---

[4] At the end of a Folger Shakespeare Library copy of 29 in an 18th-cent. binding is an 8-page advertisement, *Books Printed for Thomas Astley at the Rose in St. Paul's Church-Yard, 1728.* The date suggests that the binder inserted the advertisement by mistake; it remains uncertain that Astley sold 29.

[5] See Pat Rogers, 'The Phantom Moore', *Bibliography Newsletter*, 1, no. 11 (Nov. 1973), 9–10; comments by Terry Belanger, ibid. 10; comments by David Foxon, *Bibliography Newsletter*, no. 12 (Dec. 1973), 6–7; and Foxon, *English Verse*, ii. 172.

[6] Appendix I; *Corresp.* v. 257.

LONDON: | Printed for Francis Cogan, at the | *Middle-Temple-Gate* in *Fleet-ʃt'reet.* | MDCCXXX.

Demy 12°: A⁴ B–M¹² N²; $6 signed (− A1, 3–4, N2; L4 signed 'L3'); pp. *i–viii* 1–262 *263* 264–8. *Contents*: *i* title, *ii* blank, *iii–v* To the Reader, *vi–viii* The Contents, 1–262 The Intelligencer [nos. 1–20], *263*–8 The Pheasant and the Lark. A Fable [by Patrick Delany; compare Foxon D203], 268 Finis.

Production. Printed by W. Bowyer. Entered in the Bowyer paper stock ledger merely as 'D°' in 12°'. Bowyer used 23 reams of Holland demy to print 1000 copies of 11½ sheets set in pica type. These were all delivered to F. Cogan from 29 June to 30 July 1730.

Publication. Advertised 2 July 1730 in the *London Evening-Post*: '*This Day is published, In a neat Pocket Volume, Price 2 s. 6 d. The Second Edition, with Additions, of* THE INTELLIGENCER. By the Author of the Tale of a Tub.'

Copies collated. BL, Forster (2), OEFL, Teerink.

Facsimile. New York: AMS Press, 1967.[7]

Note. Almost without exception, *30* is printed from *29*. But in a few cases *30* introduced readings which appear authorial; see variants for no. 5. These may have been transmitted to Bowyer through George Faulkner, who by 1730 was Swift's regular printer. Faulkner, said to have formerly been a journeyman in the Bowyer shop, now was importing Bowyer's productions and sending Bowyer his own.[8]

Later Collections

Swift's *Intelligencer* papers and two of Sheridan's (by mistake?) were reprinted numerous times in editions of the Swift–Pope *Miscellanies* and of Swift's *Works*. These editions are here only summarized. I have collated only those later editions that had any probability of authorial intervention, namely the versions of the 1732 *Miscellanies* (the 'Third' volume) and the editions of the *Works* published by George Faulkner in 1735 and 1738. Furthermore, in these cases I have collated only those pages containing *Intelligencer* papers; I do not give a bibliographical account of these volumes, although I record unnoticed states if I have found them. In all cases the reader must consult Teerink–Scouten (T–S) for bibliographical descriptions. In the following listing, references to nos. 8, 10, and 15 mean that *Mad Mullinix and Timothy*, *Tim and the Fables*, and *A Short View of the State of Ireland* are included; Sheridan's introductions to these pieces are not reprinted unless specifically so stated.

[7] AMS informs me that this reproduces a copy at the University of Iowa.

[8] On Faulkner's work for Swift in 1730, see James Woolley, 'Arbuckle's "Panegyric" and Swift's Scrub Libel: The Documentary Evidence', in J. I. Fischer and D. C. Mell, Jr (eds.), *Contemporary Studies of Swift's Poetry* (Newark, 1981), 208n. On Faulkner's relations with Bowyer, see Faulkner to John Nichols, 22 Oct. 1774, in Nichols (ed.), *Biographical and Literary Anecdotes of William Bowyer, Printer* (London: by and for the author, 1782), 465–6n.; Robert E. Ward (ed.), *Prince of Dublin Printers: The Letters of George Faulkner* (Lexington, Ky., 1972), 127–8.

The 1732 Miscellanies

The 1732 collection includes *Intelligencers* 5 and 7 (combined as a single essay), 8, and 9 (all by Swift) and nos. 16 and 17 (by Sheridan).[9] The text is a reprinting of *29*, with occasional revisions generally attributable to Pope, who edited the collection. It is important because it shows how Pope handled Swift's writings. Moreover, Faulkner—presumably with Swift's approval—used this text as the basis for 35^8, thus lending authority to it. Faulkner did not, however, accept the titles Pope devised, for which see the list of unauthorized titles in Appendix L. It is striking that Pope rejected *Intelligencers* 1, 3, 10, 15 (*A Short View*), and 19, while accepting two papers by Sheridan.[10]

The collection was published in both octavo (32^8) and duodecimo (32^{12}) and is divided into two parts, prose and verse, each with separate pagination. It seems to have escaped notice that the prose part is the same setting of type in 32^8 and 32^{12}, with leading removed in 32^{12} to fit its shorter page height. On the other hand, the respective verse parts are of entirely different settings. Collation of the verse part undertaken for the present edition—no. 8, *Mad Mullinix and Timothy*, is the only poem involved—indicates that 32^{12} is printed from *29* and that 32^8 is printed from 32^{12}. For the prose part, however, 32^{12} is the later issue to be printed, as can be inferred from the correction in 32^{12} of items included in the errata list of 32^8. First publication of 32^8 occurred on 4 October 1732, as appears both from the calendar of recent publications in the *Grub-street Journal*, 5 October 1732, and from the earliest advertisement I have found (*Daily Post-Boy*, 4 October 1732). The only advertisement I know for a duodecimo edition is that in the (weekly) *Grub-street Journal* of 8 February 1732/3 ('This day is published . . .'). But since the duodecimo printing had apparently been issued the year before,[11] it seems likelier that the advertisement refers to the second duodecimo edition (33^{12}).

32^8 *Miscellanies. The Third Volume.* London: Motte and Gilliver, 1732. 8°. T–S 25(4), pp. 9–10. Printed by John Wright, according to J. McLaverty, *Pope's Printer, John Wright* (Oxford, 1977). Copies collated: BL, Bodleian, Taylor, TCD, Teerink.

32S Swift's annotated copy of 32^8 now at Trinity College, Cambridge (Rothschild 1422). Most of the corrections are incorporated in *35u*.

32^{12} *Miscellanies. The Third Volume.* London: Motte and Gilliver, 1732. 12°. Also mistakenly issued with the wrong title-page, as the 'Last' volume, 1733. T–S 27(4a or 4b), pp. 15–16. Copies collated: TCD (1732), Bodleian (1733).

[9] For Swift's role in the planning of the so-called third volume of the Swift–Pope *Miscellanies*, see Norman Ault, *New Light on Pope* (London, 1949), 248–65; Sir Harold Williams, *The Text of Gulliver's Travels* (Cambridge, 1952), 62–94; James McLaverty, 'Lawton Gilliver: Pope's Bookseller', *Studies in Bibliography*, 32 (1979), 118–20; and Ehrenpreis, iii. 743–51.

[10] Compare Swift to Pope, 12 June 1732, *Corresp.* iv. 30–1.

[11] If we trust the title-page date of '1732'; but this title-page may be a cancel replacing a title-page at first dated '1733', and the cancel may have been a literal resetting of the 32^8 title-page, neglecting to update it. See T–S 27 (4a–b), pp. 15–16.

33[12] *Miscellanies. The Third Volume.* London: Motte and Gilliver, 1733. 12°. A resetting of *32*[12]. T–S 27(4c), p. 16. Copy collated: Bodleian. This edition was erroneously reissued in 1736 with the title-page of the 'Last' volume, 1736; not listed in T–S (but see T–S 28(3), p. 17); copy examined: Rothschild 1428.

33F *Miscellanies in Prose and Verse. The Third Volume.* Dublin: Fairbrother, 1733. A resetting of *32*[8], including the same *Intelligencers*. T–S 33(3), p. 22. Copy collated: Bodleian.

36[12] *Miscellanies. The Third Volume.* Four issues, three with this title in 1736 and a fourth entitled *Miscellanies in Verse and Prose* (1742). T–S 29(4), pp. 16–17. A line-for-line resetting of *33*[12]. Copy examined: Bodleian (1742).

The Faulkner editions

35[8] *The Works of J.S, D.D, D.S.P.D. In Four Volumes.* Dublin: Faulkner, 1735. 8°. T–S 41, pp. 26–8.

Contents. Vol. i: nos. 3, 5 and 7, and 9; vol. iv: *A Short View of the State of Ireland* (reprinted in no. 15) and no. 19.

Faulkner never reprinted nos. 1 or 10; 8 was at first included in vol. ii but was cancelled before publication. See the note on *35u* below.

Copies collated. Bodleian, BL, OEFL (2), Smith College, Teerink; large paper: Rothschild, TCD. There are a number of press variants among these copies, with several lines reset, but no substantive variants, and indeed only two worth mentioning at all: vol. i, p. 290, the bottom line reads '*Schalar*' in the Bodleian, BL, OEFL 29165, Smith, and Teerink copies, but '*Scholar*' in the OEFL 29164, Rothschild, and TCD copies. On p. 282 of vol. i, the TCD copy reads 'Salary' where the others read 'Sallary'.

35[12] 12°. T–S 49, pp. 48–9. Contents as in *35*[8], from which it is printed with some corrections. The two *38* editions derive directly or indirectly from this edition. Copies collated: Chicago, Teerink, TCD, Williams.

38[8] 8°. T–S 42, pp. 28–9. Copies collated: Bodleian, Teerink, Williams.

38[12] 12°. T–S 50, pp. 49–50. Copies collated: BL, Teerink.

In his subsequent editions Faulkner never altered the selection or arrangement of the *Intelligencers*: nos. 3, 5 and 7, and 9 in vol. i, and nos. 15 and 19 in vol. iv. These editions appeared from 1742 until 1772 (T–S 43–8, 51–3).

35u The very rare uncancelled state of *35*[8], vol. ii, with the cancellanda present, including *Mad Mullinix and Timothy*, cancelled perhaps for ethical or prudential reasons. A copy of the ordinary-paper issue is in the English Faculty Library, Oxford; see Margaret Weedon, 'An Uncancelled Copy of the First Collected Edition of Swift's Poems', *Library*, ser. 5, 22 (1967), 44–56. A similar copy of the large-paper issue of *35u* is in the Beinecke Library, Yale University.

Later editions

Deriving from *35* were Fairbrother's *Vol. IV. of the Miscellanies Begun by Jonathan Swift, D.D. and Alexander Pope, Esq.* (Dublin, 1735), containing nos. 3 and 19 and

A Short View (T–S 33(4), p. 22), and the fifth volume of the Swift–Pope *Miscellanies* (London, 1735; T–S 25(5a), p. 10), reprinting nos. 15 and 19. No. 3 was in the addendum to this volume, *A Collection of Poems, &c. Omitted in the Fifth Volume of Miscellanies* (T–S 25(5b), p. 10). These three papers went into the sixth volume of the 12° *Miscellanies* (1736, 1738; T–S 28(6), p. 18, and 30(3), p. 20).

In 1739, nos. 8, 16, and 17 were reprinted in *A Supplement to Dr. Swift's and Mr. Pope's Works* (Dublin: Powell; T–S 58, p. 146). The text comes from one of the editions of the 'Third' volume of *Miscellanies*.

In 1741 occurred the first publication of Swift's letter to Pope, 12 June 1732, in which he explains precisely what his share of the *Intelligencer* had been.[12] Pope in 1732 had invented titles for those *Intelligencer* papers he had chosen to reprint; for this reason, perhaps, the editors of the 1742 *Miscellanies* failed to recognize that they had already included some of the papers Swift mentions, and they printed them again in vol. ix of their new edition.[13] The excuse for this procedure is probably that the edition was produced by two different groups of booksellers who divided responsibility for the volumes between them (T–S, p. 65). One of the owners of the new vol. ix was Davis, who was presumably still part-owner of the *Intelligencer* copyright. This 1742 series of the *Miscellanies* (T–S 66–9, pp. 65–76) contains nos. 1, 3, 5 and 7 (as combined in *32*), 5 separately, 7 separately, 8, 9, 10, 15 (as *A Short View*), Sheridan's introduction to 15, and 19. But Sheridan's nos. 16 and 17, which were brought into *32*, are now removed, and nos. 1 and 10 are reprinted for the first time since *30*. Again in 1742, the volumes supplementary to the earlier 12° series of *Miscellanies* erroneously duplicate nos. 5 and 7 and no. 9 and add no. 10, though not no. 1 (T–S 31, p. 20).

The last serious editorial attention to the *Intelligencer* papers prior to the twentieth century seems to have come in John Hawkesworth's editions of Swift's works (1754–5; T–S 87–90). He correctly included nos. 1, 3, 5 and 7, 8, 9, 10, 15, and 19. In 1779 John Nichols added no. 20 to Swift's canon in his *Supplement* to the works (T–S 90–2). Confusion about the *Intelligencer* may have been introduced in 1789 by C. Dilly, who published nos. 4, 6, and 11–14, none of them Swift's, in *Miscellaneous Pieces, in Prose and Verse. By the Rev. Dr. Jonathan Swift. . . . Not Inserted in Mr. Sheridan's Edition of the Dean's Works* (**89** (T–S 121)). The copyright was claimed for Dilly and two of Sheridan's granddaughters, Al[icia] LeFanu ('Lefanus') and Eliz[abeth] Sheridan,[14] and the volume contains both writings by Sheridan (as in the case of the *Intelligencer*) and writings by Swift that would have survived among Sheridan's papers. The omission of nos. 2 and 18 is curious, though.[15]

[12] Pope, *Corresp.* iii. 291 n.
[13] See the list of unauthorized titles in Appendix L.
[14] Stationers' Company register, 11 June 1789, BL Dept. of MSS film M455/20.
[15] That the papers are not by Swift is obliquely acknowledged on p. 147. The assertion in T–S, p. 158, that the volume was edited by John Nichols seems to be refuted by Nichols himself, who implies that between 1785 and 1801 he published no volumes of Swift's works (*Illustrations of the Literary History of the Eighteenth Century*, v (London, 1828), 396).

Various numbers of the *Intelligencer* were reprinted in newspapers, magazines, and miscellanies, *Mist's Weekly Journal* and *Fog's Weekly Journal* being the prime sources of the *Intelligencer* for the London audience before *29* appeared (see Appendix D). Such of these printings as I have found are listed in the textual notes to the individual numbers.

It is a probable assumption, though based only on my having looked at— not collated—the later editions of Swift in the Teerink Collection, that every subsequent eighteenth- and nineteenth-century text of the *Intelligencer* papers except those Faulkner published can be traced back either to the 1742 series of *Miscellanies* or to *The Works of Jonathan Swift, D.D.* edited by John Hawkesworth and first published in 1754.[16] Both these series derive from *32* and *35*. I have found no sign of authoritative variants in any text later than *35 ^{12}*.

[16] Frank H. Ellis, who has undertaken full collations in the late eighteenth-century editions, finds this relationship among them; see *A Discourse*, 182–206, and *POAS* vii. 651–2, 678–81, 686–7, 690–3. See also Hermann J. Real (ed.), *The Battle of the Books* (Berlin, 1978), 121–5.

Textual Notes to Nos. 1–20
and Appendices A–L

In the following pages the reader will find a textual note for each of the *Intelligencers* and, where appropriate, for the appendices.

Modern standards for critical editions require four kinds of textual apparatus: a historical collation, a list of emendations, a list of ambiguous line-end hyphenations, and a list of editorial notes.[17] While common practice has been to present these four kinds of information in separate lists, the reader will be better served, I believe, by a single listing of textual information keyed to line number.

Each of the following textual notes, accordingly, ends with a list of variants which includes, interfiled in a single sequence, a historical collation, editorial emendations from the copy-text, notes of ambiguous end-line hyphenation in the copy-text, and editorial notes on points of textual difficulty. (No new hyphenation has been introduced in typesetting the present edition.)

For further information, see the Textual Introduction (pp. 42–3) and the note on conventions (p. 287).

No. 1

There is no more dramatic evidence of Sarah Harding's reprintings than these seven (possibly eight) impressions, which differ in their title-pages, ornaments, and other details. No. 1 is in general more elaborate typographically than later numbers, and I assume that *28a*, which has the most elaborate title-page and also (with *28b*) the most correct text of no. 1, was first. In other issues, errors occur, especially around the edge of the type pages, as would be expected where type was tied up and then reimposed. The sequence of impressions, though conjectural, is the one that most nearly accounts for all the evidence—assuming progressive deterioration of the original setting of type, with occasional and very spotty correction. In none of the reimpressions is there any sign of authorial intervention.

28a   *The first edition, first impression*
THE | 𝕴𝖓𝖙𝖊𝖑𝖑𝖎𝖌𝖊𝖓𝖈𝖊𝖗, | [rule] | NUMB· I. | [rule] |

For		*Saturday*
May 11*th*,	[ornament: cupid]	1728. to be
continued		Weekly.

[double rule] | *DUBLIN*: | Printed by S. HARDING, next Door | to the *Crown* in *Copper-A⌐ll⌐ey*, 1728.

[17] G. Thomas Tanselle, *Selected Studies in Bibliography* (Charlottesville, 1979), 407.

Pot 8°: *A*⁴; pp. *1–2* 3–7 *8*; *1* title, *2* blank, 3 drop-head [headpiece ornament: globe] | THE | 𝕴𝖓𝖙𝖊𝖑𝖑𝖎𝖌𝖊𝖓𝖈𝖊𝖗. | [rule] | [3-line initial], 3–7 text, 7 'FINIS.' [tail-piece ornament: fountain with dolphins], *8* blank. Running head, 'The *INTELLIGENCER.*', pp. 4–7; page numbers at outer margins.
    Copies collated. NLI, RIA.

28b *The second impression*
THE | 𝕴𝖓𝖙𝖊𝖑𝖑𝖎𝖌𝖊𝖓𝖈𝖊𝖗, | [rule] | NUMB· I. | [rule] | Saturday, May 11. *To be Continued Weekly.* | [rule] | [ornament: cupid] | [double rule] | *DUBLIN*: | Printed by S. HARDING, next Door | to the *Crown* in *Copper-A*ʳ*ll*ˀ*ey*, 1728.

Collation and contents as in *28a.*
    Copy collated. Illinois.

28c *The third impression*
[Title-page as *28b* except:] . . . Sturday, May 11. *To be Continued* [first *n* in *Continnued* is turned sideways] . . .

Collation and contents as in *28a* except no full stop after headline, p. 4, and the first *I* is turned on its side; p. 7 tailpiece: arms of France; various typo-graphical errors go uncorrected.
    Copies collated. TCD, Yale.

28d *The fourth impression*
[Title-page as in *28b*, except:] . . . *N*UMB. I. | . . . [ornament: arms of France] . . . Door to | the *Crown* in *Copper-Alley*, 1728.

Collation as in *28a*, except: 3 drop-head: . . . THE | INTELLIGENCER. No full stop after headline on p. 4 (but no letters are turned).
    Copy collated. ULC. Possibly signalling another impression, a variant state of the outer forme has the flower basket rather than the arms of France as a title-page ornament; copy collated: Rothschild.

28e *The fifth impression*
Title-page as in *28b*. Collation and contents as in *28a*, except: 3 drop-head: . . . THE | INTELLIGENCER. | No full stop after headline on p. 4 (but no letters are turned); headline on p. 6 has number at inner rather than outer margin; p. 7 is unnumbered.
    Copy collated. TCD.

28f *The sixth impression*
[Title-page as in *28b*, except:] . . . *N*UMB. I. | [rule] | Saturday, May, 11. *To* . . . [ornament: arms of France] . . . Door to | the *Crown* in *Copper-Alley*, 1728.

Collation and contents as in *28a* except: 3 drop-head: . . . [ornament: thistle-crown-rose] | THE | INTELLIGENCER. | [rule] | [3-line initial]. Full stop missing from headline on p. 4, p. 6 numbered at inner margin, and p. 7 unnumbered.
    Copies collated. NLI, Rothschild.

28g *The seventh impression*

[Title-page as in *28b*, except:] THE | 𝕴𝖓𝖙𝖊𝖑𝖑𝖎𝖌𝖊𝖓𝖈𝖊𝖗. | [rule] | NUMB. I. | [rule] | Saturday. May, 11, *To be Continued Weekly,* | [rule] | [ornament: arms of France] . . . Door to | the *Crown* in *Copper-Alley,* 172

Collation and contents as in *28f* except that p. 3 has a short display initial (slightly taller than 2 lines), p. 4 headline ends with a full stop, p. 5 is un-numbered, pp. 6–7 are numbered at inner margin, and p. 7 is misnumbered '8'. Many errors are introduced around the inner edge of p. 4.

    Copies collated. Forster, RIA, Taylor.

Later editions

No. 1 was reprinted in *29* from one of the Harding impressions, and *30* was reprinted from *29*. The essay first appeared among Swift's collected works in the 1742 *Miscellanies,* ix. 32–5, reprinted from *30*. Faulkner never reprinted it, despite Swift's explicit claim of authorship (*Corresp.* iv. 30).

Copy-text: *28a*, NLI copy. The all-caps paragraph openings are silently reduced to caps and lower case. *Variant readings* in the following editions and impressions are recorded in the following order:

        28a–28b–28c–28d–28e–28f–28g–29–30

DATELINE. To] to *28a*
DATELINE. For *Saturday May* 11*th*, 1728.
  To be continued Weekly.] Saturday,
  May 11. *To be Continued Weekly. 28b–g*
  [*see bibliographical descriptions*]
  8. Numbers,] ~ₐ *28c–g*
13. Information:] ~ₐ *28g*
15. *Play-house,*] ~ₐ *28c–e*, *28g*

16. *Assemblees,*] ~ₐ *28c–g*; *Assemblies, 29–30*
18. *College,*] ~ₐ *28g*
18. *Mayor*ₐ] ~, *28g*
19. and toₐ] ~ ~, *28g*
20. *Brandy-Shops,*] ~ₐ *28g*
46. over-charged] over-|charged *28*
48. shall have] have *30*
53. whatever] what-|ever *28*

No. 2

28a *The first edition, first impression*

THE | 𝕴𝖓𝖙𝖊𝖑𝖑𝖎𝖌𝖊𝖓𝖈𝖊𝖗, | [rule] | NUMB· II. | [rule] | *Occurſare capro, cornu ferit ille, caveto.* Vir. | [rule] | [ornament: cupid] | [double rule] | *DUBLIN*: | Printed by S. HARDING, next Door | to the *Crown* in *Copper-A⌐ll⌐ey,* 1728.

Pot 8°: *A*⁴; pp. *1* 2–8; *1* title, 2–8 text; 8 '*FINIS*' (no full stop).

    Copies collated. Illinois, NLI, RIA, TCD, Yale.

28b *The second impression*

[As *28a* except:] . . . NUMB. II. . . . *carnu* . . . *i⌐ll⌐e,* . . . [ornament: basket] . . . Door to | the *Crown* . . . *Copper-Alley* . . .

    Copy collated. Rothschild.

28c *The third impression*

[As *28b* except:] . . . *N*UMB· II. . . . [ornament: cupid] . . . Door | to the *Crown* . . . *Copper-A⌐ll⌐ey* . . .

Copies collated. TCD; ULC copy has variant states of both formes, with 'drin' erroneously given for 'dri-' four lines from the bottom of p. 2 and a different setting of the page number on p. 5.

28d *The fourth impression*
As *28c* except that the ornament is the arms of France.

Copies collated. Rothschild, with ornament slightly to left of centre; a variant state has the ornament slightly to right of centre: Forster, NLI, RIA, Taylor.

These four impressions are from standing type, with title-pages reset. Sequence of the impressions is inferred from progressive deterioration of the edges of the type pages.

Later editions
From one of the Harding impressions *29* was printed; *30* was printed from *29*. The essay was next printed in Scott (1814), i. 367–72n.

Copy text: 28a (NLI copy). *Variant readings* are recorded from the following editions and impressions in the following order:

28a–28b–28c–28d–29–30

MOTTO *cornu*] *carnu 28b–d*
19. *fore-horses*,] ~ₐ *28b–d*
39. to!] *too! 28*
65–6. a *long*] *along 30*

70. Fortnight] Fort-|night *28*
88. Ferry-boat,] ~ₐ *28d*
95. Blank's ... *Boatman's 29–30*] *Blank's ... boat-man's 28*

No. 3

28a *The first edition*
THE | 𝕴𝖓𝖙𝖊𝖑𝖑𝖎𝖌𝖊𝖓𝖈𝖊𝖗, | [rule] | NUMB· III. | [rule] | *Ipſe per Omnes ibit Perſonas*, | [slightly indented] *Et turbam reddet in uno.* | [rule] | [ornament: basket] | [double rule] | *DUBLIN:* | Printed by S. HARDING, next Door to | the *Crown in Copper-Aˡlˡey*, 1728.

Pot 8°: *A⁴*; pp. *1–2* 3–8; *1* title, *2* blank, *3* drop-head: [double rule] | The *Intelligencer.* | text, 3–8 text; 8 '*FINIS*' without period following.

Copies collated. TCD, ULC.

28b *A later impression*
[Title as *28a* except:] ... *NUMB. III.* ... *turbam redet* ... [ornament: arms of France] ... *Crown in Copper-Alley*, 1728.

Collation as *28a*; second line of the title-page motto indented. A reimposition of the type from *28a*, with occasional lines reset and title-page reset; some dislocation of type in the outer forme. On the last line of the title-page, the 't' of 'the' is under the 'ed' of 'Printed'.

Copy collated. Rothschild.

28c *Another impression of* 28b
Description as for *28b*, but a different imposition of both formes. The dis-

located type on pp. 4–5 of *28b* has been replaced. On the last line of the title-page, the 't' of 'the' is under the 't' of 'Printed'.

Copy collated. NLI.

28d *A later impression than* 28b–c
Description as for *28c*, except that the second line of the motto is not indented, and *reddet* has two *d*s. Ornament: basket. The title-page and p. 8 are reset; on p. 8 '*FINIS*' is followed by a period.

Copies collated. NLI, Rothschild.

28e *Second edition*
[Title as *28a* except:] . . . NUMB· III. | [rule] | *Ipfe per Omnes ibit Perfonas*, | [not indented] *Et turbam reddet in uno.* | [rule] | [ornament: cupid] | [double rule] | *DUBLIN*: | Printed by S. HARDING, next Door | to the *Crown* in *Copper-Alley*, 1728.

Collation as before; on p. 8 '*FINIS*' is followed by a period. An entirely different setting of type from *28a–d*.

Copies collated. Illinois, Yale.

28f *Another impression of* 28e
'THE' at the head of the title-page is markedly to left of centre, and the setting of the page numbers is different, indicating a different imposition of the type; otherwise identical to *28e*.

Copies collated. RIA, TCD.

28g *Third edition*
[Title-page as *28a*, except:] . . . *N*UMB· III. | [rule] | *Ipfe per Omnes ibit Perfons*, | [not indented] *Et turbam redet in uno.* | [rule] | [ornament: arms of France] | [double rule] | *DUBLIN*: | Printed by S. HARDING, next Door | to the *Crown* in *Copper-A⌐ll⌐ey*, 1728.

Collation as before, with a period following '*FINIS*' on p. 8. An entirely different setting of type from the other two editions, *28a–d* and *28e–f*.

Copies collated. Forster, NLI, RIA, Taylor.

Evidence is slight as to the priority of the three Harding editions. With some variation, the two latter editions reprint the first edition line for line. Nevertheless, assuming that all editions published have been accounted for, the sequence may be conjectured from the textual notes to the motto and lines 17, 26, 80, 96, 102, 150–1, 153, and 163. Considering first the four impressions of the first edition, it is clear from progressive deterioration of the type page that *28b* follows directly from *28a*. Impressions *28c* and *28d* must therefore either precede or follow that pair, and since page 6, line 6 is in the same setting in impressions *28b*, *28c*, and *28d* but in a different one in impression *28a*, the sequence must be *a–b–c–d* and not *d–a–b–c*. Impression *c* shares some of *b*'s errors and some of *d*'s. The pattern of the indentation in the motto is most nearly accounted for if *e–f* follow rather than precede *a–b–c–d*. Variants in the motto and line 79 suggest that *g* was printed from *b*. The order of *e* and *f* is indifferent; I conjecture that *g* was published later than they (see Diagram A).

DIAGRAM A. Early transmission of no. 3.

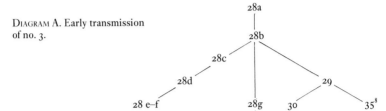

Later editions

From one of the Harding editions, *Mist's Weekly Journal* published the essay 6 July 1728; see Appendix D. *Mist's* softens the satire in several respects, and the softenings are entered among the variants (**Mi**) as an indication of what seemed dangerous about the essay. The essay was reprinted, probably from *28b*, in *29*, and from *29* in *30* and in Faulkner's editions (vol. i). Pope omitted it from *32*; it made its way into the *Miscellanies* from *35*, via *A Collection of Poems, &c. Omitted in the Fifth Volume of Miscellanies* (London: Davis, 1735); and from *35* it was also reprinted in Fairbrother's *Miscellanies*, iv. Thomas Birch quoted it at considerable length from *29* or *30* in his article on John Gay in Pierre Bayle, *A General Dictionary, Historical and Critical*, v (London: Bettenham, 1737), 406–8 n. A French translation, 'The Intelligencer. Ou Le Gazettier. Num. 3', appeared in *Choix de petites pieces du théâtre anglois, traduites des originaux* (A Londres. Et se vend, à Paris, chez Prault Fils, 1756), vol. ii, pp. iii–xi (Folger Shakespeare Library copy). The essay is edited in Geoffrey Tillotson, Paul Fussell, Jr, and Marshall Waingrow, *Eighteenth-Century English Literature* (New York, 1969), 444–6.

Copy-text: *28a* (ULC copy). *Variant readings* are recorded from the following texts in the following order:

$$28a–28b–28c–28d–28e–28f–28g–29–30–35^8–35^{12}–38^8–38^{12}$$

A selection of variants from *Mist* is also included.

MOTTO. *Personas*] *Persons 28g*
MOTTO. *reddet*] *redet 28b, 28g*
MOTTO. *uno.*] *unam. 29–38; second line not indented 28d–g; lines rearranged 29–38, breaking '. . . omnes | Ibit'* . . . rather than *'Personas | Et'*.
HEADING. *35–38 add note*:
  Written in *Ireland* in the Year 1728.
2. this] the *35–38*
4. Subject,] ~∧ *35–38*
4. the manner,] the Manner∧ *29–30*; Manner, *35–38*
7. *London*] *Londen 28a–d*
16. *Italian,*] ~∧ *28g*

17. *Tast*] *Taste 28e–f*
17–18. a Hundred] an ~ *35–38*
21. whatever] whatsoever *38^{12}*
25. *Eloquence,*] ~∧ *28g*
26. *Tast*] *Taste 28e–f*
27. succeeds] succeed *35–38*
55. Corruption] Corruptions *35–38*
58. personal] the private *35–38*
68. those,] ~∧ *28g*
72. Duty,] ~; *29–38*
74. an high] a ~ *29–38*
77–8. (whom I never think on, but with the most profound Veneration)] *ital. 35–38*

79. obtains,] ~ ∧ *28g*
80. Reflections] Reflection *28b, 28g–38*
82. Mr. *GAY*, the Author] the Author *Mi*
86. *Friends*, he *Mi*] *Friends* ∧ *28–38*
88. M——] Minister. *35–38, adding footnote*:
  Sir *Robert Walpole*.
89. M——] Minister *35–38*
90. Mr. *Gay*] ~ ∧ ~ *28a*; ~. *GAY 28g*
92–3. great M——] Prime Minister *35–38*
93. Chastity of] Chastity *35 ¹², 38¹²*
96. *Gay's*] *Gay's 28a–d; GAY's 28g*; this Author's *Mi*
97. Pieces,] ~ ∧ *28g*
98. *D.*] *Duke 29–38*
99. Reward;] Reward (and no Doubt has had it) *Mi*
100. *Courtiers*] the *Courtiers 35–38*
100. is] be *35–38*
102. considering,] ~ ∧ *28g*
102. people] People *28e–f*
105. Mr. *Gay*] ~. GAY *28g*; this Author *Mi*
107. *Humor*] Humour *28g*
110. *Ranks*,] ~ ∧ *28g*
113–14. more immediately] *om. 35–38*
123. among] with *35–38*
123. would] might *35–38*
124. and at such lewd *Comedies*] at such *Comedies 35–38*
125. *Tragedies* ∧] ~, *28e–f*
131. goes] comes *35–38*
134. P——te] Prelate *35–38*
137–8. COURT-CHAPLAIN] *35–38 add footnote*:

Dr. Herring, *Chaplain to the Society at* Lincoln's-*Inn.*
139–40. Sermons of so stupid, so injudicious, and so prostitute a Divine] bad Sermons *Mi*
141. of Mr. *Gay*] ~ ~ *GAY 28g*; ~ ~ GAY's *29–38; om. Mi*
149. these] those *35–38*
150–1. it doth] itdoth *28a–c*
150–2. although it doth by no means affect the present Age, yet might have been useful in the former and may possibly be so in Ages to come.] without enquiring whether it affects the present Age, may possibly be useful in Times to come. *35–38*
152. former ∧] ~, *28d–g*
153. takes] taekes *28a–c*
153. occasion] the ~ *35–38*
153–4. *common Robbers to Robbers of the Publick*;] *Common Robbers of the Publick, 29–38*
161. that many Years ago,] many years ago, *30*; many Years ago, that *35 ¹²*
162. grew so frequent . . . that many] grew frequent . . . and many *35–38*
163. sure] Sure *28b*
163. a Fore-runner] the Fore-runner *29–38*
163. Singers] singers *28b*
164. want] have *35–38*
168. reasonable] reason|able *28a–c*
169. Moral-performance] moral Performance *29–38*
169–70. of the CELEBRATED MR. GAY.] *om. Mi*

No. 4

The Harding edition

There were three and possibly four separate impressions, reimposition of the type being suggested by resettings of the drop-head title, the page numbers, and the concluding 'FINIS.' The order of impressions is uncertain. Pages 4–5, the upper part of 6, the lower part of 7, and all of 8 are set in smaller type than the rest of the pamphlet. There is no direction line on p. 3. Perhaps the compositor set most or all of the essay in the larger type before realizing he had too much for eight pages, whereupon he awkwardly tried to fit the space by a partial resetting in smaller type, attempting to avoid mixing type sizes within a page or, failing that, within a paragraph. It is also possible that the large-type passage on pp. 6–7 (the illiterate letter and the previous paragraph) represents a late shortening of a passage that had been longer in small type.

28a *Uncorrected state*
[drop-head title:] [double rule] | THE | 𝕴𝖓𝖙𝖊𝖑𝖑𝖎𝖌𝖊𝖓𝖈𝖊𝖗, | [rule] | NUMB. IV. | [rule] | *Quando alea hos animos* ? Juv. | [rule] | [text]

Pot 8°: *A*⁴; pp. *1* 2–8; *1* drop-head title; *1*–8 text.
   Copy collated. Illinois.

28b *A corrected state*
Drop-heading and collation as for *28a*; for differences from *28a* see textual variants.
   Copies collated. NLI (cropped), TCD, Yale.

28c *Another impression*
Drop-heading and collation as for *28a*, except that a period, not a comma, follows '𝕴𝖓𝖙𝖊𝖑𝖑𝖎𝖌𝖊𝖓𝖈𝖊𝖗' in the drop-head title.
   Copies collated. Rothschild, TCD, ULC.

28d *Another impression*
Drop-heading and collation as for *28a*, but without the double rule beginning the drop-head title.
   Copies collated. Forster, NLI (2), RIA (2), Taylor. A variant—possibly indicating a reimposition of the type and therefore another impression— occurs in the other Rothschild copy, where the rule above 'NUMB. IV.' on p. 1 occurs in a different position.

Later editions
The illiterate letter was excerpted in the *London Evening-Post*, 6 Aug. 1728, as part of a pretended dispatch from Tunbridge Wells. In 'the present Dearth of News', the essay was reprinted, slightly abridged and modified, in instalments in the *Daily Post-Boy*, 19, 20, and 21 Nov. 1728. In *29* the essay was reprinted from *28b*, *c*, or *d*, and in *30* from *29*. It was abridged, as 'A Short Essay on the Folly of Gaming, by Way of Application. Extracted from the Dublin Intelligencer', to accompany [Daniel Bellamy]'s poem *Back-Gammon: or, The Battle of the Friars* (London: Wilford, 1734), 17–22. From *30* it was anonymously reprinted as 'Some Serious Reflections on the Fatal Consequences of Gaming, by Way of Application to the Two Preceding Tales' in *The Agreeable Companion* (London: Bickerton, 1745), 67–73, omitting the Latin and substituting London for Dublin references. Finally, *89* reprinted it from *29*. (BL copies of all of these have been examined.)

Copy-text: *28b* (NLI copy, with some details taken from the TCD copy). *Variant readings* are recorded from the following texts in the following order:

28a–28b–28c–28d–29–30

6. nor] or *28–30*	*12.* Losses, *29–30*] ~. *28*
8. figure.] Figure? *30*	*22.* Eo.] *Ergo 29–30*

25. *a good*] *good 30*
30. *Bishop*; *29–30*] ~, *28*
60. *Stephen's*] *Stephen's 28–29*
61. *Ear-Rings*, *29–30*] ~. *28*
71. *Snuff-box*] *Snuff-|box 28*
80. Inconveniences] Inconveniencies *29–30*
96. nearer] nearer to *30*
104. described] disribed *28*
105. ——*Ergo*] ——*Ergo*—— *28a*
107. *Saltet*] *saltat 30*
116. Humane] human *29–30*
129. of] off *29–30*
129. upon] upoh *28*
133. Class] Glass *30*
137. αἰσχροκερδεῖς] ἀισχροκερδεις ̄ *28*
147. yet] ye *28a*
148. her. Soon] ~, soon *28*
148. on] or *28a*

150. Years] Yours *30*
151. Minutes; *29–30*] ~, *28*
151. good-natured] good-|natured *28*
164. wich *29–30*] with *28*
164. *losst*] *lospt 28a*
169. borrow the] borrow *30*
169. this,] ~ˌ *28a*
173. Virtuosi] Virtuoso *28*; Virtuoso's *29*; Virtuosos *30* [*Note*: *Virtuoso*, an obvious error, seems likelier to have been a misreading of *Virtuosi* than *Virtuoso's* or *Virtuosos*—all forms in current use.]
182. Blows,] ~ˌ *28a*
182. some of *29–30*] some *28*
183. bring] bringing *29–30*
187. for] after *30*
188. and as] and *30*
193. Inventor] *om. 28a*

No. 5

28a

THE | 𝕴ntelligencer, | [rule] | NUMB· V. | [rule] | Defcrib'd it's thus: De⌐fi⌐n'd would you it have? | Then the World's hone⌐ft⌐ Man's an errant Knave. | BEN. JOHNSON | [rule] | [ornament: cupid] | [double rule] | *DUBLIN*: | Printed by S. HARDING, next Door | to the *Crown* in *Copper-A⌐ll⌐ey*, 1728.

Pot 8°: *A*⁴; pp. *1–2* 3–8 (misprinting 4 as '3'); *1* title, *2* blank, 3–8 text; 8 'FINIS.'

Copies collated. Rothschild, TCD (−*A*4), ULC. A variant state of the inner forme misnumbers p. 3 as '2' and fails to space between 'The' and '*Intelligencer*' in the dropped title on p. 3 (copies collated: Gilbert, Illinois, Yale). A different state of the inner forme occurs in the Forster copy and another TCD copy, with p. 3 numbered '2' but 'The *Intelligencer*' correctly spaced. The same copies have a variant state of the outer forme in which p. 4 is correctly numbered.

28b *Another impression*

[Title as *28a*, except:] THE | 𝕴ntelligencer, | *N*UMB. V. | Defcrib'd it's thus: De⌐fi⌐nd'd would you have? | . . . [ornament: arms of France] | . . . Door to | the *Crown* in *Copper-Alley*, 1728.

Pages correctly numbered; no rule after 'Intelligencer' in title-page; no space between 'The' and '*Intelligencer*' in the dropped title on p. 3.

Copies collated. Harvard, Rothschild.

28c *Another impression*

[Title as *28b*, except:] ... *N*UMB· V. | ... Defind'd would you have: | ... [ornament: arms of France] | ... Door | to the *Crown* in *Copper-A*ʳ*ll'ey*, 1728.

Pages numbered correctly; proper spacing in the dropped title, p. 3; the first 'i' of 'within' has slipped from line 20 to line 21 on p. 3.

   Copies collated. NLI (2), RIA (2), Taylor.

The three impressions of *28*, perhaps issued in the sequence listed, are from standing type with different settings of the title-page.

Later editions

Apparently *29* derives from *28b* or *28c*, judging from the faulty emendation of the motto in *29*; *30*, printed from *29*, has some variants that may be authorial. From *29* was printed *32⁸*, in which, and in texts deriving from it, nos. 5 and 7 are combined as a single essay; this arrangement was continued in *35* and derivative texts. From *32* the combined 5 and 7 were reprinted in *33a*, *33b*, and Fairbrother's vol. iii (*33F*); from *33F*, in turn, Faulkner reprinted it in *35*, vol. i. More than half the manuscript revisions Swift made in his copy of *32⁸* (**32S**) are *not* followed in *35*.

Copy-text: *28a* (Rothschild copy). *Variant readings* are recorded from the following texts in the following order:

$$28a–28b–28c–29–30–32^8–32S–35^8–35^{12}–35^8–38^{12}$$

HEADING. *32 adds title*:
   AN ESSAY ON THE *Fates of Clergymen.*
MOTTO. *rom. 28*; *om. 32–38*
MOTTO. *Defin'd*] defind'd *28b–c*
MOTTO. *would you it*] would you *28b–c*; it would you *29–30*
MOTTO. *have?*] have: *28c*
MOTTO. *World's*] town's *Jonson*
MOTTO. *honest*ₐ] ~, *30*
MOTTO. *an*] her *Jonson*
MOTTO. *errant*] arrant'st *Jonson*; arrant *29–30*
HEADING. *35–38 add note*:
   Written in the Year 1728.
2. reach] rech *28*; Reach *29–38*
3. People] Men *35–38*
3–4. and in common *32 errata*] and is in common *28–32*; in common *35–38*
10. greatest *35–38*] gratial *28*, *an obviously corrupt reading*; Greatest *29–32*
13. present] the present *32–33F*
16. that share] the Share *35–38*
17–18. means to meddle] Means, meddle *35–38*
18. require] reqnire *28*
28. further] farther *29–38*

28. t'other] the other *35¹²–38*
30. nor] or *30*, *35*, *38¹²*; to *38⁸*
31. and indeed *29–38*] and and indeed *28*
31. to do so] *om. 35–38*
33. Courts 32S, *35–38*] the *Courts 28–32*
44. great] *om. 30*
45. a One] an One *29–32*
45. occurs. For, if] occurs; if *29–38*
46. certain] *35–38 add footnote*:
   Vide *the Author's Thoughts on various Subjects.*
46. true,] ~, that, *28–38*
46–7. when a great Genius appears in the World, the] When a true Genius appears in the World, you may know him by this Sign, that *Thoughts 1711.* [*The Faulkner text of* 'Thoughts' (*1735*) *inserts* 'infallible' *before* 'Sign'.]
47–8. And thus although he imploys] And, if this be his Fate, when he employs *35–38*; *marked* '\' *for correction in margin of 32S*
49. Avarice; what must he expect] Avarice, he is sure to raise the Hatred of the noisy Croud, who envy him the quiet Enjoyment of himself. What must such an one expect *30*

51. and every] every *30*
51. ready] will be ready *30*
52. when] as soon as *30*
52. And in] In *30*
57. this.] ~,. *28*
58. it's] its *29–38*
61. Reading] *marked '\ for correction in margin of 32S, then marked* 'stet'
63. Stations] Station *35–38*
68. Promotions] Promotion *35–38*
70. Regulations] Observations *35–38*; *marked '\ for correction in margin of 32S*
74. *Discretion 29–38*] Diseretion *28* (*foul case*)
75. World *29–38*] Word *28*
78. Man] Men *29–35, 38⁸*
78. A.B.C.T.] an Archbishop. *32–38*; *35–38 add footnote*:
  Dr. Tenison, *late Archbishop of* Canterbury.

79. Clergy-Man] Clergymen *30*
82. *S—rs*] *Summers 35*; *Somers 38⁸*; *Sommers 38¹²*
84. *Pr—*] Prelate *32–38*
88. *—Shire*] *Yorkshire 35–38*
88. a Gentleman *29–38*] a Gentlemen *28*
89. understanding] nnderstanding *28*
100. heartly] heartily *29–38*
102. happen] happens *29–38*
102. uppermost] upper-|most *28*
103. usually] generally *30*
103. be] me *29–38*
110. Resty] resty *32S, 35–38*; Rusty *28–32*
111. In some following Paper, I will give] I will here give *32–38*
112. *Clergy-Men*] *Clergyman 35⁸*
113–14. worldly Discretion] this Discretion *32S, avoiding repetitious* World . . . worldly

No. 6

28a *The first edition*
[drop-head title:] THE | 𝕴𝖓𝖙𝖊𝖑𝖑𝖎𝖌𝖊𝖓𝖈𝖊𝖗. | [rule] | NUMB. VI. | [rule] | *O patria! o divum domus!* | [rule] | [text]

Pot 8°: *A⁴*; pp. *1* 2–8; *1* drop head, *1*–8 text, 8 'FINIS.' Text of pp. 1–6 and the first line of p. 7 are set in larger type, the remainder of p. 7 and p. 8 in smaller type.

Copies collated. Forster, Taylor.

28b *Corrected edition*
THE | 𝕴𝖓𝖙𝖊𝖑𝖑𝖎𝖌𝖊𝖓𝖈𝖊𝖗, | [rule] | *N*UMB· VI. | [rule] | *O patria! o divum domus!* | [rule] | [ornament: flower basket] | [double rule] | *DUBLIN*: | Printed by S. HARDING, next Door to | the *Crown in Copper-Aˡlˡey*, 1728.

Pot 8°: *A⁴*; pp. *1–2* 3–8; *1* title-page, *2* blank, 3–8 text, 8 'FINIS.' The smaller type is used for the entire text, with pp. 7–8 reset line for line from *28a*; the change of size also permits the usual title-page to be employed. A garbled passage from *28a* is put right, and there are several corrections, possibly authorial. Differences from *28c–d*: the comma after 'HARDING' is slightly to the left of the top of the *ˡlˡ* in *Aˡlˡey*; the vertical stroke of the page number '4' is directly above the second '*o*' in '*Mythologists*'; the left parenthesis before the page number '6' is above the 'av' in 'have'; the right parenthesis after the page number '7' is above the second 'n' in 'Demonstrations'; numerous other small differences emerge from optical comparison. The order of the impressions of the corrected edition is conjectural.

Copies collated. NLI, RIA (2), Rothschild, Yale.

28c *Another impression of* 28b

Description as for *28b*; the comma after 'HARDING' is directly above the ⌐*ll*⌐ in '*A*⌐*ll*⌐*ey*'; the page number '4' is over the '*gi*' in '*Mythologists*'; the left parenthesis before the page number '6' is directly above the 'a' in 'have'; the right parenthesis after the page number 7 is—in the one complete TCD copy— above the second 'o' in 'Demonstrations'.

Copies collated. TCD (2, 1 lacking *A*4).

28d *Another impression of* 28b

Description as for *28c*, except that the 'N' in 'NUMB·' is roman and the right parenthesis after the page number 7 is above the second 'on' in 'Demonstrations'.

Copies collated. Illinois, Rothschild, ULC.

Mi

The essay was reprinted, probably from *28b*, in *Mist's Weekly J.*, 27 July 1728; a few of the substantive variants cast light on the essay and are recorded below. For the ironic preamble from *Mist's*, see Appendix D.

Copy collated. BL.

Later editions

The source of *29* is *28a*, and *30* derives from *29*. The essay was next reprinted in *89*, pp. 156–63.

Copy-text: *28b* (copy: RIA Haliday Tracts 179). *Variant readings* in the following editions and impressions are recorded in the following order:

28a–28b–28c–28d–29–30

1–2. Kingdom (and] Kingdom, and *28a*, *29–30*

5. Favour] F— *Mi*

6. *Compassion*] *Passion 29–30*

10. these] the *28a*, *29–30*

18. *vocant*] *vocart 28a*

20. entertain'd,] ~ₐ *28a*, *29–30*

21. Day.] ~, *28a*

24. Rancour] Rencour *28a*

26. *Mythologists*, *29*] ~ₐ *28a*; ~. *28b–d*

34. *Knuckle-Bones*] ~ₐ~ *28a*

34. *Guts*] Guts *28–30*

35. Down:] ~. *28a*, *29–30*

51. *Droghedah*] Drogheda *28a*, *29–30*

51. Town,] ~ₐ *28a*

61. *Mardonius*] Mardonuis *28*

64. all,] ~ₐ *28a*

70. fond *29–30*] found *28*

72. *Cromwell*] Cormwell *28a*

77. Politicks] Politick *28a*

78. of *Ireland*,] ~ ~ₐ *28a*; in - - - - - *Mi*

79. the defacing] defacing *29–30*

79. Churches,] ~ₐ *28a*

96. Megara,] ~. *28a*

97. *round about*] round *30*

106. People,] ~ₐ *28a*

106–7. Hunger and Cold, *rather appearing like Spectres than Men 29–30*] *In 28 only the words* 'and Cold . . . Spectres than' *are italicized, leaving* 'Hunger' *and* 'Men' *in roman, probably following a carelessly underlined MS*

108. Fellow-Creatures] ~ₐ~ *28a*, *30*

109. Reflections] Reflection *28a*, *29–30*

110–11. Sights and Occurrences which I had in this my last Journey, have so] my last Journey sights and Occurrences which I had in this so *28a*, *garbled probably from an interlined MS; emended in 29–30 (presumably conjecturally) in the same manner as the present edition, except that* 'have' *does not appear.*

114. upper-most *28a*] upper-|most *28b–d*

119. First] Frst *28a*

125. it's] its *29–30*
128. infallibly] hardly *Mi*
134. Garrons] *Mi adds footnote*:
    A poor lean Horse so called in *Ireland*.
134. before.] ~∧ *28a*
139. others] other *28–30*
142. barefoot.] ~, *28*

144. white;] ~, *28*
145. Hay.] ~∧ *28a*
153. single∧House] ~–~ *28a*
158. done.] ~, *28a*
170. rise, it] ~. *It 28a*; ~. It *28b–d*
173. it's] its *29–30*
174. it.] ~∧ *28a*

No. 7

The Harding edition appeared in two impressions whose priority cannot be determined and whose texts are identical:

28a

THE | 𝕴ntelligencer, | [rule] | *N*UMB· VII. | [rule] | ———*Probitas laudatur &* *alget.* | [rule] | [ornament: flower basket] | [double rule] | *DUBLIN*: | Printed by S. HARDING, next Door to | the *Crown in Copper-A⌐ll⌐ey*, 1728.

Pot 8°: *A*⁴; pp. *1* 2–8; *1* title-page, 2 drop-head: [double rule] | The *Intelligencer·* | [text]; 2–8 text; 8 'FINIS.'

    Copies collated. Forster, Illinois (cropped), RIA, Rothschild (2), TCD (cropped), Yale. All copies have the basket ornament to left of centre—some more so than others.

28b *Another impression*

An entirely different setting of the title-page, differing from that of *28a* in that it is headed by a double rule, 𝕴ntelligencer is followed by a period, the period after 'NUMB' is on the line, and the 'N' is roman, as is 'in' in the last line. Collation as for *28a*.

    Copies collated. NLI, RIA (cropped), Taylor.

Later editions

In London the essay was first reprinted, with minor variants, in *Fog's Weekly J.*, 26 Oct. 1728. For the headnote, see Appendix D. From *28* the essay was next reprinted in *29*, and from *29* in *30* and (with *Intelligencer 5*) *32*. See textual note for no. 5.

    The essay was imitated in *Gespräch zwischen einem Römisch-Catholischen Priester und zweyen Herrenhutern die Frage betreffend: Ob die Protestantische Pfarrer eine der Größesten Landplagen auf der Welt seyn? Nebst einem Unterricht des berühmten D. Swift, worinn denen geistlichen Studenten gewiesen wird, wie sie gar leicht zu einem Pfarrdienste gelangen können* (Frankfurt and Leipzig: Traiano Machiavelli, 1752), 11–41 (copy: BL).

Copy-text: *28a* (the Rothschild copy with basket less nearly centred). *Variant readings* from the following texts, recorded in the following order:

$$28a–28b–29–30–32^8–32^{12}–32S–33^{12}–33F–35^8–35^{12}–38^8–38^{12}$$

1. an] at *30*
8. dagling] dragling *29–38*

16. *perceived*] perceive *29–38*
17. *spoke*] speak *38¹²*

18. *Sir*,] ~∧ *28*
19. *Man's*] Man's *28*
20. and got] got *29–38*
20–1. Orders, having by the most extreme Parsimoney] *marked '\for correction in the margin of 32S*
22. Fellowship,] ~∧ *28*
23. Waiting-woman] a Waiting Woman *30*
25. fourteen] Ten *35–38*
30. House] Houses *35–38*
31. beside] besides *35¹²–38*
42. his] his own *30*
49. disposed] disposed of *29–38*
52. starched,] Starched∧ *28*
53. Promotion. *29–38*] ~, *28*
54. high] great *32S*
57. *Corusodes, 29–32*] ~∧ *28*
72. their faults.] the ~, *28*; their Faults: *29–38*
74. *Ministries,*] Ministers; *38⁸*
78. and *Quod 29–38*] and quod *28*

78. *nihil*] nil *32–33*
81. Popery] *Popery 32–38*
84. his] in *30*
86. Mitre,] Mitre, (in which he succeeded) *32S*
95. most] must *35¹²*
96. Nephews, or] ~: Or *35⁸*
96. be not] be *30*
109. Streets] Street *35–38*
112. a good] good *32S*
113. fortune,] Estate; *35–38* [*avoiding the repetition of* 'Fortune']
114. Church∧ *29–32*] ~: *28*
116. the Men] Men *29–38*
132. late,] ~∧ *28*
133. this] the *35–38*
135. his] this *35–38*
135. Words.] ~, *28*
138. had] he had *38¹²*
138. Father∧] Father's, *29–38*
139. pound] Pounds *35–38*
139–40. Lincoln-shire] Lincoln-|shire *28*

No. 8

28a *The first edition*
[drop-head title:] [double rule] | THE | 𝕴𝖓𝖙𝖊𝖑𝖑𝖎𝖌𝖊𝖓𝖈𝖊𝖗. | [rule] | NUMB. VIII. | [rule] | *Par coeatque pari.* | [rule]

Pot 8°: *A⁴*; pp. *1* 2–8.
   Copies collated. Huntington, Illinois, Rothschild (2), RIA Haliday Pamphlets 78, TCD, Yale.

28b *Another impression or state*
Description and collation as for *28a*. The bottom third of p. 7 is a different setting of type, as is the uppermost portion of p. 8; the first line of p. 3 is wrongly indented, and p. 5 lacks a catchword. See also the variant readings.
   Copies collated. Forster, NLI, RIA Haliday Tracts 179, Taylor.

Later editions
As usual, *28* is the source for *29*, and *29* is the source for *30* as well as *32*. Pope prepared a text without Sheridan's introduction, which seems not subsequently to have been reprinted. As outlined in the General Bibliographical Note, *32¹²* derives from *29* and at least in this case is the source of *32⁸* and *33¹²*. Fairbrother's Dublin edition of 1733 (*33F*) copies *32⁸*.
   Swift complained to Motte that errors in *32* 'quite alter the sense in those indifferent verses of mine' (*Corresp.* iv. 83), and while as regards *Mad Mullinix and Timothy* Swift's assessment seems overstated, he did enter a number of

emendations in his own copy of 32^8, now in the Rothschild Collection at Trinity College, Cambridge (*32S*).

Faulkner's uncancelled text (**35u**) was lost until Margaret Weedon reported an uncancelled copy in the English Faculty Library, Oxford, in 1967 (*Library*, 5 ser., 22 (1967), 44–56). The same year David Woolley, finishing Herbert Davis's posthumous edition of Swift's *Poetical Works*, emended the text of *Mad Mullinix and Timothy* with readings from *35u*. There is interesting if not quite conclusive evidence that for this poem, *33F* was Faulkner's copy-text, while some of Faulkner's extensive emendations derive from Swift's annotations in *32S*. In the eleven instances where *33F* differs from its source (32^8), Faulkner's *35u* agrees with *33F* as against 32^8. Even though Faulkner and Fairbrother observed similar conventions of style, 100 per cent agreement between them seems too great to be coincidental. (But if it is coincidental, *35u* is derived from 32^8, as would have been supposed.)

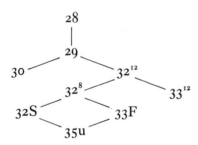

DIAGRAM B. Early transmission of no. 8.

The poem was printed in vol. iii of the *Miscellanies* in 1736, and in vol. iv in 1742, 1749, and 1751. It was also published in *A Supplement to Dr. Swift's and Mr. Pope's Works* (Dublin: Powell, 1739), pp. 308–15, in a text deriving from 32^{12} (i.e., not from 32^8 or 33^{12}). The important modern edition is that of Harold Williams, in *Poems*, iii. 772–82; but see also Joseph Horrell's in the *Collected Poems* (London, 1958), ii. 527–34, 781, and Rogers, 336–43, 776–8. The poem was included by C. H. Sisson in his *Jonathan Swift: Selected Poems* (Manchester, 1977), 53–60.

Date of composition. Probably only a few weeks before publication, on the evidence of the references to recent Dublin events. The headnote in *35u*, 'Written in the Year 1727', is probably one of the errors of chronology characteristic of Faulkner's edition.

Copy-text: *28a* (RIA Haliday Pamphlets 78 copy). *Variant readings* are recorded from the following texts in the following order:

$$28a\text{–}28b\text{–}29\text{–}30\text{–}32^{12}\text{–}32^8\text{–}32S\text{–}33F\text{–}35u$$

In addition to strictly substantive variants, I list as well variant readings which affect rhythm, pause, emphasis, or pronunciation, as explained in the Textual Introduction.

29–35u begin a new line whenever there is a change of speaker in mid-line.
MOTTO. *om. 32–35u*
PROSE INTRODUCTION
1–16. *om. 32–35u*
3. while] whilst *29–30*
7. well-wishers] well-|wishers *28*
POEM
TITLE. MAD MULLINIX and TIMOTHY] A DIALOGUE between MAD MULLINIX and TIMOTHY *32–35u; 35u adds note:*
   Written in the Year 1727.
4. *Jacobits*] *Jacobites 29–32*
7. *Priests . . . Fryers*] Priests . . . Fryers *32⁸–35u*
8. me‸] ~, *29–35u*
9. *Tories*] Tories *32⁸–35u*
9. over‸] ~. *30*
13. Earl] *35u adds footnote:*
   Earl of Barrymore.
15. Debts? *29–35u*] ~. *28*
16. Lord,] ~‸ *28*
17. Statesman] Statesman Bishop *30;* Statesman-B—— *32–35u*
18. up?] ~‸ *29–35u*
23. 'tis] in *35u*
24. *Avignion*] *Avignon 29–35u; 35u adds footnote:*
   A mid-land City in France.
25–34. *om. 32–35u*
29. But‸ *Tim‸*] ~, ~, *29–30*
31. you‸] ~, *29–30*
33. Z—ds‸] ~, *29–30*
33. serious;] ~‸ *28b;* ~, *29–30 (the semicolon is visible only in the RIA copy of 28a, Haliday Pamphlets 78/7)*
34. us.] ~; *29–30*
35. These] *M.* These *29–35u*
35. brangling] wrangling *30*
37. Wrong, 'tis certain, *32–35u*] ~‸ is ~‸ *28;* ~‸ is ~, *29–30*
41. you‸ . . . past‸] ~, . . . ~, *29–35u*
43. *Martin Marrall*] ~ *Marall 30;* ~ *Marral 29, 32; 35 adds footnote:*
   A Play of Dryden*'s, called Sir* Martin Marrall.
44. was] is *32–35u*

45. are] were *29–30*
47. Leaders‸] ~, *33F–35u*
48. Plunder.] ~, *29–33F;* ~; *35u*
49. past, *29–35u*] ~‸ *28*
51. And, . . . *Grecian‸*] ~‸ . . . ~‸ *29–33F;* ~‸ . . . ~, *35u*
57. peevish‸ *29–35u*] ~, *28*
58. Plots, *29–35u*] ~; *28*
59. busy, *29–35u*] ~‸ *28*
64. Stink‸)] ~.) *33F–35u*
65. Presence, *29–35u*] ~‸ *28*
69. Friend‸ *Mullinix, 32–35u*] ~‸ ~‸ *28;* ~, ~, *29–30*
69. forbear.] ~, *29–35u*
72. Advice‸] ~, *29–35u*
73. But‸ . . . Blood,] ~‸ . . . ~‸ *28;* ~, . . . ~, *29–35u*
76. *Glorious*] *old Glorious 35u*
80. Prance] *praunce 35u*
80. the] his *32–35u*
80. Statue] *35u adds footnote:*
   A Statue of King William *in* College Green, Dublin, *round which his Adorers, every Year of his Birth, go on Foot, or in their Coaches: But the Number is much lessened.*
81. Safety, *29–35u*] ~‸ *28*
88. Delight] *ital. 32–35u*
89. act‸ . . . diff'rent] ~, . . . ~ *28;* ~‸ . . . different *29–35u*
90. wise,] ~ — *32–35u*
90. Heart. *32–35u*] Hearts‸ *28;* Heart: *29–30*
92. Puppet-show] *ital. 32–35u*
96. rejoice.] ~! *29–35u*
99. *Pretender,*] ~; *32–35u*
102. Stage‸] ~, *29–35u*
103. Punch] Punch *28*
105. again,] ~; *32–35u*
107. You‸ . . . moment‸] ~, . . . ~, *29–30*
107. ev'ry *29–32¹²*] e'ry *28;* every *32⁸–35u*
108. appears] appear *35u*
109. clap‸ *29–35u*] Clap, *28*
112. Punch 29–35u] Punch *28*
112. roar'd.] ~; *29–30, 35u;* ~, *32–33F*
113. Reviles] Revil'd *32–33F*
114. sells] sold *32–33F*
117. Kicks, *29–35u*] ~‸ *28*
119. Nose, *29–35u*] ~‸ *28*

120. why, *29–32 ^{12}, 35u*] ~$_\wedge$ *28, 32 ^{8}–33F*
121. Scenes, . . . break] ~, . . . breaks *28*;
  ~$_\wedge$ . . . break *29–35u*
122. Punch 29–35u] Punch *28*
127. share;] ~, *29–35u*
128. hear,] ~$_\wedge$ *29–35u*
130. Saint, . . . Snake.] ~$_\wedge$ . . . ~, *29–33F*;
  ~$_\wedge$ . . . ~; *35u*
132. plagues] plague *32*
133. Thus$_\wedge$] ~, *29–35u*
135. petulant,] ~$_\wedge$ *30–35u*
137. So$_\wedge$ . . . Booth,] ~$_\wedge$ . . . ~$_\wedge$ *32*; ~, . . .
  ~, *35u*
138. Tim$_\wedge$] ~, *29–35u*
139. Rout, *29–35u*] ~$_\wedge$ *28*
140. Brother] *ital. 35u*
141. a] one *32S, 35u*
143. grin, . . . clatter,] ~, . . . ~$_\wedge$ *28*; Grin$_\wedge$
  . . . Clatter, *29–33F*; Grin, . . . Clatter,
  35u
146. you, . . . Man;] ~$_\wedge$ . . . ~; *30–33F*; ~$_\wedge$
  . . . ~. *35u*
147. then$_\wedge$ . . . Tories$_\wedge$] ~, . . . ~, *29–35u*
152. Coy] Toil *30*
155. Blood,] ~, *29–35u*
156. place,] Place$_\wedge$ *29–35u*
158. time,] Time$_\wedge$ *29–35u*
158. P—] Peer *30*
159. got] get *35u*
160. peace] Pace *29*
163. Tories$_\wedge$ Jacks] *Tories, Jacks 29–33F,*
  35u; *35u adds footnote*:
  A Cant Word for Jacobites, *or those who*
  continued in the Interest of King James II.
  after King William *got the Crown, and now*
  are for his Son, commonly called the
  Pretender.
166. stare *29–35u*] stair *28*
169. constant,] ~$_\wedge$ *32–35u*
170. self,] ~$_\wedge$ *29–35u*
171. Death,] ~; *35u*
172. Breath,] ~; *35u*
175. Vitals! *32–35u*] ~$_\wedge$ *28*; ~, *29–30*
176. so; *32–35u*] ~, *28–30*
178. Than *30, 32 ^{8}–35u*] Then *28–29*,
  32 ^{12}. [*Note*: In Swift's hand, 'e' and 'a'
  are easily confused, and he inveighs
  against the misuse of 'then' for 'than';
  see H. Real and H. Vienken, "'A Pretty
  Mixture'", *BJRL* 67 (1984), 527.]
179–80. endure$_\wedge$ . . . renown'd$_\wedge$] ~, . . . ~,
  29–35u

181. cry$_\wedge$] ~, *29–30*
182. Nimble Tim] nimble Tim *29–35u*
187. Bl—s . . . W—ds] Bloods . . .
  Wounds *32–35u*
191. roar$_\wedge$ a Plot, a] ~, *a Plot, a 29–35u*
194. Spy] *Spy 32–35u*
195. new paragraph 32–35u
196. beg,] ~; *35u*
196. nice. *35u*] ~: *29–33F*; Nice, *28*
201–2. Reward, . . . guard,] ~, . . . *Guard.*
  32–33F; ~; . . . ~: *35u*
203. 'Prentice] *'Prentice 32–35u*
205. Air$_\wedge$] ~, *29–35u*
206. Cinder-picking Fair] *ital. 32–35u*
207. Affection$_\wedge$] ~, *29–35u*
209. Your] Thy *32–35u*
209. deny'd,] ~; *35u*
214. ephippia.] Ephippia— 35u
215. $_\wedge$There's] (~ *32–35u*
215. too$_\wedge$] ~, *29–35u*
216. I *32S, 35u*] much *28–33F*
216. Dr. ——$_\wedge$] ~ ——) *32–33F*; ~ Lee)
  35u, adding footnote:
  A deceased Clergyman, whose Footman he
  was.
217. you$_\wedge$ may$_\wedge$ try] ~-~-~ *32–35u*
223. oyly,] ~$_\wedge$ *32–35u*
225. prepar'd$_\wedge$] ~, *29–35u*
226. and] or *32–35u*
228. is which,] ~ ~$_\wedge$ *30–35u*
228. know.] ~, *29–33F*; ~; *35u*
231. careful,] ~$_\wedge$ *29–35u*
231. behind,] ~; *32–35u*
232. mind.] ~; *29–30, 35u*; ~, *32–33F*
233. imitate$_\wedge$ *28b–35u*] ~, *28a*
234. Mien,] Mein$_\wedge$ *29–35u*
235. Style,] ~: *35u*
239. our] your *29–33F*
240. City: *29–35u*] ~$_\wedge$ *28*
247. Some] *35u adds footnote*:
  Chimney-Sweepers.
248. *Zenith*] Zenith *32–35u*
249. Some] *35u adds footnote*:
  Scavengers.
251. Some] *35u adds footnote*:
  Coblers.
251. us$_\wedge$] ~, *29–30*
252. upright] *ital. 35u*
253. Some$_\wedge$] ~, *32 ^{12}, 33F, 35u*; *35u adds*
  footnote:
  Keeper of Bridewell.

255. Some,] ~∧ *30–33F, 35u*; *35u adds*
  footnote:
    Porters.
256. to *29–35u*] too *28*
257. Weight,] ~∧ *32–35u*
258. M—rs] Ministers *35u*
259. We] *new paragraph 35u, adding foot-*
  note:
    —*Non de domibus rebusve alienis, &c.*
  Hor.
260. Of] of *28*
262. Manners *32S, 35u*] Mannors *28*;
  Manours *29–32, 33F*
263. Our] *35u adds footnote*:

  —*Sed, quod magis ad nos,* | *Et nescire
  malum est, agitamus, &c.* Id.
265. Life,] ~; *35u*
269. Cheese,] ~∧ *29–35u*
270. Another∧] ~, *35u*
273–4. *om. 32–35u*
273. *Audoin*] *Audouin 29–30*
275. How by the *Almanack*] Or how by
  Almanacks 32–35u
278. Time,] ~∧ *32–35u*
279. Ends,] ~: *35u*
281. Birth] Bɪʀᴛʜ *35u*
283. *new paragraph 35u*
283. you,] ~. *35u*

No. 9

28a *The Harding edition*

THE | 𝕴ntelligencer, | [rule] | NUMB· IX. | [rule] | [ornament: flower basket] | [double rule] | *DUBLIN*: | Printed by S. HARDING, next Door to | the *Crown in Copper-A⌐ll⌐ey*, 1728.

Pot 8°: A⁸; $3 signed; pp. *1–2* 3–16; *1* title, *2* blank, *3* drop-head: [double rule] | The *Intelligencer*. 3–16 text, 16 '*FINIS.*'
   Copies collated. Illinois, NLI, Rothschild, Yale. An uncorrected state of the inner forme gives 'Gentlemen' for 'Gentleman' on p. 11, line 8, and 'Le⌐ff⌐n' on p. 11, line 25: copies collated: NLI, RIA, TCD.

28b *A less correct impression*

THE | 𝕴ntelligencer, | [rule] | *N*UMB· IX. | [rule] | [ornament: arms of France] | [double rule] | *DUBLIN*: | Printed by S. HARDING, next Door | to the *Crown* in *Copper-A⌐ll⌐ey*, 1728.

Collation as for *28a*. A different setting of the title-page and a different, prob-ably later, imposition of the rest of the type. *28b* may be identified by the following additional points: it lacks the full stop after *Intelligencer* in the drop-heading on p. 3; it inserts an unwanted space ('Equipage ,') on p. 8, line 30; it lacks the 'a' before 'Patron' on p. 13, line 31; and it prints ';the' (with no inter-vening space) on p. 15, line 15.
   Copies collated. Forster, NLI, RIA, Taylor.

Later editions
The essay was first reprinted, in instalments, in *Mist's Weekly J.* (**Mi**), 10 and 17 Aug. 1728 (see Appendix D). Bowyer reprinted *29* from *28a* or *28b*, and *30* from *29*. The text in *32* was printed from *29* and was corrected both by an errata list (*32e*) and by Swift's marginalia in his own copy (*32S*). Both the 12° *Miscellanies* of 1733 (*33¹²*) and Fairbrother's *Miscellanies* of 1733 (*33F*) reprinted *32* (see Textual Introduction). Faulkner's *35⁸* is an edited version of

32, taking account of most of Swift's revisions in *32S*. It appears that *35¹²* and *38⁸* were printed from *35⁸*, with *38¹²* being printed from *35¹²*. In 1745 a translation, 'Ein Versuch über die heutige Auferziehung', was published as an appendix to [Johann Georg Sulzer]'s *Versuch einiger vernünftigen Gedancken von der Auferziehung u. Unterweisung der Kinder* (Zürich: Orell, 1745), 111–25 (copy: Universitätsbibliothek, Trier). Vera Philippović attributes the translation to Heinrich Waser in her Zürich dissertation, *Swift in Deutschland* (Agram, 1903), 14.

Copy-text: *28a*, corrected state (Rothschild copy, supplemented on one or two points by the Yale copy). *Variant readings* are recorded from the following texts in the following order:

$$28a–28b–29–30–32^8–32e–32S–35^8–35^{12}–38^8–38^{12}$$

HEADING. *32 adds title*:
    AN ESSAY ON *Modern Education.*
3. thereof] there-|of *28a*
4. worse] *ital. 32–38*
5. Wealth and Grandeur] *Wealth* of and *Grandeur 32*; *Wealth* and *Grandeur 32e–38*
6–7. one Monarch] *ital. 32–38*
7. where] *ital. 32–38*
11. I] *new paragraph 32–38*
13. a] at *38¹²*
28. some Additional] *some 35–38*
33–4. a Neighbouring Kingdom, from whence the Chief among us are descended, and whose manners we most affect to follow.] *England. 32–38*
36. in that Kingdom] *om. 32–38*
36. the Hands of] *om. 35–38*
37. very few] few *35–38*
38. having] have *38¹²*
39. supported] supplied *35–38*
43. Ormonde] *Ormond 29–38*
43. had] have or had *28–32*; having *35–38* [*a grammatically corrupt passage in 28*]
49. chief Conduct of publick Affairs] highest Employments of State *35–38*, [*avoiding repetition of* 'Chief Conduct of Affairs']
50. Ministers,] ~; *35–38*; ~∧ *38¹²*
52. though] although *35¹²–38*
53. sometimes] some-|times *28a*
54. good Estates] ample Fortunes *35–38*
56. Bridgman] *Bridgeman 32–38*
56. Coventry] *Coonuley 28–30*; *om. 32–38.* [*Note*: 'Coonuley' would be a misreading of the handwritten 'Coventry'; *32*

and therefore its successors simply admitted defeat.]
58. Summers] *Sommers 29–35*, *38¹²*; *Somers 38⁸*
58. Churchil] *Churchill 35¹²–38*
58. Vernon] *Vernor 28–30*
58. Harry Boyle] *Boyle 32*
59. St. John] St. John *28*
59. Harcourt] *Harcout 35–38⁸*
59. Trevers 28–30] *Trevor 32–38*
61. last] following *32*
61–2. understood for many Years, to be] for many years *32–38*
62. happily] HAPPILY *35–38*
64. Craiggs] *Craggs 29–38*
64. Allyance *32S–38*] allowance *28–32*
69. share] a Share *35–38*
69. important *32S–38*] compatent *28*; competent *29–32*. [*Note*: Against this line in *32S* Swift first placed the marginal symbol '\' as a reminder that revision was needed. Given Swift's handwriting, it is not improbable that 'compatent' was a misreading of 'important'. *OED*, citing this instance only, defines *competent* as '?Requiring competence. *Obs.*']
71. Omissions,] ~∧ *29–38*
74. natural Parts] *ital. 35–38*
76. Children∧] ~. *30*
76. Noble and Wealthy] noble wealthy *35–38*
77. Body] Bodies *30*
81. Birth; *32S–38*] ~. *28–32*
81–2. a universal] an universal *30*; a *35–38*
83. on] in *32S*. [*Note*: To charge something *on* somebody is idiomatic—see

OED under *charge*, *v.*, 16; in haste Swift mistakenly deemed *fault on* unidiomatic and revised it, disregarding the integrity of the larger construction.]

84–5. Ends . . . means] *Ends . . . Means* *32–38*

88–9. accomplishments . . . Time . . . Study] *Accomplishments . . . Time . . . Study* *32–38*

91. modern] *ital. 35–38*

94. publick] the publick *35–38*

106. outshine] out-|shine *28*

109. were . . . Standard-Patterns] was . . . Standard-Pattern *30–38*. [*Note*: A superficial grammatical correctness is achieved in *30–38* by throwing away the evidence that Swift meant to call all the Worthies 'Standard-Patterns'.]

110. whatever] what-|ever *28a*

113. Coffee-house] Coffee-|house *28*

121. is he] he is *28*

123. Blockado] Blockade *29–38*

124. reconoitring *35–38*, *Mi*] *recountring 28*; *rencountring 29–32*. [*Note*: rencountring may be right, but it was an old word, and I assume Swift wanted an example of the new military jargon; see *OED*.]

128. contempt of Learning] *Contempt 30*

128. without] with-|out *28a*

129. many, and some even in this Kingdom] many *32*; a few *35–38*

135. that] the *35^{12}*

135. Nobility] *ital. 32–38*

136. been likewise] likewise been *29–38*

137. a humorous] an humorous *30*

138. Le-Sac] Le-Sack *32*; Le Sac *35–38*

141. Well] *35–38 add footnote*:
  The Author's Friends have heard him tell this Passage as from the Earl himself.

145. any,] ~; *35–38*

149. till] until *38^8*

149. other] othet *28*

150. Cloaths,] ~: *35–38*

150. the Dancing-master *28, 30, 32S–38*] Dancing-master *29, 32*

151. does] doth *35^{12}–38*

154. Gentleman] Gentlemen *28a variant state*

155. Age adding only to *29–38*] being *28* (*obviously corrupt*)

156. Vice] Vices *32S–38*

157. Boyhood] Boy-|hood *28*

160. posture] the Posture *35–38*

160. change] Changes *35–38*

161. knowledge] knowlidge *28*

163. Nursery] Nursary *28*

168. Lord] *35–38 add footnote*:
  The Author is supposed to mean the Lord Viscount Montcassel, *of* Ireland.

176. Great 29–38] great *Great 28*

177. own] one *28*

180. removal,] Removal to the University; *35–38*

182. very Worthy] *om. 35–38*

184. singular] *ital. 35–38*

186. acquired *29–38*] required *28*

187. should] shall *35^{12}*

189. important . . . Gentleman] important . . . Gentlemen *28*

199. them to] ~ in *35–38*

201. Quality] *ital. 30*

202. that] who *35–38*

204. a Patron] Patron *28b*

207. Schools 28–30, 38^{12}] *School 32–38^8*

212. are, *29–38^8*] ~_∧ *28, 38^{12}*

217. out of] by *35–38*

219. for] But *35–38*

222. never] ever *32*

222. misled *32S–38*] Mild *28–32*; wild *32e*. [*Note*: 'Mild' may have been not a misprint but Swift's original intention; if so, he would have been trying to develop the idea that education trained one to moderate the 'Excesses' of 'Warmer Blood' but not to be 'Mild' in exercising the 'noble Gifts of the Mind'. The unsatisfactory 'wild', presumably Pope's revision, would have prompted Swift to change the wording.]

228. Miracle, *32*] ~_∧ *28–30*; ~; *35–38*

235. be] to be *38^{12}*

238. Maintenance?* 29–38*] ~. *28*

241. Course *35–38*] cause *28–32*

244. calls] calleth *35–38*

247. Wealth? *29–38*] ~: *28*

248. Spendthrift] Spend-|thrift *28*

251. Mushroom] Mush-|room *28*

257. the] their *35–38*

258. enervated] enervate *30*

258. thorough] through *29–38*

No. 10

28a *The first edition*

THE | 𝔍𝔫𝔱𝔢𝔩𝔩𝔦𝔤𝔢𝔫𝔠𝔢𝔯, | [rule] | NUMB. X. | [rule] | *Magnas Componere lites.* | [rule] | [ornament: basket] | [double rule] | *DUBLIN:* | Printed by S. HARDING, next Door to | the *Crown* in *Copper-Alley*, 1728.

Pot 8°: *A*⁴: pp. *1–2* 3–8; *1* title; *2* blank, 3 drop-head [ornament: thistle-crown-rose] | The *Intelligencer.* | 3–8 text; 8 [tailpiece ornament: fountain with dolphins] | *FINIS.*

   Copies collated. Illinois, NLI (2), Rothschild, RIA (2), TCD, Yale.

28b *Another impression*

[Title-page as in *28a*, except for imprint:] *DUBLIN* | Printed by S. HARDING next Door to | the *Crown i n Copper-Alley.*

Description as in *28a*, with these exceptions: On the title-page, the basket ornament is to left of centre, whereas it is centred in *28a*. In the drop-heading on p. 3, the full stop is missing; and the page numbers on 3 and 4 are in different positions from *28a*. The order of the concluding elements on p. 8 is reversed: *FINIS.* | [tailpiece ornament: fountain with dolphins]

   Copies collated. Forster, Taylor (2).

Reissue?

To fill out the Taylor set, which lacks no. 15, someone has overprinted a second copy of no. 10 so that its title-page reads 'NUMB. X.V'. See also the textual notes to no. 11.

Later editions

No. 10 was reprinted from one of the Harding impressions in *29*; and *30* reprinted *29*. The piece was next reprinted in the 8° *Miscellanies* of 1742, x. Williams edits it in *Poems*, iii. 782–3.

Copy-text: *28a* (Rothschild copy). *Variant readings* are recorded from the following texts in the following order:

28a–28b–29–30

MOTTO. *Lucass*'s] *Lucas's 29–30*	POEM.
30. Advantages∧ beside,] ~, ~∧ *28*	*3. Lucass*'s] *Lucas's 29–30*
36. Monkey∧] ~, *28*	*22.* for't] fort *28*

No. 11

LJ *Source of Smedley's letter*

[drop-head title:] The LONDON JOURNAL. | [rule] | SATURDAY, *April* 6. 1728. NUMB. 453. | [rule]

[colophon:] *LONDON:* Printed by *W. WILKINS*, at the *Dolphin* in *Little-Britain*; and fold by *J. PEELE*, at *Locke*'s *Head* in *Pater-noſʃ'er-|Row*; where Advertiſements are taken in. Advertiſements for *this Paper*, and for the

Whitehall Evening-Po⌐ſt⌐, are alſo taken in by | *N. BLANDFORD*, at the *London Gazette*, *Charing-Croſs*.

2°: 4 pp. unnumbered, 3 columns. The letter from Smedley is the lead article and occupies most of the first page.
    Copies collated. BL, Yale.

Proposal
A revised version of the announcement was published 9 Nov. 1728 as *Proposals for Printing by Subscription, An Universal View. . . .* By the Reverend Jonathan Smedley, Dean of Clogher. Copy collated: Bodleian (John Johnson). For the date, *A Register of Books, 1728–1732, Extracted from The Monthly Chronicle*, ed. D. F. Foxon (London, 1964).

28a *The Harding edition, first impression*
THE | **Intelligencer,** | [rule] | NUMB· XI. | [rule] | —*Ut dehinc Specioſa miracula promat.* Hor. | [rule] | [ornament: basket] | [double rule] | *DUBLIN*: | Printed by S. HARDING, next Door to | the *Crown in Copper-A⌐ll⌐ey*, 1728.

Pot 8°: A⁸; $2 signed; pp. *1–2* 3–16; *1* title, *2* blank, 3–16 text; 16 '*FINIS.*'
    Copies collated. Illinois, NLI (3), Rothschild, RIA (2), TCD, Yale (2).

28b *A later impression*
[Title-page as *28a* except for the last two lines:] Printed by S. HARDING next Door to | the *Crown i*n *Copper-Alley.*

A new setting of the title-page, with the basket right of centre, with sporadic resetting elsewhere and many typographical errors around the edges of the type pages, suggesting that standing type had been tied up and then re-imposed.
    Copies collated. Forster, NLI P600, Taylor.

Reissues?
Someone seems to have attempted to alter remainders of the two preceding impressions in order to pass them off as other numbers, probably to fill out sets. Indeed the Yale set has two copies of *28a*, one of them inserted in place of no. 12. Both Yale copies have a blind impression in the shape of an 'I', just after 'XI' on the title-page, as though someone had once attempted to change 'XI' to 'XII'. In the NLI copy of *28b*, 'XI' has been overprinted by adding 'III', so that the first of the added *I*s covers the original *I*, resulting in an apparent 'XIII'. To this someone has added a further 'I' by hand to make it 'XIIII', and someone (else?) in an apparently nineteenth-century hand confirms this, writing above it 'N° 14'. Thus this copy, which until 1914 was in the RIA Haliday Collection, came to be catalogued at NLI as no. 14. Cf. the reissue of no. 10.

Later editions
As usual, *29* reprints from one of the impressions of *28*, probably *28a*, and *30* and *89* reprint from *29*. No. 11 seems not to have been otherwise reprinted.

Copy-text: for Smedley's letter, *LJ* (BL copy), of which *28* attempts a verbatim transcription. For the remainder, *28a* (Rothschild copy). I have silently raised *LJ*'s small capitals to capitals whenever *28* does so. *Variant readings* from the following texts are reported in the following order:

LJ–28a–28b–29–30

Since for Smedley's letter *28* is not the copy-text, accidental variants between *28a* and *28b* are not recorded for the letter. These consist mainly of the deletion of a number of commas in *28b*; they tend to show that *29* was printed from *28a*.

MOTTO. *dehinc Speciosa*] *speciosa dehinc 30*
INTRODUCTION
  21. *S---d---l---y*] S---d-----y *28b*;
  S---d---y *29–30*
  86. others.] ~_∧ *LJ*
  98. Vols.] Volumes *28–30*
  130. Work is] Work *30*
  134. that] the *30*
  143. curious, *28*] ~_∧ *LJ*
POEM
  2. *Journal,*] ~_∧ *28b*
  15. anew] *a new 28*
  17. *prophane,*] ~_∧ *28b*
  22. *Debate,*] ~_∧ *28b*

  23. *Ale,*] ~_∧ *28b*
  25. *Learning,*] ~_∧ *28b*
  26. *discerning,*] ~_∧ *28b*
  27. *Confusion,*] ~_∧ *28b*
  29. *this,*] ~_∧ *28b*
  30. *amiss,*] ~_∧ *28b*
  82. of *29–30*] if *28*
  105–6. Popery . . . *Rope a wry*] Pop'ry . . .
  Rope 'wry 29–30
  109. *Remember*_∧] ~, *30*
  123. *two*] *too 30*
CONCLUDING COMMENT
  2–6. quotation marks at left margin *28–30*
  8. *Intelligencer.*] ~_∧ *28b*

No. 12

This anonymous poem first appeared in the *Craftsman*:

CJ *The first edition*
[drop-head title:] The COUNTRY JOURNAL: Nᵒ 109. | OR, THE | CRAFTSMAN. | [rule] | *By* CALEB D'ANVERS, *of* GRAY'S-INN, *Esq*; | [rule] SATURDAY, AUGUST 3. 1728. | [rule]

[Colophon:] *LONDON*: Printed for R. FRANCKLIN in *Covent-Garden*, where Advertisements and Letters to the Author are taken in.

2°: *A²*; pp. *1–4*.

'The Progress of Patriotism' is on pp. *1–2*, mostly *2*. The inner forme of this four-page newspaper exists in two settings of type with numerous differences, largely in accidentals. A copy of the earlier setting (**CJa**) is at Harvard; copies of the later (**CJb**) are at BL, Bodleian (2), and Yale; the Yale copy has early but sometimes erroneous manuscript annotations. The resetting appears in no way occasioned by the poem (one item of new news appears in *CJb*). Sheridan republished the poem from *CJa* in *Intelligencer* 12:

28 *The Harding edition*
[drop-head title:] [double rule] | THE | 𝔍ntelligencer. | [rule] | NUMB. XII. | [rule] | [text]

Pot 8°: A^4; pp. *1* 2–8; *1* drop-head, *1*–8 text, 8 'FINIS.'
    Copies collated. Forster, Illinois, NLI (2), RIA (2), Taylor, TCD.

Later editions
29 derives from *28*, and *30* from *29*. The text in *89*, pp. 176–83, is also printed
from *29*. The poem alone is reprinted from *CJa* in *Robin's Panegyrick. or, The
Norfolk Miscellany* (London: Tims, [1729]), 99–103, not to be confused with
Robin's Panegyrick, or, The Norfolk Misselany (London: Tims, 1729). The poem
appears with possibly authorial emendations in *A Collection of Poems on Several
Occasions; Publish'd in The Craftsman* (London: Francklin, 1731), 43–52. From
the latter is derived the text in *The Craftsman*, vol. v of the collected edition
(London: Francklin, 1731), 326–31. An eighteenth-century manuscript miscel-
lany, Harvard MS Eng. 629F, pp. 156–8, presents a text perhaps derived from
CJb. The poem is reprinted from *28* in *Lloyd's Evening Post, and British
Chronicle*, 26 Mar. 1759, tentatively but mistakenly attributed to Swift; see also
the discussion in *Lloyd's*, 17 and 28 Feb. and 12 and 19 Mar. 1759.

    The poem has nothing to do with *The Progress of Patriotism: A Poem* (London:
L. B., 1731).

Copy-text: for the introductory note, *28* (NLI S.C. 99b copy); for the rest,
beginning '*From my own Chambers*', the copy-text is *CJa* (Harvard copy), which
Sheridan intended to follow literally. I have recorded only substantive
variants, and those only for *CJ*, *28*, *29*, and *30*, with this exception: I have
recorded *all* variants of *28* from *CJa*, since they provide some index of the
(in)accuracy of Harding's typesetting. I have silently adopted *28*'s characteristic capitals where *CJ* uses small caps.

INTRODUCTION
    5. 1728, the] ~. The *28*
POEM
    7. Preach'd] Preach *28*
    19. approv'd] approv*l*d *28*
    35. *Party*] party *28*
    59. Condescensions] Condescentions *28*
    64. human] humane *28*
    65. yield] yeld *28*
    73. Favour] favour *28*
    77. premis'd] permis'd *28*
    77. part,] ~. *28*
    88. *Townly*] *Townley CJb*
    89. Place;] ~: *28*
    94. *Bub-ble*] *Bubble 29–30*

    117. promiscuous *CJb*, *28-30*]
        promiscous *CJa*
    118. or] of *28*
    169. That] That That *28*
    169. *Whig-Direction*] ~∧~ *28*
    173. Friend] friend *28*
    180. censure] ensure *28*
    180. *Treason.*] ~, *28*
    181. *no paragraph 28*
    182. *wrong,*] ~∧ *28*
    188. Man] Men *CJb*; man *28*
    193. assiduous Art,] assidous ~. *28*
    194. *Damon*∧] ~, *28*
    199. Sheets,] ~. *28*
    200. Man] man *28*

No. 13

28a *The first Harding impression*
THE | 𝕴𝖓𝖙𝖊𝖑𝖑𝖎𝖌𝖊𝖓𝖈𝖊𝖗, | [rule] | NUMB· XIII. | [rule] | *Sermo datur cunetis animi
fapientia paucis* | Cato | [rule] | [ornament: basket] | [double rule] | *DUBLIN*: |
Printed by S. HARDING, next Door ot | the *Crown in Copper-A⌐ll⌐ey*, 1728.

Pot 8°: *A*⁸; pp. *1–2* 3–14 *15–16*; *1* title, *2* blank, 3 drop-head: [double rule] |
The *Intelligencer·* | [text]; 3–14 text, 14 'FINIS.', *15–16* blank.
   Copies collated. Forster (−*A*⁸), Illinois, Rothschild, RIA.

28b   *Corrected impression*
[Title-page as *28a*, except:] ... NUMB. XIII. | ... *cunctis* ... *DUBLIN* |
Printed by S. HARDING next Door to | the *Crown in Copper-Alley.*

   Copy collated. NLI.

28c   *Another impression with a few more corrections*
[Title-page as *28a* except for the motto:] ... *Sermo datur cun⌐ct⌐is animi ſapientia
paucis* | Cato. | ...

Collation as *28a*.
   Copies collated. RIA, Yale.

28d   *Reissue of* 28c *with reset title-page*
THE | 𝕴𝖓𝖙𝖊𝖑𝖑𝖎𝖌𝖊𝖓𝖈𝖊𝖗, | NUMB· XIII. | *Sermo datur cun⌐ct⌐is animi ſapientia pauci.s* |
Cato | [ornament: basket] | *DUBLIN*: Printed by S. HARD ING, next Door | to
the *Crown in Copper-A⌐ll⌐ey*, 1728.

Note the absence of rules. Collation as *28a*.
   Copies collated. Taylor, TCD.

Later editions
The corrected version, *28b–d*, has not hitherto been reprinted. The uncorrected *28a* was first reprinted in *Fog's Weekly J.*, 16 Nov. 1728 (see Appendix
D), and next in *29*. In turn *29* was reprinted in *30*, and *30* was reprinted
28 Jan. 1736/7 in the *Virginia Gazette*. No. 13 was reprinted without acknowledgement as 'An Humorous Essay on Story-telling, by Way of Introduction'
in *The Agreeable Companion; or, An Universal Medley of Wit and Good-Humour*
(London: Bickerton, 1745), 1–9; and as 'The Art of Story-Telling' in *The Wit's
Magazine; or, Library of Momus*, 2 (Jan. 1785), 7–10, signed 'E.' The essay also
appears in *89*, pp. 184–93.

Copy-text: *28c* (RIA copy), one of the impressions Sheridan apparently corrected and emended, though inadequately. No. 13 is probably among the
numbers Swift had in mind when he told Pope that the *Intelligencer* had been
'most horridly mangled in the press' (*Corresp.* iii. 314). Extensive emendation
has been necessary to prevent misreading. *Variant readings* are recorded from
the following texts in the following order:

28a–28b–28c–28d–29–30

I record all variants between the copy-text and *28a*; otherwise I list substantives only. For the quotation from *A Tale of a Tub* (**T**), the pre-1728 editions of
the *Tale* are, for this passage, too similar to say which of them Sheridan used.

MOTTO. *cunctis*,] ~∧ *28b–d*; *cunetis*∧ *28a*   MOTTO. *Cato*.] ~∧ *28a–b*, *28d*
MOTTO. *paucis*.] ~∧ *28a–c*; *pauci.s 28d*   1. kind] knd *28b*

5. *True*] rue *28b*
8. made very uneasy;] ~ ~ ~ ∧ *28b–d*; dis-oblig'd; *28a, 29–30*
8. the] they *28a*
8. it is] is *30*
12. Compelled] Compell'd *28a*
16. off *29–30*] of *28*
18. Contemptible] Contemptable *28a*
20. whatsoever ∧] ~, *28a–b*
23. Repetitions] Repetions *28a*
25. Protraction] Psotraction *28b*
26. hour] Hour *28b*
28. Hearer.] ~, *28*
33. were] was *28a, 29–30*
34. solid] soild *28b*
36. hence;] ~, *28*
39. purpose;] ~, *28*
47. them.] ~, *28*
49. has] has a *29–30*
53. Contemptible] Contemptable *28a*
56. Assembly, the] ~. The *28*
58. privilege] priviledge *28a*
61. *Mantua*] the *Mantua 28a*
65. *Bird.* At] ~, at *28a*
66. Hollow-tree] Hallow-tree *28a*
69. ran] run *28a*
71. one,] ~ ∧ *28a*
72. Words;] ~, *28*
75. are six] ~ Six *28*
75. Councellors ∧] ~, *28a*
75. sixty] fixty *28 (foul case)*
76. Alderman ∧] ~, *28*
77. Nation,] ~ ∧ *28a*
77. one,] ~. *28*
77. all] All *28*
77. Gentlemen,] ~ ∧ *29–30*. [*Note: 28* can be read as meaning all ladies, young or old; *29–30* cannot.]
78. exception, five *28a*] ~. Five *28b–d*
78. College ∧] ~, *28*
86. stay *29–30*] stay'd *28a*; stayd *28b–d*. [*Note:* 'stay'd' is illogical; if there had been anyone to stay him, the midwife would not have needed him to keep her company.]
87. before,] ~ ∧ *28a*
89. to] till *30*
90. three] Three *28a*
91. one Mr.] on ~ ∧ *28a*
94. Words,] ~ ∧ *28a*
94. than *29–30*] then *28*

102. reason,] ~ ∧ *28a*
103. is] *not present 28–30*
105. no] *om. 28a, 29–30*
105–6. it. And beside, there is some kind of Amusement in seeing a] *om. 28a, 29–30* [*presumably Harding's compositor dropped a line from Sheridan's MS*]
106. Amusement] Amusemment *28b–d*; *om. 28a, 29–30*
106. Person] Persons *28–30*
110. Sir,] ~ ∧ *28a*
112. Ours,] ~ ∧ *28a*
112. Traveller. Very strange,] ~, very ~ ∧ *28a*; ~, very ~, *28b–d*
113. Hives?] ~, *28a*
117. or else] otherwise *28a, 29–30*
118. Country-Men] ~ ∧ ~ *28b*
124. three-score] three-|score *28*
126. compass,] ~; *28*
127. Touch.] ~ ∧ *28*
131. Puppy,] ~ ∧ *28*
131. all?] ~. *28*
133. Ball?] ~; *28*
134. *Ides*,] ~ ∧ *28a*
135. *China*] Chinæ *28a*
136. *Cows*, to yell] ~? toyell *28a*
139. relates] relats *28a*
140. within] with in *28a*
146. nits] knits *29–30*
148. bites] bits *28*
149. Table,] ~ ∧ *28a*
149. Money.] ~, *28a*
152. *Carp*, . . . Pond ∧] ~ ∧ . . . ~, *28a*
156. handle;] ~, *28*
160. again. Now,] ~, ~ ∧ *28a*
160. Cook-maid] Cook-|maid *28*
165. Day. And *28a*] ~, and *28b–d*
168. Cannon-ball,] ~ ∧ *28*
169. River] River's *30*
176. Facts.] ~, *28a*
177. every] ever *30*
181. expletives] explatives *28a*
184. qualifyed] quallifyed *28a*
187. little;] ~, *28*
188. desires] deserves *28a, 29–30*
188. Applauded;] ~, *28b–d*; Applanded, *28a*
189. shews] shhews *28a*
190. thing ∧ *28a–b*] ~, *28c–d*
192. *Bucephalus.* Such] ~ ∧ such *28*
194. own,] ~ ∧ *28b*
194. is,] ~ ∧ *28*

194. Detestable,] ~‿ *28*
199. him;] ~, *28*
201. together?] ~, *28a*
202–3. Weaver, . . . him,] ~‿ . . . ~‿ *28a*;
   ~, . . . ~‿ *28b*
204. who,] ~‿ *28a–b*
204. Devil's‿ *Name,*] ~‿ ~‿ *28a–b*; ~, ~‿

28c–d
204. helps] *I wonder, helps T*
206. fit] *free T*
207. Damnd] Damn'd *28a*
210. Country-men] Country-|men *28*
211. Story-telling,] ~‿ *28a*
220. inuendoes] inuendos *28a*

No. 14

28a *The Harding edition*
THE | 𝕴ntelligencer, | [rule] | NUMB· XIV. | [rule] | *Naturam expe^rll^as furcâ licet ufque recurret.* | Hor. | [rule] | [ornament: basket] | [double rule] | *DUBLIN*: | Printed by S. HARDING next Door to | the *Crown* i n *Copper-Alley.*

Pot 8°: *A*⁸; pp. *1–2* 3–14 *15–16*; *1* title, *2* blank, *3* drop-head: [ornament: thistle-crown-rose] | THE | 𝕴ntelligencer, | [text]; 3–10 prose part, 11 drop-head: [rule] | THE | TALE. | OF THE | T——D· | [rule], 11–14 verse, 14 heading: [rule] | THE | MORAL. | [text]; 14 'FINIS.', *15–16* blank.
   Copies collated. Forster (−*A*8), Illinois, NLI, Rothschild, RIA, TCD (−*A*8), Yale.

28b *An incorrect reissue*
[Title-page as *28a*, except:] THE | 𝕴ntelligencer. | [rule] | NUMB. XIV. | [rule] | *Naturam expe^rll^as fuerâ lice*e *ufqu^rae^recurret* | . . . | *DUBLIN* | . . . S. HARDING, . . . *Crown* in *Copper-A^rll^ey* 1728

Drop-head on p. 11 differs: [no rule] . . . OF | THE . . .

Largely the same setting as *28a*, but with reset title-page and several reset patches. There are abundant typographical errors around the edges of the type pages, suggesting that standing type, having been tied up, is now re-imposed.
   Copy collated. Taylor.

Later editions
Both *Fog's Weekly J.*, 23 Nov. 1728, and the *Maryland Gazette*, 11 Mar. 1728/9, reprint *28*, though *Fog's* omits the verse (see Appendix D). Among reprinters, the *Maryland Gazette* is unusual in acknowledging its source: 'The following Piece is taken from a Pamphlet entituled, THE INTELLIGENCER. (*Dublin* Printed, in 1728.)' Bowyer and Davis take the *29* text from the error-ridden *28b*, emending frequently; *30* reprints *29*. In *The Agreeable Companion; or, An Universal Medley of Wit and Good-Humour* (London: Bickerton, 1745), 11–18, no. 14 is reprinted as 'Prometheus; or, The Grecian Potter'; after the prose part is inserted a twelve-quatrain paraphrase entitled 'Nature Will Prevail', followed in turn by Sheridan's verse, introduced as 'The Same Story Paraphras'd, by Another Hand, under the Title of The Tale of a T—d'. No. 14 was also

reprinted as 'The Story of Prometheus' in the *Wit's Mag.*, 1 (Oct. 1784), 382–4 (without the moral); and in *89*, pp. 193–8.

Copy-text: *28a* (Forster copy). Heavy emendation has been necessary. Some paragraphs open with a word in all caps; these words have silently been reduced to caps and lower case. *Variant readings* (substantives only) are recorded for the following texts in the following order:

28a–28b–29–30

INTRODUCTION
5. *Blue* and *Red*] *Blue Red 28b–30*
6. Hardships] Hard-|ships *28*
11. not₍ₐ₎] no, *28b*
20. *Leg-shaper*] *Leg-|shaper 28a*
25. because] is the cause *28b*
26–7. *Master-Workman*] *Master-Work-|man 28*
30. wanting] way|ting *28b*
31. Oily Pith] Oil-Pith *28b–30*
44. not *28b*] ot *28a*
49. Offender] Offend *28b*
50. *Fear* did] *Fear*did *28a*
60. joy,] ~₍ₐ₎ *29–30*
63. long,] ~₍ₐ₎ *28*
64. small, or awry₍ₐ₎ *29–30*] ~₍ₐ₎ ~ ~, *28*

84. Jibers] Jibbers *29–30*
86–7. even their] eventheir *28*
92. his] hist *28b*
109. *Animals.*] ~; *28*
117. restrain] refrain *29–30*
121. first,] ~₍ₐ₎ *28*
POEM
TITLE. TALE₍ₐ₎] ~. *28*
1. T—] T—d *28b*
20. *Cake.*] ~, *28*
24. *Pan-Cake,*] ~₍ₐ₎ *28–30*
26. fumes] fnmes *28*
30. *bak'd*] *back'd 28*
32. *Jakes*] *Jake 28b*
32. *came.*] *a*₍ₐ₎ *28b*

No. 15

No. 15 reprints Swift's anonymous pamphlet *A Short View of the State of Ireland* with an introduction by Sheridan.

28a *Uncorrected state*
A | Short VIEW | OF THE | STATE | OF | IRELAND. | [ornament: arms of France] | *DUBLIN*: | Printed by *S. HARDING*, next Door to | the *Crown* in *Copper-A⌐ll⌐ey*, 1727-8.

Pot 8°: A⁸; $4 signed; pp. *1–2* 3–15 *16*; *1* title, *2* blank, 3–15 text, *16* blank; p. 3 misnumbered '1'.
Copies collated. BL, Goldsmiths', ULC.

28b *Corrected state of the outer forme*
Description as for *28a*.
The two states of the outer forme are distinguished as follows: title-page ornament left of centre (*28a*, facsimile in *Prose*, xii. 3), or more nearly centred (*28b*); p. 8, line 29 'unconverted' (*28a*) or 'uncontroverted' (*28b*); p. 12, line 11 'Journey' (*28a*) or 'Irony' (*28b*); p. 12, line 14 '*Island*' (*28a*) or '*Ysland*' (*28b*). The corrected state (*28b*) was unknown to Herbert Davis (*Prose*, xii. 323).
Copies collated. Teerink, TCD.

According to *Mist's Weekly J.* (30 Mar. 1728), *A Short View* was published 19 Mar. 1727/8 (see Appendix D); I have found no support for the publication date assigned by T–S, 'ca. Jan. 28, 1728'. The essay had probably been composed not long before it was published, though *35*, often unreliable as to dates, says it was written 'in 1727'. Since dozens or hundreds of pamphlets regularly appeared in this format in Dublin, one should not read special significance in the fact that *A Short View* appeared 'in the same format as the first *Drapier Letter*' (*Prose*, vol. xii, pp. x, xix).

The next edition was probably:

Daniell

[within double rules] A | Short VIEW | OF THE | STATE | OF | IRELAND | [ornament] | [rule] | Printed for, and Sold by *Combra* | *Daniell*, Bookſeller, oppoſite the Main | Guard.

8°: A⁸; $4 signed; pp. *1–2* 3–15 *16*. A very careless reprint of *28b*. Daniell was a bookseller in Cork. Copy collated: ULC.

Mi

From *28a* the essay was excerpted, by a combination of transcription and summary, in *Mist's Weekly J.*, 20 Apr. 1728 (see Appendix D). In 1729 Swift claimed that because of Mist's reprint 'his press-folks were prosecuted for almost a twelvemonth, and, for ought I know, are not yet discharged' (*Prose*, xii. 122). This claim cannot be supported.

Copy collated. BL.

Mist pamphlet

The *Mist's Weekly J.* version was shabbily and not quite completely reprinted in:

[drop-head title:] [headpiece] | THE | Preſent STATE | *IRELAND*; | BEING | Political Reᵣflᵣeᵣctᵣions by Mr. *MIST*, | on a Pamphlet lately publiᵣfhᵣed at | *Dublin*.

8°?: *A⁴*; pp. 1–8; p. 5 unnumbered, or the number cropped; 'FINI' on p. 8; no indication of place, date, or publisher.

Copy collated. BL.

28c *The Harding* Intelligencer

From *28b* the essay was reprinted, with an introduction by Sheridan, in:

THE | 𝕴ntelligencer, | [rule] | NUMB. XV. | Lamentations, Chap. 2. v. 19. | *Ariſe, cry out in the Night: in the begin-* | *ning of the Watches, pour out thine Heart like* | *Water, before the Face of the Lord: lift up* | *thy Hands towards him, for the Life of thy* | *Young Children that faint for Hungar, in the* | *Top of every Street.* | [rule] | [ornament: basket] | [double rule] | *DUBLIN* | Printed by S. HARDING next Door to | the *Crown* in *Copper-Alley*.

Pot 8°: A⁸; $2 signed; pp. *1* 2–16; *1* title, 2–16 text, 16 'FINIS.'

Note. The last page, containing less than half a page of text, is set in smaller type; since there was room to set these three paragraphs in larger type, the compositor may simply have run short of the larger size. This is in any case a somewhat less careful printing than *28a–b*, introducing about eighty variants, nearly all in punctuation and capitalization, without tending to alter the overall style of *28a–b* as to accidentals. None of the variants is clearly authorial; only a minority can be judged corrections, and *28c* inadvertently drops an entire line, in which it is followed by *29* and *30*.

Copies collated. Forster, Illinois, NLI (2: S.C.99a and P600), Rothschild, RIA, TCD, Yale.

Later editions

The *Intelligencer* text, *28c*, including Sheridan's introduction, was reprinted in *29*, and from *29* in *30*. Pope omitted the essay from *32*. As *A Short View of the State of Ireland*, it was reprinted from *28b*—that is, without Sheridan's introduction—in *35^8* and its derivative editions: the Swift–Pope *Miscellanies. Volume the Fifth* (**35M**); Fairbrother's *Miscellanies*, vol. iv (1735), 65–75; and most notably, in *35^{12}*. The preponderance of evidence (including accidentals not listed among the textual variants) suggests, contrary to what one might expect, that *38^{12}* was printed from *35^8* and that *38^8* was printed from *38^{12}*. It is possible, however, that *38^{12}* was set from a copy of *35^{12}* that had been corrected from *35^8*.

Sheridan's introduction was reprinted from *30* in *Miscellanies*, vol. ix (1742) and its reprints.

A Short View was excerpted as 'Causes of a Country's Growing Rich and Flourishing. By Dean Swift', in the *Worcester* [Massachusetts] *Mag.*, no. 13 (Last Week in June, 1786), 155. The essay served later political causes; it was reprinted in *Irish Political Economy*, no. 1 of the Irish Confederation tracts, ed. John Mitchel (Dublin, 1847), 7–16; and, with some abbreviation, in *Dean Swift on the Situation* (Dublin: Cumann na mBan, 1915), 22–6.

Among modern editions of *A Short View* may be mentioned John Hayward's in *Gulliver's Travels and Selected Writings in Prose & Verse* (Bloomsbury, 1934) and Herbert Davis's in *Prose*, vol. xii. Both unfortunately failed to collate *28b*, *28c*, and *30*. The essay has frequently been edited in anthologies and collections of Swift's writings, including translations into Czech, French, German, Italian, Russian, Spanish, and no doubt other languages.

Copy-text: *28b* (Teerink copy) for Swift's essay; *28c* (Rothschild copy) for Sheridan's introduction. On the whole Sheridan clearly intended in *28c* simply to reprint *28b*; I have accepted a few of *28c*'s changes, though whether either Swift or Sheridan made them himself is impossible to say. *Variant readings* are recorded from the following texts in the following order:

$$28a\text{--}28b\text{--}28c\text{--}29\text{--}30\text{--}35^{8}\text{--}35^{12}\text{--}38^{8}\text{--}38^{12}$$

2. honour to] honour of *30*
11. neglected. *29–30*] ~$_\wedge$ *28c*
14. Intitled] intiled *29*

19. Whereas] Where-|as *28c*
20–1. Corporation-town] *Corporation-|town 28c*

56. Vice-roys~ *29–30*] ~, *28c*
TITLE OF THE ORIGINAL PAMPHLET:
A Short VIEW OF THE STATE OF
IRELAND. *28a–b, 35–38*
HEADNOTE ADDED *35–38*:
Written in the Year 1727.
59–60. practised~ . . . Court,] ~, . . . ~~
28c–30
59. method] METHOD *38⁸*
65. happens] happen *35–38*
67. Contradictors *28a–b catchword*]
Con-|dictors *28a–b* [*error at page break;
catchword correct*]
68. cordially] *ital. 35–38*
68. or] and *29–30*
68. obligingly] *ital. 35–38*
77. Conveniencies] Conveniences *35¹²*
78. into other] ~ others *28c*; to other *30*
83. manufactured, *28c–35*] ~~ *28a–b*
89. Liberty] Priviledge *35–38*
89. Countries~] ~, *28–38* [*leading to syn-
tactic confusion which 30 attempted to
remedy*:]
90. them,] them~ to export their Goods
over the World, *30*
94. Applications~ *29–38*] ~, *28*
100. Eighth] Eight *28c*
100. Prince . . . Administrator *35–38*]
Princes . . . Administrators *28–30*
109. Country~] ~, *28c–30*
116. publick] pub- *29 variant state*
118. the People *35–38*] a People *28–30*
[*35–38 avoid repetition*]
123. recollect; *30–38*] ~, *28–29*
124. these, *30*] ~; *28–29*; ~: *35–38*
144. manufactured. *35–38*] ~, *28a–b, 29–
30*; ~~ *28c*
144–5. of which however we are only
defective in] *line om. 28c–30*
149–50. bestowed us so liberally]
bestowed on us so liberally *29–30*; hath
bestowed so liberally on this Kingdom
35–38
152. this Kingdom] *Ireland 35–38*
154. hath] has *35¹²*
159. this~] this Privilege, *35–38*
160. Power~] ~, *28c–38* [*emphasizing*
'Power']
164. unto] on to *29–30*
167. uncontroverted] unconverted *28a*
167. Name, *28c–38*] ~~ *28a–b*
167. my L— C— J— *W*—'s] my

L—C—J—W—'s *28*; my L— C— J—
W—d's *29–30*; Lord Chief Justice
Whitshed's *35–38*
168. LIBERTAS] *35–38 add footnote*:
Liberty and my native Country.
169. Perjuring] —— *35M, cancelled state*
170. Patients~] ~, *28c–38*
173. decide *28c–38*] divide *28a–b*
174. whole] *om. 35¹²*
177. leave] leaves *35¹²*
191. Court] Courts *28c–30*
196. Silver;] ~, *28a–b, 29–30*; Sliver, *28c*;
Silver; 35–38
206. in great quantity] *om. 35–38*
211–12. Liberty, Trade, Manufactures,
Inhabitants, Money] *ital. 35–38*
212. privilege of Coining] *ital. 35–38*
212–13. Industry, Labour] *ital. 35–38*
213. Improvement of Lands] *ital. 35–38*
213. half of] half *35–38*
216. North, 28c–38] ~~ *28a–b*
216. casual, *28c–38*] ~~ *28a–b*
220. C——rs] *Commissioners 35–38*
227. Dyet~] ~; *29*
229. Seaport-Towns, the] ~. The *28*; ~;
the *29–38*
232. these] those *35–38*
235. Irony] Journey *28a, Mi.* [*Note*:
'Journey' is an error, from the compositor's eyeskip. *Mi*, however, admiringly
describes the unauthorized metaphor as
'this pathetick Expression'.]
237. travelling in] ~ into *35¹²*
237. Ysland] Island *28a*; Iceland *30*
243. Butter-milk] *ital. 28c–30*
243. Potatoes] *ital. 28c–30*
244. a Shoe] Shoe *35¹²*
249. magnus] magna *35–38*. [*In the*
Miscellanies, *vol. ix (1742)*, 'magna' is corrected to 'magnus' in a list of errata.]
253. Tenants, *28c–30*] ~~ *28a–b*
254. Interest, *29–35, 38¹²*] ~~ *28, 38⁸*
254. Countries~ *28a–b, 29–35⁸*] ~, *28c,
35¹²–38*
254. Wealth, 28c–38] ~~ *28a–b*
260. themselves *35–38*] they *28–30*
[*causing an ambiguous pronoun reference*]
261. Buildings] Building *35¹²*
264. Country] Countty *35¹²* [*foul case*]
266. Gold; *29–38*] ~, *28*
273. Custom-house] Custom-|house *28*
274. that] who *35–38*

279. *Pharoah*] *Pharoach 28c*; *Pharaoh 35^12*,   283. and_∧] ~, *35^8, 38*
    38^12   290. Town_∧ *28c–30*] ~, *28a–b*
282. these] those *35–38*   297. Kingdom] Kindgom *28a–b*

No. 16

28 *First edition*
[drop-head title:] THE | 𝕴ntelligencer. | [rule] | NUMB. XVI. | [rule] | *Sed virum verâ virtu⌐te⌐ vivere animatum addecet,* | *Fortiterq; innoxium vacare adverſum adverſarios.* Enn: | [rule] | [text, pp. 2–8]

Pot 8°: *A⁴*; pp. *1* 2–8; *1* drop-head, *1*–8 text, 8 'FINIS.'
    Copies collated. Forster, Illinois, Taylor, TCD, Yale.

Fg
Mrs Harding's edition (*28*) was reprinted anonymously in *Fog's Weekly J.*, 11 Jan. 1728/9 (see Appendix D). *Fog's* softened the references to the Father and George. I have recorded important substantive variants both as evidence of the felt danger of Sheridan's language and to show the text to which two contemporary replies were directed (Appendix G).
    Copy collated. BL.

Later editions
28 was reprinted in *29*, which in turn was reprinted in *30* and *32*. In turn, *32* was reprinted in the 12° *Miscellanies* (*33^12*), in Fairbrother's *Miscellanies*, vol. iii (*33F*), in the 12° *Miscellanies* of 1736, vol. iii, and (again as though Swift's) in *A Supplement to Dr. Swift's and Mr. Pope's Works* (Dublin: Powell, 1739). The fol-lowing record lists substantive variants (only) for *29*, *30*, and *32*, the latter text of interest because presumably edited by Pope.

Copy-text: *28*, Forster copy. *Variant readings* are recorded from the following texts, listed in the following order:

28–29–30–32

MOTTO. *vacare*] *vocare 29–30*
MOTTO. *adversum*] *adversos Fg*
MOTTO. om. *32, adding title*:
    A LETTER TO THE
    INTELLIGENCER.
1. Mr. *Intelligencer.*] SIR, *32*
3. *Son . . . Father*] Stranger . . . Flesh and
    Blood *Fg*
4. meet with from mine] receive from
    my Brothers *Fg*
10. oftentimes] often- | times *28*
23. with an Account of my *Father's*
    behaviour,] om. *Fg*
28. *Kick-shaws*] Kick-|shaws *28*
29. dispose] dspose *28*
34. are_∧ *32*] ~, *28–30, Fg*

37. quitted] qnitted *28*
38. Manly] many *Fg*
39. *Pitching*] Piching *28*
46. he] and paying Interest for great
    Debts, he *Fg*
59. easily] om. *Fg*
75. School] Shool *28*
77. my *Father* uses all his Interest] all
    Interest is used *Fg*
83. prevailed upon my *Father*, to join]
    join'd with —— *Fg*
89. Presbyterian] *Presbyteryean 28. [Note:
    this spelling, if not a misprint, may show that
    Sheridan accented the penult.*]
97. Project;] ~_∧ *28*
104. a] in *32*

105. unkindness] Forgetfulness *Fg*

110. Intercepted.] *32 adds signature*: PATRICK.

118. way,] ~∧ *28*

119. your *Father*] —— *Fg*

125. last *Fg, 29, 30, 32*] least *28. [Note: the reading 'least' does not logically support the rhetorical thrust here.*]

128. Father] —— *Fg*

132. detected). You may find∧] detected)∧ you ~ ~, *28* [*garbled here, perhaps because the compositor omitted something in the manuscript*]

141. Witchcraft] Witch-|craft *28*

146–7. I am . . . *Intelligencer.*] I am, yours, *&c. Fg*

No. 17

28a *First edition, first impression*

THE | 𝕴ntelligencer. | [rule] | NUMB. XVII. | [rule] | *Quan⌐ſi⌐um ⌐st⌐agna Tagi rudibus ⌐ſi⌐i⌐ll⌐antia veni | E⌐ffl⌐uxere decus! quanto pretioſa meta⌐ll⌐o | Hermi ripa micat; quantas per Lydia culta | Deſpumat rutilas dives Pa⌐ct⌐olus arenas.* | Claudian. | [rule] | [ornament: fountain with dolphins] | [rule] | *DUBLIN:* | Printed by S. HARDING, next Door to | the *Crown* in *Copper-A⌐ll⌐ey* 1728

Pot 8°: *A*⁴; pp. *1–2* 3–8; *1* title, *2* blank, *3* drop-head: [double rule] | The *Intelligencer·* | [text], 3–8 text; 8 'FINIS.'

Copies collated. Illinois, NLI, TCD. The TCD copy is 12°—i.e., with horizontal chain lines; apparently Mrs Harding was using the portion of a sheet left over from another job.

A corrected state of the outer forme has the last line of the title-page reset, with a period after '1728', and some resetting at the top of p. 5, but no variants affecting the text.

Copies collated. Forster, Huntington, RIA.

28b *Second impression*

[Title-page as *28a*, except:] THE | 𝕴ntelligencer, | . . . | Claudian, | [rule] | [ornament: fountain with dolphins] | [double rule] | *DUBLIN:* | . . . next D or to | [last line omitted]

Title-page almost entirely reset; some resetting on other pages and considerable deterioration around the edges of the pages. A careless production even by Mrs Harding's standards.

Copy collated. Taylor.

Later editions

28 was reprinted in *29*, which in turn was reprinted in *30* and *32*. In *32* there are no substantive variants, except for the addition of a title, 'A Second LETTER TO THE INTELLIGENCER', and the deletion of the concluding reply. *32* was reprinted in *33¹²*, *33F*, and *36¹²*, and (again as though Swift's) in *A Supplement to Dr. Swift's and Mr. Pope's Works* (Dublin: Powell, 1739).

Copy-text: *28a* (NLI copy). *Variant readings* (substantives only) are listed for the following texts in the following order:

28a–28b–29–30–32

MOTTO. *Quantum . . . venis 29–30*]
  Quanstum . . . veni 28
8. of] *om. 28b*; in *29–30*
9. than ever∧ *29–30*] then ~, *28*
14. Counter; 29–30] ~, *28*
16. But] But But *29*
24. unnecessary] unecessary *28*
30. especially;] ~∧ *29–30*; specially; *28b*
56. Coaches,] ~? *28*; *emended from 28 catch-*
  word on previous page
57. Neighbours?] ~∧ *28*
58. Great-Brittain] *Great-Brittæin 28*
61. says,] ~. *28*

62. it,] ~. *28*
62. out.] ~, *28*
72. when] When *28*
74. unhabited] uninhabited *29–30*
77. expensive?] ~. *28*
79. Man∧ say] ~, ~ *28*
81. where] were *30*
82. business?] ~∧ *28*
86. Beggary?] ~. *28*
98–106. *om. 32*
103. Treasure.] ~, *28*
103–4. Gold-Finder,] ~. *28*

No. 18

28 *The first edition*
THE | 𝕴ntelligencer, | [rule] | NUMB. XVIII. | [rule] | *Hic dies anno redeunte*
feᵣſtˀus. | Hor: | [rule] | [ornament: fountain with dolphins] | [double rule] |
DUBLIN: | Printed by S. HARDING next Door to | the *Crown* in *Copper-*
Aᵣllˀey

Pot 8°: *A⁴*; pp. *1* 2–8; *1* title, 2–8 text, 8 '*FINIS.*'
  Copies collated. Forster, Illinois, RIA, Taylor, TCD.

Later editions
28 was reprinted in *29*, and *29* in *30*.

Copy-text: *28* (Forster copy). *Variant readings* (substantives only) are listed
from the following texts in the following order:

                         28–29–30

28. Merchants] poor Merchants *29–30* [*a*
  perverse corruption]
31. from] of *30*
53. Represented] Representd *28*
58. therewith] there-|with *28*
78. endeavour] endavour *28*
81. Barbarous] Babarous *28*
87. inhumanly] inhumanely *29–30*

90. We] *no paragraph 28–30*
91. Time.] ~∧ *28*
114–15. cheap, and considering that]
  cheap, and that *28*; cheap; especially
  since *29–30* [*clearly 28 is corrupt*]
126. that] the *29–30*
131–7. *POSTSCRIPT. . . . in General.*]
  om. 29–30

No. 19

28 *The first edition*
THE | 𝕴ntelligencer. | [rule] | NUMB. XIX. | [rule] | *Having on the* 12th *of*
Oᵣctˀober *laᵣſtˀ, receiv'd* | *a LETTER Sign'd* Andrew Dealer, *and* | Patrick
Pennylefs; *I believe the following* | PAPER, *juᵣſtˀ come to my Hands, will be* | *a*
fuᵣffiˀcient Anfwer to it. | [rule] | *Sic vos non vobis vellera fertis ovos.* | Virg. | [rule] |
[ornament: basket] | [rule] | *DUBLIN* | Printed by S. HARDING, next Door to
| the *Crown* in *Copper-Aᵣllˀey* 1728

Pot 8°: A⁸; $4 signed; pp. *1–2* 3–15 *16*; *1* title, *2* blank, *3* drop-head: [double rule] | THE | Intelligencer, &c. | [text]; 3–15 text, 15 '*FINIS.*' *16* blank.

Copies collated. Forster, Illinois, NLI (2), Taylor, TCD. The last line of the title-page does not print in the Forster and Illinois copies.

Later editions

The essay was reprinted, apropos of 'the unhappy Condition of the Protestants of the Northern Parts of' Ireland, in *Fog's Weekly J.*, 1 Mar. 1729 (see Appendix D; BL copy collated). By that time the pace of emigration from the North had stepped up, and public concern over it had heightened. As usual, *28* was reprinted in *29* and *29* in *30*. Pope omitted the essay from *32*, and it next appeared in Faulkner's editions, vol. iv: *35⁸* was copied from *29*, with considerable emendation, at least some of it authorial. Then *35¹²* was printed from *35⁸* with only a few changes. The available evidence suggests that *38⁸* was printed from *35¹²* and was itself the source for *38¹²*. The essay appears also in the usual derivatives of *35⁸*, including Fairbrother's fourth volume (1735).

During the Irish coinage debates of 1736–7, *Intelligencer* 19 attracted what must have been, to Swift, unwelcome attention. In no. 19 Swift had dealt with the disparity in the value of gold and silver by recommending that the value of gold be lowered. When in 1736–7 he opposed lowering the gold and instead recommended raising silver, *Intelligencer* 19 was on at least two occasions reprinted to taunt him:

A | LETTER | FROM THE | Revd. *J.S.D.S.P.D.* | TO A | Country Gentleman | IN THE | *North* of *IRELAND.* | [rule] | [ornament] | [double rule] | Printed in the Year, MDCCXXXVI.

8°: *A⁴*; pp. *1–2* 3–8. Reprinted from *35⁸*; the printer was, on the evidence of the title-page ornament, S. Powell. (For this information I am indebted to the TCD file of Irish printers' ornaments.) Teerink's supposition (T–S 667, p. 331) that this pamphlet replies to *A Letter from a Gentleman in the North of Ireland, to His Friend in Dublin, in Relation to the Regulation of the Coin* (Dublin, 1736) is incorrect. Copy examined: BL.

[drop-head title:] THE | *Hibernian* Patriot: | OR, A | VINDICATION of Dean *Swift*, in a LETTER to | Mr. *G. F.* in *DUBLIN.*

½°: 2 sides, one column. The last five paragraphs only of the essay are reprinted from *35⁸*. The letter, dated '*Belfast, Sept.* 15, 1737', reads as follows:

> Some malicious Persons among Us have been so ungrateful to that truly worthy Patriot *J. S. D. S. P.* as to give out, upon the long wish'd-for Reduction of our Gold Coin, he hung out a black Flag on the highest Pinacle of St. *Patrick*'s Steeple.
>
> As We of the Linen-Manufacture have particular Obligations to that Gentleman, I hope you'll be so kind to print the following Paper, which will be a sufficient Vindication of him, and an Obligation to *M. B.* Linen-Draper.

(For the black-flag episode, see *Poems*, iii. 840–1, and *Corresp.* ed. Ball, vi. 47.) Copy collated: Gilbert.

The essay was quoted, to much the same derisory effect, in *Some Reflections, Concerning the Reduction of Gold Coin in Ireland. Upon the Principles of the Dean of St. Patrick's and Mr. Lock: Humbly Submitted to the Good People of Ireland* (Dublin, 1737), 9–12. See also *An Unprejudic'd Enquiry into the Nature and Consequences of the Reduction of Our Gold* (Dublin, 1737), 5. Fourteen years later Swift's 1737 turnabout was remembered, though hazily, by Richard Pococke as 'a strong proof of his want of principle and integrity'. (Pococke to Lord Orrery, 31 Dec. 1751, in one of Orrery's copies of his *Remarks*, Harvard 16423.3.4*, p. 87 of the leaves added at end.)

Copy-text: *28* (NLI S.C.99b copy). *Variant readings* (substantives only) are listed from the following texts in the following order:

$$28\text{–}29\text{–}30\text{–}35^8\text{–}35^{12}\text{–}38^8\text{–}38^{12}$$

HEADING. *prefatory note added in 35–38*, above the note beginning 'Having on the':
N. B. *In the following Discourse the* Author *personates a Country Gentleman in the North of* Ireland. *And this Letter is supposed as directed to the* Drapier.
MOTTO. *oves*] *ovos 28*
MOTTO. Virg.] *om. 35–38*
BELOW MOTTO, *note added in 35–38*:
Written in the Year 1728.
5. till] until *35–38*
6. to be not] not to be *29–38*
12. Shop-keepers] Shop-|keepers *28*
14. Conveniencies] Conveniences *35*
16. kinds] Kind *35–38*
17. till] until *35–38*
18. among us] us *35–38* [*avoiding repetition of* 'among']
19–20. *Ale-house . . . Brandy shop*] Ale-houses . . . Brandy-shops *38¹²*
29. other] *om. 35–38* [*avoiding repetition of* 'other']
29. though] although *35–38*
34. least] last *38⁸*
35. of] They consider not *35–38*
36. of half] that half *35–38*
37. sent annually] are annually sent *35–38*
37. and] with *35–38*
38. excepted for our Sins] except ~ ~ ~ *29–30*; *om. 35–38*
38. keeps] keep *29–38*
40. so often] soo ften *28*
47. too] so *35–38*

49. inconveniences] Inconveniencies *29–30*, *38*
49. greater] great *35¹²–38*
50. timely] tamely *35–38*
55–6. the Lord Lieutenant] *35–38 add note*:
The Lord Carteret.
59. *easy*] made easy *35–38*
59. *that*] this *35–38*
64. came] come *38⁸*
66. *Shop-keepers*] Shop-|keepers *28*
70. easy] uneasy *38⁸*
72. 6 *d.*] and 6 *d. 35–38*
74. dare] dares *29–30* [*spoiling the ironic subjunctive*]
77. in *thirty 35–38*] to ~ *28–30*
106. will] will I *35¹²–38*
116. Tooth-ach] Tooth-|ach *28*
116. lest our *35–38*] lesty our *28*; least our *29–30*
116. politick] Politicks *30–38*
117. Disaffection.] ~ₐ *28*
118. Crowley] Cowley *28*; Crawley *29–38*
120. Exigence] Exigency *38*
125. degree] Degrees *30*
128. till] until *35–38*
*132. Money*ₐ *29–38*] ~, *28*
133. conveniences] Conveniencies *30*, *38*
138. would never] could never *35–38*
149. Farmers, *30*] ~ₐ *28*
149. Bargainsₐ *29–38*] ~, *28*
150. Rack-rent] Rack-|rent *28*
159. ago, *29–38*] ~; *28*
159. to] of *30*
161. Landₐ *29–35*] ~, *28*

166. Price‸ *29–35*] ~, *28*
168. at all] all *30*
175. as of our] as our *38¹²*
176. come *30–38*] came *28–29*
188. satisfactory] satisactory *28*
193. Tract of] Tractof *28*
199. Insults] Insulst *28*
201. pay‸] ~, *28*
202. Now] now *28*
203. inclines] incline *30*, *38*

204. false] fair *38¹²*
205. so,] *om. 35–38*
206. have] have also *35–38*
214. discourage] discourse *30*
215. Yet] *new paragraph 35¹²–38*
216. effects] Effect *35–38*
219. Enemy] Enemey *28*
227. false,] false, and *38¹²*
228. beside] besides *35¹²–38*
239. Obedient] Obidient *28*

No. 20

28 *The first edition*
THE | 𝕴ntelligencer. | [rule] | NUMB. XX. | [rule] | Dean Smedley | Gone to ſeek
his | FORTUNE. | [rule] | *Per varios caſus pertot diſcrimina rare Rum·* | [rule] |
[ornament: cherub's head with wings] | [rule] | *DUBLIN*: Printed in the Year,
MDCCXXIX.

Pot 8⁰: *A*⁴; pp. *1–2* 3–8; *1* title, *2* A ⌐ſh⌐ort HISTORY of the *DEAN*, by
way of i⌐ll⌐u⌐ſt⌐ration., 3 drop-head: [headpiece: FIVE SHIL.] | THE |
INTELLIGENCER | [rule], 3–6 character and poem, 7 head: row of type orna-
ments; 7–8 text, beginning '**ALL** Gentlemen'; 8 tailpiece: cock and '*FINIS.*'

Production. The new typographical style and the absence of a printer's name
and address suggest that this number was produced after Mrs Harding left
Copper Alley and combined forces with Nicholas Hussey.

Copies collated. Forster, Huntington, NLI (2), Rothschild, RIA, TCD.

Textual history of the character of Smedley
The character was first printed in the (London) *Daily Post* (**DP**), 13 Feb.
1728/9 (copy collated: BL); it was reprinted in the *Pol. State* (**PS**), 37 (Feb.
1728/9), 209, with minor variants, nearly all accidentals. Copies collated: BL
(4: 3 of the first issue and 1 of the second), Institute of Historical Research,
London.

The character, though the *Daily Post* attributes it to Smedley, survives in a
clean, uncorrected copy of a later version, in the handwriting of Smedley's
then assistant Thomas Birch (see introductory note to no. 20):

> *Reverendus Decanus, Jonathan Smedley, ultramque expertus Fortunam; Theologiâ
> instructus, in Poesi exercitatus, politioribus excultus Literis*[,] *parcè pius, impius
> minimé, invisus multis, exosus quibusdam, amicus omnibus, Veritatis indagator,
> Libertatis, opinione, Scriptis, et cultu Dei, Assertor; per varios Casus, per Famam,
> atque Infamiam; mente sanâ, Corpore sano, volens, lætusque, Quinquagenarius et
> ultra, ad Res Familiares restaurandas, augendasque et ad prædicandum Indos inter
> Orientales, in Civitate Maderas, et Arce Sancti Georgii, Evangelium, transfretatus
> est.* | *Feb. 15th 1728/9* | *Fata vocant, revocentque precamur.* | *Saturday.*

(Abbreviations expanded. Thomas Birch collection of biographical anecdotes, BL MS Add. 4223, fo. 198; I am indebted to Margaret Nickson of the

BL Dept. of Manuscripts for the opinion that the handwriting is that of the young Birch.)

The eighteenth-century antiquary Michael Lort's somewhat careless transcript of the character, from a printed text, is on the flyleaf of the Bodleian copy of Smedley's anonymous *Poems on Several Occasions* (London: Richardson, 1721).

Later editions of Intelligencer 20

From *28* were reprinted both the very rare **29a** (see the General Bibliographical Note) and *30*. No. 20 was next reprinted in 1776 (from *30*) in John Nichols's *Supplement to Dr. Swift's Works* (London: Bowyer and Nichols), 561–3n. This is T–S 88, the large 8° edition, examined in A. C. Elias's copy. Here Nichols prints the character and poem in a long footnote to ?Swift's *Epistle upon an Epistle* and attributes the poem only to 'the author of *The Intelligencer*'. By 1779, Nichols tentatively decided that the poem was Swift's; it appears, entitled 'Inscription Intended for a Mezzotinto of Dean Smedley, Written by Himself. With a Burlesque Translation by Dr. Swift', in the so-called small 8° edition of the *Supplement*, iii. 251–3 (T–S 90, vol. xxvi, or T–S 91, vol. xxvii) and in the 18° edition (T–S 92, xxvii. 262–5); Teerink copies examined. However, Nichols now prints the texts in his catchall section for doubtful material, 'Poems by Dr. *Swift* and His Friends', and in a footnote he retains his original noncommittal attribution 'to the author of *The Intelligencer*'. Neither the character nor the poem is present in the 4° edition of the *Works* or in its *Supplement* (T–S 87).

Copy-text: *28* (Forster copy). Substantive variants only are noted, except that all departures of *28* from *PS* are recorded. I suspect that in *28* the character was set from a manuscript transcription of the *PS* text. The quotation marks beginning each line of the Latin character are silently omitted. In *30* the character is displayed in centred phrases, like a monumental inscription. *Variant readings* from the following texts are recorded in the following order:

DP–PS–28–29a–30

MOTTO. *per tot 30*] *pertot 28–29a*
MOTTO. *rare Rum*] *rerum 29a–30*
INTRODUCTION
 4. to] in *30*
16. himself.] *After this, 28 begins a new page, inserting a headpiece and the drop-head*
 THE | *INTELLIGENCER.*
17. From] **F**ROM *28–29a*; *This from 30 (no new paragraph)*
18. **A**BOUT] **A**Bout *28*
18. time∧] ~, *PS*
18. published] publish'd *PS*
18. *Dayly*] *Daily PS*
18. of] *om. 29a*
19. that] We hear that *DP* [*this is the beginning of the DP account*]

19. *Mezzotinto*] Mezzotinto *PS*
20. *Dean*] Dean *PS*
20. Written] said to be written *PS*
21. Himself] the Dean *PS*
22. **R**EVERENDUS] **R***Everendus 28*
22. Smedley: *PS*] ~∧ *28*; *Smedly∧ 29a*
22. *instructus DP*] *iustructus 28*; instructus *PS*
25. *Author*] Auctor *30*
26. VETULÆ.] ~: *PS*
29. *Corpore*;] ~, *PS*
29. *plus quam*] plusquam *PS*
30. *et*] & *PS*
31. *Februarii*] Februariis *PS*
31. *Sancti*] Sanctæ *29a*
32. *Æquinoxium*;] ~, *PS*

POEM
1. **THE**] The *28*
19. of] off *29a*

CONCLUSION
21. the] *om. 30*

Appendix C

Reprinted from the *London J.*, 20 Apr. 1728 (BL copy); the *Dublin Weekly J.* text, which Swift may have seen, differs only in a few accidentals.

Appendix D

Mist's, *Fog's*, and *Brice's* are quoted from the BL copies, the *Flying-Post* from Bodleian copies.

Appendix E

[drop-head:] THE TRUE | CHARACTER | OF THE | INTELLIGENCER. | [rule] | Written by *PADY DROGHEDA*. | [rule] | [text]

[colophon:] Printed in the Year 1728. *FINIS.*

$\frac{1}{2}$°: 1 side, 1 column.
    Copy transcribed. Huntington.

Appendix G

(*a*)

Printed from the only known copy, that in the Beinecke Library, Yale University:

A | LETTER | TO THE | INTELLIGENCER | [rule] | *HONOS ALIT ARTES.* | [rule] | Written by a Young GENTLEMAN, of | *Fourteen* Years Old. | [rule] | [ornament: fountain with dolphins] | [rule] | *DUBLIN*: Printed by S. HARDING, next | Door to the *Crown* in *Copper-A⌐ll⌐ey*, 1728.

Pot 8°: A⁴; $2 signed; pp. *1–2 3–7 8*; *1* title, *2* blank, *3–7* text, *8* blank.

I have silently emended the accidentals to prevent misreading. Substantive emendation:

46. that 'tis] 'tis

(*b*)

The Weekly Journal: or, The British Gazetteer, no. 191 (18 Jan. 1728/9).
    Copies collated. Bodleian, BL.

Emendations:

127. Masquerades] Masqurades
154. Brouge] Bronge

156. gloss∧ *over*,] *gloss, over*∧
180. than] that

(*c*)

The Daily Journal (London), no. 2523 (8 Feb. 1728/9).
  Copy transcribed. BL.

Emendations:
285. reinstated] re-|*instated*

Appendix H

The *Jntelligencer.* | [rule] | NUMB. XX. | [rule] | *A Po⌐ſt⌐hum⌐us⌐* Worke
Communicated, | [rule] | [rule] | [ornament] | [rule] | *DUBLIN:* | Printed for the
Author. 1728.

8°: *A*⁴; pp. *1* 2–8. The printing is crude, with two sizes of text type.

  Copies collated. TCD; Forster 8545 (leaf *A*1 only). The Forster leaf is
described in Teerink as 'another Number XX' and 'the second No. XX' (T–S
666, p. 330).

  Publication. Printed by Christopher Goulding and published during the
week 23–8 Dec. 1728. The *Old Dublin Intelligence* reported on 31 Dec., 'We
hear Complaints have been made to some of our Magistrates against one
Goolden, a Romish Printer in this City, for publishing a Vile and Flagitious
Paper, last Week, under the Title of D—n Sw—ts Intelligencer, No: XX. for
which 'tis Expected he will, if possible, be Punish'd.' The same paper
reported on 14 January 1728/9,

> Yesterday one *Golden*, (Famous, for being the *Editor* of the Flagitious
> Paper, publish'd under the Title of the *Intelligencer*, No. XX,) publish'd a
> *Scandalous, Nonsensical and Affrontful Copy of Verses*, on the Death of the
> above Mr. *Wingfield* and his Lady, for which, 'tis expected, he will be
> call'd to an Account, and punished, as well as for the forementioned,
> *Intelligencer* for which due Prosecution is commenced against him, by
> some Persons in Power; The said *Golden* is the Person who Printed the
> Scandalous Elegy on the Death of the late Mr. *Fortune* . . .

—i.e., *An Elegy on the Much Lamented Death of Mr. Robert Fortune, our Lord Mayor's
Clerk, who Departed this Life on Monday the 18th of this Instant December 1727. At his
House in Loftis's Lane* (copy: TCD). Not much is otherwise known of Goulding,
but I am indebted to M. Pollard for the information that he was in 1735
admitted as a quarter brother to the Guild of St Luke the Evangelist, the
Dublin stationers' guild, and that his will was proved in 1746. Goulding's
spurious *Intelligencer* is mistakenly listed as *No. 99 D—n Sw—ts Intelligencer* in
R. L. Munter's *A Handlist of Irish Newspapers 1685–1750* (London, 1960), 20,
whence the error is carried to the *New Cambridge Bibliography of English
Literature*, ii. 1384.

  In the colophon of Swift's *Journal of a Dublin Lady*, published in Jan. or early
Feb. 1728/9, Sarah Harding mentioned that at her shop 'Gentlemen may be
furnished with the *Intelligencer*, from No 1, to No 19.' This note was probably

designed as a repudiation of Goulding's pamphlet. The true no. 20, published in May 1729, of course also served to discredit Goulding, if further discrediting were needed.

Copy-text. TCD. Several obvious misprints are silently corrected. Above the motto, the original has 'To the Intelligencer'. Other emendations:

22. *pine;*] ~,
22. *Arts*] *Art's*
51. Afflictions,] ~_∧

124. succeeded] succeed
132. Historicrittical] Historicrillical

Appendix I

Copy-text is the 1729 edition; there are no substantive variants in *30*.

Appendix J

Copy-text: Rylands English MS 659, items 9–10 (fig. 3). The manuscript is in a hasty, sometimes small, and occasionally almost illegible jotting hand. I have not tried to reproduce all the resultant oddities; for example, when Swift writes hastily he uses a mark which looks like 'te' for 'the', and I am content to reproduce it as 'the'. (I am grateful to David Woolley for sharing his notes on the MS with me.)

(*a*) On two sides of half a folded sheet, endorsed 'Hints | Educ^{tn} de dames | pour une Intelligencer'. On the other half is 'Gay Maitre d'hotel', Swift's draft of *To Mr. Gay*. See George Mayhew, 'A Draft of Ten Lines from Swift's Poem to John Gay', *BJRL* 37 (1954), 257–62.

TITLE. Education of Ldyes] *seems to have been added later*
35. balast] *Swift first wrote, then crossed out* 'ball'

(*b*) A single leaf, endorsed 'Intelligenc^{rs}'.

Appendix K

[drop-head title:] [four rows of type flowers] | To the Author of those Intelligencers | printed at *Dublin*, to which is pre- | fix'd the following Motto, | *Omne vafer vitium ridenti* Flaccus *amico* | *Tangit, & admi^rſſ^rus circum pr^rae[⌐]cordia ludit.* | *Perſius.* | Being a Defence of the Plantations again^rſt[⌐] the | virulent Aſperſions of that Writer, and such | as copy after him. | [one row of type flowers] | [motto; factotum and text begins]

[colophon on p. 10:] NEW-YORK, Printed and Sold by *J. Peter Zenger.* 1733.

2°: *A*–B² C1; pp. 1–10.

Copy collated. New York Public Library. Quotation marks have been silently deleted; quoted and indirectly quoted matter is amply marked by the italics of the original, here retained.

Emendations:

35. Villains,] ~ .
50. because] *bocause*
53. Bedstead] *Beadstead*
110. their Ruins] thier ~
129. to] *om.*

161. Continent] Countinent
180. thereby] there-|by
184. which] whhich
228. abandon'd] *abondon'd*

Index

The text, introductions, appendices, and notes are indexed. Members of the nobility are entered under their best-known names—ordinarily their highest titles (but see Bacon, Carteret, Harley, Orrery).

Important subject headings: *Dublin, England, London,* Intelligencer, *Ireland, Sheridan,* and *Swift.*

TS = Thomas Sheridan (1687–1738); JS = Jonathan Swift

Abercorn, James Hamilton, 6th Earl of 115
Acheson, Anne, Lady 25, 31, 84, 206
Acheson, Sir Arthur, Bt. 25, 84, 206
Addison, Joseph 115, 116, 119, 127, 234, 266
  Cato 67
  Old Whig 116
  see also Tatler; Spectator
Aeacus 215
Aelian 91
Aesop 91, 195, 196, 210, 212, 282
Agreeable Companion (1745) 306, 323, 325
aldermen 48, 79, 81
ale 53, 95, 98
Alexander the Great 161, 163
Allestree, Richard 127
almanacs 111, 143
ambition 79
American colonies 276–82
  coinage 210–11
  Irish immigrants 195, 280; *see also* Ireland: emigration from
  postal service, to Ireland 212, 216
  see also Delaware; Maryland; Massachusetts; New Jersey; New York; Pennsylvania; Virginia
Americans, Native 211
Amhurst, Nicholas 147
Anacreon 264
anger 165, 166
Anne, Queen 94, 119, 121, 192, 278
Anthony, 'Doctor' 101
apes *see* monkeys
Apollodorus 56, 91, 168
Arabic language 20
Aratus of Soli, *Phaenomena* 215
Arbuckle, James 77, 112; *see also Tribune*
Arbuthnot, John, *History of John Bull* 192

architecture, English 188, 191
Aristophanes, *Clouds* 157
Aristotle 120
  Nicomachean Ethics 73, 77
  On the Heavens 82
  Physics 194, 196
  Politics 175, 182
Arklow, Co. Wicklow 51
Armagh, town 216
Armagh Royal School 14
army 171, 178, 192, 198, 200
  as source of fashionable clothing and diction 120, 318
  barracks 48
  pay 87, 91
  standing 152, 155
  see also Ireland: militia
Artaxerxes 72, 76
Ashe, St George, Bishop of Clogher 67
assemblees 48, 49, 272; *see also* assemblies
assemblies 120, 122
Astley, Thomas 292
Astrea 210, 215
astrology 62
Athena 173, 181
Athens 87–8, 91, 173, 181
Atterbury, Bishop Francis 81
Audouin, John 110–14
Aughrim, Battle of 174, 181
Augustus, Caesar 72, 158
avarice 79, 123
Avianus, fables of 186
Avignon 104, 111, 314

Backsterus *see* Baxter, William
Bacon, Sir Francis, *Essayes* 79, 81, 119, 127, 129
Badgers, a 'great rogue' 275

Baker's News: or, The Whitehall Journal 135
balls 48, 122; *see also* masquerades
Ballyspellan spa, Co. Kilkenny 30
bankers *see* Dublin: bankers
Barber, John 237
Barbon, Nicholas 249
Barlow, Thomas 145
Barrymore, James Barry, 4th Earl of 111,
        314
Bath, order of the 58, 154
Baxter, Richard 186
Baxter, William 264
Bayle, Pierre, *General Dictionary* 304
Bedford, Arthur 67
Bedford, Lucy Russell, Countess of 73,
        77
bees 105, 112, 159
beggars 89, 92, 123, 180, 195
Belfast 205
Bellamy, Daniel, *Back-Gammon* 306
Benefit of Farting (attributed to ?William
        Dobbs) 246
benevolence 167; *see also* charity
Bettesworth, Richard 21
Bible:
    commentaries on 136–46
    Genesis 56, 138, 192, 214
    Exodus 129, 186
    Deuteronomy 174, 192
    1 Samuel 112, 192
    1 Kings 112
    2 Chronicles 112
    Psalms 114, 181, 202
    Proverbs 114
    Ecclesiastes 129
    Jeremiah 232
    Lamentations 173
    Matthew 146, 192, 202, 223
    Luke 192
    Romans 202
    Galatians 186
    Ephesians 186
    Colossians 186
    1 Thessalonians 68
    1 Peter 192
bibliotheques 138, 139, 145
Bill of Rights 215
Bindon, Francis 245
Bingley, Edward 237
Birch, Thomas 136, 145–6, 217, 219, 304,
        335–6
bishops *see* clergy
Blackburne, Archbishop Lancelot 94

Blackmore, Sir Richard 75
blasphemy 75
Blenheim palace 191
Blunder of All Blunders (attributed to TS)
        246
Blunder of All Blunders (Teerink–Scouten
        1217) 246
Bolingbroke, Henry St John, 1st
        Viscount 81, 115, 119, 126–7, 147,
        155
Bologna 111
Bolton, Charles Paulet, 2nd Duke of
        183, 214
bonnyclabber 110, 114
Book of Common Prayer 68, 181
Borneo 159
Boston: Irish immigrants 205
Boswell, James, *Life of Johnson* 146
Boulter, Archbishop Hugh 145, 184
    letters quoted or cited 111, 115, 204,
        205, 214
Bowyer, William, jun. 267, 289, 292, 293;
        see also Intelligencer: Bowyer-Davis
        editions
Boyer, Abel 99
Boyle, Hon. Henry, afterwards Baron
        Carleton of Carleton 118, 126
Boyle, John *see* Orrery
Boyne, Battle of the 174, 181
Bradford, Bishop Samuel 94
Brasidas 157
Bray, Co. Wicklow 51
Bray, Thomas 69
bribery 147, 148, 152, 153
Brice's Weekly Journal 4, 241–2
Bridgeman, Sir Orlando, Bt. 118, 124
Bristol 160
Brooking, Charles, *Map of the City and
        Suburbs of Dublin* (1728) 250
Browne, John, of the Neale 30, 171, 173,
        186, 214
    Essay on Trade in General 182
    Letter to the Author of the Short View 171
    *Lucubrations of Sallmanazor Histrum,
        Esq.* 30
    Plain Dealer's Intelligencer 30
    Scheme of the Money-Matters of Ireland
        172, 184, 196
    Seasonable Remarks on Trade 170, 182
    Temple-Oge Intelligencer 1, 27, 29, 30
Browne, Bishop Peter 112, 203
Buckingham, George Villiers, 2nd Duke
        of 81

Bull, William 216
Burnet, Bishop Gilbert 82, 159, 162, 236
Butler, James *see* Ormonde
Butler, Theophilus *see* Newtownbutler
butter 89, 179
buttermilk 179

Calmet, Augustin 139, 140, 142, 143, 145
Cambridge University 122, 178
Camden, William, *Annales* 201
Camillus, Marcus Furius 199, 202
Campbell, Archibald 146
Campbell, Colen 191
canaries 160
cannibalism 197, 198, 201–2
cards, playing 70–5; *see also* gambling;
    quadrille; whist
Carew, Thomas 77
Carey, Henry 69
Carleton, Baron *see* Boyle, Hon. Henry
Carlisle, Lucy Hay, Countess of 73, 77
Carmarthen, Marquess of *see* Danby
Carnarvon, Robert Dormer, 1st Earl of
    73, 76
Caroline of Ansbach, consort of
    George II 13, 57, 58, 67, 185
carp 160
Carrick ferry, Wexford 54, 56
carrs 89, 92
Carson, James, *Chronology of Some
    Memorable Accidents* 114
Carte, Thomas 13
Carteret, Frances, Lady 13
Carteret, John, 2nd Baron (afterwards
    Earl Granville) 184, 208–9, 214,
    218, 255, 260, 279
    and TS 11, 12, 101
    and Wood's halfpence controversy
    202
Castle Howard 191
Catholic Church:
    in England 97, 140, 143, 236, 278
    in France 140, 146
    in Ireland 102, 104, 189
    in Scotland 188
Cato, Distichs of 156, 162
Cato the younger 72, 76
Cattle Acts 182, 192, 258
Cavan, county 14–15, 21
Cavan Royal School 14
Cavanagh family 198, 201
Cervantes Saavedra, Miguel de 61, 66
chancellors, lord 64

chaplains 95; *see also* clergy
charity 48, 96, 123, 167, 228
charity schools 53, 55–6, 94, 239
charity sermons 239
Charles I 79, 88, 91, 93, 118, 124
    sermons on, as royal martyr 88, 91–2,
        99
Charles II 118, 124, 278
Charles Fort, Kinsale 135, 223
Chelsea *see* London
Chichester, Sir Arthur 198
chimney-sweeps 114
China 160
chinaware 164
Chios 165
Choix de petites pieces du théâtre anglois
    (1756) 304
Church of England 188; *see also* clergy
Church of Ireland 68, 189; *see also* Book
    of Common Prayer; Ireland:
    clergy; preaching
Church of Scotland 188
Cicero 199, 202, 264
    letters 88, 92, 185
    Tusculan Disputations 260
Civil War 118
Clarendon, Edward Hyde, 1st Earl of
    81, 118, 124
Clarke, Henry 128
Claudianus 193, 196
clergy 64, 68, 120
    at the theatre 64, 67–8
    bishops 87, 116
    careers 78–83, 93–9
    see also Ireland: clergy; preaching; TS:
        as clergyman; JS: as clergyman
Clifford, Thomas, 1st Baron Clifford of
    Chudleigh 118, 125
climate 65, 66, 117
Clogher, rectory and deanery of 135,
    136, 218, 223
clothing and dress 109, 120, 121, 128; *see
    also* Ireland: clothing; wigs
coffee houses 120; *see also* Dublin: coffee
    houses; London: White's
    Chocolate House; London: Will's
    Coffee House
Cogan, Francis 244, 247, 293
Coghill, Marmaduke, letters 26, 27, 29,
    32, 204, 216, 230, 231
coinage *see* American colonies: coinage;
    Ireland: coinage; Wood's
    halfpence controversy

coins, cutting and clipping 28, 210–11, 215–16

Coleraine, Co. Londonderry 205

Collection of Poems on Several Occasions; Publish'd in The Craftsman (1731) 322

Collins, Anthony, *Discourse Concerning Ridicule and Irony in Writing* 236

comedy 61, 66

commedia dell' arte 66

Compton, Sir Spencer 154

Congress of Soissons 154–5

Congreve, William:
  Concerning Humour in Comedy 60
  Way of the World 113

Connaught 205

Conolly, William 185

Considerations on Two Papers Lately Published (1728) 171

Constitution Explain'd, in Relation to the Dependency of the House of Lords 116

conversation 59–60, 63, 72–3, 75, 156–62, 273

cookery 167–8; *see also* diet; Ireland: diet

Coonuley 317

Corinth 175, 182

Cork, city 85

Cork, county 179

Cork and Orrery, 5th Earl of *see* Orrery

Country Journal: or, The Craftsman 57, 136, 152, 231, 292, 322
  and *Intelligencer* no. 12: 27, 29, 33, 147, 321

courtiers 63, 78

Court of Requests (Palace of Westminster) 149, 153

Coventry, Sir Henry 118, 125

cows 160

Craftsman see *Country Journal*

Craggs, James, the younger (1686–1721) 119, 127

Creech, Thomas 232

crime and criminals 57, 64, 71, 73, 194, 234; *see also* bribery

Cromwell, Oliver 85, 87, 88, 102, 278, 279

Cromwellians 84, 102
  desecration of Irish churches 84–8

Crowley, Sir Ambrose 210, 215

cruelty 167

Cuilcagh, Co. Cavan *see* Quilca

Cumberland, Duke of *see* William, Prince

Cumpstey, Andrew 246

cursing 72, 75

Cypselus 175, 182

Daily Journal 145, 196, 256, 292

Daily Post 219, 220, 292, 335

Daily Post-Boy 292, 294, 306

Dalrymple, James, 1st Viscount Stair 192

Damascus 159

Danby, Sir Thomas Osborne, Earl of (afterwards Marquess of Carmarthen and Duke of Leeds) 118, 125, 147

dancing 97, 119, 121, 128; *see also* balls

Daniell, Combra 327

D'Anvers, Caleb, nominal author of the *Craftsman* 68, 147, 153, 321

Davenant, Sir William 76, 77

David (Welsh representative) 253–6

Davies, Sir John 13, 22, 77

Davis, Charles 289, 292, 296; *see also Intelligencer*: Bowyer–Davis editions

Dean Swift's Intelligencer (bibliographic ghost) 338

debt, public 104, 148, 154

Declaratory Act (1719) 183, 214, 215

Defence of the Conduct of the People of Ireland in Their Unanimous Refusal of Mr. Wood's Copper-Money 201

Defoe, Daniel:
  Tour through the Whole Island of Great Britain 185
  True-Born Englishman 69

deism 68, 162

Delany, Patrick 113, 275
  and TS 7, 17, 22
  and the *Intelligencer* 244, 248
  Humanist 244
  Observations upon Lord Orrery's Remarks 156
  Pheasant and the Lark 18, 293

Delaware, Irish immigrants to 205

Demosthenes 199, 202

Dennis, John 60, 66, 69, 145

Derbyshire 98

Derry 205
  Siege of 174, 181

Devil (puppet character) 106, 112

Devonshire, Charles, Earl of *see* Mountjoy

Devonshire, Christian Cavendish, Countess of 73, 77

Devonshire, William Cavendish, 1st
    Duke of 93
dice 70, 75; *see also* gambling
diet 188, 192; *see also* drinking; gluttony;
    England: diet; Ireland: diet;
    Scotland: diet
Dilly, Charles 296
Dingley, Rebecca 22
Diodorus Siculus 56, 91, 215
Diogenes 158, 162
Diomedes 54, 56
Dion of Syracuse 199, 202
discretion 25, 78–81
Distress'd State of the Poor of Ireland (1728)
    249
Dobbs, Arthur 171
Dobbs, ?William, a surgeon 246
Dodington, George Bubb 150, 154
Dodsley, Robert 15, 16
dogs 87, 91, 160
Donatus, Tiberius Claudius 213
Donne, John 77
Dorset, Lionel Cranfield Sackville, 1st
    Duke of 279
Down, county 213
Drapier, cult of 24
    see also JS, as Drapier; JS, Works:
        Drapier's Letters
Drayton, Michael 77
drinking 53, 114, 122, 194, 208; *see also*
    ale; temperance; wine
drinking to the memory of the dead 112,
    200, 202–3
Drogheda 84, 87, 278
    Siege of (1649) 85, 87
Drogheda, Patrick 244–5, 248
dropsy 71
Drumlane manor, Co. Cavan 12
Dryden, John:
    *Author's Apology for Heroic Poetry and
        Poetic License* 60
    *Discourse Concerning the Original and
        Progress of Satire* 66
    Essay of Dramatick Poesy 77
    Evening's Love 66
    Sir Martin Mar-all 105, 112, 314
Dublin, city:
    Abbey Street 250
    aldermen 48
    Anglesea Street 250
    Aungier Street 250
    Bachelor's Walk 250
    balls 48; *see also* assemblees

bankers 51, 172, 180, 185, 209; *see also*
    Ireland: banknotes
barracks 48
Black Dog Prison 114
Blind Quay 38
Bolton Street 250
brewers 249–50
Bridewell Prison 114, 315
building in 195, 249–50, 275
Capel Street 101
charity school movement 55
Christ Church Cathedral 183
Christchurch Place 202
Clarendon Street 250
clergy 64
coffee houses 47; *see also* Dublin:
    Lucas's Coffee House
College Green 72, 112; *see also* Dublin:
    William III, statue of
College of Physicians 269
Copper Alley 38
Cork Hill 77
Cork House 77
courts of law 48, 183
Dawson Street 70, 72, 76, 250
Dublin Castle 82, 250; *see also* Dublin:
    Groom Porter's house; TS,
    Works: *Ode*
Essex Street 246
Foundling Hospital 186
Grafton Street 250
Groom Porter's house 74, 77
Guild of St Luke the Evangelist 338
Henrietta Street 250
houses 249–50
Jervis Street 72
Kildare Street 250
labourers 204
lord mayor of 48
Lucas's Coffee House 4, 74, 77, 131–3
migration to, from the country 249
Molesworth Fields 250
Molesworth Street 250
Newgate Prison 114
Parliament House 48, 275
poorhouse 196
poverty 204, 228; *see also* beggars
St Patrick's Cathedral *see* St Patrick's
    Cathedral (separate entry)
St Stephen's Green 72
Skinner's Row 202
Smock Alley 101
South William Street 250

Dublin (*cont.*)
  'state days' 171
  street life 101, 108–10, 244–5
  streets, new 195
  theatre 48, 61–5, 68
  Tholsel 200
  Trinity College *see* Trinity College,
    Dublin (separate entry)
  weavers 228, 269–70
  William III, memorial celebrations of
    200, 202
  William III, statue of 106, 112, 314
  York Street 250
  see also Ireland
Dublin, county 84
Dublin Intelligence 244
Dublin Journal (Faulkner) 9, 14, 15, 16,
  20, 245, 292
Dublin University *see* Trinity College,
  Dublin
Dublin Weekly Journal 59, 77, 112, 234,
  239, 337
Ducasse, Paschal 218, 223
Dudge, Amos (pseud.) 236
duelling 75
Dun, Lady 269
Dun, Sir Patrick 269
Dunboyne parish, Co. Meath 14
dunces, Irish 31, 222
Duncombe, William 59, 68; essay on *The
  Beggar's Opera* **234–5**
Dundalk, Co. Louth 84, 87, 92
Dunkin, William 244, 248
Dunleer, Co. Louth 84
Dunster, Samuel 19
Dunton, John 7, 69
Du Pin, Louis Ellies 145
Dutch *see* Holland

East India Company 136, 218, 219
economics, mercantile 92, 170, 214
education 9–11, 72, 167, 176, 241–2,
    251–3
  corporal punishment 119, 127
  grammar, study of 8, 120
  languages, study of 241–2, 272; *see also*
    French; Greek; Latin
  moral 116–17, 122–3
  music, study of 272
  of government leaders 123
  of legislators 123
  of nobility and gentry 115–29

  of princes 115
  of women 263–5, 269–75
  'pedagogues' 121, 128
  philosophy, study of 120
  public schools 119
  sex instruction 72, 264–5
  trigonometry, study of 120
  see also Cambridge University; Oxford
    University; Trinity College,
    Dublin
effeminacy 65, 119, 123, 188, 254
*Elegy on the Much Lamented Death of Mr.
  Robert Fortune* (1727) 338
elephants 159, 162
Elizabeth I 198, 199, 201–2
Endor, witch of (puppet character) 106,
  112
England:
  and British Crown 187–92
  and Ireland 257–60; *see also* Ireland:
    and England
  colonies *see* American colonies;
    Fort St George
  crime 194
  diet 188
  Irish in 194, 228
  nobility 116, 120, 124, 127
  office-holders 116, 118
  Parliament 115–16, 124, 147–55, 183;
    see also laws, English and British
  poverty 240–1
  Privy Council 102, 205
  religion 188
  tourism into 178
English language:
  capitalization 40–1
  pronunciation 39, 41, 42, 255
  punctuation 41
  spelling 41
English people:
  in Ireland 227–8
  national character of 61, 65–6, 188,
    254–5
enmity *see* friendship
Enniscorthy, Co. Wexford 51
Enniskillin, Co. Fermanagh 174, 181
Ennius 187, 191
Entertainer (1746) 244, 247
Epicurus 99
Erasmus:
  Adagia 99, 113, 168, 260
  Apophthegms 76
excrement 167–8

exercise 71, 75
Exeter 4

fables 87, 91; *see also* Aesop; Avianus;
Gay, John, *Fables*; Poggius
Fairbrother, Samuel 21, 295
Falkland, Lucius Cary, 2nd Viscount 73,
76
farce 61, 66
Farquhar, George, *Inconstant* 101
Faulkner, George 292, 293
and William Bowyer, jun. 267, 293
and JS 38, 39, 66, 81, 181, 297; *see also*
JS, Works: *Works*
on the *Intelligencer* 5
see also Dublin Journal
Faustina: or The Roman Songstress (Henry
Carey) 69
Faustus (puppet character) 106, 112
fear 165
Felltham, Owen 75
fencing 119
Ferns, deanery of 218
Finch, Sir Hineage (afterwards 1st Earl
of Nottingham) 83
Fitz-Baker, Dick *see* Tighe, Richard
Fitzgerald family 198, 201
Fleetwood, Bishop William 68
Florus 182
Flower, William 231, 232–3
Flying-Post; or, Post-Master 239, 241
Fog's Weekly Journal 206, 236, 292
Intelligencer reprints 4, **242–3**, 260,
297, 311, 323, 325, 330, 333
reply to 253–6
Folly of Punns (1719) 17
food *see* diet
Ford, Charles 78, 231
Fort St George, Madras 136, 218, 220,
221, 223, 335
foxes 166, 210
fox-hunting 53
France 61, 140, 152
franking privilege 108, 113
Frankland, Sir Thomas, Bt. 185
Frederick, Prince of Wales 124
freedom of the press 210, 236
French language and manners 20, 120,
121, 122, 272
friendship 48, 79, 167
Fuller, Francis 75
*Funeral Procession of the Chevalier de St.
Patrick* (1734) 245

gambling 24, 47, 70–7, 120, 194, 223
garrons 92, 311
Garter, Order of the 154
Gay, John 234
and JS 22, 130, 131
and Walpole 58, 63
Beggar's Opera 3, 25, 47, 57–69
morality of 234–5
performed in Dublin 239
Fables 58, 63, 130, 132, 134
quest for preferment 67
Gellius, Aulus 146, 191
generosity 48, 79
genius 79, 97
Gentleman's Magazine 93
Geoghegan, Francis 55, 231
George I 58, 278
George II 1, 58, 111, 236, 279
George, St. (puppet character) 107, 113
*Gespräch zwischen einem Römisch-
Catholischen Priester und zweyen
Herrenhutern* (1752) 311
gesture 156
Gherardi, Evaristo 65
Gibbons, Grinling 112
Gibson, Bishop Edmund 94
Gilliver, Lawton 294–5
Glasnevin, Co. Dublin 84
Glastonbury thorn 179, 185
gluttony 166
God 123
Godolphin, Sidney, 1st Earl of 118, 125
Godwin, Bishop Timothy 12
Golden Legend 113
good humor 167
good sense 122, 156
Gorey, Co. Wexford 51, 55, 84, 231
Goulding, Christopher 338–9
gout 71, 213
Grafton, Charles Fitzroy, 2nd Duke of
184
Grashoper (poem on TS) 17
gratitude *see* ingratitude
Grattan, Richard 162
Grattan family 22
Gravesend, Kent 223
gravity 79
Great Britain *see* England
Greece, ancient 91
nobility 117
Greek language 8, 9, 10, 20, 97, 119, 127,
251
Greenwich 221, 223

Greer, John, *Bathyllus Redivivus* 17
Grierson, George 36
Grub-street Journal 294
Guardian 266
Guarini, Battista 14

Hale, William 15
Halifax, Charles Montagu, 1st Earl of
    118, 126
Hammond, Henry 139, 143, 146
Hanoverian Succession 101, 102
Harcourt, Simon, 1st Viscount 115, 119,
    127
Harding, John 35–6, 39, 183, 201, 203
Harding, Sarah 31, 35–9, 49, 288
    and the *Intelligencer* 4, 24, 38, 50, 288–
    9, 299–335 *passim*
    as object of charity 29, 197, 201, 203,
    232
    printing 35, 41, 288, 290–1, 299–335
    passim, 337
Hardwicke, 1st Earl of *see* Yorke
hares 160
Harley, Edward, 2nd Earl of Oxford 231
Harley, Robert, 1st Earl of Oxford 81,
    115, 116, 120–1, 128
    ancestry 119, 126
Harrison, William 185
Hawkesworth, John 296–7
Hawkins, John 114
Hawksmoor, Nicholas 191
Hearne, Thomas 94
Hebrew language 20
Helsham, Richard 7, 22
Henry VIII 267
heraldry 255, 260
Herbert, Robert Sawyer 185
Hercules 54, 56
Herring, Thomas 68, 305
Hervey, John, Baron 154
Hibernia, figure of 195
*Hibernian Patriot: or, A Vindication of Dean
    Swift* (1737) 333–4
Historiae Augustae Scriptores Sex 56
Hoadly, Bishop Benjamin 135–6
Hoey, James 292
hogs 166
Holland 193, 198
Homer:
    Iliad 112
    Odyssey 72, 76
homosexuality 65, 69

honour 119, 122, 123, 181
honours 197, 200, 260; *see also* statues
hospitality *see* Ireland: hospitality
Horace 19, 62, 66, 264
    Creech's translation 232
    Ars Poetica 136, 144, 261, 266
    Epistles 109, 111, 113, 168, 260
    Odes 197, 201, 232–3, 265, 266
    Satires 73, 77, 114
horses 52, 54; *see also* garrons
Howard, Henrietta, Countess of Suffolk
    57, 59, 184–5, 230
Howth, William St Laurence, 14th
    Baron 111
*Hue and Cry after the Letter to the Lord-
    Mayor* (1729) 38
Humanist (Patrick Delany) 244
Hume, David 185
humour 25, 59–60, 61–2, 65–6, 94
    and conversation 59–60, 156
    low 62, 235
humours 71, 129
hurling 191
Hussey, Nicholas 38, 39, 335
Hutcheson, Francis 77, 159, 162
Hyde, John 38
Hyginus, *Poetica Astronomia* 215
hyphens (pauses in speech) 161, 163
hysterics (medical symptom) 71

Iceland 179
Ides, Ysbrant 159–60, 162–3
idleness 123, 195
India *see* East India Company; Fort St
    George
Indians (Native Americans) 211
informers 49, 50
ingratitude 59, 190
injustice 123; *see also* justice
Innes, Alexander 140–1, 144, 146
Inns of Court *see* London
INTELLIGENCER
    *Adventures of the Three Brothers, George,
        Patrick, and Andrew see* no. 16
    and Dublin 1–2, 47
    and Ireland 47
    Art of Story-Telling see no. 13
    authorship 3, 5, 24, 32–3, 336
        no. 2: 2–3
        no. 10: 130
        no. 12: 147
        no. 20: 217, 336

Bowyer–Davis editions 236, 270, 276, 289, 292–3, 301–36 *passim*
  copy-text for later publications 39–40, 42, 217, 301–36 *passim*
  emendations in 65, 99, 162, 191, 222, 301–36 *passim*
  preface 2, 164, **267–8**
cessation of 23, 31, 70, 270
characters in:
  Andrew 187–9, 253, 255, 256–7
  Andrew Dealer 206, 207
  Augustus 159
  Bluestring, Sir 149–54
  Brasidas 157
  Bryania the virago 74, 77
  Bub-ble 150, 154
  Burnet, Dr. 159
  Corusodes 93–8
  Damon 153
  Diogenes 158
  Eugenio 93, 97–8, 99
  George 187–9, 253–6, 256–60, 330
  Morisda 74, 77
  Mullinix 101–11, 131–3
  North, A. 206–13
  Patrick 187–9, 253–6, 256–60
  Pennyless, Patrick 206, 207
  Ralph, Sir 148–53
  Socrates 157
  Timothy 131–3
  Townly 150, 154
Characters of Corusodes and Eugenio see no. 7
comment on:
  published **236–48**, **250–60**
  unpublished **230–3**
copyright 292, 296
Description of What the World Calls Discretion see no. 5
Dialogue between Mad Mullinix and Timothy see no. 8
Essay on Modern Education see no. 9
Essay on the Fates of Clergymen see nos. 5 and 7
Folly of Gaming see no. 4
Foolish Methods of Education among the Nobility see no. 9
Harding editions 267, 276, 288–91, 299–336
  capitalization 40
  edition sizes 43
  price 43
  reissued 319, 320

Hardships of the Irish Being Deprived of Their Silver, and Decoyed into America see no. 19
'hints' for 25, 31, 76, 92, **269–75**, **339**
Inhospitable Temple of Squire Wether see no. 2
Letter to the Intelligencer see no. 16; *see also Letter to the Intelligencer* (separate entry)
manuscripts, putative 41, 43; *see also Intelligencer*: 'hints' for
Marks of Ireland's Poverty, Shewn to Be Proofs of Its Riches see no. 17
names named in 49
newspaper reprints of 29, 147, 187, 236–43
no. 1: **47–50**
  printing and publication 26, 27, 32, 230, 296, **299–301**
no. 2: 2–3, 24, 32, 47, **51–6**, 84, 231
  printing and publication 32, 296, **301–2**
no. 3: 3, 47, **57–69**, 191, 240
  printing and publication 32, 43, 295, 296, **302–5**
no. 4: 19, 24, 27, 47, **70–7**, 114, 164
  printing and publication 32, 296, **305–7**
no. 5: 25, 27, **78–83**
  printing and publication 32, 293, 294, 295, 296, **307–9**
no. 6: 3, 24, 47, 51, **84–92**, 130, 133
  and other *Intelligencer* papers 170, 196, 214
  printing and publication 27, 32, 43, 84, 236, 296, **309–11**
  reaction to 230, 240, 276, 277–9
no. 7: 25, 27, 32, 83, **93–100**, 242
  printing and publication 32, 294, 295, 296, **311–12**
no. 8: 3, 30, **101–14**, 244
  and other *Intelligencer* papers 32, 77, 131–3, 202, 217
  and Tighe 26, 47, 101–3
  printing and publication 32, 293, 295, 296, **312–16**
no. 9: 3, 47, **115–29**, 241
  printing and publication 32, 294, 295, 296, **316–18**
no. 10: 47, 102, 114, **130–4**
  printing and publication 26, 27, 29–30, 32, 293, 294, 296, **319**
no. 11: 24, 25, 47, **135–46**, 217

INTELLIGENCER (*cont.*)
    printing and publication 29, 32, 41, 296, **319-21**
    no. 12: 27, 29, 41, 125, **147-55**, 231
    printing and publication 27, 29, 32-3, 41, 147, 174, 296, **321-2**
    no. 13: 18, 24, 25, **156-63**, 243
    printing and publication 33, 296, **322-5**
    no. 14: 24, 33, **164-9**, 243, 267
    printing and publication 4, 296, **325-6**
    no. 15: 27, 33, 41, 47, 92, **170-86**, 230, 237-9, 275
    and other *Intelligencer* papers 24, 91, 130, 133, 171, 196, 204, 214, 249
    printing and publication as *A Short View* 36, 236, 237, 295, 296, **326-7, 328-30**
    printing and publication as an *Intelligencer* paper 33, 41, 170, 293, 296, **327-30**
    no. 16: 24, 47, 91, 170, **187-92**, 196, 214, 243
    printing and publication 33, 294, 296, **330-1**
    reaction to 251-60
    no. 17: 24, 47, 170, **193-6**, 214, 249, 250, 275
    printing and publication 33, 43, 293, 296, **331-2**
    no. 18: 24, 25, 36, 47, 112, 170, **197-203**, 214
    printing and publication 28-9, 33, 296, **332**
    reaction to 197, 232, 233
    no. 19: 3, 47, 170, 173, **204-16**
    printing and publication 26, 28, 29, 31, 33, 205, 295, 296, **332-5**
    reaction to 231, 232-3, 243, 276, 277, 279-82
    no. 20: 25, 47, **217-23**
    printing and publication 26, 28, 31, 33, 38-9, 41, 296, **335-7**
    no. 20 (spurious) 5, 33, 231, 232-3, **261-6, 338-9**
    planning for 25, 47; *see also Intelligencer*: 'hints' for
    Prometheus's Art of Man-Making see no. 14
    proofreading for 42, 288
    Proposals in Prose and Verse for, An Universal View of All the Eminent Writers on the Holy Scriptures see no. 11
    publication of 3-6, 24, 26-33, 43, 204; *see also Intelligencer*: Bowyer-Davis editions; *Intelligencer*: Harding editions; *Intelligencer*: proofreading
    reception 3-6, 29, 51, 147, 187, 276; *see also Intelligencer*: comment on
    Representation of the Present Conditions of Ireland see no. 6
    St. Andrew's Day, and the Drapier's Birthday see no. 18
    Second Letter to the Intelligencer see no. 17
    Services the Drapier Has Done His Country see no. 15
    Sir Ralph the Patriot Turned Courtier see no. 12
    Tale of the Turd see no. 14
    Tim and Gay's Fables see no. 10
    Vindication of Mr. Gay, and the Beggars Opera see no. 3
interest rates 99, 185; *see also* usury
Ireland:
    agriculture 87, 132, 170, 171, 176, 178, 179, 182, 240, 249; *see also* Ireland: famine; Ireland: soil
    and England or Great Britain 176, 187-92, 208-9, 236
    appeals from, to the British House of Lords 183
    as a conquered nation 89, 209, 214
    as flourishing 86, 89, 90, 131-2, 193
    refuted by Archbishop King 91, 170, 182, 227-8
    refuted in *Intelligencer* no. 15: 91, 170, 175, 179, 181, 182
    as Hibernia 195
    bankers *see* Dublin: bankers
    banknotes 193, 196, 215
    butter 89, 179
    charities 228
    church buildings 84-8
    clergy 115, 132, 182, 194, 232, 269
    climate 177, 179, 182
    clothing 25, 89, 176, 178, 179, 180, 269; *see also* clothing and dress; wigs
    coinage 28, 189, 199; *see also* coins; Ireland: gold and silver; Ireland: mint; Ireland: money; Wood's halfpence controversy
    commerce 172, 175, 179, 189, 198
    Commissioners of Revenue 179, 185

constitutional status of 192, 253–60
Court of Common Pleas 183
Court of King's Bench 183
crime 194, 195
custom-house officers 180
debt, public 104
depopulation of 177; *see also* Ireland:
     emigration from; Ireland:
     populousness
diet 25, 40, 53, 86, 110, 114, 176, 179,
     205, 227–8; *see also* Ireland: eating
     blood; Ireland: famine
eating blood 86, 91
economy 84–92, 130–3, 170–86, 193,
     207; *see also* Ireland: agriculture;
     Ireland: as flourishing; Ireland:
     commerce; Ireland: emigration
     from; Ireland: exports; Ireland:
     famine; Ireland: housing; Ireland:
     imports; Ireland: interest rate;
     Ireland: landlords, absentee;
     Ireland: land tenure; Ireland:
     manufacturing; Ireland: money;
     Ireland: poverty; Ireland:
     taxation; Ireland: unemployment
emigration from
     to America 195, 204, 205–7, 211, 216,
          249, 279–82, 333
     to the West Indies 25, 89, 92
English in 26, 86, 193–5, 198, 227–8
exports 175, 177, 182, 258
famine 4, 26, 170, 204, 208, 239
     in Queen Elizabeth's reign 198
forestry 178, 179, 275
gentry 52, 132, 171, 180, 227–8
gold and silver, rate of exchange
     between 172, 209, 214, 333–4
hospitality 51–6, 180–1, 189, 195, 228,
     242
housing 87, 88, 89–90, 179, 180, 195,
     227, 249–50
immigration into 176
imports 171, 175, 176, 178, 193, 239
inns 52, 54, 90
interest rate 185
Jacobites in 104, 111
landlords, absentee 132, 184
land tenure 171, 175, 179–80, 194, 205,
     207, 211, 213–14, 249
     confiscations (1641, 1691) 102
     land prices 171, 175, 179, 185
     leases 171, 211, 240
laws *see* laws, Irish

lawyers 132, 178, 184, 194
linen manufacture 179, 204
Lord Lieutenant 178, 183
Lords Justices 205
manufacturing 175, 179, 182, 204
militia 51, 52
mint, lack of 176, 178, 179, 184, 209–
     10, 239
money 132, 172, 180, 211, 214
     exchange rate 172
     shortage of 28, 172, 174–5, 185–6,
          193, 205, 210
     see also Ireland: banknotes; Ireland:
          coinage; Ireland: gold and silver;
          Ireland: mint
natural resources 176
nobility 26, 132, 194
northern *see* Ireland: Ulster
Parliament 4, 48, 214, 275
     acts *see* laws, Irish
     House of Commons 102–3, 111,
          171, 192
     House of Lords 111, 115
political parties 101–11
populousness 182; *see also* Ireland:
     emigration; Ireland: immigration
ports *see* Ireland: shipping and
     shipbuilding
poverty 89–90, 174, 179, 193, 239, 249,
     275; *see also* beggars; Ireland:
     emigration; Ireland: famine;
     Ireland: housing; Ireland:
     unemployment
Privy Council 101–2, 113, 214
rents *see* Ireland: land tenure
ruins 84, 88, 185
rural-urban migration 89, 249
shipping and shipbuilding 175, 177,
     179, 182
silver, value of *see* Ireland: gold
soil 175, 177, 179, 182
squires 52, 171, 180
taxation 170, 171, 227–9
tillage *see* Ireland: agriculture
tourism from 178
tourism into 176, 178
Ulster 194, 198, 205, 232, 243, 275
     see also Ireland: land tenure
unemployment 91, 132, 194, 208, 252
     because English are preferred 11,
          26, 87
union with England proposed (1703)
     192

Ireland (*cont.*)
  weaving 178, 184
  wit in 238, 239
  see also Dublin; Catholic Church;
    Church of Ireland; Presbyterian
    Church; Wood's halfpence
    controversy
Irish Confederation tracts 328
Irish language 17
Irish people:
  industry of 177
  like ancient Israelites 180
  like Scythians 178, 183–4
  national character 189, 242, 253–6
  pronunciation 255
Ironside, Nestor, putative author of the
    Guardian 262, 266
Ironside, Roger (pseud.) 265, 266
irony 179
Isaac (dancer) 128
Italian language 20, 272
Italian opera *see* opera
Italians 61, 62, 69

Jackson, Daniel 246
Jacobites 113, 133, 236
  in Ireland 51, 102, 104, 105, 111, 112,
    181, 203
  in Scotland 191, 192
James, Old Pretender 104, 111
James II 113, 118, 181
Jenney, Henry 248
Jerome, St 99
Johnson, Esther (Stella) 19, 22, 99, 101,
    113
Jones, Inigo 191
Jones, John 7
Jonson, Ben 77, 78, 81
Julius Capitolinus 53, 56
Jupiter 54, 56, 215
justice 48, 122, 123, 176; *see also* injustice;
    law
Juvenal:
  compared with Horace 62, 66
  quoted or cited 70, 73, 75, 77, 98, 223

Keif, Margaret 114
Kennett, Bishop White 93–4
Kilbride parish, Co. Meath 14
Kilcommon Erris parish, Co. Mayo 223
Kildare, William Fitzmaurice, 2nd Earl
    of 111

Kilkenny: St Canice's Cathedral 85
Killala, deanery of 135, 223
Kilmore, deanery of 14
King, Archbishop William 10, 91, 172,
    183, 204
  *Some Observations on the Taxes Pay'd by
    Ireland* 7, 170, 182, **227–9**
King, Peter, Baron King of Ockham 68,
    172
King, William, of Christ Church 196
  Swan-Tripe Club 77
Kin[g]sale, Gerald Courcy, 24th Baron
    135
Kinsale, Co. Cork 51, 135, 141
Knockmark parish, Co. Meath 135, 223

Lactanius 99
Ladies Opera (?1728) 70, 82, 163
Landen, Battle of 160, 163
land tenure 123; *see also* Ireland: land
    tenure
languages, learning *see* education
Lapland 179
Larne, Co. Antrim 205
Latin language 8, 9, 10, 20, 97, 119, 127,
    251
Laud, Archbishop William 79, 81
laughter 62, 63, 95, 234
law:
  British: effect in Ireland 228
  civil 188, 192
  Irish *see* Dublin: courts of law; laws,
    Irish
  see also justice; laws; injustice
laws, English and British:
  Magna Charta 215
  3 Edw. I (West.), c. 34 (*Scandalum
    magnatum*, 1275) 124
  15 Chas. II, c. 7 (Navigation Act, 1663)
    177, 182
  18 Chas. II, c. 2 (Cattle Act, 1666) 182,
    192, 258
  32 Chas. II, c. 2 (Cattle Act, 1680) 182,
    258
  1 Will. III, sess. 2, c. 2 (Bill of Rights,
    1689) 215
  7 & 8 Will. III, c. 22 (Woollen Act,
    1696) 182, 192, 258
  10 & 11 Will. III, c. 10 (Woollen Act,
    1699) 182, 258
  6 Anne, c. 11 (Act of Union, 1707) 191
  1 Geo. I, stat. 2, c. 54 (Disarming Act,
    1715) 192

6 Geo. I, c. 5 (Declaratory Act, 1719) 183, 214, 215
11 Geo. I, c. 26 (Disarming Act, 1724) 192
19 Geo. II, c. 39 (Disarming Act, 1746) 192
see also libel; paraphernalia; primogeniture
laws, Irish:
  10 Hen. VII (Poynings's Law, 1494) 260
  33 Hen. VIII, sess. 2, c. 3 (Attorneys, 1542) 184
  8 Anne, c. 3 (Quakers, 1709) 163
  6 Geo. I, c. 5–6 (Quakers, 1719) 163
  1 Geo. II, c. 5 (Quakers, 1727) 163
laws, Scottish:
  Act of Security (1703) 192
lawyers 78, 79, 157; *see also* Ireland: lawyers
Layfield, Patrick (pseud.) 206
laziness 71, 119, 123, 166, 195
Leeds, 1st Duke of *see* Danby
Leeson, Joseph 250
LeFanu, Alicia 296
Leigh, Thomas 109, 113, 315
Le Sac (dancing master) 120, 128
Letter from a Dissenting Teacher to Jet Black, attributed to TS 10
Letter from a Nobleman of Scotland to a Gentleman of England 116
Letter from the Revd. J. S. D. S. P. D. to a Country Gentleman in the North of Ireland (1736) 333
Letter to the Intelligencer. Written by a Young Gentleman (1728) 91, **251–3**
Letter to Tom Punsibi (1721) 17
libel 118, 124, 216; *see also* blasphemy; freedom of the press
Libertas et natale solum (motto) 174, 177, 181
Lincolnshire 98
Lindsay, Archbishop Thomas 13
Lindus 181
Livy 182
Lloyd, David, *Memoires* 76
Lloyd's Evening Post 322
Locke, John:
  Some Thoughts on Education 127
  Two Treatises of Civil Government 182
London:
  Bethlehem Hospital 186
  Change Alley 96

Church Street, Soho 137
Court of Requests 149, 153
Covent Garden 100
French community 128
Gerrard Street 135
homosexuals 69
Inns of Court 68, 178, 184, 305
Leicester Fields 161
Lincoln's Inn 68, 305
Lincoln's Inn Fields Theatre 68, 237
Middle Temple 184
Romilly Street 145
Royal Academy of Music 68
Royal Hospital, Chelsea 154
St Botolph's Aldgate 67, 92
St James's Street 128
St Paul's Cathedral 191
St Stephen's Chapel (Palace of Westminster) 150, 154
theatre 67; *see also* London: Lincoln's Inn Fields Theatre
Westminster, Palace of 149, 150, 153–4
White's Chocolate House 120, 128
Will's Coffee House 97–8, 99–100
see also Greenwich
London Evening-Post 223, 292, 293, 306
London Journal 59, 234
  and Smedley 136, 137, 141, 145, 319–20
lord mayor's feast 165, 168
Lorraine, Charles V, Duke of (puppet character) 106, 112, 113
Lort, Michael 336
Loughgall, Co. Armagh 248
Lough Larne 204, 205
Louisa, Princess (daughter of George II) 59
love 165
Lowther, Anthony 185
L'Sac *see* Le Sac
Lucas's Coffee House *see* Dublin
Lucretius, *De Rerum Natura* 82, 196
Lucubrations of Sallmanazor Histrum, Esq. see Browne, John
lust 124
luxury 119, 123, 166, 195
Lycurgus, *Against Leocrates* 91
lying 72
Lyon, John 156, 182

McFadden, Anne 8
McFadden, Charles 8

Macrobius, *Saturnalia* 72, 76, 157, 158, 162
Maculla, James 184, 215
Magna Charta 215
Maittaire, Michel, *Opera et Fragmenta Veterum Poetarum Latinorum* 65
Man, Isle of 178, 180, 184
Mandeville, Bernard, *Fable of the Bees* 146, 159, 162
Manilius, *Astronomica* 65
Maple, William 214
Mardonius 88, 91
Market Hill, Co. Armagh 25, 28, 84, 206
Marlborough, John Churchill, 1st Duke of 118, 120, 126
marriage 71, 72, 262–6, 272; *see also* sex
Maryland colony 215, 216
Maryland Gazette 4, 5, 325
masculinity *see* effeminacy
Mason, W. Monck 289
masquerades 188, 191
Massachusetts, province of 215–16; *see also* Boston
Massareene, Clotworthy Skeffington, 4th Viscount 111
mathematics 22, 120, 188, 192
Mathews, Sir Tobie, *A Collection of Letters* 77
maxims *see* proverbs
Mayo, Theobald Bourke, 6th Viscount 111
Mead and Curtis, Dublin bankers 196
Meath, Chaworth Brabazon, 6th Earl of 111
Meath, county of 84
Memoirs of the Life and Writings of Jonathan Swift, D.D. (1752) 245
Memorial Address'd to the Reverend Dean Swift 239, 240
Middle Temple, London 184
military *see* army
Minerva 173, 181
Minos 215
Minucius Felix 99
Miscellanies see JS: Works by or attributed to
Mist, Nathaniel 237, 327
Mist's Weekly Journal 128, 297
and the *Intelligencer* 4, 29, 32, 153, **236–42**, 304, 310, 316
and *A Short View* 185, 237–9, 327
prosecuted 236, 242, 327
Mithridates VI, king of Pontus 142, 146

Molesworth, Robert, 1st Viscount 116
Molloy, Charles 237
Molloy, Neale 237
Molyneux, John 101, 103–11, 113
Molyneux, Samuel 172
Molyneux, Sir Thomas 75
Molyneux, William 182, 214, 260
monkeys 131, 159, 166
Moor(e), A. (fictitious London imprint) 292
Moryson, Fynes 25, 198–9, 201
Moscow *see* Muscovy
Motte, Benjamin 131, 294–5, 312
mottoes 181–2
Mountcashel, Catherine Davys, Viscountess 13
Mountcashel, Edward Davys, 3rd Viscount 10, 13, 26, 128, 318
Mountcashel, James Davys, 2nd Viscount 13
Mountjoy, Charles Blount, 8th Baron (afterwards Earl of Devonshire) 198, 201
Mullinix *see Intelligencer*, characters in
Mummius, Roman consul 182
Muscovy 160
music 61, 65, 66, 68–9, 272

Napier, John 192
Naul, Co. Dublin 84, 91
Navigation Act (1663) 177, 182
Newborough, Co. Wexford 51
Newcastle, Thomas Pelham-Holles, 1st Duke of 150, 154, 204, 205
New Gingle on Tom Dingle (1726) 18
New Jersey colony 281
Newry, Co. Down 198, 201
Newtownbutler, Battle of 181
Newtownbutler, Theophilus Butler, 1st Baron 21
New York 4, 276, 279, 281
Nichols, John 93, 146, 244, 248, 293
and *Intelligencer* no. 20: 217, 296, 336
Nimrod 210, 214–15
nobility 115
Greek and Roman 117
see also England: nobility; Ireland: nobility
Nottingham, 1st Earl of *see* Finch

oaths:
Quakers' affirmations 160, 163
see also blasphemy; swearing

O'Brien, Sir Edward, Bt. 10
O'Byrne family 198, 201
Old Dublin Intelligence 338
Old Whig 116
On Wisdom's Defeat in a Learned Debate (1725) 36, 38
opera 61, 65, 68–9, 120, 188, 191, 254
oratory 157; *see also* preaching
Ormonde, James Butler, 1st Duke of 118, 124
Orrery, John Boyle, 5th Earl of Cork and 13, 19, 22, 244, 246, 334
Osborne, Sir Thomas *see* Danby
O'Toole family 198, 201
Oughton, J. 6, 8, 14, 181
Ovid, *Metamorphoses* 215
Oxford, 1st Earl of *see* Harley, Robert
Oxford, Edward Harley, 2nd Earl of 231
Oxford University 76, 93, 95, 97, 122, 129, 178
    Christ Church 98
    Hart Hall 129
    St Edmund Hall 93

Palmerston, Henry Temple, 1st Viscount 231
paradox 181
paraphernalia 71, 76
Parke, Robert 216
Parker, Samuel 145
parliament *see* England; Ireland; Scotland
parliamentary privilege 115
Parthenon (Athens) 173, 181
passive obedience 189, 192
Patrician 116
patronage 62, 122; *see also* TS: quest for patronage and preferment; JS: quest for patronage and preferment
Pausanias 181
peacocks 166
Pearce, Sir Edward Lovett 275
Peele, J. 319
peerage *see* nobility
Peerage Bill debate (1719) 115–16
Pennsylvania: Irish immigrants 205, 216
pensions 62, 147, 152, 178
Persia 159
    army 91
Persius, *Satires* 196, 234, 235, 267, 268, 276; *see also* TS: Works
Petau, Denis 139, 142, 145

Petavius, Dionysius *see* Petau
Peterborough, Charles Mordaunt, 3rd Earl of 170
Peterborough, deanery of 94
petition, right of 210, 215
Petty, Sir William, *Political Anatomy of Ireland* 183
Pharaoh of Egypt, compared to English oppressors of Ireland 180, 186
Philadelphia, Irish immigrants in 216
Philips, Ambrose 145
Phocion 199, 202
Pilkington, Laetitia 162
Pindar, *Odes* 173, 181
pin-money 72, 76, 272
Pistorides 102
Plain Dealer's Intelligencer see Browne, John
Plato:
    Apology 202
    Gorgias 215
    Laws 113
    Phaedo 202
    Phaedrus 75, 77
    Republic 113
    Symposium 72
plays *see* theatre
Pliny, *Natural History* 146, 160, 163, 168
Plutarch:
    Alexander the Great 163
    Artaxerxes 76
    Caesar 67
    Camillus 202
    Cato the Younger 76
    Cicero 67
    Dion 202
    Moralia 157, 162
    Phocion 202
    Themistocles 202
Plutus 195, 196
Pocklington, John 12
Pococke, Richard 334
Poem to the Whole People of Ireland, Relating to M. B. Drapier, by A. R. Hosier 35
poetry 61, 66
Poggius, fables 196
Political State of Great-Britain 219, 335
Pomfret, Thomas 77
Poole, Matthew 138, 139, 142, 143, 145, 146
Pope, Alexander 3–5, 101, 145
    and TS 19
    and *The Beggar's Opera* 57

Pope, Alexander (*cont.*)
  and the *Intelligencer* 223, 230, 231
  and Voiture 145
  as editor of Swift 294, 318; *see also* JS,
    Works: *Miscellanies*
  attacked in *Gulliveriana* 29
  Dunciad 65, 136, 145, 218, 222, 223
  Miscellanies see JS: Works
  Peri Bathous 145
Porter, Endymion 73, 76
portreeve (of Irish towns) 56
postal service, America–Ireland 281–2
Powell, S. 41
Poynings's Law 260
preaching 157, 275; *see also* charity
    sermons; Charles I
Presbyterian Church 189
Present Miserable State of Ireland (1721) 36
Pretender, Old *see* James, Old
    Pretender
prime ministers 118
primogeniture, law of 252
printers' ornaments 39, 288, 290–1, 333
printing 35–43 *passim*, 288–340 *passim*
prisons *see* Dublin: Black Dog Prison;
        Dublin: Bridewell Prison;
        Dublin: Newgate Prison
Prior, Thomas 171
  List of the Absentees of Ireland 173, 184,
    185
  Observations on Coin in General 172, 173,
    184, 196
Procrustes 54, 56
Progress of Patriotism. A Tale see
    Intelligencer no. 12
Progress of Patriotism: A Poem (1731) 322
Prometheus 164, 165–7
pronunciation 255
  indicated by spelling 39, 41, 42
property *see* land tenure; paraphernalia
Protestants 135; *see also* Church of
    Ireland; Presbyterian Church
proverbs 274
  quoted or cited 67, 77, 91, 97, 99, 112,
    129, 146, 163, 181, 196, 202, 223; *see*
    also mottoes
prudence 48, 78; *see also* discretion
Psalmanazar, George 146
public spirit 48, 62
Pulteney, William 147
Punch (puppet character) 106, 107, 131
Punchinello *see* Punch
puns 16–17, 55

pun-sibi 17
puppet shows 106–7, 112–13
Pyle, Edmund 68

quadrille 48, 49, 70, 71
Quakers 160, 163
Queen of Sheba (puppet character) 106,
    112
Quilca (Cuilcagh), Co. Cavan 8, 9
Quintilian 146

Rabelais, François 61, 66
racing 194
raillery 235
Ram, Abel (1669–1740) 47, 51–6, 231
Ram, Sir Abel 51
Ram, Andrew 54, 56
Ramus, Peter 95, 98–9
Rathfarnham, Co. Dublin 15
reputation 71; *see also scandalum*
    magnatum
Restoration, immorality during 118
revenge 166
reverend, as title for judges 64, 68
Rhadamanthus 215
Rhodes 181
Rhône river 111
Richardson, Samuel 135, 136
Rincurran parish, Co. Cork 11, 12, 14,
    51, 135, 203, 222
Ringrone parish, Co. Cork 135
Robin's Panegyrick. Or, The Norfolk
    Miscellany (1729) 322
Robin's Panegyrick, or, The Norfolk
    Misselany (1729) 322
Rochfort family 22
Rome, ancient: nobility 117
Roman invasion of Britain 91
Roque, John, *Exact Survey of the City and*
    Suburbs of Dublin (1756) 250
Roscommon, Wentworth Dillon, 4th
    Earl of 276
Rosse, Richard Parsons, 1st Earl of 111
Rufus, Servius Sulpicius 92
rum (a poor country clergyman) 222
Russell, Thomas 11, 12
Russia *see* Muscovy

Sabra of Silene (puppet character) 107,
    113
Sacheverell, Henry 192
St Canice's Cathedral, Kilkenny 85
St. James's Journal 135

St John, Henry *see* Bolingbroke
St Patrick's Cathedral, Dublin 85, 113,
     135, 197, 239, 333–4
St Stephen's Chapel *see* London
satire 25, 59, 62, 64, 66–7, 235
Savage, Richard, *Bastard: A Poem* 41
Sawbridge, Thomas 218
scandalum magnatum 118, 124
Sciron 56
Scotland 117, 132
     Act of Security (1703) 192
     and British crown 187–92
     arms-bearing 191–2
     diet 192
     Jacobites 191
     national character 188
     nobility 115
     parliament 192
Scott, Sir Walter 101, 128, 244, 271
Scythians 178, 183–4
secret service money 147, 148
sermons *see* clergy; preaching
servants 48, 62, 72, 90, 121
sex 72, 263–5; *see also* homosexuality
sex roles *see* effeminacy
Shaftesbury, Anthony Ashley Cooper, 1st
     Earl of 118, 125
Shakespeare, William 10
     King Lear 196
     Troilus and Cressida 112
Sharp, Archbishop John 82–3
Sharpe, Isaac 94
Sheridan, Elizabeth (granddaughter of
     TS) 296
Sheridan, Elizabeth McFadden (wife of
     TS) 8, 9
Sheridan, Patrick (father of TS) 6
Sheridan, Patrick, Bishop 7
SHERIDAN, THOMAS (1687–1738)
     and Cavan 14, 21
     and friendship 20
     and the *Intelligencer* 1–6, 24–6
     and Esther Johnson 22
     and Ambrose Philips 145
     and Pope 19
     and Swift 15, 19, 20–3, 161, 200; *see
         also* JS: and Sheridan
     and theatre 10, 12, 25
     and Richard Tighe 101–2
     and women 23, 71–5, 164, 166–7
     as almanac writer 246–7
     as clergyman 11–12, 14, 25, 101, 203
     as linguist 20

     as poet 16
     as proofreader 42
     as punster 55
     as schoolteacher 8, 10–11, 16, 18, 26,
         128
     play performances 10, 12
     Cavan Royal School 14
     Dublin schools 9, 11, 14, 15, 30, 192
     attacked 5, 18, 29, 244–7
     birth and ancestry 6–7
     canon 244
     death 15
     education and degrees 6–8, 11
     health 15
     income 11, 23, 202
     library and reading 15, 20, 65, 75, 181,
         201
     manuscripts of 15–16, 19
     marriage and family life 8–9, 15, 23,
         164
     personality 21, 22–3, 78
     poems on 17–18; *see also* TS: attacked
     pun-sibi his *nom de guerre* 17
     quest for patronage and preferment
         11–14
     style 217
     travel 30, 47, 51, 84–90
     WORKS BY OR ATTRIBUTED TO:
     Alexander's Overthrow 18
     Anglo-Latin exchanges with JS 18
     Ars Pun-ica, sive Flos Linguarum 16–
         17, 156, 244
     Ballyspellin 16, 23, 30
     Blunder of all Blunders (attributed to
         TS) 246
     bons mots collection 14, 18–19, 156,
         162
     Cobbler to Jet Black 248
     Easy Introduction of Grammar 8, 16,
         17, 90–1
     Essay upon the Immortality of the Soul
         22, 23–4
     Historical Relations (Sir John Davies),
         ed. TS 111
     Intelligencer see nos. 2, 4, 6, 11, 13,
         14, 16, 17, 18
     Juvenal translation attributed to 19
     Latino-Anglicus exchanges with JS
         102, 222
     *Letter from a Dissenting Teacher to Jet
         Black* 10, 17, 244, 246
     *Letter of Advice to the Right Hon. John
         Earl of Orrery* 13

SHERIDAN, THOMAS (*cont.*)
  Montaigne translation 19
  New Simile for the Ladies 16, 164
  Numb. II. The following fable ... 102
  *Ode to Be Performed at the Castle of
    Dublin* 13, 23, 39
  On Paddy's Character of the Intelligencer
    (possibly by TS) 248
  Pastor Fido (Guarini), translated by
    TS 14, 15
  Philoctetes (Sophocles), translated by
    TS 13
  poem on Dan Jackson's nose 246
  Poem on the Immortality of the Soul (Sir
    John Davies), ed. TS 13, 162
  Punch Turn'd School-master 18, 246
  Satyrs of Persius (translated by TS)
    13, 16, 17, 19, 26, 128
  *Sermon Preached at St. Patrick's Church
    on St. Caecilia's Day* 18, 21
  Sheridan's Master Piece 18
  'Sufficient unto the day' sermon 12,
    22, 23, 26, 101
  Tasso translation 19
  Tom Punsibi's Letter to Dean Swift 16
  To the Dean of St. Patricks 16
  To the Dean When in England 16
  To the Honourable Mr. D. T. 38, 102
  *To the Right Honourable the Lord
    Viscount Mont-Cassel* 26, 36
  Wonder of All Wonders (attributed to
    TS) 246
  works, publication of, proposed 15
Sheridan, Thomas the younger (1719–
    88), son of TS 14, 15, 67
Sheridan, William, Bishop 7
Sheridan's Master Piece (1721) 18
Shrovetide pancakes 168–9
Sican, Elizabeth 22
Sicily *see* Syracuse
singing 272
Sinis 56
Sinon 90, 282
Sir Ralph the Patriot see Intelligencer no. 12
Sisyphus 54, 56
slavery 123, 182, 183, 214
Sligo, town 205
sloth *see* laziness
Smedley, Jonathan 21, 24, 47, 335, 336
  career 135–6, 217–23
  death 218
  Gulliveriana 25, 29, 136, 217, 230, 244,
    246

His Grace's Answer to Jonathan
    (sometimes attributed to
    Smedley) 217
Letter from D. S—t to D. S—y (sometimes
    attributed to Smedley) 217
London Journal letter 136–46
Poems on Several Occasions 335
portrait (mezzotint) 219, 220
*Proposal for Printing by Subscription, An
    Universal View* 320
*Universal View of All the Eminent Writers
    on the Holy Scriptures* 25, 136–46,
    217, 220
Smeglicius, Martinus 264
Smiglecki, Marcin *see* Smeglicius
smoking 122
Society for the Promotion of Christian
    Knowledge 94
Society for the Propagation of the
    Gospel 94
Socrates 99, 157, 199, 202
soil 66, 117; *see also* Ireland: soil
Soissons, Congress of (1727) 154–5
Solomon, King (puppet character) 106,
    112
*Some Considerations Humbly Offer'd,
    Relating to the Peerage of Great
    Britain* 116
*Some Reflections, Concerning the Reduction of
    Gold Coin in Ireland* (1737) 334
Somers, John, 1st Baron Somers of
    Evesham 80, 82, 115, 118, 125, 215
Southampton, Thomas Wriothesley, 4th
    Earl of 118, 124
Southwell, Edward, Secretary of State
    for Ireland 26–7, 216
sovereign (of Irish towns) 56
Spain 61, 62, 154
Spain, king of (puppet character) 106
span-farthing 121, 128
Spanish language 20
Spectator 1, 76, 128, 234–5
Speech of a Noble Peer (Earl of Abercorn?)
    (1728) 115
Spence, Joseph 57, 66
Spenser, Edmund, *View of the State of
    Ireland* 183, 201
sport 188
squires 52, 171, 180
Stair, James Dalrymple, 1st Viscount 192
Stationers' Company registers 289, 296
statues 174–5, 181, 182, 188
statutes *see* laws

Steele, Sir Richard 135, 234, 266
  Letter to the Earl of Oxford 116
  Plebian 116
  see also Tatler; Spectator
Stella *see* Johnson, Esther
storytelling 156–63
Strafford, Thomas Wentworth, 1st Earl
  of 79, 81
Stratford, William 230
Suckling, Sir John 73, 77
Suetonius, *Augustus* 76
Suffolk, Countess of *see* Howard,
  Henrietta
Sulzer, Johann Georg, *Versuch einiger
  vernünftigen Gedancken von der
  Auferziehung u. Unterweisung der
  Kinder* (1745) 317
Sunderland, Charles Spencer, 4th Earl
  of 135
*Supplement to the Papers, Writ in Defence of
  the Peerage Bill* 116
*Supplement to the Works of the Most
  Celebrated Minor Poets* (1750) 247
Supremus (representative of the united
  kingdoms of England, Scotland,
  and Ireland) 257–60
Swan-Tripe Club in Dublin 77
swearing 72, 75
Swift, Deane (cousin of JS) 250, 271
SWIFT, JONATHAN (1667–1745)
  and America 210–12
  and *The Beggar's Opera* 57–69
  and charity schools 56
  and friendship 20
  and Gay 22, 57, 130, 131
  and Halifax 126
  and his audience 66
  and the *Intelligencer* 1–6, 27–8, 30–1,
    47, 204, 217, 269–75
  and Esther Johnson 1
  and John Jones 7
  and White Kennett 94
  and Thomas Leigh 113
  and Marlborough 126
  and *Mist's Weekly Journal* 236–43
  and music 61, 66
  and opera 61, 65, 68–9
  and Ambrose Philips 145
  and Pope 3, 223
  and Quilca 9
  and Shaftesbury 125
  and Sheridan 11, 14, 15, 20–3, 24, 28,
    31, 248; *see also* TS: and Swift

  and Sheridan's school 10
  and Smedley 135
  and Somers 125
  and theatre 64, 67
  and Tighe 101–3
  and Voiture 145
  and Walpole 58, 67
  and whist 82
  as clergyman 21, 25, 135
  as Drapier 35–6, 174, 197, 199, 209,
    334; *see also* Wood's halfpence
    controversy
  as proofreader 39, 42
  as punster 55
  as storyteller 156, 161, 163
  as Whig 103
  at Market Hill 28, 30, 31, 206
  at Oxford 122, 129
  attacked 29, 236, 242
  attributions to 236–7, 247; *see also*
    Intelligencer: authorship
  birthday celebration 28, 197
  diction and style 217
  English reputation 238
  governor of Bethlehem Hospital,
    London 186
  governor of Foundling Hospital,
    Dublin 186
  handwriting 315, 317, 339
  income 182
  library and reading 65, 66, 81, 82,
    130, 275; *see also* JS, Works:
    marginalia
  motto 181
  on fiction and drama 57–69, 272
  on marriage 64, 272–5
  philanthropy 232
  praised 161, 163, 174, 197–200, 242
  proofreading 39; *see also* *Intelligencer*:
    proofreading
  quest for patronage and preferment
    57, 67, 82, 83, 93, 126, 230
  travel 28, 31, 47, 51, 84
  WORKS BY OR ATTRIBUTED TO:
    account books 10, 182
    *Ad Amicum Eruditum Thomam
      Sheridan* 18, 20
    Altho a great Dunce I be 21
    Anglo-Latin exchanges with TS 18
    *Answer of William Pulteney to Sir Robert
      Walpole* 275
    Answer to a Paper, Called A Memorial
      36, 171, 173, 183, 185, 230, 240

SWIFT, JONATHAN (*cont.*)
Answer to Several Letters from Unknown Persons 173, 206, 207, 269
Answer to Several Letters Sent Me from Unknown Hands 173, 269
Answer to the Ballyspellin Ballad 23
Answer to the Craftsman 91, 183, 216
Author upon Himself 78, 82
Bons Mots de Stella 19
Cadenus and Vanessa 81, 217
Causes of the Wretched Condition of Ireland 92, 185, 186, 202
Character of Doctor Sheridan 9, 10, 19
Character of Sheridan as Lilly 23
Character, Panegyric, and Description of the Legion Club 102, 112
Collection of Poems, &c., Omitted in the Fifth Volume of Miscellanies (1735) 296, 304
Compleat Collection of Genteel and Ingenious Conversation 156, 217
Considerations about Maintaining the Poor 92
Considerations on Two Papers Lately Published (sometimes attributed to JS) 171
Dean and Duke 217
Dean Smedley Gone to Seek His Fortune see Intelligencer no. 20
Discourse of the Contests and Dissentions 82, 125
Discourse, to Prove the Antiquity of the English Tongue 270
Drapier's Letters 19, 35, 41, 170, 181, 183, 184, 185, 201, 203, 232, 327
Enquiry into the Behaviour of the Queen's Last Ministry 81, 117, 126
Epigram on Fasting 19
Epistle upon an Epistle 336
Examiner 1, 115, 116
Grand Question Debated 128, 222, 271
Gulliver's Travels 9, 22, 38, 50, 91, 99, 115, 246
Hints: Education of Ladies **269–75**
Hints for *Intelligencers* 25, 31, 76, 92, **269–75**, **339**
Hints on Good-Manners 156, 270
Hints toward an Essay on Conversation 156
History of the Four Last Years of the Queen 116, 125
History of the Second Solomon 12, 23, 31, 78

Humble Address to Both Houses of Parliament 170, 172, 184, 185
Intelligencer see nos. 1, 3, 5, 7, 8, 9, 15, 19, 20
Journal of a Dublin Lady 31, 36, 38, 41, 70, 271, 338
Journal of a Modern Lady see Journal of a Dublin Lady
Latino-Anglicus exchanges with TS 102, 222
Letter . . . Concerning the Sacramental Test 135
Letter Concerning the Weavers 173
Letter on Maculla's Project about Halfpence 173, 215, 270
Letter to a Young Gentleman, Lately Entered into Holy Orders 66
Letter to Mr. Pope (1721) 50, 183
Letter to the Archbishop of Dublin, Concerning the Weavers 206, 269, 270
Letter to the Lord Chancellor Middleton 173, 185
Letter to the Whole People of Ireland (1724) 35
Libertas et Natale Solum 183
list of friends 115
Mad Mullinix and Timothy see Intelligencer no. 8
marginalia in Burnet's *History* 82
marginalia in Clarendon's *History* 76, 125
marginalia in Davila's *Historie* 69
marginalia in Macky's *Characters* 125
Mary the Cook-Maid's Letter 18
Maxims Controlled in Ireland 92, 173, 214, 249–50, 270
Memorial to Harley about the first-fruits 86
Miscellaneous Pieces, in Prose and Verse (1789) 296, 306, 310, 320, 323
Miscellanies 3, 5, 16
Miscellanies (1727) 59, 67
Miscellanies (1732) 39, 42, 93, 293–5, 312, 316, 328, 330, 331, 333; copy-text 39
Miscellanies (1735) 296, 304, 328
Miscellanies (1736) 313, 330, 331
Miscellanies (1742) 296, 297, 301, 319, 328
Miscellanies (Fairbrother) 21, 295, 304, 312, 316, 328, 333

Modest Proposal 24, 25, 36, 38, 92, 197, 227
On False Witness 50
On Good-Manners and Good-Breeding 270
On Mutual Subjection 115
On Paddy's Character of the Intelligencer (sometimes attributed to JS) 244, 247–8
On the Bill for the Clergy's Residing on Their Livings 85
On the Education of Ladies 270
On Wisdom's Defeat in a Learned Debate (possibly by JS) 36, 38
Polite Conversation 77
Portrait from the Life 8–9
Preface to the Bishop of Sarum's Introduction 112
Proposal for Correcting the English Tongue 129
Proposal for Giving Badges to the Beggars 92
Proposal for the Universal Use of Irish Manufacture 183, 184–5
Proposal for Virtue 270–1
Proposal that All the Ladies and Women of Ireland Should Appear Constantly in Irish Manufactures 173, 183, 270
remarks on Gibbs's *Psalms* 237
Satirical Elegy on the Death of a Late Famous General 126
Seasonable Advice (1724) 183
Short View of the State of Ireland see *Intelligencer* no. 15
Simile, on Our Want of Silver 172
Story of the Injured Lady 187
Strephon and Chloe 112
Supplement to Dr. Swift's and Mr. Pope's Works (1739) 296, 313, 330, 331
Supplement to Dr. Swift's Works (Nichols) 217, 248, 296, 336
Supplement to the Works of Dr. Swift (1752) 247–8
Tale of a Tub 78, 82, 163, 187, 292, 293, 323; quoted or cited 59, 66–7, 81, 99, 112, 215, 216
Tatler no. 230: 128
Thoughts on Various Subjects 82
Three Sermons 16
Tim and the Fables see *Intelligencer* no. 10
To Doctor Delany, on the Libels Writ Against Him 78, 98

To Mr. Delany 59, 60
To Mr. Gay 339
Tritical Essay 168
True English Dean to Be Hang'd for a Rape 218
Upon Giving Badges to the Poor 92
Upon the Martyrdom of King Charles I 85, 91
Verses on the Death of Dr. Swift 49, 58, 131, 156, 248
Vindication of His Excellency the Lord Carteret 12, 102, 103
Wonder of All Wonders 246
Works (1735) 39–40, 185, 214, 217, 246, 295, 304–35 *passim*; Swift and 39, 42, 293, 294; uncancelled copies of vol. ii 313
Works (1738) 295
Works (1762) 81
Works (Hawkesworth edn.) 296, 297, 336
Sydenham, Thomas, MD 75
Synge, Bishop Edward 162
Syracuse 182, 199, 202

Tacitus 91, 99, 216
Taffy, nickname for a Welshman 253
Tartars 171
taste 61, 97, 234, 254
Tatler 1, 128
taxation 148, 175, 280; *see also* Ireland: taxation
temperance 122, 123
Temple, Henry, 1st Viscount Palmerston 231
Temple, Sir William 61, 65–6, 67
Of Poetry 60, 66
Temple-Oge Intelligencer see Browne, John
Tenison, Archbishop Thomas 80, 82, 309
Tertullian 99
theatre 188, 254, 272
see also comedy; Dublin: theatre; London: theatre; TS: and theatre; JS: and theatre
Theatre Italien 61, 65–6
Themistocles 199, 202
Thersites 105, 112, 131
Theseus 54, 56
Theuth 75
Thistle, Order of the 154
Thompson, Edward 185
Tibullus, Albius 264

Tickell, Thomas 22
tigers 160
Tighe, Richard 21, 25, 113, 131–3, 134
  and TS 12
  career 101–3
Tindal, Matthew 162
Tisdall, William 10, 13, 21, 113, 248
  Tom-Punsibi Metamorphosed 13–14, 18,
    244–7
  True Character of the Intelligencer 18,
    244–7
toads 166
Toland, John 162
Tonson, Jacob, II 132
Tories 86, 101–11
*To the Author of Those Intelligencers Printed
  at Dublin* (1733) **276–82**
*To the Reverend Dean Swift. A Reply, to the
  Answer Given to the Memorial of the
  Poor Inhabitants, Tradesmen, and
  Labourers, of the Kingdom of Ireland*
  (1728) 171, 182
*To the Reverend Dr. Jonathan Swift. The
  Memorial of the Poor Inhabitants,
  Tradesmen, and Labourers of the
  Kingdom of Ireland* (1728) 170–1
toupees 50, 109, 114
Townshend, Charles, 2nd Viscount 135,
  150, 154
Trevor, Capt. 202
Trevor, Sir Thomas, Baron Trevor of
  Bromham 119, 127
Tribune (ed. James Arbuckle) 292
Trinity College, Dublin 76, 112, 113,
    124, 132, 135, 194
  Mountcashel at 122, 128
  TS and 6–9, 11, 20
Troy, Siege of 105
True Character of the Intelligencer (1728) 18,
    245–7
Trueman, Andrew (pseud.) 206
Turco-Judaeo-Machia (1733) 20
Turks, at Siege of Vienna 113
tympany (medical condition) 71, 76
tyranny 123; *see also* slavery
Tyrone's rebellion 260

Udall, Nicholas, *Thersites* 112
Ulster *see* Ireland: Ulster
Union, Act of (1707) 191
United East India Company *see* East
  India Company
Universal Spectator 17

Upon Mr. Sheridan's Turning Author (1716)
    18
urinary calculi 71
usury 99

Valentine, Mary 216
Vanbrugh, Sir John 191
Van der Gucht, Gerard 131, 134
vapours (medical symptom) 71
Velleius Paterculus 182
Verner, Edward 216
Vernon, James 118, 126
Vernor 317
Verus, Emperor 53, 56
Vienna, Siege of 113
Virgil 95
  Aeneid 90, 153, 215, 222, 282
  Eclogues 51, 55, 133
  'sic vos non vobis' anecdote attributed
    to 207, 213
Virginia colony 216
Virginia Gazette 323
Voiture, Vincent 137, 145

Wake, Archbishop William 12
Wales, national character of 253–6
Waller, Edmund 73, 76, 77
Walpole, Horace (afterwards Baron
    Walpole of Wolterton) 119, 127,
    150, 154
Walpole, Sir Robert (afterwards Earl of
    Orford) 119, 127, 154, 164, 202,
    260, 305
  and Gay 57, 58, 63, 67
  and JS 57, 58, 170
  as connoisseur 150–1, 154
  as Sir Bluestring 149, 154
  opposition to 57, 147, 187, 236–7
  use of bribes 147, 152
Walter, Peter 275
Ward, James, dean of Cork 244
Warner, T. 292
War of the League of Augsburg 163
War of the Spanish Succession 120, 126,
    128
Waterford, bishopric of 82
Waters, Edward 183
Weekly Journal: or, Saturday's Post (Mist)
    128; *see also Mist's Weekly Journal*
Weekly Journal: or, The British Gazetteer
    197, 236, 253
Westminster, Palace of *see* London

Wexford, town and county 51, 84; *see also* Carrick ferry
Whalley, John 246
Wharton, Philip, 1st Duke of 236
Whigs 103; *see also* Ireland: political parties
Whimsical Medley 21
whisk and swobbers *see* whist
whist 80, 82
Whitehall Evening-Post 146, 218, 292
Whitehall Journal 135
Whiteway, Martha 22
Whitney, Thomas 204
Whitshed, William 171, 177, 181, 183, 329
Whitshett's Ghost Appears to the Reverend Dean Swift (1728) 171
Whole Duty of Man (? Richard Allestree) 127
Wibsey, nr. Bradford, Yorks. 83
Wicklow, town 51
wigs 50, 109, 114, 168
Wilkins, W. 319
William III 82, 118, 181, 200
    anniversary commemorations of, in Dublin 200, 202–3, 314
    as 'Glorious' 106, 112
William, Prince, Duke of Cumberland 58, 63
Williamites 203
Williams, Archbishop Gruffith 85
Willis, Bishop Richard 94
Will's Coffee House *see* London
Wilmot, William 36
Windsor castle 94
wine 171
Winstanley, John 101
wisdom 115, 119

wit 25, 59, 61–2, 80, 94, 238, 239
Witch of Endor (puppet character) 106, 112
Wit's Library 323
Wit's Magazine 326
wolves 166
women *see* marriage; paraphernalia; pin-money; TS: and women; JS: on marriage
Wood, William 36, 192, 199
Wood's halfpence controversy 19, 101, 173, 182, 198, 199, 201, 202; *see also* JS: as Drapier; JS, Works: Drapier's Letters
Woollen Acts 182, 192, 258
Wooton, John 130–1, 134
Worcester Magazine 328
Worrall, John 22
Worrall, Mary 22
Wortley, Francis, *Characters and Elegies* 76
Wren, Sir Christopher 191
Wright, John 294
Wylde, Thomas 185
Wyndham, Thomas, Baron Wyndham 68

Xenophon 72, 157, 162

Yonge, Sir William, Bt. 150, 154
Yorke, Sir Philip, afterwards 1st Earl of Hardwicke 68
Yorkshire 309

Zacynthia 199, 202
Zenger, John Peter 276
Zeno of Citium 261, 266